W9-BRN-429

St Antony's Series

General Editor: **Richard Clogg** (1999–), Fellow of St Antony's College, Oxford

Recent titles include:

C. W. Braddick
JAPAN AND THE SINO-SOVIET ALLIANCE, 1950–1964
In the Shadow of the Monolith

Isao Miyaoka
LEGITIMACY IN INTERNATIONAL SOCIETY
Japan's Reaction to Global Wildlife Preservation

Neil J. Melvin
SOVIET POWER AND THE COUNTRYSIDE
Policy Innovation and Institutional Decay

Juhana Aunesluoma
BRITAIN, SWEDEN AND THE COLD WAR, 1945–54
Understanding Neutrality

George Pagoulatos
GREECE'S NEW POLITICAL ECONOMY
State, Finance and Growth from Postwar to EMU

Tiffany A. Troxel
PARLIAMENTARY POWER IN RUSSIA, 1994–2001
A New Era

Elvira María Restrepo
COLOMBIAN CRIMINAL JUSTICE IN CRISIS
Fear and Distrust

Julie M. Newton
RUSSIA, FRANCE, AND THE IDEA OF EUROPE

Ilaria Favretto
THE LONG SEARCH FOR A THIRD WAY
The British Labour Party and the Italian Left Since 1945

Lawrence Tal
POLITICS, THE MILITARY, AND NATIONAL SECURITY IN JORDAN, 1955–1967

Louise Haagh and Camilla Helgø (*editors*)
SOCIAL POLICY REFORM AND MARKET GOVERNANCE IN LATIN AMERICA

Gayil Talshir
THE POLITICAL IDEALOGY OF GREEN PARTIES
From the Politics of Nature to Redefining the Nature of Politics

E. K. Dosmukhamedov
FOREIGN DIRECT INVESTMENT IN KAZAKHSTAN
Politico-Legal Aspects of Post-Communist Transition

Felix Patrikeeff
RUSSIAN POLITICS IN EXILE
The Northeast Asian Balance of Power, 1924–1931

He Ping
CHINA'S SEARCH FOR MODERNITY
Cultural Discourse in the Late 20th Century

Mariana Llanos
PRIVATIZATION AND DEMOCRACY IN ARGENTINA
An Analysis of President–Congress Relations

Michael Addison
VIOLENT POLITICS
Strategies of Internal Conflict

Geoffrey Wiseman
CONCEPTS OF NON-PROVOCATIVE DEFENCE
Ideas and Practices in International Security

Pilar Ortuño Anaya
EUROPEAN SOCIALISTS AND SPAIN
The Transition to Democracy, 1959–77

Renato Baumann (*editor*)
BRAZIL IN THE 1990s
An Economy in Transition

Israel Getzler
NIKOLAI SUKHANOV
Chronicler of the Russian Revolution

Arturo J. Cruz, Jr.
NICARAGUA'S CONSERVATIVE REPUBLIC, 1858–93

St Antony's Series
Series Standing Order ISBN 0–333–71109–2
(*outside North America only*)

You can receive future titles in this series as they are published by placing a standing order. Please contact your bookseller or, in case of difficulty, write to us at the address below with your name and address, the title of the series and the ISBN quoted above.

Customer Services Department, Macmillan Distribution Ltd, Houndmills, Basingstoke, Hampshire RG21 6XS, England

Japan and the Sino-Soviet Alliance, 1950–1964

In the Shadow of the Monolith

C. W. Braddick
Professor of International Political History
Musashi University, Tokyo

一枚岩の影に—日本と中ソ同盟

Palgrave/Macmillan
in association with
ST ANTONY'S COLLEGE, OXFORD

First published 2004 by
PALGRAVE MACMILLAN
Houndmills, Basingstoke, Hampshire RG21 6XS and
175 Fifth Avenue, New York, N. Y. 10010
Companies and representatives throughout the world

PALGRAVE MACMILLAN is the global academic imprint of the Palgrave Macmillan division of St. Martin's Press, LLC and of Palgrave Macmillan Ltd. Macmillan® is a registered trademark in the United States, United Kingdom and other countries. Palgrave is a registered trademark in the European Union and other countries.

ISBN 1–4039–1778–7

This book is printed on paper suitable for recycling and made from fully managed and sustained forest sources.

A catalogue record for this book is available from the British Library.

Library of Congress Cataloging-in-Publication Data

Braddick, C. W. (Christopher William), 1961–
Japan and the Sino-Soviet Alliance, 1950–1964: in the shadow of monolith=
[Ichimaiiwa no kage ni, Nihon to Chu-[So]]/C. W. Braddick.
p. cm.
Latter part of Japanese title missing; last word in Japanese title supplied by cataloger.
Includes bibliographical references and index.
In English; table of contents also in Japanese.
ISBN 1–4039–1778–7 (cloth)
1. Cold war. 2. Japan–Foreign relations–China. 3. China–Foreign relations–Japan. 4. Japan–Foreign relations–Soviet Union. 5. Soviet Union–Foreign relations–Japan. 6. Soviet Union–Foreign relations–China. 7. China–Foreign relations–Soviet Union. 8. Japan–Foreign relations–1945–1989. 9. China–Foreign relations–1949–1976. 10. Soviet Union–Foreign relations–1945–1991. I. Title: [Ichimaiiwa no kage ni, Nihon to Chu-[So]]. II. Title.

DS849.C6B63 2004
327.52051'09'045–dc22 2003062249

10 9 8 7 6 5 4 3 2 1
13 12 11 10 09 08 07 06 05 04

Printed and bound in Great Britain by
Antony Rowe Ltd, Chippenham and Eastbourne

To my Lover

'To live at all is miracle enough,
the doom of nations is another thing...'

(Mervyn Peake, 1911–68)

Contents

List of figures and tables

Figures

Tables

Glossary, abbreviations and conventions

Ajia Mondai Kenkyūkai	Asian Problems Research Association, LDP
Ajia–Afurika Mondai Kenkyūkai	Asian–African Problems Study Group, LDP
AmConGen	American Consulate General
AmEmbMos	American Embassy, Moscow
AmEmbTok	American Embassy, Tokyo
Anpo (*NichiBei Anzen Hoshō Jōyaku*)	Japan–US Security Treaty
AusEmbTok	Australian Embassy, Tokyo
AusEmbWash	Australian Embassy, Washington D.C.
Bōeichō	Defence Agency, Japan
BrEmbTok	British Embassy, Tokyo
CCP	Chinese Communist Party
CEC	Central Executive Committee
CFR	Council on Foreign Relations, US
ChiCom	Chinese Communist
CHINCOM	China Committee of Paris Group
CIA	Central Intelligence Agency, US
CITPC	China International Trade Promotion Committee
COCOM	Coordinating Committee of the Paris Group
COMECON	Council for Mutual Economic Assistance
CPSU	Soviet Communist Party
CRO (*Naikaku Chōsashitsu*)	Cabinet Research Office, Japan
DDRS	Declassified Documents Reference System
DEA	Department of External Affairs, Australia
DOS	Department of State, US
DSP (*Minshatō*)	Democratic Socialist Party, Japan
Enc.	Enclosure
EPA (*Keizai Kikakuchō*)	Economic Planning Agency, Japan
FARC (*Gaikō Chōsakai*)	Foreign Affairs Research Council, LDP
FED	Far Eastern Dept., FO
FO	Foreign and Commonwealth Office, UK
FRUS	Foreign Relations of the United States

Gaikō Mondai Kondankai	Foreign Policy Problems Deliberation Council
Gaimushō	Ministry of Foreign Affairs, Japan
Gensuikyō (*Gensuibaku Kinshi Nihon Kyōgikai*)	Japan Council Against Atomic and Hydrogen Bombs
GOJ	Government of Japan
GS (*Gaimushō Shiryōkan*)	Foreign Ministry Archives, Japan
Heiwa Dōshikai	Peace Comrades Association, JSP
Ichimai iwa	Monolithic (unity)
IISS	International Institute for Strategic Studies, UK
IR	Intelligence Report
JCP (*Nihon Kyōsantō*)	Japan Communist Party
JCTPA (*NitChū Bōeki Sokushinkai*)	Japan–China Trade Promotion Association
JITPA (*Nihon Kokusai Bōeki Sokushin Kyōkai*)	Japan International Trade Promotion Association
Jiyūtō	Liberal Party, Japan
JSP (*Nihon Shakaitō*)	Japan Socialist Party
JT(W)	*Japan Times* (*Weekly*)
Keidanren (*Keizai Dantai Rengokai*)	Federation of Economic Organisations, Japan
Keizai Dōyūkai	Japan Committee for Economic Development
KMT	*Guomindang* (Chinese Nationalist Party)
Kōan Chōsachō	Public Security Investigation Agency, Ministry of Justice, Japan
Kokusai Shiryōbu (RAD)	Research and Analysis Division, MOFA
L–T Trade Agreement	Liao–Takasaki Trade Agreement
LBJ	Lyndon B. Johnson National Security Files, US
LDP (*Jiyūminshutō*)	Liberal Democratic Party, Japan
MC	Memorandum of Conversation
MITI (*Tsūshō Sangyōshō*)	Ministry of International Trade and Industry, Japan
MOFA (*Gaimushō*)	Ministry of Foreign Affairs, Japan
NA	National Archives, Washington DC
NAA	National Australian Archives, Canberra
NATO	North Atlantic Treaty Organisation
n.d.	No date
NEA	Office of North–East Asian Affairs, DOS
NHK (*Nihon Hōsoku Kyōkai*)	Japan Broadcasting Corporation
NIE	National Intelligence Estimate, US
Nihon Kaishintō	Progressive Party of Japan
Nihon Minshutō	Democratic Party of Japan

Nihon no Koe Dōshikai	Voice of Japan Comrades Association
Nisshō (*Nihon Shōkō Kaigisho*)	Japan Chamber of Commerce and Industry
NisSo Kyōkai	Japan–Soviet Society
NitChū Bōeki Sokushin Giin Renmei	Diet Members' League for the Promotion of Japan–China Trade
NitChū Kokkō Kaizen Kenkyūkai	Japan–China Diplomatic Relations Improvement Study Group
NitChū Mondai Kenkyūkai	Japan–China Problems Study Group, LDP
NitChū NisSo Kokkō Chōsei Sokushin Dōmei	Alliance for the Promotion of Normalised Diplomatic Relations with China and the Soviet Union
NitChū NisSo Kokkō Kaifuku Kokumin Kaigi	National Council for the Reestablishment of Diplomatic Relations with China and the Soviet Union
NSC	National Security Council, US
Ōa Kyōkai	Society for the Study of Communism in Europe and Asia
OCB	Operations Coordinating Board, NSC
OEEC	Organisation for European Economic Cooperation
OIR	Office of Intelligence and Research, DOS
OSS	Office of Strategic Services, US
PARC (*Seimu Chōsakai*)	Policy Affairs Research Committee, LDP
PRC	People's Republic of China
PRO	Public Records Office, Kew, London
PTBT	Partial Nuclear Test Ban Treaty
RAD (*Kokusai Shiryōbu*)	Research and Analysis Division, MOFA
RC	Record of Conversation
ROC	Republic of China
Rōnōtō	Labour–Farmer Party
Rtd.	Retired
Ryokufūkai	Green Breeze Society
SCAP	Supreme Commander Allied Powers
SDF (*Jieitai*)	Self-Defence Forces, Japan
SEA	Secretary for External Affairs, Australia
SEATO	South–East Asia Treaty Organisation
seikan	wait and see (policy)
seikei bunri	policy of separating economic from political relations
Shakaishugi Kyōkai	Socialist Association
Sōhyō (*Nihon Rōdō Kumiai Sōhyō Gikai*)	General Council of Trade Unions of Japan

Soren Kenkyūsha Kyōgikai	Council of Sovietologists
Soren Mondai Kenkyūkai	Soviet Problems Research Association
SOS	Secretary of state
Tairiku Mondai Kenkyūjo (*Taiken*)	Continental Problems Research Institute
UK	United Kingdom
UN	United Nations
UPA	University Publications of America
US	United States of America
USSR	Union of Soviet Socialist Republics
Zenrō (*Zenkoku Rōdō Kumiai Dōmei*)	Japanese Confederation of Labour

Conventions

The following conventions have been observed in this book:

1). Japanese names follow Japanese practise, that is, with the family name first and the given name second.

2). Romanisation of Japanese words generally follows the Hepburn system.

3). Romanisation of Chinese words generally follows the *pinyin* system, except in the case of quotations and certain famous names, for example, Chiang Kai-shek.

4). English spellings follow the Oxford English Dictionary, unless they are quotations.

5). All materials from the US National Archives (NA) are from Record Group 59, unless otherwise stated.

6). All newspaper references are to morning editions unless otherwise stated.

7). All Japanese materials were published in Tokyo unless otherwise stated.

Preface

This book examines Japan's relations with the former Communist bloc or the 'Second World', as it was occasionally called. I envisage that it will ultimately form part of a trilogy to which I have given the overall title: Japan in the Cold War: the Cold War in Japan, or perhaps, Japan and the Three Worlds. As the title implies, the aim is to understand both Japan's role in the development of the Cold War and the influence of the Cold War on Japanese politics and society. The second volume will focus on the forging of Japan's ties to the Western Alliance, the so-called 'Free World'. A third book, exploring Japan's interaction with the Non-Aligned Movement, and the influence of neutralism will complete the series.

Somehow, the writing of this first book has managed to absorb twelve years of my life: almost as long as the period of history it covers. I would not have been able to sustain this effort without the support of many friends and colleagues. For my intellectual development, I owe a great debt to three people whom I am proud to call my mentors. To David Steeds, whose wonderful lectures first opened the eyes of a naïve young undergraduate to the fascinating political history of China and Japan. Secondly, to Ian Nish, who, in his quiet dignified manner, introduced me to the joys and value of diplomatic records, and who has watched over my career ever since. And last, but not least, to Arthur Stockwin, who taught me the interconnectedness between Japan's domestic and international politics, and who with an admirably light touch guided an often absent 'student/professor' through the labyrinthine doctoral process at Oxford.

There are, of course, many others who have contributed to my research in more specific ways. I would especially like to thank Rosemary Foot, Julie Gilson, Reinhard Drifte, Hugo Dobson, Tanaka Takahiko and the anonymous reviewers for reading and commenting on earlier versions of this book, and David Walton and John Swenson-Wright for locating useful documents. I would also like to thank Harald Fuess, Purnendra Jain, Verena Blechinger and Tianbiao Zhu for offering me the opportunity to have my work appear before a wider audience, and *arigato gozaimasu* Kawazoe-sensei for teaching me Japanese. I owe a special debt to Moreen Dee for improving my manuscript in so many ways. To the editors at St. Antony's College and Palgrave/Macmillan, I extend my thanks. I am grateful to Kibata Yoichi, Maureen Todhunter, Peter Berton, Ohnishi Hitoshi, Richard Sims, Ishii Akira, Roger Buckley, Kweku Ampiah, Tohmatsu Haruo, Goto-Shibata Harumi, David Williams, Daqing Yang, Susan Hoyler, Adam Kabat, Inoguchi Takashi, Ingolf Simon, Pauline Bosman, Tanaka Kazuo, Katalin Ferber,

Suzuki Shogo, Lynne Payne and everyone at St. Antony's College, the Nissan Institute, and Mejiro-Kōpo for their assistance wide and varied. Being married to a member of the profession, I must not forget to thank the many librarians and archivists who put their vital skills at my disposal. I would also like to thank the SSRC and *Monbushō* (as they were then called) for scholarships which enabled me to begin my postgraduate studies, to my colleagues at Musashi University for allowing me a fifteen-month study leave to get this book underway, and to my friends and colleagues in the Research School of Pacific and Asian Studies (ANU) for granting me a visiting fellowship to complete it. My apologies to anyone that I have forgotten to thank. All errors of grammar, typography, fact and interpretation are my own.

I would also like to remember those who will not see the results of my labours, Annie Olive and Peter Hein, Edith Braddick, Peter and David Fincham, and Michael Turner.

To my Mum and Dad (and Mum-in-law) thank you for your constant support and love. To my wonderful and brave children Izumi and Kizaki a big hug for all the times when I was too busy to play with you. Finally, I come to the real reason for all of this, my wife Josie. I can only say thank you Lover for without you I am nothing.

Ekoda, Japan
June 2003

1

Japan in a bipolar world: an introduction

The 50th Anniversary of the signing of the Sino-Soviet Alliance went unnoticed in most Asian capitals. This included Tokyo, where ironically the Russian Foreign Minister, Igor Ivanov, was concluding an official visit. In February 1950, however, all eyes had focused upon Moscow, where Josef Stalin and Mao Zedong were concluding a 30-year pact to unite the strategic 'heartland of Eurasia'.[1] A 'Communist bloc' now stretched from Berlin to Beijing. Little more than a decade later, however, as the outside world watched in astonishment, this 'eternal and indestructible' alliance slowly crumbled under the weight of its internal contradictions.[2]

As its title implies, the Sino-Soviet Treaty of Friendship, Alliance and Mutual Assistance was much more than simply a defence pact. This multifaceted agreement also embodied a Marxist–Leninist union, a foreign policy coalition, an economic partnership, a boundary settlement and even a putative cultural community. Hence, despite its relatively short life span, the subsequent disintegration of this relationship had serious strategic, ideological, diplomatic, commercial, territorial and social implications. It divided not just the Chinese and Soviet communist parties, but their governments, armed forces, economic infrastructures and peoples. In short, there were many Sino-Soviet conflicts.

The consequences of the making and breaking of the Sino-Soviet Alliance were not confined to the Communist bloc. Just as the cementing of the alliance was a crucial step in the spread of Cold War bipolarism to East Asia, its subsequent collapse helped to propel the international system towards the multipolarisation that characterised the 1970s and 1980s. The historian John Gaddis has argued that the outcome of the Cold War was ultimately determined by the fact that, 'democracy proved superior to autocracy in maintaining coalitions'.[3] It is a central premise of this study that the demise of the Sino-Soviet Alliance alongside the survival of the Japan–US Security Treaty, crucially affected the outcome of the Cold War in East Asia.

Of all the so-called 'Free World' states, Japan—by virtue of its geographical proximity, strategic significance, and potential for political and economic instability—was peculiarly vulnerable to the machinations of both Moscow and Beijing. Article 1 of the Sino-Soviet Alliance explicitly targeted Japan, pledging joint action to prevent 'the resumption of aggression and violation of peace on the part of Japan or any other state that may collaborate with Japan directly or indirectly in acts of aggression'.[4] The treaty predated Tokyo's secret security pact proposal to Washington (which ultimately produced the Security Treaty of 8 September 1951), but the presumption—probably correct—that the US was the alliance's main *bête-noire* has long overshadowed its importance for Japan both domestically and internationally. The terms of the Sino-Soviet pact were remarkably similar to its predecessor, concluded with the Republic of China in 1945, which was directed against Japan alone. Moreover, a longer historical perspective reveals that the 1950 Sino-Soviet Alliance was but the latest in a series of anti-Japanese coalitions between Russian and Chinese governments stretching back to the secret Li–Lobanov Agreement of 1896.[5] In Northeast Asia, as Allen Whiting has observed, a 'regional triangle of tension had pitted Russia, Japan, and China against each other through…three-quarters of a century of confrontation and conflict'.[6]

The rise and fall of the Sino-Soviet Alliance managed to transect almost every major issue in Japanese domestic and foreign affairs during the 1950s and early 1960s: from reparations, repatriations and rearmament to nationalism, neutralism, and normalisation. Initially, it influenced some sections of Japanese society more than others. As Sino-Soviet relations deteriorated, so the range of Japanese affected increased. Four groups felt the impact most keenly: the foreign policy-making elite (the conservative ruling party and government bureaucracy); the business world; the ideological Left (Communists, Socialists, neutralists and pacifists); and finally, the informed public (especially opinion shapers in the intellectual community and the media.)

During its 15 years of active existence, the Sino-Soviet Alliance veered from weak to strong and back again before ultimately being adjudged impotent by most Japanese observers. As the alliance imploded, four main interpretations can be identified. It is important to recognise, however, that these do not represent discrete phases. Rather their emergence was gradual, cumulative and overlapping, each one enriching the existing image. Thus, somewhat akin to Kurosawa Akira's technique in the film *Rashōmon*, we have the same story of the rift told from different perspectives. What was initially perceived as a diplomatic division of labour, added an ideological dispute, an economic schism, and a struggle for bloc leadership, until finally the conflict appeared all consuming and the alliance was generally regarded as a dead letter. In short, the Japanese were also aware of the multifaceted nature of the Sino-Soviet conflict afflicting the Communist bloc.

It is contended here that in the mid-1960s, Japan reached a crossroads, but the path to independence was not taken. Instead, non-involvement in the Sino-Soviet strategic conflict, which resulted from the collapse of the alliance, became a central tenet of Japanese foreign policy—at least until the 1970s—alongside a deepening interdependence with the US. Yet, the manner in which this minimalist response emerged exposed an array of deep policy cleavages both within and between Japanese ruling and opposition groups, as well as between Japan and its superpower 'protector', the US. As such, an examination of the heterogeneous Japanese response to the rise and fall of the Sino-Soviet Alliance offers important insights into Japan's political history and the evolution of East Asian foreign relations.

Analytical framework

This is a study in the International Political History of East Asia. The methodology combines insights from the disciplines of International History, International Relations, and Asian Politics. The result is empirically based research that is theoretically open. In attempting to apply Western social scientific theory to the study of this region, however, one confronts a familiar dilemma: how to balance the Trans-Atlantic Universalism implicit in most of the international relations literature with the particularism prevalent in East Asian and especially Japanese historical studies. A pragmatic approach is adopted here that describes the workings of Japan—a historically, geographically, culturally, and socially defined nation state—in a language intelligible to students of history, politics and international relations, while proposing modifications to that body of theory to make it more relevant to the Japanese experience.

The starting point is a multidimensional, external phenomenon—the evolution of the Sino-Soviet Alliance between 1950 and 1964—and the impact that it had on Japanese politics and East Asian foreign relations. Covering a 15-year period counters the tendency in foreign policy analyses to concentrate on the, by definition, atypical big decision or crisis while neglecting a consideration of the imperatives of foreign policy-making on a day-to-day basis. It also broadens the focus in another sense, that is, to move beyond the conventional state-centric approach to international relations. Domestically, the analysis here examines the impact of this external event on Japanese society as a whole—across the political spectrum from ultra-Left to extreme right, and from the policy-making elite at the top to the ordinary citizen at the bottom. Externally, it is not restricted to official state-to-state diplomacy, but incorporates informal channels of Japan's interaction with international society.

The analytical complexities revealed in the preceding discussion indicates that a full comprehension of the Japanese response to the Sino-Soviet Alliance is impossible without first undertaking a detailed examination of the intricate interplay between Japan's external and internal environments. The former—the external environment—corresponds to the international system level of analysis. Here it is analysed in three stages: the *status quo ante*—the international politico-economic structure when the alliance was concluded—provides the background; the influence of the waxing and waning of the Sino-Soviet Alliance between 1950 and 1964 on this Cold War international environment supplies the dynamic; and most significantly for this work, the consequences of any change in the external environment for Japan's internal environment constitutes the outcome. In taking this approach, the study encompasses such issues as the degree of Sino-Soviet unity on policies towards Japan, the influence of Marxism–Leninism in Japan, and the effect of Washington's responses to the Sino-Soviet Alliance on Tokyo's policy-making processes.

Before setting out the method taken in examining Japan's internal environment, it is necessary to refer briefly to the debate on the relative importance of environment and perception in the process of foreign policy-making, which has been ongoing between the 'realist' and 'behaviourist' schools of international relations since the 1960s. It is reminiscent of the age-old dispute between those who believe human behaviour to be socially constructed (mediated by culture) and those who believe biological programming (genes) plays the more significant role. In practice, there is a complex interaction between environmental pressures and personal propensities. To relate this to the study of foreign policy-making necessitates drawing a distinction between the psychological and operational milieux.[7] The psychological sphere of the external environment is largely beyond the scope of this study, but when applied to an analysis of the internal environment, this differentiation allows the disjunction between the mental and physical reality of the Japanese to be explored. It is noted, however, that even if the validity of such a model is accepted, a dispute over which sphere takes precedence will continue. With the interaction between the human senses and their physical environment still not fully comprehended by the natural sciences, it seems unreasonable to adopt a doctrinaire stance in applying the distinction elsewhere. Opting for the pragmatic approach, it is assumed here that either path is possible (see Figure 1.1.)

Concerning the more cerebral aspects of the Sino-Soviet Alliance, for example ideology or national identity, it could be expected that the primary impact would be on Japan's psychological sphere, and thus any effect on the operational sphere would only be indirect. On the other hand, such concrete aspects of the alliance as the trading or military relationship, most likely would alter Japan's operational environment—both internal and external—directly, without necessarily first penetrating the psychological sphere, although it may, of course, feel the consequences. The internal operational environment is thus examined in three parts: fixed or material factors, fluid or manipulating factors, and human factors.[8] In Japan's case, the first element must take into account a long history of relative isolation interspersed with brief bouts of expansion, a meagre endowment of natural resources, and a location off the east coast of Asia. The second ingredient includes a rapidly rising level of economic development and broad-based educational system, but with minimal military capabilities. The third component embraces a factionalised political structure with competing elites and interest groups, an influential media, and an insular culture. The starting point for this analysis is again the existing structure—here the domestic sources of policy—which helped to condition responses. When and where this structure felt the impact of the Sino-Soviet Alliance most keenly—how it influenced Japan's economic and military capacities, political structure and civil society—are considered, followed by an examination of the constraints this imposed on the psychological sphere and the decision-making process, thereby limiting policy options.

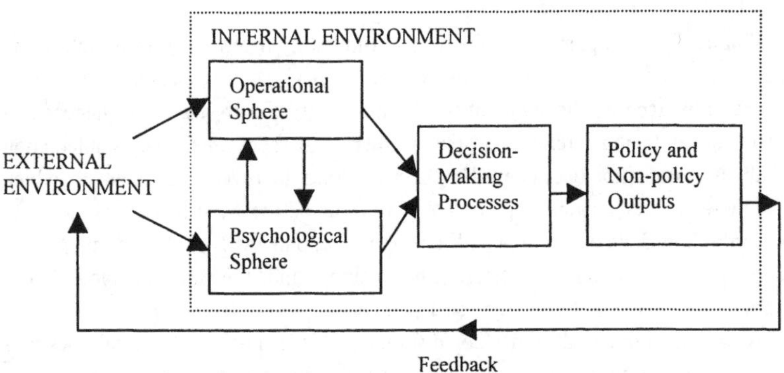

Figure 1.1 Analytical framework

The consideration of the internal psychological sphere attempts to dissect the cognitive processes of the Japanese—their perceptions of the situation (images of China and Russia, views on international relations and on Japan's role therein), and their belief systems (ideologies, ideals, identities, norms, values and objectives). Both factors filter the necessarily incomplete incoming information and motivate actions.[9] The next step is to assess the impact of the Sino-Soviet

Alliance on this mental 'template', and finally to investigate the altered psychological sphere's influence on the operational sphere, decision-making processes and outputs. This necessitates employing three levels of analysis: micro, macro, and mezzanine. Most studies equate the psychological sphere with the individual wherein subjectivity resides. Yet the notion of national identity—a shared sense of cultural, political and psychological self-awareness—is also influential.[10] On the other hand, Japanese society is far from homogenous, and groups often attempted to create their own belief systems. In Japan's case, for instance, it is important to differentiate between mass and elite perceptions. This study focuses on four perspectives—those of the foreign policy establishment; the business world; the left-wing opposition, and the informed public—although, as will become clear, competing visions coexisted within each group. Nonetheless, these actors felt the impact of the Sino-Soviet Alliance most strongly.

All of these inputs—operational and psychological, internal and external—influenced the decision-making processes that formulated Japan's official policy and other responses during the period under review. It is essential, therefore, to examine the impact of the Sino-Soviet Alliance on Japan's post-Occupation decision-making systems and the effects that this had on Japan's policy and non-policy outputs. Such an analysis reveals the processes by which decisions were reached and also the institutions, groups, and individuals—politicians, bureaucrats, businessmen, left-wing activists, intellectuals and journalists—who most influenced them.

Finally, when implemented, the decision-making processes result in policy and non-policy outputs: a product of the interaction between established positions and changes induced by the status of the alliance. This in turn has consequences that feed back into the international environment and represents Japan's interaction with the international system. This section seeks to reveal the extent to which Japanese actively sought to influence the fate of the Sino-Soviet Alliance; to describe how Japanese policy and non-policy outputs evolved during this period; and finally to ascertain whether the making and breaking of the alliance stimulated Japan's independence or dependence.

Armed with this multidimensional framework, the three fundamental questions inherent in the study can be addressed: how influential Japanese reacted to the Sino-Soviet Alliance; why they responded in the way that they did; and what were the implications of their responses for Japan and the wider world.

A note on sources

In order to encompass the full impact of the Sino-Soviet Alliance on Japan in all its complexity and diversity, it is essential to draw on a wide range of source materials. Contemporary diplomatic records offer the most reliable guide to the foreign policy elites' thinking. During the period under scrutiny, public statements of Japanese policy were relatively frequent, but MOFA's reluctance to open its archives on relations with China and the Soviet Union presents historians with a major problem. Other ministries and government institutions are even less forthcoming. Happily, governments in Australia, Britain, Canada, New Zealand and the US take a more enlightened view on such matters. Relevant agencies in these countries have in recent years declassified a large amount of material from the 1960s, and since intelligence relationships forged with Tokyo at that time led to the exchange of a range of sensitive material, many important Japanese foreign policy documents have quietly entered the public domain.

Diplomatic records, however, cannot adequately explain the importance of domestic factors in the foreign policy-making process. Although the secretive culture of Japan's bureaucracy also pervades its political parties, fortunately, for the researcher, over the years much important political information has been leaked to the Japanese press. The media is also useful as a window on public opinion. Polling has long been a national obsession in Japan, and although it has serious limitations, the results do offer some insights into the domestic political environment in which decision-makers have to operate. This study has also made extensive use of other contemporary Japanese materials, including party and think-tank publications—sometimes called 'grey literature'—intellectual journals and monographs, popular weekly magazines, and newspapers. Furthermore, while often unreliable, various forms of statistics (including bilateral trade figures) have been considered as major primary resources, as have the memoirs of the period left by some of the key political and bureaucratic actors, despite their even more doubtful credence.

Finally, a wide array of English and Japanese secondary sources have been consulted. The 1960s saw the publication of many penetrating studies of the Sino-Soviet rift, but relatively little then appeared until the ending of the Cold War when Soviet documents held in Russian archives became available for research.[11] Although a definitive history of the entire alliance period has yet to be published, many scholars are engaged in a re-examination of various aspects of the alliance in the light of this invaluable newly released Soviet information. Some have examined the origins of the alliance, while others have attempted to uncover the causes of its demise and the consequences for China and the Soviet Union.[12] A few academics have also considered the international impact of the rift.[13] However, very few of them have broadened this to include non-socialist states, with the notable exception of some fine studies of US policy towards the Sino-Soviet Alliance.[14] All the literature to date, however, fails to give any real consideration to the impact of the alliance on Japan. The limited research that exists on this subject—two doctoral theses from the early 1970s, a short chapter here and there, some contemporary articles in Japanese journals—concentrates almost exclusively on the opposition parties' point of view. This has created the misleading impression that the impact on Japan was purely ideological.[15]

On the other hand, the literature on post-war Japanese politics and diplomacy is voluminous. But many questions remain unasked, many answers remain unproven, and myths abound. The role played by the Sino-Soviet Alliance in Japanese foreign policy-making, in particular, has attracted scant attention. Scholars have generally preferred a bilateral approach to a multilateral one, which has resulted in Japan's post-war relations with the Soviet Union and China being treated as virtually two separate stories. This disjunction has accentuated the importance of a territorial dispute over the Kurile Islands in the former case, and of Taiwan in the latter.[16]

Outline of the study

The main body of this book consists of a series of eight paired chapters arranged chronologically and organised according to the four dimensions or perspectives—diplomatic/strategic, economic, ideological, and ideational—outlined above. As the changes wrought by the Sino-Soviet Alliance in each case were gradual and far from synchronous, the erection of any historical partition is inevitably somewhat arbitrary. In this study, the dividing line is drawn where the emergence of the Sino-Soviet conflict first had both a substantive and perceived impact on that particular dimension.

This introduction is followed by two chapters that examine the diplomatic and strategic dimensions, and thus concentrate on the role of Japan's foreign policy elite. Chapter 2 shows that, although the monolithic view of the Sino-Soviet Alliance was often challenged by predictions of an inevitable split, the spread of the Cold War forced every state in East Asia to 'lean to one side'. Nevertheless, Japan's four premiers of the 1950s adopted distinctive approaches to the Sino-Soviet Alliance. Chapter 3 reveals how Tokyo gradually came to accept that Moscow and Beijing were engaged in a struggle for power. Divergent Sino-Soviet strategic priorities forced Japanese policy makers to revise their threat perceptions. China and the Soviet Union were now 'unmistakably divided', but the Japanese government sought to avoid intervening in their strategic rift.

The focus of the next two chapters is on the economic dimension, in which, for this study, government–business relations form the core. Chapter 4 details how Japan for a long time attempted to separate its trading relationships with China and the Soviet Union from its political (or lack of political) ties. This policy reached an impasse in 1958, when China suspended all economic relations. Chapter 5 describes how a disagreement over development strategy led to a sharp deterioration in Sino-Soviet economic relations. This was to have positive side effects for Japan as the two Communist states sought to attract Japanese businesses and strengthen connexions with the government in Tokyo. Their responses varied but by late 1964, rapidly expanding Japan–China and Japan–Soviet economic exchanges were overtaking plummeting Sino-Soviet trade.

The nature of Japanese domestic politics in the period under study dictates the consideration of the ideological dimension carried out in Chapters 6 and 7. Since the political parties that governed Japan during the 1950s were all Conservative and anti-Communist, an examination of the ideological impact of the Sino-Soviet Alliance on Japan primarily entails a study of left-wing opposition politics. Chapter 6 relates how, despite Communist claims to the universality of Marxism-Leninism, the idea of an 'ideological dispute' slowly emerged. Many Japanese on the Left, however, continued to dismiss it as merely 'a quarrel between brothers'. After a considerable gestation period, as Chapter 7 records, the dilemmas the dispute posed for the Japanese Left took on a truly nightmarish quality. Many organisations proved unable to withstand the intense pressure that arose as the CPSU and CCP fiercely competed for the allegiance of Japanese Marxists.

The last two chronological chapters focus on the ideational dimension and look at the interaction between the Japanese people as a whole and the prime shapers of public opinion—the media and the intellectuals. Chapter 8 recounts how early predictions of a Sino-Soviet rift were frequently dismissed as 'wishful thinking' by these two groups, and goes on to discuss the emergence of a grudging acceptance of the alliance's existence as a permanent feature of the East Asian political landscape. Mainstream Japanese journalists were therefore slower than were their colleagues in the West to appreciate the significance of the Sino-Soviet dispute. The only exceptions were the occasional translation of foreign analyses and the outpourings of small anti-Communist think tanks. The way in which the Japanese public learned of the existence of an open Sino-Soviet breach is the subject of Chapter 9. Reflecting the sweeping nature of the rift, a broad cross-section of the Japanese intelligentsia, not just specialists in international relations or Communist politics, but economists, historians, philosophers, even novelists and artists joined the debate. For a long time, however, they all seemed more concerned with identifying the causes of the dispute and its significance for Marxism rather than considering its practical consequences for Japan. It was only once the serious racial and territorial dimensions of the dispute were recognised that the split was generally accepted to be irreversible, and opinion leaders argued that Japan should adopt 'independent thinking'.

Finally, Chapter 10 uses the results of the examinations undertaken in Chapters 2–9 to evaluate the relative merits of the analytical framework outlined above, and to briefly reassess the degree and nature of the Sino-Soviet Alliance's influence on Japanese politics and foreign relations. Japan may not have been a major player in the bipolar global system that characterised the 1950s and early 1960s. Yet this study will show that given its vulnerability to international events, Japan could not remain unaffected by issues arising out of the Sino-Soviet split. Moreover, Japan had a significant influence on the course of international relations in East Asia during the Cold War era.

2

Leaning to one side: Japanese diplomacy and the Sino-Soviet Alliance, 1950–60

The origins of the Cold War lay not in the post-war division of Asia but in superpower disagreement over the future of Europe. Stalin's demand for a strategic buffer zone to prevent another invasion from the West caused President Harry Truman to respond with a policy of containment and deterrence. To this end, the US concluded a series of alliances aimed at preventing the spread of Communist power, resulting in much of the world being divided into two antagonistic blocs. Each superpower was able to exploit its hegemonic status to impose loyalty within its own bloc: increasing the costs of defection by encouraging economic and strategic dependence.

The global strategic Cold War that by 1955 neatly divided most of Europe between the NATO and Warsaw Pact alliances took rather more complicated forms in the Northeast Asian region. Instead of these overarching multilateral organisations, a series of bilateral treaties linked the superpowers to their respective client states in the region. The most important of these were undoubtedly the Japan–US Security Treaty and the Sino-Soviet Alliance.

When confronted with the challenge of how to respond to the Sino-Soviet Alliance, policy-makers in Tokyo, Washington, London and elsewhere, initially came up with remarkably similar prescriptions. Emphasis on improving relations with China, as the more vulnerable of the two to seduction by the West, enjoyed the support of mainstream anti-Communist opinion. However, this concordance of views did not survive the outbreak of the Korean War in June 1950. Thereafter, a number of contradictory approaches to the Communist alliance competed for support on both the domestic and international levels.

It is worth emphasising that the Sino-Soviet Alliance was signed less than five years after Japan's defeat in World War II. Although overlain and partially obscured by the new Cold War structure, the painful legacy of these deeper lines of conflict continued to be felt in the region. Memories of the war would seriously hinder Japanese leaders' pursuit of an activist foreign policy.

For Japan, three political heavyweights—Hatoyama Ichirō, Yoshida Shigeru and Kishi Nobusuke—came to dominate this process. Ideologically speaking, all were Conservative and strongly anti-Communist, yet the policies they adopted vis-à-vis the Sino-Soviet Alliance exhibited significant differences. Hailing from a political family, Hatoyama Ichirō had long been a powerful figure in the pre-war Diet. Following Japan's surrender in 1945, he was quick to rebuild his political machine. Hatoyama's *Jiyūtō* (Liberal Party) won a plurality of seats in the April 1946 general election and he was widely expected to become the next prime minister. At this point, however, the Supreme Commander for the Allied Powers (SCAP) intervened and ordered his purge.[1] In response, Hatoyama approached a reluctant Yoshida Shigeru and persuaded him to serve as a 'temporary substitute'. After a long and distinguished diplomatic career (including seven years service in China), Yoshida was still a relative political novice when he was suddenly elevated from the post of foreign minister to *Jiyūtō* president, and hence prime minister, in May 1946. However, when Hatoyama was finally deemed fit to re-enter the world of democratic politics in August 1951, he found that the diplomat-turned-politician had grown attached to the premiership and refused to relinquish it. Thereafter the two men engaged in a bitter feud, Yoshida clearly gaining the upper hand until December 1954, when an aged and infirm Hatoyama led a coalition of radical conservative forces which, with Socialist help, finally succeeded in toppling him.

The third central figure, Kishi Nobusuke, was if anything an even more controversial premier than his predecessors. He had been a leader of the nationalistic 'renovationist bureaucrats' from the 1920s, a senior official in the *Manchukuo* government and minister of commerce and industry in Tōjō Hideki's wartime cabinet. Following Japan's defeat he was imprisoned for three-and-a-half years as a Class 'A' war criminal, although never formally charged. He returned to politics in 1952, and rose rapidly until Yoshida expelled him from the Liberal Party in 1954. A year later, however, he returned to become the first secretary-general of the newly merged *Jiyūminshutō* (Liberal Democratic Party, LDP). Narrowly defeated in the battle for the party presidency by Ishibashi Tanzan, he was compensated with the foreign minister portfolio. Just two months later, in

February 1957, Kishi inherited the premiership from the ailing Liberal. Despite growing disquiet at home and abroad (except in the US), he managed to hold on to power for the next three-and-a-half years.

Occupied Japan

The birth of Yoshida's China Thesis

As early as November 1948, Yoshida Shigeru—recently restored to the premiership after a 17 month Socialist interregnum—was reportedly 'without any anxiety' regarding the possibility of a Communist take-over of China. He believed that the 'Chinese Communists were Chinese first and communists second.' A Communist Chinese regime, Yoshida felt, would soon prove as nationalistic and xenophobic as had its predecessors, and thus rather than contributing to Soviet power in Asia would actually diminish it. He also thought that Sino-Japanese ties could be rebuilt to the benefit of both.[2]

American thinking at this time tended to confirm Yoshida's assessment that 'Titoism in China' (following the independent path of the Yugoslav leader) was a realistic prospect. Even after the establishment of the PRC on 1 October 1949, Washington appeared, at least in theory, willing to allow Tokyo to 'maintain normal political and economic relations with the communist bloc and, in the absence of open hostilities, resist complete identification either with the interests of the United States or Soviet Union.'[3] During the next 12 months, however, the conclusion of the Sino-Soviet Alliance, the outbreak of the Korean War, and the subsequent Chinese intervention therein, caused the earlier American optimism to evaporate. In its place arose a fear of losing Japan as well, to what was now perceived as an ever-expanding Communist monolith.[4]

Yoshida's thinking did not undergo any such transformation. Commenting on the freshly minted Sino-Soviet Pact, he told the House of Representatives Foreign Affairs Committee: 'I do not think it will affect Japan very much'. At worst, he thought it might delay the conclusion of Japan's peace treaty.[5] Yoshida remained convinced that, 'China would never become a slave to the Kremlin.' Prescient though this later appeared, his reasoning seemingly owed more to racial prejudice than rational analysis:

> Referring to centuries of Chinese history, the character of the Chinese people, their consistent successes in the past in thwarting efforts at domination or absorption, and their superiority to the Russians in intelligence, cleverness and political astuteness, he declared that he had every confidence in the outcome. The Chinese, he concluded, will be "too much for the Russians".[6]

Under mounting domestic pressure to restore Japanese sovereignty, in May 1950 Yoshida secretly despatched Finance Minister Ikeda Hayato to Washington in an effort to persuade the Americans to comply with these popular demands. He offered US forces the right to remain in post-Occupation Japan, but also hinted that Japan might prefer a Soviet peace treaty if it included a favourable territorial settlement. The proposal was discussed in Washington at the highest levels, but no official response was forthcoming.[7] Hence, on 1 June, the Japanese government issued a White Paper declaring its 'willingness to sign a peace treaty with any nation that recognised its independence'.[8]

The outbreak of the Korean War on 25 June 1950 caused the Truman Administration not only to revise its thinking on prospects for a Sino-Soviet rift, but also to question its own ability to influence the process.[9] Japan's reaction lacked such uniformity. MOFA issued a statement that presupposed the existence of a 'monolithic Communism' by implying that a link existed between North Korea's invasion of the South and the earlier signature of the Sino-Soviet Alliance. It spoke of the Communists viewing Japan as a 'special prize' and referred to the 'war threat' they posed to Japan.[10] Yoshida, on the other hand, continued publicly to downplay the seriousness of any Communist threat to Japan. Even after November, when large numbers of Chinese 'volunteers' turned the tide in Korea, he reassured the Diet: 'We do not have the slightest expectation that the communist countries will invade Japan.'[11]

Such talk made the Americans more nervous about a future sovereign Japan, which the Central Intelligence Agency (CIA) had already labelled as 'opportunistic'.[12] Thus, on 23 April 1951, US Special Ambassador John Foster Dulles extracted an oral pledge from Yoshida not to sign a separate peace treaty with the mainland.[13] Yet, right up until his departure for the San Francisco Peace Conference in September, Yoshida continued to preach his China Thesis to anyone who would listen: Japan, he claimed, could help to 'wean the Chinese away from Moscow'.[14]

Two peace treaties: San Francisco and Taipei

Although carefully stage-managed by the Americans, the San Francisco Peace Conference could not escape the influence of the intensifying Cold War conflict. Festering Anglo-American differences over recognition of the PRC or the transplanted ROC regime meant that neither Beijing nor Taipei was represented. Yoshida carefully avoided the issue of which Chinese regime Tokyo would recognise, although in private talks with British diplomats, he continued to argue that, 'Japan's role would be to "democratize" China'.[15] In contrast to London and Washington, Moscow and Beijing maintained a united front. Both Communist governments had insisted that a peace settlement was impossible without their participation. This apparently coordinated approach extended to mutual support for their respective territorial claims vis-à-vis Japan. Thus, after the Americans spurned every amendment proposed by the Soviets, the three Communist delegations present at San Francisco refused to sign the treaty. Consequently, Yoshida signed a 'one-sided' Peace Treaty with the Western allies and reinforced this stance by simultaneously concluding a Security Treaty with the US that allowed it to continue occupying bases in Japan.

On his return to Tokyo, however, Yoshida still appeared willing to place relations with the two Chinas on an equal footing. Specifically, he expressed an interest in opening an official overseas office in Shanghai (like the one about to open in Taipei) and added that he would welcome a Communist Chinese office in Tokyo on condition it avoided propaganda- or conflict-related activities.[16] The 'China Lobby' in Washington was reportedly furious, believing that Yoshida had reneged on his earlier promises not to establish ties with the mainland.[17] State Department officials feared that a Sino-Soviet rift might ultimately lead to the development of a Sino-Japanese 'third-force'.[18] Dulles had no choice but to undertake a fourth trip to Tokyo.[19]

The two men soon reached a compromise on the diplomatic front: Japan would recognise the ROC as *a* government of China rather than *the* government, and any treaty would be restricted to the area under actual Nationalist control.[20] However, Japanese and American approaches to the Sino-Soviet Alliance were now poles apart: Yoshida remained wedded to the belief that, 'Japan might be able to play an important role in weaning China away from domination by the Soviet politburo'. This was something Dulles regarded as no better than 'political fantasy'.[21] In his view, with Communist China representing the primary threat to Japanese security, 'containment' was the only realistic option.[22]

For Yoshida, the resulting eponymous letter setting out the terms of his agreement with Dulles represented a postponement of his China Thesis not its abandonment.[23] His sole contribution to the Dulles authored draft was a reference to the Sino-Soviet Treaty—'virtually a military alliance aimed at Japan'—as an additional justification for Japan's action.[24] This was disingenuous to say the least, for until this point the alliance had never particularly perturbed Yoshida. The statement appears to contradict his fundamental belief in the inevitability of a Sino-Soviet rift. However, if Yoshida anticipated the letter being made public, it may be seen as a useful weapon with which to defend an unpopular policy reversal at home.[25]

Yoshida in fact continued to seek to avoid a total commitment to Nationalist China (ROC). He hoped to maintain working relations with both Chinas. The US would not permit this, and with the election of a Conservative government in Britain, Yoshida found himself isolated on the issue.[26] Following US Senate ratification of the Japanese Peace Treaty, Nishimura Kumao, a close advisor to Yoshida, met with US Embassy officials. He explained to them once again

'Japan's conviction that the Peking Regime is not and will not be really Communist, in the sense of being directed by Moscow.' Nishimura thus characterised the Taipei talks as 'simply...a local, minor settlement', where the US should not force the pace 'at the cost of prejudicing a possible comprehensive settlement in East Asia.'[27] He followed up this contact two weeks later, when he pointed out how Yoshida:

> had many times expressed the view that Japan as an old nation familiar with the Far East, could assist and even guide the US, which is inexperienced in foreign policy and has got itself in a "circle" on the China question.[28]

These diplomatic probes produced no concrete results. Ultimately Japan signed a 'peace settlement' which went beyond the 'Yoshida Letter' and recognised Taipei's jurisdiction over territories that in future might fall under its control. The Japanese public, which strongly favoured recognition of the PRC, concluded that the Yoshida government had turned its back on Beijing.[29]

Post-Occupation Japan

Yoshida's China Thesis in abeyance

During the succeeding two years, Yoshida largely maintained a judicious silence vis-à-vis the Sino-Soviet Alliance. This did little to calm Western diplomats' fears regarding his China policy, however. Disregarding the Japan–ROC Peace Treaty concluded only a few days earlier, Robert Murphy, America's first postwar ambassador to Japan, warned Washington about 'the indigenous policy tendency'. While recognising the constraints that its overwhelming dependence on the US imposed on Japan, he asserted that,

> the Yoshida–Nishimura group...is determined to pursue a positive policy toward Peking, with a view to establishing a relatively normal commercial *and* diplomatic intercourse as soon as possible...argu[ing it] would be highly advantageous to long-range US interests because it would be accomplished by Japanese subversion of Chinese obeisance to the Kremlin.

Yet at the same time, Murphy did not rule out the possibility that Yoshida was using such tactics cynically as a 'gambit in bargaining for increased economic assistance from the US.'[30] Such confusion was not unique to Murphy. In conversation with Malcolm MacDonald (British High Commissioner for Southeast Asia), Yoshida continued to 'belittle the danger of communism' in Japan. MacDonald concluded that the premier 'appears incapable of appreciating the reality of the communist menace.' The Australian diplomat T.W. Eckersley on the other hand believed that 'the Prime Minister's apparent indifference [to the threat] is largely a pose.'[31]

While Western diplomats continued to probe for the real intentions of the deliberately enigmatic Yoshida, the Japanese government's public position was becoming clearer. MOFA had not softened its hard line stance. It still adjudged both Communist powers to pose a 'political and military threat to Japan.'[32] Similarly, the newly appointed foreign minister, Okazaki Katsuo, was quick to point out that the aim of the Sino-Soviet Alliance, 'remains destructive words and actions like the overthrow of the [Japanese] government.'[33] Moreover, Yoshida himself, when asked by a journalist in mid-September about prospects for convening a peace conference with the PRC, replied that the Beijing government first had to 'stop its aggression in Asia', revise sections of the Sino-Soviet Alliance, cease assisting the JCP, and return all Japanese internees.[34]

Within MOFA, the alliance was perceived as strong and growing stronger. In November 1952, Niizeki Kinya (chief of the Eastern Europe Desk) claimed that Moscow was concentrating its energy on 'strengthening ties with its satellites, including Communist China'.[35] Yet, Suma Yakichirō, an influential retired diplomat, noted that despite the firm promises to establish a new Sino-Soviet axis made at the Moscow Conference in mid-September, the Soviets had postponed the return of its base at Port Arthur (*Lushun*) until both parties had concluded peace treaties with Japan. Suma's sound analysis was as critical of those anticipating China's imminent Titoisation as it was of those arguing that China was becoming a Soviet satellite. In his view, the Korean War gave the Communist allies a common foe and as long as it continued, the Soviets could dominate the Chinese. However, Suma noted, there were already problems in Sino-Soviet trade relations and he was certain that 'China would never abandon its national pride.' Although firmly anti-Communist, Suma recommended that his former colleagues cautiously pursue diplomatic normalisation with both Moscow and Beijing.[36]

The death in March 1953 of Josef Stalin, one of the Communist alliance's founding fathers, sparked renewed interest within MOFA at prospects for a rift. Wada Shusaku (chief of the South Asia Desk) asserted that one strong school of thought supported Yoshida's view that 'it would be possible to wean China away from Moscow'. However, this group believed that Japan first had 'to sever its ties with the Chinese Nationalist and French-controlled Vietnamese regimes and to seek to form a "cooperative bloc" with the Peiping Government.'[37] Three months later, Wajima Eiji (director of the Asian Affairs Bureau) claimed that, 'the Chinese Communist leaders had been and still were taking their orders, at least in [the] foreign affairs field, from Moscow.' Nevertheless, he felt that, 'it was only a matter of time before the Chinese reached the point when they would no longer find it to their advantage to cooperate so closely with the Soviets.'[38] Such views were not confined to MOFA. For example, Suma Yakichirō—now a *Kaishintō* (Progressive Party) Diet member—was quick to note China's abandonment of its pro-Soviet Liu Shaoqi line following Stalin's death.[39]

In Washington, American officials drew different conclusions. Here it was recognised that, 'the death of Stalin will create many problems of adjustment in China–Soviet relations', and that their entente was vulnerable ideologically and nationalistically. Nevertheless, US diplomats felt that 'the Mao regime will continue its allegiance to the Soviet Union.'[40] Remarkably, in view of subsequent developments, State Department officers were worried that, 'the Soviet Union now may have a closer, more productive alliance with Communist China than we do with Japan.'[41]

Yoshida's China Thesis revived

The conclusion of the Korean War armistice in July 1953 had no immediate perceptible effect on American attitudes towards China. Japanese public opinion responded more positively, and in September the opposition Japan Socialist Party (JSP) put forward its view that a joint security guarantee should replace both the Sino-Soviet Alliance and Japan–US Security Treaty. Instead, Yoshida again despatched Ikeda Hayato to Washington the following month, where a compromise was reached on Japanese rearmament that resulted in the conclusion of the Mutual Security Assistance Agreement six months later.[42]

Meanwhile in Tokyo, John M. Allison (the new US Ambassador) complained to Washington that the Japanese government 'still basically holds to the theories of the durability of [the] communist capture of China and of the possibility of facilitating the alienation of Peking from Moscow.'[43] In fact, MOFA officials were in two minds on prospects for a Sino-Soviet rift. In late October, Chinese Vice-Premier Guo Moruo told a Japanese trade mission that people who regarded the 'peaceful' Sino-Soviet Alliance and the 'war-like' Japan–US Security Treaty as sharing the same character lacked understanding. Guo also hinted at the possibility of signing a Sino-Japanese non-aggression pact once Japan became a 'peace-loving and independent nation.'[44] The China Desk interpreted Guo's speech as a clear signal. In an internal report officers argued that as a subordinate system of the Cold War this two treaty structure was unlikely to disappear in the near future, but for the sake of peace within the region both Japan and China now sought 'independence' (*jiritsu*) from it.[45] The head of the section, Takeuchi Harumi, was not convinced and in talks with the Americans a few weeks later took a rather different line. He stated that he 'did not think that there was any chance at [the] present time or in [the] foreseeable future of Japan or any other nation weaning Communist China away from its intimate ties with Moscow.'[46] His superior, Wajima Eiji, lacked Takeuchi's confidence. While he basically concurred with the majority view within MOFA that: 'a general mutuality of interests in the Far East made continued Sino-Soviet ties a strong probability for some time to come', he also believed that if the Soviet Union resisted the emerging 'peaceful coexistence' strategy of China, 'the opportunity would present itself to approach Peking in an effort to widen whatever crack developed.' To support his argument, Wajima cited other diplomats who 'had considered significant the different manner in which the repatriation of Japanese had been handled during the past year by the Chinese Communist and Soviet governments'.[47] Moreover, they also 'detected certain differences in the approach taken by the Soviet and Chinese representatives at [the] Geneva [Peace Conference]' in April 1954.[48] Nevertheless, MOFA officials speculated that: 'Russia might have given Peking pretty much of a free hand in the Far East and might in particular have allotted her the leading role in implementing communist bloc strategy toward Japan.'[49] This 'division of labour' theory was later to prove very popular as a way of explaining away conflicting Sino-Soviet policies in East Asia without recognising the emerging rift.

To the Japanese, in bringing peace to Indochina, the Geneva Peace Conference held out the prospect of a new era of East Asian détente. Opinion polls reported strong support for trade and even diplomatic relations with China from all corners of Japanese society.[50] Perhaps it is not surprising then that Yoshida chose this moment to revive his China Thesis.[51]

In late May, Yoshida ordered both MOFA and his intelligence agency, the *Naikaku Chōsashitsu* (CRO), to undertake a high priority study of the immediate prospects for a Sino-Soviet rift and what steps Japan might take to hasten the process.[52] After ten weeks labour, this detailed report expressed 'many doubts about whether Sino-Soviet relations are [characterised by] brotherly love, but they are mutually beneficial.' Hence, it predicted that only 'when they are economically equal will it be possible [for China] to become "independent".' Finally, the authors concluded rather pessimistically that: 'Mao Zedong is totally committed to the Soviet Union...[and] as long as Mao Zedong is alive Communist China will not become a second Yugoslavia.'[53] Impatient for the report to appear, however, Yoshida returned to his old China Thesis and informed Ambassador Allison that:

> by a judicious combination of diplomatic persuasion and pressure exerted from the Western Pacific island chain Peking could be weaned away from its dependence upon and alliance with the Soviet Union and the stage might even be set for the unseating of the Chinese Communist Regime...The Japanese... because of their long experience on the mainland could play a valuable role in promoting these desirable developments by working to reconcile American and British policies towards China.[54]

It is noteworthy that Yoshida now advocated the use of diplomatic and strategic means to achieve what he had earlier felt trade alone could accomplish. A US Embassy official, however, dismissed this as a mere 'restate[ment of] the hoary thesis, so dear to Japanese "Old China Hands".'[55] A former Japanese diplomat, Hirasawa Kazushige confirmed this assessment, when he unfavourably contrasted:

> the older generation of Japanese diplomats and politicians...[with] younger informed Japanese bureaucrats [who] are aware that there is little possibility of splitting Communist China from the USSR in the next few years [because] Communist China's economy and its plans for industrial development are closely geared to the Soviet economy...[56]

The generation gap was not the only dimension to the split on Yoshida's China Thesis within the Japanese government. An 'interesting difference of opinion' was also said to exist 'within the Foreign Office between the Soviet and China Desks'. According to Niizeki Kinya, head of the former:

> All signs indicate that the Soviet Union and Communist China are currently bound by the closest ideological, economic and national security ties; there is nothing to indicate that any significant parting of the ways can be expected in the foreseeable future.[57]

Niizeki also predicted that a unilateral Russian initiative to normalise relations with Japan would occur 'before long'. The new man in charge of the China Desk, Ogawa Heishirō—a close ally of Ikeda Hayato—argued that, 'The possibility should not be ruled out, even within the next few years, of a real divergence of Sino-Soviet interests, in the economic field at least'. These differences in view should not be overdrawn, however. In the first place, Ogawa was the principal author of the pessimistic MOFA report commissioned by Yoshida on the Sino-Soviet rift. Second, Niizeki also conceded that in the long term, 'serious potential tensions undoubtedly exist and Russia, for her part, probably feels real concern about the growth of Chinese military and industrial power.'[58] Still, such intra-ministry differences were probably a factor in the decision by a gathering of Japanese diplomatic envoys in Europe that summer to improve the system for collecting information on Russia and China.[59]

Opinion among Diet members was similarly divided. In July, a multi-party Japanese delegation returned from a peace conference in Sweden via Moscow and Beijing. Nishimura Naomi, the *Jiyūtō* leader of the group, was surprised at the 'wide differences' he observed between the two Communist states. He suggested this might reflect differences between Europe and Asia, or the fact that, 'the Soviet Union is a grown-up country, whereas Communist China is a young one.'

Not every member of the team shared this view, however. Nakasone Yasuhiro (*Kaishintō*), for example, concluded that 'The Soviet Union and Communist China are one and undivided and have organised a strong united front.'[60] Nonetheless when Soviet Deputy Foreign Minister Vyshinsky told the mission that Moscow hoped to restore diplomatic relations with Japan even before a peace treaty was signed, the response from Foreign Minister Okazaki was surprisingly positive.[61] Reversing the logic of Yoshida's China Thesis, he argued that because of the Japan–ROC Peace Treaty it was 'much easier for Japan to normalise relations with the USSR than with Communist China'.[62] It was generally assumed at the time that this would have angered Yoshida.[63] Even more controversial, however, was the speech made to party leaders two weeks later by Ikeda Hayato, newly appointed *Jiyūtō* secretary-general, allegedly in response to the Chinese proposal for a non-aggression pact first raised by Guo Moruo the previous October. Describing US foreign policy as a failure and suggesting that Japan should instead follow Britain's diplomatic line, he reportedly asserted that: 'This is not the time for Japan to choose outright between West and East'. Ikeda felt that 'Japan's attitude should be characterized by greater flexibility in foreign and economic policy'.[64] Ambassador Allison reacted scathingly, advising Washington that 'Japan is for sale to the highest bidder'.[65] This proved to be overly alarmist as Ikeda's 'trial balloon' was soon deflated. A report by his party's FARC issued in late August specifically excluded early diplomatic recognition of Beijing.

The following month, Soviet Foreign Minister Molotov kept up the pressure by sending a letter to the Japanese government again proposing normalisation talks and emphasising Moscow's view that the Sino-Soviet Alliance was not aimed at Japan, being merely a defence against aggression. Tokyo responded by repeating its standing offer to conclude a peace treaty along the lines of the one the Soviets refused to sign at San Francisco, but perhaps for the first time, the conditions it attached did not include revision of the Sino-Soviet Alliance.[66]

The Sino-Soviet Joint Declaration and the fall of Yoshida

On 12 October 1954, Mao and Khrushchev signed a seven-part joint declaration reaffirming, inter alia, 'their readiness to take steps to normalize their relations with Japan.'[67] In itself this was nothing new, and Ikeda dismissed the approach as 'dogs barking in the distance (*inu no tōboe*)', but in Tokyo it now served as the locus for a Conservative–Socialist marriage of convenience to topple the premier. Shigemitsu Mamoru, president of *Nihon Kaishintō* (Progressive Party of Japan), one of the leaders in this plot, publicly interpreted the declaration as primarily aimed at the 'integration (*ittaika*) of Sino-Soviet relations'. The Japanese government saw it as part of a Communist 'peace offensive' designed to separate Japan from the US. In Rome on a diplomatic world tour, Yoshida repeated this message, graphically comparing the Joint Declaration to 'a thief insisting that all locked doors be removed.' Yet he continued to claim that 'The entente between Russia and China is far from complete'.[68] In every capital city that he visited Yoshida asserted that: 'Our aim must be to detach the Chinese from the Russians who were not natural friends.'[69] At official talks in London, he astonished his hosts, and 'surprised and embarrassed' the Japanese diplomats present, by proposing a new scheme to help realise his goal.[70] His plan called for 'some sort of organisation in Singapore' to which 'the US, UK, French, and the Japanese would send representatives to exchange information and discuss means for countering communist propaganda.' The British refused to support the scheme.[71] When Yoshida repeated the proposal in Washington, Dulles politely called it 'a very interesting suggestion'.[72] However, with the passage of the no-confidence vote that removed Yoshida from office in December, the scheme was quietly buried, until resurrected by Yoshida's protégé, Ikeda Hayato, in April 1963.[73]

Hatoyama's 'Window to the East'

The road to Bandung

Following the death of Stalin, the cease-fire in Korea, and the settlement in Indochina, the mid-1950s experienced a thawing in the Cold War: an era of 'peaceful coexistence' produced a 'loose bipolar' international system. In Asia and Africa this allowed scope for the emergence of the Non-Aligned Movement. In Tokyo, Hatoyama Ichirō—the second dominant figure in Japanese politics during the 1950s—rode to power on a wave of popular support from an electorate grown weary of Yoshida and enthused by the relaxation of international tensions. If the underlying theme of Yoshida's premiership had been his unsuccessful effort to temper America's harsh 'containment' strategy with his China Thesis, the big idea of Hatoyama's two-year term was to 'open a window to the East'. This meant improving relations with Moscow and Beijing to promote regional détente and to counter what was widely seen as Yoshida's cringing subservience to the US.

Hatoyama had called publicly for the 'prompt normalisation' of relations with Moscow as early as September 1952.[74] Shortly before taking office in mid-December 1954, he published an article in which he advocated a kind of 'bridge strategy', with Japan spanning the East–West divide while remaining firmly anchored to the US. Tokyo should start, he asserted, by 'confirming the termination of the state of war between the Soviet Union and Communist China on the one hand and Japan on the other.'[75] In his first press conference as premier, Hatoyama, troubled by the crisis in the Taiwan Straits then nearing its peak, provocatively 'stressed the priority of opening peaceful relations and economic intercourse with the Soviet Union and China.'[76] The following day, 11 December, his reputedly anti-Soviet foreign minister (and deputy prime minister) Shigemitsu

Mamoru felt the need to 'clarify' Hatoyama's comments, thereby establishing a reactive pattern between the two men that would persist until they left office two years later.[77] Shigemitsu confirmed that the new government intended to establish diplomatic relations with both Moscow and Beijing, but only 'on mutually acceptable terms with the free nations.'[78]

Hatoyama aroused further controversy a few days later, when in a radio broadcast he explicitly declared his support for a 'two Chinas' policy. He described both Beijing and Taipei as 'fine, independent regimes', and expressed bafflement as to 'why [political] relations could not be established with both.'[79] Shigemitsu again intervened, declaring the next day that while *de facto* recognition could not be withheld from Beijing and trade with the mainland should be promoted, Japan did not intend to sacrifice its diplomatic relations with Taipei.[80] Conscious that Hatoyama's actions would be making waves in Washington, the foreign minister then met with the US Ambassador in Tokyo and 'assured him that [Hatoyama's] statements were primarily designed for public consumption.' He convinced Allison that the government had 'no concrete plans for regularising relations with [the] communist bloc', and promised prior consultation with the US were it to consider any.[81]

In an officially inspired article on the Hatoyama Cabinet's Asian policies published at the beginning of January, the *Asahi Shimbun* reported:

> Opinion is divided on whether Communist China will break away (*rihan*) from the Soviet Union and choose the path of socialism in one country, but in the near future the likelihood of Titoisation in Communist China is slim. Thus, it would be premature to take into account this possibility...in working out a policy toward Communist China.[82]

That same day, Hatoyama proposed proceeding towards normalisation of relations with the USSR and PRC in stages, beginning with the removal of travel restrictions.[83] One week later, with a new sense of urgency, he reportedly set a target date of mid-March for signing peace treaties with both countries.[84]

Hatoyama's former aides later insisted that their leader had always differentiated between the two Communist states.[85] However, in January 1955 informed sources were suggesting otherwise.[86] In part, such confusion may reflect the inconsistency noted above. Definitions of the government's foreign policy goals under Hatoyama seemed to vary from person to person and sometimes from day to day. Contemporary commentators complained of Japan having 'eight foreign ministers' or 'three Foreign Offices'.[87]

Shigemitsu was not the only member of the newly formed *Nihon Minshutō* (Democratic Party of Japan) to be concerned about the potentially harmful consequences of Hatoyama's public statements for Japan's relations with the West. Secretary-General Kishi Nobusuke, also claimed that he had had to 'lecture' his premier at the beginning of February, 'warn[ing] him in the strongest possible terms against continuing to talk so freely about relations with the USSR and Communist China.'[88] In the event, the Democratic Party platform for the February general election modestly committed the leadership to 'endeavour to coordinate Japan's relations with Russia and China on the basis of maintaining friendly relations with the Free World.'[89]

Critics were quick to accuse the Democrats of timidity, but the changes that the Hatoyama Cabinet wrought in Japanese foreign policy were not confined to mere rhetoric. Shortly thereafter, the government decided to send a delegation to the inaugural Afro-Asian Conference at Bandung, Indonesia.[90] Equally significantly, in January Hatoyama had twice met privately with Andrei Domnitsky, trade representative at the unrecognised Soviet Mission in Tokyo. Acting on advice from his officials, Shigemitsu refused to follow suit lest it be taken as *de facto* recognition.[91] Like Shigemitsu himself, MOFA's first response to Hatoyama's 'window to the East' initiative, had been damage limitation. The ministry employed every available diplomatic channel to reassure its British and American counterparts that 'Hatoyama's recent pronouncements re Japan's future relations with Peiping and Moscow should be viewed as electioneering gambits'. They represented 'a political maneuver designed to conciliate China trade proponents in the Kansai area', diplomats claimed, not 'a radical alteration in Japan's policy towards the Communist bloc.'[92] Yet, evidence suggests that with its built-in tendency towards legalism, MOFA probably preferred the idea of dealing with Moscow to contacts with Beijing.[93]

Hatoyama's 'window to the East' policy also threw policy-makers in Washington on the defensive. Robert McClurkin (director of the Office of Northeast Asian Affairs) sounded fatalistic when he wrote in January 1955, that 'over the long run there was little the US could do to prevent [the] development of direct relations between Japan and Communist China'. He thought that the best the US could hope for was some kind of 'two Chinas' policy'.[94] Secretary of State Dulles strongly disagreed. He acknowledged that, 'the existence of US relations with [the] USSR precludes strong efforts [to] persuade Japan from establishing relations with [the] USSR.' However, Dulles was by no means ready to concede this point with respect to Beijing, arguing that 'Japan's establishment of relations [with] Communist China could have a dangerous effect on the rest of Asia and its will to resist communist expansion'.[95] At Dulles' behest, Ambassador Allison passed on this 'advice': the first in an escalating series of warnings.[96]

One week later, and just ten days after Hatoyama had received his second visit from Domnitsky, Shigemitsu announced Japan's decision to commence official normalisation negotiations with Moscow alone. This did not mean that the government had forgotten about China, however. To have done so in the midst of a general election campaign would have been tantamount to political suicide: public support for the establishment of official relations with Beijing was overwhelming.[97] Without exception, the major parties sought to present themselves to the electorate as 'China friendly'.[98] On the campaign trail, Shigemitsu and Hatoyama sounded equally positive regarding relations with China.[99] Whether this stance was sincere or not, such talk had the desired effect on the electorate. The February Lower House election was a triumph for Hatoyama: the Democrats nearly doubled their representation in the Diet, mainly at the expense of Yoshida's Liberals. Yet, the poll still left Hatoyama 50 seats short of an overall majority and hence dependent on a substantial ex-*Kaishintō* faction loyal to Shigemitsu. Hatoyama was forced to reconsider his plans to replace the foreign minister with Sugihara Arata. It was clear that Hatoyama was never going to be strong enough domestically to adopt a bold foreign policy.

Parleys at Bandung, Geneva, London and Washington

On 22 April, with the premier's prior approval, the symbolically important first official contact between the PRC and Japanese governments took place at the Bandung Conference. The leader of the Japanese delegation, Takasaki Tatsunosuke (director of the Economic Council Agency, forerunner of the Economic Planning Agency) held a secret one-and-a-half hour breakfast meeting with Chinese premier Zhou Enlai. Takasaki raised the issue of the Sino-Soviet and Japan–US treaties, but suggested that neither presented a 'special problem' (*betsudan mondai*). Zhou concurred, stating that 'Japan, the US and China should all be on good terms.'[100] Three days later, Hatoyama told the Diet that in order to avoid war, Japan and the Communist powers should 'respect each other's sovereignty and thereby...open normal diplomatic or economic relations to mutual advantage without propagandizing or trying to impose one's ideology on the other.' He made it clear however, that the former referred only to Moscow: improving trade relations was now the limit of his ambition vis-à-vis Beijing.[101]

In the meantime, the US sought to maintain the balance of power in East Asia in the face of the dramatic changes shaking the region. In February 1955, both Eisenhower and Dulles were convinced that serious disagreements between the Chinese and the new leadership in the Kremlin headed by Bulganin and Khrushchev had emerged over the Taiwan Straits question. However, in its dealings with Tokyo, the US continued to play down any indications of an emerging Sino-Soviet rift.[102] Continuing anxiety over improving Sino-Japanese relations and the threat this posed for its containment policy motivated such deception.[103] MOFA reportedly saw these developments within the Communist bloc in a rather different light. 'Ministry sources' predicted that the Soviet change of leadership would result in the 'relative influence of Red China, and in particular Mao Tse-tung…becom[ing] stronger in the Communist camp'. Others within the ministry, paying special attention to Molotov's statement that Taiwan was a 'part of China', felt that Moscow's first priority was 'to cement its ties with continental China'.[104]

On 6 April, Hatoyama attempted to reassure the Americans via his deputy cabinet secretary, that Japan was not about to join the Communist bloc, and nor did it deliberately set out to antagonise the American government.[105] Dulles' response was to reject a request from Shigemitsu to visit Washington to explain in person the new government's policy towards China and the Soviet Union.[106] Furthermore, the US government on 28 April formally reminded the Japanese government that:

> The United States continues to oppose political relations between Japan and Communist China such as a treaty opening relations or a non-aggression treaty. It therefore hopes that the negotiations with the Soviet Union will cause no impairment of Japan's relations with the Republic of China.[107]

Undaunted by these obvious displays of American displeasure, Hatoyama told the Diet in May, that although his government had ruled out diplomatic recognition, it 'might consider' exchanging consuls with China. Yet again the task of explaining the legal ramifications of the premier's pronouncement was left to MOFA. Within 24 hours, the ministry declared this 'impossible' pointing out that such an action would 'amount to *de facto* recognition.'[108] Hatoyama was not discouraged. In June, he told Noel Barber of the *Daily Mail*: 'I believe firmly in the possibility of two Chinas'.[109] He again expressed his 'personal' support for the opening of Japanese consulates in China, although he acknowledged that relations with the US would make this 'difficult'.[110]

Meanwhile, though publicly committed to correct diplomatic procedure, MOFA was by no means united in its opposition to Hatoyama's China policy. Ogawa Heishirō (head of the China Desk) described three distinct views as coexisting within the ministry at this time. One group favoured 'moving rapidly toward expanded economic and cultural relations with China, leading to diplomatic recognition in the not too distant future'. A second camp, reversing the order, instead proposed 'following the British course—establishing political relations and using them to promote trade'. This idea was in turn criticised by a third faction. It held that 'the British position can have little in common with Japan, particularly in view of the fact that the U.K. is not under the same military and economic pressure the way the Japanese would be as Peking grows stronger (sic).'[111] Realising the dangers this factionalism posed for Japanese foreign policy making on such a vital issue, an attempt was made to promote consensus by establishing an advisory body including outsiders: the China Problem

Investigation Committee (*Chūgoku Mondai Kentōkai*).[112] A week later, secret diplomatic contacts with the PRC began in Geneva.

This rather less public form of diplomatic exchange took place as the world's attention focused on the Four-Power Summit that was about to open. On 15 July, the Japanese Consul General in the Swiss city sent his Chinese counterpart a proposal for official talks concerning the repatriation of some 47,000 Japanese.[113] Ten days later, Premier Zhou Enlai replied that he would like to meet Hatoyama or his representative to discuss the normalisation of diplomatic relations.[114] After Hatoyama responded that his government would 'fully study' the Chinese invitation, Zhou moderated China's conditions for normalisation.[115] Although secret exchanges continued intermittently over the next few months, they made little progress.

A number of factors complicated the picture. On the Japanese side, merger talks between Hatoyama's *Minshutō* and Yoshida's *Jiyūtō* commenced in July. Their respective views on the Sino-Soviet Alliance remained far apart. That month, Hatoyama told the Diet: 'Russia's way of thinking has somewhat changed, thoughts of world domination and world conquest have abated completely.' He had equal 'confidence in the peaceful intentions of...Communist China...[which] has suppressed its desire for war with the Nationalist Government.'[116] The New Party Foundation Committee, however, did not share his optimism. It published a report in August claiming that, 'Although international Communism has been forced into a change of tactics by the rapid development of atomic science, world domination remains unaltered as its ultimate goal'.[117] More perceptive was Suma Yakichirō, now *Minshutō* secretary-general, who predicted that:

> Until 1957 when the first five-year-plan ends, I do not think that Sino-Soviet relations will be broken. After 1960, however, some form of crisis will probably occur...the Chinese bear a grudge against the Soviets, and until this racial feeling dies out, I do not think Sino-Soviet relations will be truly solid.[118]

In the intense manoeuvring that preceded the conservative parties' merger, the Japan–Soviet peace talks—which had opened in London on 1 June—became a political football. Yoshida continued to promote his China Thesis and to oppose relations with Moscow.[119] Shigemitsu intervened to block an early agreement with the Soviets that would have met Tokyo's minimum demands.[120] The foreign minister then embarked on his delayed visit to Washington in late August. While Dulles praised Japan's handling of the normalisation negotiations with Moscow, he stated that Beijing's policies did not entitle it to recognition. Shigemitsu in turn stressed the domestic Communist threat Japan faced and raised the issue of revising the Security Treaty.[121] Dulles simply dismissed such hopes as 'premature' and Shigemitsu returned home empty-handed.[122]

Since 1 August, the Americans had in fact been engaged in their own ambassadorial talks with the Chinese Communists in Geneva. Not surprisingly, this prompted intense speculation in Japan that a major shift in Washington's China policy was in the offing.[123] On 3 October, Ogawa Heishirō made an extraordinary request of an American Embassy official: 'if the United States is planning to recognize Red China…[would it] allow Japan to take the lead in this role.'[124] The Americans moved quickly to quash any such thoughts. Two days later, on a visit to Japan to discuss an economic development plan for Asia, Under-Secretary of State Herbert Hoover Jr, met with Hatoyama. Hoover had no objections to make when told that Tokyo's negotiations with Moscow 'would be settled soon', since Japan would be content simply with the 'return [of] Habomai and Shikotan without conditions'. China was a different matter. Hoover stressed to Hatoyama that 'US public opinion [was] very sensitive on [the] question [of] Communist China and that any indication Japan intended [to] enter into relations with [the] mainland government would create [an] unfavorable reaction.' Hatoyama could do little more than reassure Hoover on this point.[125]

The China issue was too important in Japanese politics for such approaches to resolve anything. The following month, Ogawa attended a secret four-day conference in Bangkok, organised by MOFA for working level officials in the region to discuss the China problem. Although details remain classified, the tenor of the conference can be gauged by the participants' startling prediction that Beijing would be in the UN by the spring of 1957, and that Japan would extend recognition the same year.[126] An intelligence study produced soon after by MOFA's Research Section drew on the findings of this conference. It argued that Communist China, having abandoned its 'adventurous expansionism' of the Korean War period, was winning the battle for 'hearts and minds' across the Taiwan Straits. The mainland Chinese had the 'utmost trust and confidence' in their government, whereas, according to Ogawa, 'the National Government of China can not exist under the present leadership more than two years longer.'[127]

Coming on top of visits to China by four separate Japanese political delegations during the previous three months, the leadership in Washington reacted to this study by issuing a more explicit warning.[128] A six-point 'Oral Statement' was presented to Ambassador Iguchi Sadao on 11 November. It is worth quoting at length:

> 1). The combination of unrestricted informal contacts with Communist China and North Korea can only have [the] effect of building up strong domestic pressures over which [the] Japanese Government may have little control.
> 2). [The] present friendly posture of [the] Communist Chinese regime was designed to lull free nations into a relaxation of pressures without the

> abandonment of subversion and aggression and with no renunciation of [the] use of force on [the] part [of the] Communist Chinese.
> 3). The Sino-Soviet Treaty of 1950 is perhaps the most illuminating documentary evidence of Peking's true attitude toward its neighbors and the world at large.
> 4). Japanese rapprochement with [the] Communist China regime or with North Korea will inevitably affect adversely trade relations with [the] ROK, Taiwan and other free nations and can not help but lead public opinion in [the] US to question [the] reliability of Japan as [a] member [of the] free world.
> 5). [The] US Government...believes that until Communist China indicates by [its] actions a sincere desire not to settle disputes by force, the modification of present trade controls constitutes a risk to [the] security of [the] US, Japan and other free nations.
> 6). The US Government has received indications that possibly [the] Japanese Government believes that [the] US is considering recognition of the Chinese Communists. This is completely erroneous...In [the] Ambassador level talks at Geneva [the] US effort has been directed to influencing the Communist Chinese in keeping with [the]...policy of conserving and exploiting all possible pressures...No step toward recognition of Communist China or its seating in [the] UN has been implied.[129]

Obviously stung by the American intervention, Foreign Minister Shigemitsu 'candidly observed [that] for geographical and historical reasons, it is impossible for Japan to maintain as aloof and incompromising (sic) a posture toward Communist China as [the] US may think desirable.'[130] Nonetheless, he did not ignore the implications behind the 'oral statement'. The following week, Shigemitsu warned the new LDP Cabinet that the Chinese 'aim at building up a fait accompli in establishing a closer relationship between [the] two nations on [the] non-governmental level'. Hence, he recommended that the Japanese government 'should take some measures to control this undesirable trend.'[131]

The US was not the only source of external pressure that Japan had to contend with; in mid-December 1955 events at the UN served to further expose Tokyo's delicate international position. Japan's ambitions to join the world body were again frustrated by a Soviet veto, although significantly most Japanese blamed Taipei for stubbornly blocking Outer Mongolia's admission and thereby unravelling a carefully crafted East–West package deal. Hence, when the Japan–Soviet negotiations resumed in London on 17 January 1956 (after a four-month break) agreement was quickly reached on the UN question, as well as all other outstanding issues except for the territorial dispute over the Kurile Islands. The talks were then postponed, allowing the chief Soviet delegate, Ambassador Yakov

Malik, to attend the Twentieth Congress of the CPSU in Moscow. It was at this historic meeting that Khrushchev made his famous 'secret speech' denouncing the crimes of Josef Stalin, which would later be cited by the Chinese as the starting point for their rift with the Soviets. MOFA officials, however, failed to anticipate the deeper significance of these events. On the eve of the conference, the Asian Affairs Bureau produced a top-secret report. It acknowledged that China was 'different from the East European satellite countries...[since] being on the path to Great Power status encouraged China's very strong sense of nation.' Moreover China's earlier 'dissatisfaction with the Soviet Union', especially over the route to economic construction, was said to have led to a change in the bilateral balance of power. Since the October 1954 Joint Declaration, 'the Soviet Union appeared to appease Communist China on many points.' However, it also recognised that 'Sino-Soviet relations have to date been extremely close (*kiwamete missetsu*)...[and] Communist China's level of dependence on the Soviet Union remains very high'.[132] A follow-up study simply concluded that Khrushchev's speech would not cause Moscow to change its policy towards the negotiations with Japan. Indeed a mere 12 days after the resumption of the Japan–Soviet talks on 8 March, they were again suspended, this time indefinitely.[133]

On 30 January 1956, while plenipotentiaries Matsumoto Shunichi and Malik were still haggling in London, Chinese Premier Zhou Enlai took a hand. Disappointed by the lack of progress in the secret Sino-Japanese exchanges in Geneva, he publicly referred to the three Chinese proposals for talks on normalisation made since June 1955, and repeated the offer. Speaking in the Diet later that same day, Foreign Minister Shigemitsu denied having received any formal overtures from Beijing and rejected Zhou's latest invitation. The Chinese Foreign Ministry promptly published all of the relevant documentation, forcing Shigemitsu into an embarrassing public retraction. Yet, he stubbornly maintained that 'the time is not yet ripe' for formal talks like those with the Russians.[134]

Despite American misgivings and the best efforts of Shigemitsu to preserve the legal distinction between establishing diplomatic relations with the two Communist powers, members of the Japanese government were still toying with the idea of opening normalisation talks with a reinvigorated PRC. They had been distracted for over a year by the intermittent negotiations with Moscow, but with only a seemingly small territorial compromise needed to bring this frustrating process to a successful conclusion, the opportunity to move ahead with Beijing was now looming. Dulles decided that only his personal intervention could save the situation for US interests.

The Dulles intervention

Assurances from both governments notwithstanding, there remained a distinct lack of mutual trust between Japanese and Americans on the China issue. Tokyo feared a pre-emptive Sino-American rapprochement.[135] Washington was equally concerned about the activities of Japanese politicians and diplomats vis-à-vis their mainland neighbour.[136] A State Department intelligence report, dated 29 February 1956, concluded that:

> The Foreign Ministry evidently regards [the] mainland of China as a potentially promising field for diplomatic activity; the Ministry feels assurance in its competence on Chinese affairs and is anxious to utilize it for purposes of enhancing Japan's security, diplomatic prestige and economic stability.[137]

When the number of Japanese visiting China increased four-fold during 1955, Washington proposed a tightening of Japanese passport controls.[138] Foreign Minister Shigemitsu obliged in late March, but differences with the Justice Ministry apparently rendered the scheme 'inoperable'.[139]

By this time, however, Dulles had already decided to make a personal visit to Tokyo. Upon arrival on 18 March, he assured Shigemitsu that, '[the] rejection of Stalinism at [the] Twentieth Party Congress...was a tactical one, Soviet objectives remained [the] same.' He then turned his attention to 'expansionist' China, and drew a 'moral' distinction between recognising the fact of her existence and extending diplomatic recognition. Dulles dismissed Yoshida's China Thesis as too risky.[140] The following day, however, when Hatoyama joined the discussions, Dulles broached the China issue in unusually conciliatory terms. 'Japan has had greater experience than we in dealing with the Chinese', he conceded, 'and we would be most happy to cooperate in determining the best policy with which to cope with China.' Hatoyama responded with the usual pledge of loyalty.[141] Dulles was touched. He later told a colleague that for the first time he felt Japan was becoming a true ally. Unfortunately for Shigemitsu, the afterglow was soon extinguished as his arch rival, Fisheries Minister Kōno Ichirō, launched his own diplomatic initiative.

The following day, the stalemated Japan–Soviet talks were broken off in London, and 24 hours later Radio Moscow responded by announcing the imposition of severe restrictions on the Japanese fish catch in northern waters. Kōno flew to Moscow at the end of April and an interim agreement was soon reached, but only on condition that the normalisation talks would resume before 31 July. Kōno allegedly orchestrated the whole episode.[142]

This linkage disturbed Dulles sufficiently for him to issue—the very next day—his first veiled public warning on the Japan–Soviet negotiations. 'Anything which will restore a juridical state of peace between those countries is to be desired as long as it is done on terms consistent with the sovereignty and dignity of Japan', he stated.[143] Kōno responded by flying on to Washington, where he informed Dulles that, 'Bulganin had suggested resumption of Japan–Soviet relations on the

Adenauer formula, [normalising relations without a territorial settlement] and that this course [of] action appeared inevitable to the Japanese.' Dulles did not object, but instead pointed to 'some evidence that internal changes in [the] Soviet Union indicate a greater degree of nationalism and a lesser degree of emphasis upon international communism.' Kōno concurred.[144]

Shigemitsu complained bitterly at the apparent success of his great rival.[145] He had consistently supported the US line, but, Shigemitsu warned the Americans, 'continuing rumors in Japan of a shift in US policy toward Communist China following the November [presidential] election' was undermining his stand against recognising Beijing.[146] The Asian Affairs Bureau was predicting that sooner or later Washington would drop its opposition to Japan's policy of 'engagement' with China. It also expected Sino-Soviet relations to remain 'close' (*kinmitsu-na kankei*) for a considerable time.[147] Yet, within Japan's diplomatic corps various shades of opinion on these issues coexisted. In late May, Takeuchi Harumi (chief of the North America Desk) told US Embassy officials that rapid Japan–Soviet normalisation was now 'all but inevitable'. He also described the 'tremendous popular pressure for normalization of relations with Peking' which could be expected to follow. Takeuchi then rashly inquired of his American colleagues: 'How would the US react if Japan were to send a mission to Peking to negotiate the establishment of diplomatic relations?' He was told that it would 'probably be more violent than he could even imagine'.[148] Nevertheless, contemplating a temporary increase in US criticism and even the breaking off of diplomatic relations by Taipei with equanimity, the China Desk, on 21 August, recommended the public opening of inter-governmental contacts with Beijing, leading to official diplomatic relations. Section chiefs on the China Problem Investigation Committee soon vetoed this proposal, however, concluding that, 'It is better for Japan to be a partner or advisor rather than an object of America's Asian policy.'[149]

On 31 July, the Japan–Soviet peace talks had reopened as promised. After much argument within cabinet, Shigemitsu himself led the Japanese delegation to Moscow. He failed to persuade the Russians to improve on their 'two island' (Shikotan and the Habomai islets) offer, but determined to sign a formal peace treaty, the foreign minister surprised many observers by suddenly agreeing to the Soviet terms. The next day, however, the Japanese cabinet overrode Shigemitsu's provisional acceptance and again the talks were broken off.[150]

Shigemitsu then met Dulles in London, who tried to convince the foreign minister that his approach was misguided. Under the terms of the San Francisco Peace Treaty, Dulles posited a potential legal threat to Japan's 'residual sovereignty' over Okinawa should it cede the disputed Kurile Islands to Moscow.[151] Despite the tenor of this intervention, Dulles later asserted that he was merely attempting to strengthen Tokyo's bargaining position. In a sense this was true, but the overwhelming Japanese popular reaction to the so-called 'Dulles threat' remained one of outrage.[152] Hatoyama now resolved to go to Moscow to finalise the process himself. He proposed simply to accept the 'Adenauer formula' adopted for the Bonn–Moscow normalisation, leaving territorial problems to be sorted out by his successor.

Yoshida meanwhile led the fight to prevent this outcome, working in part through the FARC. His motivation for doing so was not just that he saw a future Soviet Embassy in Tokyo 'serv[ing] as the Communist headquarters in Japan', but also that he still believed China to be the key to breaking the Sino-Soviet Alliance.[153] A variety of influential Japanese continued to share Yoshida's faith in a forthcoming rift, including Nakasone Yasuhiro, a member of the Kōno faction, who wrote that China's 'turn to Titoism…[wa]s only a matter of time.'[154] This view was contradicted by Ogawa Heishirō (head of the China Desk), who, reversing his earlier stance, now 'believe[d] the two work[ed] in almost complete harmony.' He admitted, however, that not all of his subordinates agreed with him.[155]

As the Moscow talks entered their end game, the Americans were well aware of this renewed Japanese interest in Yoshida's China Thesis.[156] A major Office of Intelligence and Research (OIR) study completed on 12 September, noted that:

> there is a solid conviction in Japanese official and popular thought based upon [the] view that communism is merely a transitory phase in China's long history, that fundamental differences between Peking and Moscow exist and can be *exploited* to Japan's advantage.[157]

In his submission to the report, Ambassador Allison in Tokyo had written of 'the Sov[i]et Union and Communist Chinese *competing with each other* and with us for influence in Japan'.[158] In its final version, however, the OIR report rejected his prescient view. Instead, its authors asserted that,

> Even apart from [the] bonds of international communism, Peking and Moscow share a common aim in their policies toward Tokyo; to neutralize and weaken Japan as a military threat, primarily by drawing Japan away from alignment with [the] US.[159]

Ambassador Allison responded by calling for 'a fresh start with Japan', and warned that, 'Japan is beginning...to reappraise her whole relationship with [the] US, and to consider the advantages to be gained by following a more detached role in future.' In part, he attributed this trend to 'the partial breakup of polarized world tensions into more complex patterns'. More importantly, Allison believed that, 'Japan feels taken for granted and deeply resents it.' In evidence, he cited a pungent comment by Ogawa: 'We are not a partner, but merely an object of your China policy'.[160]

To sum up, in the wake of Khrushchev's 'secret speech' many Japanese were looking forward to dealing with their Communist neighbours on a one-to-one basis. Dulles' hard-line tactics seemed to have backfired, but as time would show, for Tokyo an opportunity only half-grasped can be an opportunity lost.

Resolution and resignation

Meanwhile conversations between Chinese leaders and Japanese visitors showed that Beijing had still not given up totally on hopes for early normalisation.[161] On 14 October, Zhou Enlai invited Hatoyama to visit Beijing on his way home from the Moscow peace talks.[162] This was a blatant attempt to piggy-back on the impending Japan–Soviet normalisation. Hatoyama ignored the offer, but still expressed a wish to mediate between the 'two Chinas'.

Hatoyama in fact had expended the little political capital he still possessed to win cabinet backing for a last bid to normalise relations with the Soviet Union. After weeks of bitter party infighting in which he eventually had to promise to resign the premiership, Hatoyama finally arrived in Moscow on 13 October 1956. Using Kōno as the main negotiator, a joint declaration normalising relations on the 'Adenauer formula' was signed after just four days of talks.[163] At the time most Japanese, including Hatoyama, saw it as a *precursor* to Sino-Japanese normalisation, implying a general inability to recognise Moscow's unilateral action as indicative of early problems in the Sino-Soviet relationship.[164] Deputy Cabinet Secretary Matsumoto Takizō, however, noted on his return from Moscow how 'Bulganin had not pressed Hatoyama to accept the Chinese Communist invitation to return by way of Peking'. Yet Matsumoto found little support for his suspicions about Russian attitudes. When, on 25 October, he told visiting Assistant Secretary of State for Far Eastern Affairs Walter Robertson that he 'suspected there was jealousy between Moscow and Peking', the American was dismissive.[165]

Ignoring the crisis then engulfing Warsaw, two days earlier Foreign Minister Shigemitsu had announced that Japan intended next to normalise relations with Poland. Moreover, although recognising 'it will be extremely difficult', he added that, 'Japan should consider resuming relations with Communist China'.[166] For the Eisenhower Administration, this remained the primary concern.[167] When Robertson asked Hatoyama three days later about the possible development of new relationships with China, 'Mr Kono interrupted to say no emphatically and asserted that Japan would not change its policy without consulting Mr Dulles.'[168] Strangely, Kōno and Shigemitsu seemed to have exchanged roles.

Yoshida did not undergo any such conversion. He even threatened to quit the LDP if it supported ratification of the Japan–Soviet Joint Declaration. Ultimately he stayed, but when the agreement received Diet approval at the end of November, members of the Yoshida faction were conspicuous by their absence. According to Satō Eisaku, one of his deputies, 'Yoshida and his colleagues believed that eventually relations would have to be normalized with Peking, [but] they would never think of acting independently or contrary to [the] wishes of [the] US in this regard.'[169] Japan would have to await the emergence of a more enlightened policy in Washington.

Some Japanese diplomats lacked Yoshida's patience. In late November, at the regular monthly meeting between 'middle-level' MOFA officials and US Embassy representatives, Takeuchi Harumi spoke out against Japanese policy being 'fettered by the unseen hand' of the US when pursuing its 'natural' and 'essential' goal of normalised relations with Communist China. He complained that 'American interference...is deeply resented' and that a 'two Chinas' policy should take care of US strategic concerns. Warning that, 'normalization of relations with Peking could not be postponed indefinitely', Takeuchi again posed the question: 'What would US reactions be...if Japan were to go ahead and normalize relations with Peking on her own?' The American response failed to impress the Japanese. All present 'agreed with China expert Ogawa that a change in US policy toward China and [the] admission of Communist China to [the] UN were "only a matter of time".'[170]

Right up until the day he left office in December 1956, Hatoyama continued to speak of his 'desire [for] normal relations with the Peking government.'[171] That month he even sent messages to Beijing and Taipei proposing informal talks between Zhou Enlai and Chiang Kai-shek.[172] However, it was nothing more than an empty gesture, for Hatoyama was by this time the lamest of lame ducks.[173] Nevertheless, expectations were high that his successor would complete the process.

The Ishibashi interlude

That a man of Ishibashi Tanzan's genuinely Liberal and 'pan-Asianist' persuasions should have made it to the top of the LDP's greasy pole speaks volumes for the pluralism of Japanese politics before the stultifying '1955 System' became entrenched. It also indicates the discomfiture still widely felt at Japan's role in the US security structure. When this former journalist and trade minister narrowly defeated Kishi Nobusuke in the LDP presidential election in December 1956, many assumed that he would move rapidly towards at least *de facto* recognition of the PRC.[174]

At its inaugural meeting on Christmas Day 1956, the new cabinet did in fact agree to allow the PRC to open a permanent trade mission in Tokyo. Nevertheless, Ishibashi also recognised that 'The restoration of relations with China will be very hard for the time being', given the widely divergent views held within the ruling party on the issue.[175] Yoshida reportedly lent his support, with Cabinet Secretary Ishida Hirohide passing on Yoshida's message that 'China and Russia say their alliance is as tight as a knot, but they are bound sooner or later to split up.' Although welcoming this as 'a good piece of advice, an insight becoming a diplomat of Yoshida's maturity', Ishibashi was unable to use Yoshida's support to his advantage.[176] In an effort to preserve party unity, Ishibashi was forced to give the foreign minister's portfolio to Kishi Nobusuke, a long-time opponent of Yoshida, who represented a strong faction of the LDP that was closely associated with Nationalist China.

Opposition to Ishibashi's policies was not confined to the LDP. In January 1957, a conference of Japanese ambassadors based in the Asia–Pacific region concluded that Tokyo should avoid establishing closer relations with the PRC.[177] Moreover, American disappointment at Ishibashi's elevation was manifest, for here was a Japanese leader that they might not be able to control. Even before Ishibashi's cabinet was announced, Assistant Secretary of State Walter Robertson was back in Tokyo browbeating the new LDP president. Subjected to the usual diatribe against 'international communism', Ishibashi merely responded with the standard assurances of Japanese loyalty.[178] Robertson was not persuaded and concluded that the 'era of more or less automatic Japanese compliance with American wishes on China was over'.[179] One can only speculate as to whether Ishibashi would have overcome internal and external resistance had ill health not forced him to resign after just 65 days in office.

Kishi and the disguised strategic rift

Kishi's foreign policy agenda

While still serving as acting prime minister, Kishi had declared in his policy address to the Diet that, 'relations with the Communist countries...will be handled...in accordance with the best interests of Japan.' This was qualified by his assertion that, 'cooperation with the Free World should be the basic principle of Japanese foreign policy.'[180] Nonetheless Kishi continued to promote a more independent foreign policy line after his confirmation as premier, although, as was soon apparent, his definition of 'independent' differed markedly from that of Ishibashi. For Kishi, independence entailed accelerated rearmament and a less paternalistic security treaty for Japan rather than attempting to balance the American relationship with Japan's desire for strengthened ties with its Communist neighbours.

In April 1957, during a meeting with the newly appointed US ambassador, Douglas MacArthur II, Kishi read from a discussion paper, which concluded bluntly:

> many Japanese have come to believe that [the] foreign policy of [the] US is ultimately a policy of war aiming at the overthrow by force of the Communist bloc, and that Japanese–American cooperation under [the] existing formula amounts to subjugation [of] their country to US policies that may lead...to war.[181]

Kishi quickly pointed out that he personally did not share such views, but he was using them to support his contention that the 'Security Treaty arrangements should be reviewed'. As premier, Kishi soon earned MacArthur's 'seal of approval'.[182] The following month, the Americans committed themselves to the total withdrawal of their remaining ground troops from Japan. In return, Kishi agreed to draw up a 'Basic Policy for National Defence' and the 'First Defence Build-up Plan', which envisaged a continuing, albeit slowly diminishing, dependence on US military protection.[183]

Kishi also pleased Washington by dismissing the idea of normalising diplomatic relations with Beijing in the near future. Although Kishi saw 'no reason why we should not make friends with communist states overseas' and welcomed 'peaceful coexistence' with them, he excluded China, which he continued to label an 'aggressor'.[184] More controversially, during his unprecedented visit to Taipei in early June, Kishi reportedly told a friendly Chiang Kai-shek that he would welcome the Nationalists' recovery of the mainland. He also warned that because of the difference in the way ordinary Japanese felt about their two Communist neighbours 'Communist infiltration from Communist China rather than from the Soviet Union was more to be feared.'[185] Kishi clearly lacked his predecessor's affinity with mainland China.

A solid Sino-Soviet Alliance?

The first public hint of unilateralism regarding China's Japan policy came in April 1957. In response to a proposal from JSP Secretary-General Asanuma that a four-power collective security system replace the two major hostile alliances in Northeast Asia, Mao Zedong reportedly said:

> I wish gradually to change the USSR–China Treaty of Friendship and Alliance into a treaty centered on economic and cultural friendship, eliminating those parts of the treaty concerning military agreements. This is already being done in fact, since Soviet naval forces are no longer stationed in Port Arthur even though they have the treaty right to do so.[186]

Rather than lauding this as a potential first crack in the 'Communist monolith', however, conservative Japanese commentators dismissed it as a Soviet plot. For example, Suma Yakichirō, now a senior member of the FARC, felt it was 'no mere coincidence' that Marshal Kliment Voroshilov of the Soviet Presidium was in Beijing for the occasion.[187] The *Japan Times* was more blunt, attacking the Socialists for 'showing subservience to plans which have originated in the first instance from Moscow.'[188] These conservative suspicions were seemingly confirmed two months later when Nikita Khrushchev, in an interview with the editor of *Asahi Shimbun*, 'offered to urge the Chinese to revise [the Sino-Soviet] treaty in return for Japan's recognition [of the] PRC and North Korea and development of trade with them.'[189]

On 15 October 1957, Japan's recently retired ambassador to Washington, Tani Masayuki, offered a slight corrective to this trend. Somewhat surprisingly he predicted that,

> It is unthinkable that a revolt will not break out in Communist China, when one broke out in Poland and Hungary...and if the Soviet Union intervenes, the Chinese people will surely oppose the intervention. The Soviet Union will not be able to suppress the revolt.[190]

Whether this was his personal assessment or whether such views were more widely held within MOFA at this time is unclear, but the Eisenhower Administration definitely did not share them.[191] Nor had Kishi given any indication that he held similar views. During his June visit to Washington, neither side had directly broached the subject of Sino-Soviet relations. Kishi seemed more concerned with preventing a rift developing with his hosts than in provoking one between the Communists:

> The Soviet Union, Communist China and JCP...tried at first to communize Japan. They have failed in that, and now they are trying to alienate Japan from [the] US. If even a small crack is opened between Japan and [the] US, [the] communists will drive a wedge into it. We must endeavour to prevent any such crack from being opened.[192]

Kishi also warned of 'a rising tide of nationalism...in Japan, which insists upon Japan's independence.' Hence, there were aspects of the Security Treaty that he wished 'to see reconsidered.' The Americans did no more than agree to establish a joint-committee on security problems to study the matter.[193]

Asked about prospects for a Sino-Soviet split at a Los Angeles press conference on his way home, Kishi's reply was cautiously optimistic: 'China is a country with a long history. I do not think that it will act together with the Soviet Union forever. However, from current Communist thinking, I do not think that they will split soon.'[194] In San Francisco the following day, Dulles conceded that there were 'basic power rivalries between Russia and China in Asia', but in his view

Yoshida's China Thesis remained misguided. Dulles contended that even if both states ceased to be allies, their Communist ideology would continue to pose a threat to US interests. He was also concerned that a softer line towards China might lead inevitably via a kind of 'domino effect' to the loss of Japan: a fear shared by President Eisenhower.[195]

On his return home, Kishi undertook a major cabinet reshuffle. The new foreign minister, Fujiyama Aiichirō, a business leader and old friend, was quick to make his mark, declaring on 8 August:

> the nucleus of Japanese diplomacy will be close cooperation with the US and other Free World countries on an equal footing. [But a]s a member of the Asian family, Japan must also maintain close and sympathetic ties with the other Asian nations.[196]

More controversially, he expressed the belief that, 'Japan should assume the role of a "bridge" between the two ideologies' dividing the international community.[197] In so saying, he was somewhat ahead of Japanese public opinion and indeed MOFA.[198] When the ministry announced the 'three basic principles' of Japan's foreign policy in its first 'Blue Book' at the end of September, Fujiyama's 'bridge' idea was replaced by 'support for the UN'.[199]

Meanwhile, that autumn, a series of events seemed to tilt the global strategic balance in Communism's favour. August saw the first successful test of a Soviet intercontinental ballistic missile overfly Japan. The even more dramatic launch of the world's first artificial satellite, *Sputnik*, followed just two months later. A secret 'New Defence Technical Accord', wherein Moscow agreed to help Beijing to develop its own nuclear weapons, was also signed.[200] Mao Zedong, on his first visit to Moscow since the signing of the 1950 alliance, summed up the euphoric mood by declaring that 'the East wind has prevailed over the West wind.'[201] In retrospect, however, this represented the high water mark for the alliance. The overall tenor of the Moscow Conference of Communist Parties—the purpose of Mao's visit—was one of solidarity, but it also witnessed the first open foreign policy dispute between the CCP and CPSU. On this occasion, Mao seemed to get his way: Khrushchev conceded that the non-peaceful road to Socialism was also valid and that the US was the centre of world imperialism.[202]

These recent developments in the Communist bloc coincided with the Kishi cabinet proposing a major expansion in the funding and personnel of its intelligence arm, the CRO.[203] They were also high on the agenda for the fourth meeting of the Japan–US Committee on Security scheduled for 19 December.[204] Foreign Minister Fujiyama opened the discussion by declaring that, in Tokyo, 'Communist China–Soviet ties are viewed as very close.' He particularly emphasised their military ties, describing China as 'a *de facto* member of the

Warsaw Treaty', and noted the Soviet agreement to cooperate in developing a Chinese nuclear weapon.[205] Ambassador MacArthur no doubt was pleased with this apparently firm Japanese view and responded by summarising a State Department assessment that:

> [the] solidarity [of the] Peiping–Moscow alliance [has been] strikingly demonstrated during [the] year. Any belief in [the] existence [of] serious Soviet–ChiCom differences and [the] possibility of [a] rift in the foreseeable future [has been] discredited by [the]...Moscow meetings in November.[206]

However, not content simply to debate the existing state of relations, Fujiyama expressed interest in 'further discussion of ways and means to divide [the] ChiComs and USSR.' His attempt to revive Yoshida's China Thesis merely angered MacArthur.[207] In short, the Japanese and American governments still agreed in their basic assessment of the situation in the Communist bloc, but differed over how best to proceed.

There was some suggestion of Japan following through on Fujiyama's policy proposal in hints of a substantive MOFA initiative to open ambassadorial talks with Beijing around this time, but nothing came of it.[208] Instead, Kishi resisted Chinese and domestic pressures to grant *de facto* recognition to Beijing as part of a fourth unofficial trade agreement, resulting in the PRC imposing virtually a total embargo on contacts with Japan in early May 1958.

On 13 May, one week before a general election, Japan launched a major foreign policy initiative that called on the world's three existing nuclear powers—the US, UK and USSR—to cease all nuclear testing, production and stockpiling.[209] London and Washington rejected Tokyo's proposal outright. The positive Soviet reaction implied a lack of commitment to Chinese acquisition of an independent deterrent, but speculation instead centred on differing Sino-Soviet economic policies towards Japan. Similarly, MOFA officials interpreted Beijing's latest tirade against Yugoslavia as a warning to Chinese revisionists rather than Soviet ones.[210]

The LDP comfortably won its first general election, with, it has been suggested, a little help from the CIA.[211] In his victory press conference Kishi declared that the government 'would not change [its] policy of non-recognition [of the] ChiComs, but would seek to expand trade with them.'[212] The majority of Japanese favoured a more balanced foreign policy.[213] That the government appeared willing to ignore this fact is evident from Fujiyama's assurance to Ambassador MacArthur that:

> [The b]asic position of [the] Japanese Government is that some form of long term security ties with [the] US are, under present circumstances, essential

> given [the] huge power of [the] Sino-Soviet bloc. This was Kishi's view last year and there has been no change since then.[214]

However, speculation was rife in Tokyo—not least amongst cabinet ministers—that the US hard line against China was softening and Japan might find itself isolated.[215] At a conference of Japanese ambassadors and senior officials on 10 July, Asakai Kōichirō (ambassador to Washington) categorically rejected such a possibility.[216] When he conveyed these fears to Dulles on 1 August, the secretary of state also dismissed any such suggestion.[217] Nevertheless, in an effort to dissuade the Japanese from approaching Beijing, a detailed explanation of US non-recognition policy was passed to the Japanese Embassy on 6 August. It stressed Washington's view that: 'The Chinese Communists are part of the international communist movement.'[218]

Kishi still hoped for a twin-track strategy: revising the security relationship with the US while re-establishing contact with Beijing. On 1 August, he told MacArthur that Japan favoured a completely new security treaty and, in the meantime, JSP Diet member Sata Tadataka was asked to discover China's price for reopening talks.[219] Unfortunately for Kishi, these foreign policy goals were to prove mutually exclusive.

Renewed tension in the Taiwan Straits

When Mao provoked the second Taiwan Straits Crisis on 23 August, he was probably aiming to derail Khrushchev's 'peaceful coexistence' policy and reveal the feebleness of Washington's commitment to its East Asian allies.[220] Ironically, he merely succeeded in exposing the limitations of Moscow's strategic support for Beijing.[221] War was narrowly averted, but the Sino-Soviet Alliance had been dealt a fatal blow. In this context, Japan–US Security Treaty revision took on a whole new meaning. In early September, fear of being dragged into a Sino-American war prompted the FARC to express reservations for the first time about the desirability of a revision in the near future. Hence it recommended to Fujiyama that he not discuss the matter on his forthcoming mission to the US.[222] Yoshida Shigeru was apparently the force behind these moves. According to Fujiyama, the former premier was still busily promoting his China Thesis, even suggesting to the foreign minister that a consulate general be opened in Shanghai.[223] Publicly, however, Yoshida warned that, 'The sinister and unpredictable operations of the Moscow–Peking Axis are a constant menace to the free world.'[224] Yoshida's determination to pursue his China Thesis seemed to hinge on his conviction that the Americans did not understand the Chinese.[225] What he and others in the LDP anti-mainstream feared was the realisation of Dulles' long-standing ambition to incorporate Japan into an integrated American-led multilateral East Asian alliance system via a revised treaty.[226]

Meeting Fujiyama in New York on 11 September 1958, Dulles took the lead, telling his guest that the Soviets were probably responsible for the Chinese aggression in the Taiwan Straits. Moreover, he added, that with Soviet nuclear threats to contend with, 'there is no alternative for the free non-communist nations but to unite their strength.'[227] Later that day, they announced a shared desire to revise the existing Security Treaty. During their second day of talks, however, Fujiyama repeated his suggestion that, 'opening windows in [the] iron curtain upon [the] free world would hasten native opposition to Communist dictatorships.' Dulles, however, showed no interest, although he was no doubt aware of the findings of a State Department intelligence report acknowledging for the first time that Beijing and Moscow were pursuing different approaches towards Japan. He argued that this would be difficult in practice and concluded by emphasising Moscow and Beijing's shared hostile objectives in the region.[228]

On his return to Tokyo, Fujiyama expended considerable energy in trying to rally the LDP behind the banner of treaty revision. Yet, when the first round of formal negotiations opened on 4 October, the ruling party remained divided.[229] At this stage the dispute centred on the proposed treaty area: whether it should include US-controlled Okinawa or not.[230] The domestic political crisis provoked by the authoritarian Police Duties Performance Bill, which Kishi eventually was forced to withdraw in mid-November, led to some hardening of attitudes across the ideological divide. Kishi blamed Chinese Communist plots for this setback to his Conservative agenda. On 27 November, he angrily informed Harry Kern, a close friend and influential founder of the right-wing American Council on Japan, that, 'communism must be fought by all means both in Japan and throughout Asia.'[231] Fujiyama's view of China also seemed to undergo some adjustment. Now, for the benefit of US Senator William Fulbright, he criticised the 'many Japanese familiar with old China [who] continued to believe that, because of [the] nature and character of Chinese people, [the] Communists [were] unlikely to succeed in creating [a] state like [the] USSR.'[232] This sounded like a veiled attack on Yoshida, but then the ex-premier himself was sounding rather out of character at this time. According to Kern, Yoshida had told him on 17 November that, 'It is impossible to make a deal with Russia or Communist China. They are out to Communize Asia—especially the Chinese. The Chinese are more to be feared than the Russians because they are smarter.' He restated his 'fifth column' strategy, and also declared that, 'Japan must join SEATO'. Finally, and most extraordinarily, he supported Dulles' 'domino theory', claiming that, 'The US must never recognize Communist China...[because] Japan and other Asiatic countries would follow suit and they would all be lost…The Japanese are a very foolish people and they need guidance.'[233] If Kern's report is to be believed, perhaps Yoshida now feared that the very survival of the Security Treaty itself and not just its revision was at risk, and thus went to Kishi's aid.[234]

The Taiwan Straits crisis prompted further questions about the solidity of the Sino-Soviet Alliance, but they remained unanswered as the Security Treaty revision negotiations finally got under way.

The Sino-Soviet campaign against Security Treaty revision

The opening of the negotiations on Security Treaty revision soon provoked bitter denunciations from Japan's Communist neighbours. On 19 November, Chinese Foreign Minister Chen Yi accused Kishi of attempting to 'revive Japanese militarism' and called on the Japanese people to force Kishi to abrogate the Security Treaty. He warned that Japan only had a future as an independent, peaceful, democratic and neutral country. This was the first time that Beijing had called on Japan to adopt a policy of neutrality.[235] MOFA issued a swift rebuttal and China Desk Chief Okada Akira correctly predicted that, 'it will backfire with critical reaction among [the] Japanese public (sic).'[236] Nevertheless, similar declarations followed from Pyongyang, Hanoi, and most importantly Moscow, at the start of December. The Soviet note offered to respect Japanese neutrality but also emphasised Japan's vulnerability to nuclear attack. It drew a distinction between the 1951 Security Treaty, which Yoshida had been forced to sign, and the proposed revision, which was at Kishi's request.[237] Ambassador Kadowaki Suemitsu in Moscow was not alone in thinking that '[the] Russians had taken their cue from the Chinese.'[238] Niizeki Kinya, briefly his predecessor as ambassador and now a counsellor in the European Affairs Bureau, offered a slightly different interpretation of events. Asked why Moscow had joined a plainly unpopular Chinese campaign, he replied that, '[the] Soviet bureaucracy is not geared to resist proposals for propaganda statements of this kind even if their specialists in Japanese affairs knew that [the] campaign would prove counterproductive.'[239] The US Embassy in Tokyo concluded that these were the first shots in 'a *coordinated* Soviet–ChiCom campaign with the apparent objective of hampering the Security Treaty negotiations and forcing Japan's neutrality.'[240]

In the wake of the second Taiwan Straits Crisis, the American view of the Sino-Soviet Alliance had in fact undergone some revision. In early November, President Eisenhower was wondering 'if the Soviets weren't really becoming concerned about Communist China as a possible threat to them in the future.'[241] Such speculation carefully avoided the present tense, however. For now, Dulles remained convinced that his line was the correct one. In mid-January 1959, he acknowledged that, 'you could very well have a struggle between...Mao Tse-tung and Khrushchev as to who would be the ideological leader of International Communism'. Nevertheless, reflecting the general pessimism prevailing amongst America's professional China-watchers, he concluded that there was 'no early prospect of a division there which would be helpful to the West.'[242] Walter Robertson, Dulles' hard-line assistant, shared his apocalyptic vision with LDP right-winger Kaya Okinori: 'The leaders of the national Communist parties were not nationalists but members of an international conspiracy trying to take over the world.'[243]

Dulles' views appeared to be vindicated by the outwardly cooperative proceedings at the CPSU's 21st Congress.[244] Shortly thereafter, in late February, Soviet Ambassador Nikolai Fedorenko suggested to JSP leaders that the conclusion of a peace treaty with the Soviet Union should perhaps have priority over a basic settlement with China. Nevertheless, by March, China was not only publicly supporting Khrushchev's call for an Asia–Pacific nuclear-free zone, but also making the annulment of the Sino-Soviet Alliance's anti-Japanese clauses conditional on Tokyo's conclusion of non-aggression pacts with both Moscow and Beijing.[245]

Throughout the first half of 1959, Moscow and Beijing kept up a constant barrage of statements urging Japan to abandon the Security Treaty revision process and adopt neutrality. In response, MOFA made some minor efforts to sow seeds of discontent by playing up various potential problems in the Sino-Soviet relationship: territorial disputes; economic exploitation; Korean War expenses, and the international status of China.[246] Prime Minister Kishi, however, still having to contend with divisions within his own party, was more concerned with this 'intensified Sino-Soviet campaign to turn [the] country toward neutralism.'[247] After Khrushchev offered Japan bilateral, trilateral, quadrilateral and multilateral options to guarantee its neutrality—following which the Sino-Soviet Alliance would be 'amended'—Ambassador MacArthur informed Washington that, 'Japan is now the main target of Sino-Soviet campaigns in Asia.'[248]

In June 1959, on the eve of Khrushchev's historic US visit, the second major step towards the Sino-Soviet strategic rift was taken. While the Soviet leader was boasting of delivering missiles to the Chinese capable of hitting the US, Moscow secretly informed Beijing that because of the test-ban negotiations then underway in Geneva, they would not be receiving any nuclear weapons after all.[249] If the Japanese were aware of this development, there were no outward signs. Three days later, on 23 June, Ambassador Kadowaki in Moscow claimed that, 'basic Communist objectives remain [the] same and there will be constant...probing to try to widen any divisions or differences of opinion between [the] Western powers.'[250] The following month, Kishi, on an 11-nation European tour, summed up the official Japanese view by telling British Prime Minister Harold Macmillan that, 'There were some uncertain problems in Sino-Soviet relations but he could not see a split.'[251] Two weeks later in a pamphlet entitled 'Why the Security Treaty Should be Revised', the LDP again sought to justify the treaty as a counter weight to the Sino-Soviet Alliance.'[252]

Despite the superior intelligence resources at its disposal, the US government also continued to hold essentially the same views concerning the Communist alliance. In the spring, a CIA report prepared for the National Security Council (NSC) had described Sino-Soviet policy toward Japan as fundamentally unaltered.[253] In July, Ambassador MacArthur, in a long and detailed despatch from Tokyo, contrasted the distinct, but 'parallel' approaches represented by the Soviet and Chinese neutralisation campaigns.[254] Although by this time, President Eisenhower was said to be aware of deepening Sino-Soviet ideological differences, the CIA was still warning in September that it would be 'grave imprudence' to assume major discord within the 'Moscow–Peking axis'. Later that month, a second NSC report concluded that China was 'unlikely to be...alienated from the Soviet Union'.[255]

The September 1959 visits by senior LDP Diet members Miki Takeo and Ishibashi Tanzan to Moscow and Beijing, respectively, elicited the merest hints of Chinese and Soviet dissatisfaction with each other. These were overlooked at the time, but Sino-Soviet differences soon became more pronounced.[256] At the end of the month, Khrushchev proceeded immediately from his successful US visit to Beijing, for the PRC's tenth anniversary celebrations. The Soviet leader failed to persuade his Chinese comrades that they should employ only peaceful means in their campaign to reunite with Taiwan.[257] His departure without issuing a joint-communiqué prompted intense speculation in the US and Western Europe that something was amiss in Sino-Soviet relations. Within MOFA, however, the general reaction was more cautious.[258] Referring to Khrushchev's statement in Beijing, the Japanese Ambassador in Canberra told the Australian Secretary of External Affairs that,

> Whether or not there was any difference of approach on the part of the USSR and Communist China to the question of use of force in support in of foreign policy objectives, the Communist bloc would continue to make use of the weapon of subversion.[259]

Similarly, Fujiyama told Dulles' replacement, Christian Herter, that 'Soviet or Communist Chinese policies had to be regarded as a unity and differences between them were only on matters of detail.'[260] There were some exceptions. Vice-Foreign Minister Yamada Hisanari hinted that 'China might not be very pleased', after Khrushchev issued a joint-communiqué in the US which upheld the principle that international problems should not be resolved by force.[261] Similarly, Yoshida Shigeru, on a tour of Southeast Asia and Australia, felt that the absence of a Mao–Khrushchev communiqué 'was significant'. He argued that 'There was clearly a division between Moscow and Peking', and that the 'democracies should work together to drive a wedge between Soviet Russia and Red China.' However, the ageing Yoshida had no new solutions to offer and could only rehash his 'Singapore Plan'.[262]

By the end of October, Foreign Minister Fujiyama had secured final approval from the LDP for a ten-year revised Security Treaty, but dissent within the party continued.[263] Anti-mainstreamer Utsunomiya Tokuma claimed: 'the argument that it is necessary for Japan to reinforce the Security Treaty with the US because of the existence of the Sino-Soviet Alliance does not hold water'. However, his conclusion was not based on awareness of an emerging Sino-Soviet rift, rather he pointed to 'Article 2...[which] provides that this treaty is only a temporary one to remain effective until China and Japan resume normal diplomatic relations.'[264] Utsunomiya argued that, 'any revision in the Japan–US Security Treaty should be made in parallel with the abrogation or revision of its Sino-Soviet counterpart.'[265] Then on 10 November, Fujiyama told the Diet that although the new Security Treaty was specifically designed to defend Japan, US troops based in Japan guaranteed the security of the 'Far East'—an area that included the Taipei-controlled islands of Quemoy and Matsu, and even the Soviet Maritime Province. The thought that Tokyo would have a veto over their deployment only made the resulting storm of media criticism all the more ferocious.[266] Moscow and Beijing seized the opportunity to step up their campaigns against revision. Japanese public opinion became more deeply divided.[267]

Disregarding his many critics, Kishi went ahead and signed the new Security Treaty and Administrative Agreement in Washington at 2.30 p.m. on 19 January 1960. That morning, Kishi told Eisenhower, '[W]e should not expect the collapse of Communist China', adding that, 'Japan also assumes the Sino-Soviet alliance will hold together despite [the] reported differences between these two communist powers.' Like Yoshida in 1951, he specifically cited this as one of three reasons 'why the government had entered into the new agreement.' In reply, the president expressed optimism regarding his forthcoming summit with the Soviet leader and indicated that, 'Khrushchev might fear a strong Red China would challenge the USSR.'[268] In short, both governments were by now clearly aware of the Sino-Soviet dispute's existence, but believed that it was not serious enough to cause a split, and hence the revised Security Treaty was deemed necessary.

Ratification and resignation

The response from Moscow and Beijing was predictably both swift and harsh. A note from Foreign Minister Gromyko arrived on 27 January. It stipulated that since the new treaty deprived Japan of her independence and was directed against the USSR and PRC, Shikotan and the Habomai Islands would not now be returned until all foreign troops had been withdrawn from Japanese territory. Japan's vulnerability to nuclear attack was also mentioned, and to reinforce the point, the Soviets carried out another missile test overflying Japan.[269] Meanwhile on 24 January, Beijing extended the scope of its critique to include those Japanese friends of China who 'still hold an incorrect view which puts the Sino-Soviet alliance on a par with the Japan–US alliance.' Retreating from their long-standing support for a four-power pact, the Chinese again claimed that the two treaties were 'of an entirely different nature. The Sino-Soviet alliance is an alliance to safeguard peace'.[270]

The Communist allies appeared equally incensed by Japan's actions, yet a subtle difference existed between them. The Chinese would not have anything to do with the 'Kishi clique of war criminals', but the Soviets had not abandoned hope for better relations.[271] In Tokyo, however, there was as yet little awareness of such diplomatic nuance. On 28 January, according to Deputy Vice Foreign Minister Shima Shigenobu, MOFA had planned to issue a statement which asserted that: 'Obvious coordination existed between Soviet efforts to interfere with Security Treaty ratification and those of the Chinese Communists.'[272] Niizeki Kinya was more perceptive. He at least:

> did not think that there had been any prior consultation between the Soviet Union and China before the [27 January] Russian aide-memoire was handed over, particularly as China and Russia did not seem to be on very good terms.[273]

More generally, Niizeki believed that while 'the immediate national interests of Russia and China might...conflict...their basic ideological harmony was likely to prove to be the predominant factor...[and] in the immediate future there was little prospect of a break between the two countries.'[274]

The fissures within the LDP over Japan's defence policy widened as Kishi attempted to secure Diet ratification of the revised Security Treaty in the face of growing popular discontent. The premier attempted to mollify the opposition by promising that, 'The fear among the free nations that Japan might tilt toward neutralism will be eradicated by treaty revision and we can henceforth open a dialogue with the Communist powers.'[275] Still, Miki Takeo, Ishibashi Tanzan and others from the party's anti-mainstream repeatedly called on the cabinet to change its China policy. Foreign Minister Fujiyama responded by placing the onus for revision firmly on Beijing's shoulders.[276]

Throughout that spring, the Chinese maintained a steady stream of invective against the Security Treaty.[277] Moscow and Tokyo also exchanged a series of temperate diplomatic notes between January and July. The third Soviet memo, dated 22 April, was notable for the way in which it revived the earlier proposal to reconsider the provisions of the Sino-Soviet Alliance, if Japan annulled the Security Treaty and closed all foreign military bases. It even claimed that the Chinese were willing to cooperate.[278]

The temperature of debate was further raised when the Soviets shot down an American U2 spy plane deep inside their territory on 1 May.[279] Kishi resorted to strong-arm tactics to secure Diet ratification of the Security Treaty in the early hours of 20 May. His undemocratic methods, however, led to Japan's largest post-war street protests, forcing the cancellation of Eisenhower's planned state visit to Japan and nearly splitting the LDP in two. As decreed by the Japanese Constitution, the ratification process was completed automatically one month later. A few hours later Kishi resigned the premiership.[280] In Japan, the dispute over revision of the Security Treaty had effectively disguised the emerging Sino-Soviet strategic rift. This situation was soon to change.

Interpretative comments

Input: external environment

Geographical proximity to China and the Soviet Union meant that Japanese leaders could not afford to simply ignore the Communist Powers: being neighbours accentuated the potential military threat that they posed to Japan. The conclusion of the Sino-Soviet Alliance in 1950 represented the formal establishment of a strategic 'united front' against Japan, although somewhat conflicting perceptions of Tokyo endured. The alliance also represented an unspoken admission by the signatories of their failure to shape developments in Occupied Japan. Moreover, Moscow's subsequent refusal to sign the San Francisco Peace Treaty—in part because of Beijing's exclusion—left both Communist states without official diplomatic representation in Tokyo.

Three years later, the 1954 Sino-Soviet Joint-Declaration publicly reaffirmed Moscow and Beijing's shared peaceful intentions vis-à-vis Japan, but the post-Stalin Soviet leadership apparently chose to pursue its diplomatic courtship of Tokyo unilaterally. The gap between Soviet and Chinese approaches towards Japan became more salient after 1956, when Khrushchev's success in normalising diplomatic relations with Tokyo placed Moscow's ties on a different level. Beijing's unilateral imposition of an embargo on Japan eighteen months later confirmed the disparity. However, the launching of Soviet and Chinese campaigns against the revision of the Japan–US Security Treaty helped to disguise the divergent trend for the next few years.

For most Japanese, however, the relationship with the US was the more important. American influence over Japan was transcendent from 30 August 1945: the day that General Douglas MacArthur arrived to launch the Allied Occupation. Although Japan was weak, isolated from its neighbours, and susceptible to external pressures, for Washington it was the 'super domino': vital to the strategic and economic balance of power in East Asia. The Sino-Soviet Alliance, by cementing China into the bipolar Cold War structure, strengthened American determination to remain the predominant force in Japan, even after sovereignty was restored to Tokyo. The Japan–US Security Treaty was one method Washington employed to guarantee that this would be so, and over the next decade, the Americans worked to prevent their wartime allies from acquiring influence in Tokyo.

Nevertheless, before the outbreak of the Korean War, the idea that China was not firmly committed to the Soviet Union was widespread in virtually all non-communist countries—with the notable exception of Taiwan. From 1951, however, under the influence of US Special Ambassador (and later Secretary of State) John Foster Dulles, American strategy to promote a Sino-Soviet rift departed dramatically from that advocated by Yoshida. Although there were always voices within the US government willing to speak out in favour of Yoshida's China Thesis, after the outbreak of the Korean War they were a shrinking minority. Fearing Yoshida's 'soft wedge' approach towards China would weaken US–Japan ties, a 'hard wedge' strategy that sought to increase rather than decrease Beijing's dependence on Moscow, became the official US line.

Washington believed that Beijing represented a more virulent strain of Communism than Moscow. Although divided on the issue, the Eisenhower Administration offered only limited opposition to the idea of Japan–Soviet normalisation, being more concerned to prevent a positive knock-on effect on Japan–China relations. There is ample evidence of the persistence with which the US sought to persuade Japan not to normalise relations with Beijing, but Dulles really only objected to the territorial aspect of the proposed settlement with Moscow. In short, Washington was willing to tolerate the Hatoyama government 'opening a window to the East', as long as a 'bamboo curtain' prevented any light shining in from Beijing.

The Americans were happy when Ishibashi Tanzan was removed from office before he could deflect the course of Japanese foreign policy. They found his successor, Kishi Nobusuke, much more to their liking and rewarded him publicly with a more balanced Security Treaty, and secretly with millions of CIA dollars to help ensure the LDP's continued electoral success. The US was unrelenting in its efforts to play up the threat from the Communist bloc and play down evidence of Sino-Soviet disagreements in order to maintain the solidarity of its own Cold War alliances, especially that with Japan.

Internal environment: operational sphere

Japan was still under foreign control when the Sino-Soviet Alliance was signed. The postwar Constitution had established a new democratic political structure but it remained vulnerable and untested. The 'reverse course' in SCAP policy reflected the onset of the Cold War in Europe, and tilted the balance against progressive forces. This right-wing bias became entrenched after the consolidation of the conservative and socialist parties respectively in the so-called '1955 system': a diffuse but rigid bipolar political structure.

During the 1950s, Japan remained virtually powerless in the strategic sense, despite the establishment of the National Police Reserve in 1950, which by 1954 evolved into the Self-Defence Forces. The Constitution, in particular the pacifistic Article 9, presented a major barrier to Japan's development of military power. Yoshida's policy, which gave priority to economic development over rearmament, reinforced this state of affairs. However, Japan began gradually to upgrade its defence capacity during the mid-1950s, with the Sino-Soviet Alliance providing a useful, if tacit, justification for this. Nonetheless a decade later Japan remained seriously under-powered relative to its neighbours. The decision to minimise rearmament limited Tokyo's options when it came to participating in regional power politics.

Psychological sphere: belief systems

In the 1950s, as citizens of a fledgling democracy, a wide range of ideologies, ideals, norms, values and objectives motivated the Japanese political elite. Bilateralism and multilateralism, capitalism and Communism, Confucianism and developmentalism, internationalism and nationalism, pacifism and realism, pro-Westernism and Pan-Asianism each attracted disciples. The desire for peace, prosperity and security, or in other words, the fear of war, poverty and insecurity, were perhaps universal values. Yet, when it came to specific foreign policy choices—like how to cope with the Sino-Soviet Alliance—priorities varied across the political spectrum. The Cold War meant that ideology was a quite important factor in Japanese politics, especially at the extremes, but it tended to be expressed in negative terms: politicians were either anti-Communist or anti-Capitalist, anti-militarist or anti-pacifist. Pecuniary motives may have been even more decisive: structural corruption was endemic and each of the major political parties was secretly receiving funds from foreign governments in the 1950s and early 1960s. Given the nature of the Japanese electoral system, however, for most of the politically active money was only a means to an end: power. But to what extent did Japanese premiers of the period share these values?

Yoshida Shigeru is widely credited with laying the foundations of post-war Japanese foreign policy during his seven-year reign as premier, yet he remains an enigma. Why did he align Japan with the US? The Sino-Soviet Alliance cannot have been the main motive for signing the Security Treaty with Washington, since his decision to side with the US predated negotiation of the Communist pact. The rationalist explanation is that Yoshida was selecting the best option for achieving Japan's unchanging core national interests—security, peace, and prosperity—and all at minimum risk to Japan. According to such logic, compromising national sovereignty was a small price to pay for this 'special relationship'. Does Yoshida's knowledge that US troops would remain in Japan explain his public nonchalance when confronting Chinese and Soviet power, or did it stem from some deeper conviction? If the latter was the case, then the primary function of the Security Treaty with the US cannot have been to deter Communist attack. Was it perhaps the minimum price that Tokyo had to pay in order to safeguard relations with Washington, to prevent the US from regarding Japan as a potential enemy? This would suggest that Tokyo's security relationship with Washington was more the result of fear of US power than fear of Communism. In Stephen Walt's terms, Yoshida was 'bandwagoning' not 'balancing', that is, aligning with the chief source of danger not allying with others against the prevailing threat.[281]

The crushing Japanese defeat in World War II had reinforced Yoshida's hostility towards the military, yet it did not prevent him from thinking of Japan as a Great Power. During his years as pre-war ambassador to London, he had imbibed deeply of the English superiority complex vis-à-vis the Americans. Although he was enough of a realist to acknowledge Japan's physical (military and economic) dependence on the US, he was convinced that the Japanese understood China better than did the Americans. Yoshida still hoped for some degree of diplomatic independence, at least vis-à-vis relations with China. Yoshida believed that a 'clash of civilisations' made a Sino-Soviet split inevitable. Closer relations with China were a means to that end: a way to accelerate the collapse of the Communist alliance, build a bridge between East and West, and weaken the Soviet Union. Yoshida's policy towards the Sino-Soviet Alliance, his China Thesis, was rooted in three firmly held convictions: the Japan–US Security Treaty was stronger than the Sino-Soviet Alliance. In other words, inverting Mao Zedong's famous aphorism, Yoshida believed that the 'West wind would prevail over the East wind'. Secondly, he felt that the Chinese Communists were more Chinese than Communist. Thirdly, through trade and cultural exchanges, Yoshida was convinced that the West could infect Communist China with the values of capitalist democracy, and thereby bring about a rift with Moscow. During Yoshida's term in office and for many years thereafter these proved to be misconceptions. In short, the picture of Yoshida that emerges from this study is of a moderate pragmatist, an advocate of 'soft power', pursuing a doctrine of suppressed nationalism.

Hatoyama Ichirō did not share Yoshida's 'culturalist' conception of international relations. In all likelihood, Hatoyama originally supported the idea of 'opening a window to the East' as a stick with which to beat Yoshida. Once *Minshutō* was in power, however, it acquired a new function: helping to maintain popular and Diet support for what was, until November 1955, a minority government. He also hoped that it would produce a major diplomatic coup to compare with Yoshida's achievement at San Francisco. Hatoyama was a functionalist whose greatest fear was a Third World War. He was more anti-Communist and nationalistic than Yoshida, but he was able to separate ideological differences from normal diplomatic and economic relations. Hatoyama sought peaceful coexistence with the Communist states. Japan's role was still to help build a bridge, but between the two camps, not merely between China and the 'West'. Shigemitsu Mamoru considered himself the diplomatic expert in the Hatoyama cabinet and did not see eye to eye with the prime minister on all aspects of foreign policy, in particular over the degree of deference accorded to the Americans. However, one should not exaggerate their disagreements. The basis of their political alliance was a set of shared goals that included improved relations with the Communist bloc. Often the difference between them is more one of style than substance: Hatoyama, sometimes indiscreet, often tailoring his pronouncements to fit his audience; Shigemitsu, more cautious, usually preferring the gradual approach lest Washington take offence.

Although hailing from the same wing of the LDP as Hatoyama, Kishi Nobusuke focused on fighting Communism not accommodating it. He was a realist who believed in a balance of power between the two camps and distrusted neutralism. He was also a 'Pan-Asianist' of the prewar kind, who felt that Japan was the natural leader of Asia. Fujiyama Aiichirō suppressed his pro-China sentiments during his term as Kishi's foreign minister. He emerged as a leader of the pro-Beijing faction within the LDP during the 1960s.

Japanese premiers represented the mainstream conservative values of their time, but many of the ruling party's Diet members did not share them. Even more so than its antecedents, the LDP was a pragmatic, not an ideology-based, party: a party that owed its existence primarily to a lust for power. Consequently, it embraced a broad church of beliefs. Leaders of the anti-mainstream 'pro-China' wing, like Matsumura Kenzō or Utsunomiya Tokuma, were emotional 'Pan-Asianists' for whom the Sino-Soviet Alliance did not represent an insuperable obstacle to restored friendship between Asian neighbours. They sought fully normalised relations with the Chinese mainland, thereby hoping to promote stability in the region and Japan's independence from the US. They were particularly alarmed at the prospect of a Sino-American war.

Turning to the bureaucrats, the attitude of MOFA diplomats was generally cautious and legalistic. A number of factors combined to produce diplomatic timidity in their external dealings: an exaggerated sense of Japan's limited diplomatic, military and economic resources; a hypersensitivity to reactions in Washington (and Taipei); a fear of making mistakes, and a limited understanding of the complex, emerging multipolar regional/international environment. Certainly, there was a general desire not only to maintain, but also to improve the relationship with Washington. At the same time, however, on the issue of relations with China and the Soviet Union, differences were deeply ingrained. A 'pro-US' wing sought to obstruct progress on both fronts, although in line with its American sponsors, it opposed the approach to Beijing more strongly. A second 'Asianist' group was more critical. Heads of the China Desk like Ogawa Heishirō and Takeuchi Harumi, stand out—although they were far from being alone—as men resentful of US policy towards China: convinced that it must and would change.

Psychological sphere: perceptions

Yoshida did not take the Sino-Soviet threat seriously, since he was convinced that their alliance would soon collapse. He was more afraid of domestic sources of Communism. Hatoyama must have assumed that the Sino-Soviet Alliance was solid for he did not appear to draw any distinction between Moscow and Beijing. Later, when force of circumstance made it unavoidable, Hatoyama seemed to differentiate between them only reluctantly. By the mid-1950s, within Japanese governing circles, the accepted view of the Sino-Soviet relationship was of a firm alliance, growing stronger day by day. Under Kishi, early suggestions from MOFA that differences existed between Chinese and Soviet policies towards Japan, were submerged beneath a tidal wave of Communist disapproval of the Security Treaty revision process. Evidence of serious Sino-Soviet disputes over China's conduct of the Taiwan Straits crisis, and Moscow's subsequent reneging on its promise to supply Beijing with a sample nuclear bomb, were virtually ignored by the Kishi government.

Decision-making process

Formally speaking, MOFA was Japan's central agency for implementing the foreign policies decided by the democratically elected Diet. In practice, however, for a variety of reasons, including diplomats' superior knowledge and experience, partisan disagreement on foreign affairs, and the emergence of a one-party dominant political system, MOFA usually assumed both functions. Thus when it came to foreign policy, the Diet was frequently reduced to little more than a talking shop.

During the Occupation, Japan had no 'foreign policy' as such. Although a rump MOFA continued to exist, its primary function was to liase with SCAP, which bore responsibility for the day-to-day management of Japan's external relations. Even after the San Francisco Peace Treaty restored its sovereign independence, Japan still lacked diplomatic relations with most of its neighbours, including China and, until 1956, the Soviet Union. Japan was rightly dubbed the 'orphan of Asia'. Thus when it came to developments within the Communist bloc, MOFA found itself suffering from a dearth of reliable information. Regular meetings of Japanese heads of mission from the region helped to broaden perspectives, but could not plug every gap in the ministry's knowledge.

MOFA was happy to establish various principles to govern Japan–China and Japan–Soviet relations, but its approach to policy making was essentially piecemeal and reactive. MOFA was divided—both within and between bureaux—over how to respond to developments in the Sino-Soviet Alliance. Strict, legally defined divisions of responsibility reinforced such differences. With a 'bottom-up' and subsystem oriented decision-making process even 'middle-ranking' officers at the ministry were influential, but presumably higher-ranking diplomats or their 'political masters' quashed the activism prevalent at these lower levels.

Competition with other ministries weakened MOFA's influence. MITI was the most important of these rivals (see chapter 4). The Justice Ministry, on the other hand, particularly when in the hands of the pro-Taiwan right-winger, Kaya Okinori, adopted a rigidly legalistic approach to China. There is no evidence to suggest that the Defence Agency exerted significant leverage even on explicitly defence matters. Finally, although often overlooked, the influence of intelligence agencies like the CRO and *Kōan Chōsachō* should not be underestimated.

Bureaucrats may have dominated foreign policy-making in Japan during the 1950s, but MOFA was not immune to political pressure. For Japan's ruling party, policy towards the Sino-Soviet Alliance was potentially too significant an issue with the electorate to leave entirely in the hands of the diplomats. The lack of official diplomatic ties with Moscow and Beijing enabled politicians, both within the government and without, to pursue their own agendas. All were examples of 'amateur diplomacy' in the eyes of MOFA professionals, but were none the less effective for that.

Politicians relied on MOFA for expert advice, but they did not necessarily follow it. Normally, the ministers responsible for foreign affairs worked in tandem with the diplomats, but there were occasional conflicts when the premier or foreign minister tried to stray from the familiar path. On such occasions, MOFA usually brought the unruly politician into line. However, when Hatoyama Ichirō, a leader with strong popular appeal, chose to ignore official channels and conduct his own diplomacy, MOFA was unable to derail it, although the ministry certainly helped to limit his success.

Yoshida, Hatoyama and Kishi were all unusually active Japanese premiers in the field of diplomacy. 'One man' Yoshida became famous for his 'un-Japanese' autocratic decision-making style. He considered foreign policy his personal prerogative, serving as his own foreign minister under the Occupation, and thereafter giving the post to an ex-diplomat and loyal subordinate, Okazaki Katsuo. Like Janus, Yoshida had two faces, one for the Japanese and one for the Americans. This was necessary since he had two masters: he needed the confidence of the US government as much as, if not more than, that of the Japanese electorate and his party colleagues.

Despite his popularity, Hatoyama was unable single-handedly to dominate the foreign policy agenda as his predecessor had. Hatoyama had to endure a collective party presidency, including Yoshida supporters, until March 1956. Hatoyama even lacked the authority to have his first choice installed as foreign minister. Other members of the cabinet, in particular, Agriculture Minister Kōno Ichirō and Trade Minister Ishibashi Tanzan, clashed more openly with Foreign Minister Shigemitsu Mamoru, but their factional base within the ruling party was never strong enough to have him replaced. Following the establishment of the LDP, the Yoshida faction probably represented the most serious limitation on Hatoyama's room for manoeuvre, and vice versa. Yoshida slowed the pace of normalisation with Moscow, but in the end, he was unable to prevent it.

As a former bureaucrat and head of a substantial LDP faction, Kishi's position in the policy-making process was somewhat stronger. He was his own foreign minister until July 1957, and for the next three years Fujiyama Aiichirō, a close friend, filled the post.

It has become a commonplace of Japanese political studies to state that the country has usually lacked a strong leader or leadership: the so-called 'truncated pyramid' model. This is at best an oversimplification. Japanese prime ministers of this period were at least able to set the tone or general direction for foreign policy. However, official LDP organs, like the FARC, possessed an effective veto on foreign policy innovation. Furthermore, unofficial structures like the factions and issue groups further limited the premiers' room for manoeuvre.

Output: official diplomacy

Under Yoshida Shigeru, Japan, which was still technically at war with the two Communist allies, consciously spurned any direct contact with the Soviet and Chinese governments. Washington (and to a lesser degree, London) were the main targets of Yoshida's China and Soviet policies. He tried to exploit the differences between Britain and the US regarding China policy, but without success.

Yoshida's seven-year reign can be divided into three unequal segments, according to the degree to which he actively pursued his China Thesis. The first phase spanned most of his second term as prime minister of Occupied Japan. During this time, Yoshida tried to persuade the Americans to allow Tokyo to keep open a channel to Beijing, in order to accelerate its disenchantment with Moscow. China was thus the focus of Yoshida's interest in the Communist bloc. Moreover, for him, 'Japanese diplomacy was economic diplomacy'. By channel, therefore, Yoshida meant primarily trade relations, although he did attempt to fashion a Peace Treaty with Taipei that would afford Tokyo the option of later signing a separate treaty with Beijing. He was unsuccessful. Yoshida's China Thesis was increasingly dismissed at home and abroad as mere 'wishful thinking'. The second spell, a two-year hiatus, lasted until May 1954, and the final stage, covering Yoshida's last eight months in office, saw him make a futile attempt to revive his thesis. In short, when the China Thesis directly conflicted with Japan's political or economic survival, it simply was not his highest priority.

Hatoyama Ichirō's two-year term as premier described a similar trajectory. He set out to counteract Yoshida's over-dependence on Washington with a more independent foreign policy. Unlike his predecessor, there is no evidence that Hatoyama sought to split the Sino-Soviet Alliance. Rather, he resolved to blunt its claws by making peace with both Moscow and Beijing. In practice, this proved impossible. Hence, reversing Yoshida's priorities, Hatoyama chose to emphasise relations with the Soviet Union over China. While concern with Soviet normalisation was a constant, his interest in China apparently waned after an initial burst of enthusiasm, only to be rekindled when it was too late. Hatoyama succeeded in restoring diplomatic relations with Moscow, before ill health and internal opposition forced his retirement. A similar fate prevented his successor, Ishibashi Tanzan, from completing the task.

Although never clearly articulated, Kishi Nobusuke's basic approach was to counter the Sino-Soviet Alliance by strengthening defence and collective security ties with the US (and perhaps Southeast Asian states.)

External environment: feedback

Japan and the US never saw eye to eye on China. The Japanese thought that they understood China well for cultural and historical reasons: US views of China they regarded as blinded by ideology. The Americans, on the other hand, felt that Japanese views of China were emotional and irrational: their own realistic. Yet while the Japanese government usually preferred to tell Washington only what it thought the Americans wanted to hear, the latter preached to the Japanese what they thought would be good for them. This did not reflect cultural differences so much as their relative power positions, distinct historical experiences, and a still limited measure of mutual trust. Yoshida's persistence with his China Thesis merely heightened American suspicions of Japanese loyalty. The line taken by Yoshida's successor, Hatoyama Ichirō, was even less compatible with the US approach. If his intention was to pressure Washington into conceding a more balanced relationship, then in the short-term at least, he failed. The US regularly consulted with its allies, including Japan, but there is no evidence to suggest that Tokyo's views carried much weight in the policy processes of Washington. Kishi was the first postwar Japanese premier to be able to consistently elicit the desired response from the Americans. Yet even under Kishi, Tokyo remained little more than a semi-detached member of the Western Alliance. Consequently, the US government never stopped fretting about the danger of losing Japan, and offered both carrots and sticks to minimise the risk.

Watching Japanese–American bonds strengthen and the steady development of Soviet–Japanese ties, China was doubtless frustrated by the relative lack of progress in Sino-Japanese relations. In addition to the Chinese domestic political environment, this helps to explain Beijing's increasingly hard-line responses to Tokyo's conciliatory policies.

3

Fire across the sea: Japanese security and the Sino-Soviet strategic rift, 1960–64

対岸の火事

In the wake of President Dwight D. Eisenhower's cancelled visit to Tokyo, Ikeda Hayato's first priority as Japan's new premier was to reassure the stunned Americans of his government's unshakeable commitment to their bilateral relationship.[1] Yet as a Yoshida protégé, determined to avoid the mistakes of his predecessor, it should come as no surprise that from the very beginning Ikeda would take a close interest in the Sino-Soviet Alliance, and especially China.[2] On 19 July 1960, in his first press conference as prime minister, Ikeda declared: 'The most important thing for us is to increase our credibility in the Free World.' However, at the same time he also wanted Japan to 'become a country that will be taken seriously by the Chinese Communists, that will not be easily manipulated by them…We are watching China carefully and quietly.'[3] The Japanese public expected no less.[4]

Ikeda's 'low profile' diplomacy

In the last days of Kishi's premiership, the sixth meeting of the heads of Japanese missions in the Asia–Pacific had judged that 'the mutual interdependence of Moscow and China is such that China is unlikely to commit any act of overt aggression which might precipitate world war.'[5] Now, however, in a repeat of Yoshida's May 1954 request, MOFA was asked to make a special study of prospects for a Sino-Soviet rift. According to Endō Matao (head of the China Desk) the general feeling within the ministry remained pessimistic:

> recent publicized differences were superficial only...[and w]e should not be misled by journalistic wishful thinking...There were many fields for possible Sino-Soviet friction and disagreements could be expected from time to time to come to the surface, but the basic unity remained.[6]

Official American assessments of the state of the Sino-Soviet Alliance were very similar to those of Japan.[7] In the wake of the *Anpo* crisis, however, this did not prevent Washington from worrying about relations with its ally.[8]

Following Kishi's departure, the anti-Security Treaty protests in Tokyo quickly dissipated, but this was not the case in Moscow or Beijing. Encouraged by a sense of achievement, in late July the Chinese government sent its first delegation to Tokyo for two years.[9] However, Beijing did not halt its verbal assault on the Security Treaty that bound Japan to 'US imperialism'.[10] Similarly, Khrushchev tied the return of the 'Southern Kurils' to Japan adopting a 'neutral and truly independent stand'.[11] Then on 1 October, the Soviet leader, claiming to speak on behalf of an absent Beijing, told the UN General Assembly that:

> The government of China actively favors the creation of a peace zone in Asia as well as a zone free from atomic weapons in the Pacific. It proposes a peaceful nonaggression treaty between all countries of Asia and the Pacific coast, including the United States.[12]

Such presumptuousness may in part account for the first open airing of Sino-Soviet foreign policy differences over Japan at the secret Moscow Conference the following month. A compromise eventually emerged: they would place equal emphasis on Japanese resistance to the American alliance on the one hand, and 'peaceful coexistence' and disarmament on the other. Nevertheless, Beijing continued to stress the former and Moscow the latter.[13] Another indication of the continuing importance Beijing attached to 'the liberation of Japan' came on 9 February, when Mao Zedong told a delegation of Japanese workers that 'The first revolution was the Russian Revolution...The second revolution was the Chinese Revolution...The third revolution will be in Japan. When Japan is liberated, the East will be liberated and then the whole world will be liberated.'[14]

The widely leaked reports of Sino-Soviet clashes at the Moscow Conference revived the idea in Western government circles that a strategic rift was a realistic possibility. In the US, this revelation coincided with a change in leadership. After a high-level meeting on 11 February, President John F. Kennedy ordered a major study of the 'Sino-Soviet dispute'.[15] Significant differences of opinion soon emerged between the CIA and State Department.[16] Still, the view conveyed to Tokyo in advance of the Ikeda–Kennedy summit scheduled for June 1961 was little altered from the 'Dulles line', circa 1959:

> While Peiping's dispute with Moscow may reflect serious strains within the Sino-Soviet alliance, each is clearly aware of the advantages which lie in that alliance, and neither has revealed any diminution of its desire to replace free world societies with communist societies.[17]

In Japan too, 1961 saw the first stirring of what would later become a vigorous debate within the ruling party on the strategic dimension of the Sino-Soviet rift. Takasaki Tatsunosuke, the former trade minister, who visited China in October 1960, attributed Sino-Soviet foreign policy disputes to the differing vintages of their revolutions: 'Khrushchev advocates peaceful coexistence 43 years after the Russian Revolution. I optimistically think that China, too, will follow in the Soviet Union's footsteps.'[18] However, this 'time lag' theory did not convince Nakasone Yasuhiro, another leading member of the Kōno faction, who believed that 'Despite the solid front they present to the US, Communist China and the Soviet Union are opposed to each other within the communist bloc.' He seemed to share Washington's threat perceptions, asserting that:

> The Soviet Union is afraid and wary of Communist China for a variety of reasons—among them China's population of 650 million people, the Soviet Union's own guilt feelings at having snatched a portion of former Chinese territory...and the Chinese people's traditional pride, which sees all other races as barbarians. Furthermore, where China's traditional expansionism is involved...the Soviet Union seems anxious to forestall any catastrophic collision with the United States.'[19]

Many others on the LDP right wing, however, shared Kishi Nobusuke's view that Moscow still led 'an unwavering bloc of countries pliant to its wishes.'[20]

Such discussions were not confined to the LDP. On 16 August 1960, Ikeda invited 36 individuals representing a range of opinons on the China issue from the right to the moderate left to join a *Gaikō Mondai Kondankai* (Foreign Policy Problems Deliberation Council). Seven months later it suspended activities, having been unable to reach any agreement except that the problem was 'complicated' and Japan should adopt an 'independent course…neither blindly follow[ing] the US nor yield[ing] to Communist Chinse threats.'[21]

MOFA also formed a very active intra-ministry China Study Group under the chairmanship of Deputy Vice-Foreign Minister Shima Shigenobu. Shima himself presumed that Sino-Soviet relations remained intimate, but Hōgen Shinsaku (director of the European Affairs Bureau) seemed willing to go along with Takasaki's 'generation gap' theory. That spring, he responded to a question about rumours of a Sino-Soviet estrangement by saying that he thought 'it natural that there should be a difference of opinion between them'. Although aware of the disputes at the previous November's Moscow Conference, Hōgen also noted that both of the Communist powers have recently 'been emphasising aspects where they are in agreement.'[22] The ministry's official line was contained in August's annual *Diplomatic Blue Book*: 'At this [November 1960] meeting the Sino-Soviet ideological rift was said to have ended, but differing opinions not about Marxism–Leninism, but actual policy [continue]. The stages of their revolutions and international standpoints are different, it seems.'[23]

Meanwhile, the Defence Agency had also been keeping a close eye on strategic developments that might affect Japan. In a situation analysis prepared for Ikeda's Washington trip, it predicted increased Sino-Soviet tension. However, the report concluded that, 'direct Chinese Communist aggression in the [Far East] area is not likely for some time to come and that for the present the Communist emphasis is on indirect aggression and exploitation of unstable conditions and popular discontent and apathy.'[24]

While both Japanese and American officials continued to underestimate the seriousness of the emerging Sino-Soviet strategic rift, the issue which threatened the maintenance of Ikeda's diplomatic 'low profile' was the long dormant but related question of China's UN seat.

The battle over China's UN seat

In January 1961, Ikeda opened the new Diet session by declaring that, 'Although we want to normalize relations with Communist China, the Communist China problem can not be settled only...between Tokyo and Peking...Japan must see what other free nations intend to do concerning the problem'.[25] In private, Chief Cabinet Secretary Ōhira Masayoshi was more explicit:

> nobody knew how the Peking regime would behave in the UN and there seemed no point in having it in unless we could all be assured that its behaviour would be reasonable. Besides Japan had good and close relations with Formosa.[26]

Within MOFA, although a large group supported abstaining if the US were to reintroduce a moratorium resolution at the UN, consensus remained elusive. Deputy Vice-Foreign Minister Shima, discussing a 'one China, one Taiwan' solution, concluded that it was 'essentially the US attitude which stood in the way of a change that was increasingly favoured everywhere.' Nevertheless, he envisioned both superpowers playing a mediatory role, with Washington responsible for pressuring Chiang Kai-shek into accceptance, while 'the Russians [were] to sell it to Peking.'[27] Asian Affairs Bureau Chief Iseki Yūjirō was more impatient. He favoured 'some method of seating Communist China in the UN...[after which] recognition of the Peking Government by Japan would follow automatically.'[28] Ambassadorial and even ministerial talks with Beijing were under active consideration, but many Japanese diplomats remained opposed to taking any initiative and pinned their hopes on an Anglo-American compromise.[29]

In May, in an overt effort to influence Ikeda's agenda for his forthcoming summit meeting with the US president, FARC's China Problem Subcommittee—established by Kishi in April 1960—published an 'interim report'. Although the LDP group took into account the report of the *Gaikō Mondai Kondankai*, as well as the views of MOFA, MITI, Takasaki Tatsunosuke, Taipei and other interested parties, its in-built conservative majority held sway. Preaching caution, the report continued to rule out diplomatic recognition for the time being and advised the government to follow the US line over the UN seat, whatever it might be. It also declared a strategic interest in preventing Taiwan from being absorbed into the Communist sphere, and even asserted that there was no guarantee that Beijing did not pose a military threat to the region.[30]

At Ikeda's June summit with Kennedy, China emerged as the focus of discussion. In preparatory documents, both sides agreed that the moratorium procedure was unlikely to succeed at the 16th UN General Assembly that autumn.[31] Moreover, while the two leaders were aware of the substantial perception-gap between Japanese and American popular perceptions of China, their governments intended to cooperate on a new approach that would keep Taiwan in the UN.[32] Secretary of State Dean Rusk and Foreign Minister Kosaka Zentarō also agreed that, 'recognition of the PRC was not contemplated by either country'. However, significant differences remained. While Ikeda offered no objections to a General Assembly seat for Beijing once Taiwan's was secure, Kennedy merely sought: 'a formula *which appears* to indicate a willingness to take Communist China into the UN and to embrace in effect a "two-China" policy'.[33] In the words of Deputy Vice-Foreign Minister Shima: '[The] United States was prepared to contemplate offering membership to Peking only on terms that Peking could not accept, [whereas] Japan was prepared to accept Peking membership and was not thinking specifically of ways of keeping Peking out.'[34]

Contrary to earlier reports, documents declassified to date do not indicate that the state of Sino-Soviet relations was raised during the summit itself.[35] The following day, however, at the National Press Club in Washington, Ikeda declared: 'Today, the communist world is united under the ideology of Marx–Leninism...Openly and covertly, it is conducting a sustained campaign against Japan and other nations of the non-communist world'.[36] It has been suggested that Ikeda's goal had been nothing less than to 'persuade Washington to change its traditional orientation toward China': if so, then he failed.[37] As Ikeda himself later admitted: 'American feelings towards Communist China and towards the Soviet Union are very different. They hate the Chinese Communists.'[38]

Ikeda returned home to face demands from pro-normalisation factions that he fulfil his election promises. That summer, LDP Diet member Nakasone Yasuhiro was not the only influential Japanese suggesting that, 'Japan should look to the example of Britain' in the matter of diplomatic relations with China.[39] Foreign Minister Kosaka, however, still hoped for trilateral coordination. Discussing the problem of China's UN seat with Prime Minister Macmillan during a visit to London in early July, he repeated that 'Japan felt it most important that there should be a policy concerted between [the] UK, US and Japan.'[40]

Japanese public opinion overwhelmingly favoured Beijing's admission to the UN.[41] Yet, when the issue finally came to a vote in New York on 6 December, Japan joined Britain and the US in co-sponsoring a resolution to make a change in the government representing China an 'important question', thus requiring a two-thirds majority. Despite the carefully worded speech of UN Ambassador Okazaki Katsuo, pro-China opinion in Japan was shocked and Beijing itself was outraged.[42] Whether Rusk had needed to twist Japanese arms or whether, 'The Japanese...played an active part, much of it behind the scenes, in the manoeuvres over the "China seat" at this last [General] Assembly session', remains unclear.[43] Rusk certainly complimented Ikeda on 'Japan's increasing willingness to take the initiative in foreign affairs both in the UN and in other fields.'[44] Whichever is the case, it seems that Tokyo's increasing awareness of the Sino-Soviet strategic rift had not yet caused it to pursue an independent diplomatic line on China.

Japanese and American views on the strategic rift diverge

In January 1962, the JSP undertook a controversial mission to China. The loud LDP protests that ensued obscured something of greater importance. Beijing revived its proposal that, 'with the conclusion of a Sino-Japanese [Treaty] of Friendship and Mutual Non-Aggression, the provisions of the Sino-Soviet Treaty of Friendship, Alliance and Mutual Assistance for prevention of the resumption of Japanese militarism will *automatically* become null and void.'[45]

In the light of such statements, the first few months of 1962 saw official American views on the state of Sino-Soviet relations undergo a sea change, thus resulting in a growing divergence between official assessments of the Communist alliance in Tokyo and Washington. Until this time, the Americans had concluded that in the last resort the Communist alliance remained operational.[46] Now, the US virtually abandoned its earlier scepticism regarding the strategic nature of the rift, and outstripped Japan in appreciating the serious implications of the schism. At least four major reports on the subject appeared in quick succession. While differences remained as to the potential benefits of the rift for the US, a basic consensus accepted that the ideological schism was now complete and that the dispute was fundamentally a clash of 'national interests'. The CIA predicted that provided the leadership of both parties remained unchanged until mid-1963, 'a Sino-Soviet break...in either party or party and state relations—is more likely than not'. Similarly, the State Department's Policy Planning Staff concluded that, 'monolithic unity and control no longer exist in the communist camp.'[47]

How much of this information Washington passed on to Tokyo remains unclear, but recent developments in Sino-Soviet relations prompted MOFA's European Affairs Bureau to organise a Committee for the Coordinated Study of All Aspects of Communism to be chaired by Niizeki Kinya. This was not a sudden awakening on the Japanese government's part. As already noted, Tokyo had been ahead of Washington in recognising a possible Sino-Soviet rift. Reports such as that from London Ambassador Ōno Katsumi in November 1961 had recognised that Soviet public censure of Albania was 'really directed against China.'[48] By the summer of 1962, the Ikeda government seemingly accepted that the rift was no longer simply an ideological or economic phenomenon. On 8 July, a report on China with contributions from MOFA, the CRO, and others noted that 'since the spring China has ceased its attacks on the Soviet Union, but this is because of its own economic crisis, not because their ideological dispute has been resolved.' Moreover, the authors of the report also argued that 'Sino-Soviet policy differences were inevitable (*shukumeiteki*), the result of their differing experiences of Communist politics, levels of national power, geographic and strategic positions.'[49]

If the American and Japanese governments now concurred on the increasing seriousness of the rift, Tokyo still did not share Washington's assessment of its strategic consequences. In May, a conference of Japanese ambassadors from the Asian region concluded that the international influence of China had peaked, at least for the foreseeable future.[50] In other words, China was considered a diminishing threat if one at all.

No doubt this evaluation was unwelcome in Washington and in an effort to induce Tokyo to reconsider, at the second meeting of the Japan–US Security Consultative Committee on 1 August, a US report was presented on the rapid progress of China's nuclear weapons programme.[51] For the US, further evidence of Chinese 'aggressiveness' came with China's launch of a full-scale offensive in the Himalayas on 20 October 1962, over its border dispute with India. Japanese reaction, however, was restrained. Ikeda wrote to Indian Prime Minister Nehru describing the Chinese military action as 'a grave threat to the peace of Asia and indeed of the whole world', but refusing to take sides, he did no more than express the Japanese people's 'deep sympathy' for India's plight.[52] Shiga Kenjirō (director general of the Defence Agency) was less reticent. In mid-November, when Assistant Secretary of State for Far Eastern Affairs Averell Harriman suggested to him that China now posed 'a greater danger than that emanating from the Soviet Union', Shiga made no attempt to disguise Japan's 'considerable resentment' against India and sympathy for China.[53] China won more friends in Tokyo by unilaterally calling off its offensive and withdrawing its forces after just one month.[54] Any lingering Japanese concern with China's strategic ambitions was soon overshadowed by the much more serious superpower confrontation that erupted on 22 October 1962 over the construction of a Soviet nuclear missile base in Cuba. Khrushchev's decision to withdraw the Soviet missiles on 28 October, thereby avoiding almost certain war, marked another milestone on the road to the Sino-Soviet strategic split, and had a profound effect on perceptions of the rift throughout the world.

In the immediate aftermath of the Cuban missile crisis, China was very critical both of Khrushchev's recklessness in provoking the confrontation and of his cowardice in backing down when the stakes became too high. At a meeting with Takasaki Tatsunosuke in late October, Zhou Enlai even hinted at a new strategic alignment: 'Forgetting our grudge, let us strengthen Asia by joining hands. An Asia strengthened in such a way would not challenge others militarily, but should there ever again be pressure from outside Asia we might (be able to) defend ourselves.'[55]

In London, meanwhile, Japanese Ambassador Ōno was busy preparing for an official visit from Prime Minister Ikeda. In a 'proposed outline for Ikeda's talks with [British Prime Minister Harold] Macmillan', Ōno stated that:

> the Sino-Soviet rift occurring in the Communist bloc is an ideological problem and a leadership struggle which will have a big influence, but as long as the Cold War continues I do not think it will directly profit the West. The trend towards polycentrism is linked to the Communist bloc's stage of development. The Sino-Soviet rift is having a direct influence on Communist China, Soviet aid has been reduced, but if one thinks that the Soviets themselves are in economic difficulties, then even without the Sino-Soviet rift one can see Soviet power is reduced.[56]

Ikeda paid little attention to his ambassador's advice, although he agreed with Macmillan that relations were steadily getting worse. 'China and the Soviet Union were at very different stages in their political and economic evolution and as recent events had shown, the partnership was by no means an easy or happy one', Ikeda explained. He proposed reviving Yoshida's China Thesis, but dismissed the possibility of recognising Beijing, at least 'for the time being'. However, when Foreign Secretary Lord Home pointed out that, 'The Soviet economic squeeze on Communist China has seriously retarded its military preparedness', Ikeda disagreed. Nevertheless he made his threat perceptions very clear: 'I fear Communism, but I do not fear China.'[57]

With Washington increasingly concerned about the growing Communist threat in Indochina, the Pacific allies' perspectives on China diverged further. At the end of November, Roger Hilsman (director of the State Department's Intelligence Bureau) offered the first public admission by the US government of the seriousness of the Sino-Soviet split.[58] At the same time, he dismissed the probable impact of a Chinese nuclear test stating that: 'it will not change the balance of power in Asia, much less throughout the world'.[59] Yet, when the Japan–US Committee on Trade and Economic Affairs met on 3 December, Kennedy pointedly warned Ōhira (now foreign minister) that: 'The major problem facing us today is the growth of communist power in China, and how to contain communist expansion in Asia.'[60] Rusk elaborated further that afternoon. Stressing that Beijing was now the major threat in the 'far Pacific'—even more so if nuclear armed—'very discretely' he expressed the hope that Tokyo would accelerate its rearmament programme. The Japanese response was apparently positive. However, the next day when the secretary of state again inquired about Japan's stance on China following its dispute with the Soviet Union, Ambassador Asakai Kōichirō responded that, whereas Americans tended to like Russians and hate Chinese Communists, 'in Japan the situation is exactly reversed.' He spoke of the pressure Tokyo felt to 'make a deal with Communist China before it becomes a nuclear power.' Ōhira advised Rusk that, 'the US should leave Communist China alone. Making too much fuss about it only served to raise its prestige.'[61] Two days later, Ikeda publicly offered Japan's support for US strategy, but only if the target was 'Stalinist expansionism'.[62]

The argument resumed on 19 January 1963, this time within the framework of the Japan–US Security Consultative Committee. In the intervening weeks, Washington had aroused further resentment by calling on Tokyo to strengthen its defence efforts and offer port visitation rights for US nuclear-powered submarines. The Kennedy Administration had also received additional evidence of the deterioration of Sino-Soviet relations.[63] The CIA now claimed that ideological and policy differences were 'so fundamental that for most practical purposes, a "split" has already occurred.' The agency felt this was a positive development, but feared 'the emergence of a separate Asian Communist bloc under the leadership of China...because of Peiping's militant and intensely anti-Western line'.[64]

Many details of the Joint Security Consultative Committee meeting remain classified, but it is clear that there was a serious disagreement over how to handle China in light of the escalating strategic rift. The Americans reportedly stressed the danger of underestimating the threat—including the potential nuclear threat—posed by China in Asia.[65] The report from the Japanese Defence Agency, in contrast, apparently highlighted the weaknesses of the Beijing regime, even going so far as to suggest that counter-revolution was a distinct possibility.[66] Following the meeting, Ōhira publicly confessed that there were some 'discrepancies in nuance' between the two sides' evaluation of China and put it down to their historically contrasting relationships with Beijing. He expressed optimism, however, that, 'these discrepancies can be narrowed in future talks.' According to the foreign minister, Japanese and American assessments of Moscow's conciliatory policy since the Cuban Missile Crisis were consistent. Moreover, Ōhira proclaimed, they agreed that the Sino-Soviet 'dispute was centred primarily on means to achieve the same goal and not on a conflict of purposes', and therefore, 'the free world must not expect to gain substantially from the dispute.'[67] In short, Ōhira now seemed to be implying that both Moscow and Beijing should be regarded as a threat.[68]

Washington maintained the pressure by sending Deputy Defense Secretary Roswell Gilpatric to Tokyo in February. He caused a further stir in government circles by repeating US demands that Japan play a greater role in defending itself, as part of a Pacific defensive chain to contain latent Chinese power.[69] Although the Americans reportedly played no role in its writing, Washington's stance may have been a factor in the decision that month of the SDF's highest military organ, the Joint Staff Council, to commission the '1963 General Defence Plan of Operation'. A group of senior officers under Lieutenant-General Tanaka Yoshirō was asked to produce a secret contingency plan detailing Japan's military response in the event of a serious crisis arising on the Korean Peninsula. Better known as the '*Mitsuya kenkyū*' or Three Arrows Study, it is noteworthy for the 'potential enemy' status accorded to both the Soviet Union and China.[70]

In light of the Sino-Soviet strategic split, Japanese–American differences of opinion regarding the Communist threat in Asia continued, but during 1963, these disagreements were augmented by an escalating divergence of views within the Japanese government itself. Before the year was out, one young scholar, was suggesting that, 'the debate being conducted in Japan on the Sino-Soviet dispute...could amount...to an "agonizing reappraisal" of Japan's strategic position in the Far East and her attitude to nuclear weapons.'[71]

Japanese views on the strategic rift diverge

Yoshida Shigeru started off the New Year in typically provocative fashion by declaring in the *Tokyo Shimbun* that 'Marxism has collapsed. I think this is one of the reasons for the current Sino-Soviet confrontation. The controversy between the Soviet Union and China is something like "dusting off one's coat in the dust".'[72] In other words, it was an exercise in futility that could never produce a Communist revival.

Within the LDP views on China had never been uniform, but under the impact of what was now seen as a strategic Sino-Soviet rift, its long-standing 'East–West' cleavage was becoming increasingly prominent. On 19 January, *Sankei Shimbun* reported that 'pro-US' groups in the party were claiming that since the 'world trend was to make approaches to the Soviet Union and isolate China' then Japan should follow suit. On the other hand, 'pro-China' Asianist factions felt that for traditional reasons of history, geography, and trade, Japan should resist American pressure and attempt to strengthen ties to the mainland.[73] An anonymous article in *Chūō Kōron*, a leading intellectual journal, described the LDP clash as 'A deep, quiet dispute that has been carried on between a "Communist China faction" and a "Soviet faction"'. Yet unlike the ideological quarrels dividing the opposition parties, the LDP fight was said to be more policy-oriented. Alongside his mentor Yoshida Shigeru, Ikeda Hayato was depicted as the foremost member of the 'China camp' because of his 'forward-looking' attitude towards Beijing. Also included, albeit with rather different perspectives, were Matsumura Kenzō and Takasaki Tatsunosuke. In the so-called 'Soviet faction', Kaya Okinori (chairman of the PARC) and Funada Naka (chairman of the FARC) aimed to exploit China's increasing international isolation and domestic near-collapse, resulting from the Sino-Soviet rift. Although anti-Communist (and pro-Taiwan), they were said to be willing to 'compromise with the Soviet Union' as long as Japan 'assumed a high-handed attitude towards Communist China.' Other important supporters supposedly included Kishi Nobusuke, Satō Eisaku, and Ishii Mitsujirō.[74]

The results of a questionnaire contained in the same issue of *Chūō Kōron* confirmed the existence of internal disagreements over the causes of the rift. Aichi Kiichi (from the 'pro-Soviet' Satō faction) noted that, 'Attached to the ideological covering [of the dispute] is a nationalist rivalry that appears to have reached a stage where neither can easily retreat from its claim to leadership [of the bloc].' Aichi predicted that, 'Sino-Soviet antagonism will become more serious and the Communist world will move towards polarisation or polycentrism.' Representing the 'pro-China' camp, former Foreign Minister Fujiyama Aiichirō, replied that, 'Today's political disputes and antagonisms between China and the Soviet Union are ascribable to differences in their development of Communism, but also to...their national characters'.[75]

MOFA too was closely observing recent developments. In January it published a detailed analysis of the state of Sino-Soviet relations by Hōgen Shinsaku (head of the European Affairs Bureau). He noted how the Cuban Missile Crisis and the Sino-Indian border dispute had 'deepened the antagonism between Communist China and the Soviet Union.' Moreover, Hōgen seemed to lay most of the blame for the continuing rift at Beijing's door:

> Since the Soviet Union needs Communist bloc unity to conduct its foreign policy successfully...Moscow probably does not desire to perpetuate its dispute with Communist China...However, the Communist Chinese are not likely to "surrender" easily. They presumably have nothing more to lose through continuing the dispute.

Hōgen questioned whether recent Chinese moves to settle the dispute represented 'a change in their basic attitude.' In his view, 'Sino-Soviet relations will not be improved easily, even though they may not be broken off completely.'[76] Similarly, a meeting of Europe-based Japanese ambassadors held in Vienna during January reached the unanimous conclusion that, 'the causes of the [Sino-Soviet] dispute…were considerable and went very deep, and there were no signs of any significant reconciliation. Basic Soviet policy was aimed at achieving an ideological isolation of Communist Chinese leaders'. On the other hand, it was thought that the 'Communist Chinese leaders were aiming at assuming leadership by opposing the peaceful coexistence policy of the Soviets.' The ambassadors predicted that the 'campaigns by both parties to win support for their views among other world Communist parties would aggravate and intensify differences between the two countries.'[77]

A secret MOFA research report on 'recent Sino-Soviet relations', written in early March, essentially followed the same line. Beijing's attitude was described as 'cold and arrogant', while Moscow was seen as aiming to 'isolate China, but with some moderation in tactics in the hope of preventing further worsening of relations.' It concluded that the 'present exchanges may lead to [a] temporary improvement in relations, but disagreement on fundamental questions is so deep that no early final solution is in sight.'[78] Even after the Soviet and Chinese parties agreed later that month to hold a bilateral conference, according to press reports, the ministry's general view remained that 'shallow-rooted differences in views may be eliminated easily, but...the Sino-Soviet rift [will] be increasingly complicated in future.'[79]

In Canberra, meanwhile, Ambassador Ōta Saburō argued that 'the Chinese were becoming more and more isolated not only from the Western world but from other parts of the Communist world and that some Chinese had misgivings about this isolationism'.[80] Rumours circulating at the time suggested that, 'a number of [Japanese] Foreign Office officials known from prewar days for their pro-Western sympathies are said already to sympathize with the "containment school of thought"'.[81] In short, MOFA seemed to be aligning itself with the 'pro-US' wing of the LDP.

Aware of the growing significance of the Sino-Soviet rift, at the end of March, the government finally gave its approval for MOFA to establish a *Kokusai Shiryōbu* ('Research and Analysis Division' or RAD). First announced as early as September 1959, it constituted a significantly upgraded version of the Committee for the Coordinated Study of All Aspects of Communism. With an initial staff of 30 and Niizeki Kinya from the European Affairs Bureau in charge, this represented the first coordinated effort to assess the significance of the rift for Japanese foreign policy.[82] As Niizeki himself declared: 'the Foreign Ministry regarded Sino-Soviet activities in other countries, and the effects of these activities and of the Sino-Soviet dispute on those countries' foreign policies, as one of the most important problems affecting Japanese foreign policy.'[83]

Niizeki was soon quizzed by Australian diplomats on the veracity of a report that had recently appeared in the *Yomiuri Shimbun*. The paper had claimed—allegedly on the basis of official CCP documents obtained by the Japanese government from a former CCP Central Committee member—that MOFA believed the antagonism between Moscow and Beijing was far more serious than had been assumed. Niizeki denied that the Japanese had access to such sources, but he was convinced that the Russians were being subjected to 'widespread criticism' in China, some of it directed against the central authorities in Beijing for relying too much on Moscow for aid. MOFA also had reports that Khrushchev had been personally involved in intrigues against Mao.[84]

The launch of the new section coincided with the arrival of British Foreign Secretary Lord Home, who started a new European trend by flying to Tokyo to discover Japan's views on current international issues, especially Sino-Soviet relations.[85] Questioned by journalists, Home asserted that despite the existence of 'a deep cleavage of views in regard to war as a means to achieve Communist ends...the objective of all Communist countries is to bury capitalism sooner or later, by one method or another.' Nevertheless, although Britain continued to regard the matter as an 'important question', London supported Beijing's claim to a seat at the UN.[86] At their meeting on 3 April, Ikeda contrasted Washington's illogical policies towards China, with the 'very much more sensible and wise' policy of London. He regretted that due to 'internal political reasons' and 'the added complication that she recognised the regime on Formosa', Japan could only pursue improved relations in all areas short of full diplomatic recognition. In addition, he again proposed reviving a modified 'Singapore Plan': establishing a US/UK/Japan agency headquartered in Tokyo, but with offices in Hong Kong and Singapore, aimed at 'coordinat[ing] plans for preserving stability in India, Pakistan, Malaysia and Thailand'. The British dubbed it the 'Ikeda Plan', but it was never to be realised.[87]

At the 12th meeting of Japanese ambassadors stationed in the Asia–Pacific region, held in mid-June 1963, there was reportedly a 'lively exchange of opinions' between the heads of mission and Tokyo-based officials, including Foreign Minister Ōhira. The dominant view was that while the forthcoming Sino-Soviet conference might achieve a superficial and temporary reconciliation, a resolution of the basic rift would be very difficult.[88] Differences remained, however, over how Japan should respond: 'Some of the envoys apparently came out firmly in favour of Japan's taking a more definite position as a member of the free world.'[89] In other words, they supported Washington's strategic 'containment' of China. In Tokyo, however, many policy-makers still tended to share a low estimation of Japan's diplomatic skills and were more keenly aware of Japan's limited strategic resources.[90] The issue was no longer simply a matter of how Japan should respond to the Sino-Soviet split, but also the more practical issue of what it was capable of doing about it. This debate further intensified following the conclusion of the Partial Nuclear Test-Ban Treaty (PTBT) on 25 July.

Japan debates the implications of the strategic rift

Following Khrushchev's sudden *volte-face* on 7 June, trilateral negotiations on the PTBT opened on 14 July: the same day that the CPSU launched a hard-hitting attack on the CCP redolent of nineteenth century 'yellow perilism'. To American eyes the treaty represented the first dividend accruing from the Sino-Soviet strategic rift. Its signature coincided with the break down of critical Sino-Soviet talks aimed at reversing the deterioration in the alliance.[91] In Washington, opinions were divided as to the extent to which the Sino-Soviet Alliance still represented a strategic threat.[92] Beijing seemingly harboured few such doubts. Its first reaction to the resumption of the PTBT negotiations was to accuse Washington of 'wooing the Soviet Union, opposing China, and poisoning Sino-Soviet relations.'[93] After failing to prevent the Soviets from signing the agreement, the Chinese government issued a harshly-worded statement denouncing them for their 'surrender to imperialism', and appealing for global nuclear disarmament (while secretly redoubling efforts to produce its own bomb.)[94]

The Soviets countered by arguing that the PTBT was in the interest of all Socialist countries, including China, and claimed that their primary motive had been to prevent the possible nuclear arming of West Germany and Japan.[95] According to Khrushchev, however, Japan was no longer an important target of Soviet military strategy. On 5 August, he told a group of Japanese news editors: 'Japan is free to choose allies to suit her taste and we are [in] no way against her having good relations with other countries including the US.'[96]

Less obvious, perhaps, was the way in which the signing of the PTBT also tested the Japan–US alliance. Tokyo had long claimed a place at the forefront of the nuclear disarmament movement, and in March 1962, it had officially protested at Kennedy's decision to resume atmospheric nuclear testing. At the end of July 1963, however, Ikeda was reportedly unhappy at the US presumption of unconditional Japanese support for the new treaty.[97] The government adopted a 'wait and see' attitude, claiming that it had not been kept fully informed of the background to the negotiations and hence wanted to study international and domestic reactions to the pact.[98]

Japanese public opinion strongly supported the PTBT.[99] However, the government's temporising statement reflected the vigorous discussion of the strategic rift then preoccupying decision-makers in Tokyo. At the beginning of

July, the LDP's Security Problems Deliberation Council (a right-wing, anti-Communist group formed two years earlier) published an interim report. Its authors pessimistically predicted that 'encroachments on Japan of Communist influence is expected to increase as strife between the two Communist countries intensified (sic).' They therefore called for the consolidation of government efforts to study Communism into an organ akin to the CIA.[100] At a meeting on 11 July, MOFA's likely contribution to any such organisation, the RAD, concluded that 'the result of the present talks in Moscow would be the creation of two distinct international communist groups.' Its new head, Ogawa Heishirō, felt that 'in the immediate future Japan probably would not be seriously threatened by either the Soviet or Communist China' since both countries would follow 'soft-line' policies vis-à-vis Japan.[101] A few days earlier, an anonymous 'Foreign Office source'—now identified as Sono Akira (MOFA's chief spokesman)—revealed a very similar line of thinking. He began by challenging the prevailing view in the West, which blamed the 'bad', 'unbending' Chinese and not the 'innocent', 'flexible' Russians for their rift. Sono felt that racial prejudice might account for the split. He was at pains to describe how in practice, despite its fiery rhetoric, the rift left Beijing with no alternative but to pursue a cautious foreign policy:

> at present and in the foreseeable future, it is unlikely that Communist China will become capable of entering into a military adventure without the help of the Soviet Union...[and] there is no longer a possibility for Communist China and the Kremlin to reconcile.

In Japan's view, he asserted, the Soviet Union was still regarded as far more threatening than China because of its military power and industrial capacity. The main difference between the US and Japan lay in their differing estimations of China's 'potential threat.' Finally, the outspoken diplomat declared that 'Japan neither wants nor feels the necessity for taking advantage of or promoting the Sino-Soviet dispute, although it welcomes the split'. This was because it hoped that Beijing, freed from Moscow's influence, would be easier to deal with. Ogawa (RAD) privately criticised his colleague for being 'indiscreet', although he conceded that some members of his division might share Sono's views about the shortcomings in Western understanding of China.[102]

On 19 July, in what seems to have been his first public assessment of the rift, Ikeda told reporters gathered at his official residence that 'while it may well influence Japan, Communist China's moves towards Southeast Asia are more significant.' Japan would, he promised, help to strengthen these countries. The premier also asserted that 'the Sino-Soviet rift is becoming increasingly serious', since it had 'gone from being an ideological problem, to being a nationalist (*minzokushugi*) one.'[103] According to some reports, Ikeda seemed willing to blame Beijing for this, since 'Communist China's nationalism has recently become stronger domestically, even arguing about the [1858] Treaty of Aigun.' Other accounts, however, claimed that the prime minister concluded the interview by reminding the journalists, 'We must not forget the possibility that Communist China may turn to the free nations now that it has split with the Soviet Union.'[104]

At the beginning of August, Ōhira attended what appears to have been a hastily arranged meeting with Kennedy.[105] There is no record of them having discussed the PTBT. However, upon returning to Tokyo on 7 August, the foreign minister announced that Japan would be joining the treaty. If Ōhira thereby hoped to stifle further debate on the issue he was to be disappointed. A few weeks later, Shima Shigenobu, recently promoted to vice foreign minister, published his thoughts on the conclusion of the PTBT. He went along with the widely held view that Sino-Soviet relations were poor and the treaty was the result of Khrushchev's 'peaceful coexistence' policy. He did not, however, share the optimism of the 'pro-US school', claiming 'the hasty conclusion cannot be necessarily accepted that the Soviet Union will make friends with, or assume a mild attitude towards the West because of the Sino-Soviet dispute'. As far as Shima was concerned, there had been 'absolutely no change in the final objective of international Communism to Communise the whole world.'[106]

Genda Minoru also joined the debate—a man with a rather different perspective on Japan's Communist neighbours. He had been the 'best pilot' in the Imperial Navy Air Force, served as chief of staff of the Air Self-Defence Force, and latterly had become an influential right-wing LDP member of the House of Councillors. Genda repeated the by now common observation that 'behind the Sino-Soviet ideological dispute lie struggles over leadership of the international Communist movement, of nationalism or racism.' His primary concern, however, was with the threat from Beijing. Identifying a Chinese bid for leadership of the 'coloured nations', Genda predicted that in future the Cold War would be supplemented by 'struggles among races.' He also highlighted the danger posed by a nuclear-armed China:

> if Communist China should carry out a nuclear test in the near future, this would not only have a great effect on the Sino-Soviet dispute and the Partial Nuclear-Test Ban Treaty but also bring about a dreadful change in the strategic situation in the Far East...At present, when the Japan–US Security Treaty exists, it is impossible for Communist China to directly apply strategic pressure on Japan with her nuclear arms...[but] the nuclearisation of Communist China will have very great psychological effects on the surrounding countries.

Genda worried that this might lead to a future Japanese government 'taking a neutral stand'.[107] For him, the Chinese threat was real and growing.

Recently returned from an extensive tour of the Soviet Union and Eastern Europe where he had 'witness[ed] at first hand the latest issue between Moscow and Peking—racialism', Ogawa (RAD) agreed with Genda's first point. Moreover, according to Ogawa,

> MOFA was increasingly concerned at the way Japan was being involved in the issue of racialism by the tactics of Soviet propaganda. Moscow had twice attacked Matsumura [Kenzō] for his alleged "conspiracy" to support Peking's leaders' aim to unite all coloured peoples against the white race.

Contrary to Genda's main point, however, Ogawa stated that 'the Ministry's assessment quite definitely named the Soviet Union as presenting the greatest threat.'[108]

On 1 September, five months after setting up the RAD, MOFA published its first major analysis of the Sino-Soviet rift. It contained some important findings. The report began by declaring that, 'their rift is now decisive (*ketteiteki*), it has gone beyond an ideological dispute, becoming an open leadership struggle in the international Communist movement, and increasingly a state and national rift.' Even the possibility of a complete break in diplomatic relations and/or the suspension of economic ties was not discounted. In short, the report concluded that, 'a return to the so-called "monolithic unity" of the past is impossible.' The authors thought that the CCP was convinced of the correctness of its own revolutionary line and would promote 'national liberation movements'. However, they felt it improbable that the Chinese government would adopt a radical policy in partner countries, preferring a soft-line to promote a pro-Chinese mood. The report also anticipated no change in Khrushchev's 'peaceful coexistence' line, and foresaw a steady increase in Soviet power. Finally, it addressed the question of how Japan should respond to the rift. For the first time, MOFA publicly announced that it would 'basically maintain the same policy, but could no longer concur with the influential US policy of isolating Communist China.' This decision was justified on two grounds. First, the report argued that 'With the Sino-Soviet rift's intensification, whether one liked Beijing or not, it had become a centre of international relations impossible to ignore'. Second, it claimed that 'while one cannot expect Communist China's attitude towards the West to undergo a basic change...in the long-run...it would be useful to lead Communist Chinese policy in a realistic direction.'[109]

September proved a busy month for Japanese diplomacy. As Ōhira and Ikeda were to discover on landmark visits to Europe/North America, and Australasia respectively, Western governments were showing an even greater interest in

Tokyo's view of the Sino-Soviet rift. Playing down Chinese aggressiveness continued to be Japan's central message. In Stockholm, when asked whether in future 'Japan would side with Red China…as a result of the dispute with Soviet Russia', Ōhira replied that 'Japan had "no intention whatsoever" of taking any policy decisions based on racial considerations.'[110] In Scotland, on 3 September, Ōhira told British Foreign Secretary Home that, 'the Japanese Government never considered [the rift] as a primarily ideological question, they had thought that considerations of national interest were more decisive.' In retrospect, he dated its inception to 'three or four years ago', and looking ahead felt 'it was obvious that the split could not be healed in the foreseeable future'. Ōhira then renewed the Japanese critique of US China policy, insisting that 'neglect of China' rather than 'containment' was the better line to take. Finally, he highlighted three main factors motivating the rift: 'distrust of Chinese Communist leaders by the Russian leaders'; 'competition for leadership of the world Communist movement'; and a territorial dispute, specifically over Outer Mongolia. 'The Soviet Union, more than any other nation had to contain China', Ōhira concluded.[111] In Paris on the final leg of his European tour, French Foreign Minister Couve de Murville advised Ōhira 'not to interfere on one side or the other in the Sino-Soviet dispute but rather to let the two parties face their own difficulties. The relations between Moscow and Peking might one day change again. The West should therefore keep its own position open and uncommitted.'[112] In New York for the opening of the UN General Assembly, Ōhira met Secretary of State Rusk on 19 September, informing him that Beijing 'lacked the capacity for any major military adventures'. In a somewhat diluted version of Yoshida's China Thesis he also argued that Japan would be able to 'exercise a helpful influence on China by means of trade and [other] contacts'. Rusk urged caution and requested closer exchanges of information on China.[113]

The message Ikeda conveyed to Canberra at the end of the month echoed Ōhira's. He told Australian Prime Minister Robert Menzies that, 'China is unlikely to make aggressive moves in Southeast Asia' and similarly predicted that 'there is unlikely to be war, although [Sino-Soviet] relations are near breaking point.'[114] In Wellington a few days later, Ikeda related to New Zealand Premier Keith Holyoake details of a recent discussion with the Soviet Ambassador in Tokyo on the significance of the Sino-Soviet dispute. The Soviet Ambassador had told Ikeda that 'it was quite usual for husband and wife to fight until their golden jubilee, but the Ambassador was silent when he asked whether the parties were still "man and wife".' Ikeda concluded that Sino-Soviet differences were 'serious' since 'China was now claiming territories which had long been recognized as part of the Soviet Union.'[115]

Ikeda and Ōhira both returned to Tokyo in time for the fourth meeting of the Japan–US Security Consultative Committee on 10 October. In marked contrast to the previous meeting in January, Ōhira now claimed that the two sides reached 'a basic consensus' on security questions.[116] MOFA sources unofficially expressed their gratification at the convergence of views on Beijing's inability to become a major military menace in the region in the near future. Details remain sketchy, but the Japanese side apparently contended that when China carried out its first nuclear explosion, its effect on her neighbours—including Japan—would be psychological rather than military, and even this would soon pass. US Ambassador Edwin Reischauer evidently agreed.[117] In his foreign policy speech to the Diet one week later, Ōhira again posited a connexion between the Sino-Soviet rift and Moscow's relaxed foreign policy:

> the distrust and division that has been developing between Communist China and the Soviet Union over the last several years have suddenly revealed their seriousness since last year. Thus, the Communist bloc which has boasted of its iron unity is showing stronger signs of polarization: and it cannot be denied that this is one of the factors which is compelling the Soviet Union to push more actively its professed policy of so-called peaceful coexistence.[118]

International tensions had eased in consequence, but Ōhira the 'realist' maintained that with peace still dependent on a fragile balance of power, Japan had no alternative but to continue its existing security arrangements.[119]

Despite the improved international atmosphere, within MOFA long held suspicion of the Russians was slow to fade. Conciliatory steps towards Japan taken by Moscow during the latter half of 1963 were frequently dismissed as manifestations of a superficial '*bishō gaikō*' (smile diplomacy.)[120] One week after Ōhira's speech, Ogawa Heishirō (RAD) 'could not help having reservations about the sincerity of the Soviet's initiative leading up to the partial nuclear test ban'. Analysing the forthcoming Communist Party conference in Moscow, he predicted that China would continue to 'promote...subversive militant movements' in the Third World, while the Soviet Union was 'preparing, behind the scenes, to relax her previous hostility [towards China].' Japan's Embassy in Moscow reinforced this assessment. It reported the views of a Soviet Foreign Ministry official who claimed that 'Sino-Soviet antagonism is a temporary phenomenon and from the long-term point of view the two countries should have a common destiny.'[121]

MOFA was not the only branch of the Japanese government to have been scrutinising the deteriorating Sino-Soviet relationship. The Public Security Investigation Agency (*Kōan Chōsachō*), the anti-subversion organ of the Justice Ministry, was likewise concerned. In November 1963, a senior agency official, Hirotsu Kyōsuke, contradicted the general trend by re-emphasising the ideological dimension of the rift:

> It is unwarrantable to overlook the serious ideological dispute between Communist China and the Soviet Union because there is a contradiction in their national interests...To a Marxist..."theory" and "practice" are united dialectically and are regarded as one.

Hirotsu warned his fellow Japanese that, 'whether we like it or not, we shall be unable to evade the influence of the Sino-Soviet dispute.' He concluded with a virtual call to arms. 'In order to defend freedom and democracy at this violently changing time', he declared, 'it is necessary for us to strengthen our own independent standpoint and conduct a brave struggle on its basis, regardless of developments in the Sino-Soviet rift'.[122]

Hirotsu may have been reacting to the first evidence of the rift having consciously influenced a concrete policy decision. At the beginning of August, the Justice Ministry had refused entry to a Chinese reporter wishing to attend the Ninth *Gensuikyō* Congress. Justice Minister Kaya Okinori, a leading member of the so-called 'Soviet faction', later conceded that the decision 'had been due to a Soviet request' that the Chinese mission not outnumber their own.[123]

By this time, it seemed that every LDP Diet member with a passing interest in foreign affairs was publishing their views on the rift. In October, Kaya's ideological soul mate, Funada Naka (chairman of FARC) contrasted the 'maturity' of the Russian revolution and the Soviet desire for 'peaceful coexistence' with the 'callow youth' (*aonisai*) that was the Chinese revolution, with its 'self-delusions of grandeur' and blasé attitude towards nuclear weapons. He was also at pains to dispel the *dōbun dōshu* myth, asserting that 'communised Chinese...are no longer the same as the pre-war Chinese with whom we shared a written language and ethnic origin'. Funada noted that 'In some quarters, it is even being said that the Sino-Soviet military alliance has lost its power' and he welcomed the fact that this had 'finally compelled the Beijing government to take conciliatory measures towards Japan'. However, Funada also warned that the rift's effects, especially in East Asia, were 'very grave' and he recommended that Japan should keep a 'close watch on developments'.[124]

Although hailing from an opposing sect of the LDP's 'broad church', Takasaki Tatsunosuke (chairman of the Japan–China Overall Trade Liaison Council) similarly characterised the Sino-Soviet rift as 'like a quarrel between father and son', but unlike Funada, Takasaki considered the 'child's' view equally valid.[125] Ikeda Masanosuke, a defector from the 'pro-China' wing, was equally convinced that Moscow's 'conciliatory policy (*kanwa seisaku*) towards Japan' was a direct result of its rift with China. Continuing to mirror what had become the conventional wisdom, Ikeda predicted that, 'Even if there should be a lull, they will not come to terms, absolutely not.'[126]

While most LDP Diet members seemed content merely to analyse the emerging rift, former premier Ishibashi Tanzan choose this moment to attempt to effect a Sino-Soviet reconciliation.[127] In an interview with Zhou Enlai on 10 October, Ishibashi rather naïvely tried to 'talk some sense' into the Chinese premier by pointing out the absurdity of the issue. Zhou, while subtly placing the blame for their dispute on Moscow, reassured his guest that despite their 'clash over principles...the Sino-Soviet Alliance remains very much alive...and there is no danger of the conflict between the two nations worsening.' Ishibashi was not entirely convinced. On his return home, he issued a warning to those 'people who think that the dispute between China and the Soviet Union is advantageous to Japan.' Ishibashi reiterated his support for Moscow's 'peaceful coexistence' line, believing that it symbolised a gradual convergence between Communism and capitalism.[128]

Ishibashi's fruitless mediation efforts garnered some media attention and confirmed his standing as one of the LDP's leading 'heretics', but it may also have cost him his seat in the general election held on 21 November.[129] Overall, the poll held out the prospect of a strengthened 'pro-China' group, with the Kōno faction gaining ground at the expense of the Satō faction. In the event, however, the resulting cabinet reshuffle produced an anti-Kōno backlash within the Miki and Fujiyama factions.[130]

The assassination of President Kennedy on 22 November led Ikeda and Ōhira to make an unplanned visit to Washington. At a necessarily brief meeting, Rusk spoke blandly of the need to 'make an accurate and thoughtful assessment' of the meaning of the Sino-Soviet rift 'avoiding naïveté and illusion on the one hand and blindness to the significance of developments on the other hand.' He believed that it was still impossible to predict whether its outcome would be beneficial and worried lest Japan misinterpret US efforts to probe for areas of agreement with the Communists. Rusk reassured Ikeda that America's commitment to the 'alliance with Japan is utterly fundamental'.[131]

The Japanese government had come to understand the changing nature of the Sino-Soviet Alliance, but thus far, the effect on Tokyo's foreign policy had been minimal. This was about to change.

Ōhira leans towards China

The New Year opened with dramatic evidence that Sino-Soviet rivalry vis-à-vis Japan was extending into the strategic sphere. With France about to announce its diplomatic recognition of Beijing, the *People's Daily* introduced a significant strategic innovation: the theory of the 'intermediate zones'.[132] In talks with Japanese guests a few days later, Mao Zedong assigned 'Japanese monopoly capital' to the 'second intermediate zone'. This he did on the premise that although still dependent on the US, 'some of its representatives openly come out against the US'. Mao predicted that in time Japan 'will throw off the American yoke.'[133] Western scholars have viewed this as the point when Beijing began to see Japan as 'a separate though hostile entity in the American-sponsored containment of China' and thus started to fear its potential rapprochement with the Soviet Union.[134] The new Chinese theory targeted Moscow as well as Washington and Zhao Anbo (secretary of the China–Japan Friendship Association), on a visit to Tokyo in February 1964, asserted: 'We do not consider the Soviet Union a partner since the Soviet leaders have lapsed into racial egoism.' This constituted the first official Chinese denunciation of the Soviet leadership on Japanese soil.[135]

Ōhira responded to news of France's policy switch by cautioning the Diet on 21 January that 'the relaxation of tension does not mean that we may immediately change the basic aims of our foreign and defence policies.'[136] Public support for recognition of the PRC received a substantial boost, however, although a narrow majority still favoured a 'two Chinas' policy.[137] The latter remained the predominant view within the upper echelons of MOFA. Moreover, the idea that it was 'meaningless and impossible to contain Communist China' still enjoyed near unanimous support within the ministry.[138] Pro-Taiwan members of the LDP, like former premier Kishi, worried about the impact of the French decision on ordinary Japanese:

> [They] had no difficulty in rejecting Communism, such was the inherent Japanese dislike of Russia [but]...As Chinese Communism acquired more respectability...the Japanese because of their traditional links of culture and sentiment with China could find it increasingly difficult to preserve the strength of their anti-Communist convictions.[139]

Ikeda called a crisis meeting of foreign policy advisors at his official residence on 22 January. They agreed that maintenance of Taiwan's seat in the UN remained more important than blocking Beijing's entry.[140] This did not bode well for the third meeting of the Japan–US Committee on Trade and Economic Affairs rearranged for 26–27 January.

Although still heavily censored, the latest account of the meeting hints at continuing differences on the China issue. While Secretary of State Rusk did not completely rule out the possibility of friendly relations with China, he insisted that 'it had to be a two-way street.' He roundly condemned President de Gaulle's recent action in terms of American efforts 'to relieve Asian countries from the danger of the Chinese Communist threat.' On the other hand, Rusk approved of the 'new Soviet caution' which he attributed to the Cuban Missile Crisis, and regretted that, 'Peiping unfortunately did not share in that experience.' In an effort to counter Japan's lean towards China, Rusk ascribed Moscow's signature of the Test Ban Treaty to its 'anxiety over the prospect of a country of 800 million people armed with nuclear weapons.' Foreign Minister Ōhira accepted that 'there seemed to be a possibility for adjustment' of relations with Moscow and he claimed that Tokyo had attempted to dissuade Paris from recognising Beijing.[141]

At an official luncheon on the second day, however, Ikeda spoke of the enormous significance of the strategic rift for Japan:

> Japan, as you know, is in the singular position of being encircled by three great world forces—the US...and two large Communist powers which in recent times have been wallowing in the luxury of disagreeing on their views and policies. Fortunately, we are an island nation. The shock of the political upheaval and change in continental Asia is not as strongly felt in Japan as in countries on the continent. But even so, *the impact on Japan is far greater than countries outside of Asia could possibly imagine.*[142]

Ōhira later appeared to praise the French action, claiming that rather than damaging Free World solidarity, as widely believed in the US, the popular Japanese view was that 'France has provided an opportunity for more contacts with the Chinese mainland.' In an attempt to elucidate further, he described how:

> A sense of guilt still remains from Sino-Japanese hostilities preceding World War Two, and the public does not yet feel directly involved in conflicts in south–east Asia and on the border of Communist China and India. There is a deeper feeling of enmity against Soviet Russia than against any other country while hostility toward Communist China is not great.

In these circumstances, Ōhira warned that, 'to try to force the public to accept an American-type policy would produce a sharp and unfavorable reaction.' Rusk's response sounded ominously like a threat: 'If the United States pulled out of Southeast Asia today it could take care of itself, but could Asia?' Nonetheless, the secretary of state suggested that Tokyo 'think of its own interests in this part of the world…think in Asian terms and…consider Asian relations with Peking'. Ōhira was more than happy to agree that, 'Japan should give the fullest attention to its individual interests and responsibilities in Asia.'[143]

At first, Rusk's comment sounded like a major US concession, but as a series of statements by Japanese leaders over the next month made plain, the two sides were talking at cross-purposes. On 30 January, three days after the meeting concluded, Ōhira announced that should the UN admit the PRC, Tokyo would have to normalise its relations with Beijing. One week later, on 6 February, he went further by declaring that Beijing's foreign policy 'was not adventurous but rather based on a realistic and cautious appraisal of the international situation.' On 12 February, he repeated his statement linking recognition to UN actions, although he added that until Beijing's admission Tokyo would continue to support the 'important question' resolution. Ikeda also entered the fray, citing the rift in support of Yoshida's belief that Chinese Communism was different: 'In China they have a feeling of kinship and closeness to the Asian nations. Nationalism has transcended ideology. Does not the Sino-Soviet dispute show this?' This lean towards China culminated on 18 February in Ōhira's most controversial statement to date, when he told the Upper House Foreign Affairs Committee that China was 'not a threat to Japan, either militarily or economically.'[144]

In the wake of Beijing's new strategic thinking, Ōhira appeared to test the limits of anti-Chinese sentiment at home and abroad. He was to find that the constraints had not significantly eased and the remaining months of 1964 witnessed a steady erosion of Ōhira's lean towards China.

Balance restored

For the LDP right wing and its international allies, Ōhira's statement was the final straw. Confronted by a hail of criticism Ōhira was forced to effect a tactical withdrawal. Through diplomatic channels, he soon let it be known that Japan would only reconsider its attitude towards Beijing if it were admitted to the UN 'with the support and blessings of the great majority of countries'—notably US recognition was not explicitly mentioned. Japan's action in recognising Beijing was also to be premised on prior agreement 'on the separate future of Taiwan'. Regarding the Chinese threat, Ōhira claimed he had been talking from a Tokyo perspective, and 'this did not mean that the Japanese government did not recognize Communist China as part of the *general threat* of world Communism or as a threat to the security of South and South East Asia.'[145] Under pressure in the Diet, Ōhira introduced further qualifications. Addressing the Foreign Affairs Committee on 20 February, the foreign minister implied that a nuclear-armed China would change Japan's threat perception. Nor did he rule out the 'possibility of aggression by the Communists'. He made the point, however, that even though the US was 'Japan's best friend', this did not mean that both had to agree on every issue, citing the current differences over China as one such example.[146]

Summoned to defend his views before the conservative-dominated FARC one week later, Ōhira reiterated his belief that although China posed no military threat to Japan this did not mean that it was a proponent of peace. He even claimed that, 'there was no discrepancy between Japan and the US in regard to the Communist China issue.'[147] This was at best optimistic, at worst deliberately misleading. In fact, Secretary of State Rusk was at that very moment telling Ambassador Takeuchi Ryūji in Washington that, 'Peiping offers the most immediate threat to the peace.' He would not even rule out the possibility of war breaking out in Asia within the next six months. The contradictions in Rusk's position first revealed at the Tokyo conference remained in evidence. On the one hand, he again argued that, 'Japan's China policies should not be viewed as a problem of US–Japan relations...[but] as a key factor in the determination of Japan's own Asian policies.' On the other hand, he still insisted that Japan 'not take any steps which might encourage Peiping to believe that its aggressive policies could pay dividends.'[148]

When Ikeda and Ōhira appeared before the House of Councillors Budget Committee on 4 March, Ikeda criticised Beijing for its negative attitude towards the Japan–US Security Treaty and confirmed that Japan was under 'no obligation' to recognise the Communist regime, even if the UN did so. Ōhira, however, again asserted Tokyo's independence proclaiming that 'Japan itself must determine its policy for coping with international Communist activities.'[149]

The following day, in what appears to have been an attempt to contain the growing rifts within both MOFA and the ruling party, the former distributed a 'Unified View' on China policy to all cabinet ministers. Addressing the key question of 'the threat posed by Chinese Communist aggressiveness', the statement began by declaring that 'The Communist Chinese regime's ultimate goal is to Communize the world.' It went on to emphasise that 'Peiping denigrates Moscow's peaceful coexistence policy in the Sino-Soviet ideological dispute, opposes the limited nuclear test-ban treaty and is going ahead with its own nuclear test preparations.' This was balanced, however, by the observation that China was in practice cautious in dealings with its neighbours and 'a direct, armed invasion against Japan' was deemed improbable, if only because of the Japan–US Security Treaty. In MOFA's view therefore Mao Zedong's long-term goal—'to drive a wedge between Japan and the US'—called for continued vigilance. On the second crucial issue, diplomatic relations, normalisation was ruled out on the grounds that it would 'result in the complete rupture of relations with Taiwan...jeopardise the peace and stability of Asia, and impair the solidarity of the Free World'. At the same time, the policy statement noted that geographical proximity and history meant that Japan's position vis-à-vis China was 'fundamentally different' from that of the US, which could avoid relations altogether if it chose to. In short, the 'Unified View' reasserted the validity of the *seikei bunri* (separating politics from economics) line. Finally, on the matter of the UN seat, the ministry said that it was too early to decide on a policy for the autumn. The impact of the French decision on sovereign 'world opinion' was as yet unclear, and Japan was carefully observing trends.[150]

During the weeks that followed, with the Soviets resuming their public criticism of China, Moscow and Beijing stepped up their strategic competition over Japan. An April mission to Tokyo led by Nan Hanchen (chairman of the China International Trade Promotion Committee), although ostensibly economic in nature, attempted to strengthen ties with senior LDP politicians including Satō

Eisaku. Then when Matsumura Kenzō again visited Beijing to sign important agreements on trade and the exchange of journalists, Chinese Foreign Minister Chen Yi sought to draw a distinction between Beijing's confrontation with Moscow and its positive attitude towards Japan. Matsumura returned home declaring of the Sino-Soviet rift that 'what is done cannot be undone'.[151]

The Soviets responded with a full-fledged diplomatic offensive that saw Soviet diplomats approaching their Japanese counterparts in posts across Europe and Asia—an unusual occurrence—and attempting to 'explain' the Sino-Soviet situation. In Rangoon, it was claimed that 'the attitude of Communist China is undemocratic, dogmatic and interferes with the domestic affairs of other states', and that Japan 'as the only country which has suffered nuclear damage should support Russia positively' on the importance of avoiding nuclear war. In Yugoslavia, a Soviet diplomat went so far as to state that 'the Soviet Union would prefer to have American cooperation in limiting the national strength of China.'[152] The Soviet Ambassador to Japan, Vladimir Vinogradov, sought Japanese support from Vice-Foreign Minister Shima Shigenobu against Chinese efforts to exclude the Soviets from the planned second Afro-Asian Conference. The next day, Vinogradov surprised MOFA by announcing that Deputy Premier Anastas Mikoyan would make a second visit to Japan during the latter half of May. Ministry officials reportedly concluded, 'the Soviet Union now counts Japan as a major power in Asia as against Red China and that improved ties with Japan have become important in the face of the current feud with Peiping.'[153]

Just after Mikoyan's arrival, the RAD issued 'Analysis No.12', its most detailed study of the Sino-Soviet confrontation to date. The division still did not expect that 'the relations between the countries will be formally ruptured or that the Sino-Soviet alliance treaty will be broken.' However, it did acknowledge that 'the tendency towards pluralism within the international communist movement is gaining strength.' As regards its impact on the Cold War, the report asserted that 'Since the Sino-Soviet confrontation implies a fragmentation of forces opposed to the West, it is of profit to the West.' It listed four main advantages: the challenge to Soviet prestige; Khrushchev's inevitable continuing support for peaceful co-existence; retardation of Chinese military and economic modernisation (resulting in an improved attitude towards trade with Japan); and the confusion sown amongst the Communist parties in the West. The report concluded with the dramatic admission that:

> The Sino-Soviet confrontation has given rise to a feeling of complacency in the West, and there is danger from certain national movements which could threaten Western unity. However, the overall weakness of the Communist bloc should easily compensate for this. In the case of Japan, in particular, the Soviet

> Union's attitude, in that it is slowing the development of China, both militarily and economically, is something we would like to see continued.[154]

During his two-week stay, however, Mikoyan refrained from public attacks on Beijing and even claimed that the Soviet Union would welcome closer Sino-Japanese relations. Yet at the same time, he dismissed the JSP's long-standing proposal for a four-power non-aggression pact as unnecessary and agreed with Satō Eisaku that the Soviet–American policy of 'peaceful coexistence' was playing an important role in world peace. Although briefed to introduce the topic, the state of Sino-Soviet relations was not raised during Ikeda and Ōhira's meetings with the Soviet deputy premier.[155]

Not to be outdone, Mao Zedong made a further attempt to draw Tokyo into the strategic rift in July when he reportedly suggested that 'Japan and China must come together by forming an alliance and acting in common'. Even more controversially, he also declared China's support for Japan's claim to the strategically important Soviet-occupied Kurile Islands. An enraged Moscow struck back with frenzied verbal attacks on the Chinese leader. More constructively for Tokyo, however, Mao's statement also prompted the Soviets to begin 'making suggestions [to the Japanese] about reaching a satisfactory solution to the problem of the Kuriles.'[156]

Japan's friends in the West were watching these developments with interest and some concern. In a meeting with Ōhira in early April, French Foreign Minister Couve de Murville had expressed 'doubts that [the] USSR was as enthusiastic as it pretended to be over France's recognition of [the] ChiComs'. Moreover, 'concerning the Sino-Soviet dispute,' he again emphasised, 'the necessity of avoiding intervention to assist either side.'[157] The British advocated the same passive stance at official level talks held on 1 May. Ogawa Heishirō (RAD) 'agreed generally with this assessment', but Hōgen Shinsaku (director of the European Affairs Bureau) saw wider implications in the rift and was more impatient. Since 'the dispute would develop further', he asserted, 'the Eastern European and other satellites must be encouraged to assert their independence.' Indeed, according to Hōgen, Tokyo was already actively pursuing such a policy, for example, by giving 'VIP treatment to visiting trade delegations from Eastern Europe.'[158] British Embassy officials concluded that the Japanese were aware of the Sino-Soviet dispute strengthening their hand vis-à-vis Moscow, but that 'They dislike the Russians and will not readily give them any support against China.'[159]

In Washington, meanwhile, the CIA produced a special report entitled 'The China Problem in Japanese Politics'. The agency recounted the fear and nonchalance traditionally exhibited by the Japanese when confronted by the Russian and Chinese threats respectively. It then pointed to the PTBT, US grain sales to Moscow, and French recognition of Beijing, as having 'encouraged [the Japanese] to move ahead, toward closer ties with mainland China'. Aware of both Ikeda's growing dependence on the 'leftist' Kōno Ichirō in the run-up to the party presidential election and Satō's efforts to disrupt their alliance, the report also noted how 'China policy has...become deeply embroiled with struggles for leadership in the LDP.' It mentioned rumours that the premier 'wanted to go down in history as the prime minister who "normalised" relations with Communist China', before predicting that the only question remaining was 'merely the manner and timing of [Japan's] inevitable approach to Peking.'[160] A few weeks later, the State Department compiled a secret policy paper on 'The Future of Japan'. Contemplating the coming decade, it characterised Japan as a kind of East Asian 'super domino'. While not anticipating Japanese diplomatic recognition of China, at least not 'under present international circumstances', it noted that 'most Japanese will continue to feel an instinctive desire to "normalise" relations with mainland China.'[161]

The report virtually coincided with a meeting in Tokyo on 24 June between the recently promoted Vice-Foreign Minister, Ōda Takio, and the Australian Ambassador Lawrence McIntyre. In a remarkably frank interview, Ōda confirmed that Tokyo was 'being wooed by both Moscow and Peking' and that 'Japan's natural sympathy lies towards China, Communist or not'. Nonetheless, he went on to say that Japan's preference was to avoid any 'aggravation of current Sino-Soviet differences'. Ōda, however, was 'simply not sure how Japan would decide if the breach between Moscow and Peking should become irreparable and Japan should be forced to choose between them'. He thus felt that Japan would 'do its best to put off any decision as to which side it might be compelled to take between the two', claiming that the government, 'while closely interested', had given no thought to 'what possible role Japan might play either to widen the rift or to profit from it'.[162]

In an article published the following month, Ōhira noted the significance of the 'Sino-Soviet split' as being 'the most conspicuous example of...the tendency among nations of both camps toward self-assertion and independent action.' Nevertheless, he maintained that it still amounted to no more than:

> an internal wrangling over the succession to Marxism–Leninism, and it has not yet affected the East–West balance of power. However furiously Moscow and Peking may fight over the Communist leadership, the overthrow of the free world is their common goal.

In other words, he was arguing that the rift could undermine the vertical Cold War structure on the Communist side without affecting its horizontal East–West dimension. Yet Ōhira also warned, somewhat contradictorily, that Moscow and Beijing were 'now competing with each other in penetration of the non-communist world.' He welcomed Beijing's recent tolerance of Japan's 'separation of political affairs from the economic'. Nevertheless, he ruled out recognising China on the grounds that, 'such a step on our part at this moment is prejudicial to the peace in Asia and to the solidarity of the free world.'[163]

The uncertainty prevailing among Japanese policy-makers vis-à-vis its powerful neighbour was clear. As Ōhira had told British Foreign Secretary Rab Butler on 2 May, Japan did not necessarily know China better than other countries did despite its geographical proximity: 'the darkest spot is at the foot of a lighthouse', he observed.[164] That August, the RAD produced two further analyses: 'Communist Chinese and Soviet Approaches to Japan' (number 13) and 'Effects of the Sino-Soviet Dispute on Conditions in Southeast Asia' (number 14). The former contained few surprises, but the latter was important for highlighting the two-edged nature of the rift. On the one hand, it 'weakened their [Sino-Soviet] influence' in the region and produced a 'more reasonable Soviet attitude', but at the same time the report acknowledged, 'Communist China has tended to show interest in spontaneous local movements which has increased the danger to the security of Southeast Asian countries.'[165]

That same month, the CRO too published a major study of the impact of the Sino-Soviet rift on Japan. It noted that, 'the scale and strength of its influence was deeper and bigger than expected', but predictably stated that Japanese 'reformists' were the most strongly affected. It recognised that, 'China and the Soviet Union have both acted positively to get closer to Japan', but predicting that the rift would become 'increasingly serious', the report felt it warranted Japan's 'deep concern'.[166]

Following his narrow victory in the mid-July LDP presidential election, Ikeda replaced Ōhira as foreign minister with the rather less impressive Shiina Etsusaburō (Kishi faction), but Tokyo's view of the international situation remained essentially unaltered. Tension mounted with the alleged Tonkin Gulf 'clash' of 2 August, which heightened fears of Chinese intervention in the Vietnam conflict. Washington immediately escalated its participation in the war. At the time, the Japanese government publicly accepted the (later discredited) US version of events and offered its full understanding. The result was to strengthen the hand of the pro-US wing of the LDP in its anti-Chinese stance.[167]

The following day, Rusk met Shiina in India at Nehru's funeral. The secretary of state shocked his Japanese counterpart by informing him that because of the 'seriousness of the situation in Laos and Vietnam…the US was prepared to react in whatever way necessary to meet a threat…[and] did not exclude bombing Peking itself.' Moreover, he claimed that 'the US had had indications that the

USSR would not intervene in that eventuality.' Rusk wanted the Japanese to communicate to the Chinese how seriously the US regarded the situation.[168]

Concern for potential Chinese aggression was also the focus of the fifth meeting of the Japan–US Security Consultative Committee held on 31 August. Participants—who included Shiina, Koizumi Junya (director general of the Defence Agency), Ambassador Reischauer and Admiral Grant Sharp (commander-in-chief of US Pacific Forces)—agreed that

> whilst cessation of Russian military and economic aid to Mainland China weakened Peking's potential influence in the [Southeast Asian] area, there was a danger that relaxation of Russian restraints on the Chinese might lead to their entertainment of aggressive initiatives in the area.[169]

In the main, however, Japanese officials were more concerned with how the rift was affecting Japan's interests. In September, Ogawa (RAD) informed an Australian diplomat that 'competition between Communist China and the Soviet Union to improve their public image was, at least for the time being, operating in Japan's favour.'[170] Hōgen Shinsaku (director of the European Affairs Bureau) remained more sceptical. He 'failed to see in all this anything more than minor tactical changes on the part of the Russians…the fundamental Soviet objective was still the same—to get rid of American bases in Japan as soon as possible.'[171]

At the same time, the Canadian secretary for external affairs suggested to Shiina that the split had 'provided the Free World with opportunities for new policies and ha[d] made the Soviet Union more amenable to concluding specific agreements'. Shiina countered that the rift was largely responsible for 'a stalemate in East–West relations.' Moreover, he 'poured cold water' on Ottawa's view that, 'the Peking Government's policy is likely to become increasingly aggressive following the removal of Soviet restraints'. Tokyo had noted 'recent conciliatory gestures' from both Moscow and Beijing, but their contrasting positions on the Kurile Islands led Shiina to recommend that: 'every attempt should be made to open additional Chinese [not Soviet] windows to the world'.[172]

Three weeks later, Shiina appeared even more confident in his reading of the situation and of Japan's place in it. While publicly acknowledging that the fundamental pattern of Cold War confrontation remained in operation, he also noted the recent 'polycentralization of power within *both camps* of East and West'. Making a classic 'neo-realist' argument, Shiina claimed that, 'the intensification of the opposition between the Soviet Union and Communist China' was accompanied by 'Japan–US relations...enter[ing] a new phase of *independent* participation in international society…where the two nations will *share* the responsibility...to establish a new world order'.[173] This optimistic assessment of

Japan's diplomatic 'coming of age' was somewhat premature. A series of major developments in the autumn of 1964 soon drove Tokyo back under Washington's wing.

The turning point

The Kennan affair

George F. Kennan was a former ambassador to Moscow who, as head of the State Department's Policy Planning Staff in the late 1940s, devised America's 'containment' strategy. On a research trip to Japan in the summer of 1964, Kennan said that it would be 'a mistake to over-dramatize Sino-Soviet differences', predicting that relations would return to the 'traditional, pre-revolutionary pattern'. Although claiming that the dispute 'was not necessarily useful to peace', he still believed that, 'it will be easier for nations to live together in an atmosphere of polycentrism'.[174] Kennan subsequently questioned the continuing validity of the assumptions on which the Japan–US security relationship was founded in an article that appeared in the October 1964 edition of the American journal *Foreign Affairs*. He pointed out that, 'Japan has two possible opponents, not one, on the mainland of Asia'. Yet, in light of the Sino-Soviet strategic rift he dismissed any possibility of either invading Japan, even if US forces were withdrawn. Kennan was not immediately recommending such a course of action to Washington; rather he hoped to persuade US policy-makers that it was in America's interest to allow Japan to develop closer relations with Communist Asia. He even proposed a joint US–Soviet security guarantee for Japan and added that with differing needs and interests, 'There is no reason why Japanese policy toward Communist China should be identical with that of the United States.' In short, Kennan the neorealist believed that Japan was entering into a new polycentric world, one in which she would have greater room for manoeuvre in her relations with both the Communist powers and the US.[175]

Ambassador Reischauer was so concerned that the Japanese would misinterpret Kennan's article as foreshadowing a change in official US policy that Washington immediately despatched Assistant Secretary of State for Far Eastern Affairs William Bundy to Tokyo to disabuse them.[176] Addressing an audience of academics, Bundy said,

> We recognise the profound implications of the Sino-Soviet rift…but let us recognise always that differences between the Soviet Union and Communist China are still concerned primarily not with their basic objectives but rather with the degree of violence to be employed to achieve those objectives.

He went on to claim that the PRC still represented the 'most immediate source of danger in the world today.'[177]

Japanese reactions to the Kennan affair were mixed. On the left, the JSP and former premier Ishibashi Tanzan welcomed Kennan's acceptance of their ideas.[178] On the right, Genda Minoru demolished Kennan's 'incomprehensible' (*ryōkai shigatai*) thesis, which did 'more harm than good.' Genda saw the rift in personal terms and had 'no doubt that in the event Stalinists replace Khrushchev, the Soviet Union and China will recover their iron solidarity and push, in concert, an offensive policy against the US and Japan.' He agreed that Beijing obviously lacked the military capacity to invade Japan, but feared Chinese 'ideological aggression under the veneer of friendship'. Genda predicted that a joint US–Soviet security guarantee would eventually 'lead to the stationing of US and Soviet troops in Japan, turning it into another...Germany or Korea.' He preferred to see Japan contribute more to its own security.[179]

MOFA and the CRO also prepared secret critiques of the Kennan thesis. MOFA officials were particularly 'upset' with Kennan's article, as they believed they had succeeded in persuading the American of the 'errors' in his analysis during his earlier visit to Japan. The CRO report essentially followed Genda's logic. It emphasised the fragility of the current US–Soviet détente and pointed out that although Soviet policy-makers were not at present considering 'full-scale aggression, there is no guarantee that it will be so forever.' Neither did the authors fear 'direct military aggression' by China, but they claimed that Kennan 'overlook[ed] how dangerous the basic character, tactics and strategy of the Communist Chinese regime are to our country'.[180]

On the basis of these reports, the US Embassy in Tokyo concluded that, 'by eliciting such strong adverse responses Kennan may in the long run have contributed to the strength of those advocating closer ties with the US.'[181] However, in writing the analyses, the Japanese officials admitted that they had been influenced by news from the Kremlin and from Lop Nor of two contemporaneous events of even greater significance.

The fall of Khrushchev and the Chinese nuclear test

It was generally felt in Tokyo, that the enforced resignation of Nikita Khrushchev on 16 October would have little long-term effect on the course of Sino-Soviet or indeed Japanese–Soviet relations. In the spring of 1963, when the press had prematurely reported Khrushchev's demise, MOFA sources predicted that, 'Moscow diplomacy would revert to its old hard line.'[182] No one was publicly suggesting such a scenario now that Khrushchev had actually been ousted. The JSP expressed regret at the news and Ishibashi Tanzan went so far as to describe Khrushchev's 'peaceful coexistence' policy as 'the greatest discovery since the

Communist Manifesto.'[183] Most reaction, however, was more restrained. The effect on the Tokyo Stock Exchange lasted but a few hours.[184] Chief Cabinet Secretary Suzuki Zenkō initially accepted official reports that Khrushchev had resigned due to poor health, but he did note the existence of protracted quarrels with China. LDP Secretary-General Miki Takeo ruled out the possibility of Moscow deviating from its basic principle of 'peaceful coexistence', but thought there would be changes in US–Soviet and Sino-Soviet relations.[185] The first reaction from MOFA was to confess that 'it had insufficient information to determine the significance of the change of Soviet Government'.[186] Nevertheless, three days later, in a hastily produced report, the RAD concluded that:

> There will be no immediate improvement in Sino-Soviet relations as a result of Khrushchev's fall. No doubt there will be some modification of tactics on both sides, but ideological reconciliation would be extremely difficult...there is a strong probability that Chinese and Russian leaders will sooner or later take steps to improve relations between their parties and countries...But the antagonism between them is not a mere rivalry between leaders, or even merely ideological. It is rooted in economic and social differences and conflicts of national interest. This being so, there is no chance of a fundamental solution to the quarrel. At the most, the two sides will simply maintain a relationship of equality and independence.[187]

Hōgen Shinsaku (director of the European Affairs Bureau) and Ushiba Nobuhiko (deputy vice foreign minister), informed the FARC on 21 October that the emotional rivalry between Moscow and Beijing would probably soften and open the door to negotiations. Nonetheless, they expected no great change in Soviet domestic or foreign policies under Leonid Brezhnev and Alexei Kosygin and hence no reconciliation.[188] Ogawa Heishirō (RAD) shared the American view that the cause of Khrushchev's removal was his 'handling of the Sino-Soviet dispute and the resulting disunity in the Communist movement'. His head of research, Hasegawa Takaaki, was more explicit, pointing the finger at members of the secretariat, especially Mikhail Suslov, who had been in charge of the negotiations with the CCP. He even speculated on a link between the 'palace coup' and the Chinese nuclear test, which took place just a few hours later.[189]

As early as 29 September, Secretary of State Rusk had warned the world that a Chinese nuclear test was imminent. On 10 October, Khrushchev had informed ex-Foreign Minister Fujiyama Aiichirō that based on Soviet nuclear aid supplied until 1960, China should now be capable of conducting a test. Qualifying this statement, however, Khrushchev added that China would not have an operational nuclear weapon for several years and therefore it posed no real threat. Foreign Minister Shiina passed on these warnings to the Diet, emphasising that it would take up to a decade before Beijing would have an adequate delivery system. The only real problem at this time, Shiina declared, was how to deal with the psychological impact on the Japanese people of a nuclear China.[190] Within MOFA two schools of thought contended on this question. The optimistic view, held by Ogawa (RAD) and most senior officials, predicted that 'thinking Japanese would appraise the event realistically and quickly appreciate that…[it] would not give mainland China a significant military advantage for quite some time.' The pessimistic view, supported by most section heads and especially Inada Shigeru (Southeast Asia Section), claimed that the test would have 'a tremendous emotional impact amongst the Afro-Asian group dramatically increasing the influence [of]…mainland China'. This would have serious repercussions in Japan, although left-wing Japanese might be alienated by China's action.[191]

Chinese scientists successfully detonated a Hiroshima-size nuclear device at Lop Nor in Xinjiang Province on 16 October. The Soviets immediately reassessed China's potential as a military threat.[192] The Japanese and American governments, however, conspired to publicly play down the explosion's strategic importance. Piqued at the way Beijing had upstaged the Tokyo Olympics, Chief Cabinet Secretary Suzuki Zenkō issued a strongly worded protest to the Chinese government. At the same time, he reassured the Japanese public that, 'this initial experiment can have no influence on nor pose any threat to our country as long as the US–Japan Security Treaty remains in force.'[193] In a further attempt to minimise the military significance of China's actions, Foreign Minister Shiina later added that he saw no need for Japan to alter its nuclear policies because of the test, and that Japan would not even change its stance on the entry of China to the UN.[194] He was supported by US Defence Secretary Robert McNamara who kept referring to China's 'primitive test device', and continued to insist that it would be many years before Beijing would have an operational nuclear weapons system.[195]

Earlier that year, the French nuclear strategist General Pierre Gallois, architect of the '*Force de Frappe*' (France's independent nuclear deterrent), had visited Tokyo. He gained some notoriety by predicting that following Chinese development of a practical nuclear capability, Japan would become 'the second nuclear power in Asia.'[196] If not, Gallois argued, Tokyo had only two other options. It must either seek a strengthening of the US nuclear umbrella, thus heightening dependence on Washington, or adopt a neutralist foreign policy and promote stronger ties to Beijing.[197] In the event, support for all three alternatives was strong, albeit from different quarters. Although the JSP immediately came out in opposition to the test, there was also a sense that China had raised its status in the world—even a sneaking admiration for the first Asian nuclear power. Arguing that Beijing's action necessitated a reconsideration of Japan's policy alternatives, Matsumura Kenzō claimed that China's possession of a nuclear device meant the need to normalise Sino-Japanese relations had become 'greater than ever.'[198] Another member of the pro-China camp, Ishibashi Tanzan, wrote:

> It is the height of foolishness for Japan to follow in America's wake and say that even though Communist China has conducted a nuclear test Japan is safe, as long as the Japan–US Security Treaty exists. Today, the Security Treaty is more a source of danger for Japan.[199]

By contrast, within MOFA, some officials optimistically suggested that a more secure Beijing might even adopt a more flexible foreign policy. Defence Agency sources, on the other hand, interpreted Chinese intentions as primarily political, and in direct contradiction to MOFA's official line, linked the timing of the test to the overthrow of Khrushchev.[200] Agency Director Koizumi Junya insisted that he had no intention of re-examining Japan's defence plans because of the test.[201]

There is evidence to suggest that beneath all this bravado and the calm public exterior lay the fear that a century of Japanese diplomatic, psychological and military superiority over China had been erased overnight.[202] On 18 November, the LDP's right-wing Security Problems Research Council published a report claiming that even if the Chinese did in time develop some form of nuclear weapons system, the threat to Japan would 'increase only slightly' that currently posed by 'Soviet military might.' As countermeasures, the report recommended strengthening conventional defences, asking Washington to reaffirm its security guarantee, and developing civilian nuclear and space technology to overcome any popular sense of inferiority emerging vis-à-vis China.[203] The CRO, however, went much further, stating that:

> [China's] political threat, enhanced by her nuclear explosion, is greatly increased toward all Asia including our country…Compared with the Soviet threat, Communist China's threat to our country is much greater...[and] Communist China will become more dangerous as time passes.'[204]

The Americans, who were seriously concerned that Chinese development of nuclear weapons would cause Japan to follow suit, subsequently produced their own report on 'Japan's prospects in the nuclear weapons field'. In common with many others, it concluded that the Chinese nuclear experiments 'appear to have had little impact in Japan, long accustomed to the nuclear weapons of its traditional enemy, the USSR.' Nonetheless, it went on to predict:

> The appearance of a deliverable nuclear weapons capability in Communist Chinese hands will unquestionably, however, provoke a stronger reaction. A significant proportion of Japanese, led by right-of-center conservatives such as

> Satō already leaning in this direction, will undoubtedly favor expanded Japanese defenses including a nuclear element.

In support of this contention, the report first quoted Satō Eisaku's press conference of 31 December 1964, where he claimed: 'Japan has no intention whatsoever of having nuclear weapons in the future', and second, his radically different statement made to Ambassador Reischauer just two days earlier:

> If the other fellow has nuclear weapons, its only common sense to have them oneself. The Japanese public is not ready for this, but would have to be educated. The younger generation is showing hopeful signs of going this way...Nuclear weapons are less costly than is generally assumed, and the Japanese scientific and industrial level is fully up to producing them.[205]

Perhaps Satō's views could have been simply dismissed as those of the LDP right-wing fringe, but for the fact that he was by this time the prime minister.

Satō Eisaku and the origins of 'equidistance'

Ikeda's resignation on 26 October, after doctors had diagnosed his cancer as terminal, represented the final stage in Japan's reversal of its lean towards China. On the advice of Yoshida, the ailing premier named Satō Eisaku as his successor. The State Department, in its analysis of the prospects for the new premier, noted that 'Of all the conservative political leaders Satō may be the least attracted by the idea of political relations with Peiping.' Nevertheless, it warned: 'There appears to be a growing momentum within the Japanese Government and in conservative political circles toward establishing some form of official relations with Peiping [and] Satō can bring himself to bend with the political wind.'[206] There was also the problem that Japanese public opinion continued to support diplomatic normalisation.[207] This American concern was not misplaced.

In his first policy address to the Diet as premier, on 21 November, Satō expressed his 'heart-felt regret' over the Chinese nuclear test and strongly urged Beijing to refrain from conducting any more. Nonetheless, he went on to announce that the test would not cause him to alter Ikeda's *seikei bunri* policy. Still, this statement marked a considerable retreat from Satō's position the previous summer, when he had ridiculed Ikeda's weak-kneed China policy.[208]

Satō's status quo stance on China's UN seat was soon under threat, however. Foreign Minister Shiina openly admitted that the 'important question' formula supported by the Japanese government would inevitably be interpreted as a means of preventing or delaying Beijing's admission. To counter Shiina's public blunder, Satō was forced to retreat from his earlier position and tell the same Diet session that Japan's China policy might well change in the future. In addition, he denied ever assuming a hostile attitude towards China, supporting its 'containment' or blindly following the lead of others. Addressing the same committee on 3 December, Satō went even further in declaring his readiness to initiate ambassador-level contacts with China, and announcing that Shiina would have to retract or revise his statement. This produced a brief flurry of press speculation over a possible split between the two men and also prompted fears in pro-Taipei quarters that Satō was moving towards revision of Japan's China policy.[209]

The Satō–Shiina partnership in fact endured for another two years. This element of stability, however, could not avert a much broader schism opening up within the ruling party. With the intention of preventing any policy change before Satō's upcoming summit meeting with President Johnson, leading members of the LDP's pro-Taiwan faction held the inaugural meeting of the *Ajia Mondai Kenkyūkai* (Asian Problems Study Group) on 16 December. They criticised Satō for sowing confusion within the party and declared themselves 'very concerned with the threat to Japan's security posed by the Communist regime in China.' Some within this group held the 'senior Gaimushō officials' who were briefing Satō for the summit, responsible for the prime minister's stance.[210] They promptly drew up an 'interim report on foreign policy' which the FARC approved and passed on to Satō on Christmas Day. It demanded that Satō defend Taipei's seat at the UN and block Beijing's admission as it had rejected peaceful coexistence.[211]

In response the LDP's 'pro-China' group immediately revived the long-dormant *NitChū Mondai Kenkyūkai* (soon renamed the *Ajia–Afurika Mondai Kenkyūkai* or Asian–African Problems Study Group).[212] With Satō already en route to Washington, a leading member of this group, Utsunomiya Tokuma, departed for China to view at firsthand the current state of Sino-Soviet relations. Utsunomiya's talks with Foreign Minister Chen Yi soon convinced him that the situation had not improved. Nevertheless, on his return to Tokyo he sounded optimistic, expressing the hope that, 'in due course a distinguished [Soviet] leader would emerge and the peoples of China and the Soviet Union would once more join hands.'[213] Japanese ambassadors meeting in Hong Kong at this time adopted a more cautious stance. They saw 'no immediate prospect of reconciliation between Moscow and Beijing', but nor did they anticipate 'any further deterioration'.[214]

Satō opened his first summit in Washington on 12 January 1965, by declaring that 'the Communist China question is of an even more urgent nature than the Vietnam problem.' Although some details of the meeting remain secret, it is known that the leaders discussed most aspects of the China issue—Beijing's 'aggressiveness'; the impact of its nuclear explosion on Japanese public opinion; Sino-Japanese trade, and post-Khrushchev Sino-Soviet relations—and that President Johnson pledged:

> [Japan] could depend on us fully for defense in the Pacific area...since Japan possesses no nuclear weapons, and we do have them, if Japan needs our nuclear deterrent for its defense, the US will stand by its commitments and provide that defense.[215]

Johnson also promised that the US would 'consult closely with Japan before making any crucial decisions involving policy changes on the China problem and matters of comparable importance.'[216] In response, Satō did little more than confirm Tokyo's long-standing position that, 'politics and trade are differentiated in Japan's contacts with mainland China.' Later that day, he again raised the issue of future Sino-Soviet ties with Rusk. While conceding that the public positions of China and the Soviet Union remained unaltered despite the change in Soviet leadership, Rusk was nevertheless concerned about a possible improvement in the relationship given that 'the temperature of their language has been reduced.' Satō dismissed this view, claiming that it was 'clearly unlikely that Communist China and the Soviet Union would draw closer together.'[217]

Upon his return to Tokyo, Satō's subsequent statements exposed the contradiction that had lain at the heart of Japanese foreign policy, namely, the belief that Tokyo could adopt a fully independent China policy while still relying on the US for defence. On 20 January, he told the press that, 'Japan would pursue its own policy toward Communist China.' Yet when asked whether Chinese nuclear development would necessitate revision of the Security Treaty, he replied: 'The existing Security Treaty takes all possible contingencies into consideration. I think it is because this Security Treaty exists that Japan has not become nervous about China's nuclear test.'[218] Five days later, reporting on the Washington summit to the Lower House Budget Committee, Satō insisted that he had made no concessions to Johnson on China, and that Japan's China policies were in no way bound by their joint-communiqué. He predicted a second Chinese nuclear explosion in the near future, and declared that, 'while it was inconceivable that Red China should be aiming at Japan, this country should be ready to defend itself.' At the same time, however, he welcomed Johnson's reaffirmation in the joint-communiqué of 'the US determination to abide by its commitment under the [Security] Treaty to defend Japan against any armed attack from the outside.' Finally, Satō claimed that:

> [It] was not necessary for Japan to differentiate between Communist China and the Soviet Union in carrying out its policy toward Communist bloc countries...[since] peaceful coexistence with the two countries would be possible if they both understood Japan's position and do not adopt expansionist policies.[219]

In late April 1965, Walt Rostow, chairman of the State Department's Policy Planning Council, visited Japan and held meetings with senior Foreign Ministry officials and LDP politicians. Upon his return to Washington, he reported that:

> the impression the Japanese leaders gave [was] that, despite their abhorrence of the regime in mainland China, they retain a basic respect and sympathy for the Chinese; moreover, they are apparently not so concerned about Communist China's expansionist tendencies (...) as they are about the expansionist designs of the Soviets viz-a-viz Asia, including mainland China'.[220]

MOFA experts present reportedly argued that increasing pressure on China or pro-Chinese regimes would not necessarily serve to intensify the Sino-Soviet rift. According to a US diplomat who had accompanied Rostow, the main difference between MOFA and American views was over whether or not 'escalation of the Vietnam War would heal the Sino-Soviet rift.' He believed that the Japanese were most concerned 'lest China and the Soviet Union come together again.'[221] In May, MOFA tried to use the split to justify its opposition to Soviet participation in the follow up Afro-Asian Conference to be held in Algiers. Some Diet members apparently felt that Russia's entry could act as a useful counterweight to mainland China, but most officials disagreed.[222]

Six months later, however, Satō's perspective on China was shifting. In October, he told British Foreign Secretary Michael Stewart that 'The Soviet Union was not really any longer a serious problem…the real nuclear threat came from China.'[223] Shortly thereafter, Satō became the first Japanese prime minister publicly to refer to China as a direct military threat: 'a China with a nuclear capacity is, as far as Japan is concerned, a nuclear threat.'[224] He was not alone in this view. Other members of the defence establishment shared his assessment.[225] By year's end, some MOFA officials had even concluded that 'Russia wanted to cultivate [Japan] as her partner in Asia in place of China.'[226] Nevertheless, Satō continued a policy of non-involvement in the rift, maintaining a balance or 'equidistance' between relations with Moscow and Beijing, until the early 1970s, when pressure from the domestic 'pro-China' camp and US policy changes finally compelled Tokyo to choose sides and forced Satō from office.[227]

Interpretative comments

Input: external environment

The Sino-Soviet split was ultimately a major element in the global trend towards multipolarisation, widely canvassed in the mid-1960s. Mulitpolarisation weakened the superpowers' dominance of their respective camps and hence of the international system generally. However, it seems that scholars at the time exaggerated both the pace and scope of this process. The dispersion of power within the structure of international relations occurred only slowly, and, reflecting the differing degrees of Sino-Soviet split, initially affected the economic and political dimensions far more than the central strategic balance.

If signature of the Sino-Soviet Alliance had reduced Japan's room for diplomatic manoeuvre, then logically its collapse should have increased it. The evidence, however, is mixed. Objectively speaking, Sino-Soviet rivalry diluted the direct military threat to Japan, or in other words, the rift strengthened Japan's strategic position vis-à-vis the Communist powers. By the end of 1964, Beijing's first nuclear test and its increasingly vociferous expressions of irredentism led the Soviets to commence the redeployment of forces along their enormous mutual border with China. The strategic rift had become so fundamental that Moscow assigned a higher priority to preventing the development of closer Sino-Japanese relations than to loosening Japan's security links with the US. The Soviets relied mainly on economic incentives rather than ideological appeals or strategic threats in its haphazard efforts to influence Japan's international alignment. The Kremlin was never audacious enough to offer to settle the territorial dispute over the Kurile Islands on Japanese terms in order to cement bilateral ties.

Alarmed at the way in which the split with Moscow was increasing its international isolation, in 1964 Beijing launched a futile campaign to lure the Japanese (and others) into an 'intermediate zone' from where it was hoped they would oppose both superpowers. Two years later, such foreign policy goals were abandoned as China descended into the madness of the Cultural Revolution. It also severely curtailed Chinese involvement in Southeast Asia, and thus increased Japan's room for diplomatic manoeuvre at the regional level. The period culminated in Beijing's development of medium-range nuclear weapons and serious fighting breaking out along the Sino-Soviet frontier in 1969, which increased the risk of major regional conflict. In short, the onset of the strategic Sino-Soviet rift injected an additional element of instability into East Asian politics. Consequently, the need to balance relations with Moscow and Beijing meant that in this respect constraints on Japanese foreign policy strengthened rather than weakened.

Meanwhile, distracted by the escalating conflict in Indochina, the US was slow to comprehend the new strategic options presented by the rift. The Vietnam War led the Americans to conclude that China represented the primary threat to Western interests in Asia. Hence, by late 1963, Washington was openly telling Tokyo that it should increase its contribution to the containment of 'aggressive' Chinese Communism, and thereby become more zealous in exploiting the Sino-Soviet rift.

The Johnson Administration tried a different tack, encouraging Japan to base its policy towards the rift on its own national interests, but as Tokyo was soon to discover, only within strictly defined limits. Washington continued to worry that it might lose Japan. The US therefore permitted Japan a sense of increased equality, but only in order to further Tokyo's integration into the Western Alliance.

Internal environment: operational sphere

Japanese democracy emerged from the 1960 *Anpo* crisis bruised and battered but fundamentally sound. However, all attempts at reforming the system, for instance by revising the Constitution or abolishing the party factions ended in failure.

For Japan, the Sino-Soviet rift added a new dimension to the conservative versus progressive Cold War that had afflicted domestic politics since the late 1940s. Now an internal Sino-Soviet rift pitted pro-Soviet Japanese against their pro-Chinese compatriots. The two groups fought every bit as fiercely as did their sponsors in Moscow and Beijing. The rift increased polarisation within the domestic political structure. It cut across the traditional factional alignments, and even threatened LDP unity in the short-term. On the other hand, such turmoil also meant that additional policy alternatives could be offered within the framework of 'one party rule'.

Psychological sphere: belief systems

The LDP was a union of several old parties and remained a broad church, embracing Liberals, Conservatives and right-wing nationalists. On critical foreign policy issues like China the contradictory beliefs occasionally threatened a schism.

Ikeda Hayato was a realist who saw the international environment in essentially bipolar terms. The Sino-Soviet split strengthened Ikeda's confidence in his pro-Western policies. However, as a disciple of Yoshida, he felt that Japan—a 'pillar of the free world'—was strong enough to sway international events, including relations with China. Satō Eisaku, another Yoshida protégé, held rather similar views, although with a less pronounced anti-Soviet bias.

Psychological sphere: perceptions

After the Security Treaty was revised, and especially following Kishi's resignation, Japanese perceptions of the Sino-Soviet Alliance began to change, albeit slowly at first. No consensus view was to emerge within the LDP, or the wider policy establishment, as to whether China and/or the Soviet Union represented a security menace or not. Four radically different threat perceptions coexisted (Figure 3.1). Ikeda Hayato reasserted the traditional Japanese view: Russia and Communism were to be feared, but China, while it might pose a threat to 'Asia', did not represent a menace to Japan. Ōhira Masayoshi, his second foreign minister, did not share Ikeda's confidence. Despite his famous declaration that China posed 'no threat' to Japan, he felt that even after the rift both Communist powers still shared the same ultimate goal: a Communist world order. Nor did the gap between Ikeda and Ōhira by any means embrace the whole range of perceptions coexisting within the LDP at this time. For while a 'pro-US' wing agreed with the Americans that Beijing now represented a greater threat than Moscow, a 'pro-China' wing held precisely the opposite view. Others on the left of the party, like former premier Ishibashi Tanzan, felt that neither country threatened Japan, whereas some on the right, for example Genda Minoru, considered them both to be menacing.

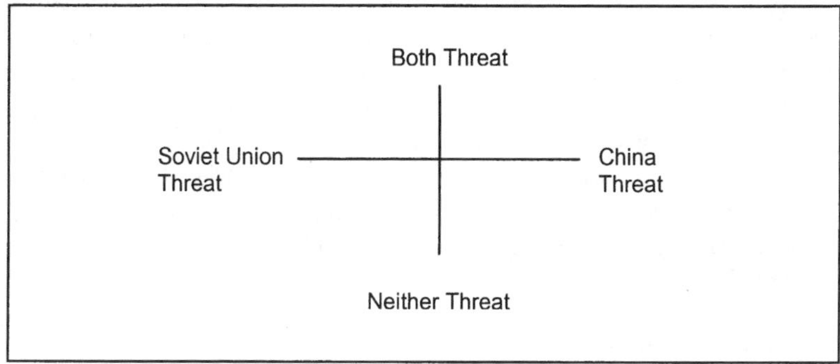

Figure 3.1 Japanese threat perceptions

Within MOFA, opinions were similarly divided. Diplomats were among the first to recognise the emerging Sino-Soviet rift but, with a few notable exceptions, they were slow to appreciate the full implications of the split. Higher officials within the ministry tended to follow Ōhira in pointing out that both Communist powers still shared the same long-term goals, and emphasised Beijing's criticism of Moscow. The China Desk, however, repeatedly claimed that Chinese foreign policy was cautious in practice, despite its bellicose rhetoric in the rift. The Soviet Desk, in contrast, remained suspicious of Moscow's 'smile diplomacy', arguing that the Soviets would not necessarily be friendly towards Japan because of the rift. Meanwhile the Defence Agency, which based its estimates on military capacities rather than political intentions, maintained a very cautious attitude. It still believed that China and the Soviet Union could quickly revive their alliance given a sudden policy change in Beijing.

Satō Eisaku's accession to the premiership coincided with a number of crucial developments in the Sino-Soviet strategic rift. The replacement of Khrushchev was not expected to lead to an early Sino-Soviet reconciliation. Subsequent visits by Premier Zhou Enlai to Moscow and Foreign Minister Andrei Gromyko to Beijing confirmed the impression that their alliance was crippled, if not dead. Equally significant was the explosion of China's first nuclear device. Although Washington and Tokyo conspired to play down its impact, it is clear that in some quarters it led to a significant amplification of the Chinese threat. The CRO concluded in December 1964, that while the Soviets were untrustworthy, China now represented the primary threat. Unlike Ikeda, Satō himself apparently shared this view, and personally favoured a nuclear capability for Japan.

The Japanese government gradually came to realise that Sino-Soviet tension derived not just from contradictory interpretations of Marxism–Leninism, or disagreements over development models, but also a struggle for power based on incompatible national interests. The whole debate revealed a quite sophisticated understanding of the origins and nature of the rift. However, it seems that most members of the Japanese government did not believe that the collapse of the Sino-Soviet Alliance had strengthened Japan's strategic position. If anything, the resulting instability and uncertainty left them feeling rather less secure than before. Even if the Communist threat was reduced, this was not seen as sufficient to permit Japan military independence: Tokyo still needed its American security blanket.

Decision-making process

The elevation of Ikeda Hayato to the premiership signalled the return to power of the 'Yoshida School'. But although he was the head of the largest LDP faction and assembled a very strong cabinet, Ikeda's position was not unassailable. Hence, on policy towards the Sino-Soviet Alliance, he could not afford to ignore the views of other powerful party faction bosses such as Kōno Ichirō or Satō Eisaku. Furthermore, in recognition of the growing influence of the factions, Ikeda was also the first post-war premier to require the services of more than one foreign minister: initiating a system of approximately biennial rotation that limited their influence.

The various policy groups seemed to embrace like-minded officials, politicians and businessmen. These horizontal alliances or 'sub-governments' can be reduced to five basic schools of thought, if one factors in uncertainty. Since each group corresponds to a threat perception, they can be superimposed on Figure 3.1 (Figure 3.2).

The horizontal axis separates the Sinophiles from the Sinophobes. Those who believed that Beijing represented the primary threat tended to favour Japan adopting a more active role in US East Asian strategy, supporting the American (and increasingly the Soviet) policy of isolating China. Although traditionally anti-Communist, they came to see improved ties with Moscow (in addition to their existing friendly bonds to Taipei) as useful for curbing strengthened Japan–China relations. In direct opposition another group continued to see the Soviet Union as the only real threat to Japan. It is generally described as 'pro-China', and its membership revealed a shared antipathy for Washington's 'containment strategy'. Members of the 'Yoshida School'—including Prime Minister Ikeda Hayato and most of the China Desk at MOFA—criticised Washington's hard-line policy against Beijing. The ministry's Soviet Desk was a hotbed of anti-Communism.

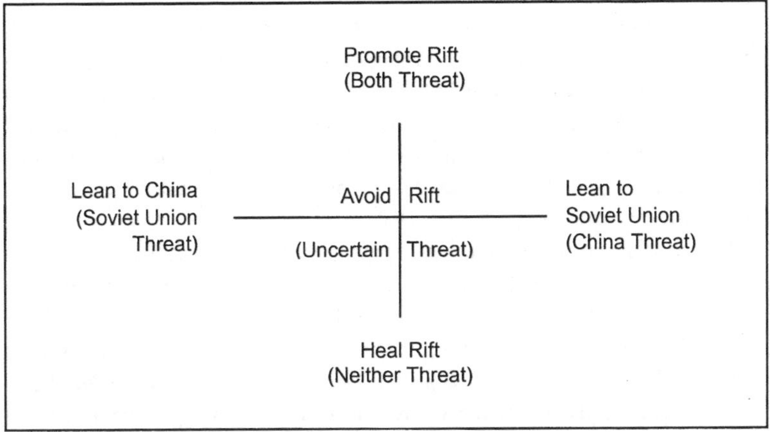

Figure 3.2 Japanese responses to the Sino-Soviet rift

The vertical axis ranges from the restorative to the incendiary, from helping to mend the Sino-Soviet rift at one extreme to encouraging it at the other. Those who considered that China and the Soviet Union posed a serious threat to each other but not to Japan tended to be healers. Admittedly, outside of the JCP few Japanese wished to see the Sino-Soviet Alliance restored to its former glory. However, signature of a 'four-power pact' remained official JSP policy, and even the LDP was not immune to such idealism. Ex-premier Ishibashi Tanzan's efforts at reconciliation proved futile, but he maintained a small support base within the ruling party. By the end of the decade, many Japanese (and Westerners) shared his fear that the split would result in war, and they recognised the desirability of at least constraining the deterioration in Sino-Soviet strategic relations.

At the opposite extreme a small group of LDP members and diplomats—self-proclaimed 'Gaullists'—regarded both China and the Soviet Union as threatening, and did not even completely trust the US security guarantee. They wanted Japan to exploit the room for strategic manoeuvre created by what they saw as a more multipolar international system. As 'realists', they spoke of 'tilting' or 'balancing', that is, leaning alternately towards Moscow and Beijing, and using the links thus established as leverage to advance the cause of a strong and independent Japan. A minority advocated acquisition of nuclear weapons to underpin an 'independent' Japanese foreign policy.

Finally, where the two axes intersect, one finds the remaining policy-makers. Undecided about the direction of the strategic threats, if any, to Japan, and uncertain about the permanence of the Sino-Soviet rift, they lacked a common policy preference except to 'wait and see'. In the meantime, these waverers felt it best, as far as possible, to maintain the status quo and avoid any involvement in the rift. Essentially passive, the most that they were willing to contemplate was the purely commercial exploitation of the rift. Later, when total aloofness proved impossible, they sought to minimise political involvement by adopting a policy of 'equidistance' or 'neutrality', aimed at insulating relations with Moscow from those with Beijing. Of the five main schools of thought, this proved to be the most influential.

The popular, immobilist theorem suggests that the Japanese policy-making system was characterised by inertia, stemming from the traditional emphasis on consensus, the factional structure of the LDP, and the relative weakness of the office of prime minister. Here it seems that a different variety of immobilism has been unearthed, one in which established LDP factional conflicts played little or no part, whereas the premier was influential. There was a compartmentalised decision-making system, partitioning responsibility not just between institutions but within them. Nevertheless, this did not preclude turf fights. The effect of the Sino-Soviet rift on this process was both magnetic (attracting more actors wishing to influence relations), and schismatic (intensifying discord within and between the bureaucracy, Diet, business community, media, intelligentsia, and the public.) This greatly complicated the whole procedure. The 'activists' were not strong enough to impose their views, but were able to veto any rapid movement in the opposite direction, thus tending to cancel each other out. There were too many competing conceptions of Japan's national interests to allow a clear definition to emerge. Issues like the Sino-Soviet rift threatened to overload the system. The lack of reliable information on China, the Soviet Union and Sino-Soviet relations, and/or the inability to process the available data, also injected a high degree of uncertainty into proceedings. Indeed this prompted MOFA to establish secret intelligence exchange relationships with Britain, Australia and others, and devote ever-increasing resources to the problem; ultimately setting up its first entirely new section since the Occupation (the *Kokusai Shiryōbu*). Nevertheless, the result was at best a diffused, and at worst a virtually paralysed, decision-making system.

Yet, the quite significant policy variations observed between 1950 and 1964 should not be overlooked.

Output: official diplomacy

Japanese diplomacy was surprisingly active while the Sino-Soviet Alliance appeared strong, but appeared less so as the rift escalated. The more the parties to the Sino-Soviet Alliance tried to pressure Japan into playing an active international political role, the more earnestly its government sought to avoid one. Ikeda Hayato adopted a 'low profile' (*teishisei*) foreign policy that emphasised economic development and broadening relations with the West. However, Ikeda also applied Yoshida-style logic to the Sino-Soviet question and declined every American invitation to increase Japan's strategic activism. Since a passive stance would certainly have led to Japan being drawn into the dispute, active non-involvement in the strategic rift became a guiding principle of Japanese foreign policy. The result was at best a prudent, and at worst a timid, foreign policy.

Satō accepted that the Sino-Soviet alliance was dormant and fearing the consequences of involvement in their dispute, sought to avoid taking sides. Satō hinted at a policy of 'equidistance', although in practice Moscow was to receive more attention than Beijing.

External environment: feedback

Japan went from being an occupied country effectively excluded from the international system in 1950, to become a regional power by the mid-1960s, but the influence of its foreign policy upon the international environment remained limited. Japan helped to preserve US political influence in the East Asian region and in a wider sense to preserve the unity of the Western alliance. If Japan could not end dependence on the US; the next best alternative was to encourage American dependence on Japan. Political ties with the US matured and the relationship became a little more symmetrical. However, although Western leaders visited Tokyo in greater numbers and listened to government views on Sino-Soviet relations, there is no evidence to suggest that Japanese perspectives had a particularly strong impact on policy-makers in Washington.

Ikeda's 'low profile' foreign policy had the effect of internalising the Sino-Soviet rift, accentuating its influence at the domestic level, and not without cost. However, the government was unable to completely prevent the rift from affecting Japan's external relations. Tokyo's refusal to choose sides—to play the great power game—at least until the 1970s, led to intensified Sino-Soviet rivalry over Japan and helped to delay the onset of a balanced multipolarisation.

When Sino-Soviet relations began to deteriorate in the early 1960s, the US and Japanese governments responded in very different ways. The Americans were slow to recognise the significance of the rift, and even slower to exploit it. However, the problem was not that Washington clung to an outmoded vision of Communist 'monolithic unity', whereas Tokyo clearly distinguished between Moscow and Beijing, for by early 1963, they were in basic accord as to the rift's seriousness. At issue were its consequences and how best to deal with them. This led some members of the Japanese government to question the relationship with the US, but such misgivings never became serious enough to undermine the Security Treaty. For a while Ikeda Hayato seemed to be leaning towards improved relations with Beijing even as Kennedy—lulled by Khrushchev's post-Cuban Crisis 'peaceful coexistence' rhetoric—decided that he could do business with the more cautious Soviets. The events of late 1964—China's nuclear test, the fall of Khrushchev, and the promotion of Satō Eisaku—helped to narrow the gap, but significant divisions between Japan and the US (and Taiwan) over policies towards the USSR and PRC persisted.

In a sense, Japan was both more independent of, and closer to the US by the mid-1960s. Perhaps the way out of this conundrum is to recognise that autonomy and dependence can coexist. The Sino-Soviet rift, by strengthening America's claim to global hegemony, reinforced Tokyo's dependence on Washington. The Japanese and American military structures became ever more firmly integrated. Sheltering under the US strategic umbrella, Japan probably enjoyed greater leverage vis-à-vis the Soviet Union and China than it would have had standing alone. The umbrella also allowed the Japanese the luxury of disagreeing on defence issues secure in the knowledge that it would have little impact on the outside world. Unlike Paris, Tokyo did not defy Washington's wishes and normalise relations with Beijing, nor develop a close relationship with Moscow. Japan did not downgrade its alliance with the US, nor develop an independent nuclear deterrent. Each of these options was certainly explored, and all attracted supporters, but ultimately, as with the Left's neutralist alternative, the Right's Gaullist approach was rejected. In short, the rift created an opportunity for Japan to increase its independence, and it was recognised as such in Tokyo, but it was in no way deterministic. Japan's putative freedom of manoeuvre proved illusory, for the Cold War continued, with the Sino-Soviet rift merely adding to its complexity.

4

Separating economics from politics: Japan's trade with two planned economies, 1950–60

Following its unconditional surrender Japan lost control over its foreign trade to SCAP. Such scrutiny, in addition to the disjunction caused by World War II, brought Japanese trade with China and the Soviet Union to a virtual standstill. A slightly more liberal trading regime appeared from 1947 onwards with the beginnings of the 'reverse course'. As late as March 1949, official US policy still aimed to 'augment, through permitting restoration of ordinary economic relations with China, such forces as might operate to bring about serious rifts between Moscow and a Chinese Communist regime.'[1] Just two months later, however, Washington extended US export controls to include China—albeit less severe than those imposed on the Soviet Union—and General Headquarters in Tokyo applied these to Sino-Japanese trade.[2]

Trading under the Occupation

For Prime Minister Yoshida Shigeru, economic relations with the Soviet Union held little or no interest, but he repeatedly declared his support for Japan–China trade. In February 1949, he told an American journalist that:

> Japan could establish trade relations with Communist China since the latter needed machinery and manufactured goods which it could not produce itself or obtain from Russia. The Communists were realists and would trade with Japan

> if it were profitable for them to do so. Japan could not afford to neglect any market and China was a "natural market", whether Communist or not.[3]

Three months later Yoshida went even further:

> I don't care whether China is red, white or green, we are willing to do business with her. China is our neighbor. There is a danger that trade between our countries might be permanently cut, but I believe that we shall eventually transcend ideological differences and progress together.[4]

It was noted in Washington: 'how distinctly assertive, unified, and confident the Japanese appeared on this issue, as compared to the almost cowering remarks on foreign policy that usually emanated from Tokyo.'[5]

That summer, on Kansai initiative, Japan's pro-mainland trade lobby was busily getting itself organised. The non-partisan *NitChū Bōeki Sokushin Giin Renmei* (Diet Members' League for the Promotion of Japan–China Trade) was established on 24 May with *Kaishintō* Secretary General Tomabechi Gizō as chairman and an initial membership numbering about 90. One week later, the JCP-dominated *NitChū Bōeki Sokushinkai* (JCTPA), led by Sugi Michisuke of the Ōsaka Chamber of Commerce, was formed. Meanwhile, the Chinese Communists revealed their own enthusiasm for establishing economic relations by sending a small trade mission to Japan. It left empty-handed. Yoshida, not wishing to hand the initiative to Beijing or to his domestic political rivals, accused the JCP of exploiting the trade issue for propaganda purposes and protested that it should not be discussed 'as if Japan will go bankrupt unless she trades with Communist China.'[6] By year's end, however, Trade Minister Inagaki Heitarō confidently set a target for China's share of total Japanese foreign trade at between one quarter and one third, roughly the same as that during the 1930s.[7] US Secretary of State Dean Acheson was not unsympathetic, describing Japan and China in December 1949, as 'natural trade partners' that 'should be encouraged to revive economic relations.'[8] Even the formation of the Sino-Soviet Alliance did not stop the State Department from finally freeing Japanese traders from General Headquarters' control in March 1950. In theory, they could now trade without restriction.[9] This prompted the House of Councillors to adopt a multiparty resolution at the end of April, calling on the government to: 'leave aside ideological and political differences and…exchange economic missions with the new China'.[10] More concretely, it spurred a rapid increase in Sino-Japanese trade to more than double the previous year's total.

In the meantime, under the terms of the new alliance, the outbreak of the Korean War that June produced a substantial transfer of resources—economic, financial and technical—from Moscow to Beijing, as well as rapidly expanding levels of Sino-Soviet trade.[11] China also adopted a Soviet model of collectivised, heavy-industry-centred development. In addition to consolidating Sino-Soviet ties, the onset of the war reinforced Japan's economic dependence on the US. In December 1950, when China intervened militarily in support of the North Koreans, Washington embargoed all exports to the mainland. A SCAP directive ordered the Japanese government to halt exports of strategic goods not only to China, but also to Manchuria, North Korea, Hong Kong and Macao.[12] Not surprisingly, Yoshida raised the embargo question with Special Ambassador John Foster Dulles when the two men met at the end of January 1951, and the American record notes:

> [Yoshida] spoke of the long-term necessity of trading with China, and while he realized that in view of [the] present communist domination of that country it would not be possible to expect great results in the near future, nevertheless, he believed that in the long run the Chinese would adopt the attitude that 'war is war and trade is trade' and that it would be possible for a reasonable degree of trade to take place between Japan and China.[13]

This was the first time that Yoshida introduced the concept later termed *seikei bunri* (separating politics from economics.) It is important to note, however, that he was recommending such a policy for China, not Japan. Tokyo was to use trade for covert, ideological purposes: 'Japanese businessmen because of their long acquaintance with and experience in China, will be the best fifth column of democracy against the Chinese communists'.[14] Yoshida retracted this formulation within a month, but in August he revived it with a subtle twist, claiming that 'by trading with the Chinese, the Japanese might…wean the Chinese away from Moscow, even if they did not undermine their brand of Communism.'[15] In other words, Yoshida believed a Sino-Soviet rift was inevitable, and he hypothesised that promoting Sino-Japanese trade would accelerate the process.

Nonetheless in his speech to the San Francisco Peace Conference in September 1951—extensively rewritten by the Americans—Yoshida stated that, 'the role of Chinese trade in [the] Japanese economy...has often been exaggerated.'[16] Once back in Tokyo, however, he reasserted his belief that trade and politics were separate entities. Unfortunately for Yoshida, a State Department paper now inverted the logic of his China Thesis to create the so-called 'hard wedge' strategy. It argued that '[increasing Chinese] dependence on the Soviets for economic necessities is more likely to work in our favor than against us by hastening the day when China becomes disillusioned with Russian aid.'[17] Yoshida now recognised that he had to place trade issues on hold. Nothing could be done to jeopardise the anticipated US Senate ratification of the Peace Treaty and the restoration of Japanese sovereignty.

Japan joins COCOM

As the formal conclusion of the Occupation drew near, the Japanese government assumed responsibility for implementing their own trade embargo. It agreed to maintain current control levels until peace was restored on the Korean peninsula. On the day that Japan regained sovereignty, MOFA even issued a 15-page pamphlet entitled 'Japan in the World of Today', which sought to justify America's 'hard wedge' strategy. Nevertheless, resentment in other quarters at the US-imposed restrictions on Japan–China trade strengthened. An American report noted that while the textile manufacturers and exporters of the Ōsaka area were in the forefront of the pro-China trade campaign, the Japanese challenge to the trade embargo was now much broader.[18] Communist leaders sought to take advantage of such sentiments in Japan and elsewhere using the Moscow International Conference of April 1952. An invitation from Beijing in early January for a Japanese delegation to attend this meeting led to the formation of an International Economic Council. Its elite membership included two post-war finance ministers and several other influential politicians and business leaders critical of the government's cautious approach.[19] The cabinet did not support Japanese participation in the conference and succeeded in persuading some prominent members to withdraw.[20] Yet, even a refusal to issue passports could not prevent three opposition members of the Diet from eventually reaching Moscow. Stopping in Beijing on their return journey to Japan, they signed the first unofficial Sino-Japanese Trade Agreement on 1 June 1952. It was a modest effort, aiming for a total of £60 million in balanced trade.[21] The reaction from the Japanese government was hostile. MITI issued a policy statement imposing strict conditions on trade with the mainland—although it was couched in superficially positive language. MOFA went even further, denouncing the export of production materials to China as a security threat; it attacked the unofficial trade agreement; and accused Beijing of aiming to drive a wedge between Japan and its friends.[22]

The situation was further complicated by the fact that MOFA was engaged at the time in delicate negotiations to relax trade restrictions by gaining admission to the Paris Group (COCOM) rather than be part of a proposed separate East Asian version: the option preferred by Washington and MITI.[23] Multilateral talks opened in Washington in July. A compromise ultimately emerged whereby a sub-committee on China was established (CHINCOM) and on 5 September, Japan gained admission to the Paris Group. This would have represented a significant victory for Yoshida—putting Japanese trade with China on an equal footing with the Europeans—but for the fact that Japan's chief negotiator, Takeuchi Ryūji, succumbed to American pressure and promised to enforce additional bilateral restrictions.[24] US fears of Yoshida's China Thesis were based on the belief that:

> Japan may try to take advantage of [the] US–USSR conflict; desiring to restore Japanese influence on the continent of Asia and to regain [the] advantages of China trade, Japan might conclude that an accommodation with communist-controlled areas in Asia would serve Japanese interests.[25]

The New Year brought a change of leadership for both superpowers, but Yoshida's cautious trade policy seemed unaffected. The death of Stalin in March 1953 sparked off an intense power struggle within the Kremlin, but it did not lead to an immediate Japanese reassessment of prospects for economic relations with the Soviet Union. MOFA was not anticipating any kind of 'favourable offer' from Moscow. It still perceived Soviet strategy as aiming at Japan's 'economic collapse'.[26] Meanwhile, Japanese businessmen returning from China were reporting 'evidence [of] strong Chinese nationalistic feeling' and consequently they recommended taking a 'calculated risk' on Yoshida's China Thesis.[27] Washington's response remained uniformly discouraging, although this masked deep divisions within the newly inaugurated Eisenhower administration.[28]

More immediately threatening to Yoshida, however, was the domestic alliance being forged between business groups interested in trade with the Communist countries and his conservative political rivals: Shigemitsu Mamoru's *Kaishintō*, and the breakaway Hatoyama faction from Yoshida's own *Jiyūtō*.[29] China twice extended the unofficial trade agreement with Japan, prompting the revival of the Diet Members' League—mothballed since the outbreak of the Korean War—and the subsequent spread of similar trade promotion organisations to all levels of government.[30] On the eve of the signature of the Korean Armistice, League members helped to pass a Diet resolution demanding that the government temporarily reduce its embargo to a level 'as low as the Western European countries.'[31] Although intended as an attack on the prime minister, Yoshida was to use this domestic pressure to good effect in his ongoing low-intensity struggle with Washington over the China trade.

The split within the conservative camp over how to promote trade with China became ever wider. In October, while Ikeda Masanosuke, head of the Diet Members' League and a close associate of Hatoyama Ichirō, led a mission to China to assess trade prospects, Yoshida sent his protégé Ikeda Hayato to Washington.[32] The attitudes each encountered were quite different, despite relative calm having returned to the Korean Peninsula. China, embracing *seikei bunri*, surprised Ikeda Masanosuke with a second unofficial trade agreement.[33] The US in contrast merely reinforced its hard-line against China.[34] Ikeda Hayato, however, had some success in Washington with a new line of argument: 'Even if there were no security restrictions…given the nature of the present communist regime in China no great volume of trade would develop in any case.'[35] On 8 March 1954, Japan and the United States signed the Mutual Security Assistance Agreement and a few days later, the US finally agreed to release Japan 'gradually, as appropriate' from its obligations under the September 1952 agreement on China trade controls.[36] It is not difficult to imagine that the former acted as some kind of quid pro quo for the latter. Yoshida's success produced a 75 per cent jump in Sino-Japanese trade, but this was not sufficient to satisfy his critics at home, let alone Beijing.

While the negotiations for the new Japan–US agreement were in progress, a statement from Foreign Minister Okazaki Katsuo at the end of November 1953 sought to clarify the government's position on the China trade. In contrast to MOFA's criticism of the first unofficial trade agreement, he now acknowledged that the second agreement was 'something of deep significance'. Furthermore, in light of the July Diet resolutions, he promised that the government would 'continue its efforts' to liberalise this trade, if only 'to the extent that the ties with the free nations are not broken'.[37] The following month, Wajima Eiji, until recently the head of the Asian Affairs Bureau, informed the Americans that, 'the Government did consider it desirable and important from the point of view of Japan's interests to explore the possibility of expanding trade with China.' However, despite this and 'the strong pressures exerted by the Kansai businessmen', he claimed that Japanese businessmen generally were losing interest in mainland China as they became more aware of its development strategy, and were looking instead to Southeast Asia.[38] This view was directly contradicted by Ōhashi Chūichi, a former 'foreign minister' of *Manchukuo* and a founding member of the *Dōyūkai*, a loose grouping of independent Diet members. Although right-wing and anti-Communist, he claimed in early June 1954 that, 'pressures for increased trade with both China and the Soviet Union are becoming increasingly strong especially in the Kansai area.' MITI supported this view and responded accordingly, planning for increased trade with the Communist bloc in anticipation of a successful outcome to the Geneva Peace Conference.[39]

Ogawa Heishirō, the new head of MOFA's China Desk, thought that China might 'make a serious, large-scale trade bid [to Japan] within the next year or so.' He predicted that Russia's 'apparent inability…to supply all the equipment and services which China desires in order to carry out her industrialization plans...would lead Peking to adopt a more conciliatory policy toward Japan and the West.' At the same time, however, Ogawa also recognised that, 'security considerations and the reluctance of Peking to carry out a major readjustment of the country's foreign trade, now so overwhelmingly oriented toward Moscow, could operate to prevent the Chinese leaders from proceeding far in [Japan's] direction.'[40]

That summer, Communist interest in Japanese trade intensified. With Khrushchev tightening his grip on power, the Soviet Union pursued a more active role in establishing commercial relations with Japan. A whole series of visits took place. In May, Moscow invited Hiratsuka Tsunejirō, president of the Japan Fishery Association and a close associate of Hatoyama, for talks.[41] In July, when Nishimura Naomi of *Jiyūtō* led an all-party delegation to Moscow and Beijing, his Soviet hosts offered, inter alia, to promote economic exchanges. Foreign Minister Okazaki surprised journalists by announcing that if the Soviets offered Japan 'presents' then Japan should not hesitate to accept them.[42] During August, while three Soviet trade representatives were in Tokyo, Fukunaga Kazuomi (*Jiyūtō*), accompanied by Ushiba Nobuhiko (counsellor in MOFA's Inspection Section) visited the Soviet Union to discuss trade and fisheries problems.[43] Progress at the talks was slow, however, and it was not helped by MITI's alleged instruction to shipbuilders to set the unit price for ships at double the norm.[44]

Beijing was no less active. In September, a report by the Liberal Party's FARC expressed support for increased trade with Beijing and associated visits.[45] The following month, a multiparty Diet mission led by Yamaguchi Kikuichirō, a pro-China member of the Kōno faction, visited China to discuss economic issues. This coincided with the arrival of a Chinese Red Cross delegation in Japan. It discussed trade matters with Murata Shōzō (president of the *Nihon Kokusai Bōeki Sokushin Kyōkai* or JITPA): an important new body formed in late September to coordinate the efforts of non-Communist firms interested in promoting trade with the Communist bloc.[46] These Soviet–Japanese and Sino-Japanese exchanges achieved few concrete results. They did, however, help to pave the way for the Sino-Soviet Joint Declaration of 12 October, in which the two powers in addition to strengthening their bilateral economic ties, confirmed their support for the development of broad trade relations with Japan.

Reflecting his contradictory responsibilities, the reaction to the declaration from Trade Minister Aichi Kiichi was ambiguous. On the one hand, he reassured the Americans that despite the 'considerable pressure within Japan for expanding trade with China, Japan would continue to observe COCOM restrictions'. On the other hand, he warned that it was 'only a question of time…[before] Japan will be forced by events to make every effort to expand its commerce with the Chinese mainland.'[47] Moreover, with China then accounting for a mere two per cent of Japan's global trade, the reported aim of MOFA's China Desk to restrict it to ten per cent of the total, revealed high expectations.[48]

Within the Japanese business world, there were three general reactions to the Sino-Soviet Joint Declaration. On the left businessmen such as Yamamoto Kumaichi (deputy head of JITPA) positively approved of the statement and thought that Japan should respond quickly, while right-wing executives simply denounced it as another example of the Communist 'peace offensive'. The vast majority, however, lay somewhere in between, supportive of expanded economic exchanges, but cautious about political moves. Takemura Tadao, managing director of the *Nihon Keizai Fukkō Kyōkai* (Japan Economic Revival Association) and a member of the third group, appreciated that the Joint Declaration represented a shift towards a more balanced Sino-Soviet Alliance. In particular, he pointed to the fact that the negotiations were held in Beijing; the joint ventures established in 1950 were to be transferred to exclusive Chinese control; and that Soviet troops were to be withdrawn from their bases in Manchuria. He also mentioned the demotion of the pro-Soviet Liu Shaoqi.[49]

Most Japanese financial and business leaders nonetheless now agreed that to compensate for the post-Korean War decline in US procurements, Japan needed to increase trade with its Communist neighbours. American and Taiwanese sanctions against individual companies for trading with China were losing their effectiveness and large Japanese trading companies started entering the mainland market. Government policy was increasingly out of step with the demands of business. In Washington, on the last leg of his world tour, Yoshida attempted to persuade Secretary of State Dulles to reverse the China containment policy and instead channel the 'inevitable forces leading to a greater understanding between China and Japan into a road open to friendship and trade.'[50] Any concessions on Dulles' part, however, would have been too late to save Yoshida. In early December, he was unceremoniously removed by a temporary coalition of left and right wing Diet members.

Yoshida's cautious methods met with some success during his post-Occupation years as premier, but it ultimately failed because Japanese businessmen lost patience. Many felt that he prevented them from taking full advantage of the increased trading opportunities that resulted from the changing attitudes of Moscow and Beijing. The new government promised a more active approach.

Hatoyama changes tack

In opposition, Hatoyama Ichirō had called for free trade with the Communist bloc; once in power he immediately set about achieving this goal. On 4 January 1955, he proposed relaxing COCOM/CHINCOM regulations on trade in strategic goods.[51] This view enjoyed broad support. In mid-December, a group of 67 conservative lawmakers, academics and businessmen including Labour Minister Chiba Saburō, had signed an open letter requesting 'some relaxation of the Communist China embargo.' The following month, the Democratic Party's *Seimu Chōsakai* (PARC) in its first foreign policy recommendations called for increased trade with China.[52] The House of Representatives also approved a resolution urging the government to invite a Chinese trade mission to visit Japan and negotiate a third trade agreement. MOFA reluctantly offered its blessing.[53]

Foreign Minister Shigemitsu Mamoru, conscious of American sensitivities, justified the government's action by claiming that it aimed 'to undercut…that portion of anti-American opinion which blames the US for the Japanese not being able to have any sort of contact with what they consider a most important Asiatic neighbor.'[54]

Hatoyama's new approach was soon to bring results. Murata Shōzō (president of JITPA and an advisor to Hatoyama) embarked on an 'inspection tour' of China in late January as an 'unofficial representative of the Japanese Government.' There he described US interference in Sino-Japanese relations as 'a great nuisance', but was surprised to hear Premier Zhou Enlai hinting at difficulties in Beijing's relationship with Moscow. '[Soviet] material assistance is not as great as you might think', Zhou confessed, '[but still w]e consider the Soviet Union our elder brother.' Nevertheless Murata felt that 'China's attitude towards Japan has changed', and on his return, he discussed with Hatoyama the possibility of exchanging trade missions.[55]

What was to prove a groundbreaking official visit by a Chinese trade mission went ahead at the end of March. Despite discouraging remarks from some mainstream business leaders such as Ishikawa Ichirō (president of *Keidanren*) and discrete threats of economic sanctions from Washington, large Japanese companies participated in negotiations for the first time.[56] Progress at the talks, however, was slow. In an attempt to facilitate agreement, Hatoyama ignored deep divisions within his cabinet—especially between Trade Minister Ishibashi Tanzan and Foreign Minister Shigemitsu—and proffered his personal 'assurance' that the government would provide 'support and assistance' to the third unofficial trade agreement with China. This proved sufficient to induce the politically ambitious Chinese finally to sign an agreement on 4 May. It included a call for the exchange of permanent trade representatives.[57]

Having cleared this important hurdle, Hatoyama pressed ahead. The Japanese premier soon announced that his government was 'considering' signing an official trade agreement with China, and in June, he described the stationing of a Chinese private trade representative in Japan as 'desirable'.[58] Some Japanese diplomats were already interpreting Beijing's enthusiasm for a trade agreement with Tokyo as evidence of a desire to 'avoid complete dependence' on Moscow.[59] However, an early indication that MOFA was no longer interested in exploiting such sentiments came with its rejection—reputedly at Taipei's insistence—of a request from the Chinese trade delegation to extend its stay.[60] MOFA officials nonetheless recognised that they lacked the legal authority to prevent the opening of a private PRC trade office in Japan.[61] *Kyōdō News* soon reported that the ministry had reconsidered its opposition to the exchange of trade missions with China as long as they had 'no diplomatic status'.[62] Some diplomats within MOFA were prepared to take a more radical approach. In mid-November, at a secret MOFA conference held in Bangkok, Iseki Yūjirō (consul general in Hong Kong) proposed that the 'government should send some of its China experts to [the] mainland to appraise the situation for themselves' and that it 'should set up [a] permanent official trade liaison center in Peiping.' Ogawa Heishirō (China Desk) offered his support, believing that such action would help the Japanese government to 'take contacts with [the] Chinese Communists out [of] leftist hands and exert some control over snowballing unofficial relations between [the] two countries.'[63] Nevertheless, another decade would pass before Iseki's proposal was realised.

In an effort to strengthen its own influence over the burgeoning trade relationship, the following month MITI established a Japan–China Export–Import Association (*NitChū Yushutsunyū Kumiai*). This association was empowered to grant exemptions for the export of small quantities of embargoed goods. Most firms involved in the China market joined the group during the next 18 months, but it never managed to play a major coordinating role.[64] Similarly, MITI's attempt to persuade Japanese steel producers to increase their raw material imports from China was unsuccessful. However, this U-turn in MITI policy under Ishibashi prompted the State Department to conclude that Japan's China trade was now more government-led than business-driven.[65]

If bureaucratic opposition was on the wane, many other political obstacles to the pursuit of Hatoyama's Communist trade policy remained. The merger talks that had opened between the *Minshutō* and *Jiyūtō* in August represented one such constraint. The warning from ex-Labour Minister Kosaka Zentarō that 'red germs (*aka no baikin*) are infiltrating Japan on the pretext of trade', was not untypical of the Liberal attitude.[66] The Americans were no more accommodating. When Foreign Minister Shigemitsu visited Washington later that month, his request to reduce restrictions on the China trade to the level applied to trade with Moscow was rejected by Dulles.[67] Despite this setback, in October, a Diet delegation led by Democrat Kanbayashiyama Eikichi signed a joint communiqué in Beijing. They committed themselves to the 'swift abolition' of CHINCOM restrictions and to turning the offices of the trade fairs in Beijing and Tokyo into permanent trade missions.[68] Moreover, on the eve of the two parties' November merger, Education Minister Matsumura Kenzō overcame strong cabinet opposition to gain permission for Guo Moruo, president of the Chinese Academy of Sciences, to visit Japan during the Chinese trade fair in Ōsaka.[69]

From a low of $15.5 million in 1952, Sino-Japanese trade had risen ten-fold to stand at $150.9 million by 1956 (Figure 4.1). Although equivalent to only about 2.7 per cent of Japan's total foreign trade (Figure 4.2), this represented approximately 30 per cent of its trade with East Asia, and meant that Beijing was Tokyo's primary trade partner in the region. For China, it comprised 4.5 per cent of its total trade. Japan–Soviet trade on the other hand was on a much smaller scale, and totalled a mere $14.4 million for the entire five-year period 1952–56

(Figure 4.1). In August 1956, however, Soviet Foreign Minister Dmitri Shepilov optimistically predicted that Japan–Soviet trade might reach $250 million per annum within five years.[70]

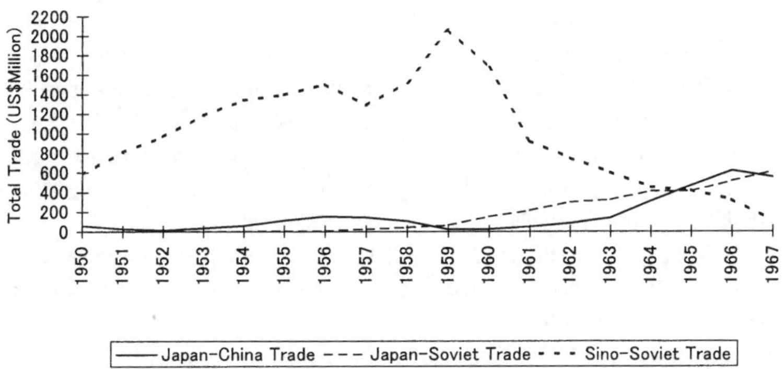

Figure 4.1 Japan–China–Soviet trade, 1950–67

Source: Japanese Ministry of Finance Customs Clearance Statistics and Soviet Foreign Trade Ministry Statistics.

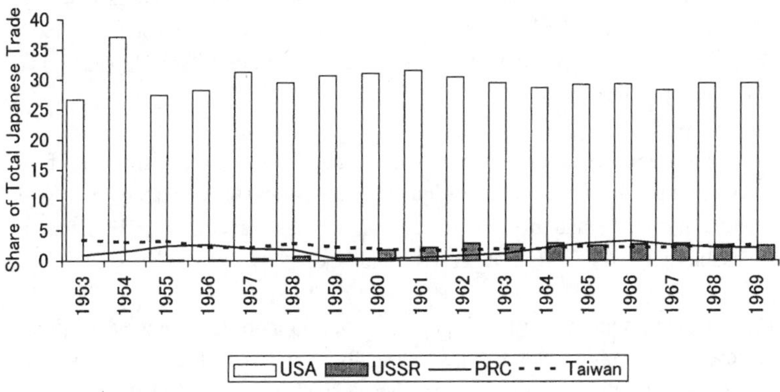

Figure 4.2 Japanese trade with selected countries, 1953–69

Source: Japanese Ministry of Finance Customs Clearance Statistics.

The buoyant nature of Japan's foreign trade inspired new confidence in the government's economic policies. In March 1956, on the eve of a visit from Dulles, the Diet unanimously passed a resolution reconfirming its June 1953 vote in favour of promoting trade relations with China.[71] Upon arrival, the secretary of state was greeted with a 'Memorandum on Current Problems', authored by Hatoyama himself. In it the prime minister described a 'new kind of offensive...in the economic and cultural fields' which the Soviets had been waging against Asian countries, including Japan, since the 'two Geneva Conferences last year and revealed more clearly this February at the twentieth communist congress'.[72] For his part Dulles declined to criticise the growth in non-strategic Sino-Japanese trade. 'We realize that this sort [of] trade may be necessary', he conceded, 'and have from time to time agreed to review our lists [of] commodities banned from export to China, in [the] hope of helping our friends.' Hatoyama welcomed this flexibility and expressed the hope that such reviews would continue.[73]

The following month, the third unofficial Sino-Japanese trade agreement was extended, and a few weeks later the Japanese cabinet finally gave its consent to the exchange of 'private-level but permanent' trade missions, albeit without any diplomatic privileges.[74] The Eisenhower Administration was still internally divided on the wisdom of Sino-Japanese trade and now hinted at withholding aid if Tokyo went ahead with this plan.[75] Hatoyama's commitment to his original goals never wavered however. He still wanted to 'work toward establishing normal ties with [the] Soviets and Red China', although in the latter case this meant, 'gradually expanding economic cooperation to create "normal relations"'.[76] Unlike his predecessor, Hatoyama wanted trade with the Communist bloc to promote peaceful coexistence, not a Sino-Soviet rift. Some sections of MOFA, however, remained wedded to Yoshida's China Thesis. In early July 1956, Hōgen Shinsaku (deputy chief of the European–American Affairs Bureau) told a British diplomat that

> based on the latest information which the *Gaimushō* had received from Communist China...the Japanese government believed…increased trade with China by Japan and other countries would have a considerable effect in weakening the links between Moscow and Peking.[77]

However, the ministry's official position was supportive of increased Sino-Japanese trade only within internationally approved limits.[78] This was unacceptable to the economic ministries. Under its first director, Takasaki Tatsunosuke, the EPA (*Keizai Kikakuchō*) published an *Economic White Paper* at the end of July, which supported the immediate relaxation of restrictions on trade with China on the grounds of economic complementarity. Trade Minister Ishibashi Tanzan meanwhile linked his demand for expanded trade with mainland China to increasing restrictions imposed by Western countries on Japanese exports.[79]

The economic ministries' campaign to ease the China embargo continued. At an inter-governmental conference held on 20 August, Japan protested to the US about its double standards on Chinese trade. Washington tried to propitiate the Japanese by accepting a list of goods the latter had earlier proposed for liberalisation, but it was too little and too late.[80] On 4 September, the Americans offered a significant concession: 'Japan may export strategic materials to Communist China to the same degree as Western European countries do, as long as she notifies the CHINCOM machinery about it.'[81] Three weeks later, Shigemitsu announced that Japan would utilise the CHINCOM special exceptions procedure to the same extent as the Western Europeans.[82] This policy change had an immediate impact: it allowed seventy per cent of the goods on the embargo list to be on display when the first Japanese trade fair opened in Beijing on 6 October.[83] Ikeda Masanosuke led a Diet Members' League delegation to the fair. There he signed a joint-communiqué which reaffirmed the goals and further extended the validity of the third trade agreement. On his return to Tokyo, despite the passage of a House of Representatives' resolution supporting the joint-communiqué, bureaucrats continued to hinder progress. Ikeda was unable to persuade those officials overseeing Sino-Japanese trade even to ease methods of payment.[84] Things took a more positive turn however, in mid-December, when the LDP narrowly selected one of its most outspoken supporters of the China trade to succeed Hatoyama as prime minister.

The Ishibashi interlude

Ishibashi Tanzan marked his promotion to the premiership by immediately informing the State Department's emissary, Walter Robertson, that the US, 'by restricting trade with China on the one hand and limiting Japanese imports to the US on the other, was "placing the squeeze" on Japan.' Unlike his predecessors, Ishibashi's case for Japan–China trade seemingly rested on grounds of economic necessity. '[T]he Japanese Government does not disagree with the general policy of the US and the Free World regarding trade with Communist China', Ishibashi conceded, '[h]owever, the US must recognize that Japan's economic position is a precarious one, and that Japan's life depends upon foreign trade.'[85] Robertson was not reassured by what he heard.

At the new cabinet's inaugural meeting on Christmas Day 1956, the policy of promoting trade with China won unanimous support. Foreign Minister Kishi Nobusuke agreed to allow the PRC to open a permanent trade mission in Tokyo.[86] Nonetheless the importance of trade ties with the US was not forgotten. Privately, Ishibashi and others continued to reassure American visitors that they 'were aware...of problems involved in trade with Communist China and they didn't wish to overstep the proper bounds.'[87] Publicly, Ishibashi promised that 'In expanding our trade with Red China...I will closely consult with the US'. At the same time he also predicted that, 'the US will gradually change its attitude toward Red China'.[88] Ishibashi's views on the issue were further clarified during the premier's traditional New Year visit to the grand shrine at Ise. Stating his intention to further ease the trade embargo against Beijing, he expressed a willingness to consider signing a payments agreement and exchanging trade representatives: both key Chinese demands since April 1955.[89] In Washington, John Foster Dulles warned that the Japanese would soon end their support for America's line on China and the Eisenhower Administration stepped up its efforts to dissuade them from doing so.

Certain sectors of Japan's business community were meanwhile trying to ensure that government policy withstood this external pressure. Increasingly this included big business. Sensing a profitable opportunity, large firms were rushing to join the relevant trade associations.[90] The government itself remained divided on the degree to which it should promote Communist trade. In January 1957, in an effort to reconcile policy differences on this point, Trade Minister Mizuta Mikio, announced that the government planned to establish an inter-ministry special economic council to review national policy on trade with both the Soviet Union and China. Later that month, however, a conference of Japanese ambassadors based in the Asia–Pacific region concluded that since the US was unlikely to relax its containment policy against China; the government should avoid direct involvement in Sino-Japanese trade. Instead, it recommended continuing to encourage the activities of private business interests.[91] Sadly for Ishibashi, illness robbed him of the opportunity to complete any of his ambitious policy agenda.

The Kishi era

The road to Nagasaki

On 23 February 1957, Kishi Nobusuke formally inherited the title of prime minister from the incapacitated Ishibashi. Having fortuitously attained the highest office, Kishi pledged to continue his predecessor's diplomatic line.[92] This was a less difficult stance for the strongly anti-Communist Kishi than it might seem. During his unsuccessful campaign for the party presidency the previous December, Kishi had promised to promote trade with both Moscow and Beijing irrespective of whether or not the latter was recognised.[93] A few days after taking over as acting premier, following Ishibashi's hospitalisation on 24 January 1957, he delivered the keynote address to the new session of the Diet. Kishi described Japan as 'economically interdependent with Communist China', and hence felt Tokyo 'must take proper measures, while cooperating with the Free World, that will lead toward the easing of the embargo against China and toward expansion of

Japan's China trade.' He also steadfastly defended the primacy of relations with the US.[94]

Kishi spent the next six months patiently working towards the elimination of the so-called 'China differential': the gap between the strict controls for exports to China and the foreshortened list imposed on the Soviet market.[95] His rationale was the same as Ishibashi's: 'It is solely under the dictate of sheer economic necessity that Japan seeks to increase her trade with mainland China.'[96] By late April, following the provocative Asanuma–Zhang joint-declaration condemning the Japanese government for its refusal to sign an official trade agreement with Beijing, *seikei bunri* was officially enshrined as the conceptual basis underlying the LDP's China policy.[97] Such a view was no longer acceptable to the increasingly ideology driven Chinese leadership. It responded by allowing the third unofficial trade agreement to lapse: business pressure on Kishi mounted.[98] Yet, when US rigidity resulted in Britain unilaterally abandoning the differential in late May, unlike most members of CHINCOM, Japan pointedly held back.[99] With Kishi en route to Taipei, and due in Washington two weeks later, perhaps such caution was understandable.[100]

The Kishi–Eisenhower summit was deemed a great success on both sides of the Pacific, although differences of opinion over China trade did not appear to narrow. Dulles told Kishi that the US would at most 'tolerate' Japan–China trade as a necessary 'evil'.[101] Privately the Americans were reconciled to their ally's abandonment of the 'China differential', but for domestic political reasons they preferred to 'force' Tokyo to take the lead.[102] Hence, in mid-July, Japan announced its decision to eliminate 207 items from the CHINCOM list and 65 items on the COCOM list.[103] Trade restrictions on China and the Soviet Union were now identical.

The recently reshuffled cabinet immediately approved the despatch of a mission to Beijing to negotiate a fourth unofficial trade agreement. It was to comprise representatives of three trade organisations—JITPA, JCTPA and the Diet Members' League—again led by Ikeda Masanosuke (chairman of the League as well as the LDP's recently established Special Committee for the Promotion of Japan–China Trade or *NitChū Bōeki Sokushin Tokubetsu Iinkai*).[104] However, this did not indicate Tokyo's abandonment of *seikei bunri*.[105] Consequently, Beijing responded negatively. The Chinese government denounced Kishi, cut the number of trade contracts signed with Japanese firms, expelled most of their 81 representatives stationed in China, and cancelled a planned Chinese trade fair in Japan.[106]

Kishi was not intimidated by the Chinese actions. He refused to bend on the recognition question, although he said that talks on the fourth trade agreement should proceed and his government was studying ways to relax immigration procedures to promote bilateral trade.[107] The following day, 9 August, Foreign Minister Fujiyama Aiichirō made his first intervention in support of Kishi's policy. An old friend of the premier's and a powerful businessman, Fujiyama had reluctantly accepted the post on condition that he was given *carte blanche*. He now repeated the 'economic necessity' argument, and promised that the ban on strategic exports to China would remain in effect.[108] Aware of the bad weather delaying the launch of China's second five-year-plan, and 'the recent reduction in economic aid from the Soviet Union', the cabinet reportedly concluded that, 'China had no choice but to promote trade with Japan'.[109] The idea that the balance of economic necessity was moving in Tokyo's favour was not confined to the cabinet.[110]

With less than a week to go before negotiations on the fourth trade agreement were due to open in Beijing, MOFA informed the State Department that Japan would approve the exchange of unofficial trade offices with China. The Japanese diplomats assured their American counterparts that this was not a step towards normalisation of relations, but inevitably this was how it was interpreted.[111] Foreign Minister Fujiyama flew to Washington to explain the policy shift. On 23 September, he offered Dulles two rationales. The trade missions were necessary because: 'the demands of trading firms must be satisfied to some extent and directed into non-injurious channels'; and 'to prevent leftists and communists from involving themselves in the trade as middlemen and steering the trade in a manner not beneficial to Japan.' Finally, Fujiyama assured the secretary of state that the trade problem was 'completely divorced from the question of political recognition.' Dulles responded with a stern warning that 'the Japanese would suffer bad political consequences if they were to open a regular trade office on the Chinese mainland'.[112]

Undaunted, Fujiyama on his return to Japan restated the *seikei bunri* line, declaring his support for the exchange of trade offices and for the Japanese team negotiating with China. He also expressed confidence in Tokyo's ability to 'explain and obtain the understanding of the [Nationalist] Chinese Government, as well as the US Government, regarding Japan's need to trade with Communist China'.[113] Despite further significant Japanese concessions, however, progress in Beijing proved difficult and on 3 November, after more than 40 days of talks, the trade negotiations were suspended.[114]

Disregarding the breakdown in the unofficial Chinese talks, Moscow pressed on with its own official trade negotiations with Japan, which had been underway since 12 September. Throughout the year, Khrushchev had been making positive statements regarding the prospects for Soviet–Japanese trade. Eventually, a five-year Treaty of Commerce and Navigation and a one-year Trade and Payments Agreement were concluded on 6 December, granting most-favoured-nation trading status and permitting the establishment of a permanent Soviet trade mission in Tokyo.[115] Moreover, unlike the stagnant China trade, economic exchanges with Moscow were booming, recording a six-fold increase over the previous year, albeit from a very low base. (Figure 4.1.)[116]

While the Kishi government had been consistently pursuing *seikei bunri* since February 1957, Yoshida's China Thesis had never disappeared completely. In December, Akashi Yasushi, the first Japanese to work for the UN, noted how some Japanese 'argue that by establishing wider economic and political contacts with mainland China and thus reducing its dependence on the Soviet Union, some kind of Tito-ization of China could be promoted'. Moreover, he felt that, 'recent pronouncements of Mao Tse-tung on the question of contradictions within the "Socialist' states" seemed to confirm this view.[117]

The thesis received more official backing when the Japan–US Committee on Security held its fourth meeting in Tokyo later that month. Foreign Minister Fujiyama began by describing Sino-Soviet ties as 'very close', but after hearing US Ambassador Douglas MacArthur II detail China's current economic woes, he questioned 'whether it might not be preferable for the free world to try to exploit these economic difficulties through increased free world trade with [the] ChiComs which would tend to separate them from the USSR.' He should have known better than to expect any revision of the American view on Yoshida's China Thesis. MacArthur was far from encouraging, asserting that 'Chinese Communist–Soviet ties are based on far more than Chinese economic dependence on the USSR'. A Sino-Soviet rift, therefore, could not 'be currently achieved through efforts to lessen ChiCom economic dependence on the USSR'.[118]

Liao Chengzhi, China's leading Japan specialist, also visited the Japanese capital in December. Although part of a Chinese Red Cross mission, he took the opportunity to meet privately with Ikeda Masanosuke and secretly with MOFA's China Desk Chief, Okada Akira.[119] Chinese conditions for a trade agreement had not softened, but Liao made it clear that Beijing wanted the talks to resume.[120]

Domestic pro-China trade pressures on the Japanese government continued to mount. By late January 1958, MOFA had received 57 petitions from major trade organisations calling for the talks with China to resume. A conference on the issue attracted participants from more than 250 economic organisations.[121] In mid-February, anticipating the imminent resumption of the talks, Kishi warned MacArthur that if an 'unofficial trade agreement...were finally concluded it was probable [that] a comm[unist] trade mission would enter Japan...[and] some privileges beyond those enjoyed by private foreign visitors would have to be accorded [to its members.]'[122]

On 25 February, the stalled negotiations on a fourth unofficial trade agreement resumed in Beijing.[123] The exchange of trade missions remained the most difficult issue. The talks nonetheless received a boost when a £200 million, five-year barter agreement was signed a few days later between the Japanese steel industry and

Chinese government corporations.[124] The fourth unofficial trade agreement was finally concluded on 5 March. It provided for £70 million in bilateral trade during the next year. In an appended memorandum, however, the Japanese negotiators substantially exceeded the list of privileges agreed to by the Kishi cabinet.[125]

Reaction to the agreement was predictably harsh in conservative circles. The FARC, long dominated by pro-Taiwan elements, immediately issued a strongly worded statement opposing the agreement.[126] An ad hoc group of six of the party's most senior officials subsequently met to consider the issue. They recommended that the cabinet not grant any diplomatic privileges to the Chinese trade representatives that could be construed as recognition. In particular, they wanted cabinet to keep the number of PRC personnel to an absolute minimum and to refuse them the right to fly their flag.[127] The Americans also preached caution.[128] Kishi and Fujiyama, however, were not immediately inclined to accept this advice. On 11 March, the premier told MacArthur that 'he was very unhappy that the Ikeda group had gone so far'. Nevertheless, he explained, 'the pressures from all sectors of Japanese national opinion, including big business, small business, conservative members of the Diet, to say nothing of the socialists, was so great that it was not possible to disapprove of the agreement.' Kishi was at pains to reassure the ambassador that, 'the private trade agreement did not in any way involve any step toward political recognition of the ChiCom regime', but, he repeated, his 'government would respect the terms of the agreement.'[129]

Just when it seemed as if the Japanese government was going to stand up to its domestic and American critics, ROC President Chiang Kai-shek dramatically raised the stakes. Despite having received a personal message from Kishi asking that he acquiesce in the deal, Taipei announced on 19 March that it was suspending trade with Japan over the flag issue.[130] At the time, its value was roughly equivalent to Japan's trade with the mainland (Figure 4.2). Kishi's response was to stall. On 24 March, he told representatives of the three Japanese trade organisations involved in the negotiations that he could not give a final reply to their request for government support of the agreement until he had settled the Taiwan problem. Three days later, Dulles asked MacArthur to convey to the Japanese government his concern 'at the apparent ability of Peiping to influence Japanese policy by threatening to limit trade', as well as over deteriorating Japan–ROC relations.[131] That evening, when the ambassador again met with Kishi, the latter seemed to shift his ground slightly. He reiterated that Japan would 'not grant diplomatic privileges' to the Chinese trade mission, and also this time specifically denied the mission's *right* to hoist the PRC flag. However, he also pointed out that 'there is no Japanese law which can be invoked to prevent the ChiComs from hoisting [their] flag.' At most, he could 'take the position that Article 92 of the criminal code which obliges the GOJ to protect the sanctity of recognized national flags will not apply.'[132]

Offers to despatch LDP Vice-President Ōno Bamboku to explain the situation to President Chiang Kai-shek were rebuffed. Taipei seemed ready to break off diplomatic relations. Kishi therefore decided to send Ambassador Horinouchi Kensuke back to Taipei with a personal letter for Chiang.[133] In the letter, delivered on 30 March, the prime minister reaffirmed his desire for friendly relations and repeated what he had told MacArthur about non-recognition of Beijing and its flag. Horinouchi added the detail about Article 92.[134] This was initially insufficient to propitiate Chiang. It was only after Ambassador Horinouchi—over the fierce objections of most senior LDP leaders—strengthened the government's commitment to prevent the raising of a PRC flag in Japan that a settlement with Taiwan was reached on 8 April.[135]

In the meantime, Beijing was outraged and immediately denounced the Kishi letter as 'a deliberate attempt to destroy the trade agreement.'[136] On 9 April, in an open letter to the three Japanese trade organisations that had negotiated the unofficial agreement, Kishi attempted to mollify all concerned by promising to 'respect the spirit' of the trade pact. He offered his support and cooperation 'within the limits of relevant Japanese laws, on the basis of the understanding that [Tokyo] did not recognize [Beijing], and considering existing international relations.'[137] It was Chief Cabinet Secretary Aichi Kiichi who announced that '*the right* of the trade mission to raise its flag will not be recognized.'[138] The three trade organisations conveyed the government's views to Beijing and not surprisingly received an angry reply from Nan Hanchen (chairman of CITPC) on 13 April. The subtleties of the Japanese position were apparently lost on Beijing. Nan declared that, 'so long as the various obstacles put up by the Japanese Government remain, the implementation of the agreement is impossible.'[139] Despite the suspension of the agreement and the negative popular reaction this invited at home, Japanese government circles remained optimistic that something could yet be salvaged from the situation. Their hopes were soon dashed.

On the last day of April, a small touring exhibition of Chinese postage stamps opened in a Nagasaki department store. The Taiwanese consul in Kōbe requested that the local government remove a small PRC flag that was flying over the exhibit. The sponsors refused, but on 2 May, only hours before the exhibit was due to close, a young Japanese tore down the flag. He soon apologised and the flag was restored to its original position.[140] The next morning's newspapers made no mention of it, but on 5 May, several Chinese mainland papers warned that Beijing was 'taking a grave view of the incident.'[141] To Kishi, this seemed like a gross overreaction to a youthful prank. The following day, he told reporters that 'Communist China should stop trying to use [the] fourth private trade agreement issue as [a] *de facto* political springboard for making Japan recognize her.'[142] He was not about to change his position, but hoped that the Chinese would calmly reconsider theirs.[143] They did just the opposite. In the course of the next seven days, China launched verbal broadsides directed at Kishi personally, and undertook a series of retaliatory measures against Japanese business interests. Foreign Minister Chen Yi attacked the Japanese government for having 'openly sabotaged' the trade agreement and accused Kishi of personally conniving in the Nagasaki flag incident and seeking to revive Japanese militarism. China did not depend on trade with Japan, the *People's Daily* scoffed. A Chinese warship seized fourteen Japanese fishing boats and their 170 crew members. 1262 contracts worth approximately £35 million and involving about 110 Japanese companies directly (and perhaps ten times that number indirectly) were cancelled. A Chinese steel mission was withdrawn and the remaining 40 Japanese businessmen stationed in Beijing were expelled.[144] Within a month, all Chinese ports were closed to Japanese vessels and the Sino-Japanese fishing agreement was allowed to expire.[145] Nor were the Chinese economic sanctions confined to purely bilateral channels. China started 'dumping' textiles and manufactured goods on the markets of South and Southeast Asia, substantially undercutting Japanese prices and grabbing market share.[146] The fact that China imposed an embargo on Japan following its formal abandonment of the Soviet economic model (the so-called Great Leap Forward), cannot be regarded as coincidental. However, most Japanese were slow to make the connexion.

The Japanese response to Beijing's actions was contradictory. Ambassador MacArthur rather perceptively described it as 'characterized by dismayed annoyance tempered to a large extent by a cautious desire to find means of placating [the] ChiComs without losing face.'[147] MOFA let it be known off-the-record that it felt 'the Chen statement, which was issued during an election campaign in Japan...was aimed at lowering the prestige of the Kishi Government in the eyes of the Japanese people'. Such Chinese behaviour was to be treated as a case of 'meddling in Japan's domestic affairs.[148] As far as the government was concerned, the best strategy was thus to stand firm until after the elections, when, it was believed, things would gradually return to normal. In a fine example of political double-speak, MOFA declared that Japan's official policy was one of 'active wait and see' (*sekkyokuteki seikan*).[149] Big business, in the shape of the steel and agro-chemical industries, agreed with the government, convinced that eventually China would have to come back to them.[150]

However, some members of the ruling party were more sceptical. On 15 May, Miki Takeo, now chairman of the PARC, told voters that he believed 'Communist China's suspension of trade with Japan was not a gesture aimed at influencing the Japanese election, but was because of a change in the foreign policy of the Beijing regime.'[151] Meanwhile the LDP's pro-China wing was reportedly considering sending a party representative to Beijing after the elections. Privately, even some diplomats expressed concern at the possibility of China turning to alternative sources to supply its import needs.[152] The JSP was more outspoken. Apparently oblivious to the true state of Sino-Soviet economic relations, the Socialists claimed that, 'economic cooperation has been strengthened so much within the Communist bloc that Communist China's decision to suspend trade with Japan is not a mere threat.'[153] On 12 May, the LDP spurned a JSP offer of a joint conference to seek a solution to the problem.[154] Thereafter, the leading opposition party berated the government for its incompetence and proposed that it compensate firms affected by the Chinese sanctions (many of whom had ties to the JSP.)[155] Thrown onto the defensive, the LDP struck back by accusing the Socialists of encouraging the Chinese to take their tough stand on the trade agreement.[156]

Pro-China business groups reportedly suffered 'a deep psychological shock' from the Chinese boycott. The NGOs that represented their interests sent abject apologies to Beijing, but to no avail. On 20 May, a National Convention for Discussion of Countermeasures Concerning Japan–China Relations was organised by the Japan–China Friendship Association, and joined by various business groups, it demanded that the government support the unofficial trade agreement.[157] On 3 July, the Diet Member's League passed a similar resolution, but following the LDP's 22 May election victory, most party members followed informal instructions to withdraw. Without its bipartisan following the organisation lost much of its influence.[158]

Confusion over Japan's China policy remained. Kishi repeated the 'wait and see (*seikan*)' policy line in his Diet policy speech on 17 June, but the very same day he was contradicted by Takasaki Tatsunosuke, his new Minister of International Trade and Industry. Takasaki told the press that because it was financially very important to Japan, he hoped to restore relations with the mainland as soon as possible. Two days later, a member of Kishi's own faction, Chief Cabinet Secretary Akagi Munemori, received Takasaki's support when he suggested that the 'cumulative method (*tsumiage hōshiki*)' be employed to resolve the problems with China, starting with the despatch of a special envoy to Beijing to 'positively promote' friendly relations.[159] Akagi was soon forced to withdraw his statement, however, and in a rather obvious slight, LDP Secretary-General Kawashima asked that Akagi himself enforce a strict 'gag' rule on cabinet ministers concerning China policy.[160]

The first debate over a Sino-Soviet economic schism

If the Japanese reaction to the Chinese embargo was confused and contradictory, the Soviet response was clear-cut. Pyongyang joined the boycott against Japan on 20 May, but Moscow seemed oblivious to Beijing's actions. The Soviets calmly proceeded to renew their bilateral fisheries agreement (22 April); put into effect the Japan–Soviet Trade Agreement signed the previous December (9 May); offer an aviation agreement and a cultural agreement, and conclude a Navigation Treaty (3 June).[161]

By mid-June, Ambassador MacArthur was reporting that there was 'much speculation in Japanese political and other circles re [the] vastly different attitude which [the] Soviet Union on [the] one hand and [the] ChiComs on [the] other are displaying toward Japan.' He identified three viewpoints. There were sceptical Japanese who felt that 'Peking and Moscow are closely collaborating with each other re policy toward Japan and are dividing work on the basis of some agreed tactics'. At the opposite extreme, a second group wondered whether 'ideological differences' lay behind the disparity. In between were those who believed that the differing approaches of Moscow and Peking were 'based on [a] difference of views between them on tactics to neutralize Japan'.[162]

Hara Katsu, the political critic, tended towards the more serious end of MacArthur's scale. On 18 June, Hara had told a US Embassy official that, 'the ChiCom severance of trade and cultural relations with Japan was not done in concert with or under the direction of Moscow.' Moreover, he felt that, 'there...probably is a feeling of competition and rivalry between Peiping and Moscow in terms of attempting to achieve an influence in Japan'. Indeed, according to Hara, 'Far from using the Chinese Communists to promote Soviet goals in this country, the Soviets probably are highly suspicious of all Chinese Communist activities here and want to keep their influence to a minimum.' He suggested that, 'backed up by the strength of the U.S. and the rest of the free world...the Japanese, if they are clever, could exert considerable pressure on the Chinese Communists in the conduct of their trade relations.' 'Unfortunately, however,' Hara lamented, 'Japanese politicians, diplomats, and businessmen are [not] skillful enough to exploit these possibilities.'[163]

When Vice-Foreign Minister Yamada Hisanari questioned MacArthur regarding US views on the subject, Washington's response was dismissive. Dulles informed the US Embassy in Tokyo that the State Department believed 'policy differences [were] less radical than [those] advanced by [the] GOJ and probably ascribable to allowable Chinese Communist tactical initiative in [a] matter [of] their primary interest rather than to Chinese Communist's operating on [their] own.' Concerning the 'division of labour' hypothesis, Dulles thought it 'conceivable' that there was an 'agreement providing for [a] division [of] responsibilities in pursuing bloc objectives [vis-à-vis] Japan with each partner concentrating [on] Japanese vulnerabilities most exploitable by it.' However, he maintained that the Department

> considers unlikely any possible ideological differences [which] would disturb [their] essential solidarity on foreign policy which [was] demonstrated in [the]

> November 1957 Declaration of Communist parties... Specifically [it] considered this solidarity extends to [the] two countries' policies toward Japan.[164]

Dulles was exaggerating the solidity of the Sino-Soviet Alliance in order to keep Japan in line. This was the message that MacArthur conveyed to Fujiyama when the two met on 9 July.[165] It was the main topic of discussion when the foreign minister conferred with senior Japanese ambassadors and ministry officials in Tokyo the next day. After a lengthy debate, participants 'endorsed' the government's 'wait and see' approach. The difference between hard-line Chinese and 'superficially' soft-line Soviet attitudes towards Japan was adjudged to be 'tactical' not 'strategic'. This 'discord (*kuichigai*)', however, was seen to reflect the disparity in Moscow and Beijing's diplomatic status rather than any divergence in their basic line.[166] This fundamental assumption would guide official Japanese policy for the next two years.

Not everyone within MOFA agreed with this assessment, however. That autumn, the Hong Kong Consulate General reported that, 'Gromyko and Mikoyan have expressed displeasure to [the] ChiCom Ambassador over [the] failure to consult them when [the] abrupt change over took place from soft to hard tactics vis-à-vis Japan.' Their view was that Beijing's action was part of a wider policy change: the Chinese hard line attitude was not limited to Japan, but extended to Socialist Yugoslavia and even to the Soviet Union. According to Hong Kong's analysis, Moscow's new-found determination to preserve a more stable international environment had left Beijing with a deepening sense of international isolation and a strong impulse to overturn the status quo.[167] However, with revitalised Sino-Soviet bilateral trade disguising evidence of Communist economic differences, Kishi decided to wait quietly for China to bend under the mounting Soviet pressure. Unfortunately for Kishi, the Chinese leadership proved to be more patient than the Japanese public.

The struggle to restore the China trade

The next two years—mid-1958 to mid-1960—were marked by low-intensity internal conflict as various members of the Japanese government set out to overturn Kishi's stubborn insistence that Japan could only 'wait and see' what China would do. Powerful faction leaders like Kōno Ichirō, believed that Japanese politicians could and should take the initiative to resume trade with China. More moderate in their views were Foreign Minister Fujiyama and others within MOFA, who employed unofficial diplomatic channels to explore the range of possible interaction with China. In the end, despite all of the intrigue and political manoeuvring, China's unrelenting hard-line and Kishi's political prejudices combined to block any policy change.

Defying Kishi's prediction of a gradual post-election return to normality, on 7 July 1958, Beijing named a high price for its economic cooperation. Having first appealed to overseas Chinese to join the boycott against Japanese goods, the *People's Daily* outlined 'three political principles' that Tokyo must observe if it hoped to see the embargo lifted. Japan would have to abandon its 'hostile attitude' towards China; work earnestly for the normalisation of Sino-Japanese relations; and refrain from promoting the 'two Chinas plot'.[168]

In a report to Dulles at the end of July, Ambassador MacArthur described Beijing's cessation of trade with Japan—and its 'obvious determination to maintain [the] closest partnership with Moscow'—as having had a triple impact on Japanese thinking:

> (1) Japanese hopes for a vastly expanded export trade with the mainland have been undermined; (2) concern has been created about ChiCom politico-economic competition in Asia, and (3) a sobering awareness has taken root (sic) of the naked power of the "new China".

This accounted for Kishi's suspension of *seikei bunri* and adoption of a 'wait and see' policy in its stead. However, MacArthur warned of growing 'pressures within Japan and within [the] LDP itself to find a way of appeasing the Chinese Communist regime.' Noting that there was 'no significant body of opinion in Japan that views trade relations with Communist China as other than an entirely desirable thing', he concluded that 'Exploratory efforts to find out...Communist China's price for renewed trade...[were] likely.'[169]

MacArthur's prediction was correct. With Japanese business already suffering from a worldwide recession, Okada Akira (China Desk) confessed that, 'his section was under heavy pressure from business and political circles to "do something" about [the] China trade issue.'[170] At the same time, the business daily *Nihon Keizai Shimbun* reported that the government was again sounding out Chinese intentions via the Consul General in Geneva. Furthermore, Sata Tadataka of the JSP met secretly with Okada, Itagaki Osamu (Asian Affairs Bureau director) and Foreign Minister Fujiyama before departing on a mission to China at the end of July.[171] A week later, Itagaki informed the US Embassy that, '[the] cabinet has decided [to] attempt [to] reopen talks with [the] ChiComs in regard to Japanese still held on [the] mainland and possibly explore [the] fisheries question.'[172] By mid-August, Okada was discussing 'prospective site[s] for potential ambassadorial talks with [the] Chinese Communists'. Neither Okada nor Itagaki sounded particularly enthused at the prospect, however, implying that pressure was now being exerted from above and beyond—by influential figures both within and without MOFA.[173]

On 15 August 1958, the Japanese government announced another large cut in the COCOM list, leaving just 118 restricted items.[174] Trade Minister Takasaki Tatsunosuke, commenting on the commercial opportunities thereby created, told journalists that he 'thought [the] Government should send special representative[s] to Peking to try [to] resolve [the] trade deadlock.'[175] However, three days later, on 23 August, China provoked the second Taiwan Straits Crisis. Within a week, Okada informed the US Embassy that MOFA was now 'reconsidering its tactics' and had 'decided not to attempt any new approach for the time being'. According to Okada, however, the primary reason for this sudden change in attitude was not Chinese military action, but rather,

> the deep dismay and vexation felt in [MOFA] at the highest level over the exceedingly harsh terms for resolving the current impasse between Japan and Communist China laid down by the ChiComs to socialist Dietman Sata during the latter's recent visit [to] Peiping.[176]

Sata in fact delivered his full report to Fujiyama on 29 August. In addition to the 'three political principles' outlined by the PRC on 7 July, there were three new conditions. The Kishi government had to formally apologise for the Nagasaki Flag Incident, make amends, and officially start working to restore Sino-Japanese relations. When all the conditions stipulated were satisfactorily fulfilled, Beijing decreed that the Japanese government could send an official delegation to the mainland to discuss 'future problems'. For Okada Akira, acceptance of these harsh terms would have been 'tantamount to unconditional surrender'. His colleagues referred to them (only half in jest) as 'China's Twenty-one Demands.'[177]

While Sata's report may have temporarily chastened MOFA supporters of an initiative aimed at restoring trading links with China, within the LDP it merely served to sharpen existing divisions. Disagreement centred not on whether to resume trade, but on how far Japan should go in pursuing improved relations. According to commentator Hara Katsu, Kōno Ichirō attempted to get the LDP's Executive Board, which he now chaired, to consider the Sata Report. Ikeda Masanosuke blocked him, however, for although he was chairman of the LDP's Japan–China Trade Promotion Committee, Ikeda was close to Kishi. Reportedly scheming for Fujiyama's job, Kōno then met privately with Soviet fisheries expert A. A. Ishkov, in a bid 'to enlist Soviet help in breaking the Japan–Communist China impasse.'[178] This suggests that Kōno believed some warmth remained in Sino-Soviet relations.

Foreign Minister Fujiyama occupied the middle ground in this LDP debate on China. Through the autumn, he continued to speak of an 'active wait and see' policy and to hint at the possibility of ambassadorial talks with China.[179] In mid-September, at the UN, Fujiyama promised Dulles that there would be:

> No change in Japan's policy of recognizing only the [ROC] nor in Japan's position as [a] member [of the] free world community, but, with respect to Red China, Japan must pursue [a] different course from [the] US in trade, fisheries and movement of persons.[180]

Miki Takeo (director of the EPA) was typical of the LDP centrists who had thus far given Kishi the benefit of the doubt. In late October, Miki felt that if Kishi were removed China would soften its attitude, but he remained resigned to the 'wait and see' approach: 'Everybody in Japan wants to trade with China...but matters are now in Peiping's hands.'[181] Embroiled in a domestic crisis over the Police Duties Bill, Kishi seemed to go out of his way to alienate such moderates. Resentful of Beijing's endless personal attacks, in an interview on 14 October, the premier referred to China as an 'aggressor nation' and bluntly declared his refusal to pay the price it demanded for restored trade.[182] By late November, Kishi reportedly viewed China as 'Japan's great enemy'. Shortly thereafter, Miki Takeo and other moderates resigned from the cabinet.[183]

Meanwhile, negotiations were quietly proceeding on a second Japan–Soviet trade pact. After less than a month of talks, an agreement was reached on 4 December that aimed at increasing two-way exchanges by 40 per cent within a year.[184] Soviet Ambassador Fedorenko later followed this up with a 'wish-list' of Japanese manufactures Moscow desired to import to promote Siberian development.[185] State Department officers speculated that, 'the Japanese today are finding the Russians much easier to live with than the ChiComs.'[186]

The New Year opened with renewed efforts in various quarters to restore trade links with China. A January 1959 article written by China Desk Chief Okada Akira (under the pseudonym Yamamoto Michio) sparked a particularly interesting episode.[187] In it, he revealed his 'strong desire for a rapid improvement in relations with Communist China' and proposed government-level talks. The article concluded, however, with what was described by one reader as 'an insultingly long recital of Sino-Soviet problems and [a] statement of "sympathy" for Communist China which is "forced to stand on an unequal footing with [the] Soviet Union".' Okada did not have to wait long to see his 'trial balloon' shot down. In February, he received a personal letter from Liao Chengzhi describing him in rather unflattering terms as a 'human pepper'. When later that month *Sōhyō* Secretary-General Iwai Akira met with Zhou Enlai, the latter reportedly felt 'particularly incensed with Okada's jabs at Sino-Soviet relations', describing the article as further evidence of 'Kishi's hostile diplomacy'.[188] Okada had clearly touched a raw nerve.

Nonetheless, Secretary-General Iwai's trip to China was not a total failure. With Mao forced to resign the PRC chairmanship over the failure of the 'Great Leap Forward', the more moderate Zhou granted a special trade concession. Later called 'consideration trade' (*hairyo bōeki*), it was limited to small and medium-sized Japanese companies dependent on Chinese lacquer and chestnuts and guaranteed by *Sōhyō* or the JSP as 'not unfriendly to China.' The volume was insignificant, but China's 'splitting tactics' succeeded in dividing LDP opinion along the usual lines, with Fujiyama and LDP Secretary-General Fukuda Takeo critical of China's offer and Trade Minister Takasaki expressing gratitude.[189]

At the time, the US Embassy interpreted Okada's article as another example of his '"personal diplomacy" which has been tolerated by his immediate superiors who...are interested in devices which reveal nuances in Chinese Communist policy toward Japan'. Okada himself claimed that it had been 'reviewed before publication by [an] informal China study group in [the] LDP headed by Cabinet Secretary Akagi'.[190] Certainly, Okada was not alone in his support for high-level trade talks with China: Foreign Minister Fujiyama also seemed to be losing patience with Kishi's passive policy. In January, he established a special unit within the ministry to study events in China.[191] That same month, he told a press conference in Nagoya that Japan needed 'to take a step forward from its "wait and see" attitude towards China', and that it would be possible for Japan and China 'to sign a governmental trade agreement if talks at ambassadorial level were successful.'[192] On 3 February, Fujiyama reinforced his message, telling the Diet Foreign Affairs Committee that he was prepared to discuss 'technical agreements' with China, covering such areas as posts, meteorology and sea-rescue. His motives were called into question, however, when *Asahi Shimbun* reported that Fujiyama himself had admitted that the campaign for the June Upper House poll was seventy per cent responsible for his proposal.[193]

Still, it would be wrong to dismiss this as purely an electioneering tactic, as did Beijing when it rejected all proposals for talks in late January.[194] Three days later, Fujiyama met secretly with MacArthur and conveyed the news that the Japanese government was prepared to hold ambassadorial-level talks with Beijing 'similar to [the] talks held between [the] US and ChiComs.' In explication, Fujiyama pointed to 'electoral considerations', but he also mentioned the recent 'softening of Communist tactics' and pressure from 'Japanese trade circles', especially the 'important steel and chemical fertilizer industries'. Still, the foreign minister was not optimistic concerning the likely Chinese response, at least before the elections. Unlike Okada, he interpreted the 'ChiCom attitude of aggressiveness and intransigence' up to and including the Sata Report as 'part of [an] over-all compaign (sic) of pressure and force' by the Communist bloc.[195]

Although there is no record of MacArthur raising any objections to Fujiyama's position on this occasion, a week earlier he had met with Kōno Ichirō, who had asked him whether the US was opposed to Japan resuming trade with China. MacArthur had replied with a conditional 'no', so long as it 'consisted of items which were not on [the] strategic list and...did not involve any discrimination against [the] US or free world trade'.[196] Armed with this assurance, Kōno 'revealed' to the press a fortnight later that the climate of opinion in the US regarding recognition of China was changing. He advised Kishi to send an official LDP representative of cabinet rank to China to inquire about the possibility of resuming trade.[197] Kōno's well-known animosity towards Fujiyama ensured that this proposal was presented as a political alternative to Fujiyama's diplomatic approach, not as a complement to it. The next day, 13 February, MacArthur repeated, for the benefit of Secretary-General Fukuda Takeo, that American tolerance of Japan–China trade was conditional. He conveyed the impressions of 'certain powerful circles in the United States' that Fujiyama's proposed 'technical agreements' indicated that Japan was 'gradually moving towards political recognition of Communist China on a step-by-step basis.' Fukuda denied that this was the case, and while not excusing Kōno's 'duplicity', defended Fujiyama's behaviour in terms of the forthcoming elections. Finally, Fukuda inquired what the US reaction would be if the LDP sponsored a joint resolution with the JSP to promote trade with China. MacArthur urged caution.[198]

By this time, even Kishi's patience seemed to be wearing thin. A week later, he sent Vice-Foreign Minister Yamada Hisanari to ascertain the likely US reaction to the LDP sending an official delegation to Beijing to discuss the resumption of trade. Yamada emphasised the electoral motive and without naming names, pointed out that, 'there were very strong pressures within the Liberal Democratic Party' in support of such an option. MacArthur replied bluntly that the reaction in America 'would be very bad.'[199]

Nonetheless, Kōno and the supporters of a Japanese initiative to end the Chinese embargo appeared to be gaining the upper hand, until once more a well-meaning Socialist politician set back their plans. In mid-March, Zhou Enlai reportedly told the second official JSP mission to China that Beijing would agree to government-level negotiations as long as political issues could be discussed, and he invited Fujiyama to visit. Zhou's offer was overshadowed, however, by Asanuma's 'common enemy' statement. As the LDP propaganda machine went into overdrive attacking the JSP leader, Fujiyama denied press reports suggesting that he had sent Zhou a confidential message via the Socialists. The veracity of this information remains uncertain. It is known, however, that Okada Akira briefed the Socialist mission on government policy before its departure.[200]

Meanwhile, Fujiyama remained concerned at Chinese economic penetration of Southeast Asia, and did not abandon his efforts to restore links with the mainland.[201] At the end of March, he responded positively to a suggestion from Sone Eki—a right-wing member of the JSP mission to China—that the government should explore Beijing's real intentions towards Japan. Fujiyama apparently proposed that a group of LDP members should visit China to discuss the resumption of trade relations, although MOFA officials were quick to contradict this view. Kishi for his part stuck to a hard line, telling Sone that he was willing to sanction ambassadorial talks on this issue, but for the fact that the Chinese seemed unable to avoid linking political and economic questions.[202]

In early May, on the first anniversary of the Chinese embargo, Fujiyama told a State Department officer that Kansai businessmen were now less enthusiastic about the China trade. Japan, however, still hoped to restore economic ties and 'if private talks were resumed, he [Fujiyama] felt it would be necessary for [the] Government [to] assist [the] Japanese participants to avoid any mistakes.' Despite being warned that it was 'very difficult to separate trade from politics when dealing with communist countries', Fujiyama argued that his approach would not compromise Japan's *seikei bunri* policy.[203] On 1 June, on the eve of Upper House elections, the foreign minister told the press that Japan should reconsider its China policy. In an effort to resume trade, the LDP would, if necessary, consider sending a delegation to Beijing, leading in due course to ambassadorial talks. Japan was even willing to exchange views on political problems, he claimed.[204]

After the expected LDP election victory, speculation that Beijing might adopt a softer line resurfaced.[205] In mid-June, Fujiyama called together some senior Japanese ambassadors to discuss the China problem; the views were mixed. Ambassador Ōno Katsumi (London) argued that in light of the Geneva Conferences and changes in US leadership, now was the time for Japan to 'make great effort[s] to obtain US and UK understanding in preparation for steps toward closer relations with Communist China.' Ambassador Asakai Kōichirō (Washington) and Vice-Minister Yamada strongly disagreed, however, believing that there should be no change in policy. Ambassador Kadowaki Suemitsu (Moscow) avoided taking sides, merely expressing the opinion that Sino-Soviet economic relations were good.[206]

The Americans were uneasy at the direction in which Japanese thinking might be heading. When MacArthur called on Kishi a few days later, the ambassador fiercely attacked the idea that, '[the] GOJ or LDP might send some kind of mission to Peiping and that there should be closer cultural and other ties, etc.' In MacArthur's view: 'Japan's fundamental self-interest dictated that she should stand firm'. He assured the prime minister that there would be no change in US China policy as a result of the ailing Dulles' replacement by Christian Herter. Kishi replied that, 'he had no intention whatsoever of recognizing Comm[unist] China and did not think any serious Japanese had such [a] prospect in mind.'[207]

Perhaps Kishi no longer regarded Kōno Ichirō as a 'serious Japanese', but the latter continued to campaign for an LDP or governmental mission to Beijing. According to the pro-Taiwan right-winger Funada Naka (chairman of the FARC),

Kōno was planning either to visit China himself or to send a close lieutenant in the near future as part of a bid for the premiership.[208] In June, a public suggestion from Nakasone Yasuhiro (Kōno faction) that Japan offer aid to help China recover from extensive flood damage was eventually rejected on the recommendation of Vice-Minister Yamada.[209] In late September, Kōno suddenly dropped his proposal to send an LDP mission to China; although mounting tensions over revision of the Security Treaty further exacerbated divisions over China policy within the party.[210]

Ishibashi Tanzan was another LDP politician pursuing his own course vis-à-vis China. Three days after the June election, he wrote to Zhou Enlai seeking to visit China. He set three preconditions: Beijing had to cooperate to maintain peace; carry out political, economic and cultural exchanges; and respect each other's relations with the US and Soviet Union, recognising that such relations would not be changed suddenly.[211] Ishibashi's visit lacked official support, but privately MOFA approved.[212] Other more cynical MOFA officers believed that 'the Japanese Government would remain firm', since China's deteriorating economic situation strengthened Tokyo's hand.[213] Ishibashi returned home at the end of September with little more than a joint-communiqué conceding that politics and economics were inseparable. Ishibashi faced calls for party disciplinary action the following month, after he told a group of Ōsaka businessmen that, 'if Kishi resigned Japan–ChiCom relations would be solved in short order.'[214] By this time, however, such views were commonplace.[215]

Following in Ishibashi's footsteps, Matsumura Kenzō, another leader of the LDP's 'pan-Asianist' wing, arrived in Beijing with a much larger mission.[216] After constructive talks with Zhou Enlai, in which Matsumura promised that the Japanese government's hostility towards China would change, the Chinese leader suggested that a gradual build-up of friendly ties could lead to the full-scale resumption of Sino-Japanese trade. Diplomatic recognition was no longer a precondition. Matsumura returned home on 2 December 1959, having laid the foundations for a re-building of the economic relationship and with an invitation for former Trade Minister Takasaki Tatsunosuke to visit.[217]

Disregarding all such developments, the increasingly unpopular Kishi opened the New Year with another reaffirmation of the status quo: telling the press that Japan should not take the initiative in sending an emissary to Beijing. Three days later, on 5 January 1960, Trade Minister Ikeda Hayato spoke publicly in support of the long-standing MITI stance in favour of increased trade with the Communist countries.[218] Naturally, Matsumura Kenzō welcomed his speech, but many senior LDP members were less receptive. Hence, just two days after joining the debate, Ikeda promptly withdrew from it, 'cordially rejecting' an informal invitation he had received to visit Beijing. Other less faint-hearted politicians re-entered the fray. Miki Takeo, for instance, said that Japan could no longer afford to ignore

China, even suggesting that it was possible to resume trade without a fundamental political settlement.[219]

When Kishi arrived in Washington on 19 January to sign the revised Security Treaty, he reassured President Eisenhower that there would be no change in Japan's China policy. He told Secretary of State Herter that although 'Japan would like to resume trade with Communist China under [the] proper conditions...not much trade with Communist China is now expected by Japan.' Commenting on his domestic critics, Kishi said that along with the Socialists, Ishibashi and Matsumura caused the government difficulties on the China issue, but he still thought that the Conservatives' visits to China could be politically useful for the LDP. Finally, he mentioned the possibility of contacts with China in certain 'technical areas'. The Americans responded by insisting on prior consultations.[220]

Rumours again surfaced around this time that Foreign Minister Fujiyama had proposed visiting China in a private capacity once the new Security Treaty was ratified, although the same Chinese Foreign Ministry sources denied that any invitation would be extended.[221] On 5 March, Fujiyama publicly declared that he would not visit China 'right now'. However, he was soon hinting at his intention 'if possible this summer, to take advantage of the holding of the Moscow sample fair to visit the Soviet Union, and there grasp [the opportunity] to begin to break the Japan–China deadlock.'[222] It seems that for Fujiyama too, the path to improved Sino-Japanese relations still led via Moscow.

Although Foreign Minister Fujiyama now openly admitted that his way of thinking was fundamentally different from 'Kishi diplomacy'; other high-ranking MOFA officials maintained Kishi's passive line. In mid-January, a four-day meeting of the ministry's China experts convened in Hong Kong. Participants agreed 'it was possible that China's foreign policy would gradually become more moderate'. Nevertheless, they anticipated that, 'it would be difficult to improve Japan–China relations in the course of 1960'. Moreover, it was noted that, 'today there was little pressure from business circles for a break in the deadlock', and therefore, 'the future development of Japan–China relations would depend primarily on China.'[223]

The last observation was confirmed by Isaki Kyūtarō (president of *Ataka*, a Kansai-based company), who acknowledged that among many Kansai businessmen there also seemed to be 'a shift in interest from China trade to trade with Russia.'[224] The previous November, Ōsaka hosted a National Conference for the Promotion of Japanese–Soviet Trade. Soviet representatives present stressed the large demand for steel, oil pipes and machinery in the Siberian seven-year development plan.[225] During that same month, three separate Soviet missions arrived in Japan to discuss fish stock conservation, textile imports, and oil, coal and iron ore exports. They agreed to stage a Japanese industrial exhibition in Moscow the following summer.[226] On 15 January 1960, Japanese steel companies signed a private agreement to import nearly a million tons of Soviet coal over the next three years.[227] The conclusion of a three-year Japan–Soviet Trade Agreement followed on 2 March. The range of commodities involved was little altered, but the volumes were dramatically increased: the target for two-way trade in 1960 was set at $125 million, rising to $165 million by 1962.[228]

While economic relations with the Soviet Union seemed to be progressing smoothly, in February, LDP opposition to Kishi's China policy coalesced into two informal intra-party groups. On 5 February, the *NitChū Mondai Kenkyūkai* (Japan–China Problems Study Group) was established under the leadership of Hayashi Masao. It numbered about 30, mostly ex-Progressives and members of the Matsumura faction, although there was a sprinkling of Ikeda, Ishii, Ōno and Kishi faction members too. This was followed five days later by the *NitChū Kokkō Kaizen Kenkyūkai* (Japan–China Diplomatic Relations Improvement Study Group) comprising mostly members of the Utsunomiya and Ishibashi factions, including Utsunomiya himself, Hirano Saburō, Ide Ichitarō and Kuno Chūji. Although critical of Kishi's passivity, both groups rejected invitations to cooperate with the opposition-dominated Diet Members' League for the Promotion of Japan–China Trade.[229] The LDP leadership was not pleased. In an effort to confine all debate on the China issue to official organs, the FARC established a *Chūkyō Mondai Shōiinkai* (Communist China Problem Sub-Committee) on 11 April, to replace the old Japan–China Trade Promotion Special Committee. Ikeda Masanosuke remained chairman.[230] Its brief was to confer with officials of the various interested ministries, as well as academic China specialists, before presenting its recommended policy changes to the cabinet. Prevailing opinion on the sub-committee seemed to support Kishi's 'wait and see' policy, believing that it was 'up to China *or the Soviet Union* to take the initiative in adjusting relations between the two countries.'[231] Moscow, it seems, was still seen as a potential intermediary for restoring Japan–China trade ties. Committee members apparently had no sense of the impending crisis in Sino-Soviet economic relations.

Long before the Sub-Committee reported, however, Kishi had resigned. His downfall was primarily a result of the Security Treaty crisis, and in particular, the undemocratic methods he used to ensure ratification. However, his stubborn adherence to an unpopular China policy—based in part on a misunderstanding of the state of Sino-Soviet relations—played a significant role in his political demise.

Interpretative comments

Input: external environment

The economic dimension of the Cold War pitted the capitalist 'free market' against the centrally planned Socialist model in the struggle to reconstruct the war torn economies of Europe. By the early 1950s, there were already two distinct and largely self-contained economic systems in place, each with its own set of international institutions (OEEC and COMECON). COCOM policed the frontier.

Being neighbours theoretically increased the opportunities for China and the Soviet Union to trade with Japan. At the same time, the Sino-Soviet Alliance effectively reoriented the Chinese economy away from its traditional economic partners—including Japan—and towards the Soviet Union and Eastern Europe. Although, significantly, China did not officially join COMECON (the Soviet-led international organisation planning the international Socialist economy), the Soviet Union became the major source of Chinese imports, investment, technology, and training. Nevertheless, by 1952 at the latest, both Communist states had adopted a positive attitude towards promoting trade with Japan, although for a variety of reasons, only relatively small-scale exchanges were possible. Beijing's attitude switched dramatically in 1958 in the midst of the folly of the 'Great Leap Forward'. Moscow did not cooperate with the resulting Chinese trade embargo against Japan, but the subsequent revival in Sino-Soviet trade helped to disguise the emerging Sino-Soviet economic policy differences. The Chinese embargo did little long-term damage to the Japanese economy, although Japanese exporters temporarily lost market share in South and Southeast Asia.

Washington, on the other hand, feared that Japan was more vulnerable to Communist contamination through exchanges with the Socialist bloc than vice versa. Moreover, even if Tokyo did not withdraw into politico-strategic neutrality, the Americans believed that trade with Japan would only strengthen the Communist economies. They recognised that the Sino-Soviet Alliance rested on strategic as well as economic common interests, but saw Japan's international position as determined primarily by commercial imperatives. The US concluded that it was essential to prevent Japan from becoming economically dependent on the Communist allies, and to 'contain' the latter. The Allied Occupation, while introducing many valuable reforms, had also left the Japanese economy profoundly dependent on the US. Washington's policy was to maintain Japanese dependence on American imports while reorienting Japanese exports towards the potential growth markets of Southeast Asia.

Internal environment: operational sphere

For Japan, a relative paucity of natural resources meant that international trade was vital. However, the Japanese economy of the early 1950s was still rebuilding from the ravages of war. A severe shortage of capital and foreign exchange, outmoded technology, high trade barriers and expensive raw materials hampered recovery. Such circumstances prevented Japan from quickly restoring its extensive pre-war economic relationships with mainland China. By mid-decade, the Japanese economy was somewhat more robust, but the established trans-Pacific trade patterns proved difficult to change.

Psychological sphere: belief systems

Japan's national identity as the industrial powerhouse of Asia dates back to the Meiji period, and its identification as a trading nation has an even longer history. Amongst Japanese politicians of all parties there was always a very broad consensus in favour of trade with mainland China. The same did not hold true for Soviet trade.

Japanese prime ministers in this period were something of an exception to this general rule. After a career shot through with contradictions between words and deeds, there will always be areas of ambiguity concerning Yoshida Shigeru, but two misconceptions can now be cleared up. First, the view that Yoshida's China Thesis was simply a ruse to persuade the Americans to increase their aid to Japan or to relax the embargo against China is incorrect. If that had been the case then a statesman of his calibre would not have persisted with it long after it became clear that its effect on Washington was counterproductive. Neither would he have lectured his advisors in MOFA about the inevitability of a Sino-Soviet rift, nor expended so much domestic political capital attempting to block the expansion of Sino-Japanese Trade. The opposite view, namely that Yoshida was in Washington's pocket—making a show of resisting the US-led embargo for the sake of domestic popularity, while selling out Japanese traders behind their backs—is equally fallacious. If correct, then Dulles and others would not have found it necessary to apply such intense pressure to ensure Japan's compliance with the Western Alliance's strategic trade control regime. Moreover, on those occasions when Yoshida sought to block the expansion of Sino-Japanese trade, he did so only in an effort to prevent political opponents at home gaining control of this potentially lucrative relationship. In short, the available evidence suggests that Yoshida's belief in the efficacy of his China Thesis was sincere.

Unlike Yoshida, Hatoyama Ichirō believed that trade with the Communist bloc would lead to world peace, not a Sino-Soviet rift. Of the other two premiers, the right-wing Kishi Nobusuke was not dogmatically opposed to commercial exchanges with the Communist economies, although he lacked Ishibashi Tanzan's ardent enthusiasm. Ishibashi alone subscribed to the later popular 'convergence theory'.

Within the bureaucracy, MITI was openly critical of MOFA conservatism. Often headed by politicians from the 'pro-China' wing of the LDP, like Takasaki Tatsunosuke, Ikeda Hayato, and Fukuda Hajime, it was especially unhappy at Kishi's temporising. MITI was supportive of Japanese companies' efforts to exploit markets wherever they existed, including the Communist bloc. On this point, however, Japanese business interests were not united. Ideological prejudices were a divisive factor. During the 1950s, most sectors of big business were content to see obstacles placed in the way of trade with the Communist bloc, since this represented cheap competition for their commodity trade with the huge US market. Later Southeast Asia attracted increasing interest, leaving trade with the Communist bloc to much smaller enterprises often associated with the JSP or JCP. In part, this derived simply from the different scale of exchanges that were possible, but an unwillingness to take political risks was also a factor. Left-wing businessmen meanwhile saw trade with China as a means to counter US dominance of the Japanese economy. Local loyalties were also important. Support for the China trade centred on the Kansai region, where businessmen, especially those in the textile industry, saw mainland China as their 'natural trading partner'. They were motivated by memories of past profits, the potential for future market expansion, the substantial price differential between Chinese and American resources, and resentment at what was seen as 'American interference'.

Psychological sphere: perceptions

The signature of the Sino-Soviet Alliance did little to alter Japanese businessmen's perceptions of opportunities in the Chinese or Soviet planned economies. There had never been much interest in trade with the Soviet Union, but nostalgia for the China market remained strong. The first effect of the Sino-Soviet economic schism on Japan was probably felt as early as the summer of 1958, although few businessmen realised it at the time. Thereafter, renascent Sino-Soviet trade did much to dampen Japanese speculation.

Japanese diplomats were generally pessimistic regarding commercial opportunities in the Communist bloc, although MITI officials adopted a more positive outlook, at least vis-à-vis China. The views of politicians were determined more by their existing beliefs than any perceived changes in the state of Sino-Soviet economic relations.

Decision-making process

Within the Japanese government the basic line of conflict on the issue of trade with the Communist bloc was between a cautious MOFA and a more enthusiastic MITI. However, MITI's position on China and the Soviet Union was complicated by its conflicting responsibility for both promoting trade and enforcing COCOM restrictions. In consequence, its position was not constant. With directors like Kōno Ichirō, Miki Takeo, Takasaki Tatsunosuke, and Fujiyama Aiichirō, it is not surprising that the EPA tended to side with the pro-China elements within MITI.

The politicians reflected the concerns of certain interest groups. In Japan, the intimate relationship between big business and the state dates back to the Meiji era. During the 1950s, the Japanese government adopted a state-guided approach to economic development. However, in return for helping to finance politicians' careers and providing jobs for retiring bureaucrats, big business gained a little room for manoeuvre in the highly regulated Japanese foreign trade regime. To some extent, the government also had to respond to appeals from certain business interests for official support to increase access to the Chinese and Soviet markets, especially when MITI lent its weight to their cause. Yoshida was clearly alert to the demands of Kansai-based traders hoping to restore their pre-war relationship with China. Similarly, Hatoyama was attentive to the needs of Hokkaido's fishing industry vis-à-vis the Soviet Union (on whom his faction was financially dependent.) Even 'pro-Taiwan' Kishi lent his support to trade liberalisation with China.

One might best characterise the premier's role as a kind of safety valve. Yoshida inflated domestic pro-China-trade sentiment for the Americans' benefit while deflating expectations for China trade at home, thereby preventing a confrontation where US and Japanese national interests came most directly into conflict, namely, over China. Hatoyama, Ishibashi, and Kishi were compelled to perform the same balancing act, but they met with less success.

Small left-wing businesses likewise devoted their energy to avoiding bureaucratic controls. Unlike their larger rivals, they could not expect to pressure policy-makers directly, but they deployed their only real weapon—the manipulation of public opinion—quite skilfully. This was especially important for trade with the Communist bloc, where political or strategic considerations usually outweighed purely commercial ones.

Various NGOs like JITPA and JCTPA also played a role in encouraging the Japanese government to adopt a more positive attitude towards trade with China and the Soviet Union, although the efforts of the JSP and JCP were less successful.

Output: official diplomacy

Japanese policy on economic relations with the Communist bloc appeared to lack consistency. On the one hand, Japanese premiers from Yoshida onwards gave their personal attention to the ongoing campaign to ease the international (COCOM) restrictions on trade with the Communist states, especially the removal of the so-called 'China differential'. On the other hand, Yoshida and others sometimes placed obstacles in the way of trade with China and the Soviet Union. The desire to exert political control over Japan's economic relations with the Communist bloc was the only constant. MITI set up its own China trade association, imposed numerous regulations and offered unofficial 'administrative guidance'.

It is worth reiterating in this context that Yoshida's conception of *seikei bunri* was originally intended as a policy for Beijing not Tokyo. Hatoyama stepped up Yoshida's efforts to relax the strategic controls on trade with the Communist bloc, and at first Kishi appeared willing to continue the policy of his predecessors. Having inherited the 'economic necessity' argument from Ishibashi, Kishi subsequently deployed it under the rubric *seikei bunri*. Yet in doing so, he had something very different in mind from what Yoshida had originally intended. In Kishi's hands, it became totally divorced from strategic concerns. However, even mercantilism proved too strong for him following the Nagasaki Flag Incident, after which policy essentially retreated into a passive, inflexible 'wait and see' mode.

The lack of diplomatic relations with Beijing resulted in unorthodox channels of communication being frequently employed, ranging from opposition parties to pseudonymous articles. In contrast, following the normalisation of relations with Moscow, trade with the Soviet Union received quiet encouragement from the Japanese government.

External environment: feedback

Japanese interest in the China trade eventually helped to undermine the 'China differential', although Tokyo allowed London to take the lead in challenging Washington's discriminatory policy. The lack of Japanese interest in the Soviet market meant that despite the huge disparity in the size and level of development of the two Communist economies, the value of Sino-Japanese trade exceeded Soviet–Japanese trade until 1959.

5

Fishing in troubled waters: Japanese trade and the Sino-Soviet economic schism, 1960–64

Mid-July 1960 marked a turning point in Japan's economic relations with the Sino-Soviet bloc. The selection of former Finance Ministry bureaucrat and Yoshida protégé, Ikeda Hayato as prime minister coincided with Moscow notifying Beijing of its intention to terminate virtually all forms of economic cooperation. The Sino-Soviet economic schism was out in the open. On 16 July, the Soviets recalled all of their 1,390 experts from China and breached more than three hundred agreements, leaving innumerable projects incomplete. Coming amidst the ruins of Mao Zedong's 'Great Leap Forward' and a series of climatic disasters, this was a heavy blow indeed.

Ikeda's Communist trade policy

Ikeda did not wait long before hinting at forthcoming changes in Japan's trade policy vis-à-vis China. On 19 July, his first day as premier, he announced that:

> As far as China policy is concerned there is no need for Japan to adopt the same attitude as the US...At present...we are in a position to open cultural and economic relations. I want to encourage such relations on a large scale.[1]

Nor was this change of emphasis confined to mere statements of intent. On 26 July, Chief Cabinet Secretary Ōhira Masayoshi announced government approval for the visit of a Chinese delegation led by Liu Ningyi, chairman of the All-China

Federation of Trades Unions.[2] The following month, in another innovation, Ikeda established the *Gaikō Mondai Kondankai* (Foreign Policy Problems Deliberation Council). Comprising 36 outside experts on China from the worlds of business, the media and academia, its task was to recommend policy changes.[3]

The Americans, worried about a 'possible drift of Japan towards neutralism', wasted no time in seeking the usual reassurances from the new government concerning its policy towards the Communist states. When Ambassador MacArthur visited Foreign Minister Kosaka Zentarō, another Yoshida protégé, on 27 July, he expressed particular concern at the prospect of technical agreements with Beijing. Kosaka responded in traditional fashion:

> while there would be no changes in Japan's basic policies toward [the] ChiComs and Soviets, the Ikeda government must maintain a public posture of reasonableness and desire to improve relations with [her] communist neighbors...[But h]e was inclined personally to agree that negotiation of any technical agreements...would be well to avoid (sic) prior to the elections.[4]

The following day, MacArthur raised Washington's concern about the generous long-term credits extended to the Soviet Union and the substitution of Soviet oil for imports of 'free world oil' with Ikeda and Yoshida. Ikeda assured his guest that he was taking actions to slow the improvement of Japan–Soviet economic relations and that 'Japan's foreign policy was based on strengthening US–Japan relations, Japan's membership in the free world and its total opposition to neutralism.'[5]

Despite the Ikeda-imposed impedimenta, Japan–Soviet trade was booming: oil imports alone had risen ten-fold in the past year.[6] On 16 August, a Japanese trade fair opened in Moscow's Sokolniki Park with Trade Minister Ishii Mitsujirō in attendance. During the fair, Deputy Premier Anastas Mikoyan stressed the potential for expanding trade by linking it to Moscow's Eastern Siberia development plan. Khrushchev also expressed a desire to see bilateral trade increase in the first of a series of letters addressed to Prime Minister Ikeda on 29 August.[7] More significant, however, was the dramatic turnabout in the Chinese attitude towards trade with Japan announced by Zhou Enlai two days earlier. The revised policy took the form of three new principles presented to Suzuki Kazuo, managing director of the Japan–China Trade Promotion Association. In sum, they amounted to a reluctant willingness to allow trade to resume with Japanese firms deemed 'friendly' to China without a governmental trade agreement.[8] In mid-September, Zhou Enlai told a follow-up mission from the Japan–China Friendship Association that China also supported the conclusion of a range of technical agreements with the Japanese government.[9]

The stimulus for China's *volte-face* was much debated in Japan, but those who saw it as the result of the Communist economic split were in the minority.[10] Within MOFA, where a special study of Sino-Soviet relations was under way, the 'definite new approach' was noted, but not all 'looked upon it as a sign that the Chinese were beginning to feel isolated, perhaps owing to the aggravation of relations with the Soviet Union.' [11] Endō Matao (head of the China Desk) acknowledged that, 'Sino-Soviet trade was proving unsatisfactory', but considered that the Soviet technicians had completed their contracts 'in the normal way.'[12]

Meanwhile, the FARC had recommended in its 'Basic Policy on Foreign Affairs', that the China problem be handled 'carefully taking into account both the attitude of Communist China and changes in international conditions'.[13] Foreign Minister Kosaka seemed to ignore this advice, however, assuming a hard line posture when he met US Commerce Secretary Frederick Mueller on 16 September. He claimed that the '"clamor" for the revival of Japanese trade with the Communist Chinese by "certain" Japanese…was based on inaccurate knowledge...of the situation within Communist China'. Then when warned that Japan should not become dependent upon trade with its giant neighbour, Kosaka told Mueller that, 'the Ikeda Government should have a stronger view on this subject than its predecessor.'[14] Although not mentioned in the US record, Kosaka apparently thought also that the 'deterioration in Sino-Soviet relations and requirements of China's "Great Leap Forward" would make it necessary for Peiping to look to Japan as a source of supply for many capital goods'.[15]

Ikeda was quick to contradict his foreign minister's negative position on China trade, informally telling one-time Trade Minister Takasaki Tatsunosuke to accept an invitation to take a group of businessmen on an inspection trip of the Chinese economy.[16] More publicly, in his administrative policy speech to the Diet on 21 October, Ikeda welcomed the reopening of trade with China and expressed his government's willingness to conclude technical agreements with Beijing.[17] Earlier that month, the LDP also officially declared its support for the revival of private trade with China.[18] The *People's Daily* promptly responded to this news with a warning that resumption of large-scale trade would remain impossible, as long as the Japanese government persisted in its 'hostile' policy. The editorial did note though that individual private economic contracts were 'indispensable and necessary for the two peoples.'[19] These events coincided with the arrival of Takasaki's group in China. Meeting Zhou Enlai for the first time since their encounter at Bandung five-and-a-half years earlier, Takasaki took a firm stand. Defending the democratically elected Japanese government, and denying that it harboured any ill intentions towards China, Takasaki emphasised the desirability of concluding technical agreements at sub-government level. Zhou demurred, although he was willing for Takasaki personally to introduce 'friendly firms'.[20]

Relations failed to improve between the two during the group's three-week visit, causing Takasaki to tell a Japanese diplomat in Hong Kong that, 'towards the end of his stay he was in serious conflict with Chou En-lai'.[21] Still, the mission had been allowed to witness at first hand the half-completed projects in Manchuria abandoned by the Russians two months earlier.[22] Concretely, the visit contributed little to the development of Japan–China trade, although one scholar has asserted that Takasaki and the accompanying Japanese industrialists doubtless 'saw this [as] an opportunity for Japanese enterprises.'[23]

After comfortably winning the House of Representatives' election in December 1960, Ikeda reshuffled his cabinet, thereby weakening slightly the in-built anti-PRC majority.[24] Yet, this did not prevent the Utsunomiya, Ishibashi and Matsumura–Miki factions from reviving and merging their two separate pro-China study groups into a single Japan–China Problems Study Group (*NitChū Mondai Kenkyūkai*). The LDP mainstream requested its immediate dissolution, and surprisingly little was heard from the group for the next four years.[25]

Ikeda's was not the only important electoral triumph of that winter. One consequence of Democrat John F. Kennedy's narrow victory was the replacement of US Ambassador MacArthur. In one of his valedictory telegrams to Washington in mid-December 1960, MacArthur summarised the wisdom garnered on Japan–China relations during his four-year stay in Tokyo:

> the myth...that all Japan's economic problems would be solved if only there were close trade and other relations with [the] ChiComs is believed by numerous Japanese, many of whom also believe it is the US which prevents the GOJ developing trade and friendship with [the] ChiComs.[26]

He pointed to the growing effectiveness of the opposition's message, which he claimed was 'still calling for normalization of [Sino-Japanese] relations' and 'pressing strongly, as a first step, for "intergovernmental agreement" on trade and other matters between Japan and Communist China'. Moreover, MacArthur warned that, in addition to pressure from the Left,

> Certain industries, such as ammonium sulfate, steel, automotive, etc. which in the past have received large O[fficial] S[pecial] P[rocurement] orders [from the US government] are now actively seeking or urging trade outlets in Communist China and Russia to compensate for the loss of OSP business which they anticipate will occur.[27]

In farewell meetings, Japanese leaders were telling MacArthur a rather different story, however:

> The interest of the larger industrial firms in trade with Communist China has markedly diminished in light of the deteriorating economic situation on the mainland, [only] the marginal firms and the trading companies continue to eagerly hope for Chinese markets.[28]

This view was confirmed in mid-January by Deputy Vice Foreign Minister Shima Shigenobu: 'The industrial and commercial community would like to be free to resume trade with China', Shima said, 'but pressure came mainly from smaller interests...[t]he big firms were less interested'.[29] Later that month, Chief Cabinet Secretary Ōhira Masayoshi went further, dismissing trade with the mainland as 'likely to remain so small in quantity for some time that the difficulties associated with it made it scarcely worth worrying about.'[30]

Ironically, when Japanese big business was reportedly turning its back on China, Beijing was expressing increasing interest in trading with mainstream Japanese corporations. A JITPA mission to China in February successfully nominated 'friendly firms' for the first time. Moreover, its leader, Yamamoto Kumaichi, gained the impression that in the future Beijing was not going to limit trade exclusively to 'friendly firms'.[31] MOFA, of course, noted these indications of Chinese interest in trade, but Shima, notwithstanding Chinese statements to the contrary, remained suspicious. He speculated that Beijing's seemingly changed approach might be due to either 'the bad harvest in China', or to its 'difficulties with the Soviet Union.'[32]

MOFA was now devoting enormous energy to the resolution of the China trade problem. Shima, a diplomat with extensive experience in pre-war and wartime China, was leading intra-ministry discussions on the China problem at bureau chief level (*Kambukai*), and in the Policy Planning Committee (*Seisaku Kikaku Iinkai*).[33] In addition, the Asian Affairs Bureau was holding weekly meetings on the subject.[34] Moreover, China specialist Okada Akira (now ambassador to Warsaw) was in regular, informal contact with his Chinese opposite number.[35] All this activity spawned rumours that MOFA was considering holding official ambassadorial talks with China in the summer. On 14 March, Foreign Minister Kosaka added substance to these reports by announcing that Beijing's request for talks at ministerial level was being studied.[36]

Ikeda instituted other subtle changes in China policy before his first American trip as premier. In February 1961, he reversed Kishi's June 1959 decision and offered humanitarian assistance (in the form of rice) to help China cope with widespread famine. Then on 15 April, the government simplified procedures for importing Chinese goods.[37] In preparation for the Washington summit, on 9 May the FARC China Problem Sub-Committee, now under chairman Matsumoto Shunichi, finally published an 'interim report'. Its vague policy recommendations were of little help to Ikeda, however, reflecting as they did the sharp divisions that existed among committee members. On trade, the report predicted expansion, which would be 'to some extent useful', but which would not 'become a decisive element.'[38] The sub-committee dismissed arguments in support of an inter-governmental trade agreement on the grounds that this could imply diplomatic recognition.[39]

Ikeda's meeting with Kennedy went ahead as scheduled on 19 June. According to Endō Matao, Ikeda had intended to 'emphasise strongly Japan's need to trade with China, but would combine [sic] himself on the political side to a request for close consultation between Japan and the US in the coming months.'[40] This meshed neatly with the agreed US position: sticking to a hard-line on non-recognition and non-admission to the UN, while adopting 'a relatively relaxed attitude toward Japanese trade with Communist China.'[41] At the talks themselves, however, Ikeda took a different tack, claiming that the Japanese press exaggerated the importance of the China market, and emphasising its relative unattractiveness to big business.[42]

After the Washington summit, Beijing stepped up its propaganda attacks on Ikeda, but the response from Moscow was more positive. The first ever visit to Japan by a member of the Soviet leadership in August 1961 seemed to signal a new approach to Japan. The year had begun with the annual targets for Japan–Soviet trade again being revised upwards, and with Khrushchev once more hinting at the possibility of Japanese participation in the planned development of Eastern Siberia.[43] The Soviets had not relaxed their stiff attitude on fisheries, but when First Deputy Premier Anastas Mikoyan arrived on 14 August to open a large Soviet trade fair in Tokyo, he laid particular emphasis on the desirability of economic cooperation. In talks with *Keidanren* leaders, Mikoyan expressed the hope that bilateral trade would increase 'to $1,000 million within the next few years.'[44] He also brought a letter for Ikeda from Khrushchev in which the Soviet leader expressed his belief that, 'the volume of trade...can be increased by three- or four-fold or even more.'[45] Subsequent assessments of the impression Mikoyan made on the Japanese tend to be overwhelmingly negative.[46] One specialist concluded that this reaction perhaps reflected the unrealistically high expectations that the Japanese had placed on the visit.[47] Another adjudged that Mikoyan failed to stimulate much interest among businessmen, ignoring the fact that the 1962 annual trade target was set at 50 per cent above that of 1961.[48]

The three-way pull on Japan's trading relations with the Communist bloc continued. In early November, the inaugural meeting of the Japan–US Committee on Trade and Economic Affairs was held in Hakone near Tokyo. Ikeda, Secretary of State Dean Rusk and others discussed their economic policies towards the Sino-Soviet bloc and the Sino-Soviet economic offensive.[49] Whatever the conclusions reached in Hakone, Ikeda seemingly declared his hand in the New Year by publicly pledging to 'improve' relations with China.[50] He followed this up a few weeks later with a very confident message on China trade to the House of Representatives' Budget Committee. Apparently deciding that the time had arrived to restore a 'normal'—not JSP or JCP controlled—trade channel to China, Ikeda announced that the government was attempting to 'rebuild' the MITI-inspired Japan–China Export–Import Association, and would restore official subsidies to this body when reorganisation was completed. In addition, the premier personally guaranteed that visas would be forthcoming should China desire to send a trade mission to Japan, and spoke of further easing COCOM restrictions to the level observed by the West Europeans.[51] Ikeda was also active behind the scenes, reportedly requesting Okazaki Kaheita (president of ANA), some time during the spring of 1962, to devise a concrete trade plan to put to Beijing.[52]

Yoshida Shigeru apparently lent his support to the scheme and flew to London to discuss the reopening of the China market with Foreign Secretary Lord Home on 24 May. Yoshida argued that, 'The Free World must resume its contacts with China.' He contrasted British understanding of China with American ignorance, in an effort to persuade London 'to take the lead' on this issue. Finally, he proposed using food relief as 'the obvious card of entry' into China.[53] That same day, in Tokyo, Ikeda declared that, 'as the food crisis visiting China seems to be quite serious, we may recognise from a humanitarian standpoint a deferred payment system for China.'[54] Three conditions for such a system were announced soon thereafter: payment should be guaranteed by non-Chinese banks; Beijing must cease restricting trade to 'friendly firms'; and the terms should be in line with those offered by the Europeans.[55]

Not everyone was happy with this radical policy departure. Even well known supporters of the China trade like Suzuki Kazuo (head of JCTPA) expressed dissatisfaction. Suzuki, who had spent the first two months of 1962 in China trying to prop up the JSP's role in Japan–China trade, objected strongly to the first condition, saying that it rendered the whole scheme unworkable.[56] Kōno Ichirō was also critical.[57] Potentially more serious, however, was the reaction from Washington. Since January, the Kennedy Administration had itself been debating the idea of offering famine relief to China as a means of splitting the Sino-Soviet Alliance, but now it too objected to Japan's policy change. Assistant Secretary of State for Far Eastern Affairs, Averell Harriman, conveyed a private warning to the Japanese government.[58] On previous occasions the Japanese had usually followed such advice, albeit grudgingly, but this time things were different.[59] Despite official denials that any warning had been received, MITI indignantly announced that

> Japan's trade policy with Communist China is aimed at expanding economic exchanges between the two countries on a commercial basis on the same terms

as maintained by the European countries and will not be interfered with by the US![60]

The prime minister, campaigning in Ōsaka, followed this up two days later with a statement supporting increased trade with China and the Soviet Union and confirming that, 'Japan's trade policy will be decided independently.'[61]

Once the 1 July Upper House election was safely out of the way, Ikeda again reshuffled his cabinet. Kōno Ichirō returned, as minister of construction, Ōhira Masayoshi was promoted to foreign minister, and Fukuda Hajime (Ōno faction) became head of MITI. Importantly, all were less inclined to follow American dictates than their predecessors had been. Moreover, the pro-US character of the government was further weakened when Satō Eisaku refused to accept a post in response to Kōno's appointment.[62]

The change in the Japanese government's approach prompted a resurgence of popular pressure for restoring the China trade.[63] In early August, five trade associations, including JITPA and JCTPA, produced a wish list urging the government, inter alia, to end COCOM and other restrictions on trade, and approve deferred payments for imports and exports with the Communist states.[64] Ikeda was unwilling to go this far, but later that week he told former premier Ishibashi Tanzan that he still supported revamping the Japan–China Export–Import Association.[65] Fukuda and Ōhira promised that their respective ministries would study the reorganisation problem with a view to promoting bilateral trade. However, whether out of sensitivity for the current state of Sino-Soviet relations or US concerns, Ōhira was cautious, adding that any trade agreement concluded with China would be 'no more favorable than the existing ones with the Soviet Union and other Communist countries.'[66] This balanced approach was to be short-lived. It was soon replaced by a more pronounced 'China first' strategy.

Ikeda's 'China first' strategy

In late summer 1962, three important Japanese trade delegations were despatched: the first went to Moscow and the other two to China. The so-called 'Bolshoi Mission' was led by Kawai Yoshinari (president of *Komatsu*, the bulldozer maker), and was comprised of high-ranking representatives from virtually all major Japanese industrial sectors (except oil.)[67] In Moscow, there was again much talk of promoting trade and of Japan participating in the development of Siberia. Proposals included the establishment of a joint-airline and exchanges of management and electronic expertise. More concretely, contracts worth approximately $100 million were signed, including the long-term import of Sakhalin timber and the export of Japanese ships.[68] The mission's success caused the Japanese government to conclude that the Russians had changed tactics and 'now intend[ed] to use trade as their main political weapon here': to what end remained an unanswered question.[69] The LDP right wing was nervous, and by January 1963 they succeeded in pressuring Trade Minister Fukuda into announcing limits on the amount of credit Tokyo could extend to Moscow.[70]

If the 'Bolshoi Mission' was contentious, the second visit by Matsumura Kenzō to China in September 1962 aroused even greater controversy. Initial hopes were high, especially after Ikeda gave the mission his personal blessing: having reportedly asked the ageing Asianist to represent his 'China face.'[71] The selection of the mission's other members shows that Matsumura also had the support of the Fujiyama, Miki and Kōno factions, although Foreign Minister Ōhira was careful to stress that the politicians were all travelling in a private capacity.[72] In a brief report issued on 19 September, the two sides 'agree[d] to strive for normalisation of relations between both countries, including political and economic relations, by (a series of) gradual and cumulative measures'. Tentative agreement was also reached on the exchange of trade liaison offices and the use of deferred payments for Japanese plant exports.[73] The mission's most significant feature, however, was the change it revealed in Chinese attitudes. In his welcoming speech for Matsumura, Premier Zhou Enlai reportedly said: 'It has often been noted in the world that East is East and West is West. We two nations in the East should go hand in hand generation after generation for our coexistence and co-prosperity.'[74] Nevertheless, Foreign Minister Chen Yi subsequently denied that there were any differences between China and the other Socialist states.[75] Matsumura was not convinced by Chen's assurances on the state of Sino-Soviet relations, stating on his return to Tokyo on 25 September: 'Frankly speaking, I think that such a change is due to the fact that her relations with the Soviet Union have deteriorated.' In evidence, he cited the withdrawal of Soviet experts, the cessation of Sino-Soviet trade, an unwillingness to mention the USSR, and Zhou's 'East is East' comment, which he described as 'an indirect criticism of the Soviet Union.' In conclusion, he predicted that, 'China will adopt Communism with an Oriental flavour' (*tōyōshoku o obita[ru] kyōsanshugi*).[76] At last it seemed that a Japanese leader was giving serious consideration to the Sino-Soviet economic schism.

Matsumura's comments on Beijing's new found flexibility had touched off a brief burst of excitement within government circles. While Matsumura was still in China, Ikeda told a group of business leaders that Chinese policy towards Japan had become 'more realistic' and 'acceptable' as a result of this visit. Consequently, when Matsumura briefed the premier and other ministers on his mission on the day after his return, they expressed interest in his proposal that the government take 'positive' and 'concrete' steps to expand trade.[77] Furthermore, according to British sources in Tokyo, Japan's intelligence agency privately accepted Matsumura's interpretation of Zhou's comments: 'The Cabinet Research Office believes that the deteriorating economic situation and economic effects of the dispute with the Soviet Union are the *principal reasons* for the Chinese wish to increase trade.' The CRO apparently dated the change from August 1961, when it suspected that 'the Communist bloc and China made new, but separate, studies of Japan following Mikoyan's visit'.[78]

The US moved quickly to deflate Tokyo's confidence. At the same time as Ikeda was debriefing Matsumura, Assistant Secretary of State Averell Harriman was cautioning the Japan–US Society in Washington, repeating a warning made in Tokyo the previous May: 'Whatever trade is done with communist countries, one must recognize it might well be used later on for political purposes.' Although Ikeda specifically denied that Harriman's speech had had any effect on his attitude, he immediately went out of his way publicly to play down the prospects for trade with the mainland.[79] Other cabinet members followed suit. The effect on big business was even more dramatic. One day after Harriman's statement, Inayama Yoshihiro, the influential president of Yawata Iron and Steel, reversed his earlier decision to join a follow-up mission to Beijing to be led by Takasaki Tatsunosuke.[80] A few days later, Ishizaka Taizō (chairman of *Keidanren*) pointed out that 'Japan would stand to lose in the shape of hurt feelings in the free nations much more than it would gain from trade with Communist China.' Thus on 3 October, Chief Cabinet Secretary Kurogane Yasumi was able to announce that industrialists and businessmen displayed 'no overwhelming enthusiasm' at the prospects for China trade, and hence 'there is no need for the Government to rush into things.'[81]

Nonetheless a depleted Takasaki mission was to go ahead, and before its departure the government worked hard to produce a consensus on the precise terms of trade it was willing to condone. Interdepartmental meetings between the Ministries of Finance, Foreign Affairs, International Trade, and the EPA in mid-October were inconclusive until a joint-conference at ministerial level produced a compromise. It was decided that deferred payments for China should be offered for a list of commodities (excluding ammonium sulphate), but they should not be more generous than those offered by Western European states or those offered by Japan to third countries: the maximum term was therefore set at five years.[82] Following his briefing by government officials on these limits, the FARC China Problem Sub-Committee also reminded Takasaki that trade with China should be not be allowed to benefit the Communist bloc.[83]

It had been difficult to reach agreement in Tokyo, but Takasaki's problems did not end with his delayed arrival in China on 26 October. Although a new five-year trade agreement—dubbed 'L–T trade'—was signed by Takasaki and Liao Chengzhi on 9 November, many details were left undecided. The target for annual turnover was set at £36 million ($100 million), and the major items to be traded were specified, but actual quantities and deferred payment arrangements were to be agreed annually. For the Japanese government this was acceptable, except for the inclusion of deferred payment for plant exports, where there was no European precedent. The need for trade liaison offices in each other's capitals and national trade coordination groups was also recognised, and with MITI's support the Japan–China Overall Trade Liaison Council was established on 16 November, with Takasaki as chairman. However, another two years were to elapse before the first liaison office opened.[84]

The fact that two members of the mission returned to Tokyo to brief Ikeda just hours before his departure for Europe on 4 November clearly suggests the importance the premier now attached to trade with China.[85] However, upon arrival in Bonn, he sought publicly to distance his government from the ongoing talks, telling reporters: 'Trade with Communist China is to be conducted on a private basis, so there is no need for the government to take a formal stand.'[86] In London, Ikeda began his talks with Prime Minister Harold Macmillan by recalling Yoshida's scheme to drive 'a wedge between China and the Soviet Union', proposed during his 1954 world tour. Ikeda now reminded the British that 'Dulles had "vetoed" it', but nevertheless, stated that he 'still thought that this question should be pursued.' Reiterating Japan's 'long historical and cultural association with China' and the 'strong feeling in Japan in favour of renewing it', Ikeda argued:

> China was apparently now receiving little or no Russian economic and technical aid. This should afford the Free World countries an opportunity to increase their trade and economic ties with China. It would, however, be necessary to tread very warily, both because the Chinese were not altogether to be trusted and because of US susceptibilities.[87]

London failed to be influenced either way by this apparent effort to enlist support for a revitalised Yoshida-style challenge to US policy on the Sino-Soviet Alliance.[88]

While Britain may have preferred to maintain a guarded neutrality on the question of Japan–China relations, the US was less open-minded. On 3 December 1962, the Japan–US Committee on Trade and Economic Affairs met in the White House. President Kennedy, displaying a singular failure to appreciate Japanese sensitivities, opened proceedings by bluntly warning Foreign Minister Ōhira of the need to contain 'the expansionism of [Chinese] Communism in Asia'.[89] At Kennedy's request, Ambassador Edwin Reischauer subsequently tried to play down the remark, but as one Kennedy advisor noted, the comment 'aroused a strong and chilly reaction in Japan.' Even *Keidanren* spokesmen expressed their surprise and shock.[90] In a press conference on 6 December, Ikeda indirectly attacked the president's statement.[91] In London, just three weeks earlier, he had privately posited the existence of a strong linkage between curbing Communist power and trading with the Communist states. Now, however, Ikeda publicly asserted that, 'in dealing with Communist nations we should not mix politics and trade'. He accused the US of being 'the only country that seems to think there is a contradiction'.[92]

Despite Kennedy's later denial that 'his remarks were intended to be taken in the context of trade', Harriman told Associated Press a few days after Ikeda's statement that Japan should 'play an economic role in helping to contain Chinese Communist expansion in Asia'.[93] He also repeated his criticism of the way that Tokyo was conducting its trading relationship with Beijing, in particular the deferred payments arrangements.[94]

Washington's displeasure at Japan's ties with the Communist bloc was not confined to the improving Sino-Japanese trade relationship. In December 1961, the US government succeeded in halting the rapid growth in Japanese imports of Soviet oil. One year later, it exerted pressure on Japan to exercise 'self-control' and block exports to the USSR of large-diameter oil pipes. There was little cause for Washington's concern however. Reflecting Ikeda's 'China first' strategy and the continuing weakness of the 'Soviet lobby' in Tokyo, the Japanese government did not defend Soviet trade flows as it had those with China. For example, in January 1963, *Shinten Jitsugyō*, a Japanese trading company, was obliged to cancel a contract involving 20,000 tons of such oil pipes.[95]

In early January 1963, the negotiations in Tokyo on a new long-term Japan–Soviet Trade Treaty offered further evidence of Ikeda's pro-China bias. Soviet negotiators were frequently overheard complaining that the Japanese were 'trying to take advantage of our weakness.'[96] Then on 22 January, Trade Minister Fukuda Hajime fixed a $200 million ceiling on the outstanding balance for deferred payments exports to the Soviet Union. He blamed economic factors, claiming that the Japanese government had 'no political intention to control exports to the Soviet Union.'[97] Despite subsequent denials, MITI's move was widely interpreted as a response to US pressure.[98] Moscow, however, had its own agenda vis-à-vis Tokyo and acceded to almost all of the Japanese demands. A new three-year, $670–700 million trade and payments agreement was signed on 5 February. For the first time coastal trade was included: a particular interest of industries bordering the Japan Sea.[99] Soviet benevolence did not stop there. During the next four months, in a seemingly well-orchestrated courtship, Moscow signed a generous annual fisheries agreement (in record time) and extended the trade agreement indefinitely. It also granted Japanese fishermen permission to collect *konbu* (edible seaweed) from around Kaigara Island near Hokkaido.[100] In August, Khrushchev told a Japanese press delegation that the Soviet Union was willing to construct factories to produce goods needed by Japan if Japanese companies were willing to supply the necessary technology and capital on a deferred payment basis.[101] In the face of such largesse, it is hardly surprising that Kansai businessmen told Soviet Foreign Trade Minister Nikolai Patolichev after the signing of the February trade agreement that they had great hopes for increased trade.[102] Anxious to take advantage of the Soviet 'open door', a second large business delegation visited the Soviet Union in June.[103]

In the meantime, Japan–China trading interests continued to develop over the New Year. Three more Japanese delegations visited Beijing. The prominent pro-China LDP Diet member Utsunomiya Tokuma led the first.[104] Although relatively uneventful, the visit resulted in an intriguing analysis of the Sino-Soviet dispute.[105] Among the many reasons for the rift that he subsequently identified, Utsunomiya claimed that 'trouble of a purely commercial nature was at the bottom of the antagonism between China and the USSR.' Uniquely, he concluded that the split resulted primarily from China not having the ability to pay for Soviet imports.[106] Japanese ambassadors to Europe meeting in Vienna in January took a slightly different stance. They predicted that 'Soviet policy was not likely to be extended to include economic sanctions and isolation…[since Sino-Soviet] trade and economic assistance was now on such a small scale that any unilateral action to impose economic sanctions [on China] would be ineffective.'[107]

The limit imposed on deferred payment exports to the Soviet Union by Trade Minister Fukuda that same month appeared set to become a blanket ban when it was applied to China. An exemption was granted for the export of ammonium fertiliser worth $8 million agreed 11 days earlier: the first contract signed under the L–T Agreement. In future, however, Fukuda stated that such arrangements would not be permitted, and the export of plant equipment, including facilities for the production of vinylon (a synthetic fibre), was forbidden under any circumstances.[108] At a press conference a few days earlier, Ikeda had still sounded rather defiant: 'Japan would consider the issue of trade relations with Communist China according to [its] national interests', he declared.[109] On the day after Fukuda's announcement, however, Ikeda struck a slightly more conciliatory note. 'In trading with [Communist] countries', he told the Diet, 'there has been no change in the government's policy to conduct trade on the basis of its independent decision (sic), considering at all times its position as a member of the Free World.' Moreover, whereas in November he had privately portrayed Chinese economic woes as a positive opportunity for Japan and the West, Ikeda now reversed himself. 'Japan's trade with the Communist bloc has been steadily increasing', he noted, 'however, it is difficult to place any great hopes on the expansion of trade with them...when the economic conditions of these countries are taken into account'.[110]

With Ikeda wavering, British Foreign Secretary Lord Home arrived in Tokyo on 29 March. No longer guardedly neutral, in direct contradiction to US policy, Home claimed that free countries were free to export anything to the Communist bloc that was not on the COCOM list. He specifically included large-diameter oil pipes—which Britain and Germany had been actively selling to the Russians. Home maintained that by raising living standards, the export of non-strategic goods would help to wean ordinary people away from Communism. The American response exhibited a grudging tolerance. Later the same day, Under-Secretary of Commerce F. D. Roosevelt Jr, conceded that large diameter steel pipes had indeed been removed from the COCOM list, but emphasised their continuing embargo by the US. Turning to Japan–China trade, he described the granting of long-term credit to Beijing as 'very risky', although he accepted that this was a matter 'for Japan to decide.'[111]

At his meeting with the British Foreign Secretary on 3 April, Ikeda, without a hint of irony, criticised the way in which the Americans:

> seemed to direct their policies towards the Soviet Union and China from two totally different standpoints. They seemed to accept the fact that the Soviet Union was Communist and to conduct their policies towards that country on a tolerably rational plane. Towards China, however, they seemed to be blinded by passion and unable to pursue sensible policies because of their emotions.[112]

It was not the distinction *per se* that Ikeda objected to, but the inverted American emphasis. Sounding like an old recording of Yoshida, he opined that, 'Communism fitted the Soviet Union and had probably come to stay there, whilst the Chinese were essentially capitalist in outlook and Communism fitted the national temperament very uneasily.' He praised British policy towards China and explained how 'Japan intended to pursue policies on trade, postal and other technical matters right up to but falling short of recognition.' Home seemingly found little to argue with in Ikeda's stance, replying that 'It was up to Britain and Japan to try and make the US see the error of her ways'.[113]

In mid-June 1963, a meeting at the *Tokyo Kaikan* brought together Japanese diplomats stationed in the Asia–Pacific region and leading businessmen. In discussing the future of Sino-Soviet relations and Japanese trade with China, some of the diplomats were concerned at escalating Communist offensives in Southeast Asia, but the businessmen were more interested in the recent success of the Europeans in penetrating the Chinese market.[114] Rumours that Mitsubishi and other leading firms had established dummy companies to disguise their entry into the mainland market indicated a readiness to act on their concerns.[115]

The stage was set for a serious crisis to erupt over Japan–China trade. In late July, a Japanese company, Kurashiki Rayon, signed the first contract to export a complete plant to China on a deferred payment basis. MITI Vice-Minister Watanabe Yaeji apparently played a vital role in this decision, even overcoming resistance from his minister, Fukuda Hajime. After much debate, the government approved the vinylon contract on 20 August, with one minor amendment.[116] The

Taiwanese ambassador to Tokyo, Chang Li-Sheng, immediately appealed directly to Foreign Minister Ōhira. Chiang Kai-shek sent a telegram to Yoshida. Taiwan's friends in the cabinet—like Justice Minister Kaya Okinori—apparently tried to block the agreement, but realising that they had been outmanoeuvred, instead preached caution for the future. Defending the decision, Ikeda announced that the payment terms should follow those offered by the West European nations and government involvement via the Japan Export–Import Bank should be restricted, so as not to interfere with foreign aid to less developed nations.[117] In communicating these two principles to Taipei and Washington, MOFA added a third, namely, that the views of both governments would also be taken into account.[118] This in fact represented little more than a restatement of existing policy. MOFA hoped to mollify the US by arguing that the deal was motivated by an effort to encourage Chinese political moderation rather than economic profit. Secretary Rusk labelled it 'aid not trade': a claim reinforced by Japan's own definition of ODA. The Taiwanese remained outraged and their opposition, together with the fear that Japan and others would respond by supporting a seat for Beijing at the UN, caused the Americans to play the mediator.[119]

The diplomats' efforts at conciliation were not helped by the fact that by the autumn of 1963, MOFA had clearly concluded that the Sino-Soviet economic split was responsible for the new Chinese interest in increased trade with Japan. On 1 September, the ministry published its own report on the Sino-Soviet rift. Noting the abrupt fall in bilateral trade and in Soviet aid to China, MOFA anticipated positive approaches from the latter and recommended expanding Japan–China trade as much as possible.[120] This view was quickly passed on to Japan's friends. Foreign Minister Ōhira, in London for the second Anglo-Japanese ministerial conference of the year, told Lord Home that the decline in Russian aid and trade was the reason that China had been 'more flexible and practical than before' in its approach to Japan.[121] Similarly, on an official visit to New Zealand, Ikeda told Prime Minister Keith Holyoake that the era of good Sino-Soviet relations, which had endured for a decade after the Communist take-over of the mainland, was over. Now, the Soviets 'were asking for repayment of their loans either in cash or kind.' Consequently, both Communist powers had revised their attitudes towards Japan as they looked for new trade partners. Ikeda told Holyoake that Japan 'does not buy Communism' but would not hinder bilateral trade with Moscow or Beijing.[122] In Tokyo, Hasegawa Takaaki (RAD) told Australian diplomats that 'so long as Beijing did not impose any political conditions on present cultural and commercial exchanges with Japan the Foreign Ministry would not recommend any changes to reduce such relationships.'[123]

Upon his return to Tokyo in mid-September, Ōhira assured Okazaki Kaheita, now deputy head of the Japan–China Overall Trade Liaison Council, that MOFA would not interfere with LDP Diet members joining his planned mission to

Beijing.[124] Despite MOFA's open support for expanded Japan–China trade, relations with the ROC were not neglected. Some members of the ministry attempted to prevent two MITI-related officials from participating in the Okazaki mission, lest Taipei misinterpret it as government support. They were unsuccessful and were to suffer a further blow prior to the mission's departure.[125] On 14 September, the government announced that, contrary to the impression given just three weeks earlier, no quota would be set on Japanese deferred payments exports to the Communist bloc for the time being. The combined support of MITI and the Finance Ministry had apparently overridden the objections emanating from MOFA.[126] It proved to be a slight aberration on the government's part and in practice, limits were soon re-imposed on Export–Import Bank credits for Moscow.[127]

Public opinion was, as usual, highly supportive of trade with China, with more than 50 per cent in favour and less than four per cent against. Moreover, when asked to choose between expanding trade with China or the Soviet Union, the former respondents regularly outscored the latter by a proportion of two or three to one.[128] Moreover, within business circles, interest in the Chinese market was now at its highest level since 1957. The day after Okazaki's mission arrived in Beijing, the *Nihon Keizai Chōsa Kyōgikai* (Japan Economic Research Council) published a report entitled: 'On Trade with the Communist bloc'.[129] It had undertaken extensive consultations with government ministries as well as the financial and business communities during a nine-month drafting process. The report warned that Japan should not become too dependent on trade with the Communist bloc, yet it also clearly dismissed the need for caution based on concern for US sensibilities. Its main conclusion was that: 'it will be natural for this country to take an independent position and promote positively on a commercial basis any deal which is profitable.'[130] It is worth noting that the report did not differentiate between China and the Soviet Union. This non-discriminatory position coincided with that of an 'action group' led by the influential Kobayashi Ataru (ex-president of the Japan Development Bank and friend of the prime minister). These businessmen disapproved of the US policy of 'isolating China'. In contrast, leading members of *Keizai Dōyūkai*, such as Iwasa Yoshizane (president of Fuji Bank), preferred a hierarchical arrangement with Eastern Europe receiving top priority, followed by the USSR, and lastly China.[131]

Business interest in China also assumed concrete form. In September 1963, ten major Japanese steel companies concluded contracts to import significant quantities of Chinese coking coal and, for the first time since the war, iron ore.[132] The Okazaki mission then signed a joint-communiqué agreeing further to expand trade on the principles of the L–T Agreement. During the visit, *Dai Nihon Bōseki* (*Nichibō*) initialled a contract to export a second vinylon plant to China. Finally, the largest Japanese trade fair ever opened in Beijing on 6 October. [133]

This strong Japan–China trade promotion paralleled a strong interest in Soviet trade. In mid-August, MOFA quietly proposed a solution to Soviet claims for compensation over the unilateral *Shinten Jitsugyō* cancellation, which involved reviving the steel pipe contract early in 1964.[134] That autumn, the press was replete with stories—usually citing 'MITI sources'—anticipating future Japan–Soviet trade expansion based on the increased export of Japanese consumer goods and such things as synthetic fibres.[135] At the beginning of October, Trade Minister Fukuda announced his readiness to approve the revised *Shinten* contract. He also mentioned favourably a Soviet plan calling for the export of two million tons of such pipe to Siberia (one hundred times the *Shinten* contract), in exchange for $300 million worth of Soviet crude oil. In another apparent expression of strengthening Japanese independence, newspapers quoted Fukuda as saying that it was better for Japan 'not to rely too heavily on Anglo-Saxon oil interests.'[136] Moreover, published statistics revealed that Sino-Soviet trade flows had shrunk to less than one third of their 1959 peak (Table 4.1). Some Japanese observers were even contemplating their 'total rupture.'[137] Japanese firms reportedly expected increased prices and better profit margins on their exports to result from Sino-Soviet 'competitive bidding'.[138] The prospects for taking advantage of the Communist economic schism appeared bright.

The issue of Japanese trade with the Communist bloc was again on the agenda at the fourth meeting of the Japan–US Security Consultative Committee, held in Tokyo on 10 October. The official record remains classified, but Ōhira emerged from the meeting claiming that he 'did not think the US was against Japan's present policy on Communist China trade.' Hence, the foreign minister saw 'no need for changing Japan's Communist bloc policy.'[139] According to one diplomat, MOFA felt relieved that: 'the US Government has come to understand Japan's contention that Japan–Communist China trade is not of such a nature as to help increase the Communist Chinese menace to the peace and security of the Far East'.[140] Communist trade was scheduled for further discussion at the third meeting of the Japan–US Committee on Trade and Economic Affairs, but the assassination of President Kennedy on 22 November forced its postponement. Nevertheless, on 7 January 1964, Commerce Secretary Luther Hodges publicly confirmed that the US was not concerned at the recent growth in Sino-Japanese trade.[141]

The revival of *seikei bunri*

If a 'deepening common understanding' regarding China was emerging across the Pacific, the same cannot be said of the East China Sea. Earlier on 21 September 1963, after failing to persuade the Japanese government to reverse the *Kurashiki* decision, Taiwan had recalled its ambassador. When this did not have the desired effect, Taipei escalated its campaign, first by withdrawing its chargé d'affaires and four counsellors on 31 December, and 11 days later by suspending all new government procurement of Japanese goods.[142] Ikeda attempted to calm Taipei's wrath in his policy speech to the Diet on 21 January 1964, when he resurrected the principle of *seikei bunri*. At the same time, however, he declared that Japan had to adopt 'realistic policies' to deal with the Chinese mainland. The next day, in cabinet, Ikeda was criticised by its pro-Taiwan members for having gone too far.[143] Ikeda's position was delicate, however. While the LDP had lost 13 seats in the general election of 21 November 1963, the Kōno faction was significantly strengthened.

The LDP's pro-Taiwan wing was further put out by the French announcement on 27 January 1964, that they were extending diplomatic recognition to Beijing. Not surprisingly, de Gaulle's dramatic move prompted a fierce debate in Tokyo.[144] Japanese trading companies worried lest their government's policy of non-recognition placed them at a disadvantage in the Chinese marketplace. However, *Nisshō* President Adachi Tadashi advised caution, believing that Japan should await the reactions of other countries.[145]

The French announcement coincided with the postponed third meeting in Tokyo of the Japan–US Committee on Trade and Economic Affairs.[146] There, Rusk, after thanking Japan for its 'attitude toward strategic limitations on trade with the Sino-Soviet bloc', and declaring his hope that caution would prevail, attempted to forestall any Japanese efforts to apply Yoshida-style logic to the situation. Rusk was 'skeptical that trade will, on its own weight, or through its processes lead to a more peaceful policy' on the part of the Communists.[147] The following day, however, he appeared willing to defer to his hosts, with a surprisingly strong call for Tokyo to make up its own mind on China.[148]

Zhao Anbo, secretary of the China–Japan Friendship Association, was in Japan at this time, suggesting that China could begin exporting substantial quantities of crude oil to Japan, arguably Japan's most significant import from the Soviet Union. He also admitted that a continuing decline in Sino-Soviet trade was inevitable.[149] Meanwhile, in Beijing, Zhao's superior, Liao Chengzhi, was proposing to LDP Diet members Fujii Katsushi and Tagawa Seiichi that permanent trade representatives should be stationed in both capitals, direct airline connexions opened, and journalists exchanged.[150]

Foreign Minister Ōhira made a series of statements on the issue over the next few weeks that raised the temperature of debate still further. Giving Japan's assessment of China's current trade policy, Ōhira told Sweden's visiting foreign minister that Beijing 'appears to have shifted from dependency on certain countries to trading with numerous nations including Japan.'[151] Then on 18 February, he declared that China was neither a military nor an economic threat to Japan.[152] The storm that this statement provoked soon led to some hasty backtracking. Forced to defend himself before a hostile FARC, the foreign minister promised to place limits on trade, the exchange of reporters, and air flights to China. The government would evaluate the idea of exchanging trade representatives only at the appropriate time, and until then, Ōhira assured the committee, it would continue to follow the *seikei bunri* line. Trade Minister Fukuda was less contrite. He stated that Japan would promote normal trade with Beijing , including the exchange of 'unofficial' trade missions, and would impose no more 'political supervision' than did the Europeans.[153] In addition, the government declared that it would encourage the unification of the 'Friendship' and 'L–T trade' channels by promoting the merger of the Japan–China Export–Import Association and the Japan–China Overall Trade Liaison Council.[154]

Ikeda himself gave the impression that he had still not completely given up on Yoshida-style logic. In a television interview on 26 February, after first describing China as 'a great market for Japan', the premier claimed that:

> the United States policy of futile hostility to Communist China is unlikely to succeed. Rather by promoting economic exchange it is possible to impress upon the Communist Chinese that it is in their own interest to cooperate with the Free World and thus contribute to the easing of international tensions.

Letting his guard down even further, he confessed to a preference regarding Japan's Communist trading partners, saying that 'from the point of view of economics' he preferred 'to deal with the Chinese rather than the Russians'.[155]

Yoshida himself was in Taipei at this time. Ikeda had approved of his trip on condition that any talks would be of an abstract nature.[156] The Japanese government kept the precise status of Yoshida's 'personal goodwill visit' deliberately vague. There is little doubt though that the government sought to 'have its cake and eat it too', namely, restore trading ties with Taiwan, calm American fears, and heal the rift within the LDP, while continuing to pursue 'normal' relations with Beijing.[157] In Taipei, Yoshida skilfully took advantage of France's recognition of the PRC to win Chiang Kai-shek's reluctant acceptance of the inevitability of Japan promoting non-political relations with the mainland. In return, he assured his host that Japan did not export strategic goods to China, and 'since only limited funds were available from the Export–Import Bank of Japan, there was little scope for deferred payment exports.'[158]

MOFA was pleased with the results of Yoshida's visit, and at Ikeda's request immediately despatched Vice-Foreign Minister Mori Matsuhei on a follow-up mission. Then on 5 March 1964, in an attempt to lay to rest the political confusion over Japan–China relations, MOFA distributed a 'Unified View' on China policy to all cabinet members. The report reasserted the *seikei bunri* line and the need to maintain *de facto* relations with the mainland. Geographical proximity and history meant that Japan's position was 'fundamentally different' from that of the US.[159] Three days later, Trade Minister Fukuda nearly jeopardised this carefully crafted compromise by declaring that the government was considering approving deferred payments for the *Nichibō* contract. An official announcement was postponed however, following protests from the LDP right wing and a briefing from Mori on Taiwan's threat to break off relations completely.[160] Nevertheless, the attention being given to China policy did not diminish and on 18 March, MOFA convened a three-day conference of its China experts in Hong Kong.[161]

The following month, Matsumura undertook his third mission to Beijing.[162] This visit is best remembered for a 19 April memorandum signed with Liao Chengzhi finalising details for the exchange of trade liaison personnel and resident journalists, but Sino-Soviet trade was also discussed.[163] Furui Yoshimi, a close associate who accompanied Matsumura on each of his China trips, was told by Liao that while 'China did not intend to abrogate the Sino-Soviet Treaty of Commerce and Navigation...neither did it intend to implement it.' In other words, 'The Treaty would be allowed to sleep.' Not surprisingly, Furui concluded that, 'Sino-Soviet relations...could not be restored to the basis of intimacy that existed before the current rift opened.'[164]

Equally significant was the contemporaneous visit to Tokyo by Nan Hanchen (chairman of CITPC) to open a large Chinese trade fair. The six-week mission managed to arrange numerous meetings with senior business leaders from *Keidanren* and *Keizai Dōyūkai*, as well as with influential members of the ruling and opposition parties.[165] In terms of changing attitudes within top economic circles towards trade with China, Nan seemed to make considerable progress.[166] However, he was less successful with LDP politicians, for whom China policy was a weapon in the upcoming struggle for the party presidency. Satō Eisaku reportedly impressed Nan by denouncing Japan's *seikei bunri* policy as 'scratching an itchy foot with a shoe on'—implying that if he were premier he would adopt a less frustrating approach—but his words were motivated more by his political ambitions than any sympathy for China.[167] Yoshida Shigeru responded to this challenge to Ikeda's prospects for re-election by sending a 'private letter' (dated 7 May) to Chiang Kai-shek's chief secretary. Yoshida confirmed the agreement reached during his February visit, and offered his personal assurance that the Japanese government would not allow Export–Import Bank funds to be used to assist plant exports to China during that year. The letter's contents remained secret, but once Ikeda was informed, his chief cabinet secretary announced a reversal of the earlier decision to approve deferred payment credits for the *Nichibō* vinylon plant. It is generally assumed that the letter represented a temporary expedient on Ikeda's part, but in practice it became a binding policy commitment.[168]

Tokyo did not have long to wait for the Soviet reaction to Nan Hanchen's positive approach. In mid-May, Deputy Premier Mikoyan, accompanied by a group of businessmen from the Soviet Far East, again visited. MOFA concluded that the high calibre of the mission reflected 'Moscow's concern with Peiping's challenge for a policy hegemony in the communist world'.[169] The Soviets also met with top business leaders from *Keidanren*, as well as influential politicians like Satō Eisaku. Unlike Nan, however, Mikoyan was also received by government ministers and the emperor. Meeting with executives of the former *zaibatsu* for the first time, he again said that annual trade turnover should be in the range of one billion dollars, rather than the $320 million recorded in 1963. Mikoyan offered to supply Japan with increased quantities of timber, oil and industrial equipment, and to purchase Japanese plant and machinery worth $350 million, assuming that it could be supplied on a ten-year deferred payment basis. He also proposed the establishment of a Joint Committee on Economic Cooperation.[170]

Observing the overlapping Communist missions, the press noted how:

> The Soviet-Red Chinese competition for Japan trade is growing increasingly fierce...both Communist countries find it necessary to outdo the other in the purchasing of Japanese machinery on the one hand and to outsell each other in the export of their pig iron and coal.[171]

The indications were that both Moscow and Beijing were deliberately reducing their bilateral trade in order to sell more to Japan.[172] Examples included such commodities as oil in the case of the Soviet Union and foodstuffs from China.[173] In other words, following the collapse of their economic relationship, Moscow and Beijing did not only see Tokyo as an alternative trading partner. The similar structures of their centrally planned economies meant that they could not help but extend their ideological rivalry into commercial *competition* vis-à-vis Japan.

Unlike his previous visit three years earlier, Japanese business circles generally offered a positive assessment of Mikoyan's mission: there was even talk of a 'Mikoyan boom'.[174] The response from political circles was more mixed. Kōno Ichirō, not surprisingly, expressed a strong interest in the Siberian development projects. No less predictable was Prime Minister Ikeda's scepticism concerning Mikoyan's inflated import offers, and insistence that Japan–Soviet trade should always be conducted 'on a commercial basis.' The furthest he would go was to propose 'careful study' of the credit terms Tokyo could offer Moscow.[175]

Mikoyan's visit also inspired perhaps the first public Japanese proposal to exploit the Sino-Soviet split commercially. When talks with Mikoyan on the opening of a direct Tokyo–Moscow air link did not produce the eagerly anticipated agreement, Hirasawa Kazushige (editor of *Japan Times*), who had interviewed Mikoyan in Tokyo, suggested that:

> If the Soviet Union continues to reject Japan's proposal to establish a Tokyo–Moscow air route, Japan will have no alternative but to seek a shorter route to Europe via Peiping. In the light of current Sino-Soviet relations, it is hardly conceivable that the Soviet Union would welcome this alternate route.[176]

Moreover, it was suggested that Japanese government leaders were adopting a harder line with Mikoyan than previously, because as a result of the Sino-Soviet conflict they thought 'it is the Soviet Union rather than Japan that wants some substantial improvements in bilateral relations.'[177]

The diplomatic two-step continued. While Mikoyan was in Japan, Matsumoto Shunichi, an LDP politician and former ambassador to the UK, was in Beijing. Zhou Enlai suggested to him that Japan should establish formal ambassador-level contacts, attend the second Afro-Asian Conference (scheduled for March 1965), and promptly exchange trade liaison offices. Ōhira instructed MOFA to study Zhou's overtures, but when Japan's Asia–Pacific diplomats held their annual meeting in Tokyo at the beginning of June, Zhou's first proposal was dismissed.[178] Opposition to Zhou's third proposal was also strong in some quarters. Pro-Taiwan Justice Minister Kaya Okinori, for instance, demanded that any Chinese representatives stationed in Tokyo sign a written pledge abjuring any political activities.[179] The Chinese in fact accepted this and other impositions when the Japanese government finally approved the opening of a Chinese liaison office in Tokyo in July. Five Chinese diplomats, led by Sun Pinghua (deputy head of the China–Japan Friendship Association), arrived on 13 August. MOFA emphasised that they would not be treated as recognised representatives of the Beijing government, but in practice, both sides understood that this was what they would become.[180] Ōhira justified the decision in familiar terms: 'These exchanges will enable Japan to obtain first-hand information on new developments in Mainland China and vice versa, they help Mainland Chinese to get acquainted with Japan and the outside world.' Still, he insisted that Japan was maintaining 'the separation of political affairs from the economic.'[181] The Soviets attempted to counter this Chinese success by opening a special Export–Import Office (*Dalintorg*) in Nakhodka that autumn charged with promoting coastal trade with Japan.[182]

Meanwhile, the Johnson Administration remained stoical in the face of rapidly improving Japanese economic relations with both China and the Soviet Union. A State Department report on 'The Future of Japan' acknowledged that, 'Mainland China policy [is] the only major matter on which the US and Japanese views differ significantly.' Nevertheless, it predicted:

> Japan's economic relations with communist countries will probably continue to be a marginal element in its foreign economic relations over the next

> decade...[as] there is considerably greater realism in the Japanese business community than in the past concerning market opportunities in that area.[183]

Reassured by the 'Yoshida letter' of May, Taiwan also decided to ease the pressure a little. On 3 July, Ōhira undertook his delayed visit to Taipei, and Chiang Kai-shek responded by lifting the embargo on Japanese goods. This can only have helped Ikeda in his narrow defeat of Satō Eisaku and Fujiyama Aiichirō in the LDP presidential election later that month. Nevertheless, Ikeda's position was considerably weakened, as reflected in the ensuing cabinet reshuffle that saw the Satō faction make significant gains.

In his first press conference following the sweeping cabinet reorganisation, Ikeda was thus cautious in his statements on Japan's relations with its Communist neighbours: the *seikei bunri* policy would be firmly maintained; and there would be no ambassadorial-level talks with China or a visit to Moscow—at least for the time being.[184] The premier in fact continued to hope for increased trade with China, and in mid-August he supported Matsumura Kenzō's plan to exchange journalists with the mainland, but a combination of domestic political weakness and Taiwanese pressure would effectively debar new initiatives.[185]

The discriminatory nature of Japanese policy at the time was clearly evident when the *Nichibō* contract again came up for discussion at the end of August. The government announced that Export–Import Bank funds would not be available during the rest of the year.[186] On the other hand, however, the cabinet decided to ignore American protests and approve the export of a $10 million urea-fertiliser plant to the Soviet Union on an unprecedented eight-year deferred payment basis.[187] MITI had not completely abandoned its hard line towards Moscow, but it seemed that the government's focus was shifting from Beijing. Not surprisingly, the Soviets welcomed the change and Japanese delegations visiting Russia that autumn were warmly received.[188] In mid-September, Fukunaga Kenji, a leading figure in Ikeda's own faction, joined one mission.[189] In early October, Ishibashi Tanzan, now president of JITPA, led a business delegation to Moscow that reached agreement on a plan to hold the inaugural conference of the Japan–Soviet Committee on Economic Cooperation in Tokyo in September 1965.[190] Japanese diplomats claimed that purely commercial considerations were at work.[191]

In the final months before ill-health forced Ikeda's premature retirement in late October, his attitude towards China had not exactly been negative, but such developments presaged the revised priorities of the Satō era.

Satō Eisaku takes the reins

Competing interest groups, both inside and outside the LDP, battled to set the policy course for the new Satō administration. In mid-November, the Japan–China Export–Import Association announced that it was seeking a further significant relaxation of the COCOM restrictions. It seemed to have the implicit backing of its sponsor, MITI.[192] The long-standing battle between MITI and MOFA over economic policy towards the Communist states continued into the Satō era, with the two ministries taking stands for and against deferred payment credits to China.[193] Even more serious for Satō, however, was the increasingly open polarisation of opinions within the LDP. The pro-Taipei wing organised the *Ajia Mondai Kenkyūkai* (Asian Problems Study Group) in December. Led by Kaya Okinori, Funada Naka, Ishii Mitsujirō and Nadao Hirokichi, it brought together nearly one hundred like-minded rightists who felt that it was dangerous to expand trade with the Communist bloc. The following month, the similarly named but ideologically antithetical *Ajia–Afurika Mondai Kenkyūkai* (Asian–African Problems Study Group) attracted only a slightly smaller number. A direct descendant of the 1960 organisation, it was led by old 'China hands' Utsunomiya Tokuma, Matsumura Kenzō, Ishibashi Tanzan and Fujiyama Aiichirō.[194] During most of Satō's long reign, the former would prove the more influential.

Although the new cabinet initially seemed willing to continue or even go beyond Ikeda's line on China trade, the policy soon began to unravel. On 21 November 1964, in his first policy address to the Diet, Satō struck a cautious note, declaring that he did 'not intend to change this basic principle [*seikei bunri*] at this time'. That same day, however, the new government refused to grant Beijing Mayor Peng Chen and his delegation visas to attend the JCP's Ninth Congress.[195] Satō was said to have been planning to send Kuno Chūji, his faction's only 'China expert', to Beijing 'to explain his China policy to Chinese leaders'. Now, however, Beijing abruptly withdrew the invitation and Liao Chengzhi also cancelled an intended visit to Tokyo.[196] In damage control mode, Satō announced on 3 December, that, 'if necessary, it will be permissible to hold a Sino-Japanese ambassador-level conference in a foreign country.' In the New Year, before his departure for Washington, he hinted at the possibility of a summit with Zhou Enlai, but no such meeting was ever to take place.[197]

In contrast, the almost simultaneous changes of leadership in Moscow and Tokyo that winter did nothing to hinder the burgeoning Japan–Soviet economic relationship. In his first official contact with the Japanese government, Premier Alexei Kosygin wrote to Satō on 29 December offering increased trade and negotiations on consular and aviation agreements. Satō responded cordially in February 1965, and that month a new $350 million trade agreement was signed.[198]

Although it had initially termed the Japanese government's approval of eight-year deferred payments for Moscow 'regrettable', Washington seemed positively to encourage the development of Japan–Soviet economic ties.[199] However, US attitudes towards Sino-Japanese economic relations had hardened during 1964, especially after the Tonkin Gulf 'Incident' of 2–3 August. The following month, during the 19th annual meeting of the International Monetary Fund, US representatives urged the Japanese government to exercise restraint in promoting such sales to the 'Communist bloc'.[200] The State Department was particularly concerned with the 'Chinese component' of this trade.[201] In Tokyo, Japanese business leaders were quick to notice the change in the American attitude.[202]

Not surprisingly, China trade was discussed during the Satō–Johnson summit held in Washington in January 1965. President Johnson, however, appeared to accept the prime minister's reassurances that 'politics and trade are differentiated in Japan's contacts with mainland China.'[203] The following day, Vice President Hubert Humphrey, speaking unofficially, also sounded resigned as he told LDP Secretary-General Miki Takeo that he knew Japan 'had an economic interest in Communist China and…imagined that the Japanese would develop this trade even if we didn't like it'. Miki was even more gratified when Humphrey enquired as to

> whether through trade policy, Japan could act to reduce some of the aggressive, militant spirit of Communist China. It was clear that Mainland China needs trade. Japan might be able to modify or reduce the bite or aggressive nature of the communist government in China.[204]

Although one week after Satō's return the Japanese government disclosed that the Export–Import Bank would continue to deny credits to *Nichibō's* vinylon plant, as previously arranged, three Japanese representatives were sent to Beijing to open a trade liaison office at the end of January. The Japanese government also agreed to meet all of their expenses.[205] However, the die was cast for the new line in trade policy when Satō revealed the existence of the 'Yoshida letter' in the Diet on 8 February, and three days later he extended its application to a freighter contract with *Hitachi*. Beijing responded by allowing the *Hitachi* and *Nichibō* contracts to lapse and cancelled about 40 other plant contracts under negotiation with Japanese corporations.[206] Miki Takeo, trade minister from June 1965, repeatedly tried without success to get the 'letter' overturned.[207] In August, MOFA conceded that it was not legally binding, but Yoshida's missive remained operative and continued to cast a 'dark shadow over Sino-Japanese trade' during the remainder of the decade.[208] Without a Soviet safety net, however, Beijing could not risk cutting off economic ties to Japan, as it had in 1958.[209] Thus, even at the height of the Cultural Revolution, bilateral trade merely experienced a temporary dip.

Interpretative comments

Input: external environment

The 1960s witnessed the beginnings of a significant dispersion of economic power, from the US to Western Europe and Japan, as the latter regions fully recovered from the destructive effects of World War II and the Americans indulged in a futile effort to save Indochina from Communism.

The Sino-Soviet economic schism also conferred commercial benefits on Japan. The statistical evidence is certainly suggestive of a trade substitution effect, resulting in increased demand for Japanese goods in Communist countries. China and the Soviet Union may even have deliberately reduced their bilateral trade in order to increase their share of the Japanese market. A number of Japanese businessmen claimed to have derived significant economic advantage from Sino-Soviet 'competitive bidding', but without access to company records, the evidence remains anecdotal.

Under President Kennedy, American resistance to Japanese trade with the Communist bloc became more erratic. US grain sales to the Soviet Union effectively undermined its opposition to increased Japanese participation in the exploitation of Siberia, including the import of so-called 'red oil'. Furthermore, interventions in Japan's expanding trade relationship with China backfired, as the support of an increasingly nationalistic Japanese public prompted Ikeda Hayato to stand up to Washington's dictates more frequently than had his predecessors. The American constraint was weakening, although it remained formidable. Moreover, resistance from Taiwan seemed to strengthen to compensate. Taipei's intervention—operating via a large and vocal 'Taiwan lobby' within the LDP—may have ultimately proved decisive, forcing Ikeda to abandon his strategy of leaning towards Beijing as the best means of taking advantage of the escalating Sino-Soviet commercial competition.

Internal environment: operational sphere

Through most of the 1960s, Japan enjoyed a remarkable spell of double-digit GNP growth that by the end of the decade had produced the world's third largest economy. Such success stimulated increased economic interaction with every region of the world, including China and the Soviet Union.

Psychological sphere: belief systems

Ikeda's faith in Yoshida's China Thesis could not escape unchallenged. Ikeda soon realised that the rift was the inverse of that which Yoshida had foreseen: the Chinese revolution had become more Communistic than the Soviet one.

Business attitudes also underwent a significant change in the early 1960s. The prominence of the Kansai–Kantō distinction faded once Japan survived the Chinese-imposed economic embargo relatively unscathed. Industries located along the less developed Japan Sea coast showed particularly strong interest in building trade ties with their Communist neighbours. Large corporations also began to take the Communist markets seriously. This was in part a response to increasing North American and especially European incursions, and a consequent fear of 'missing the boat', but the emergence of the Sino-Soviet economic schism was the major factor.

Psychological sphere: perceptions

Those who suggested in the summer of 1960, that a connexion existed between Beijing's decision to restore 'friendship trade' with Tokyo and the Soviet termination of economic assistance to China a few weeks earlier, were in the minority. The situation changed two years later. Thereafter, optimists perceived increased economic opportunities for Japan, while pessimists saw greater uncertainty. For Satō, the Soviet market held greater economic potential than the Chinese.

Decision-making process

The Sino-Soviet economic schism had no major impact of Japan's economic policy-making system. It did not threaten the close business–government relationship, and may have even helped to reinforce it. The split led to a new activism in some quarters, as big business sought government help to exploit the situation. Moreover, the MITI–MOFA rivalry continued unabated. Occasionally, most notably over the deferred payments issue, the Finance Ministry expressed cautious support for MITI's position.

Output: official diplomacy

Beginning in the 1960s, MITI consciously promoted a policy of resource diversification that reduced dependence on the US and encouraged ties to China and the Soviet Union.

Ikeda appeared tempted, albeit briefly, to revive Yoshida's China Thesis. This led Japan to move towards a 'China first' policy as potentially the best means to exploit the situation commercially. It was not until after the Communist alliance had broken down that trade offices were exchanged with China, and government financial assistance was made available to plant exporters. With government support, big business attempted to muscle in on the previously opposition-controlled Communist trade. In the case of the Soviet Union, they were very successful. Concerning China, however, the establishment of the 'L–T trade' channel in 1962 represented a high point, for despite the bitter ideological disputes, 'friendship trade' steadily regained its dominant position. Internal divisions meant that Ikeda had always pursued a zigzag course, but during his last months in office the balance tilted decisively against China, forcing him to revive the *seikei bunri* line. In the end, Ikeda opted for a neutral stance, avoiding political or strategic involvement as far as possible, while exploiting the rift commercially.

In effect, this served to fossilise the existing cautious, mainstream, pro-US consensus. Satō Eisaku continued this line.

External environment: feedback

Japan's pursuit of trade opportunities with both China and the Soviet Union accentuated Sino-Soviet economic competition vis-à-vis Japan. Japanese trade volumes with China and the Soviet Union increased rapidly. Although neither the Chinese nor Soviet share of total Japanese trade exceeded four per cent during this period (Figure 4.2), Tokyo became a significant trade partner for both. By the end of 1964, in their lists of foreign trade partners Japan ranked first and second, respectively. Moreover, the balance of trade with Beijing moved firmly in Tokyo's favour, while the deficit temporarily narrowed with Moscow.

The same positive trend could be observed in the Japan–US bilateral trade balance. Tokyo and Beijing both sought an 'equal partnership' with their superpower ally, but for many years Japan's economic challenge to US leadership would prove more subtle and effective than China's blanket rejection of Soviet authority. Eventually, the 'economic miracle' of the 1960s allowed Japanese corporations to begin the construction of a capitalist international order in East Asia centred on Tokyo.

6

Monolithic unity: the Japanese Left and the Communist bloc, 1950–62

The Cold War world was for the most part dissected neatly along ideological lines that ran parallel to its strategic and economic bipolarities. During the 1950s, however, the loyalties of the Japanese people were divided. Those on the Left mostly looked to Moscow and Beijing for their inspiration. The Japanese Left comprised a vast array of interlinked institutions. At the base of this structure, however, were just three organisations: the *Nihon Kyōsantō* (Japan Communist Party, JCP); the *Nihon Shakaitō* (Japan Socialist Party, JSP), including its powerful labour federation *Sōhyō*; and the *Gensuibaku Kinshi Nihon Kyōgikai* or *Gensuikyō* (Japan Council Against Atomic and Hydrogen Bombs.)

The Japanese Left during the Sino-Soviet honeymoon

The JCP: one revolution or two?

Founded in July 1922 as a branch of the Comintern, the JCP continued to be under the sway of the Kremlin throughout the pre-war 'underground' era. In contrast to these filial ties to Moscow, the JCP's relationship with the CCP resembled that of siblings.[1] The ideological question that dominated this period was whether Japan needed a bourgeois–democratic revolution before proceeding to Socialism or not. Following Japan's defeat in 1945, the newly legalised JCP answered in the affirmative and chose to cooperate with the Occupation authorities.[2] Under the leadership of the charismatic Nosaka Sanzō the party quickly achieved a leading role in popular protests and the labour movement. It deliberately played down its ties to Moscow, with Secretary-General Tokuda Kyūichi claiming at the Fifth Party Congress in 1946: 'At present, we have no ties whatsoever with the Soviet Union…in the future as well, our party will never have relations with the Soviet Union.'[3] The JCP sought to reinvent itself as a 'loveable Communist Party' that was pursuing 'peaceful revolution'. It met with some success: by 1949, the party claimed 100,000 members, three million voters and 35 seats in the House of Representatives. In marked contrast to the majority of Japanese, the JCP 'unreservedly' welcomed the conclusion of a defensive alliance uniting the main European and Asian Communist revolutions in February 1950.[4] The party emphasised the contribution of the Sino-Soviet treaty to the cause of an overall, 'just and democratic' peace.[5] The previous month, however, the Cominform (Communist Information Bureau, successor to the Comintern) launched a bitter attack on the Japanese party line. With the backing of Beijing, Moscow demanded that the JCP follow the violent example of the CCP and direct its revolutionary struggle against 'American imperialism' rather than against Japanese 'monopoly capitalism'. The party leadership reluctantly concurred, but disagreement over the pace and depth of reform soon led to internal divisions. A radical 'internationalist' faction (led by Shiga Yoshio, editor of the party journal *Akahata*, and Miyamoto Kenji, head of the Party Control Commission) temporarily eclipsed a relatively moderate 'mainstream' faction (led by Nosaka and Tokuda).[6] In part, this may have reflected the emergence of a kind of Sino-Soviet division of labour: whereby the Soviet Union was determining the 'over-all Communist policy in Japan', but the Japanese Communists themselves were 'turning more and more for aid and advice to Communist China'.[7] Subsequent violent demonstrations by Japanese Communists against the government backfired, provoking SCAP into ordering the so-called 'Red Purge' in late 1949. This removed more than 12,000 JCP members and 'sympathisers' from politics, government, schools, the media and industry. Half-hearted attempts at guerrilla warfare also failed. Most of the party leadership either fled into exile in China or went into hiding.[8]

Following the signature of the Japan–US Security Treaty at San Francisco in September 1951, JCP publications continued to emphasise the defensive nature of the Sino-Soviet Alliance:

> Since February 1950 a false rumour has been propagated in Japan that the Sino-Soviet treaty views Japan as the enemy…but the real treaty although firmly against the revival of Japanese imperialism and invasion from Japan is not hostile towards a peaceful Japan.[9]

It was not until after the October 1954 Sino-Soviet Joint Declaration confirmed Moscow and Beijing's desire to normalise diplomatic relations with Tokyo that the JCP resumed normal activity. This revision of the Sino-Soviet Alliance prompted the JCP journal, *Zenei*, to announce, in typically hyperbolic fashion, that the alliance contained 'a mighty life force' that created a Sino-Soviet relationship 'unprecedented in history'.[10] Exiled JCP leaders started returning from China in time for the Sixth Party Congress in July 1955. The party now condemned its earlier 'ultra-Left adventurism' and reverted to the early Occupation line, with a call for a united front linking all 'progressive forces'. These efforts to resolve bitter factional infighting produced a new system of collective leadership.[11] Moreover, Nosaka emphasised 'the importance...of listening to the words of the peoples and parties of the two countries [the PRC and USSR]'.[12]

The JSP: one party or two?

With the exception of members of the extreme leftist *Rōnō-ha* ('Labour–Farmer Faction'), the JSP (established on 2 November 1945), unlike the JCP, did not inherit any special ties to the CPSU or CCP.[13] Moreover, in January 1950 the agreed party platform was support for 'neutrality'.[14] Signature of the 'anti-Japanese' Sino-Soviet Alliance the following month thus provoked mixed emotions within the party. Secretary-General Suzuki Mosaburō immediately denounced it for 'coercing' (*iatsu*) Japan. He found its targeting of Occupied Japan—a country that was entirely lacking in military power or the will to invade—'inexplicable'.[15] It was one factor in the JSP split of October 1951.[16] Of the numerous squabbles that kept the Left and Right Socialist Parties at arm's length during the next four years, three foreign policy issues were central: security against the perceived foreign Communist threat, diplomatic relations with the 'two Chinas', and trade with the Communist powers.[17] In September 1953, the CEC of the Left-JSP went so far as to propose a Sino-Soviet-American joint security guarantee for Japan to replace the existing bilateral alliances.[18]

The two parties responded differently to the Sino-Soviet Joint Declaration of October 1954. Asanuma Inejirō, secretary-general of the Right-JSP, thought it strange that in calling for the abrogation of the Japan–US Security Treaty, Moscow and Beijing did not offer to abrogate their own alliance which 'viewed Japan as a hypothetical enemy.' In contrast, the chairman of the Policy Affairs Committee (Left-JSP), Itō Kōdō, welcomed the way in which it 'strengthened peaceful coexistence'.[19] Interestingly, the joint declaration coincided with a visit to the PRC by a Socialist Diet members' fact-finding mission consisting of five representatives from each Socialist Party.[20] The mission found that the Communist regime was secure and that, 'China was neither Titoist nor a satellite, but rather a junior partner advancing toward increased equality': a new and realistic assessment of the state of Sino-Soviet relations.[21] This visit was instrumental in reconciling the foreign policy differences between the two

Socialist Parties, thereby accelerating the process of reunification, which came to fruition twelve months later. In the October 1955 manifesto, both sides agreed to demand the abolition of the Sino-Soviet Alliance (especially its anti-Japan clause) as well as the Japan–US Security Treaty. In their place, the Socialists sought the negotiation of a four-power collective security arrangement modelled on the 1925 Locarno Treaties.[22] However, the manifesto merely papered over the cracks on the other controversial questions. The reunified JSP dedicated itself both to a peaceful resolution of the Taiwan problem, and to the achievement of diplomatic relations and intergovernmental trade agreements with Beijing and Moscow.[23] It was not long before this carefully crafted compromise began to unravel.[24]

Gensuikyō: one front or two?

The *Gensuikyō* movement began life as a petition against the *Daigo Fukuryū Maru* (*Lucky Dragon*) Incident of 1 March 1954, in which high-level radiation from a US nuclear test on Bikini Island fell on a Japanese fishing boat killing one crew member. The campaign proved so successful amongst the nuclear-phobic Japanese public that by the end of the decade it had grown into 'the greatest grass roots movement in Japanese history.'[25] However, from the very first *Gensuikyō* congress in 1955, Japan's left-wing parties attempted to manipulate the movement for their own ends.[26] By 1958, a JSP–JCP–*Sōhyō* united front, with the active support of the PRC delegation, succeeded in having a resolution passed condemning only the nuclear policies of the US and Japan, thereby undermining the movement's universalist anti-nuclear credo. The following year's congress, held against the background of the intensifying anti-Security Treaty struggle, saw the influence of the left-wing alliance peak, before the emerging Sino-Soviet dispute began to undermine the integrity of *Gensuikyō*.[27] Many other left-wing organisations suffered the same fate, although some proved a little more resilient in the short-term.[28]

Discovery and denial

First hints of a Sino-Soviet dispute

When Nikita Khrushchev launched his 'secret' attack on Stalin at the CPSU's 20th Congress in February 1956, the JSP's immediate reaction was muted. Two members of the International Bureau summed up the party's confusion thus:

> JSP leaders believe [that the] 20th Congress [of the] CPSU represents an important development, but [they]...do not yet know what to make of it...Socialist leaders believe [the] CPSU has changed its policies to some extent, but they do not know why these changes were made.[29]

The same could not be said of the JCP. The first official Communist response came on 24 March 1956, with a resolution highly complimentary of the proceedings in Moscow, although it neglected to mention the attack on Stalin. At a further plenary meeting in June, the JCP Central Committee accepted Khrushchev's idea that Socialism could be achieved by peaceful means.[30] This was to become a major issue in the Sino-Soviet ideological dispute, but the JCP's actions did not indicate an early bias towards Moscow, for Beijing too initially supported Khrushchev's criticisms of Stalin.[31] Western scholars, however, were soon speculating about 'a potential rivalry between Peking and Moscow for dominant control over the JCP'.[32]

It was only after the autumn crises in Poland and Hungary that the JSP began to recognise the international significance of de-Stalinisation. When the 13th JSP National Congress opened in Tokyo on 18 January 1957, the mood was sombre. Party members argued over, inter alia, future relations with the PRC, the Japan–US Security Treaty, and the Hungarian crisis. Whereas the right wing wished to condemn the Soviet action in Hungary as 'a terrible armed oppression', the leftist factions placed the onus on the Nagy regime for bringing 'confusion', thereby lending credence to Budapest's supposed 'invitation' to Soviet troops to intervene. The final compromise version of the 'Action Policy for 1957' slightly favoured the right, in that it described the Polish and Hungarian episodes as 'liberation movements...stemming from the 20th Congress of the CPSU'. And while it conceded that they had been 'somewhat taken advantage of by reactionary forces,' it nevertheless concluded that, 'the armed intervention of the Soviet Union cannot be condoned.'[33] On other controversial questions, however, the party platform tended to reflect the increasing power of the party's left wing. Not only did the congress vote to reject 'the two Chinas plot', but for the first time it proposed to cooperate with the JCP (as well as pro-China businessmen) in a mass campaign to achieve diplomatic relations with Beijing.[34] This resulted in the establishment of the non-partisan *NitChū Kokkō Kaifuku Kokumin Kaigi* (National Congress for the Restoration of Japan–China Diplomatic Relations) on 21 July, with JSP Diet member Kazami Akira as chairman.[35] In the meantime, leftists within the party immediately formed an Ad Hoc Committee for the Restoration of Japan–China Diplomatic Relations under the leadership of Katsumata Seiichi, reportedly as a means of circumventing the party's right-wing dominated International Bureau.[36] A few weeks later, Katsumata stated:

> Some in the capitalist bloc, hoping for contradictions between the Soviet Union and China, point out a tendency to Titoisation in the "Chinese-style revolution" [but] Communist China's relations with the Soviet Union, Eastern Europe and Southeast Asia, built on proletarian unity, are very close.[37]

Equipped with such ideological blinkers, the new committee was unlikely to produce an accurate picture of the fragile Sino-Soviet relationship.

After numerous delays due to opposition from the right-wing Nishio and Suzuki factions, the arrival of the JSP's first official mission to China, on 15 April 1957, coincided with the liberating 'Hundred Flowers Movement'. Secretary-General Asanuma Inejirō (Kawakami faction) led a factionally balanced delegation, which held extensive talks with Zhou Enlai and Mao Zedong. Despite promising the Kishi government and the JSP right wing that he would not engage in 'diplomatic negotiations', Asanuma issued a joint statement with Zhang Xiruo (chairman of the Chinese People's Institute of Foreign Affairs) on 22 April. They agreed that: Tokyo should transfer its diplomatic recognition from Taipei to Beijing as soon as possible; China should have a seat in the UN; and Taiwan was a domestic Chinese problem. The statement also confirmed their united support for: increased trade and other exchanges; all 'unofficial' agreements being recognised by the Japanese government; total nuclear disarmament; and a four-power collective security pact to replace the antagonistic military blocs in Asia.[38]

Among Japanese in general, such views were not immediately seen as indicative of a weakening Sino-Soviet Alliance. This is not surprising since Soviet leaders were also making similar statements around this time.[39] By the autumn, however, the idea that all was not well in Sino-Soviet relations began to percolate through the Japanese Left. According to the later recollections of Naitō Tomochika—a leading member of the JCP's anti-mainstream—an editorial in the *People's Daily* 'caused the international faction to suspect sharp differences of opinion between the Chinese and Russians.'[40] Such suspicions had yet to infiltrate the JSP right wing. At the time, the right's leading foreign affairs expert, Sone Eki, noted 'the trend toward polycentrism apparent in the Communist bloc since the 20th Congress of the Soviet Communist Party' and China's 'reconciliatory role' in the subsequent East European crisis. He therefore no longer regarded Beijing as 'a kind of Soviet satellite'. At the same time, however, Sone concluded that 'a trend in Communist China toward Titoism or Gomulkaism…[was] unthinkable' given that China remained dependent on Soviet aid for her industrialisation and defence, and the two shared 'common ideals in the shape of Marxism–Leninism'. On Japan policy, he noted how since the October 1954 Joint Declaration 'Communist China has called the tune', but in common with many American analysts, Sone put this down to the Communist powers 'dividing the responsibility' for the Asian region. For Sone, the idea that China might emerge 'as the Soviet Union's rival in a struggle for power within the Communist bloc…[was] wishful thinking...at least in the near future.' Even in the long-term, the most he would contemplate was 'the possibility of a greater display of individuality on the part of Communist China'. In short, Sone believed, they were 'likely to maintain their unity as allies' as long as the Cold War persisted.[41] Such thinking represented little advance on the Right-JSP's October 1954 position.

There is a curious disjunction, however, between Sone's public and private views. By the time this article had appeared in early October 1957, Sone was in Washington as part of a small JSP delegation led by Kawakami Jōtarō, former chairman of the Right-JSP. When Sone introduced the Socialists' plan for 'a new general non-aggression pact' that would include the US, Japan, USSR, and Communist China, Assistant Secretary of State Walter Robertson's response was predictably dismissive, given his strongly anti-Communist views.[42] The next day Sone tried a rather different tack with Robert Murphy (deputy under-secretary for political affairs), saying that he thought a distinction could be drawn between Soviet Communism and Chinese Communism and pointing out that the latter 'favored more freedom of action.' Hence, sounding oddly reminiscent of his old enemy Yoshida Shigeru, Sone argued that, 'non-communist nations should seek to drive a wedge between them rather than forcing China into closer association with Russia.'[43] JSP leaders, however, never publicly promoted such a scheme.

While the Kawakami mission was in Washington, former premier Katayama Tetsu also led a nine-member JSP delegation to Beijing, Moscow and Warsaw to discuss economic cooperation. In talks with Khrushchev and Mikoyan, the Soviet leaders 'agreed that a collective "peace" security system, including the Soviet Union, the United States, Japan and Communist China, should be formed in the Far East.'[44] In November, the impression of Sino-Soviet unity was strengthened further during a Conference of Communist and Workers Parties held in Moscow. A China–Soviet Friendship Society was inaugurated, and more importantly, a meeting of the twelve ruling Communist parties produced the Moscow Declaration. This document reaffirmed Khrushchev's principle of peaceful coexistence and the possibility of a parliamentary road to Socialism. All 64 parties in attendance then joined in signing a 'Peace Manifesto' calling for total nuclear disarmament, peaceful coexistence and an end to military blocs.[45] Yet appearances notwithstanding, all was not well in the Sino-Soviet relationship. It later emerged that fierce arguments had taken place over the wording of the Moscow Declaration. Mao still acknowledged Soviet leadership of the bloc, but for the first time theoretical differences had been publicly revealed. Nevertheless, the hints of Sino-Soviet disagreement during 1956–7 were still very minor relative to the overwhelming evidence of Sino-Soviet cooperation and hence the Japanese Left could still safely ignore them.

Beijing's hard line and the Japanese Left's 'united front'

During the first half of 1958, the Japanese media interpreted any Soviet or Chinese action vis-à-vis Japan as an attempt to improve left-wing prospects in the forthcoming Japanese general election. On 8 May, the Chinese government turned the Nagasaki Flag Incident into a *cause célèbre* sufficiently heinous to justify breaking off all ties with Japan. The press reported that the Socialist candidates 'took full advantage of the Communist Chinese attack on the Kishi government by claiming that they alone could solve the Sino-Japanese imbroglio and promote flourishing trade with the mainland.' When the 22 May election resulted in the reunified Socialists making a net gain of only ten seats, however, the Sino-Soviet meddling in Japan's domestic affairs was deemed to have 'boomeranged'. Even JSP Chairman Suzuki, discussing the defeat later on television, sought to lay part of the blame at Moscow and Beijing's door.[46]

The JCP also did rather badly at the polls, but limited electoral appeal was not a major issue at the party's long-delayed Seventh Party Congress that convened on 21 July 1958. The main policy debates revolved around the same ideological questions that had formed the substance of the Sino-Soviet disagreements in Moscow the previous November. At issue was whether 'US imperialism' should be considered the primary enemy; whether to pursue revolution via a broad 'united front' strategy; and whether the option of a non-peaceful transition to Socialism was legitimate. To each of these questions the mainstream faction answered in the affirmative. Its call for a 'two-enemy, two-stage revolution' (*futatsu no teki, nidankai kakumei*) was opposed, however, by an anti-mainstream group led by Kasuga Shōjirō.[47] Drawing inspiration from the Italian Communist leader Palmiro Togliatti's 'structural reform theory', Kasuga argued that Japan, like Italy, was an independent, advanced, industrialised, capitalist country, and as such was ripe for an immediate, peaceful Socialist revolution.[48] The two JCP groups reflected the emerging views of Beijing and Moscow respectively, but it would be premature to label them the 'China faction' and 'Soviet faction' at this stage. Despite the recent influx of 1,500 or so young Japanese Communists 'educated' in China, the mainstream proved incapable of amassing the necessary two-thirds majority to achieve endorsement of its platform.[49] The ambiguous Moscow Declaration received the party's official blessing, however.[50]

During the May general election campaign, the JSP had promised to send a delegation to China to help restore commercial relations, at least, with the mainland. At the end of July, Sata Tadataka (former head of the party's International Bureau) undertook the mission, but Chinese terms for resumption proved exceptionally harsh.[51] The popular reaction in Japan was overwhelmingly negative.[52] Nevertheless, at a press conference following publication of his report, Sata defended Beijing's view that Prime Minister Kishi's attempt to revive Japanese imperialism was to blame for the current impasse in Sino-Japanese relations.[53] The issue sharply divided the JSP, with the right-wing Nishio faction, in particular, unhappy at the damage done to the party's public image.[54] After much debate, a new official seven-point 'Fundamental Policy Regarding Revision of Sino-Japanese Relations' was agreed upon by the CEC. In a remarkable victory for the left wing, the JSP now supported five of the six Chinese demands contained in the Sata Report, thereby accepting Beijing's linking of economic and political relations.[55] The *People's Daily* welcomed the change, lavishly praising the JSP for its efforts.[56] Sino-Japanese relations were at a standstill, but with the party falling increasingly under the spell of *Sōhyō* radicalism, the JSP–CCP connexion was going from strength to strength.

The CEC's decision to support the Chinese demands came against the background of the second Taiwan Straits crisis. Beijing's aggressive action prompted widespread fears amongst the Japanese public that US bases on their soil would drag them into a Sino-American war.[57] It also accelerated the leftward drift of the JSP. In early September, the right wing-dominated JSP International Bureau supported Foreign Minister Fujiyama's journey to Washington to commence negotiations on revision of the Security Treaty. By the time of his return, however, Socialist cooperation with the democratic wing of Japanese Conservatism, which dated back to the Katayama coalition cabinet, was in decline.[58] The second Taiwan Straits crisis, not the subsequent Police Duties Performance Law débâcle that was its consequence, sounded the death knell for the relationship. In its stead, the JSP joined with *Sōhyō*, the JCP, the Japan–China Friendship Association, and others in setting up a secretariat for the National Congress for the Restoration of Japan–China Diplomatic Relations. This was reportedly 'the first major JSP–JCP united action in regard to China'.[59] A couple of weeks later, the JSP Diet member and head of the National Congress, Kazami Akira, led a 'friendship' delegation to Beijing. A joint-communiqué, issued on 10 October, called for the 'abolition of the Japan–US Security Treaty' and blamed the Kishi government's dependence on Washington for the rupture in Sino-Japanese relations. Moreover, in a phrase that JSP Secretary-General Asanuma was to make famous the following year, it was agreed that, 'American imperialism is the common enemy of the peoples of Japan and China.'[60]

The next major step towards constructing a 'united front' on the Japanese Left came on 11 December 1958, when, following similar statements from Beijing, Moscow, Pyongyang and Hanoi, the JCP announced that it now favoured a policy of neutralism for Japan.[61] Confessing to inspiration from recent Soviet and Chinese pronouncements, a few days later the JSP's CEC declared that Japan's goal should be 'positive neutrality'.[62] This policy embraced non-participation in military blocs, withdrawal from the Cold War, active promotion of universal peace and coexistence, and the establishment of a nuclear-free zone in the Asia–Pacific region. On the Right, Nishio Suehiro spoke out against this one-sided definition. Generally, though most Socialists harboured doubts concerning the sincerity of the JCP's conversion to neutralism, they were willing to countenance Communist participation in a protest movement against revision of the Japan–US Security Treaty.[63]

On 18 January 1959, the JCP Central Committee passed a resolution calling for Japan to become neutral, promote friendly relations with all countries, and to begin by abrogating the Security Treaty and closing American military bases.[64] The following day, the JSP's 1959 Action Programme adopted 'positive neutrality' as its official foreign policy position.[65] Western commentators were quick to note that 'the foreign policy pronouncements of the Socialist Party were indistinguishable from those of the communists.'[66] However, divisions within the JCP and especially the JSP over party policy were now reaching critical proportions.

As noted in Chapter 2, the 21st Congress of the CPSU, which opened at the end of January, presented a stage-managed display of Sino-Soviet unity. Khrushchev for his part muted his criticism of China's Great Leap Forward. Furthermore, his denial of Yugoslav charges of Sino-Soviet differences was perhaps even a little overblown. Zhou Enlai, in turn, talked of the two countries' 'eternal and unbreakable' friendship and Mao's praise for Khrushchev's 'correct leadership'. The Soviet leader's support for a nuclear-free zone in the Far East and the entire Pacific Basin pleased the JSP.[67] Subsequently, JCP Secretary-General Miyamoto Kenji, returning from the congress via Beijing, signed a joint statement with CCP Secretary-General Deng Xiaoping on 4 March. It expressed support for an East Asian collective security pact and endorsed Khrushchev's proposal for an Asia–Pacific nuclear-free zone.[68]

Miyamoto's stopover, the first of three JCP missions to China during 1959, was soon overshadowed by the storm of controversy which developed over the second visit of an official JSP mission, again led by Secretary-General Asanuma Inejirō.[69] In an ill-advised speech delivered soon after the party's arrival on 12 March, he criticised US military bases in Okinawa and Taiwan—Japanese and Chinese territory respectively—and in particular their hosting of nuclear weapons. In this context Asanuma reasserted that 'American imperialism' was the 'common enemy of the peoples of Japan and China.'[70] This time the comment provoked a strong official response. At the prompting of US Ambassador MacArthur, LDP Secretary-General Fukuda Takeo cabled Asanuma, describing his statement as 'exceedingly regrettable.'[71] Thereafter, both the LDP and CCP propaganda machines sought to exploit the phrase for their contradictory ends. In the joint-communiqué issued on 17 March, Japan's largest opposition party offered its full support for Zhou Enlai's 'Three Political Principles' (concerning the resumption of Sino-Japanese trade), for the inseparability of politics and economics, and for China's 'liberation' of Taiwan. In return Beijing promised to respect the JSP's 'positive neutrality' policy, and agreed to a ban on nuclear weapons in general and those in the Asia–Pacific region in particular. In addition, the military clauses of the Sino-Soviet Alliance directed at Japan would be allowed to lapse, but only on condition that Japan first abolished the Japan–US Security Treaty and signed non-aggression pacts with both China *and* the Soviet Union.[72] These were slightly harsher terms than Asanuma had been offered on his previous visit, most notably in the way that Beijing spoke up for Moscow's interests.

Ratification of the joint-communiqué by the CEC was a foregone conclusion, although it was not obtained without the anticipated opposition from members of the right-wing Nishio and Kawakami factions. Nishio denounced it as a humiliating capitulation to the Chinese Communists, and it influenced his decision to secede from the party six months later.[73] Another determining factor in Nishio's mind was the narrowing of the ideological gap between the JSP and JCP. *Sōhyō* assisted the Chinese in the role of *omiai* or matchmaker in this marriage of convenience. Thus in March, the increasingly radical trade union federation helped to convince the JSP to grant the JCP 'observer' status in the newly established *Anpo Jōyaku Kaitei Soshi Kokumin Kaigi* (National Council for Opposing Security Treaty Revision.)[74] The first verdict of the Japanese people on this political realignment—delivered in the June Upper House elections—was negative: both left-wing parties did badly. Consequently, Nishio stepped up his attacks on JSP foreign policy, and following censure for such indiscretions, he again split the party on 18 October.[75] With 32 other JSP Diet members and the backing of *Zenrō*, the moderate labour federation, he established *Minshatō* (Democratic Socialist Party, DSP) three months later.[76] Improved JSP ties *with* Moscow and *with* Beijing certainly played a part in the party schism, but not the well-disguised ideological dispute *between* the Soviet Union and China.

The JCP meanwhile, had continued to edge ever closer to the CCP. The Fifth Plenum—held in mid-March, after Miyamoto had returned from China—saw 'independence' (implying that American imperialism was the main enemy) supplant 'peace' or 'neutrality' as the central policy plank, thereby reversing the priority of the January Plenum.[77] Khrushchev used every opportunity during the year to stress Soviet support for a multilateral security structure to guarantee Japan's permanent neutrality.[78] When JCP delegations visited Beijing in June and October, however, they heard a more partisan emphasis on abrogating the Japan–ROC Peace Treaty and the Japan–US Security Treaty. Khrushchev's failure to issue a joint-communiqué during his attendance at the PRC's tenth anniversary celebrations in October, and his studiously neutral stand in the simultaneous Sino-Indian border clashes, gave rise to intense speculation in the West that serious disagreements were emerging between Moscow and Beijing.[79] The Japanese Left, however, chose to ignore the evidence.[80]

The rise of 'structural reformism' and the collapse of the 'united front'

On 19 January 1960, despite the combined opposition of the JSP, JCP, and a variety of other groups, including a substantial minority of LDP politicians, the Japan–US Treaty of Mutual Cooperation and Security was signed in Washington.

Popular resistance to the new treaty continued, indeed grew, but when formal Diet ratification was achieved on 19 June, the common cause keeping Soviet and Chinese policy towards Japan along parallel tracks was lost. This was not immediately apparent, however, since first reactions from Moscow and Beijing were equally harsh. A Soviet memorandum delivered to the Japanese government on 27 January, contained a thinly veiled threat of nuclear destruction should war break out. It also unilaterally revised the terms of the 1956 Joint Declaration concerning a territorial settlement, making the promised return of the Soviet-held islands conditional on the closure of US bases.[81] A *People's Daily* editorial, published three days earlier, was no less severe. Pulling back from earlier concessions made to the JSP, it criticised those Japanese politicians and others, who 'still hold an incorrect view which puts the Sino-Soviet alliance on a par with the Japan–US alliance...[and] do not understand that the[y]...are of an entirely different nature.'[82] Responses from the Japanese Left varied widely. The JCP was quick to endorse the Soviet memorandum.[83] DSP Chairman Nishio Suehiro, on the other hand, claimed that the Soviets had exposed their true colours with this new demand concerning bases, and declared his support for the government's firm rejection of it. Disregarding the protestations of JSP Chairman Suzuki Mosaburō, Soviet Ambassador Fedorenko informed the Japanese Socialists in early March that the Soviet government now considered the territorial problem to have 'already been settled'.[84] The JCP–JSP 'united front' was already feeling the strain.

At the end of that month, the JSP underwent an important change of leadership. At an extraordinary party congress, Asanuma narrowly defeated his 'faction boss', Kawakami Jōtarō, to take over the party chairmanship. Eda Saburō, a little-known member of the Suzuki faction, was elected to the post of secretary-general.[85] The new team soon made its influence felt on the JSP's foreign policy line. Even before the vote, following the DSP's lead, the CEC had offered its support for a supra-party effort (including the LDP) to restore diplomatic ties with Beijing.[86] However, with the Security Treaty battle lost, a series of articles in the JSP newspaper, *Shakai Shimpō*, called for a more balanced neutralism, equally opposed to the Sino-Soviet and Japan–US alliances, and critical of the JCP's partisan neutralism. The drift back towards the political centre was becoming more pronounced.[87]

By the autumn, the trend was unmistakable. Trips to Beijing and Moscow by Hozumi Shichirō, a member of a pro-China JSP faction called the *Heiwa Dōshikai* (Peace Comrades Association), and ex-Chairman Suzuki Mosaburō, respectively, failed to improve relations.[88] Then on 13 October, with the moderate Eda Saburō assuming the leadership following the assassination of Asanuma the previous day, the JSP took another big step back towards a more even-handed foreign policy.[89] During the November Lower House election campaign, 'positive neutrality' remained the official JSP plank, but this policy was promoted with the slogan:

'Let us keep on good terms with both the US and Soviet Union.'[90] Eda himself linked the Soviet Union with the US, as a major player in Cold War power politics and hence not a 'force for peace'.[91] In so doing, the party leadership effectively 'disavowed the basic intent of the Asanuma Statement' of 1959, and reversed its stand in the ideological debate that had raged since 1954.[92] Ironically, this rendered JSP foreign policy almost indistinguishable from that of the DSP. Neither party did very well at the November polls, but this did not deter the new JSP leadership from announcing in December that it planned to send delegations to the Soviet Union, the PRC, and the US in the near future.[93]

Meanwhile in July 1960, Japan had received its first visit from a major Chinese delegation since December 1957. Led by Liu Ningyi (chairman of the All-China Federation of Trade Unions), the group's ostensible purpose was to attend the tenth birthday celebrations of *Sōhyō* at the end of July, followed by the Sixth *Gensuikyō* World Congress. However, Liu also held talks with a cross-section of Japanese political leaders, including Asanuma (JSP), Nosaka, Miyamoto, Shiga and Hakamada Satomi (JCP), and Matsumura Kenzō (LDP). Liu made China's ideological stand very clear when he insisted that *Gensuikyō* brand 'US imperialism' as the enemy of world peace. This had the effect of highlighting the growing divisions within the Japanese Left.[94] The majority of Communist delegates to the congress and a number of Socialists supported Liu's call, and an 'Appeal' was adopted which stated that only a struggle against world imperialism 'headed by the US' would lead to the banning of nuclear weapons.[95] This resulted in *Gensuikyō* suffering its first major split. DSP-influenced groups resigned and eventually formed their own anti-nuclear organisation, the *Kakuheiki Kinshi Heiwa Kensetsu Kokumin Kaigi* (National Council for Peace and Against Nuclear Weapons), in cooperation with the LDP in November 1961.[96]

By this time, the Sino-Soviet ideological schism had entered a new, more open phase. Following a war of words which began in April 1960 with the publication of a series of articles in the CCP journal *Red Flag*, matters came to a head at the June congress of the Romanian Workers' Party in Bucharest. There the CPSU and CCP aired their ideological differences in public for the first time.[97] Although they refrained from specifically apportioning blame, from now on even the leaders of the JCP's anti-mainstream 'international faction' were reportedly 'fully aware of the serious nature of the problem.'[98]

The usual anniversary celebrations for the Chinese and Russian revolutions dominated the Communists' autumn schedule. The leader of the JCP's 'structural reformists', Kasuga Shōjirō, suggested that the party establish an official line on the Sino-Soviet dispute before despatching its own delegation to Beijing. The party elite rejected his proposal. Nevertheless, Kasuga's initiative meant that the first official discussion of the rift within the JCP Central Committee took place in November 1960, after the Chinese festivities but before a special Moscow

International Conference.[99] All participants were sworn to secrecy before Miyamoto Kenji, who had led the delegation to Beijing, presented his report. He argued that the party should avoid simply choosing sides in the rift, and instead decide policy on a case-by-case basis. Miyamoto's position on the main ideological questions—the need to retain the force option while imperialism existed; the need to participate in an anti-imperialist front; the idea that Japan was advanced economically but a semi-colony politically—placed him closer to China's stance. Still, he sought the role of mediator in the dispute for the JCP. The report was approved.[100]

The Moscow Conference of the 81 Communist and Workers' Parties opened on 11 November. Two weeks of heated debate and tough bargaining ultimately produced the Moscow Statement. Although some concessions were made to the Chinese line, on paper at least the Soviet position remained pre-eminent: war was 'not fatally inevitable'; 'peaceful coexistence' was still an essential goal; as was 'general and complete disarmament'. Sections of the 1957 Declaration were simply repeated verbatim.[101] However, the committee examining revolution in non-Western countries, where Chinese delegates were said to be the most influential, drafted those passages most relevant to Japan. Hence the inclusion of the following statement: 'In some non-European developed capitalist countries that are under the political, economic and military domination of US imperialism, the working class and the people direct the main blow against US imperialist domination'.[102] The CPSU's leadership was again lauded, but it was now clear that Moscow was losing control of the international Communist movement it had founded: there was never to be such an all-embracing meeting of parties again. Under strict instruction to minimise the differences between the Chinese and Soviet positions during the conference, the JCP delegation maintained a balanced position. Subsequently, however, it became increasingly evident that the ideological sympathies of the party mainstream lay with Beijing, which shared the JCP's hostility towards 'structural reformism'.[103]

In short, the incompatible attitudes of the Japanese Left towards 'structural reform' became manifest, and hence the cracks in the JSP–JCP 'united front' became irreparable, as disagreements within the Sino-Soviet Alliance became ever more apparent in the wake of the *Anpo* defeat of June 1960.

The battle over 'structural reformism'

Although the JSP had announced in December 1960, that it would send official delegations to the PRC, Soviet Union and US in the New Year, the party found it impossible to fulfil its promise. Internal divisions were hardening. Low-level contacts continued however. In mid-January, for example, JSP Diet member Matsumoto Shichirō led a Japan–Soviet Friendship Association delegation to Moscow.[104] He then joined a *Heiwa Dōshikai* group visiting China led by Kuroda

Hisao (former head of the *Rōnōtō* or the Labour–Farmer Party).[105] Later that month, the Ad Hoc Committee for the Restoration of Japan–China Diplomatic Relations agreed to dispatch a third JSP mission to China in March. However, conscious of past precedents, the right-wing party leadership proved reluctant to lead it.[106]

The JSP's 20th National Congress in March confirmed the decision to send a mission to China, but more importantly, the congress re-elected Eda as secretary-general and approved his 'structural reform' programme.[107] Thereafter, the JSP experienced a major factional realignment. Eda and a few like-minded colleagues including Narita Tomomi, broke with the Suzuki/Sasaki faction, forming a Soviet-friendly mainstream grouping that eventually incorporated the weakened Kawakami faction (whose boss returned as figurehead chairman) and the Wada faction. A pro-China left-wing alliance comprising Matsumoto's *Heiwa Dōshikai*, Sakisaka Itsurō's *Shakaishugi Kyōkai* (Socialist Association), and crucially the Sasaki faction, opposed them.[108] The last scored a minor victory in June, when, following the successful Ikeda–Kennedy summit, it managed to persuade the CEC to postpone indefinitely, the JSP mission to the US.[109] Later that summer, however, Eda's position was significantly strengthened by events within the JCP, which led to its more liberal 'structural reformers' joining the Eda faction of the JSP.

A lull in Sino-Soviet polemics, although barely maintained at the Moscow Conference in November 1960, allowed the Japanese Left to preserve the fiction of international Socialist brotherhood for a few months more. In early July, Sone Eki of the DSP claimed that 'differences between China and the Soviet Union on the question of ideology and international policies have been largely settled'.[110] Similarly, the JSP's Wada Hiroo noted that 'Soviet relations with China actually seem more united than before.'[111] The mainstream Communist leader, Hakamada Satomi, was even more forthright, asserting that 'the Sino-Soviet dispute is a pure fabrication, a downright lie.'[112] Iwama Masao (JCP) agreed, describing 'the so-called Sino-Soviet rift' as 'an unfounded rumour', despite the fact that the Soviet delegation had failed to attend the CCP's 40th Anniversary celebrations in June.[113] Such naiveté was about to receive a strong jolt.

The JCP's Eighth Congress in July 1961 and the events leading up to it were later described, rather poetically, as 'the first ripple of the Sino-Soviet dispute to reach the shores of Japan.'[114] The ideological jousting between Kasuga Shōjirō's 'structural reform' faction and the party mainstream, which had intensified since the Seventh Party Congress in July 1958, culminated in a dramatic showdown on the eve of the Eighth. The Moscow-educated Kasuga maintained that Japan, like Western Europe but unlike the rest of Asia, had already experienced its 'democratic revolution'.[115] Hence, the party's main enemy should be 'Japanese monopoly capitalists', with 'American imperialism' as only a secondary target.

Furthermore, Kasuga believed that Japan could achieve 'Socialist revolution' without much resort to violence.[116] He attacked the party leadership for its 'dogmatism', 'ultra leftist adventurism', and 'undemocratic' Stalinist practices. Unrepentant, the mainstream faction responded by denouncing Kasuga as a 'Titoist' and 'revisionist'.[117] After losing this battle over the party platform, Kasuga withdrew from the field, tearing up his party card in the process. In the ensuing purge about four hundred JCP members either resigned or were expelled, including leading intellectuals such as Satō Noboru.[118]

Following the drama of its prelude, the Eighth Congress itself was something of an anti-climax. With the remaining anti-mainstream forces numbering less than ten per cent of the JCP membership, the mainstream platform—'the 1961 Thesis'—was adopted without incident. It differed little from the 1958 programme. The revolution would occur in two uninterrupted stages, first defeating 'US imperialism' and then 'Japanese monopoly capitalists'. Japan was recognised as being an advanced capitalist society but remained a 'semi-colony'. As such, the party could not limit itself to employing purely parliamentary methods of opposition.[119] This position accorded closely with that advocated by the CCP, but even at this late stage, the mainstream faction did not acknowledge this fact. It still preferred to perpetuate the myth that there were no significant differences between Moscow and Beijing and to claim that both offered the '1961 Thesis' their full support. Naturally, remaining members of Kasuga's 'structural reform' faction took the opposite line, highlighting existing Sino-Soviet disputes and accusing the JCP leadership of 'pretending to have the full support of foreign communist parties.' The group's only realistic hope of overcoming the pro-China majority would have been to induce the Soviets to intervene, but Moscow declined to do so. The Japanese government had in fact frustrated the plans of both the CCP and CPSU to send high-level delegations to the congress. In absentia, the CCP publicly announced its support for the JCP mainstream and attacked the dissident Kasuga, while the CPSU maintained a discreet silence.[120] Following ratification of the '1961 Thesis', however, both parties sent congratulatory messages to the congress. Certainly, 'the struggle within the JCP was developing a closer relationship with the titanic battle now preoccupying the Soviet Union and China', but the decisive split was yet to come.[121]

Having contributed to the hounding of the 'structural reformists' from the JCP, Beijing now set about the task of replicating its success with the JSP. Within days of the JCP Eighth Congress closing, Zhou Enlai informed Tanaka Toshio (*Heiwa Dōshikai*) of his displeasure at Eda's 'structural reformism' with its 'smile' towards Washington.[122] At the same time, however, the JSP's traditionally pro-CCP Ad Hoc Committee for the Restoration of Japan–China Diplomatic Relations produced a document entitled: 'Immediate Policy toward China'. It emphasised the promotion of peaceful coexistence in Asia and positive neutrality as the goals of the forthcoming third official mission to China.[123] The JSP was proving a much tougher nut for Beijing to crack.

The Seventh *Gensuikyō* Congress, which opened in early August, revealed how wide the divisions within the Japanese Left had grown. Total disarmament, including a nuclear test ban and aid for victims of the H-bomb, were the main features of the agenda agreed in advance. For the JCP, however, eager to implement its '1961 Thesis', the sole concern was to see *Gensuikyō* continue to identify 'US imperialism' as the 'enemy of peace'.[124] The JSP, with the backing of *Sōhyō* and others, now strongly contested this view. Despite being greatly outnumbered in terms of their relative national memberships, the JCP-led group proved organisationally superior, and with Beijing's vocal support the Communist line received the overwhelming backing of the Asian and African delegates.[125] As soon as the meeting concluded, the JSP-led group passed a motion of 'no confidence' in the *Gensuikyō* executive, attacking its one-sided assessment of the international situation and its undemocratic methods.[126]

The problems facing *Gensuikyō* were soon to intensify. The congress, at the insistence of the chief Soviet delegate, Yuri M. Zhukov, had also resolved that, 'the first government to resume nuclear testing [should] be denounced as an enemy of peace and the foe of mankind.'[127] When, just three weeks later, the Soviets hypocritically announced that they would be the first to break the three-year-old international moratorium on tests, the disunity of the Left was again cruelly exposed.[128] Beijing, secretly at work on its own bomb, defended Moscow's decision: the Sino-Soviet rift was still in remission.[129] The JCP, not surprisingly, backed them up, claiming that 'since the Soviet Union is a peace force, nuclear tests are a natural defensive measure'.[130] Japanese pacifists, however, were horrified. *Gensuikyō* issued a mealy-mouthed statement condemning the Soviet test, but justifying it in terms of the threat from the US and its allies. Leading liberals like Ishibashi Tanzan immediately resigned their membership of the peace organisation.[131] JSP Secretary-General Eda Saburō, in a strongly worded article, attacked the false moral distinction drawn by the Communists between their nuclear tests and those of the West: 'Fallout falls on both sides alike', he declared.[132] Caught in the middle, the *Heiwa Dōshikai* adopted an intermediate position, arguing that while there was a 'qualitative difference' between American and Soviet tests, the danger of fallout meant it was best if there were none at all.[133] The cracks in the Japanese Left were widening, but for the moment Moscow and Beijing maintained the illusion of solidarity.

The 22nd Congress of the CPSU, which opened on 17 October 1961, was an unmitigated disaster for the cause of international Communism. At the Congress, Khrushchev criticised Stalin's 'personality cult', devalued 'the dictatorship of the proletariat', and demonised the 'Albanian deviationists'. Zhou Enlai, head of the

Chinese delegation, recognised Khrushchev's speech for what it was, a thinly veiled attack on Mao and the CCP. Two days later, he defended his Albanian comrades, deplored Khrushchev's tactics, and promptly returned to Beijing.[134] When called upon to join in the chorus of anti-Albanian rhetoric, significantly Nosaka Sanzō refused. This was the first time that the JCP had publicly disobeyed an order from Moscow.[135] However, the party did not come out openly in support of the Chinese line either. Fearful of the Kasuga group's presence on its right flank, the JCP leadership sought to contain the rift, publicly proclaiming its own 'independence and autonomy' and playing down any divisions.[136] Nosaka still respected the CPSU as furthest along the road to constructing Communism and continued to urge all Communist parties to unite.[137] However, an *Akahata* editorial published in late December implied disapproval of Khrushchev's attack on Albania, thereby conceding the existence of the 'beginnings of an open dispute' between certain Communist states. The editorial also admitted that the effects of the rupture were spilling over into Japan's 'democratic movement', accusing the Kasuga group of perverting the true state of affairs for its own ends.[138] In this ultra-cautious manner, the JCP groped towards a sustainable position in the Sino-Soviet ideological schism.

Eda Saburō's views were by this time coming under the strong influence of Kasuga's former colleague, Satō Noboru, now a JSP member. For Satō, neutralism meant avoidance of war, in particular nuclear war. In all other respects, he still sided with the Socialist camp against the imperialists and capitalists.[139] This association perhaps helps to explain why Eda issued a 'political report' in November, which described US 'imperialism' as the main source of Cold War tensions. Pressure from the Wada faction soon forced the report to be amended, but it was not long before there was further evidence that the 'Asanuma spirit' was still haunting the JSP.[140]

As the eventful year 1961 drew to a close, Suzuki Mosaburō reluctantly led the long-delayed third official JSP mission to China.[141] The Chinese welcomed Suzuki with a forthright denunciation of his party leader's 'erroneous theory', equating Eda's 'structural reformism' with 'revisionism'.[142] After two weeks of reportedly difficult talks, a joint-communiqué was finally issued on 13 January. The Asanuma formula reappeared in the Suzuki Statement, albeit in slightly amended form: the struggle against 'US imperialism' was now the common task of everyone and not just the people of China and Japan. However, the statement also allowed for the peoples of these two countries to carry on 'their own struggles based on their own independent positions'. Beijing for its part again agreed to support a nuclear-free zone in the Pacific and a collective security treaty in the region to guarantee Japanese neutrality and security. The Chinese also repeated their pledge to sign a bilateral friendship and non-aggression treaty even earlier than that, provided Japan first abrogated the Security Treaty with the US and the Peace Treaty with Taiwan, closed its foreign military bases and normalised diplomatic relations with Beijing. When these conditions were met, the anti-Japanese provisions of the Sino-Soviet Alliance would 'automatically become null and void.'[143] Rather more significant for the JSP, however, were the ideas that the Chinese now rejected, namely, general disarmament, the easing of East–West tensions and total reliance on peaceful methods to resolve international conflicts. All were vital aspects of 'positive neutrality' and core issues in the Sino-Soviet ideological dispute.

The LDP predictably dismissed the collective security proposal as 'nonsensical', but surprisingly the reaction within the JSP was equally unenthusiastic.[144] Within the party views divided along established factional lines, with Sasaki and the *Heiwa Dōshikai* in favour, and Kawakami and Wada against the concept. A week later, at the party's 21st Congress, the Suzuki Statement was approved, but at the same time Eda comfortably defeated the leading leftist candidate, Sasaki Kōzō, to retain the post of secretary-general. Moreover, the congress ratified his 'structural reformist' platform.[145] After tasting defeat in the JCP, it seemed that the 'structural reformists' would at least triumph in the JSP, but this victory proved short-lived.

Beyond a Sino-Soviet ideological dispute

Throughout the spring and summer of 1962, Moscow and Beijing maintained a truce in their public polemics. Nevertheless, this could not delay a dawning realisation amongst elements within the JSP that the Sino-Soviet rift was about more than just ideological formulations. An article published in an official JSP journal in April spoke of how, 'at the moment the ideological polemics between China and the Soviet Union are attracting world attention. Ideology apart, differences between the Asia policy of China and that of the Soviet Union are an undeniable fact.' For some, this was 'not unnatural', given that China was an Asian nation and Russia a European one.[146] Such realism placed the JSP far ahead of the JCP in coming to terms with the rift. At the end of February, Ishida Seiichi (assistant editor of *Akahata*) was still insisting that Communism's enemies were exaggerating the seriousness of any Sino-Soviet differences.[147] When Chairman Nosaka Sanzō celebrated his 70th birthday in March, the JCP bathed in reflected glory as both Moscow and Beijing lavished praise on the veteran Communist leader. The fact that the former highlighted his 'struggle for peace', while the latter emphasised his combating of 'US imperialism', was ignored.[148] The splintering of the breakaway Kasuga group in May offered the JCP leadership a further source of satisfaction, but by the autumn life started to get much more difficult. The JCP mainstream's hold on neutralism was increasingly fragile, since by this time the party organisation was being rapidly colonised by young, China-trained cadres.[149]

In early August, *Gensuikyō* held its eighth annual congress in Tokyo: it proved to be the most contentious to date. In the preceding 12 months, the JSP had strengthened its influence over the organisation's leadership. Consequently, when a week before the congress was due to open, Moscow announced that it would follow Washington's lead and shortly commence another series of nuclear tests, a majority of the *Gensuikyō* Executive Committee, including the Communists, agreed to protest. However, the JCP leadership then tried to justify the Soviet decision and any hope of compromise was lost.[150]

When the congress itself convened on 1 August, it soon became clear that the Chinese delegates and their supporters were in control.[151] Eda Saburō delivered an impassioned appeal for an inclusive peace movement, firmly opposed to nuclear testing by 'any country or bloc whatsoever', and insisted that the congress send a strong protest to Moscow. The Communists, who insisted that there was a qualitative, even a moral difference between peaceful and defensive Socialist nuclear tests and those by the aggressive imperialists, rejected this approach. They demanded that 'US imperialism' again be identified as the 'enemy of peace', that military alliances and foreign bases be denounced, and that *Gensuikyō* refrain from appealing for general disarmament.[152] Hence, though the Tokyo Appeal 'regretted' the Soviet tests, its condemnation of those carried out by the US was total.[153] While the Congress was still in session, Moscow conducted a huge atmospheric test at Novaya Zemlya, north of Siberia. When an emergency meeting of the Executive Committee resisted a Socialist demand that it send an immediate protest telegram to the Soviet and American governments, the JSP and its allies resigned their offices.[154] The next day, the plenary session of the congress descended into chaos as members of the Communist and Socialist youth organisations engaged in pitched battles and the JSP and *Sōhyō* leaderships walked out. No official declaration was issued. The JCP was left in command of the battlefield, but it was to prove a Pyrrhic victory. A few days later, the JSP joined twelve other organisations in issuing a statement opposing the JCP's stand, and calling for the reform of *Gensuikyō*, in particular a reduction in its ideological and financial dependence on foreign delegations.[155] In early December, the same 13 organisations held a 'Mass Rally Against Atomic and Hydrogen Bombs' in Hiroshima. This was to prove the forerunner to a completely separate Socialist anti-bomb movement.[156]

Meanwhile, at Haneda Airport on 12 August, the departing chief of the Chinese delegation, Zhao Anbo, attacked Eda by name, claiming that he had insulted China by failing to distinguish between 'friends' and 'enemies'.[157] Eda struck back a few weeks later, accusing the Chinese of pursuing divisive policies, and stressing his own party's 'autonomous line' on the issue of nuclear weapons.[158] Despite the Suzuki Statement, relations between the JSP mainstream and the CCP remained tense.

It is worth noting that during this Sino-Japanese wrangling, the Soviet delegates in Tokyo remained aloof. As in previous years, Beijing's representatives took the lead in defending the Soviet tests. Thus, it would be fair to say that the Sino-Soviet rift was yet to make its influence *directly* felt on Japan's anti-bomb movement.[159]

Interpretative comments

Input: external environment

The Comintern played a formative role in the establishment of both the JCP and CCP, as Moscow sought to spread the Bolshevik revolution eastwards during the 1920s. Hence the ties between Chinese and Soviet Communist Parties were nearly three decades old when the alliance was signed in 1950. However, after numerous Soviet errors, the Chinese Communists ignored the advice from Moscow and pursued their own rural path to revolution according to the precepts of Mao Zedong. With the new treaty, Stalin recognised that despite the CCP's unorthodox methods, its revolution was genuinely Marxist.

In even less auspicious circumstances, the JCP had enjoyed none of the CCP's revolutionary success. However, strong personal ties, in particular a warm relationship between JCP Chairman Nosaka Sanzō and Mao Zedong developed when many Japanese cadres spent the war years in China. Consequently, whereas the CPSU treated the JCP as its subordinate, the CCP saw it more as a fraternal party. While the Soviets and Chinese were still negotiating their alliance, they lost the JCP most of its popular support at home by forcing the party to abandon its peaceful path to Communism. They did not recognise the bankruptcy of this violent policy for several years.

The relationship with the JSP was much less direct, although the party's left wing maintained good relations with Moscow and Beijing during the 1950s. The Communist Powers helped to bolster the Japanese opposition during the anti-Security Treaty struggle, but this caused the JSP to split and the JSP–JCP 'united front' began to break up soon after the successful revision of the treaty. In short, the opposition parties felt the Sino-Soviet Alliance's influence the most keenly.

The US made little attempt to court even the more moderate Socialists during this period. The Occupation had opened positively, with SCAP freeing Japanese Communists and Socialists from prison, legalising left-wing political parties and unions, and pursuing a reformist agenda with the vocal support of the Japanese Left. As the Cold War spread to East Asia, however, relations chilled, SCAP 'reversed course' and eventually supported a 'Red purge'. On the other hand, Britain's attitude towards Japanese Socialists was less hostile than America's.

Internal environment: operational sphere

The Japanese electoral system during the 1950s and 1960s operated a significant rural gerrymander, which helped to sustain a diminishing though solid conservative majority in the Diet. The JSP and JCP competed for the votes of the left-wing minority. Hence an inverse relationship developed between the electoral fortunes of the two parties. The JCP was a 'mass party' with the largest membership in Japan, whereas the JSP was weak at the grassroots level and was reliant on *Sōhyō* for mobilising the union vote. Neither party was able to maintain party unity during this period. The Communist 'structural reformers' later defected to the JSP.

Psychological sphere: belief systems

Although resident in the 'free world' zone, the sympathies of the JCP and JSP mostly lay with the Socialist states. The JCP was an ultra-orthodox Marxist party whose leadership believed that its role was to foment a revolution that would establish a 'dictatorship of the proletariat' allied to their comrades in Moscow and Beijing, although many party members preferred to pursue a non-violent path to Communism. Their conception of Japanese national identity emphasised its role as a 'lackey of American imperialism'.

Marxists dominated the left wing of the JSP too, but with intellectual debts to Britain's Labour Party and Germany's Social Democrats on the right, it is probably best described as a Democratic Socialist party. Japanese Socialists were the most firmly wedded to a national identity that revered the Hiroshima experience and treated Article 9 of the Constitution as sacrosanct. For them Japan was a peaceful model for the world. Neutralist and pacifist foreign policies held the strongest appeal for JSP members.

Psychological sphere: perceptions

Among the left-wing opposition, the JCP initially saw the Sino-Soviet Alliance as a good thing, a concrete manifestation of '*ichimai iwai*': the monolithic unity of the Communist world. The JSP, in contrast, had always had mixed feelings.

While precision is difficult, the available evidence suggests that by the autumn of 1957 at the latest, most of the Japanese Left, including the anti-mainstream factions of both the JCP and JSP, were conscious of problems in the Sino-Soviet relationship. The seriousness of their disagreements was still unclear, but what stands out are the great lengths to which Japanese progressive party leaders went in order to hide what was happening—perhaps even from themselves. Within the

JCP, the mainstream leadership—the Japanese most likely to be *au fait* with Beijing's thinking—attempted to keep any hint of a dispute from party colleagues until November 1960. Similarly, JSP leaders continued to describe the rift as 'wishful thinking' into the early 1960s. A cynic would see such behaviour as feigned ignorance motivated by fear of the potential that such an ideological conflict possessed to strengthen their enemies and weaken their already faction-ridden parties. A more sophisticated interpretation might view this as an example of what psychologists call cognitive dissonance, that is where the brain simply filters out new data that contradicts strongly held beliefs. As Marxist Internationalists, Japanese Communists initially did not consider national identity as significant, and hence most were unable to conceive of the possibility of a Sino-Soviet rift. Eventually, as evidence of a rift became incontrovertible, this conflict between image and reality caused a crisis of (Marxist) faith.

Although the official positions of the JCP and JSP remained non-committal throughout the early 1960s, this could not prevent the ideological schism from exerting an indirect influence over the two parties. However, while they crossed swords over issues fundamental to the rift, they did not fight over the rift itself. By mid-1961, the JSP and JCP were being pulled in opposite directions by Moscow and Beijing. They resisted, but the public eruption of bitter Sino-Soviet polemics following the Cuban Missile Crisis in October 1962, henceforth would make it impossible for the Japanese Left simply to deny that a serious dispute existed between Moscow and Beijing.

Decision-making process

The internal policy-making structure of the JCP reveals that its Central Committee rigidly controlled the party under the Leninist principle of 'democratic centralism'. Party discipline was very strict and Miyamoto Kenji proved to be the most powerful individual within the party. In the JSP, however, decision-making authority was more devolved. Its much more frequent party congresses were important, and allowed the affiliated unions to exert a strong influence. Like the LDP, the party suffered from chronic factionalism. The CEC carried much weight, although the rightward leaning International Bureau dominated day-to-day foreign policy making. The emergence of the Sino-Soviet rift greatly complicated policy-making for both parties. Within the JCP power became concentrated in even fewer hands.

The influence of the divided Japanese Left on official foreign policy was never strong, even at the height of its popularity during the 1950s. Acting alone the opposition parties were unable to seriously threaten Yoshida's leadership, although they did maintain a 'blocking third' in the Diet, which effectively prevented the government from revising the 'peace constitution'. More positively, they offered foreign policy alternatives, contributed to the revival of Sino-

Japanese trade, and helped facilitate the repatriation of Japanese nationals from the mainland. Hatoyama's relationship with the Socialists was rather different from Yoshida's: he only came to power with the help of the JSP's Diet votes. Thereafter, the Democrats made some progress on forging a bipartisan foreign policy. Occasionally, JSP politicians seemed willing to assist MOFA to communicate with Japan's Communist neighbours. In other words, there were cooperative and competitive elements in the relationship. However, links between the governing and opposition parties deteriorated again under Prime Minister Kishi, reaching nearly total breakdown in 1960, and recovering only slowly under Ikeda's 'low profile' policy.

Output: people's diplomacy

The JCP was in a rather strange position vis-à-vis the Sino-Soviet Alliance. Being Japanese and Communist, members were in a sense both parties to the alliance and targets of it. They were certainly the treaty's only defenders in Japan. In the early 1950s, the JCP promoted Japan's incorporation into the Communist bloc via violent revolution, but by the end of the decade, it was advocating a pro-Communist 'neutralism'. JSP foreign policy meanwhile advocated total nuclear disarmament and a four-power security guarantee for Japan to replace both the Japan–US Security Treaty and the Sino-Soviet Alliance. Into the early 1960s, the Japanese Communists and Socialists still sought to follow the path of 'non-involvement and non-alignment' in the rift.

External environment: feedback

The JCP's refusal to choose sides in the rift may have helped to preserve at least the myth of Communist unity for a while longer, but the party did not wield sufficient influence within the Communist bloc to realize this goal in practise. Excluded from government after 1948, the JSP was also unable to put its neutralist foreign policy into practice. Moreover, being out of step with trends within the European-dominated Socialist International it had surprisingly little impact on the external environment, although it did persuade Moscow and Beijing to at least pay lip service to its four-power pact idea. Only *Gensuikyō*, the Hiroshima-based nuclear disarmament movement enjoyed a broad, if diminishing appeal internationally.

7

When brothers fight: Japanese Socialism and the Sino-Soviet ideological dispute, 1962–64

兄弟喧嘩

Given their historic political and ideological disparities, it is surprising to find that the Sino-Soviet rift had such remarkably similar effects on both Japanese Socialists and Communists. In fact, the two parties passed through three relatively distinct stages between 1962 and 1966, although their moves were not always synchronous: non-involvement and non-alignment; alignment and division; and realignment and autonomy.

Non-involvement and non-alignment

The Sino-Soviet rift becomes public

A year-long lull in the Sino-Soviet rift was brought to an abrupt end by three events in the autumn of 1962, which together helped to clarify the JCP's increasingly pro-China stand. First, Khrushchev revived friendly relations with Tito's Yugoslavia.[1] The head of the JCP's Propaganda Section made his party's position abundantly clear by describing the Yugoslavs as the 'ringleaders of the revisionists of the world.'[2] Second, on 20 October, fighting broke out on the Sino-Indian border. This placed the Soviet government, which enjoyed close ties with New Delhi, in an awkward position. Moscow attempted to pursue an even-handed approach. The JCP, in sharp contrast, offered fulsome praise for the Chinese military actions.[3] Finally, the border war in the Himalayas coincided with perhaps the most serious crisis of the Cold War, precipitated by the installation of Soviet nuclear missiles in Cuba. Initially, the JCP responded with a stout defence of Khrushchev's brinkmanship, but after he had backed down, the party followed the Chinese lead with a clear expression of disapproval.[4] Later in November, the leader of the most pro-Chinese mainstream faction, Hakamada Satomi, visited Moscow and Eastern Europe, before joining other JCP leaders in Beijing. Rumours suggested that they reached wide-ranging agreement with Chinese leaders on the major ideological questions in dispute with the Soviets.[5] Publicly, the JCP still avoided openly attacking the CPSU, lest Moscow lend its support to the Kasuga group, or even encourage the defection of the Shiga group. By the end of 1962, however, doubts about where the party stood had largely vanished: the very language it used betrayed its pro-China sympathies.[6]

Divisions within the JSP were also intensifying, although here the relative strength of the mainstream and anti-mainstream camps was more finely balanced, with the pro-China forces in the minority. The debate over Secretary-General Eda's 'vision' pre-occupied the JSP during the latter half of 1962. This Socialist utopia, first outlined in August, drew on both Soviet and Western experience, but Japan's historical role model, China, was conspicuously absent. According to Eda, Japan needed its own national vision of Socialism: 'It has...become essential for our party to clarify how our view of Socialism is different from those types which exist in the Soviet Union and China.'[7] This autonomous line had the effect of crystallising the growing schism within the JSP. On the right of the party, Wada Hiroo (head of the International Bureau) maintained his support for a neutralism that looked more to the Non-Aligned Movement than to the Soviet Union or PRC.[8] On the left, members of the *Anpokai* (Diet members first elected in 1960) now signed a joint-communiqué in Beijing on 12 October, reaffirming the spirit of the Asanuma Statement. Two days earlier, speaking on the second anniversary of Asanuma's assassination, Zhang Xiruo (chairman of the Chinese People's Institute of Foreign Affairs) had forcefully reaffirmed Beijing's antipathy towards Japanese 'right-wing social democrats'. They were now placed on a par with Tito, as agents of 'US imperialism' and 'modern revisionism'.[9]

The short-term effect of such internal divisions was paralysis of the JSP's decision making process. When Chinese troops crossed the border into India on 20 October, the party was unable to agree upon a response. The moderates' views were closer to those of Nehru's India, but they dared not express their sympathy in public for fear of losing control of the pro-China left wing.[10] Beijing exercised no such restraint. The director of the China–Japan Friendship Association wrote an article praising all members of the JSP, even moderates like Chairman Kawakami Jōtarō, but singled out Eda for character assassination.[11] Eda denied the charges vigorously, but the damage was done. When the JSP's 22nd Congress opened at the beginning of November, a narrow majority approved the Sasaki faction's motion censuring the 'Eda vision'. Eda resigned as secretary-general, but two days later, the party repented and easily elected Eda's right-hand man, Narita Tomomi, to succeed him.[12] Beijing may have contributed to Eda's unseating, but Narita continued the JSP's traditional support for 'positive neutrality' and 'peaceful coexistence', which aligned the party much more closely with the Soviet than the Chinese position in the rift.

In a report approved by the CEC in late January 1963, the new secretary-general still referred to the Sino-Soviet rift as merely an ideological dispute (*ronsō*). Narita hoped that 'the two Socialist countries concerned will resolve their ideological differences so that the imperialists will not be able to take advantage of the situation' and added that the JSP would 'pursue friendly relations with both the Soviet Union and PRC.'[13] Narita's efforts to paper over the party's deep internal cracks soon collapsed. On 1 February, Ishibashi Masashi (who had inherited the International Bureau mantle from his faction boss Wada Hiroo) published in the party journal the first statement by a party leader on the Sino-Indian border conflict. He criticised Beijing and bluntly declared that, 'with regard to the Sino-Soviet dispute, we feel more sympathy with the stand of Khrushchev than that of China'. Although he qualified this statement by adding that it was also 'necessary to try to understand the stand of China'; this proviso did not contradict the main point.[14]

A fortnight later, the JSP journal carried a second article on the rift, attributed to the Editorial Department of the party's Press Bureau. The editors offered a simple defence of Khrushchev's actions during the Cuban Missile Crisis in terms of 'peaceful coexistence', while simultaneously denouncing the 'malicious propaganda of the imperialists' for describing China's behaviour as 'jingoistic'. They concluded with the observation that 'the Sino-Soviet dispute is providing progressive forces in Japan with a great opportunity to get out of (sic) the influence of international authoritarianism and establish their own independent stand as a party responsible for the people of Japan.'[15] Such an optimistic assessment was later to gain some credibility.

Meanwhile, a public consensus regarding the correct interpretation of the rift seemed to be emerging on the Democratic Socialist wing of the Japanese Left. The March issue of *Chūō Kōron*, a leading intellectual monthly, published the results of a questionnaire on China which included the responses of Sone Eki (chairman of the DSP's Foreign Policy Bureau) and Wada Hiroo (the influential JSP faction leader). The two leaders' responses revealed few differences in their views of the Sino-Soviet rift. Sone thought that, 'the basic cause…[was] a difference in the social development of the two countries', meaning that the Soviet revolution was three decades older than was the Chinese. Similarly, Wada held that it was 'natural for the policies of China and the Soviet Union to differ because they are at different stages of economic development...[and] also differ from each other in the development of Socialism.' Implicit in Sone's argument was the idea that China would mature given sufficient time. Wada, on the other hand, predicted that the dispute would be 'discussed in a calm and reasonable way in the future, [but] while China is placed under abnormal international circumstances...the difference in policy between China and the Soviet Union will not disappear.'[16] Here Wada came close to implying that the US containment of China was having its intended effect. That same month, however, DSP Chairman Nishio Suehiro publicly chastised the JSP for its handling of the Sino-Soviet dispute, claiming that its fraternal approach revealed its 'pro-Communist character.' Nishio claimed that 'the rift will not disturb trade', and that Japan should 'join the Free World for protection against Communist China's expansionist policies.'[17]

Such attacks could not disguise the fact that the resemblance between the positions of the two Socialist parties was growing more pronounced. In late July, Nishio announced the official DSP stance: 'We welcome Premier Khrushchev's realistic political line, and oppose Communist China's attitude, which has turned its back on peaceful international cooperation.' He qualified this, however, by confirming that, 'the DSP has not changed its policy of supporting efforts for Communist China to enter the UN.' On the state of Sino-Soviet relations, Nishio declared: 'The dispute has come about because of differences in ideology, stages of social development, and national standpoints. There is now a leadership struggle in the Communist bloc. Communism's boast of monolithic unity is clearly dissolved.'[18] The following month, the JSP approved a report by Wada that sought to maintain essentially the same balance.[19]

If the JSP was no longer willing or able to restrict its internal debate on the public Sino-Soviet rift, the JCP was still endeavouring to do so. On 24 January 1963, an editorial in *Akahata* described Sino-Soviet disagreements as 'temporary and limited'. It asserted that, 'An open dispute among fraternal parties does not serve the interests of the solidarity of the international Communist movement...[since] it provides enemies with material for provocation.' Finally, readers were warned that, 'No flippant comment is to be made.'[20] Three weeks later, the JCP Central Committee met to discuss developments in the rift and the party's response. Three days of secret and reportedly heated debate produced a resolution on 15 February, which conceded the rift's existence, but still sought to prohibit party members' involvement in it: 'It does not matter whether the Sino-Soviet dispute exists or not', the Central Committee declared, '[a]sking questions about it is bad, it must be based on some sinister intention.'[21] The resolution also described the CPSU and CCP as together forming the 'nucleus' of the international Communist movement, whose unity was of 'decisive importance'. The JCP recommended that they 'hold an international conference to iron out the differences in their views.'[22] At the time, some credulous scholars accepted the resolution at face value. '[I]t would be wrong...to assume...that the JCP is hostile to Moscow or firmly in the Chinese camp', one expert wrote, 'Nor is the JCP following Peking's lead in its discussion of the Sino-Soviet dispute.'[23] On the other hand, others recognised the fact that the JCP was 'feeling the effects of the rift most seriously of all'.[24] With the benefit of hindsight, the 15 February resolution has been accurately described as 'the last serious effort on the part of the JCP to maintain a neutralist stance for nearly three years.'[25]

As the worldwide shock waves from the Sino-Soviet dispute grew ever stronger, the parties of the Japanese Left could no longer sit on the fence. The JCP and JSP (with the DSP) ended up on opposite sides of the divide.

Alignment and division

The *Gensuikyō* split

Moscow chose this time to launch a last effort to heal the rift with Beijing. Having engaged in increasingly bitter mutual recrimination since the Cuban Missile Crisis, the CPSU Central Committee sent a letter to the CCP on 21 February proposing bilateral talks. The following day it sent a similar secret proposal to the JCP. The JCP delayed replying until it knew that the CCP would accept Moscow's invitation, and postponed its own meeting with the Soviets until after the proposed CCP–CPSU conference.[26]

Despite the JCP Central Committee's best efforts, further hints of internal party divisions over ideology continued to reach the public, especially via *Gensuikyō*. After the débâcle of the previous August, the peace movement's leadership had worked very hard to restore some semblance of unity to the organisation. On 21 February, five fundamental principles were agreed, including opposition to all nuclear tests and support for a nuclear-free zone in the Asia–Pacific region. The next day, however, the JCP's Central Committee denounced this hard-won compromise, and blamed the JSP and *Sōhyō* for trying to introduce its 'erroneous...positive neutrality' into the movement. Then in mid-May, the Central Committee suddenly reversed its stance again and offered to support the reconstruction of *Gensuikyō*.[27] This enabled the peace organisation's Executive Board to reaffirm the 21 February principles when it met on 21 June.[28] Ironically, the conclusion of the first nuclear arms control agreement—the Partial Nuclear Test-Ban Treaty (PTBT)—in late July 1963, dashed hopes for a revitalised Japanese peace movement, as well as for a rehabilitated Sino-Soviet Alliance.

In early July, the long-awaited CCP–CPSU talks opened in Moscow. Beijing's dispatch of an open letter on 15 June detailing every complaint against the Soviet Union back to 1956 had not improved the tense atmosphere. However, it was the successful conclusion in Moscow of simultaneous negotiations between the Soviets, British and Americans on the PTBT that sounded the death knell for the Communist alliance. On 31 July, the Chinese government issued a harshly worded statement denouncing the treaty as a 'dirty fraud' and a 'surrender to imperialism'.[29] The PTBT became a litmus test for left-wing parties everywhere: neutrality in the Sino-Soviet rift was no longer an option. The treaty immediately provoked 'a miniature Sino-Soviet dispute' at the regular *Sōhyō* congress.[30] The press recognised that it was also the first 'issue over which the Soviet Union and Communist China openly competed against each other in winning JCP support'.[31] The treaty forced the JCP, which had avoided a public declaration of its allegiance longer than any other Communist party in Asia, to choose sides.

The fact that this occurred in a number of painful stages illustrates the difficulty that the party experienced in publicly breaking with the CPSU. As late as June, pro-Soviet forces within the party were still attempting to compromise on the test-ban issue, but in the run-up to the Ninth *Gensuikyō* Congress the party line gradually hardened. At the beginning of July, an anonymous article in *Akahata* stated that, 'The policy of opposing the nuclear tests of any country is to forgive imperialism and weaken and disrupt democratic forces.'[32] A few days later, the Communist broadsheet published a two-part article by mainstreamer Ueda Kōichirō. 'If we yield to American nuclear threats because of excessive worry over the disaster of a nuclear war', he declared, 'the danger of war will only be increased'.[33] However, an editorial on 29 July, four days after the treaty was signed, was more equivocal. It spoke of the Japanese people reacting to the news with 'an outcry of joy as well as a voice of caution'. Finally, on 3 August—three days after the Chinese made their verdict public—the JCP Central Committee reasserted its authority. An official statement claimed that treating the tri-power agreement as a positive step towards total nuclear disarmament, as had the JSP, was totally misguided. It further argued that in attempting to limit the nuclear club to its existing members, the treaty actually heightened the risk of nuclear war.[34] Still dissenting voices within the party were not silenced. Two days later, *Akahata* quoted Kasuga Shōichi, a party veteran and Presidium member:

> [the JCP] has never said it favored [the] atomic or hydrogen bombs of a socialist power as desirable. We have always assumed an attitude of favoring a ban on nuclear tests and weapons by any country even if it were a socialist country... [But we] are opposed to protesting against nuclear tests by a socialist power.[35]

By this time, however, *Gensuikyō* was meeting in Hiroshima and the JCP had to put its policy into practice immediately.

The Ninth *Gensuikyō* Congress has been accurately described as 'an episode in the Sino-Soviet rift...enacted on Japanese soil'.[36] From the opening session—when members of the Soviet delegation and their supporters turned their backs on a speech by the head of the Chinese delegation—until its conclusion, the two 'allies' engaged openly in their now bitter rivalry.[37] Disagreements over the status of numerous uninvited delegates—many reputedly 'bussed in' by the JCP or exiles resident in Beijing—led the JSP and *Sōhyō* to withdraw even before the congress officially opened.[38] A Chinese delegate then proceeded to denounce the PTBT as 'an outrageous deception...completely beneficial to American imperialism'.[39] An enraged Yuri Zhukov, again leading the Soviet delegation, responded sarcastically: 'Conduct nuclear weapons tests! Contaminate the seas! Create deformed people!'[40] The debate proceeded in this vein until two resolutions, one for the Japanese delegates and a separate one for the non-Japanese, were produced in an all-night session of the drafting committee. In the end, the Soviet and Chinese delegates agreed to avoid any mention of the PTBT.[41] In most other respects, the resolutions followed the CCP/JCP line.

Before returning home Zhukov met with the JCP's *éminence grise* Nosaka Sanzō, but they could only agree that efforts to resolve their differences would have to await their anticipated party-to-party talks. Upon returning to Moscow, Zhukov published an article in *Pravda* entitled 'Hiroshima's Voice', in which he launched the first open Soviet attack on the JCP. Although relatively mild in tone compared with what would appear later, his statement that 'some JCP members attempted to ignore the positive characteristics of the PTBT at the behest of the CPR delegation' was unprecedented.[42]

Having 'lost' the JCP mainstream, Moscow now stepped up its courtship of alternative Japanese partners. Rumours circulated that Zhukov had held secret meetings with the 'structural reformist' Communists in the Kasuga–Naitō group and the surviving anti-mainstream members of the JCP Central Committee, namely Shiga Yoshio and Suzuki Ichizō.[43] Moscow allegedly pressured a delegation of the Japan–Soviet Society, which was visiting at this time, to declare its support for the PTBT.[44] The JCP responded by attempting to block the distribution of Soviet propaganda in Japan.[45] The Soviet Embassy in Tokyo counterattacked with a 'direct mail' campaign targeted at potential friends within the party membership, while embassy staff and press correspondents engaged in an intense shouting match with CCP supporters for the loyalties of the party's grass-roots.[46]

The Soviets had not confined their efforts to the JCP. On the eve of the recent *Gensuikyō* Congress, Zhukov enjoyed a 'frank talk' with leaders of the JSP and the two sides had agreed on the significance of the PTBT.[47] With the Socialists subsequently boycotting the proceedings in Hiroshima, this agreement was to no avail. The JSP called a meeting of representatives from prefectural federations, which decided that the congress was invalid and that no further efforts should be made to rebuild the 'united front' with the Communists. Instead, the party agreed to establish an independent anti-bomb movement.[48] The CEC re-affirmed this decision on 13 August. At the same time, it also agreed upon a new interpretation of the Sino-Soviet rift.

At the previous CEC meeting in June, the party had proposed that, 'In order to bring the Sino-Soviet [ideological] dispute under control the CPSU and CCP should open talks'.[49] Now, however, following the failure of the Sino-Soviet summit, a more sophisticated assessment, based on the views of Wada Hiroo, won approval. Wada claimed in the Socialist newspaper on 4 August, that the rift was in part the product of differing national interests:

> Behind the conflict are big differences between the two countries in geographical environment, historical conditions, internal political and social conditions, and therefore, if we regard the dispute as a mere ideological problem, we would be committing an irretrievable mistake.[50]

Nevertheless, the influential faction leader still believed that 'the heart of the Sino-Soviet dispute is clearly an ideological dispute based on differences over the problem of how to carry out world revolution today.' Wada also denounced the JCP for its ties to China, albeit in somewhat cryptic fashion. Asserting that, 'the Sino-Soviet conflict will last for a long time', Wada insisted that party members should 'establish [their] own independent way of thinking as socialists in Japan' rather than simply choose sides. He held up his support for both Khrushchev's 'peaceful coexistence' policy and normalised relations with Beijing as an example. In other words, he was still attempting to square the circle of Japanese public opinion.[51]

A few weeks later, Wada elaborated on his optimistic view of the rift declaring that the Sino-Soviet dispute 'has given us an unexpected opportunity'. This time he was openly critical of Beijing for its nuclear weapons programme, especially its hypocrisy in simultaneously supporting a nuclear-free zone in the region. He laid most of the blame for this, however, on the US containment policy that left China 'forcefully isolated from international society'. Japanese Socialists could no longer feign indifference, Wada warned, but still he recommended that they 'should adopt an impartial attitude toward the disputants'.[52]

Eda Saburō, now chairman of the JSP's Organisation Committee, also wrote at this time of the rift's importance: 'The outcome of the Sino-Soviet dispute will exert a serious influence upon world peace, the future path of Japan and the future of [its] reformist movement'. Eda added little to Wada's analysis, but with the avoidance of nuclear holocaust as his highest priority, he did make three recommendations:

> we must support...the Khrushchev line with a basic foreign policy of peaceful coexistence; we must completely remove international authoritarianism…and look independently for a way to Socialism most suitable to Japan; [and] we should...take the lead in restoring the international status of China.

Rather naïvely, Eda deemed the last of these suggestions 'the greatest contribution we can make to the settlement of the Sino-Soviet dispute.'[53]

Both Wada and Eda's articles bore the strong imprint of Satō Noboru's thinking, and consequently did not win universal admiration.[54] Already members of the JSP's left wing had complained of pro-Soviet bias in the CEC report of 13 August. Following mediation from Secretary-General Narita, a compromise 'unified view' emerged two weeks later.[55] In reality, the new CEC statement was little different from its predecessor. The JSP still officially supported 'positive neutrality' and 'peaceful coexistence', but now asserted that, 'the immediate task confronting Japan is to overthrow the Security Treaty setup.' In addition to friendship with the non-aligned nations, the party would seek to 'strengthen international solidarity with the forces for socialism, democracy, national independence and peace', (but not the 'peace-loving nations'.) Furthermore, while it continued to offer 'positive support' to the PTBT, the CEC stressed its incompleteness, as well as the danger of Japan–US nuclear cooperation. Finally, it repeated its opposition to the 'containment' of China.[56] Discussion of the most divisive aspects of the rift was deferred until the next meeting of the Socialist Theory Committee.[57]

When the JSP's 39th CEC meeting convened on 29 September, several right-wing prefectural party chairmen questioned the wisdom of waiting for the Socialist Theory Committee to decide on a clear JSP attitude to the rift. They also demanded to know how the CEC had arrived at the 'unified view' of 27 August. In reply, a conciliatory Secretary-General Narita asked for patience because the dispute was 'so deeply involved in the ideological field.' Yet he plainly hinted at his own pro-Soviet sympathies: 'What is fundamental is the conflict between socialism and capitalism...[not] [r]elations between colonies and the national independence movement'.[58] The final report of the meeting reflected right-wing opinion in conceding that the Sino-Soviet dispute had now 'passed the level of theoretical struggle and become a rift over national policy.'[59]

As one scholar later observed: 'Rarely, if ever, had the Japanese left been so fragmented and so frantically engaged in internal combat as it was by late 1963. And rarely had external forces impinged so directly on the Japanese left in almost all of its branches.'[60] The old issues of nuclear weapon testing and 'peaceful coexistence' had proved sufficient to fracture the Japanese Left. A more realistic view of the Sino-Soviet dispute had come at a high price and payments were still outstanding.

The JCP's split with Moscow

At the beginning of October, the JSP published a critique of the JCP's response to the Sino-Soviet rift. It predicted that when the JCP was compelled to 'make clear its stand in support of China'—which must be soon—the party would be 'rocked to its foundation, though not threatened with disintegration...[by] resistance from the pro-Soviet faction'. Somewhat strangely, the same article also claimed that, 'there exists no pro-Soviet faction worthy of the name within the JCP'.[61] In practice, the Socialists were to be proven wrong on both counts.[62]

Following the disastrous Ninth *Gensuikyō* Congress in August, the Communist mainstream had initiated a creeping anti-CPSU campaign. Another JCP delegation visited Beijing for secret talks with Chinese leaders from 3–22 September.[63] Secretary-General Miyamoto used the term '*jishu dokuritsu*' (self-reliance and independence) for the first time in public on the day after their return.[64] Three weeks later, on the eve of the JCP Central Committee's Seventh Plenum, a second confidential letter arrived from Moscow. As part of a wider CPSU effort to induce CCP agreement to an international conference, Moscow again offered the JCP bilateral talks. In the event, given the nature of the other decisions reached at the plenum, it was hardly surprising that the JCP again postponed its meeting with the CPSU. Discussion at the plenum had focused on the PTBT, and the committee easily confirmed the earlier decision to oppose the treaty on grounds similar to those cited by Beijing since 31 July. Only Shiga Yoshio, leader of the party's remaining pro-Soviet members, spoke out against the majority.[65] This opposition soon saw him replaced as leader of the JCP Diet members group. A secret resolution adopted by the Central Committee again spoke of the party maintaining an 'independent and autonomous position on the controversy within the international Communist movement'. However, unlike the 15 February resolution, it explained that 'independence' did not mean that the JCP 'intend[ed] to adopt a neutral, mediatory, indifferent, or passive attitude towards the truth.'[66] Neither the CPSU nor Khrushchev were attacked by name, but more instructive was the deletion of the few remaining positive references to the Soviet Union.[67] Contemporary commentary suggested that while 'the JCP has at last cut the umbilical cord that linked it to the Soviet Union...this Moscow tie has not been replaced...by a similar tie to Peking.'[68] Even so, any veneer of ambiguity concerning where the party stood was now effectively shed.

A few weeks later, the JCP decided to publish this Seventh Plenum resolution, together with a leading article entitled 'For True Solidarity and the Advancement of the International Communist Movement.' This *Akahata* editorial directed its wrath at 'Yugoslav revisionists' and while it denied that the party belonged to either a Soviet or a Chinese camp, it was obvious that its real target was Moscow. The rift was still seen in purely ideological terms, and the CPSU adjudged culpable for its emergence. Furthermore, the authors were particularly concerned at the CPSU's 'attempts at internal intervention' in the affairs of the JCP.[69] More of the same was soon to follow, including translations of long anti-Soviet tirades from the *People's Daily* and *Red Flag*. To the surprise of many observers, the party did not suffer for this new openness, in the short-term at least.[70] The Communists did unexpectedly well in the Lower House elections held on 21 November, garnering half a million more votes than in 1960 and two extra seats: their best result since 1949.

The JCP finally relented and agreed to meet with the CPSU at the end of February 1964, following receipt of a third request for talks on 26 November. In the meantime, the leadership set about purging pro-Soviet members from important posts in party organs and 'front organisations' like the Japan–Soviet Society.[71] Even Secretary-General Miyamoto was apparently considered ideologically suspect, and in February he began an extended stay in Beijing. Officially, he was recuperating from illness, but the rumour-mill diagnosed 'brain-washing'.[72]

If the two sides to the Moscow conference had intended to reach a compromise, the chief negotiators were singularly ill chosen. Leonid Brezhnev officially headed the Soviet delegation, but Mikhail Suslov, an influential party ideologue, played the central role.[73] Just two weeks earlier, he had signalled Moscow's abandonment of its four-month-old unilateral suspension of anti-Chinese polemics with a comprehensive critique of the CCP sent to friendly Communist parties.[74] Equally inauspicious was the selection of Central Committee Chairman Hakamada Satomi, head of the JCP's most Sinophile faction—a man who boasted of heating his *ofuro* (Japanese bath) with Soviet party literature—to lead the visiting delegation. Spurning his host's attempts to discuss the substance of their ideological differences, Hakamada repeatedly accused the CPSU of both 'supporting only those people who agree with them and do as they are told…[and] engaging in splitting operations and interfering in our internal affairs.'[75] While negotiations continued, *Akahata*, in a clear act of defiance, carried an unsigned vicarious attack on the Soviet Union and a prominent critique of 'peaceful coexistence'; the very basis of Khrushchev's foreign policy.[76] Almost two weeks of talks produced insufficient common ground to convince Hakamada to sign a joint-communiqué: an unprecedented slight. On their way home, Hakamada's group enjoyed a two-month sojourn in the Chinese capital (including side trips to Pyongyang and Hanoi), by which time the JCP had received a secret letter from the CPSU (dated 18 April) accusing it of falling totally under the CCP's spell. In particular, the missive claimed that the Japanese comrades had grossly underestimated the power of the Soviet Union and the enormous contributions Socialist states were making to the struggle against imperialism. Hence, they had incorrectly concluded that war with the imperialists was inevitable.[77] The JCP made no response. The break with Moscow was complete.

The JSP's near split with Beijing

While the CPSU–JCP relationship descended into mutual recrimination and bitterness, the strained ties between Beijing and the JSP continued to degenerate. A JSP insider highlighted the connexion between the two trends, commenting that: 'When the JCP began to favour the Chinese position, it was inevitable that the JSP would lean toward support of the Soviet position.'[78]

The New Year, 1964, began well for the PRC with France extending diplomatic recognition. This prompted most members of the JSP to sign a petition calling on the government to normalise Japan's diplomatic relations with the mainland, nullify the ROC peace treaty, and support Beijing's admission to the UN.[79] Evidence of continuing Chinese hostility towards Japan's 'soft-left' soon overshadowed this promising development, however. A New China News Agency commentary broadcast on *Radio Beijing* on 2 March accused prominent JSP leaders, by name, of conniving in a plot to create 'one China and one Taiwan.'[80] The verbal assault followed these leaders' success in reinforcing their dominant position on the party executive at the JSP's 23rd Congress held ten days earlier. The pro-China Sasaki faction responded by withdrawing into 'intra-party opposition'.[81] At the congress, the first since November 1962, a plan to send an official mission to Moscow in June faced strong opposition before it was approved. For the sake of party unity, the congress also approved the dispatch of a similar mission to Beijing. Stung by the Chinese charge, however, the JSP newspaper now warned Beijing to cease interfering in the party's internal affairs. It also reminded the Chinese that even if they regarded the JCP as their only ally in Japan, the JSP still supported a 'one China' policy.[82] Thereafter the JSP mainstream suspended contact with the Chinese government, although members of the anti-mainstream were busy planning their own mission to Beijing.[83]

JSP Chairman Kawakami, perhaps concerned that Ikeda's LDP was stealing one of his party's traditional vote-winners, tried to rebuild some bridges to China. In early April, at a rally in Ōsaka to support the restoration of Sino-Japanese diplomatic relations, he proposed that Secretary-General Narita Tomomi lead a mission that summer first to Moscow and then to Beijing. Kawakami also expressed his deep regret that the Sino-Soviet ideological dispute had assumed such serious proportions and now extended to a clash of national interests. Still, he could not resist pointing out how this had vindicated the JSP view that each country would have to find its own path to Socialism. The JSP, Kawakami reassured his audience, had no intention of taking sides in the rift.[84] A few days later he told Nan Hanchen, leader of an important PRC trade mission to Japan, that the JSP would welcome visits by any Chinese representatives, and he would press the government to promote bilateral trade. Still no date was set for a fourth official JSP mission to China.[85]

A few weeks later, Soviet Deputy Premier Anastas Mikoyan met JSP leaders in Tokyo and surprised them by announcing that Moscow saw little need for a four-power non-aggression pact.[86] Narita raised the matter again when he led a JSP mission to the Soviet Union in late June, but not before Mikoyan had witnessed the final rending of the JCP.

On 15 May, when the Japanese Diet easily ratified the PTBT, JCP Central Committee member Shiga Yoshio disregarded party policy and cast his vote in favour. He justified his action by asserting that, 'War was averted in 1962 because of the prudent policy of peace adopted by the Soviet Union in the Cuban Missile Crisis.'[87] He went on to publicly condemn China for its criticism of Khrushchev over this incident, but scrupulously avoided any mention of the Sino-Soviet rift *per se*, or the JCP's stand therein.[88] Moscow immediately announced its approval of Shiga's action and condemned his four Diet colleagues for not following his example.[89] That evening, an Enlarged Presidium of the JCP Central Committee was called into emergency session and after permitting Shiga to defend his right to free speech, his conduct was declared 'anti-party'.[90] Secretary-General Miyamoto promptly returned from Beijing and convened a plenary meeting of the Central Committee. On 23 May, members accused Shiga and his close comrade Suzuki Ichizō of 'engaging in conspiratorial activities, such as secretly contacting the Soviet Union, deceiving and betraying our party'.[91] The committee voted by a majority of 53:3 (with one abstention) immediately to expel the two men from the party.[92]

If Shiga's support base within the party had been as narrow as the Central Committee vote had suggested that would have ended the matter, but such was not the case. In mid-June, a dozen leading intellectuals and artists, who formed a so-called 'cultural group' within the JCP, submitted a petition to the Central Committee protesting the Shiga decision.[93] Eight less prominent party members were forced to join the burgeoning ranks of outcastes; others defected voluntarily. By the end of June, Shiga announced the formation of the *Nihon no Koe Dōshikai* (Voice of Japan Comrades Association), and began to publish a pro-Soviet magazine.[94]

The JSP was also close to breaking point. At the end of June, the Socialists sent rival delegations to Moscow and Beijing. The former—an official 14-member mission led by Secretary-General Narita—comprised mostly pro-Soviet mainstream delegates. The latter—an unofficial visit—consisted of the pro-China Sasaki Kōzō and five other like-minded party members.[95] Chinese leaders greeted their guests with a renewed verbal assault on the JSP's structural reformists.[96] This

Sasaki visit is best remembered for Mao Zedong's attempt to link Chinese and Japanese territorial grievances against the Soviet Union.[97] More concretely, however, China now began channelling financial assistance directly to the Sasaki 'opposition', in return for a promise to help reunify *Gensuikyō*.[98] For his part, Sasaki delivered a conciliatory letter from JSP Chairman Kawakami, which resulted in China accepting a fourth official JSP mission in October.[99]

In contrast to the controversy surrounding Sasaki in Beijing, the Narita mission to Moscow was a much more low key affair. Prior to departure, the JSP secretary-general stressed his party's desire to remain aloof from the Sino-Soviet rift, naïvely asserting that 'because we are Socialists [we] can keep away from the troubles of the Communists.'[100] He also repeated Kawakami's earlier claim that the JSP's decision to support a peaceful transition to Socialism pre-dated Moscow's policy change of 1957, and therefore did not indicate a pro-Soviet stand.[101] The mission received a warm welcome in Moscow and the various Eastern European capitals it visited. *Pravda* granted Narita the rare honour of publishing one of his articles. It praised the PTBT and condemned the JCP for not doing likewise.[102] Perhaps the most important result of a useful if not spectacular trip, was the securing of Soviet agreement to participate in the JSP-sponsored *Sankenren* (Hiroshima–Nagasaki Anti-bomb Congress) scheduled for August.[103]

Despite a further escalation in the CPSU–JCP polemics, the Soviets actually attempted to attend both the JCP-controlled *Gensuikyō* Tenth Congress and the separate *Sankenren* Congress. Frustrated by the secrecy of the JCP leadership, the Soviet Central Committee decided to appeal directly to the party membership. On 11 July, the committee published a caustic note condemning the JCP, together with its earlier one of 18 April. As mainstream leaders had kept the existence of the latter secret even from the JCP Central Committee, the impact of Moscow's action on the party was considerable. However, if Moscow had hoped to reverse the JCP's pro-Chinese tendency it was disappointed.[104] In a brief, temporising reply, dated 15 July, the JCP rebutted most of the Soviet charges and blamed the CPSU for starting the open controversy. Nine days later, it became only the third Communist Party (after the CCP and Albanian Workers' Party) to launch a direct public attack on the birthplace of the world revolution.[105]

The JCP took its counterattack a stage further at the Tenth *Gensuikyō* Congress held in early August. In addition to blocking Soviet participation in the administrative organs, party members engaged in a variety of obstructive tactics to prevent the speeches of Soviet delegates or their supporters from being heard.[106] Yuri Zhukov, the perennial chief Soviet delegate, walked out in protest. Next morning *Pravda* described those responsible for the disruption as 'Peking's pawns—malicious, berserk slanderers repeating the same speeches for the umpteenth time!'[107] Zhukov remained in Japan and on 3 August, attended the more hospitable Hiroshima–Nagasaki Congress. Subsequently, with Soviet support—both financial and moral—the congress would develop into the *Gensuibaku Kinshi Nihon Kokumin Kaigi* (*Gensuikin* or the Japanese Citizens Conference for the Abolition of Nuclear Weapons) by February 1965, a fully-fledged rival to *Gensuikyō*. The resolutions passed by the two anti-bomb organisations were on the whole remarkably similar, except for their diametrically opposite attitudes to the PTBT.[108]

The JCP finally broke off relations with Moscow on 26 August, in a detailed reply to the CPSU letter of 11 July. Point by point, the party leadership attempted to demolish the Soviet case in its dispute with China. Interestingly, it accused the CPSU of Eurocentrism for undervaluing the importance of the liberation struggles in Asia, Africa and Latin America: the 'main battleground' in the struggle against imperialism. Khrushchev had so distorted the Chinese concept of 'peaceful coexistence', the JCP charged, that it now amounted to little more than appeasement of the imperialist enemy. In short, the letter concluded, the CPSU leaders were nothing more than modern revisionists. *Akahata* published it in full one week later.[109]

Khrushchev launched a blistering counterattack against Mao's professed support for Japan's claim to the 'Northern Territories' in September.[110] In doing so, he linked the promised return of Shikotan and the Habomai Islands to the US giving up Okinawa.[111] The JSP's reaction to this latter statement provided further evidence of the party's deep internal schism. The CEC, meeting in Sapporo to prepare for the upcoming Narita mission to China, issued a statement through Chairman Kawakami declaring such a linkage unacceptable. Upon his return to Tokyo, however, Secretary-General Narita broke with the party line. Having conveyed the JSP's displeasure at the continuing Soviet occupation of the Kuriles to Moscow during his June visit, Narita now claimed that the Kawakami statement was based on a misunderstanding and the party welcomed Khrushchev's stance. At the same time, he also claimed that his forthcoming visit to China would disprove rumours that the party had split into pro-Soviet and pro-Chinese camps. He and Sasaki Kōzō agreed on the party's 'basic policies', and, Narita added, both would 'work for the promotion of friendship and early restoration of diplomatic relations with Communist China'. Nevertheless, he was careful to point out that significant differences remained between the JSP and China over evaluation of the PTBT and organisation of the peace movement.[112] At a further preparatory conference in early October, the JSP reaffirmed the need to avoid intervention in the Sino-Soviet ideological dispute, although the agenda included many issues that were major points of disagreement between Moscow and Beijing.[113]

The factionally balanced Narita mission arrived in Beijing on 14 October, just in time to hear the news from Lop Nor of China's first successful nuclear test. This placed the right-wing members of the JSP mission in a very awkward position. Narita protested, only to be told by his Chinese hosts that the test represented a great contribution to world peace. Unconvinced, Narita then proposed establishing a nuclear-free zone in the Asia–Pacific, and for a time, the JSP and CCP came close to an open breach in relations.[114] In Japan meanwhile, the CEC held an emergency meeting in response to the test, after which JSP Chairman Kawakami sent a telegram to Premier Zhou Enlai conveying the party's profound regret at the Chinese nuclear blast and asking him to cancel any planned future tests. Kawakami did however express his understanding that US containment of China and aggression in Vietnam were important factors influencing China to acquire its own nuclear arsenal. He concluded by declaring the party's absolute opposition to any attempt by the Japanese or US governments to use the Chinese test as an excuse to nuclearise Japan.[115]

The JCP predictably defended the test claiming that it should not be 'viewed as a phase in the nuclear arms race but as a means of preventing American adventurism in nuclear war.'[116] The DSP Chairman Nishio Suehiro and *Sōhyō* Secretary-General Iwai Akira both issued rather less forgiving statements. Even *Gensuikyō* described the test as 'a serious shock to the Japanese people.'[117] After difficult negotiations, a familiar-sounding JSP–CCP joint-communiqué finally appeared on 29 October, in which Narita and Zhang reaffirmed their commitment to the Asanuma Statement. Both sides concurred on the desirability of a bilateral non-aggression treaty, ultimately leading to a four-power collective security system, as well as a nuclear-free zone in the region that would serve as a precursor to global nuclear disarmament. They agreed to differ on the question of nuclear tests.[118] Narita returned home proclaiming his mission a 'great success'. Although he expressed some reservations over the joint-communiqué, he was certain that the Chinese leaders now fully understood Japanese sentiments since they had acknowledged that, 'peaceful coexistence of nations with different political philosophies' was still a valid goal.[119]

Mid-October 1964 also saw the dismissal of Premier Nikita Khrushchev, another vital development in the Sino-Soviet rift. Officially, deteriorating health and old age were responsible, but rumours circulating at the time pointed to his personal feud with Mao Zedong and his failure to predict the Chinese nuclear test.[120] Reaction in Japan divided along predictable lines. Wada Hiroo expressed his deep regret at the 'resignation' and appreciation for Khrushchev's policy of 'peaceful coexistence'. He hoped that the new leadership would continue to follow the same policies. Sone Eki of the DSP believed that Khrushchev had probably not gone voluntarily. Although he therefore anticipated a revision of Soviet policy towards China, others within the party thought the dismissal would probably not prove radical enough to revive the alliance.[121] In complete contrast, Miyamoto Kenji, recently returned from another trip to Beijing, declared that Khrushchev's removal represented 'a manifestation of the contradictions of the revisionist line.' The JCP secretary-general hoped that Soviet policies would change, but he was not very optimistic on the principle that 'history teaches us that the errors of a party cannot be corrected merely by changing the central figure of the leadership'.[122] In the event, the CPSU reaffirmed its commitment to a policy of 'peaceful coexistence', and by mid-December, *Akahata* was already lamenting the lack of positive signs from the new Soviet leadership.

Khrushchev's fall did in fact produce a temporary improvement in Sino-Soviet relations. Mao Zedong and other Chinese leaders immediately sent 'warm greetings' to the new Brezhnev–Kosygin leadership in the Kremlin. Three weeks later, Zhou Enlai led a small mission to Moscow for talks. A fragile cease-fire in the ideological bombardment ensued.[123] This, of course, placed Shiga, Suzuki and the other pro-Soviet Japanese Communists in an impossible position. In early October, they had held a press conference at which they confidently proclaimed themselves the 'true representatives' of the JCP.[124] Suddenly, their *raison d'être* seemed to be under threat. On 4 November, Shiga left for Moscow. The JCP mainstream denounced this 'conspiratorial trip' and accelerated its purge of pro-Soviet elements within the party. On 24 November, the JCP leadership finally felt sufficiently confident to hold its Ninth Party Congress, the first since July 1961. Members acclaimed the Chinese nuclear test as a victory for Socialism, for peace and for Asia. They likewise welcomed Khrushchev's removal as a serious blow to the 'revisionists'.

Expert assessments of the Ninth Party Congress differ. One has declared that it was 'essentially a repetition of the program adopted by the Eighth Party Congress in 1961.'[125] Another has stated that the congress 'all but ratified the split between the Japanese and Soviet Parties, which was to last for fifteen years.'[126] In a sense, both these views are right, but the fact that the Congress also contained the first intimation of a less than total commitment to the CCP-line should not be overlooked. A JCP Central Committee report, first released by Miyamoto in early October, contained a new chapter denouncing the Soviet Union, but it went on to state that the party's international policy was based on the principles of self-reliance, independence and equality. It also stressed the importance of uniting all of the world's Communist parties and peoples in their common struggle. Finally, it looked forward to future cooperation with the JSP.[127] The report, as adopted by the Congress seven weeks later, also expressed concern lest the party commit 'sectarian error'. This meant emphasising the fight 'against American imperialism...[to] the neglect of the struggle against Japanese monopoly capitalists'. It even gave an example of such an error, namely, the JCP's refusal to cooperate in the abortive national strike that *Sōhyō* had planned for 17 April 1964. In short, the central ideological question in Japanese Communism, far from being settled by the Sino-Soviet rift, had been reopened. The potential for a further party split still existed.[128]

Two days after the JCP Congress closed, Shiga Yoshio, who had recently returned from a two-week stay in Moscow, proclaimed the formation of the JCP (Voice of Japan): a new pro-Soviet Communist Party.[129] The mainstream JCP labelled it 'Khrushchevism without Khrushchev'. The new party never became a significant threat to the main JCP, surviving mostly on handouts from Moscow, but it did have unexpected consequences for the JSP. In deciding to strengthen its commitment to the Shiga group, the new leadership in Moscow simultaneously downgraded its relationship with the JSP right wing. Moreover, this change coincided with Beijing stepping up its support for the JSP left wing.[130] The first concrete evidence of the resulting leftward drift came with the JSP's second national congress of the year, held in December. Although Kawakami and Narita retained their posts at the head of the party, rightist Wada Hiroo and leftist Sasaki Kōzō assumed newly created posts as vice-chairmen. Even more importantly, Sasaki supporters now filled most of the junior posts on the CEC. The congress also ratified the long-awaited report on ideology from the Socialist Theory Committee entitled: '*Shakaishugi e no Michi*' (The Road to Socialism). The report came out clearly against 'structural reform', which it described as 'a form of revisionism'.[131] Despite earlier promises, it did not announce a definitive position on the Sino-Soviet rift, although Committee Chairman Katsumata Seiichi attempted to do so just before the congress opened. In a round-table discussion on 'Chinese National Interests', Katsumata declared that the Sino-Soviet conflict resulted from 'a difference in national interests derived from differences in their historical stages and in their international environments.' He conceded that 'the stage of monolithic unity has already passed', but contended that 'no conclusion has yet been reached on the question of what the new international solidarity (*rentaisei*) under multipolarism (*tachūshinshugi*) should be.'[132]

1964 therefore saw a continuation and intensification of trends set the previous year. The dramatic turn of events in mid-October appeared to have little immediate impact on the Japanese Left, but they set off a chain reaction that eventually produced a major realignment of forces.

Postscript: realignment and autonomy

Sasaki subsequently strengthened his position in the JSP, first consolidating the party's pro-China groups into the *Ajia Afurika Kenkyūkai* (Asia–Africa Research Association), and then courting centrists like Narita Tomomi and Katsumata Seiichi. Thus, when Kawakami resigned the chairmanship due to ill health in May 1965, it came as no surprise that a special congress unanimously elected Sasaki as his successor.[133] Thereafter, the JSP became increasingly sympathetic to the CCP line in the rift. The rump of the Eda faction continued to campaign for 'peaceful coexistence' and took comfort in the growing US–Soviet détente. Official party policy, however, influenced by the escalating conflict in Vietnam, saw the US–China confrontation as the locus of international contradictions.[134] Sasaki even broadened the Asanuma Statement, declaring that, 'now, American imperialism is not only the common enemy of Japan and China, but also of all mankind'. On the main ideological issue of identifying the primary enemy, he argued that the JSP should attack 'US imperialism' and 'Japanese monopoly capitalists' simultaneously.[135]

By the time of the JSP's 27th Congress in January 1966, where Sasaki narrowly defeated a revitalised challenge from Eda, there had been some factional realignment. From within the party, Sasaki was criticised for issuing a statement that appeared to approve of China's expanding nuclear test programme. The *Shakaishugi Kyōkai*, a descendant of the Worker–Farmer Party and another element in the Sasaki coalition, began openly to espouse pro-Soviet ideological positions, just as the 'pro-Soviet' Eda faction started to rediscover its 'non-aligned' credentials. Moreover, expressing some dissatisfaction with Sasaki's efforts to reunify the nuclear disarmament movement, Beijing had begun to focus its assistance on the *Heiwa Dōshikai*. In short, the Sino-Soviet rift continued to be a very sensitive topic for the JSP. The party was divided between pro-Soviet, pro-independent, and pro-Chinese groups, with the last predominant.[136] Even after the JCP–CCP schism that summer, Sasaki continued to argue that 'However bad relations may become between China and the Soviet Union and between the JCP and CCP, the JSP must continue to deepen its friendly relations with China.'[137] Until the 1990s, it was still possible to say of the JSP that: 'Factions of pro-Soviet and pro-Chinese complexion are still present...groupings [which] date from the time of the Sino-Soviet split'.[138] The effect of the rift on the JSP was not a transitory one.

After the first hints of dissatisfaction with Beijing's ideological pronouncements emerged at its Ninth Party Congress in late November 1964, the JCP concentrated on attacking the new Soviet leadership for its 'disruptive activities' within the party.[139] The bloody failure in September 1965 of the abortive *coup d'état* in Indonesia reawakened many doubts. By the end of the year, Secretary-General Miyamoto was reportedly accusing the Indonesian Communist Party of 'left-wing adventurism', and suggesting that Beijing might be held partly responsible.[140] In his 1966 New Year's Day message, Miyamoto stressed the need for organising concerted international action against US imperialist aggression in Vietnam. The following month he led a JCP mission to Hangzhou, where Mao Zedong, preparing to lead China into the abyss of the Cultural Revolution, tore up a carefully crafted compromise statement on policy towards the Soviet Union. Miyamoto left without issuing a joint-communiqué.[141] Articles soon began to appear in *Akahata* equally critical of 'left-wing dogmatism' and 'Soviet revisionism'.[142] Suddenly, Maoism and the Chinese revolutionary model were no longer considered appropriate for industrially advanced Japan. Portraits of Mao Zedong disappeared from JCP headquarters and a number of pro-Chinese party members were purged. The party attempted to forge alliances with the Korean Workers' Party and the Vietnam Workers' Party to replace the severed Chinese ties. Then at the Tenth Party Congress in October 1966, the JCP, taking a final leaf out of Mao's book, officially embarked on its own version of a 'struggle on two fronts'.[143] Thereafter, pursuing this more independent, not to say nationalistic line, the party managed to enjoy something of a popular revival with the Japanese electorate during the late 1960s.[144]

Interpretative comments

Input: external environment

The 1960s were an era of increasing ideological pluralism, inspired in part by the emergence of competing versions of Marxism. The Cuban Missile Crisis, the conclusion of the PTBT, the Vietnam War, and especially the Sino-Soviet rift were the decisive developments in the external environment affecting the Japanese Left.

The contrast between Moscow and Beijing's attitudes towards the JCP became more pronounced as their bilateral relationship deteriorated. 'Russian ineptitude'—its long neglect of the JCP, followed by the application of crude pressure, and its alleged 'splittism'—could not compete with the unwavering, fraternal concern of the CCP. When the JCP would later try to extend this spirit of cooperation onto the international stage, Mao refused to work with Moscow even in Vietnam's hour of need. This would be the decisive factor in the JCP's break with the CCP.

The experience of the JSP's 'reformist' leaders was very different: Beijing launched personal attacks, while Moscow lavished praise upon them. One element in the JSP decision to realign was the change of leadership in Moscow. This led to a loss of Soviet interest in promoting relations with the JSP, just as Beijing was stepping up contacts.

With the onset of the Cold War, Washington had adopted a hostile attitude towards the Japanese Left, but after the shock of the *Anpo* crisis, Ambassador Edwin Reischauer attempted to rebuild US ties to the Japanese progressives. The Americans also sought British and Australian assistance in this regard.

Probably more significant, however, was the American escalation of the Vietnam War. This had the effect of radicalising the JSP membership, thereby strengthening the hand of the anti-Americans at the expense of the 'structural reformists'. To some extent, the war also helped to rebuild the unity of the Japanese Left, or more accurately, to construct a 'New Left', through the agency of *Beheiren* (the 'Peace for Vietnam' Committee).

Internal environment: operational sphere

The JCP and JSP emerged from the rift relatively unscathed. They remained opposition parties with limited resources and minority support. The trend towards multipolarity at the international level led to multipolarity at the domestic Japanese level, providing opportunities for greater autonomy. Ultimately it promoted the independence of both the JSP and JCP, but by the same token, the internal squabbling and loss of ideological conviction caused by the rift left both parties weakened, at least in the short-term.

More broadly, the various labour federations, 'friendship associations', 'front organisations', and others on the Left magnified the impact of the rift but did little to shape it. The only significant exception was *Gensuikyō*, which played an important role in transmitting the rift to Japan.

Psychological sphere: belief systems

After the rift came out into the open, Beijing's policy positions were more compatible with the ideological predisposition of the JCP leadership. Meanwhile, JSP mainstream values coincided with Soviet viewpoints and contradicted Chinese ones. The party was torn between its 'norms' of pacifism and nuclear phobia on the one hand, and sympathy for China on the other. Ultimately, the rift strengthened the nationalist strain in their respective party platforms. For example, they adopted a harder line on the 'Northern Territories' issue than even the LDP.

Identities also played a part. Whether one viewed Japan as an advanced, industrialised society subordinate to American monopoly capital or a backward feudalistic one controlled by Japanese oligarchs affected one's sympathies in the rift.

Psychological sphere: perceptions

From spring 1962, leading members of the JSP acknowledged that the Sino-Soviet rift went beyond a simple clash over ideological correctness, and had developed into a conflict over policy, which derived in part from differing national interests. The JCP continued to dismiss it as merely a 'fight between brothers' (*kyōdai genka*) until 1963, when the party ceased to view Moscow as the fount of Communist orthodoxy, and Beijing inherited this mantle, albeit briefly.

Decision-making process

Although the policy-making systems of the JCP and JSP did not undergo any significant modifications during this period, at times both party machines virtually seized up because of the disagreements engendered by the Sino-Soviet split. Later, the changing distribution of power within each party produced a reversal in their respective alignments.

In general, as the Sino-Soviet rift became more serious, so the Japanese Left became less active in Tokyo's relations with Beijing and Moscow. While the LDP enjoyed enhanced communication with both the Chinese and Soviet regimes, the Japanese Socialists came close to severing their links with the CCP—as did the JCP with the CPSU—making them much less useful as potential intermediaries.

Output: people's diplomacy

The JCP resisted alignment in the rift for longer than any other Communist party in Asia. Eventually, however, the pressures resulting from the split between the progressive parties' public and private personae became too great, and the 1963 Partial Nuclear Test Ban Treaty forced a violent resolution of the contradictions. The treaty did not immediately lead the JCP or JSP to declare their loyalty to the Chinese or Soviet line, but it was now clear to most observers where their true sympathies lay. The JCP publicly abandoned its neutral position in October 1963. Siding openly with Beijing, the party began purging its pro-Soviet members. On the left of the JSP, the *Heiwa Dōshikai* and increasingly the Sasaki faction came to be seen as the pro-China wing, in opposition to Eda and the 'structural reformers'. Right-wing JSP leaders took a public position leaning towards the Soviet side in the rift, while simultaneously describing it as a good opportunity to establish an independent, specifically 'Japanese way to Socialism'. Nevertheless, the JSP policy split was less profound than that of the JCP. Even on the right of the party a residual sympathy for China endured and—Beijing's accusations notwithstanding—the Socialists never stopped officially supporting diplomatic normalisation and trade with the mainland. Moreover, unlike the JCP, the JSP's pro-China wing conceded that the PTBT was a useful first step towards total nuclear disarmament. Later, when the balance of power within the JSP shifted in favour of the left wing, the still-divided party simply leaned to the other (Chinese) side, but the ideologically united JCP developed a genuine independence and autonomy.

By May 1964, the Communist Party had expelled its pro-Soviet faction, and within three months, the Soviets were openly supporting a breakaway JCP, the 'official' Japanese Communists having severed all ties to Moscow.

With the JSP and JCP both internally divided and aligned with opposite sides in the Sino-Soviet rift by mid-1964, conditions on the Japanese Left might have been expected to stabilise for a while thereafter. Yet, both parties underwent a further major realignment after 1964.

The alternative foreign policies proposed by Japan's opposition parties—the JSP's 'four-power pact' and the pro-Communist 'neutralism' advocated by the

JCP—were discredited by the virulence of the dispute that erupted between the 'peace-loving' Chinese and Soviets.

External environment: feedback

The support of the JCP was instrumental in helping the CCP to create an 'Asian Communist bloc'—although it was to prove short-lived—and thereby loosen Moscow's grip on its East Asian allies. Similarly, the JSP's links to Moscow helped to sustain Soviet interest in the Japanese Left, although they were not strong enough to survive the overthrow of Khrushchev. Later, JSP sympathy for China reduced the Socialist International's influence in Asia. Finally, by bringing *Gensuikyō* into disrepute, the rift helped to weaken the international nuclear disarmament movement.

8

Wishful thinking: Japan's public debate on the Sino-Soviet relationship, 1950–62

Even as the terms of the Sino-Soviet Pact were being negotiated in Moscow in early 1950, Japanese were busy debating the likely objective of the alliance, its durability, and the symmetry of the relationship as defined by the new treaty. The consensus among journalists was that Sino-Soviet cooperation appeared 'very solid for the time being', but that this was only because of Beijing's current economic dependence on Moscow. Citing Mao Zedong's unprecedented two-month stay in the Soviet Union as evidence of difficult relations, many predicted that Titoisation was only a matter of time.[1] Leftist intellectuals like Iwamura Michio, director of the pro-Beijing *Chūgoku Kenkyūjo* (China Research Institute), denounced such prophecies of 'rifts' (*tairitsu*) and 'discord' (*fuwa*) as the 'bad miscalculation…[of] Western European propaganda'.[2] Indeed, in contrast to the press, many intellectuals both 'progressive' and 'conservative', claimed that the Chinese and Soviets were now a 'strong coalition' (*teikei*) and even of 'one flesh' (*ittai*).[3]

A related issue was whether China would 'become the Soviet Union's satellite and subordinate, or an equal, independent country.'[4] Each view had its supporters. Those favouring the former emphasised the scale of Soviet economic assistance and concluded that 'independent action by Communist China is impossible'.[5] Those holding the latter view argued that contrary to their 'very generous' appearance, the agreements were in fact 'cold hearted' (*reikoku*) and even 'repressive'. Members of this group often stressed the strategic dimension. Iwamura, for example, claimed that the alliance was not one-sided, as the signatories were committed to mutual defence. This camp preferred to view the time consumed by negotiations as evidence that within the Communist bloc, the 'newly joined China has shown it has a separate existence a bit different from the Soviet Union's satellites in Eastern Europe'. The PRC, therefore, would 'not become the "Kremlin's servant"'.[6] *Asahi Shimbun*, the left-leaning daily, went even further, claiming that China was 'already considering itself the leader of the union of Socialist nations in Asia', and that Beijing thought that 'this union should be independent of the Soviet Union and should stand on an equal footing'.[7]

The third issue on which opinions were divided concerned the hypothetical enemy that the alliance targeted. Some, adopting a literal interpretation of the treaty, noted that it 'said nothing about a shield against America', and concluded that, 'Japan is clearly the target of the 30-year defence treaty.'[8] Those who saw the treaty as merely a 'revision' (*kaitei*) of Moscow's August 1945 alliance with Nationalist China agreed with this view.[9] Others like right-wing economist Kusano Fumio saw Japan as merely the 'number one masquerade enemy' and the US as the real 'military target'. This group quoted 'Western reports' which saw the treaty as 'aimed at obstructing US Far Eastern policy.'[10] One writer highlighted the connections between the two: while the treaty 'targets the US', he argued, the Communist allies were also using every means 'to expel the US from Japan' hoping thereby to 'intensify the Left–Right rift within Japan.'[11]

Finally, while the Left claimed that the treaty was defensive in nature and thus a contribution to peace, the majority of Japanese did not concur. On 21 February, a poll asked 949 Tokyo residents whether the Sino-Soviet Alliance would promote peace with Japan or not. Of the 70 per cent who were aware of its existence, one half felt that it was harmful, whereas only 13 per cent responded positively.[12] During the 1950s, such perception gaps were to prove remarkably resilient.

Korean War hiatus

For the next three years, the Sino-Soviet Alliance loomed in the background as the Korean War and Japan's own peace and security treaties came to dominate the news and Japanese popular debate.[13] The issues remained unaltered: vulnerability, parity and target. The occasional sensationalist report even hinted at deep-seated insecurities. In January 1952, the journal *Kaizō* claimed that the Sino-Soviet Alliance contained secret clauses which provided for the invasion of Japan by a 'Japanese Liberation Army' of former Japanese soldiers armed by the Soviets and trained by the Chinese.[14] Such scaremongering had little apparent effect on the wider Japanese public, however. Interestingly, in spring 1953, a further poll found that for every two respondents who expected the Democratic camp to split first, five saw the Communist bloc as the more vulnerable to schism.[15] Around this time, several analysts also predicted that China 'will become less subordinate' to the Soviet Union.[16] Satō Shinichirō, a long time China resident, interpreted

Chinese intervention in the Korean War as a failed attempt by Moscow and Beijing to divert the Chinese people from their 'anti-Soviet and anti-Communist sentiment.' He criticised the US embargo for driving the Chinese into the Soviet camp, and remained convinced that China 'wishe[d] for independence and autonomy'.[17] In perhaps the most detailed Japanese analysis of the alliance thus far, the *Sekai Mondai Kenkyūkai* (World Problems Research Association) in April 1953, similarly argued that because of its size and its independent revolution, China was not 'content as a satellite country.' Moreover, the authors claimed that 'the Soviet Union has a deep wariness of Communist China.' For them too, the role of the Korean War was crucial: '[Moscow] persuaded Communist China to participate in the Korean War…to force Chinese dependency on the Soviet Union' and thus 'the continuation of the Korean War…prolongs Soviet dominance.' Nevertheless, differing Chinese and Soviet cultural traditions, topography, and socio-economic systems, were said to have produced 'dormant contradictions' and 'the method of sublimating these resulted in extremely delicate relations (*kiwamete bimyōna kankei*).' The study predicted that, 'before long the "contradictions" between China and the Soviet Union would surface or strengthen.' Finally, the authors contrasted the diametrically opposite British and American strategies for dealing with the Sino-Soviet Alliance (soft versus hard wedge), but they dismissed both approaches as 'wishful thinking'. [18]

Those anticipating an early rift were now in a minority, however. Critic Tange Gorō conceded that 'Sino-Soviet relations do not necessarily seem perfectly friendly', but felt that their shared interest in Chinese industrialisation meant that they would probably contain their differences for at least one and perhaps even two decades.[19] Foreign affairs commentator and former diplomat Hirasawa Kazushige, agreed that it was 'hardly conceivable that Communist China will be the "Tito" of the Orient at least not within ten years.'[20] Respected academics like Professor Ōhira Zengo (Hitotsubashi University) also contended that 'At present, Communist China can be called the most faithful, effective, genuine, model satellite of the Kremlin.'[21] According to Chinese economics expert Ishikawa Shigeru, one's views on the subject depended on one's background. Those who saw 'Communist China perfectly following Soviet policy' tended to be Soviet specialists, whereas the prevailing view of China researchers was that 'Communist Chinese nationalists are conscious of the rift in interests.'[22] Ishikawa's contention was no more than a rule of thumb, however. One notable exception was China analyst (and long-time former China resident) Takeda Nanyō, who argued that Western expectations of Mao's Titoisation were mistaken, as China was becoming 'more Sovietised (*Sorenka*) with every passing year.' In evidence he cited the wholesale destruction of Chinese military, economic and political traditions and in particular a series of military and economic agreements concluded during Zhou Enlai's visit to Moscow in August 1952. Still, he conceded that the Chinese people remained the final arbiters of China's fate.[23] Written during the war in neighbouring Korea, not surprisingly these early analyses often exaggerated the strength of the Sino-Soviet bond. Although a healthy measure of scepticism endured in some quarters, this all but disappeared over the next few years.

The Sino-Soviet Alliance renewed

In early 1954, Sano Hiroshi (president of the Japan Political and Economic Research Institute) noted the existence of factional rivalry within the CCP, and its establishment of ties to Asian Communist Parties independent from those of the CPSU. From this, he concluded that: Sino-Soviet relations were 'not so amicable as they appear.'[24] For most Japanese observers, however, the Sino-Soviet Joint Declaration of October 1954 confirmed the solidarity of the Communist allies.[25] Left-wing economist Takahashi Masao (Kyūshū University) felt the declaration made it clear that 'China cannot simply be a satellite of the Soviet Union.' Takahashi cited a recent report in the *Asahi Shimbun* in support of his argument. Following the lead of the British press, the paper's London correspondent had reported that 'the causes of Sino-Soviet conflicts (*funsō*)...are being removed one by one, and any attempt to estrange (*rikan*) the two countries is no more than an illusion, at least under present circumstances.'[26] Tachibana Yoshinori (*Mainichi Shimbun*) went so far as to state that they were 'inseparable (*hikihanasenai mono*). More than inseparable, they cannot easily resist being drawn closer together. The wishful thinking has become the reality.' Despite this, Tachibana believed that 'essentially Sino-Soviet policy towards Japan is unchanged.'[27]

The issue of the alliance's objectives was never far from the surface. One expert on Marxism, Hirano Yoshitarō, claimed that its 'main concern was no longer stopping an invasion from Japan but from the US imperialists.' However, the political commentator Maki Tadashi felt that its 'number one aim is to divide Japan and the US.' In a rather peculiar contribution, an editorial on the joint declaration in the *Mainichi Shimbun*, another popular daily, argued that 'Sino-Soviet relations should be much closer (*missetsu*) than Japan–US relations.'[28]

Public opinion was not consulted in this period on the state of Sino-Soviet relations, but a November 1954 poll indicated the scale of the continuing difference in Japanese perceptions of China and the Soviet Union. Both Communist states were on balance 'disliked', but the degree to which the Soviet Union was 'disliked' was clearly much greater.[29]

The debate waned somewhat once Hatoyama Ichirō replaced Yoshida Shigeru as premier, and set about trying to normalise relations with the two Communist giants. In these circumstances, only occasional comments on the alliance's prospects appeared.[30] Throughout Hatoyama's tenure, all discussion remained future-oriented; that is to say, even those who highlighted Sino-Soviet differences tended to assert that their impact would become clear only later.

While the Japanese press showed considerable interest in reports of Khrushchev's secret speech at the 20th CPSU Congress in February 1956, there was no immediate appreciation of its long-term consequences for relations with Beijing. As the Japan–Soviet peace negotiations were approaching their climax that summer, a right-wing think-tank founded in early 1952, the *Tairiku Mondai Kenkyūjo* (the Continental Problems Institute or *Taiken*), published a major study of post-war Sino-Soviet relations highlighting their areas of disagreement on Japan policy. Its major conclusion was that, 'Differing Sino-Soviet intentions concerning peace negotiations with Japan might produce a rift.'[31] The institute's director, Doi Akio, a former army general, confirmed these impressions. Having met with Mao Zedong and other leaders on a month-long visit to China in August, Doi reported that 'they absolutely never criticised the Soviet Union'. Nevertheless, he also noted: 'Communist China...is trying hard to show and make other countries believe that she is by no means a dependency of the Soviet Union, but a fine independent country on a par with it.'[32]

China specialist Takenaka Shigehisa, went even further, claiming in September that, 'anti-Soviet feelings are still dominant in the hearts of the Chinese people and may explode at any moment.'[33] Two months later, *Chūō Kōron*, an important intellectual monthly, published a debate on 'How Communist China Differs from the Soviet Union'. One of the contributors, Inoki Masamichi (Kyōto University), a leading centrist political thinker, expressed his admiration for China's Socialist construction to the extent that it differed from the Soviet model.[34] The following month, an article by the much more left-wing Yamakawa Hitoshi—founder of the pre-war *Rōnō-ha* (Labour–Farmer Faction) and the post-war *Shakaishugi Kyōkai* (Socialist Association)—supported Inoki's conclusion noting: 'In China, a Socialist government different from that of the Soviet Union has come into being and the construction of Socialism is being carried out in a different way'.[35] Similarly, *Sekai*, another significant intellectual monthly, had published in November an analysis of de-Stalinisation by the progressive intellectual Maruyama Masao. He too recognised the fact that not all Communists took their orders from Moscow, hence the need to examine 'Communist movements...in terms of the interaction between them and the given political situations'. In an important postscript added early in 1957, Maruyama was perhaps the first Japanese to borrow a term coined by the Italian Communist leader Palmiro Togliatti in June 1956 to describe the Communist movement after the 20th CPSU Congress. Maruyama forecast that 'if the Cold War should again ebb, it will be impossible to stop the Socialist countries...from following the course of polycentrism (*tasūchūshintaisei*)'.[36]

Such views, however, were by this time in danger of being overtaken by events. The Soviet invasion of Hungary on 4 November came as another painful blow for Japanese Marxist intellectuals. It too inspired a brief flurry of articles speculating on the negative implications for Sino-Soviet relations. According to the US Embassy in Tokyo:

> the Japanese press, by and large, has chosen to depend on its own imagination to deduce that Communist China is competing actively with Russia for influence in Asia, and is aloof from, if not opposed to Russian suppression of its satellites in Europe.[37]

Despite Beijing's public support for Moscow's drastic action, academics like Ōno Shinzō (Meiji University) felt certain that 'Communist China has inwardly hailed the counterrevolutions in Eastern Europe.'[38] Others pointed out how 'Recently, China's nationalistic tendency has increased remarkably compared to her unconditional 'learn from the Soviet Union' policy of the past'. Yet, it was conceded that, 'At present, there are no signs of any large-scale anti-Soviet riots breaking out in China.'[39]

The following month, January 1957, Doi Akio described the way in which Chinese and Soviet nationalisms collided militarily, economically, and territorially. He now claimed his visit to China had clearly reaffirmed for him that 'the Chinese people hate and despise the Russians'. Moreover, while conceding that Mao's commitment to world Communisation rendered a Sino-Soviet split unlikely at that stage, as a realist he argued that logically such a rift could only be to Japan's advantage and therefore its promotion should form the basis of national policy.[40] Doi's institute contended that a conciliatory speech by Mao on 27 February was only 'aimed at camouflaging the friction between Communist China and the Soviet Union' and in reality provided evidence that it was now impossible for them to reach agreement on the major questions at issue.'[41] This was still very much a minority view, however, with most analysts believing that Sino-Soviet ties were strengthening. Hatano Kenichi (*Sankei Shimbun*) was among those who interpreted Zhou Enlai's post-Hungary visit to Moscow and Eastern Europe as a sign that the Communist bloc had been reunited, and anticipated future joint Sino-Soviet action on policy towards Japan.[42]

Not surprisingly, a March special issue of *Chūō Kōron* examining Japanese reactions to de-Stalinisation failed to produce a consensus. While Okuma Nobuyuki (Kanazawa University) praised the process as a positive development for having 'made access to Socialism easier for Japanese intellectuals', critic Oya Soichi concluded that it had 'dealt a fatal blow to the JCP and many [Marxist] intellectuals.'[43]

The next 18 months saw the signature of new Sino-Soviet accords in the fields of science and technology, commerce and navigation, as well as the 12-nation Moscow Declaration of November 1957. The tone of Japanese press accounts reflected these alliance-reinforcing developments. Even the anti-Communist *Soren Mondai Kenkyūkai* (Soviet Problems Research Association or *Soken*) followed this trend. In November, Komuro Makoto, the director of two small international relations research associations, concluded:

> We cannot find any sign from analysing Sino-Soviet relations that something unusual will take place in their currently cooperative relations...Their alliance lost its main objective because of the restoration of relations between Japan and the Soviet Union last year, but its spirit remains unchanged.[44]

Despite such developments in the Sino-Soviet relationship, Japanese popular attitudes towards the Communist allies were little altered. A poll taken at that time confirmed that respondents still 'disliked' both countries more than they 'liked' them, although the gap remained much more substantial in the Soviet case.[45] However, some of the ambiguity that lay behind Japanese attitudes was revealed in the results of another—openly racist—poll conducted for *Sōrifu* (the Prime Minister's Office) in autumn 1958. When asked which peoples they considered 'superior', 20 per cent of respondents named Russians, which placed them slightly ahead of the French, if well behind Germans and Americans. Chinese garnered a mere nine per cent, roughly equivalent to Jews and Indians.[46]

During the mid-1950s, conspicuously few scholars attempted to analyse Sino-Soviet differences. The Japanese media and intellectual mainstream generally portrayed a Communist alliance in robust health. From 1958 to 1960, the balance of opinion shifted slightly, although any disagreements were still seen as confined to tactics.

Speculation on Sino-Soviet differences

During the first half of 1958, the few relevant articles appearing in the media focused on the relative merits of the Chinese and Soviet propaganda campaigns in the run-up to the Japanese general election on 22 May.[47] This changed somewhat following Beijing's virtual abandonment of its 'people's diplomacy' approach to Japan after the Nagasaki Flag Incident of 2 May. *Nihon Keizai Shimbun*, the business daily, was not alone in recognising that the Soviet Union and Communist China 'differ in the way they approach our country.'[48] Media speculation concerning Sino-Soviet foreign policy differences was further stimulated by the Middle Eastern Crisis of mid-July, Khrushchev's visit to Beijing at the end of that month, and Mao's subsequent provocation of the second Taiwan Straits Crisis. In mid-August, *Asahi Shimbun* noted what the philosopher Isaac Deutscher saw as Sino-Soviet 'discord' over the Middle East, but subsequent headlines proclaimed a 'new stage in Sino-Soviet relations', in which there was agreement on 'common interests' and 'differences of opinion are not fundamental.'[49] The following month, *Soren Kenkyū* also conceded that in Beijing, Khrushchev and Mao had reconciled their foreign policy differences, but nevertheless felt that 'differences of ideology, organisation, stage of development and national traditions are still lurking in the background'.[50]

By the end of the year, Amō Eiji, head of the recently established *Soren Kenkyūsha Kyōgikai* (Council of Sovietologists), declared: 'I do not think that at present their rivalry is so open, but I must admit the trend is in that direction.'[51] Ishikawa Tadao (Keiō University), a respected China expert, likewise noted:

> Most observers seem to agree that the [Beijing] conference demonstrates that China has...considerable influence over Soviet foreign policy...[But] while there certainly are differences of opinion between the two countries, there is no likelihood that China's independent tendencies will destroy the solidarity between them.[52]

In January 1959, the *Soken* published a 'New Year Questionnaire', which for the first time included a question asking whether Soviet and Chinese foreign policies were different. Among the 48 respondents—a mostly right-wing mixture of politicians, journalists, businessmen, veterans, academics, critics, and self-proclaimed 'experts'—the majority view held that while differences existed, they were 'tactical' rather than 'strategic' in nature. However, approximately one third remained convinced that there were no discrepancies between Moscow and Beijing whatsoever.[53]

During most of 1959, the Japanese were inundated with a barrage of intense Sino-Soviet propaganda against revision of the Japan–US Security Treaty, and appear to have forgotten the supposed disputes over tactics within the Communist bloc. Even *Soren Kenkyū* rediscovered its earlier scepticism. In April, it noted that the Soviet Union was 'unhappy at the increase in Communist China's relative importance', but dismissed a loosening of ties as 'overly optimistic'.[54]

It was not until the beginning of September that a detailed Japanese analysis of the causes of the 'Sino-Soviet leadership struggle' was first articulated. The occasion was a seminar on the Communist bloc organised by the recently renamed *Ōa Kyōkai* (Society for the Study of Communism in Europe and Asia, formerly the *Soren Kenkyūsha Kyōgikai*). A paper by Inoki Masamichi dated 'the beginning of a clear divergence between Soviet and Chinese policy towards the US' from the Second Taiwan Straits Crisis a year earlier. He offered six reasons to explain this development, including the independent nature of the Chinese Revolution; its relative youth compared to the Bolshevik Revolution; the gap between first generation (Chinese) and second generation (Soviet) revolutionary leaders, and their differing 'state interests (*shutāto rezon*)'. At the same time, he blamed US Cold War policy for helping to preserve their solidarity. On the significance of Sino-Soviet ideological differences, Inoki asserted that, 'because Stalinism has been revised to a degree there is an ideological rift (*ideorogiiteki tairitsu*)'. Inoki did not foresee this 'becoming a big obstacle', however, since he believed that their differing 'cultural traditions and social structures' were more important. His old classmate, Seki Yoshihiko (Tokyo Metropolitan University) felt that Inoki exaggerated the Chinese desire for independence, but overall most participants seemed to agree with Takahashi Masao's (Kyūshū University) view that 'international Communism's monolithic unity is just public relations'.[55]

Doi Akira (Daitō Bunka University), in a paper on economic relations, contended that while Moscow and Beijing had 'reached some agreement regarding Communist China's method of economic construction', there was still 'a possibility of the two countries clashing over their foreign policies.' He felt that China aimed to overturn the international status quo accepted by the USSR, but was constrained by its economic dependence on Moscow. Still, Doi sensed that 'both firmly believe in Marxism–Leninism. It is too early therefore, to conclude that confrontation between the two countries will be intensified.'[56]

By mid-October, Khrushchev's departure from Beijing without issuing a joint-communiqué and the subsequent replacement of the Soviet Ambassador to China prompted intense speculation in the Western media that something was seriously amiss in the Sino-Soviet relationship. In Japan too, the mainstream media began to address the issue, albeit in less dramatic terms.[57] Staff at *Asahi Shimbunsha* offered conflicting views on the subject. The newspaper had earlier hinted at future troubles: one article from mid-August focused on perceived Chinese dissatisfaction with Soviet aid, while another discussed China's rise 'from subordination to interdependence'.[58] Now, however, its London correspondent wondered whether they had reached an understanding on peaceful coexistence and the communiqué was merely postponed. The head of its Hong Kong bureau replied that a wedge had been inserted into Sino-Soviet cooperation.[59] The following day, *Asahi Jānaru*, the paper's recently established intellectual weekly, published a more cautious appraisal. The author suggested the Soviet leader's demeanour might be explained not by any 'discord with Beijing' but rather by the fact that, 'in Communist China, a Soviet ally, Khrushchev felt no need to swagger as he did in the US'. The article conceded that there was 'a subtle difference between Beijing and Moscow's approaches to the peace issue because of their very different international positions', but nevertheless it predicted that China would soon fall into line with Soviet policy.[60] Takaichi Keinosuke, an economic news reporter, likewise accepted Communist statements at face value: 'All in all, the Soviet Union and China are continuing their efforts to consolidate their brotherly unity'.[61] In contrast, Shioguchi Kiichi, from the political news division of *Asahi Shimbun*, believed that, unlike China, the Soviet Union was 'now tending to favour policies which would bring about a relaxation in international tensions'.[62]

Mainichi Shimbun also lacked an agreed 'company line'. Hayashi Takuo of the political news division dismissed the 'numerous reports saying that Communist China and the Soviet Union are presently at loggerheads with each other...[as] only wishful thinking on the part of the West.'[63] Arai Takeo, a sub-editor in the foreign news department, agreed.[64] However, the head of the department, Watanabe Zenichirō, seemed less certain, conceding the difficulties in understanding the Sino-Soviet relationship. Nevertheless, he pointed out that the removal of two former ambassadors to Moscow from their posts at the head of the People's Liberation Army, suggested that the relationship was not 'as good as Khrushchev declared.'[65] The views of the diplomatic critic Harako Rinjirō were more radical. In October 1959, he agreed that the basis of Sino-Soviet problems lay in their differing assessments of the status quo. Yet, Harako cleverly used the very lack of firm evidence to argue that 'The gravity of their rift lies in the fact that it must be kept concealed and that neither side can make unilateral concessions for its settlement.'[66]

During the first half of 1960, while the *Anpo* crisis gripped Japan, most commentators on the state of the Communist alliance tended to follow the same sceptical line. The Japanese Left was finally goaded into action by the gleeful tone of Western press reports of growing estrangement. Marukawa Tatsuo (*Asahi Shimbun*) expressed a typical view: 'The hysterical journalism of the West has been playing up the "intensification of the Sino-Soviet rift", but we cannot trust them as they are promoting their own interests.'[67] *Chūō Kōron* meanwhile published an anonymous article which noted that, 'Within the last one or two months...wishful thinking such as Titoisation in China or Sino-Soviet estrangement (*rihan*) which had concealed itself for the past few years...has [re]appeared.' It conceded that, 'one can read into Chinese and Soviet analyses of international conditions and the way they respond to international problems a subtle difference...[especially] in their attitudes towards the US.' However, the article concluded that this reflected 'China's exclusion from the stage of international diplomacy', and the gap between Soviet 'realism' and China's 'greater faith in principles.'[68]

Even on the Right, most analysts continued to understate Communist disagreements. When the *Soken* sent out its 1960 'New Year Questionnaire', it specifically asked: 'How long will Sino-Soviet brotherly unity (*kyōdaiteki danketsu*) continue?' Replies ranged from 'not long' to 'forever', but the majority thought it would last at least 'for the foreseeable future'. No one believed that it had already died, although some questioned the aptness of the adjective 'brotherly'. Two factors stood out in the reasons given for the relationship's survival—Cold War security and Beijing's economic dependence on Moscow. Conversely, the ending of the Cold War (whether through the victory of Communism, capitalism, or some reconciliation between the two), or China's acquisition of substantial economic, military and/or political power were both seen as threats to Sino-Soviet unity.[69] Similarly, a comparative study of Chinese and Soviet policies towards Japan produced by the *Taiken* in May, concluded that they probably agreed on the 'main direction of policy, but there [we]re some tactical differences.'[70] It is also noteworthy that many intellectuals in the West shared this assessment at the time.[71]

Dissenting from the majority view, one respondent to the *Soken* questionnaire, economist Kiga Kenzō (Keiō University), published an analysis of how Japanese *should* view the rift. He first explained how differing domestic political conditions and international circumstances had combined to produce a three-dimensional rift: ideological (over the socio-economic developmental stages necessary to achieve Communism); strategic (over handling of the 'imperialists'); and political (over leadership of developing as well as Communist states.) Consequently, he warned that Japan had to come to terms with a rising China, before concluding that a Sino-Soviet conflict (*funsō*) was a good thing.[72] Kiga was ahead of his time. Most Japanese continued to minimise the scope and scale of Sino-Soviet disagreements.

The beginning of open controversy

From mid-April 1960, a series of Chinese and Soviet articles published to commemorate Lenin's 90th birthday highlighted the differences between each of their thinking on the inevitability of war. This culminated in open disagreement at the Bucharest Conference in late June, although both parties refrained from attacking each other by name. Japanese interest in the problems affecting Sino-Soviet relations was suitably stimulated. At the beginning of July, *Asahi Shimbun* printed a three-part article on the dispute (*ronsō*). The analysis contained little that was new, but was significant in that this was the first time a Japanese national newspaper had directly broached the subject and thereby enlightened a wider public. Part one noted the emergence of a 'subtle rift (*bimyōna tairitsu*)', but added that the same phenomenon was observed in the mid-1950s. Part two pointed out the dangers in emphasising Sino-Soviet differences over their similarities: 'Different national conditions gave rise to divergences in foreign policies', but their 'ultimate objective' remained unchanged. Finally, *Asahi* recognised Anglo-American differences of interpretation over events at Bucharest, and hence recommended adopting a 'cautious attitude.'[73]

That same day, 5 July, two members of the *Taiken*, Hamano Masami and Shishikura Toshirō, also published an article examining the current state of 'the ideological dispute (*ideorogii ronsō*)'. They blamed its existence on 'differences in their developmental stages and international positions', and concluded that, 'one cannot expect a fundamental resolution of their rift in the near future'. It was equally 'unthinkable that the present dispute will develop into the estrangement (*rikan*) of the two nations, nor will the Soviets restrict or suspend aid to Beijing.'[74] A few weeks later, Hamano was forced to 'think the unthinkable', when Moscow did precisely that. Although believing that such a development was 'contrary to common sense', Hamano recognised Moscow's action as one of several 'signs of Sino-Soviet estrangement'. He now conceded that 'a rift is of course possible', but still not necessarily inevitable.[75]

With each succeeding issue of *Soren Kenkyū*, belief in the seriousness of the rift strengthened. In July, after examining the Lenin birthday articles, the journal found 'unconvincing' the argument that despite tactical differences there remained a fundamental unity between the two. It therefore rejected the right-wing theory that the whole thing was somehow a 'most ingenious Communist plot.' In August, *Soren Kenkyū* supported 'the theory that there is a tendency towards the rift coming into the open'. And by September, having digested the results of Bucharest, it concluded that 'the recent ideological dispute has had a big influence on Sino-Soviet relations.'[76]

In an effort to harness non-governmental expertise on East Asian international relations, in mid-August, the new Ikeda cabinet invited some of those intellectuals most interested in the emerging Sino-Soviet rift to join a 36-member Foreign Policy Problems Deliberation Council (*Gaikō Mondai Kondankai*). A prime focus was to be recent changes in China.[77] The symposium convened on 13 occasions during its six-month life span, but proved incapable of reaching agreement on any policy recommendations.[78]

However, the following month, September 1960, two important articles were published that represented a major step forward in Japanese understanding of the dispute. In the first, Maeshiba Kakuzō, a long-time Soviet expert, declared that the dispute was 'in reality directly and indirectly related to international politics' because it centred on the issue of war and peace. Maeshiba then offered a detailed study of points in contention between China and the Soviet Union, before claiming that his analysis had 'confirmed the real alienation (*sokaku*) in Sino-Soviet relations'.[79] Eguchi Bokurō (Tokyo University), a noted Marxist historian, agreed that the rift was related to international political conditions, but pointed out that there had been a natural 'gap between Chinese and Soviet opinions from the beginning'. However, Eguchi warned against a 'mechanistic understanding' of the rift as a one-way process 'simply leading to a split (*bunretsu*)'. He cautioned readers that the rift was no longer just 'a fire over the sea (*taigan no kaji*)', but a 'problem we [Japanese] must deal with.'[80]

Late summer 1960 thus marked the first peak in Japanese interest in the escalating Sino-Soviet dispute. It was notable for the way in which a few insightful scholars attempted to go beyond the confines of the 'ideological dispute' (*ideorogii ronsō*) model.

The Lake Kawaguchi Conference and after

For Japanese students of the rift, undoubtedly the highlight of 1960 was the 'Third International Conference of Sovietologists and Sinologists', which opened on 18 September. Organised by *Ōa Kyōkai*, the conference attracted nearly 50 of the non-Communist world's leading experts on Sino-Soviet relations to Lake Kawaguchi, Hakone, near Tokyo.[81] The Sino-Soviet dispute dominated proceedings.[82]

Japanese researchers authored 12 of the 38 papers delivered during the weeklong conference. Those by Onoe Masao (Kōbe University), Hirota Yōji, Kiga Kenzō, and Ishikawa Tadao were among the most interesting.[83] Onoe examined the 'factors binding the USSR and Communist China'. While recognising there was a 'difference in methodology and foreign policy concepts', he felt that Beijing's continuing dependence on Moscow for technical and economic aid, as well as national defence, would 'eventually force Communist China to adjust to the position of the Kremlin.'[84] Hirota (managing director of *Ōa Kyōkai*) took an opposing line, emphasising the 'fissures (*kiretsu*)' in Sino-Soviet relations. However, while he described their differences as 'very fundamental', Hirota deduced that they amounted in Maoist terms to a 'non-antagonistic contradiction': concluding therefore that, 'the probability that the fissures will lead to a complete rupture (*ketsuretsu bunri*) is very small.'[85] Kiga's paper—a reworking of his February article—took a more balanced approach. Going a step further, Kiga here claimed that there was 'now a rift (*tairitsu*) in the international Communist movement, Communist China and the Soviet Union are two countries with their own leaders.' Again, he saw the conflict of interests between an established power and a rising power as the basis of this rift. Still, in the short-term Kiga predicted that, '[Communist China] would not split the Communist monolith'.[86] Similarly, in his examination of 'Communist China's Japan policy', Ishikawa Tadao noted the 'subtle differences' between Chinese and Soviet negotiating methods, but felt that 'the split (*bunretsu*) between them will not necessarily lead to a fundamental rift (*tairitsu*) in their views.'[87]

One session was devoted specifically to 'the Communist bloc and Japan' and with one exception all the papers were presented by Japanese. One Western expert observed how 'most of the Japanese participants seemed to feel that Japan did indeed occupy a special place in the whole picture of Communist strategy, particularly that of Communist China.'[88] The only non-Japanese to offer a paper in this section, Paul Langer (University of Southern California), clearly shared this assessment. He described how from 1958 to 1960, Communist China and the Soviet Union 'seem to have acted toward Japan largely without reference to each other, as separate entities rather than as members of a single "socialist bloc"'. He analysed in detail the 'different conceptual base' that lay behind their 'distinctly divergent strategies' towards Japan, and the much greater importance China assigned to the 'Japan question'. Nevertheless Langer still concluded that, 'there has been no outward sign of a Moscow–Peking conflict over policy toward Japan'. Instead, he posited the existence of 'a natural...division of labor between Moscow and Peking', believing that they still shared 'a parallelism of interest insofar as elimination of US influence in Japan...w[as] concerned.'[89] Overall, however, many of those present noted a distinct methodological difference between the Western and Asian (including Japanese) scholars:

> Generally speaking, the representatives of Japan, India, and Hong Kong asserted that it is impossible to understand China's actions without considering her racial characteristics and traditions...The European participants, including the Britons and Americans, however, approached the subject from an ideological viewpoint alone. The orientals showed a willingness to understand the human aspects of Communist China's policies, but the occidentals took a stern attitude towards Beijing, in contrast to their relative leniency towards Moscow.[90]

It should therefore come as no surprise that the conference failed to produce an assessment of the Sino-Soviet Alliance acceptable to all participants:

> The broad consensus of opinion was that the divergence of views between the Soviet Union and Communist China is a reality...The conference did not always agree, however, as to the precise reasons for the differences, their sources and their implications.[91]

On a much smaller scale, the *Taiken* held an internal round-table discussion on Sino-Soviet relations later that month. After reviewing the most recent evidence, this group concluded that the surfacing of the ideological dispute, observed since late spring, had 'finally waned in September'. Still, it cautioned that without 'a basic compromise...the possibility exists that it will flare up again.' Asked about its influence on Japan, one member pointed to a potential increase in Sino-Japanese trade, but Chairman Doi Akio complained that, 'Japan is not handling the current Sino-Soviet dispute very well.'[92]

In November, *Sekai* published an anonymous article, marking the first occasion on which this 'progressive' journal entered the Sino-Soviet dispute debate. The article offered two interpretations of recent Sino-Soviet thinking on 'war and peace': either 'Both sides' theoretical views are basically the same, but naturally there are differences of emphasis and different ways to promote foreign policy', or, the disparity reflected 'something a little deeper'. Unfortunately, the author was unable to reach a satisfactory conclusion, not only declaring 'neither to be wholly correct', but also refusing to choose between the two explanations.[93]

Also in November, Zhou Jingwen, a Hong Kong based exile from the Communist regime, was more forthright in his deductions, bluntly informing his Japanese readership that, 'China and the Soviet Union are one, there is no rift, and a split is impossible.'[94] In response, Jin Xiongbo, another Chinese writing in the same Japanese weekly, declared that the 'Sino-Soviet secret feud (*antō*) continues', but nonetheless he still shared the near universal view that 'Communist China and the Soviet Union cannot break away from each other. Thus, Sino-Soviet relations will be characterised not by war or peace, but by cold war'.[95] Shortly thereafter, the brief burst of Japanese media interest in Sino-Soviet relations that had characterised the latter half of 1960 faded.

Hibernation resumed

By November 1960, representatives from 81 Communist and workers' parties had gathered for the Moscow Conference. After some heated exchanges, they produced the Moscow Statement: a 20,000-word compromise mostly supporting the Soviet line.[96] With both sides subsequently refraining from public polemics, few Japanese studies of the escalating dispute appeared during the next two years.

The Moscow Statement in fact came as no surprise to Onoe Masao, who at Lake Kawaguchi three months earlier had anticipated Moscow getting its way in the dispute. Onoe now thought that 'the Sino-Soviet ideological dispute has for the present come to a halt', but he insisted on the continuing existence of 'the disparity in their real conditions, internal and external, that produced the difference in policy'.[97] *Asahi Jānaru* also felt the fact that the conference had dragged on for three weeks was indicative of serious problems. The journal characterised the dispute in terms of Soviet 'revisionism' versus Chinese 'dogmatism', and following 'the general conclusion of most foreign correspondents', it predicted that 'in future the dispute (*ronsō*) will continue.'[98]

Members of an anonymous round-table discussion in the weekly *Ekonomisuto* reached the same conclusion. Moreover, it was suggested that Chinese influence on Japan was growing stronger, and as a result the 'labour movement and peace movement will descend into conflict'.[99]

The following month, Kiuchi Nobutane, whose *Gaikō Mondai Kondankai* was about to break up for lack of agreement on China policy, offered a very different assessment of the situation. A firm believer in the 'Communist monolith' theory, Kiuchi warned that the Soviet Union was 'trying to disturb the peace of the world', and that Communist China was 'its accomplice.'[100] This was very much the minority view by this time, however, even on the Right. The 1961 'New Year Questionnaire' from *Soken*, to which both Kiuchi and Onoe responded, this time asked: 'Can the ideological rift (*ronsōteki tairitsu*) between Communist China and the Soviet Union be resolved?' Of the 39 replies received, those answering in the negative outnumbered those who denied that there was any rift by a ratio of three to one. Admittedly, many of the former felt that a temporary or superficial settlement was possible.[101]

On the 'revisionist left' meanwhile, a few commentators bravely dared to declare the dispute a positive development. The first to do so was most likely Ōki Masato. In January 1961, he argued that the time had come to 'again creatively "revise" Marxism', and hence, 'the current "Sino-Soviet dispute" offers a very good opportunity and stimulus.' Ōki recognised that 'the imperialist camp sees even the slightest cracks in the Socialist bloc's unity as a big advance', but he rejected the simplistic interpretation given to events by the 'commercial newspapers'. For Ōki, the dispute was not an argument over 'peaceful coexistence or peaceful revolution'—as the media proclaimed—for Beijing had never denied either possibility, rather it was a debate over the 'true nature of modern imperialism', and this concerned Japan too.[102] The following month, Satō Noboru, the famous Socialist intellectual—soon to be expelled from the JCP along with the 'structural reform faction'—published an article calling for 'thorough, democratic discussion' rather than 'unprincipled compromise'.[103] He 'doubted' whether the Moscow Statement could 'solve the so-called Sino-Soviet dispute totally...[as] some theoretical problems remain'. Yet, Satō remained optimistic, believing that 'the international Communist movement can get over this transition period and can still hope to advance.'[104]

For the most part, the same familiar voices sustained the low-level Japanese debate on the Sino-Soviet rift during the fallow years of 1961–2. An exception was the well-known internationalist, Matsumoto Shigeharu (director of *Kokusai Bunka Kaikan* or International House of Japan). In April 1961, the liberal intellectual journal *Jiyū*, published a discussion between Matsumoto, Paul Langer and Fukui Fumio (*Asahi Shimbun*). The American first suggested that the Moscow

Statement represented a 'compromise' between the Soviet Union and China and that 'unless Khrushchev succeeds in his policy of peaceful coexistence, the hard-line policy of Communist China will again come to the fore.' For Langer, the period since November amounted to 'a new era' for the Communist bloc. Matsumoto agreed, and criticised the Japanese press for 'not fully recognising the importance of the Moscow Statement', as well as Japanese intellectuals for 'interpreting it in a favourable light for Communist China.'[105] Six months later, however, Matsumoto seemed to have reconsidered this view, writing that:

> while China and the Soviet Union have recently pursued independent foreign policy lines and revealed differences in their attitudes to the rest of the world, both are mainstays of the Communist bloc and remain firmly bound together in the strongest alliance the world has ever seen…[Hence] Japan's relations with both countries must be considered together.[106]

Likewise, Doi Akio reversed his position on the rift during 1961, briefly supporting Matsumoto's cautious approach for Japan. In May, Doi warned those who saw the rift as an opportunity to draw one or other of the Communist powers into the Western camp that such an exercise would not be simple. 'China and the Soviet Union would both feel good if Japan became Communist', he claimed, and thus Japan should not relax its vigilance.[107]

In the wake of the Moscow Statement, the Japanese debate on the Sino-Soviet rift made little headway, handicapped as it was by U-turns on the Right (and in the centre) and misplaced optimism on the Left.

Proxy warfare

In mid-1961, *Soren Kenkyū* saw a number of Sino-Soviet developments as affirming the discord between the two powers. In June, Moscow and Beijing signed a number of agreements on economic, scientific, and technical cooperation, but the following month they concluded separate alliances with North Korea. Meanwhile, the dispute continued by proxy, with Albania and Yugoslavia taking the parts of China and the Soviet Union respectively. *Soren Kenkyū* nonetheless rejected the view that the rift had gone beyond 'ideological contradictions' and become a 'power struggle between ordinary states'. It dismissed the idea that there was an 'absolute rift' as 'wishful thinking'.[108]

Following the open break between the Soviets and Albanians at the 22nd CPSU Congress in October, the critic Harako Rinjirō recognised that the Kremlin had made Albania into a scapegoat for China. He believed that while 'the Sino-Soviet ideological dispute remains under a truce...parallel to this, it is becoming increasingly clear that there is a Sino-Soviet struggle for hegemony over the world

Communist movement.' In Harako's view the 'only people who still deny the reality of the Sino-Soviet dispute are a few extremely thick-skinned Communists.' Also critical of both the Soviet and Chinese positions, Harako asserted that for Japan, faced with the prospect of Chinese nuclear weapons, 'the Sino-Soviet dispute can no longer be viewed as a fire over the sea (*taigan no kaji*)'.[109] Three months later, Harako pronounced the once popular expression, 'Moscow–Beijing axis (*sūjiku*)' to be part of a 'dead language'. He was now convinced that the 'basis of the Sino-Soviet rift was the discord between their national interests.'[110]

The 1962 *Soken* 'New Year Questionnaire' reflected the shifting nature of the rift by asking 'What is the real intention behind Stalin's excommunication (*tsuihō*) and the criticism of Albania?' 20 of the 48 respondents asserted that Albania was effectively a synonym for China.[111] The following month, one of this number, Watanabe Mikio (*Mainichi Shimbun*), cited both the national interest and ideological origins of the rift: 'Moscow and Beijing are unmistakably divided over their views on the status quo in the contemporary world and their interpretation of Leninism…the Beijing–Moscow road is meandering with national and racial differences sharply protruding at many points'. Still he discounted the 'possibility of a head-on Sino-Soviet collision'.[112]

As the 12th anniversary of the Sino-Soviet Alliance passed with a continuing lull in polemics, the Conservative *Japan Times*—doyen of Japan's English language press—joined the debate. Its editorial of 15 February, acknowledged that the recent 'lack of harmony' amounted to more than 'wishful thinking', but warned that the rift had been 'exaggerated'. However, like Watanabe it concluded that 'it would be foolish for the free nations to think that any strong wedge has been driven into relations between the two Communist powers'.[113] Three days later, the commentator Saitō Chū offered a rather different assessment in the same paper. He claimed that the split between the two Communist powers 'now seems too grave to put up a facade of unity and consolidation'. More unusually, Saitō also expressed 'serious doubts as to whether the break-up of the Communist camp could favorably affect the future of the Far East.' In common with some US State Department officers, he worried lest the loss of Soviet restraint upon China might ultimately lead to nuclear war.[114] A third article appeared a few weeks later suggesting that the rift was damaging Japanese popular perceptions of China. The evidence of the *Jiji* public opinion polls at that time does not support this contention at the national level (Figure 8.1). However, it is worth noting that the author cited 'the leftists who were banished from the JCP' as one of his sources for this line of thinking.[115]

Spring 1962 saw the first signs of intensifying Sino-Soviet propaganda competition vis-à-vis Japan. After an abortive attempt to conclude an agreement on cultural relations in early April, Moscow surprised Tokyo by announcing that

Yuri Gagarin, the first man in space, would undertake a goodwill visit to Japan in May.[116] Later that year, the Soviets opened an information office in Tokyo and tried to increase circulation of pro-Soviet magazines.[117] In September, Zhou Enlai responded with his famous 'East is East and West is West' comment.[118] *Pravda*, was later to interpret this as a blatant example of Chinese racism.[119]

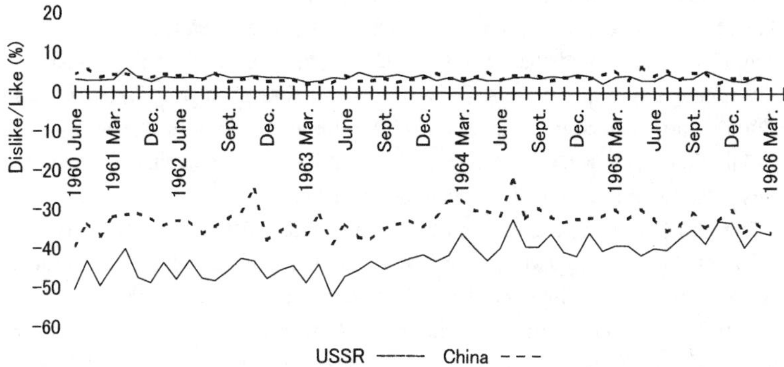

Figure 8.1 Japanese attitudes towards China and the USSR, 1960–66

Source: Yoron chōsa nenkan (1960–67).

Meanwhile, in Japan, the debate about the rift had broadened somewhat. In April, the right-wing journal *Ronsō* published seemingly the first detailed study of the dispute's influence on the Japanese Left. Rather improbably, the author, Asada Mitsuteru (Shizuoka University), concluded that debate about the rift was still confined 'to a few high-ranking executives within the JCP'.[120] Even more surprising was the economist Kusano Fumio's (Takushoku University) assertion in the same journal that 'until now there has not been much evidence of separatist trends on the economic front.' He did predict, however, that continuing Sino-Soviet discord would soon affect economic relations too.[121]

By the summer of 1962, there were three Western schools of thought on the rift—according to Sekido Tatsuzō (secretary of the *Chūgoku Sōgō Kenkyūkai* or China Comprehensive Research Association). At one extreme lay the 'division of labour' thesis beloved of politicians; at the other, the apocalyptic vision of journalists, predicting a Sino-Soviet explosion due to either 'historical experience' or 'dictatorial political systems'. In between were 'those who see the rift as serious, but think...Communist solidarity will keep the conflict within limits.'[122] Although Sekido himself belonged to the first group, most Japanese commentators fell into the last category. Sakamoto Koretada (Tokyo University of Foreign Languages) warned that 'it would be a mistake to overestimate the degree of Sino-Soviet discord…[as] the problems they are debating can probably be settled internally.' Yet he also recognised that 'the present compromise is an inadequate one...[and] there has been no change in the fundamental causes of the rift.' In Sakamoto's opinion, the rift did not arise from 'a simple disagreement over tactics', nor even from both powers' 'divergent revolutionary experiences [which] should decrease over time'. Rather the dispute arose from their 'national characters and national sentiments'.[123] Onoe Masao also employed this line of argument. He declared that the emergence of the theoretical dispute had been 'inevitable if one admits that Socialist construction should be based on each nation's particular concrete conditions.' Yet he also held that 'the unity of the Socialist bloc is necessary as long as the conflict with the capitalist bloc exists. This places a limit on the Sino-Soviet theoretical dispute.'[124]

The position of Iwamura Michio was now similar. Although he still criticised the unreliable sources used by most scholars, and doubted whether Khrushchev was the target of Beijing's attacks on Yugoslavia, he no longer denied that Sino-Soviet disagreements over imperialism and disarmament were 'serious'. He dismissed the 'division of labour' theory, and conceded that these differences were 'rooted in the Chinese and Soviet positions in international politics…and their historical backgrounds.' In short, Iwamura accepted that 'a partial rift exists', but felt 'their views are not necessarily decisively riven.' Finally, he criticised Socialists in the West, specifically Leo Huberman and Paul Sweezy, for exaggerating the inevitability of the rift and blaming China for its emergence.[125]

Harako Rinjirō, by contrast, was clearly a member of Sekido's second school. 'Sino-Soviet gestures of "unity" are essentially meaningless', Harako believed, 'in reality Sino-Soviet party-to-party relations are ruptured, and the personal feelings of hostility between Khrushchev and Mao appear to have sharpened.' He was convinced that 'the power struggle between China and the Soviet Union must soon resume, as both operate the same [domestic] one-party power structure'. Harako did not anticipate the complete 'dissolution (*kaitai*)' of the world Communist movement, but he thought a process of 'decentralisation (*bunsan*)' was already under way.[126]

By this time, Japan specialist Robert Scalapino (University of California) recognised that 'Japanese intellectual Marxists have been deeply shaken...[and] the process of fragmentation has been accelerated...[by] the widening Sino-Soviet cleavage.' Japanese scholars were not only aware of the existence of the rift but also recognised that it was more than simply an ideological dispute. The split was beginning to affect the Japanese intellectual community, but few in Tokyo would have agreed with Scalapino's provocative conclusion that, 'In socio-economic terms and perhaps in political ones as well, Japan...has passed beyond the Marxist stage.'[127]

Interpretative comments

Input: external environment

The Soviet and Chinese governments assigned a high priority to winning over Japanese public opinion to their side in the Cold War. At various stages in their history, Chinese and (to a much lesser extent) Soviet experience had each exerted an influence on Japanese thinking. Signature of the 1950 Sino-Soviet Alliance had caused many Japanese to question such links. Communist propaganda was rather crude and ineffective, but Beijing's 'people's diplomacy' or 'invitation diplomacy' brought thousands of influential Japanese to the mainland on free junkets. Moscow pursued a similar policy, albeit on a smaller scale. The popular anti-Security Treaty struggle helped the Communist powers to temporarily reach out beyond their natural support base.

In the 1950s, Japanese were in some ways quite isolated from the intellectual trends in the West. Furthermore, as the Lake Kawaguchi Conference of 1960 showed, the worldviews of Japanese intellectuals differed significantly from those of their Western colleagues. Doubts about the 'independence' of the Western media were widespread. Consequently, the US government devoted considerable resources via agencies such as the USIO (United States Information Office) and CIA to winning over the 'hearts and minds' of Japanese intellectuals, journalists and ordinary citizens.

Internal environment: operational sphere

By the 1950s, the Japanese public had already acquired the reputation of being the world's most avid newspaper readers: a reputation born out by statistics. This gave popular journalists considerable influence, and the mainstream media took its role as the fourth estate quite seriously and wasted no opportunity to criticise the government.

The Japanese intellectual community during this period was strictly divided between 'progressives' and 'conservatives', with the former in the ascendant, at least on the larger university campuses.

Psychological sphere: belief systems

Defeat in World War II and the Occupation reforms substantially redefined the Japanese national identity, although their sense of their own uniqueness did not disappear. Stripped of empire Japan became much smaller and more narrowly Japanese. Confined to just 55 per cent of their former lands, the Japanese felt constricted, resource poor, and vulnerable. Less obviously, with the loss of Taiwanese, Korean, Manchurian, Micronesian, and (temporarily) even Okinawan citizens, Japan was transformed into effectively a monocultural society. Consequently, Japanese became more insular, more 'Western', and less concerned with developments on the Asian continent. Moreover, a strong sense of victim consciousness—in part the result of the atomic bombing of Hiroshima and Nagasaki—led to an instant transformation in Japan's self-image from warrior to peace-loving nation, as evidenced by the repackaging of the emperor and the promulgation of the new Constitution.

A Cold War 'them and us' mentality afflicted most of the world during the 1950s. The Japanese people were uncertain and divided over where their best interests lay. On one point, however, there was consensus: with memories of a painful defeat still very fresh, Japanese were determined not to be dragged into another war.

The Sino-Soviet Alliance was never popular with the Japanese public, but behind this simple hostility lay a more complex jumble of feelings towards China and the Soviet Union. In 1950, historical cultural debts and racial ties (*dōbun dōshu*), war guilt, and the lure of a vast market coloured Japanese sentiments towards the 'New China'. Although this sense of 'affinity' was mixed with elements of 'fear' and 'antagonism', most Japanese felt a much deeper distrust of Russians. Traditional antipathy was reinforced by ideological and strategic considerations, and redoubled by Stalin's opportunism during the last week of the Pacific War. Admiration for Russian literature and in some quarters, respect for the 'construction of Socialism' did little to ameliorate such negative feelings. Opinion polls during these years revealed that a small handful of people liked both countries, and this number varied little as the rift emerged (Figure 8.1). A substantial minority of the population disliked both, and although dramatic swings occurred, they appeared to move in tandem, implying a dislike of Communism *per se*.

The mass media and intelligentsia could generally be relied upon to be sympathetic towards 'New China', often praising its rapid progress and distinguishing Beijing's version of Communism from that practised in Moscow.

Psychological sphere: perceptions

Initially, it seems that most Japanese—securely held in the Occupation's firm embrace—did not take the Sino-Soviet Alliance very seriously. They felt that the Chinese were culturally incapable of becoming 'real Communists' (unlike the Russians), and history had taught them that Sino-Russian relations were alwaysfragile. It was widely assumed that the alliance had been difficult to negotiate and would easily collapse.

After the outbreak of the Korean War, however, and especially as Soviet assistance to China expanded, the alliance gradually came to be accepted as a permanent feature of the international landscape. During Kishi's tenure, few 'serious' commentators dared to question its survival in public. The vast majority of observers simply submerged any hints of differences between Moscow and Beijing in their fundamental affinities. Even the rare prescient exceptions to this practice were little more than soothsayers, since they lacked hard evidence on which to base their analyses.

The growth in public understanding of the Sino-Soviet split was slow and halting. When the American (and West European) media began to publish reports of the Sino-Soviet discord, the first reaction of Japanese progressives was to dismiss these stories as mere rumour mongering. The progressives were perhaps ideologically predisposed to reject news of the dispute, but even right-wing commentators saw Communist differences in the main as being of tactical, not strategic significance. For the former, like their comrades in the opposition parties, the rift was obviously a source of confusion and embarrassment that threatened their most cherished ideals—although a handful did welcome it. For the latter, it perhaps represented a challenge to the carefully crafted 'monolithic Communist' bogey, on which the fragile support for the Japan–US Security Treaty and rearmament was thought to rest.

The Japanese mainstream media was slow to appreciate the significance of the Sino-Soviet differences. While some interested parties were conscious of increasing Sino-Soviet tensions during the later 1950s, the vast majority of Japanese only became aware of such problems after 1960. The Lake Kawaguchi Conference in September 1960 represented something of a watershed, although it too confirmed the existence of a considerable gulf between the latest Western research and the views of most Japanese participants. The Sino-Soviet dispute then appeared to enjoy a brief remission.

Decision-making process

Japan's relations with the parties to the Sino-Soviet Alliance were a source of concern to a wide cross-section of the Japanese public. However, in a dialogue of the deaf, elitist diplomats generally prided themselves on their indifference to trends in public opinion, while progressive intellectuals—self-appointed spokespersons for the latter—saw their role in society as challenging the Establishment, not collaborating with it. An ideological chasm separated the two groups and direct channels of communication were lacking. In the 1950s, many intellectuals were closely associated with either the JCP, JSP or affiliated groups. Most demanded that the government adopt neutralism and reach accommodation with the Sino-Soviet allies. Moreover, the media offered remarkably little guidance on the issue. Thus the input from a few, relatively obscure, right-leaning think-tanks had a more direct influence on the policy-making process in MOFA than the combined wisdom of Japan's more numerous and famous progressive intellectuals. Only the former enjoyed intimate contacts—financial, personal and informational—with the bureaucracy and ruling party.

Politicians could less afford to be *blasé* about public opinion. During the Occupation, however, this was less significant since SCAP and Washington represented their most important constituencies. The elitist Yoshida lacked the common touch, and apparently had little time for intellectuals. With the restoration of Japanese sovereignty Yoshida's popularity suffered accordingly. Hatoyama labelled his foreign policy '*kokumin gaikō* (people's diplomacy)', but the old political operator was an expert at manipulating public opinion. If he had genuinely respected the popular will, he would have given priority to normalising relations with Beijing not Moscow. While serving as foreign minister, Kishi paid lip service to Hatoyama-style populism, but as premier he failed to disguise a deep distrust of public opinion. Kishi's authoritarian streak proved even stronger than that of his predecessors: eventually it brought about his downfall.

Output

The Japanese mass media did little to inform the public of developments in the Sino-Soviet relationship during the 1950s. For many years, all predictions of a Sino-Soviet rift were dismissed as 'wishful thinking (*kibōteki kansoku*)'. Similarly, the under-researched and mostly second-rate analyses by intellectuals and the intermittent debates in which they engaged contributed little to enlighten an ignorant population.

External environment: feedback

Not surprisingly, Japanese views on the Sino-Soviet Alliance were of little interest to the outside world during the 1950s.

9

Independent thinking: Japanese civil society and the open Sino-Soviet split, 1962–64

The precursor to the incredible explosion in Japanese concern with the Sino-Soviet rift that occurred during 1963 was the aftermath of two events dating from late October 1962: the Sino-Indian border war and the Cuban Missile Crisis. In the wake of these incidents, Moscow and Beijing began direct verbal attacks on each other and engaged in increasingly fierce propaganda campaigns to win over 'hearts and minds' worldwide, including Japan. The effect in Tokyo was immediate, 'the dispute…[came] to attract an interest incomparably greater than before.'[1] A flood of articles appeared, dominating the headlines and academic journals throughout the next 18 months (Figure 9.1).

The Sino-Soviet rift as national infatuation

Japanese newspapers address the Sino-Soviet rift

The New Year opened with, for the first time, every major daily discussing the Sino-Soviet dispute in their editorials. Three themes stood out: recognition that the rift was now more serious; implied criticism of China's position in the dispute from a pacifist standpoint; and finally, calls for Japan to adopt an 'independent' policy towards the rift.

Mainichi Shimbun was the first, predicting: 'In international relations this year the rift (*tairitsu*) in the Communist world will be even more noticeable than the movement in US–Soviet relations.'[2] A couple of weeks later, noting that the rift centred on differing views of 'peaceful coexistence', *Mainichi* characterised Moscow's position as 'realistic', whereas Beijing's was dubbed 'belligerent' and 'idealistic'. The paper ascribed this to differences in their revolutionary stages.[3]

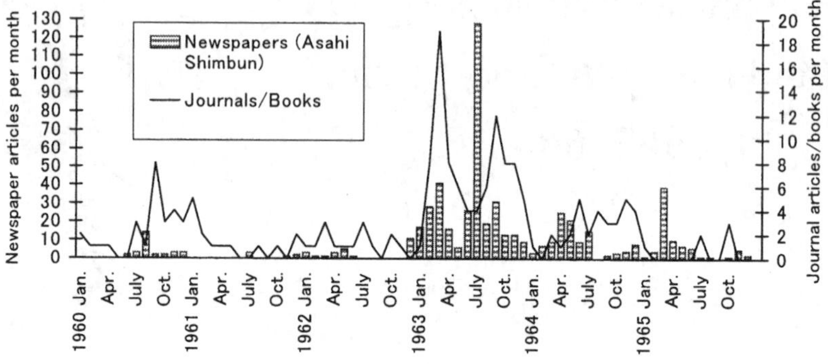

Figure 9.1 Japanese media coverage of the Sino-Soviet rift, 1960–65

Source: Asahi Shimbun and materials listed in the Bibliography.

The best-selling daily, *Asahi Shimbun*, meanwhile declared that 'the emergence of a schism (*bunretsu*) in the Communist camp is not strange'—such conflicts occurred in all religions and ideologies. It disclaimed any interest in whose interpretation of Leninism was correct but expressed concern over the consequences of Chinese support for 'just wars'. Finally, and most interestingly, *Asahi* stated: 'It is premature to view the intensification of the Sino-Soviet rift (*tairitsu*) from the narrow perspective of the Cold War and conclude that it is advantageous to the West.' Noting how 'reformist parties who believe in Communism, especially in Japan, want to think independently (*jishuteki*)', it recommended rather that the dispute be 'fundamentally re-examined from the viewpoint of mankind's benefit.'[4]

Earlier that week, the right-wing *Sankei Shimbun* had claimed that 'it is somewhat premature to see a Sino-Soviet schism (*bunretsu*) right away.' Unusually, the editorial found itself sharing some common ground with the left-of-centre *Asahi*, both when reluctantly welcoming Khrushchev's 'peaceful coexistence' line and when emphasising the necessity of Japan 'endeavouring to produce an unerringly independent (*jishuteki*) policy.'[5] *Tokyo Shimbun*, another right-of-centre daily, thought the dispute had already 'reached a climax'. It saw the Sino-Soviet rift as a 'fight over revolutionary strategy based on their respective national interests', and agreed that China was the more dangerous.[6]

In the English language press, Hirasawa Kazushige, editor of *Japan Times*, asserted that, 'The row has now become something much more serious than a "quarrel between brothers".' Yet despite the Soviet–Yugoslav reconciliation, he argued that 'Communist China cannot afford to cut off her relations with the Soviet Union...because of her economic dependence on Russia and Sino-Soviet common destiny in international politics.' Hirasawa thought there was 'a good possibility that Communist China would be driven to...[a] reshuffling of top leaders' in order to 'put an end to the doctrinal dispute with Russia'.[7] In a subsequent pair of editorials, he noted, 'The fact that Communist China now appears to be bidding for the leadership of the Communist bloc at the expense of Soviet Russia, cannot fail to interest this country'. However, Hirasawa warned that confronted by China's 'defensive expansionism...closer relations with that country must be treated with caution.'[8]

In short, the press recognised that the rift was having an effect on Japan and recommended that the country avoid choosing sides. Still, most of these journalists revealed little sympathy for the Chinese case.

Japanese intellectuals debate the Sino-Soviet rift

Japanese intellectuals shared many of the same concerns as their colleagues in newsprint. During the first half of 1963, most articles in the serious journals continued to focus on the causes of the rift, but increasing attention was paid to its consequences, especially for Japan. In addition, following the journalists' lead, there was some discussion for the first time as to how Japan should respond. Finally, there were the beginnings of a genuine dialogue as intellectuals challenged each other's views directly, either in print or at round-table conferences.

Democratic Socialist Seki Yoshihiko (Tokyo Metropolitan University) noted the surge in Japanese publications on the 'Sino-Soviet ideological struggle', but complained that 'very few of the articles are outstanding'. He blamed this on 'the paucity of reliable source materials…[and] Japanese left-wing intellectuals [who] find the present struggle an embarrassment and therefore keep silent on the subject'.[9] This assessment was a little unfair. As early as March 1961, MOFA had published a collection of more than a hundred documents from the dispute, and thereafter newspapers and magazines had supplemented these with translations of the latest materials.[10] Moreover, after Beijing criticised Moscow for its conduct of the Cuban Crisis and its rearming of India following the border war with China, not even 'progressive' Japanese intellectuals persisted in denying the existence of the rift. Realistically, one could 'no longer say that the Sino-Soviet dispute is just a groundless rumour of bourgeois journalism.'[11]

There was much talk at this time of Sino-Soviet relations having entered a 'new stage', and in discussing the current nature of the discord, efforts were made to supersede the sterile 'ideology' versus 'national interest' debate.[12] A process of convergence was underway, whereby 'conservatives' saw the rift extending from a dispute over principles to 'real politics', while 'progressives' conceded that the Communist bloc's disagreements had moved beyond 'superficial' policy issues to key questions of ideological interpretation. Satō Noboru, one of Japan's most influential Socialist intellectuals, spoke of the rift as having a 'double structure', and Mori Kyōzō (an Eastern Europe expert soon to become editor-in-chief of *Asahi Shimbun*) considered the two perspectives 'indivisible and intertwined.'[13] To some extent, the terminology writers employed reflected this trend. Although the theoretical *ronsō* (dispute) remained the norm, the more strategic *tairitsu* (rift) was gaining in popularity (Figure 9.2).[14]

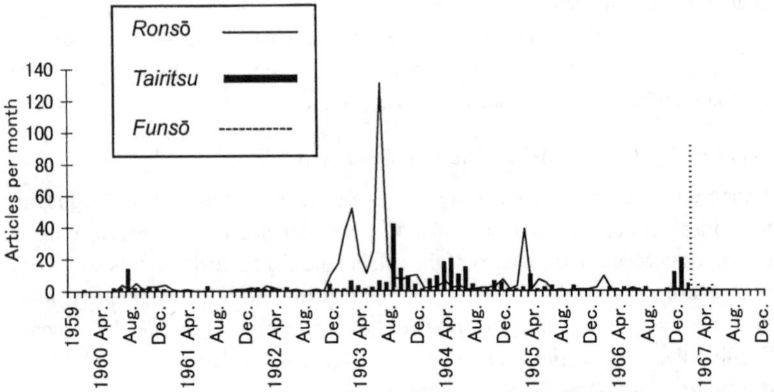

Figure 9.2 Japanese terms used to describe Sino-Soviet relations, 1959–67

Source: Asahi Shimbun (1959–67).

Others resisted this trend. Associates of the *Taiken*, for example, still held that 'the Sino-Soviet theoretical battle is a device, nothing but a deceit.'[15]

Greater differences remained, however, when it came to identifying the origins of the rift. One writer listed no less than nine separate theories as current among Japanese intellectuals at this time. The rift was said to stem from differences between their policies; state-to-state relations (since 1949); party-to-party relations (since the Comintern era); positions in international politics; stages of Socialist (economic) construction; attitudes towards power; leaders; European and Asian civilisations, or, Slav and Han races.[16] Advocates for each of these hypotheses existed, but several others could be added such as border disputes, lack of economic cooperation and attitudes towards nuclear weapons.[17] At the same time, some scholars recognised the complexity of the rift and specifically warned against relying on unicausal explanations.[18]

According to Hirota Yōji (managing director of *Ōa Kyōkai*), Japanese researchers still divided into three groups on the question of future prospects for Sino-Soviet relations. Either the Communist allies had 'finally split and there was no way to resolve the situation'; or, 'because of their huge power differential... ultimately the Soviets would overpower the Communist Chinese'; or, 'they will resolve the situation, even if only a little'. Hirota himself felt that a complete 'Sino-Soviet split is not unrealistic'.[19] Many on the Right now shared his opinion: predictions varied from 'unconditional surrender' to '20 years' before a settlement could be achieved.[20] This was by now the majority view although a number of left-wing scholars remained convinced that Sino-Soviet problems could yet be resolved.[21]

On the related question of evaluating the consequences of the rift, most analysts conceived of it as a 'zero-sum game': either it was beneficial to the West and harmful to the Communists or vice versa. Conventional wisdom supported the former view. Hirota Yōji was convinced that if the powers really split, 'the loss of Communist China will cause immense damage to the Soviet Union...and Communist China will also be humbled.'[22] Yet many Japanese held dissenting views. Mori Kyōzō declared 'interesting, but mistaken...the Cold War viewpoint [that] the development of the Sino-Soviet dispute is beneficial to the West'. In the short-term, he warned of the likely 'intensification of East–West tensions as both China and the Soviet Union try to show that their way will lead to revolution.' However, 'in the final analysis', Mori concluded that 'the Sino-Soviet dispute has a positive meaning for world history'.[23] On the Left, many continued to regard the dispute as a healthy development for Socialism.[24] Satō Noboru, for example, thought it a 'good opportunity...for the international Communist movement...to extricate itself from the "monolith".'[25] In support of their argument, some cited Maoist theory on the necessity of ideological struggle to resolve contradictions.[26]

When it came to examining the effect of the rift on Japan, commentators of all persuasions were more inclined to take a pessimistic view.[27] On the Left, Ikeyama Jūrō of the *Gendai Shakaishugi Kenkyūkai* (Contemporary Socialism Research Association) identified three influences, all negative. He claimed that the 'reactionary' Japanese government was using the dispute to 'create anti-Chinese feelings', to 'raise defence consciousness', and to foster divisions within 'the reformist camp'.[28] On the Right, the *Taiken* warned: 'If the rift becomes more violent, Sino-Soviet efforts to seize Japan will become violent.'[29] Meanwhile, *Chūō Kōron* reported that the rift was even disturbing the ruling LDP.[30]

Confronted with the problem of how Japanese should respond to the rift, seemingly only three alternatives presented themselves: lean to the Soviet side; lean to the Chinese side; or adopt an 'independent' stance. Each had its vociferous advocates, but the last view was gaining in popularity. A supporter of the first policy, Satō Noboru was unusually blunt in declaring that in the dispute, 'the Soviet position appears far and away more rational than the Chinese'. Fukuda Kanichi (Tokyo University), a professor in the history of political thought, agreed, yet both men qualified their statements with explicit support for diplomatic normalisation with Beijing. Although Satō specifically declared himself 'not anti-Chinese', this did little to shield him from his left-wing critics.[31] More numerous were the pro-China intellectuals. Mitsuoka Gen of the *Chūgoku Kenkyūjo* accused the mainstream press of 'distorting China's image' by describing Beijing as 'highhanded and belligerent'. In particular, he held Satō Noboru and Nomura Kōichi (Tokyo University), a specialist in Chinese politics, in contempt for proving susceptible to the media's 'disdain (*besshi*)' for China.[32] In a more restrained manner, Shimizu Ikutarō (Gakushūin University), a well-known ex-progressive, also appeared to sympathise with the Chinese. After criticising the pro-Soviet stance of American Socialists Huberman and Sweezy, he wrote: 'What the Sino-Soviet dispute teaches us is not that the USSR is peaceful while China is warlike, rather that there are two peaces, one for countries satisfied with the status quo and the other for those dissatisfied.'[33]

While few scholars were willing openly to choose sides, some saw a connection between the theories put forward to explain the origins of the rift and the ideological bias of the author. One writer argued that those who 'emphasised the differences in Sino-Soviet stages of development' tended to see prosperous Japan 'as nearer to the US or Soviet Union'. They reportedly found 'Khrushchev's line' in the Sino-Soviet dispute to be 'more easily understandable...[than] Mao's line'. In contrast, those who stressed the role of 'skin colour' in the rift and saw the '"white" Soviet Union and America shaking hands to counter the development of "yellow" China', leaned towards 'racial affinity with China' and 'Asian unity'.[34] Ishidō Kiyotomo, a 'structural reform' Marxist, saw the 'historical environment and national conditions' argument as 'a means to support one side in the rift', namely, the CPSU, but argued that in Japan cultural associations rendered 'the CCP's theory easy to understand and familiar'.[35]

More significant was the growing number of intellectuals who advocated that Japan should adopt an 'independent' stand, although there were subtle differences in definition. Ikeyama Jūrō offered a specifically Socialist interpretation. He pointed out that both powers had 'their weak points'. For Ikeyama it was 'not a matter of which side is the winner', rather it was necessary to 'reform one's own ideology.'[36] In one of Japan's first book-length studies on the rift, Ishidō Kiyotomo, in contrast, praised both Moscow and Beijing, but he criticised

Japanese Marxists for 'not having the courage to decide which side was right and which mistaken.'[37] Eguchi Bokurō (Tokyo University), a noted Marxist historian, broadened the scope slightly to embrace all 'theorists and researchers' lack of autonomy (*shutaisei*)' vis-à-vis the rift, without which he felt their 'discussion of the theories' rights and wrongs have no meaning'.[38] Although a close reading reveals a soft spot for Khrushchev's line, Saitō Takeshi (Tokyo University), a professor of international relations, also criticised the stands of both parties to the rift, and demanded that 'Japanese citizens must think independently (*jishuteki*).'[39] Mori Kyōzō endorsed this call, but his advice was primarily directed at the government. He thought that with the US currently regarding Communist China as its 'number one enemy', the Japanese government had a duty 'to advise the US' against continuing its 'containment' policy.[40] Political historian Fujita Shōzō (Hōsei University) blamed Japan's inability to escape the dispute's harmful effects on its 'not having an independent line (*shutaiteki rosen*)'. He insisted that, 'Japan must work to independently contribute to peace.'[41] Meanwhile, Terasawa Hajime (Tokyo University) also lamented Japan's lack of autonomy (*shutaisei*), by which he meant an independent foreign policy. Terasawa and the other members of his 'round-table' were not 'impatient' for such political independence, but they felt that in light of the Sino-Soviet rift, Japan should put its demands to China and the Soviet Union, not just the US.[42] Even more extreme were the recommendations of the *Taiken* group, which felt it 'necessary to aggravate the Communist bloc's polarization', in order to 'strengthen Japan's defence against Communisation and promote the liberation of Communist countries'.[43]

Finally, Marxist Kawabata Osamu, writing in the JCP journal *Zenei*, savaged these 'revisionist' works by Ikeyama Jūrō, Kurihara Yukio, Saitō Takashi and Satō Noboru, and those of 'realists' like Kiuchi Nobutane, Yamazaki Taketoshi, and Harako Rinjirō. He reserved particular scorn for the way in which they emphasised the need for Japanese 'independence' in the Sino-Soviet dispute, 'as if taking into account the political lessons from the CPSU and CCP's experience could harm Japan's own standpoint.'[44]

A psychological dam seemed to have burst in the first half of 1963 with the sudden flood of articles on the Sino-Soviet rift appearing in Japanese. Moreover, with the increased quantity came an improvement in quality, as Japanese intellectuals probed deeper into the origins of the split and also began to address its implications for Japan.

Public opinion on the rift

While this debate was raging among Japan's intellectuals, for the first time Japanese public opinion on the rift was consulted directly via a series of polls. The first asked respondents: 'Which do you think the most strongly united (*danketsu*), the Communist bloc or the Free World?' The results were as follows:

Table 9.1 Japanese public opinion on the unity of the Cold War blocs

	Communist bloc	Free World	Neither	Don't Know
January 1963	13.6	22.9	25.5	38.1
February 1963	11.8	20.4	23.2	44.7
March 1963	11.0	22.2	30.6	36.1
April 1963	6.5	20.3	31.3	41.9
May 1963	11.3	24.5	33.0	31.1

Source: Shūkan Jiji (various issues, 1963). Sample: 1250, nationwide. (Figures are percentages.)

Perhaps the most significant finding was the roughly two-to-one imbalance in favour of those seeing Free World unity as superior to Communist bloc solidarity.[45] Even more interesting was a poll published by *Tokyo Shimbun* that asked: 'According to recent reports, it seems as if there is a difference of opinion between China and the Soviet Union. Do you think these differences can be resolved in a friendly manner or not?' Somewhat surprisingly, 38.8 per cent still thought that the rift could be resolved in a friendly way, while a mere 15.5 per cent thought that it could not. This result appeared rather more optimistic than the general tenor of opinion current among intellectuals. A second question asked: 'Is the split in Sino-Soviet opinions helpful (*tsugō ga ii*) or harmful (*tsugō ga warui*) for Japanese politics?' and provided the following results:

Table 9.2 Japanese public opinion on the helpfulness of the Sino-Soviet split

	Helpful	Harmful	Don't Know
Company employees	17.9	28.0	54.1
Housewives	8.3	27.9	63.8
Labourers	14.3	26.8	58.9
Managers	29.2	29.2	41.6
Self-employed	20.0	40.0	40.0
Shopkeepers	33.8	27.5	39.7
Students	29.4	11.8	58.8
AVERAGE	16.3	26.6	57.1

Source: Tokyo Shimbun (4 April 1963). Sample: 800, Tokyo. (Figures are percentages.)

With the exception of the 'idealistic' students, this poll appeared much closer to the pessimism endemic in the academic community. In its own analysis of the results, the *Tokyo Shimbun* noted the relatively high response rate to the first question, which it took as an indication of 'ordinary citizens taking a strong interest in the Sino-Soviet rift problem', although 'don't know' was the most common reply. It regarded the respondents' hopefulness to be the result of 'fixed preconceptions' or 'wishful thinking'. Concerning the second question, the paper revealed that the major reason for those answering 'harmful' was that they were 'worried by Communist China's hard-line policy towards Japan based on its dogmatic rejection of Khrushchev's peaceful coexistence.' This perhaps indicated that the pacifist rather than the Asianist norm had a stronger influence on the Japanese public. From a more 'realist' perspective, the response here may also have been related to another question on the survey, which found that 68 per cent of Japanese felt Chinese nuclear tests threatened to 'jeopardise' their national security. Finally, in seeking to explain the apparent contradiction between the two main results the *Tokyo Shimbun* claimed:

> From a Cold War perspective, common sense says that the Free World should regard contradictions in the Communist world as a good thing, but in Japan's case we feel uneasy about the danger that lies behind the rift, the seriousness of its course and its influence on peace, we regard as a very dangerous condition.

By the end of the year, the Japanese public had named the Sino-Soviet rift as the number two foreign news story of 1963; only the Kennedy assassination garnered more votes. Public opinion may not have chosen sides in the rift, but it was certainly very interested in the outcome.

Sino-Soviet competition for Japanese friendship

While Japanese academics were busy trying to decipher recent developments in Sino-Soviet relations, and the Japanese people were being quizzed on their impressions, Moscow and Beijing stepped up their propaganda campaigns. In April, China granted early release to two Japanese war criminals.[46] Two months later, Moscow responded by allowing Japanese fishermen to collect *konbu* (edible seaweed) around Kaigara Island, the closest of the Soviet-held Kurile chain to Hokkaido.[47] Then on 26 August, Soviet Ambassador Vladimir Vinogradov notified Tokyo that Moscow would release all of the 141 Japanese fishermen detained in the Soviet Union. A few days later, although MOFA denied that there was any connexion, Beijing countered the Soviet move by announcing the release of another six Japanese war criminals and authorising grave visits to the mainland.[48] That same month the Japan–China Friendship Association launched a campaign to make Chinese propaganda magazines widely available in Japan, and on 4 October, a sister organisation was founded in Beijing.[49] The Russians were also attempting to flood Japan with pro-Soviet publications, but that autumn pro-Beijing JCP members seized control of the Japan–Soviet Society. This forced Moscow to fall back on the resources of its embassy and engage in a grass-roots level campaign to promote the Soviet line.[50] The fact that all Japanese employees at the Soviet Embassy's Public Information Section had been hired on the recommendation of the JCP would not have made this task any easier.[51]

Japanese newspapers reassess the rift

Any positive impressions created by such small propaganda gestures were largely negated by the violent confrontation between Soviet and Chinese delegates at the Ninth *Gensuikyō* Congress held in early August 1963.[52] This followed the resumption of harsh Sino-Soviet polemics in June, the breakdown of talks between the two parties on 20 July, and Khrushchev's initialling of the Partial Nuclear Test-Ban Treaty (PTBT) with Britain and the US five days later.[53]

The Japanese press responded to these serious developments with another spate of articles, presenting the rift as probably *the* crucial element in the changing international environment. By November, even Moscow's decision to withdraw from the race to the Moon was being blamed on the rift.[54] In early July, editorials had still described the rift as merely 'a nuisance to neighbours' and called on the Chinese and Soviets to resolve their differences through a constructive discussion of policies and revision of theories.[55] Mid-July marked a turning point, however. According to Hasegawa Saiji (managing director of right-wing media group *Jiji Tsūshinsha*): 'Yoshida's [China Thesis] was considered an old man's idle dream. The dream has come true and much sooner than expected.' He claimed that recent Sino-Soviet exchanges 'made it unmistakably clear that [they] have virtually parted...ways.'[56] Indeed, on 5 August, in reply to a questionnaire from Japanese newspaper editors, Khrushchev personally admitted that 'actual differences of view' existed between the Communist Parties of the PRC and Soviet Union.[57] *Tokyo Shimbun* acknowledged the success of Khrushchev's 'peaceful coexistence strategy in negotiations with the West', but warned that it was 'a mistake to think Communism's power is weakened by a long rift.'[58] Similarly, *Mainichi Shimbun* proclaimed: 'There is no guarantee that peaceful coexistence will be the general line of the international Communist movement forever...[since] the possibility exists that Communist China's line can grasp leadership power.'[59] In early August, *Asahi Shimbun* noted the existence of another potentially serious dimension to the escalating rift—the disputed Sino-Soviet frontier.[60] A month later, the same paper not only conceded that the rift had 'gone beyond comradely mutual criticism between two Communist parties', it also speculated on whether the 'normal state relations have become endangered.' The editor denied any desire to meddle in an internal Communist bloc affair, but stated that he felt compelled to comment now because the fate of the world was at stake. *Asahi* was 'not saying Communist China's leaders are belligerent and aggressive', but at the same time the paper expressed qualified support for Moscow's peaceful coexistence line.[61]

Concerning the dispute's consequences for Japan, *Mainichi Shimbun* not surprisingly concluded that the 'most serious influence is undoubtedly on the JCP.'[62] The more Conservative *Tokyo Shimbun* thought that Japan should be 'on guard against Communist China's Asia policy', including its trade offensive.[63] On the other hand, the right-wing *Sankei Shimbun* was unusual in arguing that as 'Japan is considered a hypothetical enemy by the Sino-Soviet Alliance, the Sino-Soviet rift is a plus.'[64]

During the autumn of 1963, Moscow renewed its efforts to suspend ideological hostilities with Beijing. The Japanese media responded by describing their rift as entering a 'calm period'.[65] This view was to prove short-lived. Hirasawa Kazushige was soon speculating that China 'must want desperately to overthrow Khrushchev...and normalize her relations with the Soviet Union. For it is obvious that without Russia's economic and technological help, Red China's pace of industrialization would suffer seriously.' In his view, this fact also helped to explain China's 'surprisingly amicable attitude toward Japan.' Hirasawa further hypothesised that 'if China adopted the realistic policy of Khrushchev, I suspect that the process of her Communist revolution might reverse itself.'[66]

The Japanese press was now acting responsibly in keeping its readers up-to-date on developments as the Sino-Soviet Alliance imploded. Some reports were a little alarmist, but overall the tone was calm and matter-of-fact. The same could be said of Japanese intellectuals.

Japanese intellectuals reassess the rift

After a relatively quiet summer, academic interest in the rift peaked again in the autumn, inspired by the abortive Sino-Soviet talks and conclusion of the PTBT. Many intellectuals now equated the split with the historic schisms in the Christian world.[67] One even described it as 'the biggest problem facing the world today.'[68] The revived debate did not display any fundamental changes from that of the spring, but trends became clearer, arguments became more sophisticated and several new themes were introduced. Furthermore, there was evidence of renewed government interest in academic views on the rift. During 2–18 September, the *Naigai Jōsei Chōsakai* (Domestic and International Conditions Investigation Association) surveyed Japanese intellectuals' perceptions of the dispute on behalf of the CRO, asking them to describe the current state of the rift (Table 9.3).

Table 9.3 Japanese intellectual opinion on the Sino-Soviet rift

Responses	Number of Responses
'It is the ages of their revolutions (stages of development) that differ'	60
'It is a nationalist/racist rift (*minzokuteki tairitsu*)'	30
'It is a struggle for the leadership of the Communist bloc'	22
'It is their consciousness and recognition of nuclear civilisation (*kakubunmei*) that differs'	12
'It is a kind of factional fight'	2
'From the viewpoint of Sino-Soviet power relations, it will absolutely not shake the [Communist] camp'	2
'There is no fundamental difference in their way of thinking'	1

Source: Naikaku Chōsashitsu, 'NisSo (sic) ronsō ni tai suru kokunai no hannō', *Chōsa Geppō* (Aug. 1964): 50–2. Sample: 102 experts, nationwide.

The responses clearly confirm overall impressions of the spring debate, namely, that the majority of Japanese scholars now felt that the rift was both very serious and no longer simply an ideological dispute.

The following month, in another example of official curiosity at outside assessments of the rift, Wakaizumi Kei, a young academic who had studied in Washington, was invited to speak to the LDP's FARC on American views of Sino-Soviet relations.[69] Wakaizumi first declared that 'the US view of the Soviet Union and Communist China is precisely the opposite to Japan's'. Yet, his description of the US interpretation of the causes of the rift was remarkably similar to the view now prevailing in Japan: Moscow and Beijing's 'stages of revolutionary development differ[ed]', and there was a large gap in their 'economic circumstances'. According to Wakaizumi, the Americans believed very strongly that 'the dispute's essence is not an ideological rift...but a national interest rift, or clash of nationalisms.'[70]

Of course, not all Japanese scholars engaged in debating the rift that autumn concurred with this analysis, but those supporting the 'comradely difference of opinion' theory were clearly fighting a losing battle.[71] Three days before the PTBT was signed, a member of the *Taiken* had already noted that 'regarding the essence of the Sino-Soviet dispute, the viewpoint that it is superficially an ideological rift, and essentially a people-to-people struggle has increased enormously.'[72] On the Left, even Iwamura Michio (director of the *Chūgoku Kenkyūjo*) reluctantly conceded that 'the central problem of their ideological dispute is closely connected with their foreign policies.'[73] On the other hand, the whole 'ideology or national interest' dichotomy was 'unrealistic' according to right-winger Kusano Fumio, since 'both are intimately intertwined.' Yet when pressed as to which took precedence, Kusano pointed to the former.[74] From a rather different perspective, Satō Noboru similarly argued:

> It is of especially vital importance to the progressive movement in Japan that the progressive camp look beyond the ideological aspects of the dispute and make a careful and objective examination of the confrontation between China and Russia as a phenomenon of international politics.[75]

Yet he stubbornly held to the view that, 'while there are nationalistic aspects to the Sino-Soviet dispute...in the final analysis...it is an ideological conflict...[centred on] two distinct views of the course that the world revolution should take.'[76] Moreover, he still insisted that: 'Far from heralding a breakdown of Marxist ideology, the dispute actually attests to the vitality and creativity of Marxism'.[77]

Hayashi Kentarō (Tokyo University), a right-wing historian, directly challenged the views of his colleagues Satō Noboru and Eguchi Bokurō.[78] Repelled by their Marxist optimism, Hayashi insisted that 'Marxist theory cannot explain a rift between two Communist states.' For him, 'Ideology [wa]s nothing more than a cover for national interests.' Yet somewhat contradictorily he also claimed that the Sino-Soviet rift was 'an expression of the self-contradictions in Communist ideology.'[79] Shimizu Ikutarō agreed that 'Marxism cannot answer the questions of how or why the dispute developed.' However, whereas Hayashi held that the '"different stages of Socialism" explanation...is not helpful', Shimizu felt the dispute proved that 'conflicts can develop between two Socialist countries when there is a disparity between their stages of economic development.'[80] Inoki Masamichi made a similar point: 'The Sino-Soviet dispute has upset the "myth" of the inevitable demise of the state'.[81]

On the related question of the origins of the rift, scholars continued to cite the same broad range of factors. Kusano Fumio, for example, mentioned differences of 'region, race, nation, economic and cultural stages of development.'[82] More original was Kamimura Shinichi, a diplomat-turned-scholar, who interpreted the rift in terms of what was just beginning to be called the 'North–South conflict': 'The Soviet–Red Chinese ideological dispute has by chance revealed the existence of antagonism between a have and a have-not country'. For Kamimura, it was a battle over 'the maintenance of the status quo.'[83] No less innovative was Mori Kyōzō, who set out to challenge the view, prevalent in some quarters, that the rift was the direct result of US policy. Mori recognised the 'close relationship' between the rift and the US–Soviet rapprochement, yet he insisted that the dispute 'sprang from the Chinese and Soviets themselves'. It was not a product of

Washington's 'containment policy', for which the rift was 'an unexpected prize (*isōgai no emono*)'.[84]

The origins of the rift would continue to provoke debate, but its consequences now attracted much more attention. Two imported 'buzzwords' dominated the conversation: 'polycentrism (*tachūshinshugi*)' and 'polarisation (*bunka* or *bunkyoku*)'. Satō Noboru and Sugita Masao saw these as distinct if contemporaneous trends. For them, the rift 'unfortunately' tended to split the international Communist movement into pro-Moscow and pro-Beijing camps, but on the 'plus' side, it also 'encouraged...national Communist parties to act more independently of both'.[85] Hayashi Kentarō insisted that in reality only the former—which he termed 'bi-centrism'—had occurred.[86] Others on the right, like Shigemori Tadashi (editorial board, *Sankei Shimbun*), used the terms interchangeably, but also considered the development a sign of Communist weakness.[87] Yet at the same time, some observers were aware of a similar phenomenon occurring in the 'Free World'. Mori Kyōzō compared the challenges of China and Gaullist France, and noted: 'In each case independent nuclear weapon development is the way they concretely realise their challenge'. He therefore felt that 'multipolarisation (*takyokuka*) and polycentrisation (*tachūshinka*)' were 'special characteristics of contemporary international politics.'[88]

Focusing on Washington's perspective, Wakaizumi Kei reported that the US government 'cannot help but think that the rift...is useful for Western interests'. For Washington, the best scenario would be for Sino-Soviet relations simply to continue as they were—'a return to friendship or a decisive split are not necessarily in the West's interest.' Wakaizumi personally favoured the US interpretation, and concluded that the Americans would persist in their efforts to 'seduce the Soviets and isolate the villainous Chinese'.[89] Such a strategy naturally upset many left-wing Japanese, like Satō Noboru, who could not see even a nuclear China as a threat, but others more to the right also thought it ill-advised.[90] Mori Kyōzō, for example, was worried that 'the West will try to take advantage of the Sino-Soviet dispute to drive a wedge into the Communist "monolith"' and possibly 'demand Japanese cooperation.'[91] Kamimura Shinichi was also dismissive of those observers who argued that 'if Communist China continues to be vociferous against the Soviet Union, the latter will try to strengthen its ties with the West'. Having spent two years in a Siberian POW camp, however, Kamimura maintained, 'Things are too complicated to justify such a cursory conclusion.'[92]

Meanwhile public concern at the impact of the rift on Japan had not diminished. However, following contending Asian tours by Liu Shaoqi and Leonid Brezhnev, the Chinese and Soviet heads of state respectively, anxiety about the consequences of the split for Japan's neighbours added a new dimension to the debate. Several analysts highlighted the extension of Sino-Soviet competition into both

Communist and non-Communist states in the region: a struggle many saw China as winning.[93] Somura Yasunobu, an area specialist, warned of the resulting threat to growing Japanese economic ties with Southeast Asia.[94]

After August's dramatic *Gensuikyō* congress, it could no longer be denied that the rift was having an impact on Japan, but opinions differed sharply as to whether it was boon or bane. Respondents to the CRO survey (cited above) pointed to both Moscow and Beijing as making 'positive approaches to Japan'. Those interested in trade saw this as advantageous, but others worried about 'Japan being unable to prevent Communist Chinese power permeating its domestic system'.[95]

On the Left, Satō Noboru, Eguchi Bokurō, and Shimizu Shinzō (Nihon Fukushi University) all lamented the rift's negative impact on Japan's progressive movement. In particular, they emphasised 'the further sharpening of the antagonism between the progressive political parties', and the way 'progressive intellectuals [like themselves!] have seen their magical powers wane, and their hold over progressive public opinion…gradually weaken.'[96] Those on the Right observed the same results with positive relish. Nabeyama Sadachika, head of the conservative *Sekai Minshu Kenkyūjo* (World Democracy Institute), wrote of the 'cowardly silence…[of] progressive intellectuals…[who] now withdraw into their shells'.[97] Shimizu Ikutarō compared the current suffering of Japanese Marxist intellectuals with that experienced by their comrades in the West during the Stalinist 1930s, before concluding that the rift 'has rubbed a substantial part of the lustre off Marxism'.[98] Similarly, members of the *Taiken* gleefully discussed the 'good education this has provided [Japan's] progressive intellectuals'.[99]

It was not all smiles on the Japanese Right, however. 'Japanese citizens' way of thinking about Communism has undergone a big revision because of the Sino-Soviet dispute,' declared Doi Akio, 'and this is a plus.' Nevertheless, he warned that 'such expectations could not be held on the political and economic fronts.'[100] Likewise, Hayashi Kentarō felt that Japanese 'should simply be happy...at such a total reversal for Communism', but he was also concerned that the upheaval might 'possibly threaten world peace.'[101] This was the inverse of the famous author and nationalist Mishima Yukio's fears. These arose from his concern that the dispute 'has unexpectedly brought about the signing of a nuclear test-ban treaty...and as a result, one feels that the peaceful era which Japan is now experiencing may last indefinitely.' For Mishima this was pernicious because it perpetuated Japan's 'psychological stagnancy', inhibiting the kind of 'spiritual satisfaction' that could only come from 'living in danger'.[102]

Looking to the future, the majority of Japanese intellectuals in fact felt that Sino-Soviet relations would further deteriorate, although a surprisingly large minority still belonged to the 'compromise' school.[103] Nor was it a simple case of political allegiance. While some right-wingers held that the Sino-Soviet 'military alliance' now existed 'in name only', others were equally confident that it would 'not collapse', even if its operability now 'depend[ed] upon circumstances'.[104] Shigemori Tadashi occupied the middle-ground, predicting 'not a total split, nor one side's surrender to the other...[but rather that] the Sino-Soviet dispute will continue as it is, mud-slinging and muckraking'.[105] Similarly, on the Left, Iwamura Michio concluded that the alliance 'will not become a dead letter'. On the other hand, Shimizu Shinzō (a former *Sōhyō* leader) thought that 'the dispute might well cause the disintegration of the Socialist world system'.[106] Nevertheless, no one was yet willing to go as far as the Americans, who Wakaizumi claimed, had 'forecast a break in diplomatic relations, the abrogation of the Sino-Soviet Alliance...and possibly frontier skirmishes'.[107]

Finally, the question of how Japan should respond to the rift remained unresolved. There was still a strong reluctance to choose sides. The CRO poll found greater support for the Soviet position in the rift than the Chinese, but the former view only accounted for one third of respondents.[108] Satō Noboru continued to argue that, 'Khrushchev's attitudes are far more rational and realistic than those displayed by the Chinese Communists.' Yet, he again qualified this statement with another expressing sympathy for Beijing's 'legitimate national interests', even finding its 'quest for nuclear weapons…perfectly understandable.' Satō called on Japan's progressive forces to help alleviate Chinese isolation 'regardless of which side one takes in the Sino-Soviet dispute.'[109] Shimizu Shinzō also addressed Japanese progressives. Of the three alternative approaches to the rift he considered open to them—'wait and see'; 'become directly involved and absorbed by one side'; or 'try to cope with the dispute as one's own problem'—he recommended the last.[110] Eguchi Bokurō similarly pointed to the need for 'independent Japanese judgement to contribute to world peace.'[111] An editorial in Ishibashi Tanzan's *Tōyō Keizai Shimpō* claimed: 'In view of the great changes in Sino-Soviet relations, Japan's role as an intermediary between Communist China and the West has become more important.'[112] Mori Kyōzō (*Asahi Shimbun*) likewise felt that Japan should continue to oppose America's China containment policy. Noting how Japanese from both extreme left and extreme right had earlier argued that Tokyo should not join the PTBT, he again called for Japan to adopt an 'autonomous foreign policy' placing 'Japan's national interests' first.[113]

Hayashi Saburō (editorial board, *Mainichi Shimbun*) also took up the issue of Japan's 'autonomous foreign policy'. He first pointed out that the 'easing of international tensions has given all of the nations under American or Soviet leadership the opportunity to assert themselves.' Nevertheless, he thought that as long as Japanese policy-makers chose a pro-US policy on 'their own initiative' this constituted 'an autonomous foreign policy'. For Hayashi, Japan had a clear-cut choice to make between 'economic prosperity' and 'political autonomy', and existing trade ties with the US ensured that he favoured the former.[114]

Hayashi Kentarō for his part found most of the above writers guilty of what he termed 'the Japanese-style approach (*Nihonteki taiō*)'. This he defined as: 'recognising both China and the Soviet Union's good and bad points...[while] not committing oneself to either side.' Hayashi felt that Eguchi's writings constituted a perfect example of this. Satō was considered the 'most praiseworthy' member of this school, but his defence of China's national interests was his 'Achilles heel': 'If Communist China's national interests are important,' Hayashi asked rhetorically, 'are not Japan's national interests more important'. Yet Hayashi also respected Mori's emphasis on 'empirical reality', and regarding the dispute, he believed Mori was

> aware that in the new situation the Soviet position is true. Not because he sees it as a means of strengthening Marxism like Satō, but because in reality Soviet Reform Marxism's way of thinking is getting closer to the Free World's.

Nevertheless, Hayashi criticised Mori for sharing Satō's opposition to US containment of China. Hayashi believed China was aggressive.[115] He exposed similar flaws in the logic of Doi Akio. On the one hand, Hayashi declared that 'Japan must play a supporting role...for US policy towards Communist China', but on the other he also said that Japan needed 'an independent foreign policy [first] and then must cooperate.'[116]

The volume of studies appearing during the autumn of 1963 was only a little less than that which had been published during the spring, and the quality of scholarship had continued to improve. Particularly noteworthy was the growing respect for empirical research methodologies at the expense of purely theoretical approaches.

Japanese passions begin to fade

The Sino-Soviet propaganda war intensifies

1964 began quietly. Sino-Soviet public restraint, which had resumed the previous autumn, endured until the end of March. A relative paucity of studies published in Japan at this time reflected this trend. The Sino-Soviet campaigns to woo Japanese public opinion, however, continued unabated. In February, Chinese leaders told visiting LDP Diet members that Beijing would allow family visits to war criminals' graves. They also proposed the opening of direct air links and the exchange of newspaper correspondents.[117] A few weeks later, the last three Japanese war criminals held in China were released.[118] Back in Tokyo, groups sympathetic to China organised a mass petition to pressure the government into normalising diplomatic relations.[119] In April, Nan Hanchen (chairman of CITPC), undertook a groundbreaking six-week visit to Japan, while in Beijing, agreement was reached on the exchange of trade liaison offices and resident journalists. This should have broadened Japanese knowledge of the situation in China, but in reality all Japanese news organisations with China correspondents subsequently abjured from reporting events in a negative light.[120]

The Kremlin responded by suddenly despatching Deputy Premier Anastas Mikoyan on a two-week visit to Japan, in a patent attempt to counter the goodwill earned by Nan Hanchen. To help pave the way for a successful tour, all 16 Japanese currently detained by the Soviets were immediately released. Upon arrival, Mikoyan delivered a letter from Khrushchev to Prime Minister Ikeda. Seeking to differentiate Soviet foreign policy from that of China, Khrushchev called upon Japan to initiate a joint-declaration aimed at extending the PTBT to include underground nuclear tests. During his stay, Mikoyan also attempted to outbid Beijing with promises of huge trading opportunities. Again seeking to out do the Chinese, Mikoyan stopped en route to Moscow and paid his respects at the graves of Japanese POWs who had died in the Siberian *gulag* after World War II. In another symbolic gesture, shortly thereafter Ambassador Vinogradov announced that Moscow would henceforth permit Japanese families to visit graves on the Soviet-occupied islands of Habomai and Shikotan.[121]

On 10 July, however, these Soviet efforts paled into insignificance when, for the benefit of visiting JSP delegates, Mao Zedong linked Chinese and Japanese territorial claims against the Soviets: ‘There are too many places occupied by the Soviet Union...In regard to the Kurile Islands, the question is clear as far as we are concerned—they must be returned to Japan.’[122] Nor was this an isolated statement. In another meeting with members of the JSP delegations nine days later, Premier Zhou Enlai claimed that he had first pressed Khrushchev to settle its territorial disputes with Japan and others as early as January 1957. He also denied that Mao’s statement was an attempt to drive a wedge between Japan and the Soviet Union, although this was how it was perceived in both Tokyo and Moscow.[123] The Soviets made desperate efforts to persuade the Chinese to retract Mao’s statement. When these proved futile, the 2 September issue of *Pravda* signalled the launch of a bitter personal campaign against Mao, accusing him of ‘supporting Japanese revanchists’ claims to part of Soviet territory.’[124] A fortnight later, in a meeting with a Japanese Diet delegation, Khrushchev even went so far as to compare Mao’s words with ‘the ravings of Hitler’.[125] The propaganda contest had descended into ‘total war’.

The Japanese press response to the Sino-Soviet split

After Beijing had resumed its verbal assault on Moscow in late March, Japanese newspaper commentators started talking about a decisive Sino-Soviet split. The *Asahi Shimbun* editorial of 1 April claimed that the rift was ‘already beyond rescue...The Communists' sham "monolithic unity" is destroyed'.[126] The next day, *Sankei Shimbun* compared the split to 'rifts in the *yakuza* which never heal.'[127] A week later, another *Asahi* editorial 'greeted the new phase in the Sino-Soviet split (*bunretsu*)', describing the 'crack in Sino-Soviet unity [as] a fatal blow to the world Communist movement.' The author blamed the rift's emergence on 'Communist parties having seized power in more than ten states' (implying increased potential for factionalism), the Soviet desire for international peace to promote further domestic construction, and especially, 'Marxist intolerance of differences in opinion'. The editorial resisted 'judging which side is correct', but concluded with a strongly pacifist message.[128] At the end of May, Hirasawa Kazushige (editor of *Japan Times*) interviewed Soviet Deputy Premier Mikoyan and appealed to the Soviet Union to patch up its differences with China. Finding his interviewee perplexed at this request, Hirasawa pointed out that while Europe, especially Eastern Europe, was profiting from the Sino-Soviet conflict, Asia was suffering from more extremist Chinese policies.[129] Then in mid-July, after Mao had expressed support for Japan's claim to the Kuriles, *Yomiuri Shimbun* accused Moscow and Beijing of trying to 'capitalise not only on the territorial issue between themselves, but also on the territorial questions of other countries.' It warned Japan and others 'not [to get] heedlessly dragged into the Sino-Soviet dispute.'[130]

Japanese media interest in the split was now on the wane as its 'news value' had declined. The newspaper editors all seemed to agree that the breach was irreparable. Few Japanese intellectuals were willing to dispute this point.

Japanese intellectuals debate the split

The origins of the rift were no longer of prime concern to the Japanese intellectuals still analysing the rift in the spring and summer of 1964. It was largely taken for granted that ideology and national differences had both played a part in its emergence.[131] There was also near consensus on the seriousness of the split. Like the journalists, most academics now agreed that 'the estrangement between the two countries has become decisive.'[132] Regarding future prospects for Sino-Soviet relations, few disputed Shimizu Ikutarō's assertion that 'henceforth the rift will become more intense'. However, not many went as far as the *Taiken*, which suggested in June that 'Sino-Soviet relations appear to be on the verge of a showdown.' The author predicted that it would be China which 'may dare to rupture relations' whereas the Soviet Union would 'look to maintain diplomatic relations, the Sino-Soviet Alliance, and all trade agreements'.[133] By September, Doi Akio saw no such distinction, declaring: 'From now on compromise is impossible, Communist China is the Soviet Union's enemy.'[134]

It was not the causes of the rift so much as its effects upon Japan, both positive and negative, that now preoccupied Japan's intelligentsia. Even discussion of the wider implications of the rift was coloured by a concern for Japanese interests. On the theoretical level, Hayashi Kentarō asserted that,

> the Sino-Soviet conflict has clearly invalidated two separate notions...that Communism represents the highest stage of development for human society, the stage where the conflict among men has been completely eliminated...[and] that democracy and Communism are totally incompatible philosophies.[135]

For Hayashi, this was a useful stick with which to beat Japan's progressive parties and intellectuals. He concluded that 'Communism is perhaps best explained as a stage within the general, historical process of industrialisation.' Hidaka Rokurō, a reformist colleague at Tokyo University, immediately rebutted Hayashi's claims, declaring that: 'while the Sino-Soviet dispute may represent a polarisation of Marxism and the Marxist world, it does not indicate that [for Japan] Marxism is a bankrupt philosophy'.[136] Mori Kyōzō felt that the hold of both Communism and capitalism on Japan was weakening. Whereas post-war Japanese values had generally been shaped by forces emanating from Washington and Moscow 'in the wake of the Sino-Soviet dispute...the number of foreign sources has increased.'[137]

Regarding the split's impact on Japan's intellectual community itself, Tsuda Michio, another Marxist philosopher, claimed that 'the Japanese discussion of the Sino-Soviet dispute has produced almost nothing of value.' He attacked the 'commercialism' of Japanese journalists, and criticised the likes of Shimizu Ikutarō and Inoki Masamichi for using the rift to launch an 'anti-Marxist campaign' in Japan.[138] In sharp contrast, Nishi Yoshiyuki (Rikkyō University), asserted that the dispute 'lays bare the decadence (*taihai*) of Japanese intellectuals.'[139] Similarly, Shimizu Ikutarō interpreted the visits of Mikoyan and Nan Hanchen as a serious blow to the Japanese Left. Both were seen as having chosen to 'go over the heads of the progressives and deal with their enemies, the government and monopoly capitalism, and even shake hands with the Emperor.'[140]

Others on the Right were more concerned with the strategic repercussions of the rift. Here the concept of multipolarisation continued to hold sway. Both the *Taiken* and Kōtani Etsuo (former head of the Materials Section of the *Kōan Chōsachō*) worried that 'the growing feud between the Soviets and Chinese will imperceptibly encourage the Western nations to feel at ease with Communism, undermining the unity of the Free World'.[141] Still, their focus was primarily on its significance for Japan. The *Taiken* felt that although 'both are dangerous...the Soviet Union represents a greater danger than Communist China which speaks honestly.' It concluded that 'the intensification of the Sino-Soviet rift is a positive development for Japan, but it is much more important not to become negligent.'[142] Doi Akio also preached eternal vigilance, believing that 'one cannot trust either of them.' Yet he still felt that the rift was a positive development: 'Some say that separate Sino-Soviet strategies are more dangerous than their being one, but it is not true.'[143] Kōtani Etsuo did not share these sentiments, noting:

> in Western Europe and America...[and] in Japan too...there is a tendency to look upon the conflict optimistically. As a generalization, such a view may hold good, but not insofar as Japan's international situation differs from that of almost all other countries.[144]

Kōtani was convinced that because of its geostrategic location, 'the Sino-Soviet conflict has a much more direct impact on Japan'. Moreover, because of its economic development, Japan was 'the biggest prize that either of them can covet in Asia...Japan today is a goal that both Moscow and Peking are struggling for.' In evidence he pointed to the competing visits by Mikoyan and Nan Hanchen. In short, he warned, 'we are faced with "two communisms"', both of which still posed a serious threat to Japan.

Mutō Teiichi, the famous anti-Communist critic, like most, agreed that Mikoyan's visit to Japan was a bid 'to promote Sino-Japanese estrangement.' He also recognised that 'the Sino-Soviet military alliance against Japan is becoming a dead letter', and did not think that China represented a threat to Japan. On the contrary, Mutō declared, 'The greater the gap between China and the Soviet Union, the greater the chance for Japan to deal with China.'[145] Similarly, Kōsaka Masataka (Kyōto University) argued that 'Although China is verbally militant...her actions...continue to be extremely prudent.' Hence, he concluded: 'What China poses to Japan today is not an immediate military and economic threat, but rather a long-range challenge of a moral and political nature.'[146]

Historian Tōyama Shigeki (Yokohama City University) was unimpressed with these pronouncements and contended: 'Since they have no solutions to offer, it is questionable whether Japanese intellectuals have the necessary qualifications to comment on...the dispute between China and the Soviet Union.'[147] For the most part, however, the analysts' foreign policy recommendations followed on logically from their perceptions of the impact of the rift on Japan. Mori Kyōzō identified three types of Japanese response to the split. First came those who 'place a higher value on Japanese power and are happy to see a split in the enemy camp.' Second, those who 'do not really feel it is a serious problem for Japan...and want to adopt a neutral position', and finally, the rest who 'have chosen one side or are at a loss as to which side to choose.' Mori continued to stress the importance of Japanese forming their own opinion on the rift, and his own position was revealed by his claim that, 'most Japanese do not agree with the CCP's belligerent strategy...[and] violent revolutionary principles.' Despite all the 'talk of *dōbun dōshu*', he made it clear that, 'by various measures the Japanese and Chinese are different.'[148]

Doi Akio obviously belonged in Mori's first category, for he bluntly suggested that 'Japan should think how she can profit from the Sino-Soviet conflict, and think about making it worse.'[149] Mutō Teiichi was no less radical, arguing, 'The two big camps have collapsed, and those countries which lived under the protection of each camp must find their own way'. For Mutō, 'France and Communist China [we]re harbingers of this new age.' He even went so far as to predict that, 'If the Sino-Soviet military alliance is abrogated, the time will also come for the Japan–US Security Treaty to meet the same fate.' Finally, sounding oddly reminiscent of Yoshida Shigeru, Mutō proposed that 'as the Chinese Communist government is so eager to reconstruct an independent state free from the Soviet yoke, Japan should cooperate as much as possible.'[150] Kōsaka Masataka at first agreed with Mutō that Japan had to adopt an independent policy towards China.[151] A few months later, however, he backtracked: 'While I feel that Japan must work to re-establish an autonomous foreign policy...I am also convinced that Japan should continue her military ties with America.' He ended up proposing a kind of 'Finlandisation' of Japan.[152]

It seems that by the autumn of 1964, the Sino-Soviet Alliance had developed from being an issue primarily of concern to Marxist political philosophers, to become a central debate in the emerging Japanese discipline of International Relations, as well as attracting scholars from a wide range of related fields.

The point of no return

Four dramatic events during that autumn exerted a decisive influence on the course of Japan's ongoing intellectual debate on the Sino-Soviet split. The combined effect of the publication of the 'Kennan Thesis', China's first nuclear test, and especially Khrushchev's fall, convinced most Japanese scholars that they were never going to see a return to the early days of the Sino-Soviet Alliance and the bipolar international order. Thereafter, the volume of reports gradually subsided: supplanted by news of President Johnson's decision to dramatically step-up US military involvement in Vietnam.

The announcement of Khrushchev's 'retirement' on 16 October came as a surprise to most Japanese and briefly led to some press speculation on the possibility of Sino-Soviet reconciliation.[153] Few accepted at face value the official Kremlin explanation blaming the premier's ill health, preferring instead to see some connexion to the rift.[154] Sino-Soviet relations did in fact enjoy a temporary improvement, symbolised by talks held in Moscow between the new leadership and Zhou Enlai in early November. However, in the New Year, tensions rose again in response to American escalation of the war in Vietnam.

Japanese intellectuals examining the likely effects of Khrushchev's demise seemed to agree with Inoki Masamichi that Sino-Soviet relations had now 'entered a new stage.' He credited the CPSU with 'removing the number one obstacle to making peace [with the CCP.]' Nevertheless, Inoki felt that while Moscow and Beijing could possibly 'compromise on their national interests', when it came to 'party-to-party relations the obstacles remained too great'.[155] Most other scholars agreed that the removal of Khrushchev would be insufficient to satisfy the Chinese, although some now identified their territorial dispute not ideology as the ultimate obstacle.[156]

Public opinion still seemed to lag far behind the 'experts' when it came to assessing the future prospects for Sino-Soviet Alliance. At the end of the year, a nationwide poll reported that those expecting relations to improve outnumbered those anticipating their deterioration by a ratio of two to one.[157] It was not until December 1965, that popular expectations reversed themselves.[158]

When it came to assessing the consequences of the rift, especially for Japan, the Chinese nuclear test and the 'Kennan Thesis' seemed more directly relevant.[159] Although the Japanese and US governments made a concerted effort to downplay its significance, press coverage of Beijing's admission to the nuclear club easily eclipsed that on the leadership change in Moscow. The former outweighed the latter by a ratio of ten to one in letters to the *Asahi Shimbun*.[160] Popular reactions seemed to comprise unequal parts of disappointment, fear, anger and a sneaking admiration. Immediately after news of the detonation, a *Jiji* poll found the public almost equally divided on whether it had increased the danger posed to Japan's security or not.[161] There was no agreement concerning how the government should respond.[162] Most intellectuals focused on the threat seemingly directed at Japan (or the US) by the Chinese test—perhaps the fact that the explosion reinforced the Sino-Soviet split was simply taken for granted. One commentator did recognise it as constituting a 'grave threat' to the Soviet Union.[163] Much later, Wakaizumi Kei claimed that the test would 'force the Soviet Union to recognise at last that there are two leaders within the Communist world.'[164]

George Kennan's proposals for a more independent Japanese diplomacy in response to the Sino-Soviet split and the newly emerging multipolar international system predictably provoked mixed reactions among Japanese intellectuals. Kennan struck a strong chord with Mushakōji Kinhide (Gakushūin University), an international politics expert who used the American's 'thesis' to attack the outdated thinking of Japanese policy makers. He agreed that: 'Japan should give more serious thought to Chinese and its own national interests', rather than always deferring to Washington.[165] Kamiya Fuji (Tokyo University), another international politics specialist, also supported Kennan's view. Kamiya agreed that 'in an age of polycentrism', Japan should look to 'Communist bloc states' in dealing with 'its own national interests.' He condemned the LDP for 'clinging to Dulles' outdated concept of "Free World unity"'.[166] The critic Irie Michimasa, on the other hand, objected to the way in which Kennan presupposed that the Sino-Soviet rift would reduce the risk of Japan being invaded by either country. Irie also questioned the outcome should they reconcile, and concluded that a continuation of the Japan–US Security Treaty was the safest policy.[167] Kōsaka Masataka fell somewhere in between these two extremes. He also accused Japanese leaders of having 'learned nothing from the recent polycentric tendencies in world politics'. Somewhat contradictorily he also supported the maintenance of the alliance with America, albeit with a greater defence role for Tokyo.[168] Participants in the *Taiken* round-table (cited earlier) added short-sightedness to the growing list of government shortcomings: 'The current LDP government...thinks of national interests one day at a time', they complained. One participant also argued that because of the split, Chinese and Soviet influence on Japan was weakening. Doi Akio himself still held that it was in Japan's interests 'to set Communist China and the Soviet Union fighting each other.' To this end, he came up with the radical suggestion that Japan both 'help to develop Siberia' and 'stop containing China.'[169] Mushakōji Kinhide fundamentally disagreed. He recognised that America was 'rejoicing at the Sino-Soviet dispute', but Mushakōji held such a view to be 'very dangerous', believing that 'the sooner they patch up their differences, the better it will be.'[170]

Of course, just as the Sino-Soviet rift did not end abruptly in early 1965, Japanese interest in their split did not suddenly evaporate. Pollsters continued to quiz the Japanese public on the issue. By 1967, for instance, nearly two thirds of Japanese were aware of the rift's existence, almost as many as understood that mainland China was a Communist state.[171] New publications also appeared, both broadening and deepening Japanese understanding of the split. The author Iida Momo, for instance, examined the poetic meaning of the dispute.[172] Major studies by Miyamoto Yoshio, Kikuchi Masanori, Kazawa Gō, Nakajima Mineo and many others analysed the rift from the perspectives of history, politics, economics and international relations.[173] However, such work was of a fundamentally different nature to the examination of the life span of the Sino-Soviet Alliance presented here. Japanese scholars now perceived the alliance to be dead in all but name and subsequent research took the form of a *post mortem*.

Interpretative comments

Input: external environment:

The 1960s witnessed a major social revolution in the West and a Cultural Revolution in China, but stagnation in the Soviet Union.

Moscow and Beijing stepped up their efforts to woo Japanese public opinion as the rift came into the open. China allowed Japanese journalists to be stationed in Beijing for the first time, while Soviet leaders granted Japanese pressmen special interviews. The growth of 'invitation diplomacy' was evidenced in the increased exchange of visitors with both China and the Soviet Union (Figure 9.3).

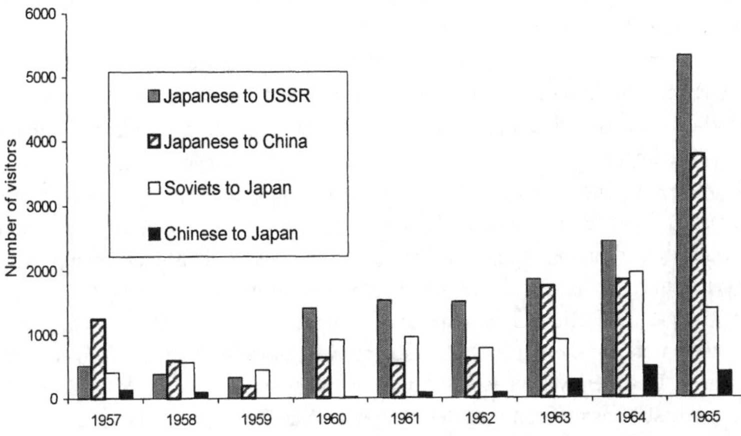

Figure 9.3 Exchange of visitors between Japan, China and the USSR, 1957–65

Source: Mori Takanosuke, 'NisSo shinzen no itsuwareru seiso', *Gendai no Me* (Aug.1966) 7(8): 113; Wolf Mendl, *Issues in Japan's China Policy* (1978) London: 129.

The US contributed to the rise of a new generation of young Japanese empiricists or 'neo-realists' trained by American universities in the latest social science techniques. This began a trend towards an increased exchange of ideas between Japanese and Western intellectuals.

Internal environment: operational sphere

The role of the Japanese media remained the same, but during the first half of the 1960s, Japan's rigid intellectual structure underwent a drastic change. Meanwhile, Japanese university campuses passed from the control of progressive intellectuals and into the hands of radical students to the detriment of their academic productivity.

Psychological sphere: belief systems

During the early 1960s, the Japanese national identity gradually regained some of its former Asian flavour, as the shame of defeat and occupation gave way to a new sense of pride in the nation's postwar achievements, and some older traditions were revived. This development coincided with a marked decline in the influence of Marxism. After 1961, increasing Sino-Soviet competition irreversibly damaged the ideological appeal of both the Chinese and Soviet models for the Japanese. On the other hand, the rift also prompted a greater interest in both Chinese and Soviet problems at the popular level.

Although the Soviets had consistently been more disliked by the Japanese public than the Chinese, opinion polls revealed that from mid-1963 onwards the gap began to narrow, until by early 1966 it had completely disappeared (Figure 8.1). The importance of China had increased in Japanese eyes because of the rift. However, Beijing's belligerent rhetoric, and especially its first nuclear test, tarnished its carefully fostered 'peace-loving' image and helped to erode the previously widespread sympathy for China. Opinions of the Soviet Union, on the other hand, improved somewhat, benefiting from Khrushchev's 'peaceful coexistence' line, which appealed to the pacifistic tendencies still prevalent among the Japanese. In short, people became more tolerant of Russia, if not exactly friendly. This then weakened anti-Soviet and Pan-Asianist norms in Japan. While a causal relationship cannot be demonstrated conclusively, it seems reasonable to assert that this was the most significant legacy of the rift for Japanese public opinion.

Psychological sphere: perceptions

The Sino-Soviet Alliance had a greater impact on Japanese popular perceptions of China and the Soviet Union when under strain than when it was thriving. The impact of the rift on Japanese thinking was the greater, not because it was unexpected, but because its timing, speed and character—associated with US–Soviet détente and not Chinese defection to the West, as Yoshida Shigeru and others had predicted—took nearly everybody by surprise. The rift produced a more 'realistic' understanding of China and the Soviet Union in Japan.

Japanese intellectuals meanwhile were engrossed in esoteric debates about whether the world was witnessing an ideological dispute or a clash of national interests. When the split came into the open, most intellectuals still evinced a reluctance to choose sides, but gradually views on the causes and nature of the Sino-Soviet split converged. The emphasis then shifted to a consideration of its consequences for the rest of the world, and especially for Japan. Most observers in the West thought that the rift would prove beneficial to Japan, whereas most Japanese commentators felt that it represented a welcome gift for the West. They worried more about the increased risk of war, and felt less secure. In this respect, there was no major divergence between elite and popular perceptions. By the end of 1964, the Sino-Soviet Alliance was generally regarded in Japan (and elsewhere) as dead, if not yet buried.

Subtle changes in the vocabulary used by the media to describe the Sino-Soviet relationship were indicative of shifting perceptions (Figure 9.2).

Decision-making process

In the wake of the onset of the rift, many progressive intellectuals broke with, or were expelled by, the JCP. They also saw their influence over public opinion drastically curtailed. Similarly, the ageing right-wing ideologues slowly retreated into the background, as Prime Minister Ikeda Hayato launched a series of efforts to reach out to moderate intellectuals, and solicit their recommendations on policy towards the Sino-Soviet Alliance. Not surprisingly, their contradictory advice proved to be of little value to policy-makers. Satō Eisaku's approach appears to have been more selective. He engaged the 'brains' of a number of favoured intellectuals and 'think tanks', but his support for the US war in Vietnam alienated many. 'Neo-realists' were now the most influential group amongst Japan's intellectuals.

The 'climate of opinion' seems to have imposed some vague limits on the policy-makers. The numerous public opinion polls commissioned by the CRO are perhaps one indication of a willingness to listen to 'ordinary Japanese'. MOFA also made available to the public many of its views on the progress of the Sino-Soviet rift. However, public activism proved incapable of pressuring the government into taking any positive diplomatic initiatives. The government, in frustrating legitimate national aspirations, perpetuated an immature conception of international relations and prompted some disillusionment with the democratic process.

Output

For the two years preceding the Sino-Indian border conflict and the Cuban missile crisis, the rift received remarkably little attention in the Japanese media. Thereafter, with the sudden deterioration in Sino-Soviet relations, it became a national obsession. In a single month, March 1963, Japanese journals published at least 20 major articles examining the dispute. In July alone, *Asahi Shimbun* contained no less than 128 stories detailing the latest developments, an average of four per day (Figure 9.1). Japanese journalists disseminated information about the rift, but offered little guidance to public opinion.

The Sino-Soviet split contributed to a change in the nature of the Japanese intellectual discourse, not just on Communist affairs but on international relations generally. It led to a paradigm shift, with the rise of realists and 'neo-realists' who saw both the Soviet Union and China as a threat to Japan. Nevertheless, 'neo-realist' scholars argued that Japan's strategic position had improved: with 'multipolarisation', they offered a theoretical rationale for a more independent foreign policy. Yet, still suffering from an exaggerated sense of Japan's limited diplomatic, political and strategic capabilities, most 'neo-realists' lacked the conviction to pursue this line to its logical conclusion. Instead, they remained generally supportive of the Security Treaty with the US—a relationship which brought so many tangible benefits—and wary of making enemies of either the Soviets or Chinese.

The split also fatally weakened Japan's traditional progressives, but they were succeeded by a smaller group of 'neo-idealists' who soon reached a consensus on the goals of peaceful coexistence and neutrality. They loudly denounced the neo-realists' balance of power theorem and sought to play down the significance of military power. Thus, the 1960s saw an unequal battle between 'realism' and 'idealism', but this was still a more pragmatic struggle than that which dominated the previous decade.

Given such a lead by the media and intellectual community, public opinion not surprisingly remained divided. Still, the majority of Japanese wished to see relations with China placed on an equal footing with the Soviet Union. Moreover, the idea that Japanese should somehow adopt an 'independent line' gained ground right across the political spectrum of Japanese civil society, but approval for alignment with the Communist bloc never exceeded two per cent. In the wake of the rift, popular support for 'neutrality' increased to equal roughly the level of support for association with the 'Free World' (Figure 9.4).

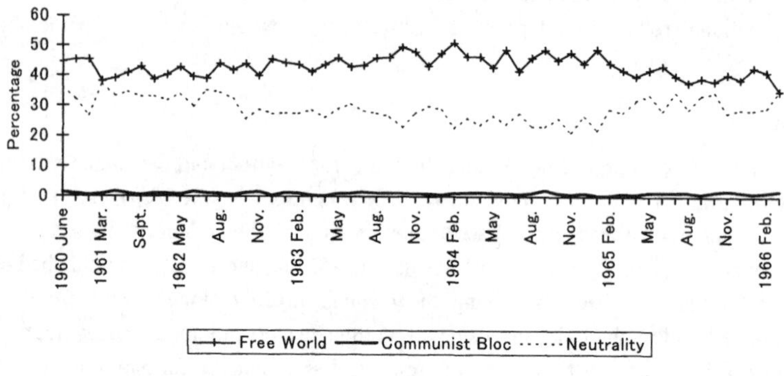

Figure 9.4 Foreign policy desired by the Japanese people, 1960–66

Source: Yoron chōsa nenkan (1960–67).

External environment: feedback

Japanese popular and intellectual views on the rift were virtually ignored by the international community until this study was undertaken.

10 Japan and the drift towards multipolarisation: concluding thoughts

Three questions warrant further attention. First, what advantages did the multidisciplinary International Political History method adopted here enjoy over more conventional approaches? This framework facilitated an in-depth analysis of the diverse impacts of the Sino-Soviet Alliance on Japan. The distinction drawn in this study between the external and internal environments permitted the complex interaction between international developments and Japanese domestic trends to be carefully dissected. It found that internal political conflicts occasionally proved more significant than foreign pressures as an influence on policy or conceptions of interest.

The flexible incorporation of both operational and psychological spheres highlighted the necessity of taking into account a wide variety of variables, rather than settling for superficially attractive unicausal explanations. The Japan–US Security Treaty and Sino-Soviet Alliance were both examples of multidimensional institutions. They demonstrate that the formation, survival or demise of Cold War pacts reflected not only diplomatic and strategic factors, but also economic, ideological, and cultural ones. However, this study has also shown that alliances can prosper despite a lack of shared threat perceptions, given sufficiently interdependent economic and military structures. Equally, they can wither despite a shared ideology, given insufficient economic and strategic integration. Nevertheless, while developments in the operational sphere created opportunities for Japan to play a more assertive role in the International System, it was primarily psychological obstacles that prevented Tokyo from advancing very far or very fast in this direction. In other words, although each of the major schools of

International Relations theory contributed to an understanding of the Sino-Soviet Alliance's impact on Japan, none could explain it fully.

The chronological structure and extended timeframe employed in this study revealed the dynamic historical processes at work along four dimensions: diplomatic/strategic; economic; ideological; and ideational. It was not a linear progression of neatly defined phases, but rather an erratic and unpredictable succession of interconnected and overlapping events. The incorporation of four levels of analysis—individual, group, national, and international—exposed the vertical and horizontal lines of conflict that characterised Japanese decision-making processes. Similarly, the inclusion of four perspectives—those of the foreign policy establishment, the business world, the left-wing opposition, and the informed public—permitted this study to go beyond state-centrism to a more diffuse model that embraced non-policy outputs and informal participation in international relations. Finally, the feedback circuit is important because it allowed the international consequences of Japanese responses to the Sino-Soviet Alliance to be assessed.

Perhaps the greatest strength of the International Political History method, however, is that it provides detailed and reliable answers to complex international questions. Unfortunately, its main weakness is that in order to do so it relies on governments granting researchers relatively free access to sensitive records. This is not generally possible in the Western democracies until 25 or 30 years after the event, and even then censorship remains a serious obstacle. In the prevailing international political climate this situation is unlikely to improve.

The second issue to consider is the extent to which the rise and fall of the Sino-Soviet Alliance affected Japanese politics and foreign relations. With potentially crucial data still classified, the views set out here must remain tentative conclusions. Nevertheless, we can deduce from the information currently available that the Sino-Soviet Alliance changed some things, while leaving many others unaltered. From Japan's point of view, the alliance's collapse did not end the Cold War division of the global system or the East Asian sub-system; it did not eliminate Japanese dependence on the US, nor hasten the demise of the Security Treaty. At the most fundamental level there was a strong degree of continuity in Japanese foreign policy: the primacy of the relationship with Washington endured. Moreover, at the domestic level, it did not weaken the LDP's grip on the levers of power.

On the other hand, reoriented lines of conflict and cooperation, revised perceptions, reorganised decision-making systems, expanded economic exchanges, and modified policies were all indicative of significant shifts induced by the Sino-Soviet Alliance. The Cold War structure was severely shaken, Japan and the US developed a more balanced relationship, and the Conservative domination of government became firmly entrenched. By the mid-1960s, the policy-making system centred on a tripartite alliance (the so-called 'iron triangle') linking the bureaucracy, ruling party, and big business, with the opposition parties, public opinion and its shapers forced to the periphery. Nevertheless, policies towards China and the Soviet Union did evolve. Despite the dominance of Conservative political parties, the Japanese government employed a number of different strategies for coping with the Sino-Soviet Alliance. Changes of direction often coincided with the arrival of a new premier.

The Sino-Soviet Alliance could not compete with the US as an external actor shaping the Japanese political, diplomatic, economic, social, and cultural order during the 1950s and early 1960s. Washington held nearly all of the trump cards. It enjoyed direct access to all levels of the Japanese decision-making process, first via the Occupation authorities and thereafter through diplomatic channels and the Security Treaty apparatus. A dense network of informal connexions augmented this official structure. However, this study uncovered evidence of serious disagreements between Japan and the US (and Taiwan) over policy towards the Sino-Soviet Alliance, which ultimately derived from differences in their perceptions of threat, national interests, and national identities. Moreover, at the global level even the Americans could not escape the influence of the Sino-Soviet rift. In other words, taken together, China and the Soviet Union represented the second most important source of *gaiatsu* during Japan's 'decisive decades'.

Finally, can it now be stated categorically whether the consequences of the Sino-Soviet split for Japan were positive or negative? Two fundamentally different lines of Japanese thinking emerged on this question. The first interpretation understood that the divisions engendered by the Sino-Soviet split in the international, regional, and domestic spheres, were evidence of multipolarity. It would allow Japan greater policy flexibility, as constraints were removed (or at least relaxed) and opportunities created. This was a necessary, but not a sufficient condition, to create an independent foreign policy. Positive incentives were also required.

Those Japanese of the alternative mindset were confused by the instability and complexity that the split produced at all three levels of analysis. They saw additional constraints resulting in aggravated risks and policy immobilism. In a rational cost/benefit analysis, they adjudged the price of an independent foreign policy to outweigh the potential gains: a higher value was placed on security than autonomy. The mainstream position was to avoid extremes. Given a choice between action and inaction this group selected positive non-involvement: a reactive strategy. Presented with the alternatives of embarking on an independent course or accepting continuing dependence on the US, they chose to pursue interdependence.

In short, at the risk of oversimplifying the issue, the formation of the Sino-Soviet Alliance was on balance detrimental for Japan and hence its collapse was beneficial. However, the alliance was more harmful to Japan on paper than in reality, and thus its demise was more helpful in theory than in practice.

Appendix 1

Nitchū NisSo Kokkō Chōsei Sokushin Dōmei
Alliance for the Promotion of Normalised Diplomatic Relations with China and the Soviet Union (established April 1953)

Founding Members

Hirano Yoshitarō	Chief, China Research Institute.
Hiratsuka Tsunejirō	President, Japan Fishery Association; ex-President, *NichiRo Gyogyō* (Japan–Russia Fishing Company.)
Itō Kesaichi	Representative Director, Japan–Soviet Trade Promotion Association.
Kanō Hisa'akira	Chairman, Hakodate Dock Company.
Kazami Akira	Independent Member, House of Representatives.
Kita Reikichi	Member, House of Representatives (*Minshūtō*); Managing Editor, *Nihon Shimbun*.
Kitamura Tokutarō	President, Shinwa Bank; ex-Finance Minister; a leader of *Minshūtō* and *Kaishūtō*.
Murata Shōzō	Chief, Japan–Philippines Friendship Association.
Nakajima Kenzō	Critic.
Ūno Shinkichi	Lawyer.
Yamamoto Kumaichi	President, Japan–China Trade Promotion Association.

Appendix 2

Gaikō Mondai Kondankai
Foreign Policy Problems Deliberation Council (established 16 August 1960)

Members

Amō Eiji	Head, *Ōa Kyōkai.*
Fukuda Kyōsuke	President, *Tokyo Shimbun.*
Fukushima Shintarō	Retired diplomat; Deputy Chief Cabinet Secretary in Ashida Cabinet; President, *The Japan Times.*
Hasegawa Norishige	Managing Director, Sumitomo Chemicals.
Hasegawa Saiji	Representative Director, *Jiji Tsūshinsha.*
Hatano Kenichi	Member, Editorial Board, *Sankei Shimbun.*
Hirasawa Kazushige	Editor, *The Japan Times.*
Honda Chikao	President, *Mainichi Shimbun.*
Horikoshi Teizō	Secretary General, *Keidanren.*
Hosokawa Ryūgen	Political commentator.
Hosoya Matsuta	Head, International Department, *Shinsanbetsu* (National Federation of Industrial Labour.)
Imazato Hiroki	President, *Nikkeiren.*
Inoki Masamichi	Professor, Kyōto University.
Iwabuchi Tatsuo	Political critic.
Iwasa Yoshizane	Representative Manager, *Keizai Dōyūkai* (Japan Committee for Economic Development).
Kamikawa Hikomatsu	Professor Emeritus, Tokyo University.
Kiuchi Nobutane	Director, *Sekai Keizai Chōsakai* (World Economy Institute.)
Kon Hidemi	Novelist and critic.
Maeda Yoshinori	Managing Director, NHK.
Matsumoto Shigeharu	Head, International House of Japan.
Mitarai Tatsuo	Political commentator.
Mizuno Shigeo	President, *Sankei Shimbun.*
Murayama Nagataka	President, *Asahi Shimbun.*
Nakagawa Mikiko	Novelist.
Nakayama Ichirō	Professor, Hitotsubashi University.
Obama Toshie	Critic.
Ōhama Nobumoto	President, Waseda University.
Ozaki Shirō	Novelist.
Rōyama Masamichi	Former President, Ochanomizu Women's University.
Sakanishi Shiho	Critic.
Sasabe Kureo	Head, Nagoya Chamber of Commerce and Industry.
Takahashi Yūsai	Vice-President, *Yomiuri Shimbun.*
Takayama Iwao	Professor, Nihon University.
Takita Minoru	Chairman, *Zenrō.*
Yamaura Kanichi	Critic.
Yokota Kisaburō	Chief Justice, Supreme Court.

Appendix 3

Soren Mondai Kenkyūkai
Soviet Problems Research Association
(established early 1952, active membership as of April 1952)

President

Satō Naotake	President, House of Councillors, *Ryokufūkai* (1949–53); Foreign Minister (1937); Ambassador, Soviet Union (1925, 1942–46), Belgium (1931–33), France (1933, 1934–36).

Chairman of Board of Directors

Morishima Gorō	Head, House of Representatives' Foreign Affairs Committee; former Minister to Soviet Union (1942–46), (postings to China).

Lecturers and research associates

Amō Eiji	Head, *Ōa Kyōkai.*
Abe Kenichi	Editor-in-Chief, *Sankei Shimbun*; Doctor of Economics.
Andō Yoshirō	Head, Political Affairs Division, MOFA (1945), (postings in China, USSR); Professor, Takushoku University.
Fuse Masaharu	Member, editorial board, *Sankei Shimbun*; Soviet specialist.
Hatano Kenichi	Member, editorial Board, *Sankei Shimbun*; China specialist.
Hozumi Nagayori	Head, *Hozumi Kenkyūjo*; ex-head, Soviet broadcast monitoring section, *Tōa Kenkyūjo*; Soviet specialist.
Hidaka Shinrokurō	Ambassador to Italy (1943–46), (postings in China, Manchuria).
Higurashi Nobunori	European–American Division, MOFA; Soviet specialist.
Ishikawa Jun	Former head Beijing office, *Mainichi Shimbun*; China specialist.
Imai Kazuo	Head, Public Works Committee; Soviet specialist.
Ibe Masaichi	Professor, Kōryū University; Soviet specialist.
Kodaki Akira	Member, House of Councillors; ex-Commercial Attaché, MOFA.
Kitazawa Naokichi	Member, House of Representatives; ex-Counsellor, MOFA.
Kubota Kanichirō	Member, House of Councillors' Foreign Affairs Committee; ex-Counselor, MOFA.
Kase Shunichi	Diplomatic commentator.
Kondō Yoshiharu	Former President, *NisSo Tsūshinsha* (Japan–Soviet News Agency.)
Kuroda Otokichi	*Mainichi Shimbun*, former Moscow Special Correspondent.
Kiyokawa Yōkichi	European–American Section, *Asahi Shimbun*; former Moscow Special Correspondent.
Miyazaki (??)	East Asia Section Chief, *Asahi Shimbun.*
Miyazaki Akira	Head, Information and Culture Bureau, MOFA; (postings to China, future Minister to Taiwan).
Maruyama Masao	Reporter, *Asahi Shimbun*; former Moscow Special Correspondent.
Maruyama Naomitsu	Journalist, (experience in Manchuria); Soviet specialist.
Niizeki Kinya	Head, Soviet Desk, MOFA.

Naoi Takeo	Correspondent, *New Leader*; Soviet specialist.
Ōkura Kinmochi	Former Deputy Head *Tōa Kenkyūjo* (East Asia Research Institute.)
Suma Yakiichirō	Head, Information Bureau, MOFA (1939–40); Ambassador to Spain (1940–46), (service in China.)
Sugihara Arata	Member, House of Councillors (Liberal Party); head, Treaty Bureau, MOFA (1945–46).
Sone Eki	Member, House of Representatives (JSP); head, First Section, Political Affairs Bureau, MOFA (1945), (service in China).
Sono Akira	Head, First Section, Information and Culture Bureau, MOFA.
Shigemitsu Akira	Head, Third Section, Treaty Bureau, MOFA.
Shimizu Jūzō	Instructor, MOFA Training Institute; China specialist.
Takeo Hajime	Member, House of Representatives; Soviet specialist.
Tsuchiya Hayato	Head, European–American Affairs Bureau, MOFA.
Takada Ichitarō	Deputy Head, Editorial Board, *Mainichi Shimbun*.
Tachibana Yoshimori	Head, East Asia Section, *Mainichi Shimbun*; China specialist.
Watanabe Mikio	Political Section, *Mainichi Shimbun*; former Moscow Special Correspondent.
Wada Toshio	Professor, Kōryū University; former diplomat; former employee of Japanese company in Sakhalin; Soviet specialist.
Yūkawa Morio	Head, Economic Affairs Bureau, MOFA.
Yūbashi Shigetō	European–American Affairs Bureau, MOFA; Soviet specialist.

Appendix 4

Tairiku Mondai Kenkyūjo
Continental Problems Research Institute
(officially established January 1952, informally spring 1951, membership as of 27 August 1952)

President

Doi Akio	Lt. General (rtd.), (formerly in charge of research and planning on the Soviet Union for the Imperial Army General Staff, and chief of intelligence and counter-intelligence field work in Manchuria); military attaché in Moscow (1938–40); postwar defence adviser to the Nationalist Government in Nanjing.

Advisors

Amō Eiji	Head, *Ōa Kyōkai*.
Ashida Hitoshi	Former Prime Minister (*Kaishintō*) (Mar.–Oct. 1948).
Gōkō Kiyoshi	Chairman, Japan Association of Defence Industries (1952–60); President of New Japan Steamship Company; President, Mitsubishi Heavy Industries (1941–45).
Hayashi Jōji	Secretary-General, Liberal Party; Deputy Prime Minister (1948–49); former President, House of Representatives (1951–52).
Murata Shōzō	Former Minister of Communications and Railways (1940–41); Ambassador to the Philippines (1943–46).
Nomura Kichisaburō	Admiral (rtd.); Ambassador to the US (Feb.–Dec. 1941; Foreign Minister (1939–40).
Ogata Taketora	Minister of State (1944–45, Liberal Party Deputy Prime Minister (1952–54), and Party President (1954–55).
Okamura Yasuji	General (rtd.)
Ōkura Kinmochi	Former Vice-President, *Tōa Kenkyūjo* (East Asia Research Institute).
Satō Naotake	President, *Soren Mondai Kenkyūkai.*
Shimomura Sadamu	General (rtd.); Minister of War (Aug.–Dec. 1945).

Trustees

Ayabe Kitsuju	Lt. General (rtd.)
Fuse Masaharu	Member, Editorial Board *Sankei Shimbun*; Soviet specialist.
Hara Tomio	Director, *Heiki Seisan Kyōryokukai* (Japan Association of Defence Industries.)
Hata Hiroshi	China specialist.
Hayashi Saburō	Colonel (rtd.); military affairs commentator.
Horiba Kazuo	Colonel (rtd.)
Horike Kazumarō	Lt. General (rtd.)
Hozumi Nagayori	Head *Hozumi Kenkyūjo*; Soviet specialist.

Iimura Jyō	Former head, *Sōryokusen Kenkyūjo* (Total War Institute); Lt. General (rtd.)
Imai Kazuo	Head, Clerical Workers' Union; Soviet specialist.
Imai Takeo	Major General (rtd.)
Ishii Masami	Major General (rtd.)
Kambayashi Tomō	Manager, *Sekai Minshu Kenkyūjo* (World Democracy Institute).
Kanda Masatane	Lt. General (rtd.)
Kawabe Torashirō	Lt. General (rtd.)
Kitaoka Juitsu	Dean, Faculty of Politics and Economics, Kokugakuin University.
Kiyokawa Yūkichi	Reporter, *Asahi Shimbun*; former Moscow Special Correspondent.
Kuroda Otokichi	Managing Director, *Soren Mondai Kenkyūkai*.
Maeda Minoru	Lt. General (rtd.)
Maruyama Masao	Reporter, *Asahi Shimbun*; former Moscow Special Correspondent.
Matsui Takuro	Lt. General (rtd.)
Miyazaki Shuichi	Lt. General (rtd.)
Mori Shōzō	Editor-in-Chief, *Mainichi Shimbun*; former Moscow Special Correspondent.
Nabeyama Sadachika	Political commentator; ex-Communist; founder of *Sekai Minshu Kenkyūjo*.
Naoi Takeo	Correspondent, *New Leader*; Soviet specialist.
Noda Yutaka	Head, *Noda Keizai Kenkyūjo* (Noda Institute of Economics.)
Ōi Atsushi	Navy Captain (rtd.); military affairs commentator.
Okazaki Kaheita	President, Ikegai Iron; Maruzen Oil.
Onouchi Hiroshi	Lt. General (rtd.)
Sano Manabu	Head, *Nihon Seiji Keizai Kenkyūjo* (Japanese Institute of Politics and Economics); ex-Communist.
Shimizu Tōzō	Technical Officer, MOFA Training Institute; China Specialist.
Takashima Tatsuhiko	Major General (rtd.)
Tanegawa Kazuo	Major General (rtd.)
Tatsumi Eiichi	Lt. General (rtd.)
Tomioka Sadatoshi	Head, Historical Truth Investigation Section, 2 Demobilisation Ministry (1945–6); Rear Admiral (rtd.)
Watanabe Mikio	Reporter, *Mainichi Shimbun*; former Moscow Special Correspondent.
Watanabe Wataru	Major General (rtd.).
Yabe Chūta	Major General (rtd.); former Military Attaché to the Soviet Union.
Yabe Teiji	Professor Emeritus, Tokyo University.
Yamaguchi Suteji	Major General (rtd.); former Military Attaché to the Soviet Union.

Appendix 5

Soren Kenkyūsha Kyogikai
Council of Sovietologists
(membership as of April 1957)
Ōa Kyōkai
Society for the Study of Communism in Europe and Asia
(changed name 2 July 1959)

Directors

Amō Eiji	Head of Association; head, UN Association; head, MOFA Information Bureau (1943–44); Vice-Foreign Minister (1941); Ambassador to Italy (1939–40), Soviet Union (1930, 1932).
Inoki Masamichi	Professor, Kyōto University.
Kiga Kenzō	Professor, Keiō University.
Maruyama Masao	Former reporter, *Asahi Shimbun*.
Watanabe Mikio	*Mainichi Shimbun*; former Moscow Special Correspondent.

Members

Asai Kinzō	*Ōsaka Yomiuri Shimbun*.
Gotō Yonosuke	EPA.
Hamada Seiichi	*Ōtoyo Kensetsu*.
Harako Rinjirō	*Jiji Tsūshinsha*.
Hasamada Shinjirō	Nihon University.
Hata Masaru	*Asahi Shimbun*.
Hayashi Kentarō	Tokyo University.
Hayashi Saburō	Researcher, MOFA.
Hiraga Kenta	Home Affairs Ministry.
Hiratake Denzō	Waseda University.
Horie Shigeo	Bank of Tokyo.
Inaba Shūzō	*Kokumin Keizai Kenkyū Kyōkai* (National Economy Research Association.)
Iwama Tōru	Tokyo Women's University.
Kaneko Yukihiko	Hitotsubashi University.
Katō Hiroshi	Keiō University.
Kimura Takeyasu	Tokyo University.
Kiuchi Nobutane	*Sekai Keizai Chōsakai* (World Economy Institute.)
Kiyokawa Yūkichio	*Asahi Shimbun*.
Kobayashi Shigezō	EPA.
Kuroda Otokichi	Former reporter, *Mainichi Shimbun*.
Maruge Shinobu	Ministry of Agriculture.
Matsui Eiichi	European–Asian Affairs Bureau, MOFA.
Miyake Masaya	*Asahi Shimbun*.
Nose Torazō	National Diet Library.
Okazawa Hidetora	Waseda University.

Ōki Saburō	EPA.
Onoe Masao	Kōbe University.
Satō Hiroyuki	*Shakai Shiso Kenkyūkai Jimukyoku* (Social Thinking Research Association Office).
Seki Yoshihiko	Tōritsu University.
Shimizu Takehisa	European–Asian Affairs Bureau, MOFA.
Sone Eki	Member, House of Councillors (JSP.)
Sugimoto Kinma	National Diet Library.
Tōhō Kōichi	*Asahi Shimbun.*
Takahashi Chōtarō	Hitotsubashi University.
Takahashi Masao	Kyūshū University.
Tomitani Hiroshi	*Kansai Keidanren.*
Tsuchiya Kiyoshi	*Asahi Shimbun.*
Uemada Yoshitada	Kansai Gakuin University.
Utsumi Yōichi	Ōsaka University.
Wada Toshio	Takushoku University.
Watanabe Zenichirō	*Mainichi Shimbun.*
Yamada Fumio	*Taiheiyō Kyōkai* (Pacific Society).
Yamaguchi Suteji	*Kyōdo Tsūshinsha.*
Yasuhira Tersuji	Tōritsu University.

Appendix 6

***Daisan Kyōsanken Kenkyū Kokusai Kaigi* Third International Conference of Sovietologists and Sinologists (Lake Kawaguchi, Hakone, September 1960)**

Official Participants

Amō Eiji	Head, *Ōa Kyōkai*.
Black, Cyril E.	Princeton University.
Brzezinski, Zbigniew K.	Research Institute on Communist Affairs, Columbia University.
Byrnes Robert F.	Director, Russian and East European Institute, Indiana University.
Dutt, Vidya Prakash	Head, Dept. East Asian History and Institutions, Indian School of International Studies, New Delhi.
Falcionelli, Alberto	Mendoza University, Argentina.
Guillermaz, Jacques	Director, Documentation Centre on Contemporary China, Sorbonne, Paris.
Halpern, Abraham M.	RAND Corporation, Santa Monica, California.
Hirota Yōji	Secretary General, *Ōa Kyōkai*.
Hoeffding, Oleg	RAND Corporation, Santa Monica, California.
Inoki Masamichi	Kyōto University.
Ishikawa Tadao	Keiō University.
Itagaki Yoichi	Hitotsubashi University.
Kerblay, Basile H.	Slavic Studies Centre, Sorbonne, Paris.
Kiga Kenzō	Keiō University.
Kirby, E. Stuart	Universities of British Columbia and Hong Kong.
Kiuchi Nobutane	Managing Director, *Sekai Keizai Chōsakai* (World Economy Institute.)
Klatt, W.	Royal Institute of International Affairs, UK.
Langer, Paul F.	Dept. of International Relations, University of Southern California.
London, Kurt	Director of Sino-Soviet Studies Program, George Washington University.
MacFarquhar, Roderick	Editor, *China Quarterly*, UK.
Mehnert, Klaus	German–East European Association, Stuttgart.
Meissner, Boris	Director, Institute for East European Politics, Society and Law, University of Kiel, Germany.
Miyashita Tadao	University of Kōbe.
Mosely, Philip E.	Director of Studies, Council on Foreign Relations, US.
Muramatsu Yūji	Hitotsubashi University.
Nakayama Ichirō	Hitotsubashi University.
North, Robert C.	Director of Studies in International Conflict and Integration, Stanford University.
Okita Saburo	Economic Planning Agency, Japan.
Onoe Masao	University of Kōbe.
Rigby, T.H.	Australian National University, Canberra.
Schapiro, Leonard	University of London.
Schiller, Otto	Indo-Asian Institute, University of Heidelberg.

Schurmann, H. F.	University of California, Berkeley.
Senirongs, Thak	President, Royal Thailand National Defence College, Bangkok.
Seton-Watson, Hugh	Head of History Dept, School of Slavonic and East European Studies, University of London.
Sherwani, Latif Ahmed	Deputy Director, Pakistan Institute of International Affairs, Karachi.
Shih, Anderson (a.k.a. Yang Chengzhi)	Company president, Hong Kong.
Takahashi Masao	Kyushu University.
Tang, Peter S. H.	Executive Director, Research Institute on the Sino-Soviet bloc, Georgetown University.
Taylor, George E.	Institute of Far Eastern and Russian Studies, University of Washington, Seattle.
Thamarit, Vibul	President, School of Welfare and Education, Bangkok.
Ueda Toshio	University of Tokyo.
Vongkomolshet, Detchard	Tulalongkong University, Bangkok.
Whiting, Allen S.	RAND Corporation, Santa Monica, California.
Yamamoto Noboru	Keiō University.

Notes

Notes for Chapter 1

1 The treaty was actually signed by Foreign Ministers Zhou Enlai and A. la. Vyshinskii. A. Doak Barnett, *Communist China and Asia* (1960) New York: 375.
2 The phrase is from Mao Zedong's speech on 17 February 1950, as he was about to depart from Moscow. Stuart Schram, *Mao Tse-tung* (1966) Harmondsworth: 256.
3 John Gaddis, *We Now Know: Rethinking Cold War History* (1997) Oxford: 288.
4 Sino-Soviet Treaty, 14 February 1950, Article 1 in Sergei Goncharov, John Lewis, and Xue Litai, *Uncertain Partners* (1993) Stanford: 260.
5 Other landmark bilateral agreements included the Treaty of Friendship, 31 May 1924, the Non-Aggression Pact, 31 August 1937, and the Treaty of Friendship and Alliance, 14 August 1945.
6 Allen Whiting, *Siberian Development and East Asia* (1981) Stanford: 3.
7 Joseph Frankel, *The Making of Foreign Policy* (1962) Oxford.
8 James Rosenau (ed.), *Domestic Sources of Foreign Policy* (1967) New York.
9 Robert Jervis was one of the first scholars to recognise the importance of images in International Relations, both those of other actors as well as self-images. Robert Jervis, *The Logic of Images in International Relations* (1970) New York.
10 Anthony Smith, *National Identity* (1991) London.
11 The classic studies are John Gittings, *Survey of the Sino-Soviet Dispute, 1963–67* (1968) Oxford; William Griffith, *The Sino-Soviet Rift* (1964) London; and Donald Zagoria, *The Sino-Soviet Conflict, 1956–61* (1962) Princeton. The Woodrow Wilson Center's Cold War International History Project has been very actively promoting such scholarship in recent years.
12 The most comprehensive to date is Odd Arne Westad (ed.), *Brothers in Arms* (1998) Stanford, CA.
13 The best known studies are William Griffith, *Albania and the Sino-Soviet Rift* (1963) Cambridge, MA; Chin O. Chung, *Pyongyang Between Peking and Moscow* (1978) AL.
14 Gordon Chang, *Friends and Enemies* (1990) Stanford; John Gaddis, *The Long Peace* (1987) New York; David Mayers, *Cracking the Monolith* (1986) Baton Rouge; Herbert Ellison, *The Sino-Soviet Conflict* (1982) Washington; Lowell Dittmer, *Sino-Soviet Normalization and its International Implications, 1945–90* (1992) Washington; Rosemary Foot, 'New Light on the Sino-Soviet Alliance' *Journal of North East Asian Studies* (fall 1991): 16–29.
15 Sei Young Rhee, 'The Impact of the Sino-Soviet Conflict on the Japan Communist Party, 1961–68' (1973), Ph.D. thesis, University of Missouri; Kim Young Bae, 'The Japan Communist Party and the Soviet Union: Pattern of Coalition and Conflict, 1945–69' (1974) Ph.D. thesis, University of Kansas. Both draw heavily on the pioneering study by Robert Scalapino, *The Japanese Communist Movement, 1920–66* (1967) Berkeley.
16 See the bibliography for numerous examples.

Notes for Chapter 2

1 For details on the background to SCAP's controversial decision see Masumi Junnosuke, *Postwar Politics in Japan, 1945–1955* (1985) Berkeley: 101–3.
2 OIR Report 4867, 24 Jan. 1949, cited in Michael Schaller, *Altered States* (1997) NY: 22; Hagiwara Tōru and Fujisaki Masato (Treaty Bureau Section, MOFA), cited in Michael Yoshitsu, *Japan and the San Francisco Peace Settlement* (1983) NY: 68–9.
3 NSC 48/1, cited in Howard Schonberger, *Aftermath of War* (1989) Kent, OH: 152.
4 Michael Schaller, *The American Occupation of Japan* (1985) Oxford: 190.
5 *Asahi Shimbun* (23 Feb. 1950); Hodgson (Tokyo) to DEA, 24 Feb. 1950, A9564, 221/1, National Australian Archives, Canberra (hereafter NAA.)
6 MC, Yoshida and Cloyce Huston, 8 Apr. 1950, *Foreign Relations of the United States, 1950* VI (hereafter FRUS): 1167.
7 John Welfield, *An Empire in Eclipse* (1988) London: 46–7; Yoshitsu (1983): 34; Schaller (1985): 257–8.
8 Schaller (1985): 258.
9 Gordon Chang, *Friends and Enemies* (1990) Stanford: 80.
10 'Statement issued by the Foreign Office for the purpose of clarifying Japan's position in the Korean conflict, 19 Aug. 1950' *Contemporary Japan* (July/Sept. 1950) 19: 463–9.
11 John Dower, *Empire and Aftermath* (1979) Cambridge, MA: 391. Following the implementation of the 'Red Purge', Yoshida was also able to declare: 'As far as the Japanese skies are concerned, the Red star is receding.' Yoshida Shigeru, 'Japan and the Crisis in Asia' *Foreign Affairs* (Jan. 1951): 179.
12 NIE-19, 'Feasibility of Japanese Rearmament in Association with US', 20 Apr. 1951, *FRUS, 1951* VI: 998–9.
13 MC, Yoshida and Dulles, 23 Apr. 1951, *FRUS, 1951* VI: 1316.
14 Casey to Tange, 'Copy Personal Diary Entry of Talk with Yoshida in Japan in [7 August] 1951', 9 Dec. 1959, A1838, 3103/10/10/2, NAA; Murphy (Tokyo) to DOS, 13 May 1952, 693.94/5–1352, National Archives, Washington, D.C. (hereafter NA.)
15 Minute by Scott, 26 Sept. 1951, FO371/92608, Public Records Office, Kew (hereafter PRO).
16 Vice-Foreign Minister Iguchi when later discussing these remarks with Ambassador Sebald termed them '"indiscreet" rather than misleading or a political sop.' According to Nishimura Kumao (Treaty Bureau Director), Yoshida had acted impulsively. Yoshitsu (1983): 71–2. Both imply that Yoshida was sincere.
17 Roger Dingman, 'The Anglo-American Origins of the Yoshida Letter, 1951–52' *Perspectives on Japan's External Relations*, David Lu (ed.) (1982): 30–1.
18 NIE-52, 'The Probable Future Orientation of Japan', 27 Dec. 1951, 794.00/12–2751, NA.
19 A fortnight before Dulles arrived, in mid-December, Yoshida met with Assistant Secretary of State for Far Eastern Affairs Dean Rusk, and promised him that Japan would not enter into 'direct negotiations' with Beijing without US knowledge. Rusk asked whether he believed that Beijing 'might be on the point of changing its policy or its alignment with the Soviet Union.' Yoshida's reply lacked its usual conviction: 'he knew Japanese who had friends on the mainland and who might be of assistance to him in finding whether there were useful steps which he might take.' MC, Yoshida, Rusk, and Sebald, 27 Nov. 1951, *FRUS, 1951* VI: 1417.
20 MC, Dulles and Iguchi, 12 Dec. 1951, *FRUS, 1951* VI: 1437–9.

21 Sebald to Acheson, 14 Dec. 1951, *FRUS, 1951* VI: 1450–1.
22 MC, Dulles and Yoshida, 13 Dec. 1951, *FRUS, 1951* VI: 1438–9.
23 See Murphy to DOS, 13 May 1952, 693.94/5–1352, NA.
24 DOS, OIR, IR 5812, 'The China Debate in Japan', Apr. 2, 1952, *OSS/State Dept. Intelligence & Research Reports, Japan, Korea, South–East Asia & Far East* (1979) Washington.
25 On several occasions that winter, Yoshida publicly cited the alliance as a justification for not normalising relations with Moscow or Beijing. *Japan News* (26 Jan. 1952); *Nihon Times* (12 Mar. 1952).
26 Richard Storry, 'Options for Japan in the 1970s' *The World Today* (Aug. 1970) 26(8): 325–33; R.K. Jain, *Japan's Postwar Peace Settlements* (1978) New Delhi: 62.
27 MC, Nishimura and Stokes, 8 Apr. 1952, 693.94/5–1352, NA.
28 MC, Nishimura and Finn, 22 Apr. 1952, *FRUS, 1952–54* XIV: 1250–1.
29 An *Asahi Shimbun* poll conducted 9–11 May 1952, found that 57% supported normalisation, with only 11% opposed, (sample, 3000). Allan Cole and Nakanishi Naomichi (eds), *Japanese Opinion Polls with Socio-Political Significance, 1947–1957* (1958) Medford: 679.
30 Murphy to DOS, 13 May 1952, 693.94/5–1352, NA. (Emphasis added.)
31 Dening (Tokyo) to SOS, 10 July 1952; Eckersley to SEA, 18 Aug. 1952, A1838, 3103/11/51, NAA.
32 Information and Culture Bureau, Foreign Ministry, 'The Trade Policy of Communist China and the so-called "China–Japan Trade Agreement"' *World Report* (7 June 1952).
33 Iwamura Haruhiko, 'Dokuritsu Nihon wa Soren to Chūkyō ni dō tachimukau ka' *Keizai Shinshi* (July 1952): 19.
34 *Sydney Morning Herald* (19 Sept. 1952).
35 Niizeki Kinya, 'Soren sekai seisaku no gendankai' *Gaikō Jihō* (Nov. 1952) 111(1): 64.
36 Suma Yakichirō, 'Tai Chū-So kokkō wa kaifuku suru ka' *Tōyō Keizai Shinpō* (20 Dec. 1952, special issue): 28–32.
37 MC, Wada and Lutkins, 5 Mar. 1953, 690.94/3–1653, NA.
38 MC, Wajima Eiji and Lutkins, 30 June 1953, 693.94/7–853, NA.
39 Suma Yakichirō, et al., 'Mō Takutō jidai to Nihon no kiki' *Maru* (Oct. 1953): 78.
40 J. Barnard to Paul Nitze, 3 Apr. 1953, *DDRS* 1993/727.
41 Young (NEA) to Robertson and Johnson (FE), 9 Sept. 1953, 611.94/9–953, NA.
42 See: Welfield (1988): 106–8.
43 Allison to DOS, 3 Sept. 1953, *FRUS, 1952–54* XIV: 1495.
44 Guo Moruo, 'Nihon ni tai suru Chūgoku jinmin no taido' *Chūō Kōron* (Dec. 1953): 28–31.
45 MOFA, China Desk, 'Gendankai ni okeru Chūkyō no tai Nichi seisaku—Guo Moruo no Chū-Nichi fukashin ron', 21 Nov. 1953, A-0133, Gaimushō Gaikō Shiryōkan (hereafter GS), cited in Inoue Toshikazu, 'Sengo Nihon no Ajia gaikō no keisei' *Nihon Seiji Gakkai nenpō* (1998): 139–40.
46 MC, Takeuchi and Lutkins, 7 Dec. 1953, 693.94/12–753, NA.
47 MC, Wajima and Lutkins, 21 Dec. 1953, 693.94/12–2153, NA.
48 Ambassador Allison feared the 'disastrous effect' that a compromise at Geneva would have on the 'emotional Japanese people'. He proposed military escalation in Southeast Asia to leave Japan 'no choice but to abandon its hope for normalisation of relations with China and the Soviet Union.' Dulles suppressed news of 'Peking's displeasure with modest Soviet support...[lest it] encourage Asian wishful thinking that China was

more Asian than communist and that a reasonable accommodation could be reached with Peking.' 10, 26 Apr. 1954, *FRUS, 1952–54* XVI: 510–2, 621.

49 MC, Wajima and Lutkins, 21 Dec. 1953, 693.94/12–2153, NA.

50 Wilbur Martin, 'Some Findings of Japanese Opinion Polls' *Japan between East and West* Hugh Borton, et al., (1957) NY: 310–1.

51 Yoshida later claimed that just after the fall of Dienbienphu (7 May 1954) he had again broached with Dulles his plan to use overseas Chinese as agents to fight the Communists in China. Kern to Robertson, 11 Dec. 1958, 611.94/12–1158, NA.

52 MC, Allison and Yoshida, 28 May 1954, 794.00/7–2054, NA. Yoshida established the CRO in 1947 and personally selected its staff from Soviet specialists of the former Imperial Army. Welfield (1988): 70–1.

53 MOFA, China Desk, 'Chūkyō no genjō to sono dōkō', 8 Aug. 1954, A-0137/10/0009–89, GS. Rumours circulating at this time claimed that the Asian Affairs Bureau's researches about the Soviet Union and Communist China were 'low-key'. The reason, it was suggested, was that anyone producing positive reports was 'blacklisted (*chūi jimbutsu*)' and in such an atmosphere 'no able officers like to remain at the China Desk and those who do keep silent.' Mukohara Tatsuzō, 'Gaimushō' *Chūō Kōron* (Nov. 1954): 98–9.

54 Berger to DOS, 11 June 1954, 693.94/6–1154, NA.

55 Ibid.

56 MC, Hirasawa and Lamb, 9 July 1954, 794.13/7–2054, NA. Nishiyama (Japanese Ambassador to India) was an example of the former, remaining convinced that 'The two countries were bound to fall apart.' Minute by Crocker (New Delhi), 17 Aug. 1954, A1838, 3103/11/147, NAA.

57 MC, Niizeki and Lutkins, 27 May 1954, 693.94/6–1154, NA.

58 MC, Ogawa Takeo (sic) and Lutkins, 1 June 1954, 693.94/6–1154, NA.

59 Memo, 25 Aug. 1954, A1838, 766/3/4, NAA.

60 Nishimura Naomi, 'Watashi wa akai kuni Soren, Chūkyō o kō mita' *Jitsugyō no Nihon* (1 Sept. 1954): 44; Nakasone Yasuhiro, 'Fukami niwa maru to yakedo', ibid.: 47.

61 Tanaka Takahiko, 'The Soviet–Japanese Normalisation and the Foreign Policy Ideas of the Hatoyama Group', *Western Interactions with Japan*, P. Lowe and H. Moeshart (eds) (1990) Kent: 108–9.

62 Allison to Dulles, 24 July 1954, 661.94/7–2454, NA.

63 Allison to Dulles, 30 July 1954, 661.94/7–3054, NA.

64 Tsuruga (Hong Kong) to Okazaki, 16 Aug. 1954, A-0133, GS, cited in Inoue (1998): 140; Allison to Dulles, 11 Aug. 1954, *FRUS, 1952–54* XIV: 1698–9.

65 Allison to Dulles, 25 Aug. 1954, *FRUS, 1952–54* XIV: 1714–5.

66 Fukui Haruhiro, *Party in Power* (1970) Berkeley: 237; *Daily Telegraph* (14 Sept. 1954).

67 Cited in Shao Chuan Leng, *Japan and Communist China* (1958) Kyoto: 7. They also agreed on the withdrawal of Soviet troops from Port Arthur by 31 May 1955.

68 *Asahi Shimbun* (21 Oct. 1954); Nomizo Masaru, 'Chū-So heiwa kōsei to Chōsen mondai no zento' *Jitsugyō no Sekai* (Dec. 1954): 22–3; 'Chū-So kyōdō sengen to hōka daihyōdan no kaiken' *Sekai Jōsei Geppō* (Nov. 1954): 9–10; Harada to Okazaki, 29 Oct. 1954, A-1503, GS.

69 'Record of Discussions at PM's Dinner for Yoshida', 27 Oct. 1954, PREM 11/3852, PRO.

70 Allen to FED, 28 Oct. 1954, FO 371/110418, PRO.

71 Blakeney (Washington) to SEA, 3 Nov. 1954, A1838, 766/3/4, NAA.

72 Minutes of Meeting, Dulles and Yoshida, 9 Nov. 1954, *FRUS, 1952–54* XIV: 1779–80.

73 The specific US objection was that 'it would cut across the aims and objectives of the Manila Pact [SEATO]', and they proposed instead 'a high-level bilateral consultative body in Tokyo'. MC, Sebald and Iguchi Sadao, 30 Dec. 1954, *FRUS, 1952–54* XIV: 1816–7.

74 Saitō Motohide, 'The "Highly Crucial" Decision Making Model and the 1956 Soviet–Japanese Normalization of Relations' *Acta Slavica Iaponica* (1991): 152. Later Hatoyama personally claimed the credit for recognising the importance of normalising relations with Moscow in order to preserve world peace. However, according to one of his closest advisors, the conversion of the hard-line anti-Communist Hatoyama to the cause of Soviet–Japanese normalisation came at the hands of two former diplomats, Sugihara Arata and Yamada Hisanari. The turnabout was rather sudden. Just two months earlier he had warned that, 'Communist aggression in Asia is very intense', and it is 'necessary for us to prevent Japan from being Communised.' Hatoyama Ichirō, *Hatoyama Ichirō Kaikoroku* (1957): 11; Sugihara Arata, *Gaikō no kangaekata* (1965), cited in Tanaka (1990): 106; Hatoyama Ichirō, 'Nihon mezasu sekishoku kakumei' *Jimbutsu Ōrai* (July 1952) 1(7): 3.

75 Hatoyama Ichirō, 'Yoshida-kun no yarikata wa machigatte iru' *Chūō Kōron* (Nov. 1954): 172–5.

76 Chae-Jin Lee, *Japan Faces China* (1976) Baltimore: 30.

77 Shigemitsu's anti-Sovietism reportedly stemmed from Moscow's insistence on his being classified as a war criminal during the Occupation. Schaller (1997): 115.

78 *Gaimushō Bulletin* (11 Dec. 1954) cited in R.K. Jain, *China and Japan, 1949–80* (1981[A]) Oxford: 14.

79 *Asahi Shimbun* (16 Dec. 1954).

80 *Asahi Shimbun* (17 Dec. 1954).

81 The State Department's Office of North–East Asian Affairs concluded that, 'Shigemitsu's assurances can and should be taken at their face value.' McClurkin to Robertson, 7 Jan. 1955, 661.941/1–755, NA. Nor were such efforts confined to the government. Ikeda Hayato and Miyazawa Kiichi, leading lights in the 'Yoshida School' and now opposition members of the Diet, expressed similar opinions to Ambassador Allison. Allison to Dulles, 11 Dec. 1954, *FRUS, 1952–54* XIV: 1804–5.

82 *Asahi Shimbun* (4 Jan. 1955).

83 *Asahi Shimbun* (4 Jan. 1955, evening.)

84 United Press (11 Jan. 1955).

85 'At that time [December 1954] the Democrat Prime Minister and his colleagues thought about normalization of Soviet–Japanese relations entirely independently and separately from the question of Sino-Japanese relations...The time was not yet ripe to take up the latter issue, as far as they were concerned.' Interview with Wakamiya Shōtarō (Hatoyama's Secretary), 23 Feb. 1966, cited in Fukui (1970): 238. Similarly, Sugihara Arata, Hatoyama's closest adviser on foreign affairs, recalled in his memoirs his recommendation at the time that: 'As a practical matter it is necessary to make a sharp distinction between relations with Communist China and with the USSR.' This meant that diplomatic relations with Beijing were out of the question, 'now or in the immediate future.' Tanaka (1990): 106.

86 A senior NHK political analyst claimed that 'the fundamental difference between the USSR and Communist China problems seems to have escaped [Hatoyama] until very recently.' MC, Hirasawa and Lamb, 13 Jan. 1955, 794.00/1–1955, NA. Tani Masayuki, Shigemitsu's right-hand-man, confirmed this assessment when he complained to the

US embassy that 'Hatoyama apparently considers normalization of relations with the Soviet Union and Communist China as being identical problems'. Hence, MOFA 'must be most careful in any action it takes [vis-à-vis Moscow] not to create in Hatoyama's mind [the] belief that the same action can automatically be taken with respect to Red China.' Allison to Dulles, 28 Jan. 1955, 661.941/1–2855, NA.

87 Togawa Isamu, 'Gaimudaijin wa 8 nin iru' *Nihon* (June 1958): 110–4; MC, Hirasawa and Lamb, 13 Jan. 1955, 794.00/1–1955, NA.

88 MC, Hara Katsu and Lamb, 4 Feb. 1955, 694.00/2–455, NA. Other cabinet members also spoke out. An open letter from (pro-Taiwan) Labour Minister Chiba Saburō, countersigned by 66 other conservatives asserted that, 'At present the Communist Empire established on the Chinese continent poses a serious threat to not only Japan but also the whole of Asia'. Signatories included Matsumura Kenzō, Nakasone Yasuhiro, Ohama Nobumoto (president, Waseda University), Professors Kiga Kenzō (Keiō University) and Wada Toshio (Takushoku University), and Gotō Hiroshi (director general, *Keidanren*). *Mainichi Shimbun* (15 Dec. 1954).

89 Fukui (1970): 238; Ishiyama Kenkichi, 'Kakutō no kōyaku o hyōsu' *Daiyamondo* (11 Feb. 1955): 12.

90 Kurt Radtke, *China's Relations with Japan, 1945–83* (1990) Manchester: 107.

91 According to two experts, it was this Soviet enthusiasm which rekindled Hatoyama's wavering interest in the issue. Donald Hellmann, *Japanese Foreign Policy and Domestic Politics* (1969) Berkeley: 57, 101; Saitō (1991): 153.

92 MC, Tanaka, Hirota and Osborn, 15 Dec. 1954, 693.94/12–1554; Lodge to Dulles, 31 Dec. 1954, 611.94/12–3154; Aldrich to Dulles, 21 Jan. 1955, 693.94/1–2155, NA. Tani Masayuki conceded to Allison that 'it will be necessary to open the window a little but not wide enough to let microbes in.' Walker to SEA, 27 Jan. 1955, A1838 3103/11/52 Pt. 2, NAA.

93 Japan's ambassadors to the UN (Sawada Renzō) and the US (Iguchi Sadao) were of this opinion. Lodge to Dulles, 31 Dec. 1954, 611.94/12–3154; MC, Iguchi and Murphy, 28 Jan. 1955, 794.00/1–2855; Dulles to AmEmbTok, 28 Jan. 1955, 661.94/1–2855, NA.

94 McClurkin to Robertson, 7 Jan. 1955, *FRUS, 1955–57* XXIII(1): 6.

95 Dulles to Allison, 19 Jan. 1955, 611.94/1–1055, *FRUS, 1955–57* XXIII(1): 5–6.

96 Dulles to Allison, 26 Jan. 1955, 661.941/1–2655; Allison to Dulles, 28 Jan. 1955, 661.941/1–2855, NA.

97 For example, in January 1955, a *Chūō Chōsasha* poll found 70% supported official relations with China, whereas only 7% did not. Martin (1957): 308.

98 Ishiyama (1955): 12–16; 'Shinten suru tai NisSo kokkō kaifuku undō' *Ekonomisuto* (26 Feb. 1955): 19.

99 Shigemitsu reportedly claimed that 'priority should be given to adjusting relations with Communist and Nationalist Chinas…rather than to normalizing relations with Soviet Russia.' Allison to Dulles, 8 Feb. 1955, 661.94/2–855, NA. This statement was soon disavowed, but on 15 February, Hatoyama told Sefton Delmer of the *Daily Express* that if returned to power he intended to officially recognise the PRC government. Echoing Ikeda Hayato's speech six months earlier, Hatoyama then expressed his desire to follow British policy towards China, there being 'no need to follow the US lead on the matter of Red China.' Walker (Tokyo) to DEA, 15 Feb. 1955, A1838 3103/11/87 Pt. 1A, NAA; Allison to Dulles, 17 Feb. 1955, 661.941/2–1755, NA.

100 Zhou also paraded the virtues of China's 'five principles of peaceful coexistence' and told Takasaki that bilateral problems could be resolved in stages. Takasaki emphasised

the constraints imposed on Japan's freedom of action by Washington, but said that trade could be a starting point. RC, Zhou and Takasaki, 22 Apr. 1955, A-0133–5–0168–82, GS. See also: Okada Akira, *Mizutori gaikō hiwa* (1983): 48–57; Kweku Ampiah, 'Japan at the Bandung Conference' *Japan Forum* (Apr. 1995): 15–24.

101 *Gaimushō Bulletin*, 25 Apr. 1955, cited in Harold Quigley, 'Japan between Two Worlds' *Far Eastern Survey* (Nov. 1956): 169.

102 MC, Tanaka and Stoessel, 2 Feb. 1955, 661.94/2–255, NA. See also: John Gaddis, *The Long Peace* (1987) NY: 185, and Chang (1990): 129–31.

103 'Recent Developments and Future Prospects of Japanese Trade with Communist China', IR 6649, 15 Apr. 1955, *OSS/State Dept. Intelligence & Research Reports, IX, China and India, 1950–61*; 'US Policy toward Japan', NSC 5516/1, 9 Apr. 1955, *FRUS, 1955–57* XXIII(1)(1): 52–62.

104 *Nihon Times* (9 Feb. 1955).

105 MC, Matsumoto and Parsons, 6 Apr. 1955, cited in Tanaka (1990): 110.

106 Walker (Tokyo) to DEA, 14 Apr. 1955, A1838, 827/3/10, NAA; Ashida Hitoshi, *Ashida Hitoshi nikki* (1986) V: 411, cited in Kataoka Tetsuya, *The Price of a Constitution* (1991) NY: 140–41. See also Douglas Johnston, 'Marginal Diplomacy in East Asia' *International Journal* (summer 1971): 485.

107 Memo handed to Ambassador Tani by Ambassador Allison, 28 Apr. 1955, 661.94/10–2055, NA.

108 Johnston (1971): 488 (n.27). MOFA recognised, however, that it lacked the legal authority to prevent the opening of a private PRC trade office in Japan. Shimizu Sayuri, 'Perennial Anxiety' *Journal of American-East Asian Relations* (fall 1995): 236–7.

109 Ledward (Tokyo) to Mayall (FED), 28 June 1955, FO 371/115233, PRO.

110 Jamieson (Tokyo) to SEA, 21 July 1955, A1838, 766/3/4, NAA.

111 MC, Ogawa and Manhard, 3 Oct. 1955, 693.94/10–355, NA.

112 Its membership included a dozen outside experts on China, including Kawagoe Shigeru (ex-ambassador to China) and Yabe Teiji (president, Takushoku University). Jamieson to SEA, 21 July 1955, A1838, 766/3/4, NAA.

113 This figure included 6,000 known civilians, 1,000 'war criminals' and approximately 40,000 MIAs. Jain (1981A): 21; A. Doak Barnett, *Communist China and Asia* (1960) NY: 267.

114 Allison to Dulles, 8 Aug. 1955, 693.94/8–855, NA.

115 Ibid.; Jain (1981A): 215–6. See also: Johnston (1971): 490.

116 Kosaka Zentarō, 'Nihon ni semaru chūritsuka seisaku' *Seikei Shishin* (Aug. 1955): 95–6.

117 Ronald Dore, 'Left and Right in Japan' *International Affairs* (Jan. 1956): 18.

118 Suma Yakichirō, 'Chū-So o eguru' *Soren Kenkyū* (July 1955): 55.

119 AmEmbTok to DOS, 10 May 1955, 794.00/5–1055, NA.

120 Hellmann (1969): 34–5, 59; Savitri Vishwanathan, *Normalization of Japan–Soviet Relations, 1945–1970* (1973) Tallahassee: 76–7; Kataoka (1991): 144.

121 In July, Tokyo had proposed signing a 25–year mutual defence pact designed 'to cope with [the] Soviet–Communist China alliance.' Robertson to Dulles, 28 July 1955, *FRUS, 1955–57* XXIII(1): 79.

122 MC, Shigemitsu and Dulles, 29–31 Aug. 1955, *FRUS, 1955–57* XXIII(1): 93–113. Suspicious of Shigemitsu's relationship with the Americans, Hatoyama sent along three confidantes—Agriculture Minister Kōno Ichirō, Kishi Nobusuke, and Deputy Cabinet Secretary Matsumoto Takizō—to keep an eye on him. Kōno and Kishi met

separately with State Department officials to denounce Shigemitsu for having 'greatly exaggerated the [Communist] danger.' Kōno advised the Americans thereafter to deal directly with Kishi, Miki Bukichi or himself rather than Shigemitsu on any important matters, since 'They were the three men who presently control [the] Japanese Government'. MC, Kōno, Kishi, Sebald and Allison, 31 Aug. 1955, *FRUS, 1955–57* XXIII(1): 105–10.

123 Chang (1990): 155.

124 MC, Ogawa and Manhard, 3 Oct. 1955, 693.94/10–355, NA.

125 Hatoyama said that his government would 'exercise caution' in dealing with China and 'did not intend [to] "go any further" than expansion [of] trade relations.' Allison to DOS, 5 Oct. 1955, *FRUS, 1955–57* XXIII(1): 128–9. According to one source, Hatoyama then received official confirmation from the Americans that 'Japan was at liberty to negotiate a territorial settlement [with Moscow] if it chose.' *Asahi Shimbun* (22 Oct. 1955) cited in Kataoka (1991): 146.

126 Rankin (Taipei) to Dulles, 21 Nov. 1955, 690.93/11–2155, NA.

127 OIR, IR 7193, 'Recent Trends in Japanese Attitudes Toward and Relations with Communist China', 29 Feb. 1956, *Confidential US State Dept. Central Files, Soviet Union, Foreign Affairs, 1945–59* (1989) Bethesda.

128 The four missions were led by Kitamura Tokutarō (Democratic Party) and Nomizo Masaru (JSP-Left), Kanbayashiyama Eikichi (LDP), Kuhara Fusanosuke (National Council for the Reestablishment of Diplomatic Relations with China and the Soviet Union), and Katayama Tetsu (JSP), respectively.

129 Judging by the amount of underlining on the original document in the MOFA archives, it was taken very seriously by the Japanese. Iguchi to Shigemitsu, 11 Nov. 1955, A-0133–5–0267–74, GS.

130 OIR, IR 7193 (1956).

131 Robertson to McClurkin, 'Relationship Japan and Communist China', 13 Dec. 1955, Box 2, 58-D-118 & 58-D-637, *Records of the Office of North East Asian Affairs: Japan, Subject Files, 1947–56, Confidential US State Dept. Special Files—Japan, 1947–56* (1990) Bethesda.

132 Ajia Kyoku, 'Chūkyō no jittai oyobi waga kuni no torubeki taido', 18 Jan. 1956, A-0356/436–53, GS.

133 MC, Hogen and Morgan, 4 Apr. 1956, Box 2, 58-D-118 & 58-D-637, *Records of the Office of North East Asian Affairs: Japan, Subject Files, 1947–56, Confidential US State Dept. Special Files—Japan, 1947–56* (1990) Bethesda.

134 Jain (1981A): 14–15.

135 'Japan's foreign policy outlook and prospects for the political future', 2 Mar. 1956, Box 8, 58-D-118 & 58-D-637, *Records of the Office of North East Asian Affairs: Japan, Subject Files, 1947–56, Confidential US State Dept. Special Files—Japan, 1947–56* (1990) Bethesda.

136 For example, when Tanaka Hiroto (first secretary in Washington) was given the delicate task of researching US China policy, he was 'read...something of a lecture' for his pains. MC, Tanaka and Leonhart, 25 Jan. 1956, Box 7, 58-D-118 & 58-D-637, *Records of the Office of North East Asian Affairs: Japan, Subject Files, 1947–56, Confidential US State Dept. Special Files—Japan, 1947–56* (1990) Bethesda. Nor had support for Yoshida's China Thesis evaporated. LDP faction boss Miki Takeo told Robert Bowie (assistant secretary of state for policy planning) that 'China cannot be ignored…to do so can only drive her closer into the arms of Russia'. Conversely, he

argued, 'if China is recognized…Contacts China then has with the Free World in Asia may lead her away from the Soviet Union.' Lamb to Bowie, 19 Mar. 1956, Box 9, ibid.

137 OIR, IR 7193 (1956).

138 847 persons (including 78 Diet members) in 1955, up from 192 in 1954. Lee (1976): 79, 95. See Figure 9.3.

139 AmEmbTok to DOS, 3 Apr. 1956, 794.00/4–356, and 7 May 1956, 794.00/5–756, NA.

140 MC, Shigemitsu and Dulles, 18 Mar. 1956, *FRUS, 1955–57* XXIII(1): 156–61.

141 MC, Hatoyama and Dulles, 19 Mar. 1956, *FRUS, 1955–57* XXIII(1): 163–70.

142 Nakasone Yasuhiro, *The Making of the New Japan* (1999) Richmond, Surrey: 127–8.

143 *New York Times* (16 May 1956).

144 MC, Kōno and Dulles, 19 May 1956, *FRUS, 1955–57* XXIII(1): 175–8.

145 Allison to DOS, 24 May 1956, *FRUS, 1955–57* XXIII(1): 179 (n.2).

146 OCB Intelligence Notes, 6 June 1956, *DDRS* (1992): 1023.

147 Ajia Kyoku, 'Chūgoku mondai taisho hoshin no ken', 20 Apr. 1956, A-0356, GS, cited in Inoue (1998): 141.

148 MC, Takeuchi and Hackler, 21 May 1956, 611.94/5–2556, NA.

149 Ajia Kyoku, China Desk, 'Chūgoku mondai no saikentō', 21 Aug. 1956, A-0356, GS, cited in Inoue (1998): 142.

150 Hellmann (1969): 37–8, 64

151 MC, Shigemitsu and Dulles, 19 Aug. 1956, *FRUS, 1955–57* XXIII(1): 202–4.

152 An aide-memoire officially confirmed that the US government supported Japan's legal claim to the four islands. Kimura Hiroshi, 'Gorbachev and the Northern Territories' *Japan Echo* (winter 1988): 20. For examples of Japanese anger see: 'Yo nimo fushigina NisSo kōshō—daresu adobarūnno imi suru mono' *Shūkan Asahi* (9 Sept. 1956): 12–14; *Sandēi Mainichi* (9 Sept. 1956).

153 In early August, Yoshida was busy preparing an article for publication, in which he stated: 'The policy of the free world should be based on the premise that the Moscow–Peking Axis is vulnerable; that it can and must be broken.' He detailed the usual historical and cultural reasons why he believed the 'unwieldy combine [wa]s bound to collapse.' Sebald to DOS, 30 Aug. 1956, 794.00/8–3056, NA.

154 'Takai to jikai' *Chūō Kōron* (autumn 1956, special issue): 164–5. See also: Emery (Kobe–Osaka) to DOS, 28 Aug. 1956, 661.94/8–2756; 10 Oct. 1956, 794.00/10–1056, NA.

155 MC, Ogawa and Coolidge, 18 Sept. 1956, 693.94/9–2656, NA.

156 A survey, conducted secretly in late June, concluded: 'There is a common notion that "Communist China" is almost a contradiction in terms...[and] Even professional Japanese diplomats believe that Peiping can be split from Moscow by peaceful means.' 'Japanese Public Opinion Mid-1956', *DDRS* (1956(77)): 334B.

157 OIR, Intelligence Report, 'The Recent and Prospective Foreign Relations of Japan (1956–61)', 12 Sept. 1956, *DDRS* (1956(79)): 194C. (Emphasis added).

158 Allison to Dulles, 8 Aug. 1956, 794.00/8–856, NA. (Emphasis added).

159 Hemendinger to Robertson, 22 Aug. 1956, *FRUS, 1955–57* XXIII(1): 205–7.

160 Allison to DOS, 21 Sept. 1956, *DDRS* (1988): 2680. To be fair, only three days earlier Ogawa had described the regular meetings that were taking place between American and Japanese China specialists in Hong Kong as 'very useful'. MC, Ogawa and Coolidge, 18 Sept. 1956, 693.94/9–2656, NA.

161 AmEmbTok to DOS, 16 Oct. 1956, 794.00/10–1656, NA; Murata Shōzō, 'NitChū keizai kōryū no tenbō' *Sekai* (Feb. 1957): 82; R.G. Boyd, 'China's Relations with Japan' *Australian Outlook* (Apr. 1960): 56.

162 AmEmbTok to DOS, 16 Oct. 1956, 794.00/10–1656, NA.

163 Vishwanathan (1973): 82–9; Hellmann (1969): 39–40.

164 See, for example: Maeda Yoshinori, 'Itashikayushi no NisSo fukkō' *Nihon Shūhō* (15 Nov. 1956): 21; Cole and Nakanishi (1958): 711; MC, Mladen Soic and Coolidge, 19 Oct. 1956, 661.94/11–2056; AmConSapporo to DOS, 794.00/10–256; and AmConNagoya to DOS, 794.00/11–1556, NA.

165 Robertson added that the US 'regarded Communist China as even more dangerous than the USSR'. MC, Matsumoto and Robertson, 25 Oct. 1956, 661.941/10–2556, NA.

166 OCB Intelligence Notes, 23 Oct. 1956, *DDRS* (1994): 1692.

167 Robertson to Dulles, 24 Oct. 1956, 661.941/11–1356, NA.

168 MC, Hatoyama and Robertson, 26 Oct. 1956, 661.941/10–2656, NA. Kōno repeated this 'categorical assurance' to Ambassador Allison, stating that party policy dictated 'resumption of relations with [the] Soviet Union would not...be followed by resumption of relations with Communist China'. Allison to Dulles, 9 Nov. 1956, 661.941/11–956, NA.

169 MC, Sato and Morgan, 9 Nov. 1956, 794.00/11–1656, NA.

170 MC, Takeuchi and Hackler, 30 Nov. 1956, 611.94/12–1156, NA. See also: A.Doak Barnett, 'The United States and Communist China', *The United States and the Far East*, Willard Thorp (ed.) (1956) Englewood Cliffs: 223.

171 *Mainichi Shimbun* (9 Dec. 1956, evening.)

172 Lalima Varma, *The Making of Japan's China Policy* (1991) Delhi: 45.

173 In retirement, Hatoyama remained active in support of improved relations with the Soviet Union, serving as president of the new Japan–Soviet Friendship Association (established in June 1957) until his death on 7 March 1959.

174 See Hosoya Chihiro, 'From the Yoshida Letter to the Nixon Shock', *The United States and Japan in the Postwar World*, Iriye Akira and Warren Cohen (eds) (1989) Lexington: 29.

175 'Ishibashi Tanzan—sono hito to seisaku' *Shūkan Asahi* (30 Dec. 1956): 8; *Asahi Shimbun* (26 Dec. 1956).

176 Wakamiya Yoshibumi, *The Postwar Conservative View of Asia* (1999): 120.

177 *Asahi Shimbun* (26 Jan. 1957); Warren Cohen, 'China in Japanese–American Relations' in Iriye and Cohen (1989): 48.

178 MC, Ishibashi and Robertson, 19 Dec. 1956, *FRUS, 1955–57* XXIII(1): 235–40.

179 de la Mare (Wash.) to Morland (Tokyo), 10 Jan. 1957, FO 371/127239, PRO.

180 Dan Kurzman, *Kishi and Japan* (1960) NY, 1960: 298.

181 MacArthur to Dulles, Apr. 10, 1957, 611.94/4–1057, NA.

182 MacArthur to Dulles, 25 May 1957, *FRUS, 1955–57* XXIII(1): 325–30.

183 Muraoka Kunio, *Japanese Security and the US* (February 1973) London: 3; Momoi Makoto, 'Basic Trends in Japanese Security Policies', *The Foreign Policy of Modern Japan*, Robert Scalapino (ed.) (1979) Berkeley: 351; and Kataoka Tetsuya (1991): 185 (n.32).

184 Kishi Nobusuke, 'Japan in 1957' *Contemporary Japan* (Apr. 1957): 555.

185 *Asahi Shimbun* (4 June 1957) cited in Doi Akira, 'Two Years' Exchanges with China' *Japan Quarterly* (Oct./Dec. 1958): 441.

186 AmConGen HongKong to DOS, 16 May 1957, 693.94/5–2957, NA.

187 MC, Suma and MacArthur, (dated) 25 April 1957, 611.94/4–2557, NA.

188 *JT* (26 April 1957).

189 Soviet Foreign Minister Dmitri Shepilov had supported a Sino-Indian idea for an Asia–Pacific collective peace treaty to replace the existing military groupings in February

1957, but in October, Khrushchev offered explicit Soviet support for the four-power pact proposal to a visiting JSP delegation led by Katayama Tetsu. DOS, 'Soviet Statements on Japan–USSR Relations', IR 8481, 6 June 1961, *OSS/State Dept. Intelligence and Research Reports, Part XI, The Soviet Union: 1950–61 Supplement* (1979) Washington, D.C.

190 Tani Masayuki, 'Amerika no Chūkyō kan' *Tairiku Mondai* (Dec. 1957): 41.

191 DRF Special Paper No. 66, 'Intelligence Estimate of Sino-Soviet Relations', (revised 6 June 1957), *Records of the Bureau of Far Eastern Affairs 1956–58, Conferences, Meetings and Visits 1957*, Lot 60 D 514, Box 3; 'US Global Policy toward Communism', 14 June 1957, *Records of the Office of North–East Asian Affairs*, Briefing Books 43–54, Box 8, NA.

192 MC, Kishi and Eisenhower, 19 June 1957, *DDRS* (1991): 3463.

193 Welfield (1988): 147.

194 *Asahi Shimbun* (28 June 1957, evening.)

195 John Gaddis (1987): 186; Chang (1990): 166–7.

196 MacArthur to Dulles, 9 Aug. 1957, 694.00/8–957, NA.

197 Ibid.

198 A CRO survey conducted in August, found that 64% of 3,000 people polled agreed with the current policy of putting cooperation with the US first, although two-thirds of those only favoured it because it was unavoidable. Asked if it was possible to combine this policy with good relations with the Communist countries, they replied: 'yes' (26%); 'no' (41%); and 'don't know' (33%). I.I. Morris, 'Foreign Policy Issues in Japan's 1958 Elections' *Pacific Affairs* (Sept. 1958): 239; 'Japanese Foreign Policy and Neutralism' *International Affairs* (Jan. 1960): 12.

199 Gaimushō, *Waga gaikō no kinkyō* (1957): 7.

200 Rosemary Foot, 'New Light on the Sino-Soviet Alliance' *Journal of North–East Asian Studies* (fall 1991): 18–19.

201 Harold Hinton, *China's Turbulent Quest* (1974) Bloomimgton: 87.

202 J.Y.S. Cheng, 'Sino-Japanese Relations, 1957–60' *Asian Affairs* (1977): 76–7.

203 *Yomiuri Shimbun* (27 Nov. 1957); *Asahi Shimbun* (2 Dec. 1957).

204 In preparatory discussions, Vice-Foreign Minister Ōno Katsumi told MacArthur that 'while [the] Foreign Ministry has not as yet prepared [a] special paper on this item, Sov[iet] bloc internal developments are under constant study and Japan welcomed discussing it.' MacArthur to Dulles, 12 Dec. 1957, 611.94/12–1257, NA.

205 MacArthur to Dulles, 20 Dec. 1957, 611.94/1–358, NA.

206 Ibid; Dulles to MacArthur, 12 Dec. 1957, 611.94/12–1257, NA.

207 AmEmbTok to DOS, 19 Dec. 1957, *FRUS, 1955–57* XXIII(1): 549.

208 For example, US intelligence reports claimed that, 'in a meeting in Tokyo in December 1957 Okada [Akira, head of the China Desk] suggested a meeting between ambassadors in early 1958 to exchange views on all issues except recognition.' The reporting officer presumed such contact must have been authorised by the vice-foreign minister, and tacitly approved by Fujiyama and Kishi, although he felt that 'enthusiastic junior officials probably exceeded their instructions...and have since been reined in'. Subsequently the Japanese reportedly withdrew the proposal for such meetings as premature and suggested that initial negotiations deal only with technical and non-political issues. Arneson (INR) to Dulles, 3 April 1958, 693.94/4–358, NA.

209 Morris (Sept. 1958): 222.

210 RC, Takase Naotomo and Brennan, 10 Oct. 1958, A1838, 3103/11/87 Pt. 3, NAA.

211 *New York Times* (9 Oct. 1994); Schaller (1997): 153.

212 MacArthur to Dulles, 26 May 1958, 794.00/5–2658, NA.
213 A Prime Minister's Office poll conducted in June 1958, discovered that 53.9% of 3,000 people thought Japan should have the same type of connexions with the Soviet Union and Communist China as she had with the US. Only 21.2% felt that Japan should focus exclusively on cooperating with Washington. *Jiji nenkan* (1959): 158.
214 MacArthur to DOS, 31 July 1958, *FRUS, 1958–60* XVIII: 43–5. On 20 June, Fujiyama told the Lower House Foreign Affairs Committee that 'Communist China must tend to strengthen its association with the Soviet Union' and 'basically recognises the leadership of the Soviet Union.' *Mainichi Shimbun* (21 June 1958).
215 *Yomiuri Shimbun* (1 July 1958).
216 Robertson to Dulles, 31 July 1958, 794.00/7–3158, NA. See also Chapter 4.
217 Dulles to AmEmbTok, 25 Aug. 1958, 794.00/8–258, NA.
218 'Fujiyama Visit Position Paper: Japan's Political Relations with Communist China', *Records of the Bureau of Far Eastern Affairs 1956–58, Conferences, Meetings & Visits 1958*, Lot 60 D 514, box 6, NA.
219 Welfield (1988): 148, and see Chapter 4.
220 According to Wang Bingnan, Chinese ambassador to the Sino-American talks in Warsaw. Chang (1990): 186–7.
221 Chang (1990): 190–1, 195–7.
222 Welfield (1988): 151.
223 Fujiyama Aiichirō, *Seiji waga michi* (1976): 94.
224 Anderson (Tokyo) to SEA, 26 Sept. 1958, A9564, 221/1, NAA.
225 'It is the British and Japanese with many years of accumulated experience in the problems of China who best understand the psychology of the Chinese people. America has not reached the point of truly knowing China.' Yoshida Shigeru, *Kaisō jūnen* (1957) 1: 270.
226 Welfield (1988): 150–1.
227 MC, Fujiyama and Dulles, 11 Sept. 1958, *FRUS, 1958–60* XVIII: 76–7.
228 DOS to AmEmbTok, 'Based on Uncleared Memorandum of Conversation (Second meeting Dulles with Fujiyama)', 12 Sept. 1958, 611.94/9–1358, NA. The report concluded that the discrepancy 'appears to stem from [the] fact that Moscow has diplomatic relations with Tokyo while Peiping does not and reflects Peiping's extreme concern over [the] "two Chinas" issue.' DOS, IR 7800, 'Divisive and Cohesive Elements in Sino-Soviet Alliance', 15 Sept. 1958, *OSS/State Dept. Intelligence and Research Reports, Part IX, China and India, 1950–61 Supplement* (1979) Washington, D.C.
229 Welfield (1988): 152.
230 *JT* (30 Dec. 1959); Welfield (1988): 154–5; Kataoka (1991): 195–6.
231 'Foreign Reports', 5 Dec. 1958, Enc. in Kern to Robertson, 611.94/12–1158, NA. For a study of Kern's role in Japan–US relations see Howard Schonberger, *Aftermath of War* (1989) Kent, OH: 134–60.
232 MacArthur to Dulles, 18 Nov. 1958, 693.94/11–1858, NA.
233 'Foreign Reports' (1958).
234 Kataoka (1991): 193.
235 Jain (1981 A): 225–6.
236 MacArthur to Dulles, 20 Nov. 1958, 794.00/11–2058, NA.
237 Morris (1960): 7.
238 Reilly (Moscow) to FCO, 4 Dec. 1958, FO 371/133590, PRO.
239 Outerbridge Horsey (Tokyo) to DOS, 23 Dec. 1958, 661.94/12–2358, NA.

240 Leonart (Tokyo) to DOS, 19 May 1959, 661.94/5–1959, NA. (Emphasis added).
241 Chang (1990): 199–201.
242 Dulles executive session testimony, Senate Foreign Relations Committee, 14 Jan. 1959, cited in Gaddis (1987): 187.
243 MC, Kaya and Robertson, 2 Feb. 1959, 611.94/2–259, NA.
244 See Chapter 6.
245 'Relations between Japan and the USSR', n.d., A1838, 3103/11/52, NAA; Cheng (1977): 79–80.
246 Yamamoto Michio (pseud.), 'Chūgoku no yūjin ni tou' *Tōa Jiron* (Jan. 1959): 9. See also Chapter 3.
247 Leonhart to MacArthur, 20 Feb. 1959, 611.94/2–2059, NA.
248 IR 8481 (1961); MacArthur to Dulles, 11 May 1959, 661.94/5–1159, NA.
249 AmEmbMos to Herter, 24 June 1959, cited in Chang (1990): 212, and Foot (1991): 20.
250 Walt (Moscow) to SEA, 23 June 1959, A1838, 3103/10/1, NAA. Earlier, Kadowaki had told the *Japan Times* that 'There has been no change in Soviet Russian–Chinese relations after Liu Shao-chi assumed the state chairmanship.' *JT* (7 June 1959).
251 RC, Kishi and Macmillan, 13 July 1959, PREM 11/2738, PRO. According to Matsumoto Shunichi (deputy chief cabinet secretary), Kishi similarly dismissed the expectations of the West German, French and Italian leaders that Sino-Soviet relations would deteriorate in the near future as 'wishful thinking'. *Tokyo Times* (12 Aug. 1959) cited in FO 371/141439, PRO.
252 Lewis (Tokyo) to SEA, 30 July 1959, A1838, 3103/11/52, NAA.
253 NSC 5516/1, 'OCB Report on US Policy toward Japan, Annex B: Relationships of Japan with Sino-Soviet bloc, 30 Mar. 1959', *DDRS* (1992): 0895.
254 MacArthur to DOS, 18 July 1959, 794.00/7–1859, NA.
255 NSC 5913/1, 'US Policy in Far East', 25 Sept. 1959, *FRUS, 1958–60* XVI: 136; Chang (1990): 209, 212.
256 Miki concluded that there was 'no basic difference of policy towards Japan' in the USSR and China. Brennan (Tokyo) to SEA, 16 Nov. 1959, A9564, 221/1, NAA; Radtke (1990): 128–9.
257 Foot (1991): 20.
258 See Chapter 8.
259 RC, Japanese Ambassador and SEA, 8 Oct. 1959, A9564, 221/1, NAA.
260 AusEmbWash to DEA, 5 Oct. 1959, A1838, 3103/7/1, NAA.
261 AusEmbTok to DEA, 29 Sept. 1959, A1838 3103/11/87 Pt. 5, NAA.
262 RC, Yoshida and Casey, 1 Dec. 1959, A1838, 3103/10/10/2, NAA. 'Like Metternich, we must divide in order to rule', Yoshida told an Australian journalist, promoting his scheme to turn overseas Chinese into 'a propaganda fifth column.' *Sydney Morning Herald* (28 Nov. 1959.)
263 Welfield (1988): 158–9.
264 In fact, Article 2 merely committed the signatories to seeking an early peace treaty with Japan.
265 Utsunomiya Tokuma, 'Seifu no "seikan seisaku" ni hantai suru' *Chūō Kōron* (Nov. 1959) 74(16): 48–9.
266 Boyd (1960): 65; and see, for example, *JT* (23 Nov. 1959).
267 For example, a poll in March 1960, found 29% of 3,000 people opposed to revision and 25% in favour. Asked about the biggest problems with revision, the fact that it 'irritated the Soviet Union and Communist China' ranked third. *Yoron chōsa nenkan* (1959): 135.

268 Kishi's other two reasons were 'neutralist pressures' at home and strengthening the 'relationship with the US.' MC, Kishi and Eisenhower, 19 Jan. 1960, *DDRS* (1986): 1402 and (1984): 1056. He also publicly proclaimed that the new treaty was necessary to counter the Sino-Soviet Alliance. Tsukui Tatsuo, 'Anpo kaitei no ato ni kuru mono' *Seikai Ōrai* (Apr. 1960): 59.

269 *Contemporary Japan* (May 1960): 593–5.

270 *People's Daily* (24 Jan. 1960) in *Oppose the Revival of Japanese Militarism* (1960) Beijing: 158.

271 Ibid.

272 MacArthur to Herter, 28 Jan. 1960, *FRUS, 1958–60* Supplement, Document 506. For reasons unknown, Tokyo's rebuttal, delivered on 5 February, omitted this statement. *Contemporary Japan* (May 1960): 603–5.

273 Mayall (Tokyo) to Dalton (FCO), 5 Feb. 1960, FO 371/ 150571, PRO.

274 RC, Masahide Kanayama, Kinya Niiseki and Keith Brennan, 23 Feb. 1960, A1838, 3103/11/52 Pt. 4, NAA.

275 Kataoka (1991): 201, 204–5.

276 *Asahi Shimbun* (12 Apr. 1960); Varma (1991): 49.

277 Mass rallies were also organised throughout the country. More than a million people turned out in Beijing on 9 May. Jain (1981 A): 44–5, 233.

278 Tamura Kōsaku, 'Sino-Soviet Arsenal' *New Leader* (28 Nov. 1960) sect. 2: 18; IR 8481 (1961).

279 Edwin Reischauer, *Japan: The Story of a Nation* (1970) NY: 281–2.

280 George Packard, *Protest in Tokyo* (1966) Princeton; Kataoka (1991): 206–11.

281 Stephen Walt, *The Origins of Alliances* (1987) Ithaca, NY: 17.

Notes for Chapter 3

1 MacArthur to DOS, 22 July 1960, *FRUS, 1958–60* XVIII: 389–90.

2 Yoshida himself never lost interest in the subject. On a visit to London at the height of the Security Treaty crisis, he asked Prime Minister Macmillan whether he believed that 'China had a great influence on the Soviet Union', and if 'China was really stronger than the Soviet Union.' RC, Yoshida and Macmillan, 2 June 1960, PREM 11/3852, PRO.

3 *Asahi Shimbun* (20 July 1960) cited in John Welfield, *An Empire in Eclipse* (1988) London: 175.

4 Asked about their hopes for the Ikeda cabinet in July 1960, 23.1% of 4,060 people replied 'restore American confidence'. This was closely followed, however, by 'adjust relations with China and the Soviet Union': 22.3%. *Yoron chōsa nenkan* (1960): 153.

5 Brennan (Tokyo) to SEA, 15 July 1960, A9564, 221/1, NAA.

6 RC, Endō and Lewis, 19 Sept. 1960, A9654, 227/10/1, NAA.

7 Rosemary Foot, 'New Light on the Sino-Soviet Alliance' *Journal of North–East Asian Studies* (fall 1991): 25.

8 NSC, 'US Policy toward Japan' (NSC 6008/1), 11 June 1960, *DDRS* (1989): 1576; MacArthur to Herter, 24 June 1960, *DDRS* (1982): 242; Herter to MacArthur, 18 July 1960, *FRUS, 1958–60* XVIII: 387.

9 Kaidray memo, 23 Aug. 1960, FO 371/150570, PRO.

10 Jain (1981 A): 45. See also Chapter 8.

11 DOS, 'Soviet Statements on Japan–USSR Relations', IR 8481, 6 June 1961, *OSS/State Dept. Intelligence and Research Reports, XI, The Soviet Union: 1950–61 Supplement* (1979) Washington, D.C.

12 Ibid.

13 Paul Langer, 'Moscow, Peking and Tokyo', *Unity and Contradiction*, Kurt London (ed.) (1962) NY: 229.

14 Hirotsu Kyōsuke, 'The Strategic Triangle: Japan' *Survey* (Jan. 1965): 127; Chu Shao-hsien, 'The Chinese Communist United Front Operations in Japan and the Future of Peiping–Tokyo Relations' *Issues and Studies* (July 1972): 75.

15 Gordon Chang, *Friends and Enemies* (1990) Stanford: 220, 229–30.

16 Chang (1990): 230–1; Foot (1991): 24–5; NIE-10–61, 'Authority and Control in the Communist Movement', 8 Aug. 1961, *DDRS* (1993): 1208; Policy Planing Council, 'US Policy toward China' [Draft], 26 Oct. 1961, *FRUS, 1961–63* XXII: 162–7.

17 The Americans also could not decide whether 'uncertainty of Soviet support' would 'act as a deterrent on Peiping' or result in 'belligerent moves'. 'Visit of Prime Minister Ikeda to Washington, 20–23 June 1961: Policy Toward Communist China', 14 June 1961, *DDRS* (1993): 2021.

18 Takasaki Tatsunosuke, 'Watashi no mita Chūgoku' *Asahi Jānaru* (15 Jan. 1961): 18.

19 He even suggested that Beijing did not desire to join the UN in part because it would mean 'submission, as a member of the Communist bloc, to the Soviet Union's control.' Nakasone Yasuhiro, 'Japan and the China Problem' *Japan Quarterly* (July/Sept. 1961): 268–9. In February 1961, Kōno sent Takasaki and Nakasone to Washington to sound out the new administration on the possibility of a change in US policy towards China. Kurt Radtke, *China's Relations with Japan, 1945–83* (1990) Manchester: 136.

20 Brennan (Tokyo) to SEA, 13 Oct. 1961, A1838, 3103/11/87 Pt. 7, NAA.

21 McIntyre (Tokyo) to SEA, 28 Mar. 1961, A1838, 3103/11/87 Pt. 6, NAA. See Appendix 2 for a list of members.

22 Hōgen Shinsaku, 'Soren to kyōsanken no jittai wa kō da' *Seikai Ōrai* (May 1961): 44.

23 Gaimushō, *Waga gaikō no kinkyō* (1961): 3.

24 'Visit of Prime Minister Ikeda to Washington, 20–23 June 1961: The Situation in the Far East', 14 June 1961, *DDRS* (1993): 2024; Welfield (1988): 176.

25 Lalima Varma, *The Making of Japan's China Policy* (1991) Delhi: 51.

26 McIntyre (Tokyo) to SEA, 30 Jan. 1961, A1838, 3103/10/10/1, NAA.

27 McIntyre (Tokyo) to SEA, 10 Jan. 1961; 28 Mar. 1961, A1838, 3103/11/87 Pt. 6, NAA.

28 Mayall (Tokyo) to de la Mare, 27 Apr. 1961, FO 371/158484, PRO; and see Chapter 5.

29 Details of a joint assessment were passed to Kosaka in June. *DDRS* (1993): 2024.

30 Welfield (1988): 177; Fukui Haruhiro, *Party in Power* (1970) Berkeley: 258; G.P. Jan, 'The Japanese People and Japan's Policy toward Communist China' *Western Political Quarterly* (summer 1969): 608; Chu Shao-hsien, 'The Evolution of Japan's Peiping Policy' *Issues and Studies* (Dec. 1971): 21.

31 By this method, the US and its allies had prevented the General Assembly from discussing the issue. See: *DDRS* (1993): 2024; McIntyre to DEA, 4 July 1961, A3092, 221/12/2/5/1, NAA.

32 MC, Ikeda and Kennedy, 20 June 1961, *FRUS, 1961–63* XXII: 680–82. According to one scholar, Ikeda conceded that China was a 'confusing' state with militant ambitions, but now he expressed fears that non-recognition fostered tensions that could lead to nuclear war. Timothy Maga, *John F. Kennedy and the New Pacific Community* (1990) Basingstoke: 90.

33 MC, Rusk and Kosaka, 21 June 1961, *FRUS, 1961–63* XXII: 680–82. (Emphasis added.)

34 McIntyre to DEA, 4 July 1961, A3092, 221/12/2/5/1, NAA.

35 Furukawa Mantarō, *NitChū sengo kankeishi* (1981): 201, claimed that Kennedy raised the issue.

36 Ikeda Hayato, 'Speech to the National Press Club, Washington' *Contemporary Japan* (Mar. 1962): 355.

37 Yung H. Park, 'The Roots of Detente', *China and Japan*, A.D. Coox and H. Conroy (eds) (1978) Santa Barbara: 357. Based on the testimony of Itō Masaya (Ikeda's secretary), Hosoya Chihiro asserted that in journeying to Washington 'Ikeda hoped to create a situation that would enable Japan to recognise the Beijing government'. Hosoya Chihiro, 'From the Yoshida Letter to the Nixon Shock', *The United States and Japan in the Postwar World*, Iriye Akira and Warren Cohen (eds) (1989) Lexington: 31.

38 Furukawa (1981): 201.

39 Nakasone (1961): 271. The 'Deputy Foreign Minister' had expressed the same desire. Australian High Commission (London) to SEA, 27 June 1961, A3092, 221/12/2/5/1, NAA.

40 Kosaka also warned of the 'danger of a deal being done between Chinese Communists and Chinese Nationalists.' RC, Kosaka and Macmillan, 5 July 1961, PREM 11/ 3407, PRO.

41 The ratio in favour always exceeded 4:1. *Yoron chōsa nenkan* (1961).

42 Okazaki told the UN: 'we cannot overlook the fact that the PRC is effectively ruling the Chinese mainland…[nor] the fact that the ROC is secure in its rule over 11 million people who detest Communism.' Ōmori Minoru, 'Nihon gaikō no kihon gensoku o tou' *Chūō Kōron* (Jan. 1963): 157–8.

43 William Nester, *Japan and the Third World* (1991) Basingstoke: 146; McIntyre to McNicol, 12 Jan. 1962, A1838, 3103/10/1, NAA; Jain (1981 A): 47–8. On 23 January 1962, in the Diet debate on the UN vote, Ikeda admitted the existence of 'two governments in China' and claimed that the Japanese Government had 'never tried to prevent Communist China's entry into the United Nations.' Lavett (Tokyo) to SEA, 31 Jan. 1962, A9564, 227/10/1, NAA.

44 'First Meeting Joint US–Japan Committee Trade and Economic Affairs', 2–4 Nov. 1961, *FRUS, 1961–63* XXII: 711. Ikeda surprised Rusk by telling him that a minority of Japanese—'including people in his own cabinet and party'—considered it 'necessary for Japan also to have nuclear weapons.' Rusk made US opposition to nuclear proliferation clear, but Ikeda replied that he 'had not been thinking so much of Japan's going into production of nuclear weapons but of the argument that the presence of nuclear weapons in Japan might be necessary for its defense.'

45 'Joint Statement JSP delegation and Chinese People's Institute of Foreign Affairs' *Japan Socialist Review* (16 Jan. 1962): 5 (emphasis added); *JTW* (10 Feb. 1962): 2. See also Chapter 6. The Soviets later accused the Chinese of making this offer without 'deign[ing] to engage in the necessary consultations with the Soviet government.' O.B. Borisov and B.T. Koloskov, *Soviet–Chinese Relations, 1945–70* (1975) Bloomington: 175.

46 Foot (1991): 27. 'Until 1961 the US nuclear war plan provided only for a comprehensive strike against all of the Warsaw Pact and China, no program option existed for sparing the PRC in the unanticipated event that it was not involved in the

Soviet aggression that would provoke US nuclear retaliation.' Desmond Ball, *Politics and Force Levels* (1980) Berkeley: 190–1.

47 CIA, 'Prospects for the Sino-Soviet Relationship', n.d. [Feb. 1962?], *CIA Research Reports: China, 1946–76* (1982) Frederick; NIE 11–5–62, 'Political Developments in the USSR and the Communist World', 21 Feb. 1962, *FRUS, 1961–63* XXII: 207–8, 229–31; Walt Rostow, 'National Security Policy and the Sino-Soviet Split', 26 Mar. 1962, *DDRS* (1962(77)): 338A; Hilsman to Rusk, 14 May 1962, *DDRS* (1962(77)): 317C; Foot (1991): 25–6; and Chang (1990): 223–4.

48 'Liaison with MFA', 15 Feb. 1962, A9564, 222/1, NAA; Lansdowne to de la Mare, 9 Nov. 1961, FO 371/18497, PRO.

49 *Nihon Keizai Shimbun* (8 July 1962, evening).

50 *Yomiuri Shimbun* (19 May 1962).

51 The committee was established after the Security Treaty revision. Welfield (1988): 177.

52 Takasaki Tatsunosuke's impending departure for Beijing to negotiate the restoration of normal trade channels may have been a factor in this decision. P.A.N. Murthy, 'Japan and the India–China Border Conflict' *International Studies* (July/Oct. 1963): 183, 185; *JTW* (10 Nov. 1962).

53 Michael Schaller, *Altered States* (1997) NY: 174–5.

54 In November 1962, Japanese who 'disliked' China reached 24.8%, the lowest level since regular surveys began in June 1960. See Figure 8.1. However, a December poll found that more people believed in India (16.5%) than China (0.9%): those who believed neither numbered 7.3%. *Yoron chōsa nenkan* (1962). See also Welfield (1988): 179–80.

55 Radtke (1990): 143.

56 Ōno to Ōhira, 29 Oct. 1962, A 0364/1449–56, GS.

57 RC, Ikeda and Macmillan, 12 Nov. 1962, FO 371/164976, PRO; Ōno to Ōhira, 14 Nov. 1962, A 0364/1495–99, GS.

58 Gerald Segal, *The Great Power Triangle* (1982) Basingstoke: 65.

59 Chang (1990): 251.

60 Furukawa (1981): 215.

61 MC, Ohira and Rusk, 3–5 Dec. 1962, *FRUS, 1961–63* XXII: 748–51. See also: Schaller (1997): 175, and Chapter 5.

62 Welfield (1988): 180–1.

63 Kohler to Rusk, 7 Jan. 1963, cited in Segal (1982): 66.

64 CIA, 'Sino-Soviet Relations at a New Crisis', 14 Jan. 1963, cited in Segal (1982): 66.

65 Welfield (1988): 180.

66 *Nihon Keizai Shimbun* (29 Jan. 1963).

67 *JTW* (26 Jan. 1963).

68 At the same press conference, Defence Agency Director Shiga Kenjirō attracted much attention by claiming that China was 'in possession of two atom bombs', until it emerged that this information did not derive from US sources. *JTW* (2, 9 Feb. 1963).

69 *JTW* (16 Feb. 1963).

70 The scenario included the SDF joining US military operations against China's east coast and Soviet Pacific territories. On 10 February 1965, JSP Diet member Okada Haruo embarrassed the government by revealing the plan's existence. Matsueda Tsukasa and George Moore, 'Japan's Shifting Attitudes toward the Military' *Asian Survey* (Sept. 1967): 614, Thomas Havens, *Fire Across the Sea* (1987) New Jersey: 28;

Albert Axelbank, *Black Star over Japan* (1972) Tokyo: 18, Welfield (1988): 204–5; Chae-Jin Lee, *Japan Faces China* (1976) Baltimore: 49.

71 J.A.A. Stockwin, 'Japanese Attitudes to the Sino-Soviet Dispute' *International Journal* (1963): 499–500.

72 *Tōkyō Shimbun* (1 Jan. 1963).

73 *Sankei Shimbun* (19 Jan. 1963, evening).

74 '"Chū So ronsō" Jimintō nimo tobihi' *Chūō Kōron* (Mar. 1963): 78.

75 Aichi Kiichi, et al., 'Watashi wa kō handan suru' *Chūō Kōron* (Mar. 1963): 149, 158–9.

76 Hōgen Shinsaku, 'Saikin no kokusai jōsei ni tsuite' *Gaisei Kenkyū* (Jan./Feb. 1963): 32–4.

77 Jamieson (Tokyo) to SEA, 26 Feb. 1963, A9564, 227/3, NAA.

78 McIntyre (Tokyo) to SEA, 16 Apr. 1963, A1838, 3103/10/1, NAA.

79 *Asahi Shimbun* (25 Mar. 1963).

80 RC, Ohta and Shaw, 9 Apr. 1963, A1838, 3103/10/1, NAA.

81 'The Sino-Soviet Dispute and Japan' *Japan Quarterly* (Apr./June 1963): 146.

82 AusEmbTok to DEA, 1 Oct. 1959, A1838, 3103/3/1/1; McIntyre (Tokyo) to SEA, 25 June 1963, A1838, 3103/10/1, NAA.

83 Other appointments included Yasui Kenji, Hasegawa Takaaki and Kataoka Aki. McIntyre to SEA, 16 Apr. 1963, ibid.

84 *Yomiuri Shimbun* (22 Mar. 1963); RC Niiseki and Wiadrowski, 4 Apr. 1963, A9564, 227/3, NAA.

85 The rift's implications were also discussed when French Foreign Minister Couve de Murville visited Tokyo a fortnight later, and in November with his West German counterpart, Gerhard Schroeder. *Asahi Shimbun* (19 Apr. 1963); *JTW* (16 Nov. 1963).

86 *JTW* (Apr. 6, 1963).

87 RC, Home and Ikeda, Apr. 3, 1963, FO 371/170759, PRO. MacLehose (head of the FED), who had accompanied Home, observed that the Japanese were 'not…impressed by the Chinese performance in standing up to the Russians in the Sino-Soviet conflict. They tend to interpret this primarily as a manifestation of Chinese pig-headedness and refusal to accept defeat rather than evidence of the emergence of China as a formidable power in its own right.' Hamilton (London) to SEA, 10 May 1963, A1838, 3103/11/51, NAA.

88 *Asahi Shimbun* (12 June 1963); *JTW* (29 June 1963).

89 Memo, 18 June 1963, A1838, 3103/10/1, NAA. By the end of the month, following Soviet demands that five Chinese diplomats leave the country, there was reportedly speculation within MOFA as to whether the planned Sino-Soviet conference would go ahead. *Asahi Shimbun* (30 June 1963).

90 'The Sino-Soviet Dispute and Japan' *Japan Quarterly* (Apr./June 1963): 146.

91 The US Embassy in Moscow later confirmed that 'the outbreak of virtually undeclared war' between Moscow and Beijing that spring 'explained Soviet acceptance of a partial test-ban agreement which it could have had at any time during the past year.' Chang (1990): 239–40.

92 CIA, 'Possibilities of Greater Militancy by the Chinese Communists', 31 July 1963, cited in Segal (1982): 68; Summary Record 516th Meeting NSC, 31 July 1963; MC, Gilpatric and Reischauer, 5 Aug. 1963, *FRUS, 1961–63* XXII: 371–4, 786–90.

93 *Peking Review* (19 July 1963) cited in Chang (1990): 242.

94 Peter Jones and Sian Kevill, *China and the Soviet Union, 1949–84* (1985) Harlow, Essex: 31–45; Morton Halperin, *China and the Bomb* (1965) London: 66.

95 Alice Hsieh, 'The Sino-Soviet Nuclear Dialogue: 1963', *Sino-Soviet Military Relations*, R.L. Gartoff (ed.) (1966) NY: 160.

96 *International Affairs* (Sept. 1963) Moscow: 3–9, cited in P.A.N. Murthy, 'Japan's Changing Relations with People's China and the Soviet Union' *International Studies* (July 1965): 15.

97 Maga (1990): 92, 96.

98 *JTW* (3 Aug. 1963).

99 A poll in August found that of those aware of the PTBT, 55% supported Japan's participation, while only 2.6% did not. The poll also revealed, however, that many Japanese supporters were dissatisfied with its provisions, a finding confirmed by another poll in October. *Yoron chōsa nenkan*, (1963): 219, 230.

100 *JTW* (13 July 1963).

101 RC, Ogawa and Wiadrowski, 12 July 1963, A1838 3103/11/87 Pt. 9, NAA.

102 Ibid; *JT* (8 July 1963).

103 *Asahi Shimbun* (19 July 1963, evening); *Nikkei Shimbun* (19 July 1963, evening).

104 *Mainichi Shimbun* (19 July 1963, evening); *JT* (20 July 1963). Two days earlier, Ambassador Ohta had discussed the need for a new form of consultations between Japan and other Pacific and Asian countries in light of the Sino-Soviet split. RC, Ohta and Shaw, 17 July 1963, A1838, 3103/10/1, NAA.

105 In response to a question from Kennedy, Ōhira explained that, 'the JCP is basically sympathetic to Communist China, but there is severe internal strife between pro-Peiping and pro-Moscow factions.' Pressed on China's future moves, the Foreign Minister predicted that China would become 'more active in promoting its ideological position, particularly in South–East Asia, but will probably remain cautious about undertaking any actions in South–East Asia.' MC, Kennedy and Ōhira, 2 Aug 1963, *FRUS, 1961–63* XXII: 783–6.

106 Shima Shigenobu, 'Kaku jikken teishi jōyaku chōin ni omou' *Kokusai Mondai* (Sept. 1963): 2–3.

107 Genda Minoru, 'Kyokutō o odokasu Chūkyō no kakubusō' *Sekai Shūhō* (20 Aug. 1963): 22–5.

108 RC, Ogawa and Wiadrowski, 9 Sept. 1963, A9564, 227/3, NAA. A few weeks earlier, Nemoto Ki (deputy director of the European Affairs Bureau) told an Australian diplomat that MOFA had 'followed the Russian line of accusing the Chinese of racialism with considerable interest…and feel that in a cooler atmosphere…the Russians would have difficulty in substantiating…these charges.' Jamieson (Tokyo) to SEA, 24 July 1964, A9564, 227/3, NAA.

109 *Asahi Shimbun* (2 Sept. 1963). See also: Ueda Toshio, 'The Outlook for Relations with Communist China' *Japan Quarterly* (July/Sept. 1966): 297.

110 *JTW* (14 Sept. 1963).

111 RC, Home and Ōhira, 3 Sept. 1963, FO 371/170757, PRO, and A 0365/1162–78, GS.

112 Dixon (Paris) to Home, 24 Sept. 1963, A1838, 3103/11/62, NAA. Vice Minister Shima also discussed this issue at the second Japan–Canada Ministerial Committee meeting on 25–6 September. Shima noted how Soviet and Chinese attitudes towards Japan had recently changed, but he remained 'apprehensive'. White (Ottawa) to SEA, 9 Oct. 1963, A1838, 229/10/4/4, NAA.

113 AusEmbWash to SEA, 20 Sept. 1963, A1838, 3103/11/87 Pt. 9, NAA.

114 RC, Menzies and Ikeda, 30 Sept. 1963, A1838, 3103/10/1, NAA. Interestingly, Deputy Vice Minister Ōda Takio, who accompanied Ikeda, told the Australians that a large-

scale Chinese attack upon India was unlikely because of Chinese dependence on Soviet oil. RC, Ōda and Tange, 30 Sept. 1963, A1838, 3103/10/1, NAA.

115 Discussion between Ikeda and Holyoake, 4 Oct. 1963, ABHS 950, W4627, 268/3/1, New Zealand Archives, Wellington.

116 *JTW* (19 Oct. 1963).

117 *JTW* (26 Oct. 1963).

118 'Ōhira Foreign Policy Speech, 18 Oct. 1963', *Gaimushō Press Releases* (1963) Tokyo: 46.

119 *JTW* (26 Oct. 1963).

120 Abe Keizō, et al., 'Nihon gaikō no jittai' *Chūō Kōron* (Jan. 1964): 117.

121 MC, Ogawa and Wiadrowski, 24 Oct. 1963, A1838, 3103/10/1, NAA.

122 Hirotsu Kyōsuke, 'Kokusai kyōsanshugi to Nihon Kyōsantō no tachiba' *Sekai to Nihon* (Nov. 1963): 23–4, 27.

123 Suzuki Kazuo, 'Shin dankai no NitChū bōeki' *Ekonomisuto* (17 Sept. 1963): 45. This even-handed policy was continued by Kaya's successor in 1964. *JTW* (1 Aug. 1964).

124 Funada Naka, 'Naze Chūkyō wa shin no kōryū o kobamu ka' *Ronsō* (Oct. 1963): 37–41.

125 Takasaki Tatsunosuke, 'NitChū bōeki futatsu no rosen' *Seikai Ōrai* (Nov. 1963): 94–5.

126 Ikeda Masanosuke, 'Chūkyō no jittai o yoku mikiwamete' *Seikai Ōrai* (Nov. 1963): 103–4.

127 Furui Yoshimi and Matsumoto Shunichi, both members of the LDP's 'pro-China' wing, were also in Beijing at this time. Liao Chengzhi told them three reasons for the Chinese attacks on the Soviet Union, namely, Moscow's 'great power chauvinism', its demand for payment for the Korean War era transfers, and 'a plot to overthrow [the] present Chinese leadership under Chairman Mao.' McIntyre to SEA, 5 Nov. 1963, A1838, 3103/10/1, NAA.

128 Ishibashi Tanzan, 'NitChū fukkō to Chū-So ronsō ni tai suru watashi no mikata' *Tōyō Keizai Shimpō* (16 Nov. 1963): 9–10. Ishibashi had also planned to visit the Soviet Union at this time, but Matsumura and Ikeda advised against it. He finally made it to Moscow in September 1964, but was unable to meet with Khrushchev. Masuda Hiroshi, *Anadorazu, kanshōsezu, hirefusazu—Ishibashi Tanzan no tai Chūgoku gaikōron* (1993): 229–30.

129 Shinohara Hajime, 'The Leadership of the Conservative Party' *Journal of Social and Political Ideas in Japan* (Dec. 1964): 44.

130 Welfield (1988): 184–5.

131 MC, Ikeda and Rusk, 26 Nov. 1963, Country Files—Japan Cables, I, 11/63–4/64, *L.B. Johnson National Security Files—Asia and the Pacific: National Security Files 1963–69* (1993) Bethesda. (Hereafter, LBJ.)

132 *People's Daily* (21 Jan. 1964) cited in Jain (1981 A): 48–9.

133 Michael Yahuda, *China's Role in World Affairs* (1978) London: 151.

134 Paul Langer, 'Japan and the Great-Power Triangles', *The World and the Great Power Triangles*, W.E. Griffith (ed.) (1975) Cambridge, MA: 304. See also Radtke (1990): 144; Dennis Yasutomo, 'Satō's China Policy, 1964–66' *Asian Survey* (June 1977): 536.

135 *JTW* (29 Feb.; 7 Mar. 1964).

136 Foreign Policy Speech Ōhira, 46th Regular Diet, *Gaimushō Press Releases* (1964) Tokyo: 10.

137 Between February and July 1964, support for recognition never fell below 31.7%, while opposition never exceeded 11.9%. During the same period, on average 20%

expressed belief in 'two Chinas', 16% in Beijing and 6% Taipei. *Yoron chōsa nenkan* (1963).

138 Abe (1964): 117–9.

139 RC, Kishi and McIntyre, 22 Jan. 1964, A9564, 221/1, NAA.

140 'France's Recognition of Peking and its Impact on Japan' *Japan Socialist Review* (1 Mar. 1964): 18–19.

141 AmEmbTok to DOS, 27 Jan. 1964, *DDRS* (1964(R)): 639C; MC, Rusk and Ōhira, 26 Jan. 1964, *DDRS* (1993): 247–8.

142 'Ikeda Speech at Luncheon in Honor US Members 3rd Meeting Joint Japan–US Committee Trade and Economic Affairs, 27 Jan. 1964' *Gaimushō Press Releases* (1964) Tokyo: 23. (Emphasis added.)

143 Communist China: Joint Economic Committee, 28 Jan. 1964, *DDRS* (1993): 3223; Rusk to Ōhira, 27 Jan. 1964, and B. Smith, 'White House Note for President', 28 Jan. 1964, Country Files—Japan Cables, I, 11/63–4/64, *LBJ*.

144 P.D. Malone, *Japan's Foreign Policy 1957 through 1967* (Apr. 1969) Geneva: 102; Varma (1991): 57; *Asahi Shimbun* (6, 13, 18 Feb. (evening), 1964); 'Taiwan o meguru sei zaikai no omowaku' *Shūkan Tōyō Keizai* (29 Feb. 1964) 3154: 38–43.

145 McIntyre (Tokyo) to DEA, 21 Feb. 1964, A3092, 221/12/2/5/1, NAA. (Emphasis added.)

146 Ibid.; *Asahi Shimbun* (20 Feb. 1964, evening).

147 AusEmbTok to DEA, 28 Feb. 1964, A3092, 221/12/2/5/1, NAA; *JTW* (7 Mar. 1964).

148 MC, Takeuchi and Rusk, 29 Feb. 1964, *DDRS* (1993): 131.

149 *JTW* (14 Mar. 1964); *Asahi Shimbun* (4 March 1964, evening).

150 Gaimushō, *NitChū kankei kihon shiryōshū* (1970): 231–2; *JTW* (14 Mar. 1964); Chu (1971): 22–3; Welfield (1988): 188.

151 *JTW* (9 May; 16 May 1964).

152 RAD, 'Our Contact with the Soviet Ambassador', Enc. Jamieson (Tokyo) to SEA, 2 July 1964; RAD, 'Informal Soviet Statements concerning Sino-Soviet Relations', Enc. Jamieson (Tokyo) to SEA, 27 Apr. 1964, A9564, 227/3, NAA.

153 Cortazzi to MacLehose, 8 May 1964, FO 371/176016, PRO; *JTW* (9 May 1964).

154 RAD, 'Analysis No. 12: The Sino-Soviet Confrontation', 16 May 1964, A9564, 227/3, NAA.

155 Rundall (Tokyo) to SOS, 4 June 1964, FO 371/176009, PRO; *JTW* (30 May; 6 June 1964); AusEmbTok to DEA, 22 May 1964, A1838, 250/10/4/4, NAA.

156 *Sekai Shūhō* (11 Aug. 1964); RC, Wiadrowski and Ogawa, 2 Sept. 1964, A9564, 227/3, NAA, and see Chapter 9.

157 Albrecht Rothacher, *Economic Diplomacy between the European Community and Japan, 1959–1981* (1983) Aldershot: 111; AmEmbTok to Rusk, 11 Apr. 1964, *DDRS* (1964(R)): 640A.

158 Cortazzi to MacLehose, 8 May 1964, FO 371/176016, PRO.

159 Rundall (Tokyo) to SOS, 4 June 1964, FO 371/176009, PRO.

160 CIA, 'The China Problem in Japanese Politics', 1 May 1964, *DDRS* (1964(77)): 22H.

161 DOS, 'The Future of Japan', 26 June 1964, *DDRS* (1995): 3262.

162 ANZUS 1964, ITEM 7, 'Japan: An Assessment', n.d. [July 1964?], A1838, 3103/10/1, NAA.

163 Ōhira Masayoshi, 'Diplomacy for Peace' *International Affairs* (July 1964): 393.

164 Record of Meeting, Butler and Ōhira, 2 May 1964, FO 371/170759, PRO.

165 Both reports are enclosed in Jamieson (Tokyo) to SEA, 10 Sept. 1964, A9564, 227/3, NAA.

166 CRO, 'NisSo (sic) ronsō ni tai suru kokunai no hannō' *Chōsa Geppō* (Aug. 1964): 44–60.
167 Welfield (1988): 190.
168 RC, Ambassador Matsudaira and Plimsoll, 3 Aug. 1964, A9564, 227/11, NAA.
169 Peters (Tokyo) to SEA, 1 Sept. 1964, A1838, 3103/11/161, NAA.
170 RC, Wiadrowski and Ogawa, 2 Sept. 1964, A9564, 227/3, NAA
171 McIntyre to SEA, 18 Sept. 1964, A1838, 3103/7/1, NAA.
172 'Third Meeting Canada/Japan Ministerial Committee, 4–5 Sept. 1964', Shiina and Martin, 11 Sept. 1964, FO 371/176020, PRO.
173 'Speech by Foreign Minister Shiina at Luncheon in his honor by Japan–America Society', 24 Sept. 1964, *Gaimushō Press Releases* (1964): 31. (Emphasis added.)
174 George Kennan, 'Polycentrism and Western Policy' *Foreign Affairs* (Jan. 1964): 173; *JTW*, (13 June 1964).
175 George Kennan, 'Japanese Security and American Policy' *Foreign Affairs* (Oct. 1964): 14–28. See also, Ole Holsti, Terrence Hopmann, and John Sullivan, *Unity and Disintegration in International Alliances* (1973) NY.
176 Reischauer to Rusk, 24 Sept. 1964, Country Files—Japan Cables, II, 5/64–11/64, *LBJ*.
177 Bundy, 'Address to the Research Institute of Japan', 29 Sept. 1964, A1838, 3103/11/161, NAA.
178 Ishibashi Tanzan, 'Kyōsanshugi o sukutta heiwakyōson' *Tōyō Keizai Shimpō* (31 Oct. 1964): 25.
179 Genda Minoru, 'Gai nomi ōkushite ri sukunashi' *Sekai Shūhō* (13 Oct. 1964): 21–3.
180 'Translation of (GOJ Unofficial Rebuttal of Kennan Article)', Enc. in Zurhellen (Tokyo) to DOS, 16 Dec. 1964; Reischauer to Rusk, 24 Sept. 1964, Country Files—Japan Cables, II, 5/64–11/64, *LBJ*.
181 Zurhellen (Tokyo) to DOS, 16 Dec. 1964, Country Files—China Cables, II, 9/64–2/65, *LBJ*.
182 *JTW* (4 May 1963).
183 Ishibashi (1964): 25.
184 *JTW* (24 Oct. 1964).
185 Just the previous month, Fukunaga Kenji, Yoshida's chief cabinet secretary, had led a 15–member parliamentary delegation to Moscow, where Khrushchev treated them to a diatribe comparing Mao Zedong to Hitler on the territorial issue. *JTW* (24 Oct. 1964).
186 Reischauer to SOS, 16 Oct. 1964, Country Files—Japan Cables, II, 5/64–11/64, *LBJ*.
187 RAD, 'Effect of Khrushchev's Resignation on Sino-Soviet Relations', 19 Oct. 1964, Enc. in Cortazzi (Tokyo) to Bently, 23 Oct. 1964, FO 371/ 176010, PRO.
188 *JT* (22 Oct. 1964). Later that day, Hōgen told Ambassador McIntyre that 'the presidium in Moscow evidently decided to remove the factor of strong personal animosity between Khrushchev and Mao in an effort to paper the rift over.' He also thought there might be 'some faintly conciliatory signs from the other [Chinese] side too.' McIntyre to DEA, 21 Oct. 1964, A1838, 3103/11/52 Pt. 6, NAA. After Zhou Enlai's visit to Moscow, however, Hōgen concluded that 'Both sides were probably waiting and watching.' They wished to 'avoid a formal rupture', but 'deep-rooted differences' existed between them which the Soviet Union 'could not solve.' Record of Discussion, MacLehose and Hōgen, 9 Nov. 1964, FO 371/176018, PRO.
189 Ogawa rejected Hasegawa's linkage theory. Cortazzi (Tokyo) to Bently, 23 Oct. 1964, FO 371/ 176010, PRO.
190 *JTW* (17 Oct. 1964).
191 Peters (Tokyo) to SEA, 13 Oct. 1964, A1838, 3103/1/1 Pt. 1, NAA.

192 Consequently, from 1965, Moscow began a major military buildup along the Sino-Soviet frontier. Allen Whiting, *Siberian Development and East Asia* (1981) Stanford: 88–9; Harold Hinton, *Three and a Half Powers* (1975) Bloomington: 98.

193 Peters (Tokyo) to SEA, 1 Sept. 1964, A1838, 3103/11/161, NAA; 'Assessing the Chinese Bomb' *Japan Quarterly* (Jan./Mar. 1965): 12.

194 *JTW* (7 Nov. 1964).

195 In fact, in June 1964, China successfully test-launched a missile (*Dongfeng-2*) capable of hitting Japan with a twenty-kiloton warhead. It did not become fully operational until October 1966, but this was much sooner than the popular estimate of ten years. It is unlikely that US intelligence was unaware of this development and it was probably not coincidental that following the Chinese test, the US deployed Polaris nuclear-armed submarines in the Pacific and attached the nuclear-powered aircraft carrier USS Enterprise to the Seventh Fleet for the first time. John Wilson Lewis and Xue Litai, *China Builds the Bomb* (1988) Stanford: 211.

196 John Welfield, 'A New Balance: Japan versus China?' *Pacific Community* (Oct. 1972): 54. Gallois held that no country could rely on another committing nuclear suicide. Fred Greene, *Stresses in US–Japan Security Relations* (1975) Washington, D.C.: 94.

197 Kōsaka Masataka, 'Kaiyō kokka Nihon no kōsō' *Chūō Kōron* (Sept. 1964) 79(9): 63.

198 *Asahi Shimbun* (20 Oct. 1964).

199 Ishibashi (1964): 25.

200 *JTW* (24 Oct. 1964).

201 *JTW* (7 Nov. 1964).

202 Rundall (Tokyo) to FED, 26 Feb. 1965, FO 371/181074, PRO; *JTW* (24 Oct. 1964); Wakaizumi Kei, 'Chūgoku no kakubusō to Nihon no anzen hoshō' *Chūō Kōron* (Feb. 1966): 77.

203 Wakaizumi (1966): 76; Welfield (1970): 8.

204 Zurhellen (Tokyo) to DOS, 16 Dec. 1964, Country Files—China Cables, II, 9/64–2/65, *LBJ*.

205 William C. Foster, 'Memo for the Members of the Committee of Principals Report on 'Japan's Prospects in the Nuclear Weapons Field', 25 June 1965, *DDRS* (1994): 1807.

206 Thomas L. Hughes (INR) to Acting SOS, 10 Nov. 1964, *DDRS* (1964(R)): 641G.

207 A *Mainichi* poll in November found that establishing diplomatic ties with China was the fourth foreign policy priority—after a comprehensive nuclear test-ban, the return of Okinawa, and promotion of economic foreign policy—but it still ranked above return of the Northern Islands, or strengthening cooperation with the Free World. *Yoron chōsa nenkan* (1964): 215. A *Kyōdō* poll in December confirmed the near 4:1 majority in favour of improved relations and China's admission to the UN. Welfield (1970): 37.

208 *JTW* (28 Nov. 1964).

209 McIntyre (Tokyo) to DEA, 4 Dec. 1964, A1838, 3103/10/1, NAA; *JTW* (5 Dec.; 12 Dec. 1964).

210 RC, Nadao and Clark, 24 Dec. 1964, A9564, 227/10/1, NAA. See also Chapter 5.

211 Lee (1976): 49.

212 Lee (1976): 50; and Zhao Quansheng, *Japanese Policymaking* (1993) Westport: 74.

213 Cortazzi (Tokyo) to Bently, 20 Jan. 1965, FO 371/181074, PRO. Prior to his trip, Utsunomiya argued that the dispute was 'taking the form of an ideological rift', but only because of 'an underlying conflict of national interests.' Yet he rejected the differing 'historical stages' and 'international environments' arguments. In Utsunomiya's opinion, Socialism 'tended to be more nationalistic', and thus the rift was inevitable. It was also 'a good thing to break down a relationship of dominator and

dominated' and he claimed that, 'the situation is being reflected back on the monolith on the other side too.' Utsunomiya Tokuma, et al, 'Chūgoku no nashonaru intaresuto' *Gendai no Me* (Nov. 1964): 81–6.

214 Peters (Tokyo) to SEA, 26 Jan. 1965, A1838, 3103/11/87, Pt. 13, NAA.

215 The following day, Vice-President-elect Hubert Humphrey took up the nuclear issue once more, arguing that, 'Japan should not enter into atomic power politics'. He added, however, that 'It would have a good effect in Communist China if you had a hand on the umbrella to be sure the rain doesn't come down on you.' MC, Miki and Humphrey, 13 Jan. 1965, *DDRS* (1965(R)): 642B.

216 MC, Satō and Johnson, 12 Jan. 1965, *DDRS* (1994): 1475, 1477.

217 MC, Satō and Rusk, 12 Jan. 1965, *DDRS* (1992): 3288. Ogawa stated that in MOFA's view 'the new [Soviet] regime, although its basic attitude to China was probably the same, was being careful to avoid taking a line that could lead to its being charged with blame for a collapse of the world Communist movement.' Jamieson (Tokyo) to SEA, 5 Feb. 1965, A9564, 227/3, NAA.

218 *Tōkyō Shimbun* (20 Jan. 1965) cited in Welfield (1970): 3; Malone (1969): 103.

219 *US Dept. of State Bulletin* (1 Feb. 1965) Washington, D.C.: 135; *JTW* (6 Feb. 1965).

220 Memo to the President from US official, n.d., *DDRS* (1993): 3123; *JTW* (8 May 1965).

221 Brady (Washington) to SEA, 14 May 1965, A1838, 3103/11/161, NAA.

222 Satō later assured the Soviet ambassador of Japan's support for Soviet attendance. Ibid; AusEmbTok to DEA, 1 June 1965, A1838, 3103/11/4; AusEmbTok to DEA, 9 June 1965, A1838, 3103/11/147, NAA.

223 Record of Meeting, Stewart and Satō, 20 Oct. 1965, FO 371/181084, PRO.

224 Evelyn Colbert, 'National Security Perspectives: Japan and Asia', *The Modern Japanese Military System*, James Buck (ed.) (1975) Beverly Hills: 207.

225 Saeki Kiichi, recently retired as head of the Defence Agency's Institute of Defence Studies (*Bōei Kenkyūjo*), likewise concluded that Chinese nuclear weapons represented 'one of the gravest threats to Japan's security'. In his opinion, however, the Soviet Union and China were 'self-acknowledged enemies of Japan [with] world revolution as their basic objective', and thus both constituted 'potential threats to Japan's security.' Saeki Kiichi, 'Nihon no anzen hoshō o dō suru' *Ekonomisuto* (10 Oct. 1965): 41–2.

226 Broinowski (Tokyo) to SEA, 15 Dec. 1965, A1838, 816/3/1 Pt. 3, NAA.

227 Ogata Sadako, *Normalization with China* (1989) Berkeley: 93, 101; A.M. Halpern, 'China and Japan since Normalization', *Dimensions in China's Foreign Relations*, Hsueh Chun-Tu (ed.) (1977) NY: 120–1.

Notes for Chapter 4

1 NSC 41, 'US Policy Regarding Trade with China, *FRUS, 1949* IX: 826–34.

2 Yasuhara Yoko, 'Japan, Communist China, and Export Controls in Asia, 1948–52' *Journal of Diplomatic History* (winter 1986): 81–2.

3 *Nihon Times* (4 Feb. 1949).

4 William Costello, 'Could Japan go Communist?' *Nation* (14 May 1949): 534.

5 Michael Schaller, *The American Occupation of Japan* (1985) NY: 189.

6 Makiko Hamaguchi-Klenner, *China Images of Japanese Conservatives* (1981) Hamburg: 71; Soeya Yoshihide, *Japan's Economic Diplomacy with China, 1945–1978* (1998) Oxford: 25–6; Fukui Haruhiro, *Party in Power* (1970) Berkeley: 241; R.K. Jain, *China and Japan, 1949–80* (1981[A]) Delhi: 26; Lalima Varma, *The Making of*

Japan's China Policy (1991) Delhi: 116–8; Leng Shao Chuan, *Japan and Communist China* (1958) Kyoto: 110–2.

7 *New York Times* (25 Nov. 1949) cited in Schaller (1985): 189.

8 Acheson memo, meeting with Bradley and others, 29 Dec. 1949, *FRUS, 1949* IX: 463–7.

9 Jain (1981 A); 27.

10 Ishikawa Tadao, Nakajima Mineo, and Ikei Masaru (eds), *Sengo shiryō: NitChū kankei* (1970): 23; Gordon Chang, *Friends and Enemies* (1990) Stanford: 73.

11 See: Lowell Dittmer, *Sino-Soviet Normalization and its International Implications* (1992) Seattle: ch. 1; P. Jones and S. Kevill, *China and the Soviet Union, 1949–84* (1985) Harlow, Essex: ch. 1.

12 From a postwar high of $19.6 million in 1950, exports fell to $5.8 million the following year, and to just $600,000 in 1952. Imports followed a similar plunging trajectory when, to Yoshida's apparent surprise, Beijing responded by banning delivery of essential materials to Japan. Chae-Jin Lee, *Japan Faces China* (1976) Baltimore: 144; Hodgson (Tokyo) to DEA, 29 Dec. 1950, A4231, 1950/TOKYO, NAA. See also: Jain (1981A): 27.

13 MC, Yoshida, Dulles and Sebald, 29 Jan. 1951, *FRUS, 1951* VI: 827–8.

14 Ibid.

15 MC, Yoshida and Sebald, 20 Feb. 1951, *FRUS, 1951* VI: 828; Casey to Tange, 9 Dec. 1959, A1838, 3103/10/10/2, NAA.

16 R.K. Jain, *Japan's Post-War Peace Settlements* (1978) New Delhi: 372.

17 David Mayers, *Cracking the Monolith* (1986) Baton Rouge: 103.

18 Eckersley (Tokyo) to SEA, 10 May 1952, A1838, 3103/7/1, NAA; DOS, IR 5935, 'Attitudes and Policies of Japan towards Trading with the Soviet bloc', 3 July 1952, *IRR*.

19 Members included Hirano Yoshitarō (Japan Peace Association), Ishibashi Tanzan (ex-finance minister), Murata Shōzō (former president of *Ōsaka Shōsen* and former ambassador to the Philippines), Kitamura Tokutarō (ex-finance minister, a leader of *Kaishintō*, and director of Shinwa Bank), Hoashi Kei (Diet member, *Ryokufūkai*), and Aikawa Yoshisuke (former president of Manchurian Heavy Industries). Kurt Radtke, *China's Relations with Japan, 1945–83* (1990) Manchester: 99.

20 Foreign Minister Okazaki told the Lower House Foreign Affairs Committee at this time that Japan would not negotiate a trade agreement with Russia unless the Sino-Soviet Alliance was revised. *Japan News* (28 April 1952).

21 The signatories were Kōra Tomi (Diet member, *Ryokufūkai*), Hoashi Kei and Miyagoshi Kisuke. Jain (1981A): 29. Immediately upon returning to Japan they helped found the *NitChū Bōeki Sokushin Kai*, chaired by former Vice-Minister of Greater East Asian Affairs Yamamoto Kumaichi.

22 DOS, IR 5941, 'Pei-p'ing "Trade Agreement" and its impact in Japan', 30 June 1952, 693.94/6–3052, NA; Radtke (1990): 99, 112 (n.52). It also described Chinese trade as 'completely dependent upon the Soviet Union.' Foreign Ministry, Information and Culture Bureau, 'The Trade Policy of Communist China and the so-called "China–Japan Trade Agreement"' *World Report* (7 June 1952).

23 Yasuhara (1986): 86.

24 Yasuhara (1986): 87–9.

25 NSC 125/2, 7 Aug. 1952, *FRUS, 1952–54* XIV: 1302. This conclusion was, in part, a reaction to the views of the emperor's brother, Prince Takamatsu. Although pro-American, he argued that since Japan's knowledge of Russia and China exceeded

America's, 'Japan, through its trade and political relationships with the USSR and Communist China, could act as a bridge between the two worlds and possibly bring about the conversion of the "red countries" or at least a split between the USSR and Communist China.' Young to Allison, 4 June 1952, 794.00/6–452, NA.

26 AmEmbTok to DOS, 5 Apr. 1953, *OSS/State Dept. Intelligence and Research Reports, Part VIII, Japan, Korea, South–east Asia and the Far East Generally: 1950–61 Supplement* (1979) Washington, D.C.

27 Steeves (Tokyo) to DOS, [12 Feb. 1953], 693.94/3–1353, NA.

28 In April, the departing US ambassador publicly warned Japanese business leaders off the China market, where 'political objectives often outweigh economic considerations.' That same month, the president had privately expressed his belief that Japan had 'no future...unless access were provided for it to the markets and raw materials of Manchuria and North China.' Secretary of State John Foster Dulles, countered that the embargo could be maintained 'for perhaps five years', while Japan was encouraged to look instead towards the markets of Southeast Asia. Jain (1981A): 30; NSC, 139th Meeting, (dated) 16 Apr. 1953, *DDRS* (1987): 2885.

29 In April, Kazami Akira, an Independent Diet member, helped to bring them together in the *NitChū NisSo Kokkō Chōsei Sokushin Dōmei*. By the autumn, it had evolved into a general coordinating body—*NitChū NisSo Kokkō Kaifuku Kokumin Kaigi*—and was led by Majima Kan, a medical doctor. Radtke (1990): 99, 101; 'NisSo kōshō to sayoku no senden katsudō' *Nihon oyobi Nihonjin* (Aug. 1955): 34–37. See Appendix 1 for a list of members.

30 Yamamoto Kumaichi, 'Trade Problems with the PRC' *Contemporary Japan* (Sept. 1958): 364; Fukui (1970): 241.

31 The League was by now the largest inter-party organisation in the Diet, comprising not only all of the Socialists, but also more than 40 Progressives, and 70 members of Yoshida's own Liberals. Qing Simei, 'The Eisenhower Administration and Changes in Western Embargo Policy Against China, 1954–1958', *The Great Powers in East Asia*, Warren Cohen and Iriye Akira (eds) (1990) NY: 127.

32 MC, Takeuchi Harumi and Lutkins, 7 Dec. 1953, 693.94/12–753, NA.

33 Chang (1990): 89–90; Jain (1981A): 30. Ikeda later credited the Chinese with originating the concept of *seikei bunri* at this time. Ikeda Masanosuke, *Nazo no Kuni, Chukyō Tairitsu no Jittai* (1969): 344.

34 AmEmbTok to DOS, 17 Aug. 1953, *FRUS, 1952–54* XIV: 1480 (n.2), 1490–1.

35 Ikeda–Robertson talks, 2 Oct. 1953, 611.94/9–2953, NA; Hosoya Chihiro, 'From the Yoshida Letter to the Nixon Shock' in Iriye and Cohen (1989): 23.

36 McClurkin to Drumwright, 14 April 1954, *FRUS, 1952–54* XIV: 1634–35.

37 Jain (1981A): 32.

38 MC, Wajima and Lutkins, 21 Dec. 1953, 693.94/12–2153, NA.

39 MC, Ohashi and Lutkins, 3 June 1954, 693.94/6–1754, NA; *Nihon Times* (31 July 1954).

40 MC, Ogawa Takeo (sic) and Lutkins, 1 June 1954, 693.94/6–1154, NA.

41 James Morley, *Soviet and Communist Chinese Policies toward Japan, 1950–57* (1958) NY: 8.

42 Allison to Dulles, 24 July 1954, 661.94/7–2454, NA.

43 'Shindankai ni haitta "Chū-So kokkō kaifuku"' *Ekonomisuto* (6 Nov. 1954): 16–7; Q. (pseud.) 'Tai So bōeki urabanashi' *Ekonomisuto* (18 Sept. 1954): 20–1.

44 Horie Masanori, 'NisSo bōeki o suishin suru mono habamu mono' *Chūō Kōron* (Dec. 1954): 207.

45 Fukui (1970): 237.

46 Other leading members included Ishibashi Tanzan, Kitamura Tokutarō, Fujiyama Aiichirō (head of JAL and the Tokyo Chamber of Commerce), Takasaki Tatsunosuke, and Suga Reinosuke (chairman, Tokyo Electric Power). Yamamoto Kumaichi and Suzuki Kazuo of JCTPA were both founding members, but plans to merge the two bodies came to naught. Since JITPA was more big business oriented, some members of JCTPA resented the newcomer. Ogata Sadako, 'The Business Community and Japanese Foreign Policy', *The Foreign Policy of Modern Japan*, R.A. Scalapino (ed.) (1977) Berkeley: 179; Soeya (1998): 28–9.

47 MC, Aichi and Murphy, 27 Oct. 1954, 611.94/10–2754, NA.

48 *Shūkan Asahi* (31 Oct. 1954).

49 'Chū-So sengen o dō uketoru ka' *Ekonomisuto* (23 Oct. 1954): 24–6. Other influential examples included Fujiyama Aiichirō and Sugi Michisuke (head of the Ōsaka Chamber of Commerce).

50 Michael Schaller, *Altered States* (1997) NY: 76.

51 William Ballis, 'A Decade of Soviet–Japan Relations' *Studies on the Soviet Union* (1964): 134.

52 Fukui (1970): 238; Ishiyama Kenkichi, 'Kakutō no kōyaku o hyōsu' *Daiyamondo* (11 Feb. 1955): 12.

53 The visit of a private Japanese fisheries delegation to China on 13 January also won official backing, and three months of talks resulted in signature of a non-governmental agreement. *Mainichi Shimbun* (15 Dec. 1954); Morley (1958): 15; Radtke (1990): 106; Jain (1981A): 37.

54 Office Memorandum, McClurkin to Robertson, 7 Jan. 1955, 661.941/1–755, NA.

55 RC, Zhou and Murata, 23 Jan. 1955, A-0133–5–0123, GS; Murata Shōzō, 'Furui Chūgokukan e no keikoku' *Bungei Shunjū* (July 1955): 60, 62; Murata Shōzō, 'NitChū kankei no genjō o ureu' *Sekai* (Nov. 1955): 19.

56 Suzuki Matsugorō, 'Kyōsanken bōeki ni odoru hitobito' *Jimbutsu Ōrai* (Apr. 1955): 53; 'Gyakuten shidashita Nichi-Bei kōshō no uchimaku' *Shinsō* (1 Apr. 1955): 16; *Japan News* (7 Mar. 1955) in A1838, 766/3/4, NAA.

57 Shimizu Sayuri, 'Perennial Anxiety' *Journal of American–East Asian Relations* (fall 1995): 235; Douglas Johnston, 'Marginal Diplomacy in East Asia' *International Journal* (summer 1971): 485–7.

58 Johnston (1971): 488 (n.27); Jamieson (Tokyo) to SEA, 21 July 1955, A1838, 766/3/4, NAA.

59 According to Yoshioka Ichirō (consul in Djakarta), 'China wanted trade relations with Japan to serve as a bargaining factor in future trade dealings with the Soviet.' RC, Yoshioka and Lee, 15 May 1955, A1838 3103/11/87 Pt. 2, NAA. Similarly, Ambassador Sawada Renzō (observer at the UN), was already predicting that 'in the long run China would…prefer to have the help of Japanese rather than Russian technicians'. Forsyth (UN) to SEA, 15 Apr. 1955, A1838 3103/7/1, NAA.

60 'NitChū bōeki kyōtei no igi' *Ekonomisuto* (14 May 1955): 23.

61 Shimizu (1995): 236–7.

62 'Japan–China Trade', 19 July 1955, A1838, 766/3/4, NAA.

63 They estimated that Sino-Japanese trade would develop only slowly, but for the first time serious concern was expressed at growing Chinese economic penetration of Southeast Asian markets. Drumwright (Hong Kong) to Dulles, 15 Nov. 1955, 693.94/11–1555; Rankin (Taipei) to Dulles, 21 Nov. 1955, 690.93/11–2155, NA.

64 Soeya (1998): 30–1.

65 'Recent Developments and Future Prospects of Japanese Trade with Communist China', IR 6649, 15 Apr. 1955, *OSS/State Dept. Intelligence & Research Reports, IX, China and India, 1950–61*.
66 Kosaka Zentarō, 'Nihon ni semaru chūritsuka seisaku' *Seikei Shishin* (Aug. 1955): 90–9.
67 MC, Shigemitsu and Dulles, 29–31 Aug. 1955, *FRUS, 1955–57* XXIII(1): 93–113.
68 Jain (1981A): 217–18.
69 Shinohara Hajime, 'The Leadership of the Conservative Party' *Journal of Social and Political Ideas in Japan* (Dec. 1964): 44. Guo apparently convinced Matsumura that the Chinese Revolution was essentially nationalist in character like the Meiji Restoration. Soeya (1998): 80.
70 DOS, 'Soviet Statements on Japan–USSR Relations', IR 8481, 6 June 1961, *OSS/State Dept. Intelligence and Research Reports, XI, The Soviet Union: 1950–61 Supplement* (1979) Washington, D.C.
71 At the same time, political commentator Inabuchi Tatsuo suggested to the Americans that, 'In future Japan may be able to compete with [the] USSR as a supplier of scientific and technical know-how to China.' Lamb to Bowie, 19 Mar. 1956, Division of North East Asian Affairs, Box 9, 58-D-118 & 58-D-637, *Records of the Office of North East Asian Affairs: Japan, Subject Files, 1947–56, Confidential US State Dept. Special Files—Japan, 1947–56* (1990) Bethesda.
72 Roger Kirk to Waddell, 22 Mar. 1956, 611.94/3–2256, NA.
73 MC, Hatoyama and Dulles, 19 Mar. 1956, *FRUS, 1955–57* XXIII(1): 163–70.
74 *Asahi Shimbun* (23 May 1956); Shimizu (1995): 237.
75 NSC, 282nd meeting, 27 Apr. 1956, *FRUS, 1955–57* XXIII(1): 174–5; Shimizu (1995): 237–8.
76 Allison to Dulles, 26 May 1956, 661.94/5–2656, NA.
77 Selby (Tokyo) to Crowe (FED), 2 July 1956, FO 371/121038, PRO.
78 AmEmbTok to DOS, 5 July 1956, 794.00/7–556, NA.
79 Varma (1991): 46; Yamamoto Kumaichi, 'Trade Problems with PRC' *Contemporary Japan* (Sept. 1958): 391.
80 General R. Collins (Joint Chiefs) to Radford, 5 Oct. 1956, *DDRS* (1956(80)): 360A.
81 Murata Shōzō, 'Nitchū keizai kōryū no tenbō' *Sekai* (Feb. 1957): 83.
82 Arisawa Hiromi, et al., 'Kokomu no kabe o koete' *Sekai* (Dec. 1956): 53; Jain (1981A): 31.
83 The Japanese government even contributed 60 million yen to help defray the costs of this 'private' exhibition and its sister fair in Shanghai. Sō Yōkichi, 'Nitchū bōeki o ugokasu mono' *Nihon oyobi Nihonjin* (Jan. 1957): 62–8; J.Y.S. Cheng, 'Sino-Japanese Relations, 1957–60' *Asian Affairs* (1977): 71; R.G. Boyd, 'China's Relations with Japan' *Australian Outlook* (Apr. 1960): 56.
84 Fukui (1970): 241; Morley (1958): 21.
85 MC, Ishibashi and Robertson, 19 Dec. 1956, *FRUS, 1955–57* XXIII(1): 235–40.
86 'Ishibashi Tanzan—sono hito to seisaku' *Shūkan Asahi* (30 Dec. 1956): 8; *Asahi Shimbun* (26 Dec. 1956).
87 MC, Masaoka and Martin, 15 Jan. 1957, 611.94/1–1557, NA.
88 AmEmbTok to DOS, 28 Dec. 1956, 794.00/12–2856, NA.
89 Hirano Yoshitarō, 'Nichi-Bei kankei no shōrai' *Ekonomisuto* (19 Jan. 1957): 26.
90 Shigemori Tadashi, 'Shiberia kaihatsu to NisSo bōeki' *Keizai Ōrai* (Feb. 1957): 40.
91 *Asahi Shimbun* (26 Jan. 1957).
92 John Welfield, *Empire in Eclipse* (1988) London: 149.

93 Kishi Nobusuke, 'Sōri kōho to iwarete' *Bungei Shunjū* (Dec. 1956): 77.
94 Dan Kurzman, *Kishi and Japan* (1960) NY: 298.
95 MacArthur to Dulles, 10 Apr. 1957, 611.94/4–1057, NA.
96 Kishi Nobusuke, 'Japan in 1957' *Contemporary Japan* (Apr. 1957): 555.
97 Lee (1976): 37. See also Chapter 6.
98 This did not signify the immediate cessation of trade, but levels soon began to fall. Morley (1958): 22; Kubota Yasutarō, 'Nitchū bōeki kōshō zasetsu no oshieru mono' *Chūō Kōron* (Jan. 1958): 130, Kimura Kihachirō, 'Daiyonji kyōtei kōshō no kihonten' *Ekonomisuto* (4 May 1957): 23.
99 Watt (Tokyo) to DEA, 9 June 1957, A1838, 3103/11/6, NAA; Warren Cohen, 'China in Japanese–American Relations' in Iriye and Cohen (1989): 49.
100 Kishi was in Taiwan from 2–4 June 1957.
101 MC, Kishi and Dulles, 21 June 1957, *FRUS, 1955–57* XXIII(1): 408.
102 Qing (1990): 136.
103 The US quietly withdrew its opposition to the elimination of the 'China differential' on 6 August, although it maintained its own embargo. Cohen (1989): 50; Jain (1981 A): 32.
104 The Special Committee was created on 9 March 1957. Morley (1958): 22.
105 *People's Daily* (30 July 1957) cited in Jain (1981 A): 18.
106 Shimizu Izō, 'Kōka shita Chūkyō no tai Nichi gaikō' *Seikai Ōrai* (Oct. 1957): 21; A. Doak Barnett, *Communist China and Asia* (1960) NY: 274.
107 MacArthur to Dulles, 9 Aug. 1957, 611.94/8–957, NA.
108 Jain (1981 A): 39.
109 *Asahi Shimbun* (15 Aug. 1957).
110 See, for example, Takami Shigeyoshi, managing director of the MITI-backed Japan–China Export–Import Association, in Uchiyama Kanzō, et al., 'Nitchū fukkō wa dō susumetara yoi ka' *Chisei* (Mar. 1957): 38. Or see the chief of MOFA's Economic Affairs Bureau, Ushiba Nobuhiko, 'Possibility of Expanding Trade with the Communist bloc' *Asian Affairs* (Mar. 1958): 74.
111 Cohen (1989): 50.
112 MC, Fujiyama and Dulles, 23 Sept. 1957, *FRUS, 1955–57* XXIII(1): 496, 499.
113 Fujiyama Aiichirō, 'Jiyūshugi jinei no tachiba de ikkan shita gaikō rosen o iku' *Daiyamondo* (22 Oct. 1957): 32.
114 'Japanese Trade Negotiations with Communist China', 2 Dec. 1957, A1838, 766/3/4, NAA.
115 William Ballis, 'A Decade of Soviet–Japan Relations' *Studies on the Soviet Union* (1964): 145; R.K. Jain, *The USSR and Japan, 1945–80* (1981[B]) New Delhi: 66.
116 This is not to suggest that the Sino-Soviet contrast was wholly in Moscow's favour, particularly on the fisheries issue. Morley (1958): 14.
117 Akashi Yasushi, 'Japan's Foreign Policy' *Yale Review* (Dec. 1957): 211–2. Akashi later headed the UN PKO in Cambodia and served as UN chief negotiator in ex-Yugoslavia.
118 MacArthur and Admiral Stump to DOS, 20 Dec. 1957, *FRUS, 1955–57* XXIII(1): 549–50.
119 AmEmbTok to DOS, 31 Jan. 1958, 694.00/1–3158, NA.
120 Kurt Radtke, *China's Relations with Japan, 1945–83* (1990) Manchester: 123.
121 AmEmbTok to DOS, 31 Jan. 1958, 694.00/1–3158, NA; J.Y.S. Cheng, 'Sino-Japanese Relations, 1957–60' *Asian Affairs* (1977): 75.

122 MacArthur to Dulles, 14 Feb. 1957, *FRUS, 1958–60* XVIII, Supplement, Document 430.
123 Radtke (1990): 124.
124 Cheng (1977): 74.
125 Boyd (1960): 58.
126 Cheng (1977): 77.
127 Lee (1976): 138.
128 Matsumoto Shigeharu, 'Japan and China', *Policies toward China*, A.M. Halpern (ed.) (1965) NY: 133.
129 MacArthur to Dulles, 12 Mar. 1958, *FRUS, 1958–60* XVIII, Supplement, Document 433.
130 Boyd (1960): 58–9.
131 Dulles to MacArthur, 27 Mar. 1958, *FRUS, 1958–60* XVIII, Supplement, Document 437.
132 MacArthur to Dulles, 28 Mar. 1958, *FRUS, 1958–60* XVIII, Supplement, Document 438.
133 Ibid.
134 Doi Akira, 'Two Years Exchanges with China' *Japan Quarterly* (Oct./Dec. 1958): 447–8.
135 MacArthur to Dulles, 9 Apr. 1958, *FRUS, 1958–60* XVIII, Supplement, Document 447.
136 *People's Daily* (3 Apr. 1958) cited in Doi (1958).
137 Fukui (1970): 231.
138 Doi (1958): 448. (Emphasis added.)
139 Doi (1958): 448–9.
140 Yamamoto (1958): 380; Naoi Takeo, 'Sino-Japanese Deadlock' *New Leader* (29 Sept. 1958): 9–10.
141 Nakano Yoshio, 'NitChū kankei no akka to shimbun hōdō' *Sekai* (July 1958): 69.
142 MacArthur to Dulles, 9 May 1958, 794.00/5–958, NA.
143 Nakano (1958): 69.
144 Cheng (1977): 76; I. Morris, 'Foreign Policy Issues in Japan's 1958 Elections' *Pacific Affairs* (Sept. 1958): 221; Fukui (1970): 231; Jain, (1981 A): 36; *People's Daily* (11 May 1958) cited in Boyd (1960): 59.
145 Doi (1958): 450.
146 Barnett (1960): 242–3; Sidney Klein, 'A Survey of Sino-Japanese Trade, 1950–66' *China Mainland Review* (Dec. 1966): 186.
147 MacArthur to Dulles, 9 May 1958, 794.00/5–958, NA.
148 *Asahi Shimbun* (10 May 1958). From this derived the now 'standard' interpretation of China's action as an attempt to influence the result of the Japanese Lower House elections, which subsequently backfired. See, for example, Lee (1976): 38.
149 Morris (1958): 221.
150 'Zenmen chūzetsu shita Nitchū bōeki' *Ekonomisuto* (24 May 1958): 6.
151 Nakano (1958): 72. Critic Hara Katsu and perhaps also Okada Akira (China Desk), dated China's 'new, more militant approach to foreign affairs' from Chen Yi's appointment as Foreign Minister in February 1958. MC, Hara and Clark, 18 June 1958, 794.00/7–158, NA.
152 MacArthur to Dulles, 9 May 1958, 794.00/5–958, NA.
153 'Zenmen chūzetsu' (1958): 6.
154 Morris (1958): 222.

155 *Mainichi Shimbun* (21 May 1958).

156 MacArthur to Dulles, 17 Apr. 1958, *FRUS, 1958–60* XVIII, Supplement, Document 451.

157 Yamamoto (1958): 384.

158 Lee (1976): 140; Fukui (1970): 241, 257; Parsons (NEA) to Parsons (FE), 8 July 1958, 693.94/7–858, NA. The LDP won 57.8% of the vote, its highest ever share.

159 AmEmbTok to Dulles, 20 June 1958, 693.94/6–2058, NA.

160 MacArthur to Dulles, 11 July 1958, 693.94/7–1158, NA.

161 Doi (1958): 449, Jain, (1981 B): 66–7; Morris (1958): 222.

162 MacArthur to Dulles, 20 June 1958, 693.94/6–2058, NA.

163 MC, Hara and Clark, 18 June 1958, 794.00/7–158, NA.

164 MacArthur to Dulles, 20 June 1958, and Dulles to AmEmbTok, 20 June 1958, 693.94/6–2058, NA. Compare: Thompson (Moscow) to Dulles, 27 June 1958, 661.94/6–2758, and AmConGen Hong Kong, 24 June 1958, 693.94/6–2458, NA.

165 MacArthur to Dulles, 9 July 1958, 661.94/7–958, NA. A week earlier the NSC had confidently reported that, 'The trend in Japanese policy has been away from neutralism and toward closer alignment with the US and free world.' NSC, OCB Report on US Policy toward Japan, NSC 5516/1, 23 July 1958, *DDRS* (1992): 0894.

166 Anderson (Tokyo) to SEA, 17 July 1958, A1838, 766/3/4, NAA; *Asahi Shimbun* (11 July 1958).

167 Hong Kong ConGen to Tokyo, 'Chūkyō no taigai seisaku no haikeitō ni kan suru kiso shiryō yōkō', Oct. 1958, A-0158, GS, cited in Inoue Toshikazu, 'Sengo Nihon no Ajia gaikō no keisei' *Nihon Seiji Gakkai Nenpō* (1998): 145; 'Foreign Reports', 5 Dec. 1958, 611.94/12–1158, NA.

168 *People's Daily* (7 July 1958) cited in Cheng (1977): 78.

169 MacArthur to Dulles, 30 July 1958, 794.00/7–3058, NA.

170 Anderson (Tokyo) to SEA, 17 July 1958, A1838, 766/3/4, NAA.

171 Clark (Tokyo) to DOS, 21 Aug. 1958, 693.94/8–2158, NA.

172 MacArthur to Dulles, 8 Aug. 1958, 693.94/8–858, NA.

173 Clark (Tokyo) to DOS, 21 Aug. 1958, 693.94/8–2158, NA; Anderson (Tokyo) to SEA, 21 Aug. 1958, A1838, 3103/11/87 Pt. 3, NAA.

174 Boyd (1960): 61.

175 Anderson (Tokyo) to SEA, 21 Aug. 1958, A1838, 766/3/4, NAA. The next day Kōno Ichirō pointed out that this was purely Takasaki's personal opinion.

176 MacArthur to Dulles, 29 Aug. 1958, 693.94/8–2958, NA.

177 Ibid. This is, of course, a reference to the infamous '21 demands' that Japan presented to China in 1915.

178 MC, Hara and Clark, 4 Sept. 1958, 794.00/9–558, NA.

179 'NitChū bōeki saikai no gensō' *Ekonomisuto* (7 Feb. 1959): 36.

180 DOS to AmEmbTok, 13 Sept. 1958, 611.94/9–1358, NA. See also Chapter 2.

181 Lawrence Olson, 'In Ten Years, in Fifty Years' *Dimensions of Japan* (1963) NY: 343–5.

182 AusEmbWash to SEA, 31 Oct. 1958, A1838, 766/3/4, NAA.

183 'Foreign Reports' (1958).

184 Among the more controversial items included were Japan's export of large-diameter steel pipes and the import of 100,000 tons of Soviet crude oil. Ballis (1964): 147; Jain (1981 B): 67–8.

185 DOS, IR 8481; 'Soviet Statements Japan–USSR Relations, 6 June 1961, *OSS/State Dept. Intelligence and Research Reports, Part VIII, Japan, Korea, South–east Asia and the Far East Generally: 1950–61 Supplement* (1979) Washington, D.C.

186 Lacey (DRF) to Stemming (INR), 29 Oct. 1958, 794.00/10–2958, NA. This may have been true but for the fisheries question which continued to plague Japan–Soviet economic relations. Boyd (1960): 62; Ballis (1964): 147; Shiratori Rei, *Peace Research in Japan* (1970) Tokyo: 39–52.

187 Yamamoto Michio (pseud.), 'Chūgoku no yūjin ni tou' *Tōa Jiron* (Jan. 1959): 4–10.

188 Clark (Tokyo) to DOS, 1 May 1959, 693.94/5–159, NA.

189 Lee (1976): 141; Brennan (Tokyo) to SEA, 26 Feb. 1959, A1838, 3103/11/87 Pt. 4, NAA. Perhaps it was merely coincidental that Takasaki also had a 'personal interest' in the lacquer trade. MacArthur to Dulles, 7 Feb. 1959, 693.94/2–759, NA.

190 Clark (Tokyo) to DOS, 1 May 1959, 693.94/5–159, NA.

191 Chu Shao-hsien, 'The Evolution of Japan's Peiping Policy' *Issues and Studies* (Dec. 1971): 21.

192 'NitChū kankei to Ikeda gaikō' *Asahi Jānaru* (15 Jan. 1961): 9.

193 Radtke (1990): 152 (n.68); *Asahi Shimbun* (3 Feb. 1959).

194 Varma (1991): 50.

195 MacArthur to Dulles, 7 Feb. 1959, 693.94/2–759, NA

196 MacArthur to Dulles, 29 Jan. 1959, 693.94/1–2959, NA.

197 Fukui (1970): 254; J.R. Maeno, *Postwar Japanese Policy toward Communist China, 1952–72* (1973) Ph.D. thesis, Univ. of Washington: 69.

198 MC, MacArthur and Fukuda, 13 Feb. 1959, 693.94/2–2459, NA.

199 MC, MacArthur and Yamada, 20 Feb. 1959, ibid.

200 Itagaki (director of the Asian Affairs Bureau) reiterated the point when he met US Embassy officials on 17 March. MacArthur to Dulles, 21 Mar. 1959, 693.94/3–2159, NA.

201 Record of talks, Fujiyama and Casey, 25 Mar. 1959, A1838, 3103/10/1, NAA.

202 AmEmbTok to Dulles, 3 Apr. 1959, 693.94/4–359, NA.

203 MC, Fujiyama and Parsons, 7 May 1959, 794.00/5–859, NA.

204 Chu (1971): 20.

205 In May, Okada Akira had been sent to Warsaw, his reputation as a mind reader of China somewhat tarnished after having repeatedly predicted that Chinese policy towards Japan was about to mellow. Ibid.; *Gaimushō nenkan* (1961): 415.

206 MacArthur to Herter, 18 June 1959, 693.94/6–1859, NA; *JT* (7 June 1959).

207 MacArthur to Herter, 24 June 1959, 693.94/6–2459, NA. A month later, Kishi told Prime Minister Macmillan in London that, 'Chinese insistence on linking political relations with economic relations made the latter impossible.' RC, Kishi and Macmillan, 27 July 1959, PREM 11/ 2738, PRO.

208 MacArthur to Dulles, 8 Apr. 1959, 693.94/4–859, NA.

209 MacArthur to Herter, 7 July 1959, 693.94/7–759, NA.

210 Ibid.; Fukui (1970): 254; *Nihon Keizai Shimbun* (27 Sept. 1959).

211 BrEmbTok to FED, FO 371/141424, PRO; Radtke (1990): 127.

212 RC, Endō Matao and Brennan, 31 Aug. 1959, A1838, 766/3/4, NAA.

213 RC, Japanese Ambassador and SEA, 8 Oct. 1959, A9564, 221/1, NAA.

214 MacArthur to Herter, 27 Oct. 1959, 693.94/10–2959, NA.

215 For example, Utsunomiya Tokuma asserted that: 'It is a mistake for Japan...to take a "wait and see" attitude until China begs for trade.' Utsunomiya Tokuma, 'Seifu no "seikan seisaku" ni hantai suru' *Chūō Kōron* (Nov. 1959): 49.

216 Participants included Diet members Furui Yoshimi and Tagawa Seiichi. Ogata (1977): 181.

217 Boyd (1960): 64–5.

218 'NitChū kankei to Ikeda gaikō' *Asahi Jānaru* (15 Jan. 1961) 3(3): 10.

219 BrEmbTok to FED, 28 Jan. 1960, FO 371/150570, PRO.

220 MC, Kishi and Herter, 19 Jan. 1960, *FRUS, 1958–60* XVIII: 277–8.

221 *Yomiuri Shimbun* (9 Jan. 1960).

222 Marukawa Tatsuo, 'Kewashii NitChū dakai e no michi' *Soren Kenkyū* (June 1960): 51–2.

223 BrEmbTok to FED, 28 Jan. 1960, FO 371/150570, PRO.

224 Emery (Kobe–Osaka) to DOS, 20 Oct. 1959, 693.94/10–2059, NA.

225 DOS, IR 8481 (1961).

226 *JT* (21 Nov.; 22, 23 Dec. 1959).

227 *JT* (15 Jan. 1960).

228 *JT* (3 Mar. 1960).

229 Marukawa (1960): 49–51; Fukui (1970): 250, 259.

230 A Soviet Problem Sub-Committee was also established under Sugihara Arata. *Asahi Shimbun* (12 Apr. 1960).

231 Marukawa (1960): 47–8. (Emphasis added.)

Notes for Chapter 5

1 *Asahi Shimbun* (20 July 1960) cited in John Welfield, *Empire in Eclipse* (1988) London: 175.

2 During their two-week stay, they met with Matsumura Kenzō and Takasaki Tatsunosuke. Official contact with the delegates was supposedly avoided, however, and an application to extend their visas was politely rejected. *Chūgoku nenkan* (1961): 55–6; Gordon Chang, *Friends and Enemies* (1990) Stanford: 82; and Kurt Radtke, *China's Relations with Japan, 1945–1983* (1990) Manchester: 133.

3 See Appendix 2 for a list of members. Chu Shao-hsien, 'The Evolution of Japan's Peiping Policy' *Issues and Studies* (Dec. 1971): 21; Fukui Haruhiro, *Party in Power* (1970) Berkeley: 243 (n.13).

4 MacArthur to DOS, 27 July 1960; Herter to MacArthur, 18 July 1960, *FRUS, 1958–60* XVIII: 387–8, 391.

5 MacArthur to DOS, 28 July 1960, ibid.: 392–4.

6 Raymond Mathieson, *Japan's Role in Soviet Economic Growth* (1979) NY: 86.

7 R.K. Jain, *The USSR and Japan, 1945–1980* (1981 [B]) New Delhi: 69; DOS, IR 8481, 'Soviet Statements Japan–USSR Relations', 6 June 1961, *OSS/DOS Intelligence and Research Reports, VIII, Japan, Korea, South–east Asia and the Far East Generally: 1950–61 Supplement* (1979) Washington, D.C.

8 Initially, only 11 small companies received the necessary recommendation from the JCTPA, JITPA, the Japan–China Friendship Association, or the JSP. However, their number grew rapidly: late 1960 (50 firms); March 1961 (67); January 1962 (108); late 1963 (300); and late 1964 (350). This included many 'dummy firms' set up by various Japanese industrial giants. Ogata Sadako, *Normalization with China* (1989) Berkeley: 11; Chae-Jin Lee, *Japan Faces China* (1976) Baltimore: 142; R.K. Jain, *China and Japan, 1949–1980* (1981 [A]) Oxford: 65; J.S. Hoadley and Hasegawa Sukehiro, 'Sino-Japanese Relations 1950–70' *International Studies Quarterly* (June 1971): 142.

9 Radtke (1990): 133; Jain (1981 A): 45–6.

10 *Asahi Jānaru*, for example, dismissed the view that 'agricultural failure and the recent deterioration of relations with Moscow' were responsible for this 'turning point in China's Japan policy', preferring to give it a 'more positive meaning.' 'Chūgoku no tai Nichi taido kawaru' *Asahi Jānaru* (11 Sept. 1960): 78. Hozumi Shichirō, a JSP Diet member and leader of the Japan–China Friendship Association mission, also categorically denied any such linkage. The *Japan Times* meanwhile suggested a 'possible desire to affect the Japanese elections'. *JT* (5 Sept. 1960). Much later, Suzuki Kazuo confirmed that after finding all of the Soviet engineers gone, he had concluded that the Sino-Soviet rift was responsible for China's change of attitude. Suzuki Kazuo, 'Shin dankai no NitChū bōeki' *Ekonomisuto* (17 Sept. 1963): 44.

11 RC, Endō and Lewis, 19 Sept. 1960, A9564, 227/10/1, NAA; Kuroda Mizuo (first secretary at the Japanese Embassy in London) made the latter comment to Henderson (FED) on 31 August. Minute by Henderson, 31 Aug. 1960, FO 371/ 150589, PRO. Matsumura Kenzō expressed an identical view on 3 September. Radtke (1990): 134.

12 When asked why China wanted a resumption of trade, Deputy Director Uryū of MITI's Bureau of International Trade replied vaguely that '"some people" think they need to trade with Japan.' RC, Endō and Lewis, 19 Sept. 1960, A9564, 227/10/1, NAA. Remarkably, as late as June 1962, Foreign Minister Kosaka was still unsure 'whether the withdrawal of Soviet technicians was due to ideological differences or had been decided on because there was nothing for the technicians to do.' Barwick (MEA) to Acting PM, 14 June 1962, A1838, 3103/7/2/1, NAA.

13 *Asahi Shimbun* (16 Aug. 1960).

14 MC, Kosaka and Mueller, 16 Sept. 1960, *FRUS, 1958–60* XVIII: 403–7.

15 AusEmbWash to DEA, 21 Sept. 1960, A1838, 3103/7/1, NAA.

16 Radtke (1990): 134.

17 Ōmori Minoru, 'Nihon gaikō no kihon gensoku o tou' *Chūō Kōron* (Jan. 1963): 157.

18 Radtke (1990): 134.

19 *People's Daily* (11 Oct. 1960) cited in Jain (1981 A): 66; Lee (1976): 42–3.

20 Hart to MacLehose, Enc. in MacLehose (Hong Kong) to FED, 24 Nov. 1960, FO 371/150570, PRO; Takasaki Tatsunosuke, 'Watashi no mita Chūgoku' *Asahi Jānaru* (15 Jan. 1961): 15.

21 McIntyre to SEA, 10 Jan. 1961, A3092, 221/12/2/5/1, NAA.

22 Takasaki Tatsunosuke, 'Shu On Rai to kaidan shite' *Chūō Kōron* (Feb. 1961): 249–51.

23 Wolf Mendl, *Issues in Japan's China Policy* (1978) London: 20.

24 Welfield (1988): 172; Kataoka Tetsuya, *The Price of a Constitution* (1991) NY: 211.

25 Lee (1976): 45–6; Fukui (1970): 250.

26 MacArthur to DOS, 16 Dec. 1960, *FRUS, 1958–60* XVIII: 413–23.

27 MacArthur to Herter, 21 Dec. 1960, *FRUS, 1958–60* XVIII, Supplement, Document 566.

28 Battle (Director Executive Secretariat) to Dungan (White House), 24 Mar. 1961, *DDRS* (1995): 1746.

29 McIntyre to SEA, 10 Jan. 1961, A3092, 221/12/2/5/1, NAA.

30 McIntyre to SEA, 30 Jan. 1961, A1838, 3103/10/10/1, NAA.

31 Soeya Yoshihide, *Japan's Economic Diplomacy with China, 1945–1978* (1998) Oxford: 64; Radtke (1990): 135–8.

32 McIntyre to SEA, 10 Jan. 1961, A3092, 221/12/2/5/1, NAA.

33 Fukui (1970): 243 (n.13).

34 Mayall (Tokyo) to de la Mare, 27 Apr. 1961, FO 371/158484, PRO.

35 One Japanese Embassy official in London claimed that Okada was 'the only person in their Foreign Ministry in direct touch with the Peking government'. Meeting between Kuroda and Wilson, 8 Dec. 1960, FO 371/158484; Dalton (Warsaw) to de la Mare, 19 May 1961; Dalton to de la Mare, 12 Sept. 1961, PRO.

36 BrEmbTok to FED, 24 Mar. 1961, FO 371/158484, PRO.

37 Tokyo dropped the compulsory barter system, allowing one-way cash settlement. Jain (1981A): 66.

38 Welfield (1988): 177; George Jan, 'The Japanese People and Japan's Policy toward Communist China' *Western Political Quarterly* (summer 1969): 608.

39 Fukui (1970): 258; and Chu (1971): 21.

40 BrEmbTok to FED, 12 May 1961, FO 371/158484, PRO.

41 'First White House Meeting with Prime Minister Ikeda—Talking Paper', n.d., *DDRS* (1995): 1505; 'Attachment 2—A Strategy for the Ikeda Visit', n.d., *DDRS* (1995): 1506. Robert Johnston noted that the Japanese favoured 'a much more overt "two Chinas" policy'. He recommended that the US 'accept the possibility of Sino-Japanese trade much more forthrightly', especially as 'The potential for trade does not seem great'. Johnson to Rostow, 19 Jan. 1961, *DDRS* (1995): 1489.

42 MC, Ikeda and Kennedy, 21 June 1961, *FRUS, 1961–63* XXII: 692–9.

43 Jain (1981 B): 69; P. Langer, 'Moscow, Peking and Tokyo', *Unity and Contradiction*, K. London (ed.) (1962) NY: 223.

44 DOS, IR 8481 (1961); William Ballis, 'A Decade of Soviet–Japan Relations' *Studies on the Soviet Union* (1964): 148–50.

45 *Contemporary Japan* (Mar. 1962): 362–5.

46 See, for example, P.A.N. Murthy, 'Japan's Changing Relations with People's China and the Soviet Union' *International Studies* (July 1965): 14; Lawrence Olson, *Dimensions of Japan* (1963) NY: 375.

47 Langer (1962): 226–7.

48 Ballis (1964): 150.

49 First Meeting Joint US–Japan Committee Trade and Economic Affairs, 2–4 Nov. 1961, *FRUS, 1961–63* XXII: 709.

50 *JTW* (6 Jan. 1962).

51 Lavett (Tokyo) to SEA, 31 Jan. 1962, A1838, 766/3/4, NAA.

52 Soeya (1998): 82–3. Matsumura Kenzō was also involved at an early stage. In April 1962, he sent his secretary, Ōkubo Masaharu, on a 'goodwill visit' to Beijing to lay the foundations for restoring economic ties. Radtke (1990): 141.

53 RC, Home and Yoshida, 24 May 1962, PREM 11/3852, PRO.

54 *Mainichi Shimbun* (24 May 1962, evening).

55 *JTW* (9 June 1962).

56 *JTW* (23 June 1962).

57 Kōno complained that, 'Despite the fact that conditions for Soviet trade are better than those for Communist China, we lean towards the latter.' Kōno Ichirō, 'NisSo kōryū ni tsuite kokumin ni uttaeru' *Chūō Kōron* (July 1962): 195–6.

58 Jamieson (Tokyo) to SEA, 7 Dec. 1962, A1838, 766/3/4, NAA; Chang (1990): 225.

59 In December 1961, when the US Defense Department began boycotting jet fuel from *Idemitsu Kōsan* because the Japanese company was buying about 30 per cent of its crude oil from the Soviets, Japanese protests were muted. 'Akai sekiyu sōdōki' *Shin Shūkan* (18 Jan. 1962): 13; Ishiyama Kenkichi Chōsashitsu, 'Soren abura no shinshutsu de sekiyukai konran' *Daiyamondo* (29 Jan. 1962): 67.

60 *Mainichi Shimbun* (31 May 1962, evening.)

61 *JTW* (9 June 1962).
62 Welfield (1988): 174.
63 In April, a public opinion poll on trade policy towards China found that 34.8% supported positive action, 26.3% a cautious examination, and only 3.7% were opposed. *Yoron chōsa nenkan* (1962): 70. In June another poll reported that 73 per cent supported trade with China. Edward Murrow to Kennedy, 11 Dec. 1962, National Security Archive, *The Cuban Missile Crisis, 1962* (1990) Alexandria: 02730.
64 *JTW* (11 Aug. 1962).
65 *JTW* (18 Aug. 1962).
66 Ibid.; Patrick D. Malone, *Japan's Foreign Policy 1957 through 1967* (Apr. 1969) Geneva: 97.
67 Seven standing directors of *Keidanren* were among the delegates, although the mission did not receive the organisation's official blessing. 'Japanese Trade Mission to Soviet Union and Development of Siberia' *Japan Socialist Review* (15 Aug. 1962): 38.
68 Ballis (1964): 151; Jain (1981 B): 35, 69.
69 Morland (Tokyo) to Home, 5 Oct. 1962, FO 371/164968, PRO.
70 Kohler (Moscow) to Rusk, 10 Jan. 1963, *John F. Kennedy National Security Files—Asia and the Pacific, 1961–63* (1993) Bethesda.
71 Furukawa Mantarō, *NitChū sengo kankeishi* (1981): 204. Ikeda sent a member of his faction, Ogawa Heiji and a key financial supporter, Tabayashi Masakichi (Japan Long-Term Credit Bank), as delegates. Welfield (1988): 178.
72 Ibid.; *Nihon Keizai Shimbun* (11 Sept. 1962). The 33–member mission included Furui Yoshimi (Matsumura-ha), Tagawa Seiichi (Kōno-ha) and Fujii Katsushi (Miki-ha). Lee (1976): 46.
73 Radtke (1990): 142.
74 This statement was made in the context of an attack on America's 'aggressive' trade policy. 'All Orientals Together' *The Economist* (29 June 1963): 1351.
75 Radtke (1990): 143.
76 Matsumura Kenzō, 'Chūkyō seikai no jinbutsu o kata[ru]' *Seikai Ōrai* (Jan. 1963): 74–5, 82. In a second article, Matsumura added that, 'Mao Zedong's way of thinking is quite Oriental and therefore different from that of Khrushchev.' Moreover, he claimed that Chinese policy was as much influenced by the reawakened 'national consciousness of the Han race' as by the works of Marx and Lenin. Matsumura Kenzō, 'Watashi no Ajia kan' *Shisō* (Jan. 1963): 153.
77 Jamieson (Tokyo) to SEA, 9 Oct. 1962, A1838, 766/3/4, NAA.
78 Trench (Tokyo) to de la Mare (FED), 28 Sept. 1962, FO 371/164985, PRO. (Emphasis added.) This represented a major change from an official MOFA report prepared just eight months earlier: it had not even mentioned the Soviet factor when attempting to explain the recent growth in Japan–China trade. Lavett (Tokyo) to SEA, 23 Jan. 1962, A1838, 766/3/4, NAA.
79 Soeya (1998): 48, 51.
80 There were also problems with participants from the steel industry because of the importance of the US market, and the fertilizer industry, which had strong ties to Taiwan and South Korea. Takasaki was eventually accompanied by a delegation of some 23 businessmen and three LDP Diet members. McIntyre (Tokyo) to Barwick, 12 Feb. 1963, A1838, 3103/10/1, NAA.
81 Jamieson to SEA, 7 Dec. 1962, A1838, 766/3/4, NAA.
82 Lavett (Tokyo) to SEA, 16, 19 Oct. 1962, A1838, 3103/11/87, NAA.

83 Hoadley and Hasegawa (1971): 145; Fukui (1970): 259. As he told the Japan Marketing Association on 11 October, Takasaki himself dreamt of an East Asian version of the Franco-German 'Schuman Plan', in which Japan and China would 'operate jointly' their iron and steel industries. Lavett (Tokyo) to SEA, 16 Oct. 1962, A1838, 3103/11/87, NAA.

84 Jain (1981 A): 67. MITI was not happy that Takasaki had included plant exports in the agreement and initially refused to approve them. Soeya (1998): 90.

85 Lavett (Tokyo) to SEA, 30 Nov. 1962, A1838, 766/3/4, NAA.

86 *Asahi Shimbun* (6 Oct. 1962, evening).

87 RC, Macmillan and Ikeda, 12 Nov. 1962, FO 371/164976, PRO; and Ōno to Ōhira, 14 Nov. 1962, A-0364/1495–99, GS. Ikeda's proposal followed a telegram from Ambassador Ōno in London to Ōhira. It recommended that the premier suggest 'Common [Anglo-Japanese] action to make Communist China less dependent on Russia (especially in the economic field) and to separate the two as far as possible, while adopting common political measures to prevent Red China from running to extremes.' Ōno to Ōhira, 18 Oct. 1962, A-0364/1441, GS.

88 'Anglo-Japanese Relations—The Ikeda Visit', 12 Nov. 1962, FO 371/164976, PRO.

89 Joint US–Japan Committee Trade and Economic Affairs, 3–5 Dec. 1962, *FRUS, 1961–63* XXII: 749 (n.1).

90 Edwin Reischauer, *My Life Between Japan and America* (1986) NY: 244–5.

91 Welfield (1988): 180–1. See also Chapter 3.

92 Jamieson (Tokyo) to SEA, 7 Dec. 1962, A1838, 766/3/4, NAA. Ōhira reinforced his premier's message, claiming that because Japan's ties to the US were strong 'there will be no problems at all even if Japan, to a degree not inimical to these relations, sorts out her affairs with Communist China, conducts trade, establishes cultural and economic ties. This is the Government's view and there will be no need to change it in the future.' *Asahi Shimbun* (12 Dec. 1962).

93 *JTW* (5 Jan. 1963); MC, Kennedy and Takeuchi, 25 Apr. 1963, *FRUS, 1961–63* XXII: 777–8.

94 Furukawa (1981): 204.

95 *JTW* (24 Aug. 1963); Noguchi Yuichirō, 'Keizai nashonarizumu ron' *Sekai* (Jan. 1965) 229: 56; Hill to Loveday, 16 Jan. 1963, A1838, 3103/11/161, NAA.

96 Kohler (Moscow) to Rusk, 10 Jan. 1963, *John F. Kennedy, National Security Files, USSR and Eastern Europe, 1961–63* (1993) Bethesda.

97 *JTW* (2 Feb. 1963).

98 See, for example, *Mainichi Shimbun* (6 Feb. 1963).

99 Cities such as Tsuruga, Niigata and Sakata had even organised a Japan–Soviet Trade and Fisheries Promotion Council. *JTW* (9 Mar. 1963); Jain (1981 B): 39; Murthy (1965): 14–15.

100 Malone (1969): 83; Jain (1981 B): 39; Murthy (1965): 14–15.

101 Jain (1981 B): 36.

102 *JTW* (9 Mar. 1963).

103 Led by Kitamura Tokutarō it comprised representatives of 18 trading companies. The mission toured Siberia and the Ukraine for two weeks and received a very enthusiastic reception. Several contracts representing a massive expansion in coastal trade were signed. *JTW* (27 July 1963).

104 The other two visitors were Suzuki Kazuo (JCTPA), who signed a protocol formalising the 'friendship trade' channel and Hiratsuka Tsunejirō (Japan–China Fishery

Association), who signed a fishing agreement. Jain (1981 A): 67, 76; Soeya (1998): 64–5.

105 Utsunomiya Tokuma, 'Watashi no mita Chūgoku' *Ekonomisuto* (5 Feb. 1963): 18.

106 Trench (Tokyo) to McKenzie Johnston, 17 Apr. 1963, FO 371/170751, PRO.

107 Jamieson (Tokyo) to SEA, 26 Feb. 1963, A9564, 227/3, NAA.

108 *JTW* (2 Feb. 1963).

109 *JTW* (26 Jan. 1963).

110 'Administrative Policy Speech by PM Ikeda before 43rd Ordinary Session of the Diet' *Gaimushō Press Releases* (1963): 3–14.

111 *JTW* (6 Apr. 1963). The following month, Roger Hilsman (assistant secretary of state for Far Eastern affairs) repeated the message. Describing deferred payments to China as equivalent to providing aid to the 'enemy', he still publicly maintained that this was a matter for Japan alone to decide. *Asahi Shimbun* (17 Apr. 1963, evening); Lee (1976): 232 (n.37).

112 RC, Home and Ikeda, 3 Apr. 1963, FO 371/170759, PRO.

113 Ibid.

114 *JTW* (29 June 1963); note, 18 June 1963, A1838, 3103/10/1, NAA.

115 Walter La Feber, *The Clash* (1997) NY: 337.

116 The 'change' was to raise the interest rate on the $20 million, five-year credit from 4.5 to 6 per cent, so that it was no more favourable than that charged to non-Communist countries, but the price was then reduced to compensate. Soeya (1998): 95–6; Jain (1981 A): 68.

117 Informally, a ten per cent limit was set. *JTW* (31 Aug. 1963).

118 Fukui (1970): 243.

119 Michael Schaller, *Altered States* (1997) NY: 176.

120 MOFA also recommended that 'Japan should increase her economic aid to Southeast Asia as a means of ensuring its stability' in the face of China's likely advance into the region. *Asahi Shimbun* (2 Sept. 1963).

121 RC, Home and Ōhira, 3 Sept. 1963, FO 371/ 170757, PRO. See also Chapter 3.

122 Discussion between Ikeda and Holyoake, 4 Oct. 1963, ABHS 950, W4627, 268/3/1, New Zealand Archives, Wellington. In Ottawa, meanwhile, Vice-Foreign Minister Shima also directly linked the deterioration in Sino-Soviet relations with their both having 'shown a more conciliatory attitude towards Japan in recent months.' Rogers to Canadian Embassy, Tokyo, 11 Oct. 1963, 20–1–2–JPN-1, Canadian Archives, Ottawa.

123 RC, Ogawa and Wiadrowski, 9 Sept. 1963, A9564, 227/3, NAA.

124 Jain (1981 A): 69.

125 Murakami Kimitaka (director, Japan External Trade Organisation) and Owada Yūji (secretary-general, Japan–China Export–Import Association) were allowed to join four LDP Diet members (Furui Yoshimi, Matsumoto Shunichi, Takeyama Yutarō and Hisano Tadaharu) and 19 industry representatives on the mission. Lalima Varma, *The Making of Japan's China Policy* (1991) Delhi: 137.

126 *JTW* (21 Sept. 1963).

127 Abe Keizō, et al., 'Nihon gaikō no jittai' *Chūō Kōron* (Jan. 1964): 118.

128 For details see: *Yoron chōsa nenkan* (1963): 219.

129 The Japan Economic Research Council was a joint research body established in 1962 by *Keidanren*, the Japan Foreign Trade Council, and others. It was headed by Uemura Kōgorō (vice-president of *Keidanren*), Nagano Shigeo (vice-president of *Nisshō*) and Professor Emeritus Nakayama Ichirō.

130 *JTW* (5 Oct. 1963); *Nihon Keizai Shimbun* (18 Sept. 1963).

131 'Attitude of Business toward Japan–China Trade' *Japan Socialist Review* (1 Dec. 1963): 24–7.
132 Jain (1981 A): 68.
133 Nearly 600 Japanese companies participated and 1.2 million Chinese visited during its 25-day run. Ishibashi Tanzan, as president of the sponsoring organisation, headed a list of more than 1000 Japanese visiting the exhibition. Welfield (1988): 182; Lee (1976): 232.
134 JTW (24 Aug. 1963).
135 See, for example, *JTW* (28 Sept. and 19 Oct. 1963).
136 Fukuda's declaration was probably influenced by his recent North American tour, where he heard US Commerce Secretary Hodges concede that 'the US should take a fresh look at trade with the Communist bloc.' He also learnt that the US planned to export surplus grain to the Soviet Union, and that Canada had already signed contracts to supply large quantities of wheat to Moscow and Beijing. *JTW* (12 Oct. 1963); Varma (1991): 52.
137 *JTW* (28 Sept.; 5 Oct. 1963).
138 *Asahi Shimbun* (30 Aug. 1963, evening).
139 *JTW* (19 Oct. 1963).
140 *JTW* (26 Oct. 1963).
141 *Asahi Shimbun* (8 Jan. 1964, evening).
142 This accounted for nearly half of total imports. Jain (1981 A): 70.
143 *Asahi Shimbun* (21 Jan. 1964, evening); Jain, (1981 A): 70.
144 Utsunomiya Tokuma and Maeda Masao reportedly clashed head-on at a meeting of the FARC China Problem Sub-Committee. Fukui (1970): 259.
145 Varma (1991): 119.
146 See Chapter 3.
147 Record of the Third Meeting of the Joint US–Japan Committee on Trade and Economic Affairs, Tokyo, 27 Jan. 1964, Country Files, Japan Cables, I, 11/63–4/64, *LBJ*.
148 Communist China: Joint Economic Committee, 28 Jan. 1964, *DDRS* (1993): 3223. See Chapter 3.
149 *JTW* (22 Feb.; 7 Mar. 1964).
150 *JTW* (29 Feb. 1964).
151 *JTW* (15 Feb. 1964).
152 See Chapter 3.
153 AusEmbTok to DEA, 28 Feb. 1964, A3092, 221/12/2/5/1, NAA; *JTW* (29 Feb.; 7 Mar. 1964).
154 AusEmbTok to DEA, 21 Feb. 1964, A3092, 221/12/2/5/1, NAA.
155 AusEmbTok to DEA, 28 Feb. 1964, A3092, 221/12/2/5/1, NAA.
156 Soeya (1998): 97.
157 Welfield (1988): 187; Zhao (1993): 139.
158 AusEmbTok to DEA, 28 Feb. 1964, A3092, 221/12/2/5/1, NAA.
159 Gaimushō, *NitChū kankei kihon shiryōshū* (1970): 231–2; *JTW* (14 Mar. 1964); Chu (1971): 22–3; Welfield (1988): 188. See also Chapter 3.
160 Canadian Embassy (Tokyo) to DEA (Ottawa), Enc. in Horne (DEA, Canberra) to AusEmbTok, 11 May 1964, A9564, 227/10/1, NAA.
161 In retrospect, the participants dated Beijing's reversion to a 'soft attitude toward Japan' to Matsumura Kenzō's autumn 1960 visit (sic). The Chinese motivation for 'the strengthening of trade relations and promotion of personal interchange' was clearly

identified as its need 'to offset the deteriorated Sino-Soviet economic relations (sic)'. Cortazzi (Tokyo) to Bently, 17 Apr. 1964, FO 371/17600, PRO.

162 In January 1964, Matsumura had again written of the importance of the Sino-Soviet rift to the positive development of Sino-Japanese relations: 'where trade just as much as normalization of relations is concerned' the dispute was 'fundamental to the problem.' Matsumura Kenzō, 'Bridging the Gap to China' *Japan Quarterly* (Jan./Mar. 1964): 27.

163 Jain (1981 A): 69–70.

164 MC, Furui Kimi (sic) and McIntyre, 15 May 1964, 10 June 1964, FO 371/17600, PRO.

165 Fukui (1970): 233.

166 People like Mizukami Tatsuzō (president, Mitsui), Usami Makoto (president, Mitsubishi Bank), and Inayama Yoshihiro (president, Yawata Iron and Steel) seemed willing to take China trade seriously for the first time. *Tōyō Keizai Shimpo* (25 Apr. 1964).

167 *JT* (19 Aug. 1964). The CIA believed that Satō was using the issue to force a showdown on China policy hoping to divide the LDP along 'former-bureaucrat' versus 'professional politician' lines, and thereby undermine the Ikeda–Kōno relationship. CIA Special Report, 'The China Problem in Japanese Politics', *DDRS* (1964(77)): 22H.

168 Soeya (1998): 98–9; Zhao (1993): 140; Welfield (1988): 189; Jain (1981 A): 70.

169 *JTW* (9 May 1964).

170 Jain, (1981 B): 38.

171 *JTW* (6 June 1964).

172 George Jan, 'Japan's Trade with Communist China' *Asian Survey* (Dec. 1969): 914; Jain (1981 B): 72.

173 Soviet oil exports to China had peaked in 1959, thereafter experiencing a steady decline. Meanwhile, Japanese imports of Soviet oil rose from near zero in 1959 to overtake Chinese imports by 1961 and continued increasing until 1967. Mathieson (1979): 86; William Griffith, *The Sino-Soviet Rift* (1964) London: 236 (n.10).

174 The managing director of Sumitomo Trading, for example, told Mikoyan that in future it would trade directly with the Soviets rather than through a 'dummy' corporation as previously. A sour note was sounded, however, by MOFA and MITI. They decided to officially investigate complaints from some Japanese traders that since early 1963, the Soviet Machinoimport Corporation had been insisting on compensatory exports offsetting 30 to 100 per cent of the value of any Japanese imports. *JTW* (30 May; 13 June 1964).

175 D.I. Hitchcock, 'Joint Development of Siberia' *Asian Survey* (Mar. 1971): 282; *JTW* (6, 13 June 1964).

176 *JTW* (23 May 1964). See also Chapter 9.

177 *JTW* (23 May 1964).

178 *JTW* (30 May, 13 June 1964). Kitamura Tokutarō (chairman of JITPA) also received an invitation to visit Beijing to coincide with Mikoyan's visit. AusEmbTok to DEA, 22 May 1964, A1838, 3103/11/52, Pt. 6, NAA.

179 Ibid.

180 Lee (1976): 146; Radtke (1990): 162.

181 Ōhira Masayoshi, 'Diplomacy for Peace' *International Affairs* (July 1964): 396.

182 Cheke to MacLehose (FED), 25 June 1965, FO371/181076, PRO.

183 'DOS Policy on The Future of Japan', 26 June 1964, *DDRS* (1995): 3262.

184 *JTW* (1 Aug. 1964).

185 *JTW* (22 Aug. 1964).

186 Nichibō chairman Hara Kichihei, having completely lost patience with the government, went ahead anyway and signed a deal offering China commercial financing at 6% per annum. Peters (Tokyo) to SEA, 14 Aug. 1964, A9564, 227/10/1, NAA; *JTW* (19 Sept. 1964).

187 The Export–Import Bank was to supply credit at 5% for the first five years and commercial banks thereafter. *JTW* (12 Sept. 1964).

188 For example, MITI persuaded steel makers to defer their imports of Soviet pig iron in order to strengthen Japan's negotiating hand in the 1965 trade talks, resulting in a massive surge in imports of Chinese pig iron. *JTW* (8 Aug. 1964); *Nihon Kōgyō* (24 July 1964).

189 Hitchcock (1971): 282.

190 *JTW* (17 Oct. 1964).

191 RC, Ōta and MEA, 14 Oct. 1964, A9564, 227/11, NAA.

192 There had been a minor revision of the COCOM list on 15 June 1964. *JTW* (21 Nov. 1964).

193 *Asahi Shimbun* (6 Feb. 1965, evening).

194 While all pro-Beijing, this group was divided on the trade issue: the Matsumura wing was committed to 'L–T Trade', whereas the more radical Ishibashi wing favoured 'friendship trade'. Zhao (1993): 74.

195 *JTW* (28 Nov. 1964).

196 Welfield (1988): 193; *JTW* (5 Dec. 1964).

197 Satō was acting on Matsumura Kenzō's advice. *JTW* (12 Dec. 1964); Okamoto Fumio, *Satō seiken* (1972): 11, cited in Dennis Yasutomo, 'Satō's China Policy, 1964–1966' *Asian Survey* (June 1977): 533.

198 Jain (1981 B): 41, 43.

199 Jain (1981 B): 42.

200 *JTW* (19 Sept. 1964).

201 DOS, 'Summary of Current Problems in US–Japan Relations', n.d., *DDRS* (1992): 3300.

202 *JTW* (12 Sept. 1964).

203 MC, Satō and Johnson, 12 Jan. 1965, *DDRS* (1994): 1475.

204 MC, Miki and Humphrey, 13 Jan. 1965, *DDRS* (1965(R)): 642B.

205 *JTW* (13 Feb. 1965); Jain (1981 A): 71.

206 Soeya (1998): 99.

207 Fukui (1970): 236.

208 Jain (1981 A): 71.

209 Warren Cohen, 'China in Japanese–American Relations' in Iriye and Cohen (1989): 54.

Notes for Chapter 6

1 Roger Swearingen and Paul Langer, *Red Flag in Japan* (1952) Cambridge, MA: 235.

2 The party was officially re-established on 4 October. Robert Scalapino, *The Japanese Communist Movement, 1920–1966* (1967) Berkeley: 54–6.

3 Swearingen and Langer (1952): 230.

4 Miyamoto Kenji, 'Chū-So dōmei to Nihon minzoku' *Atarashii Sekai* (Mar. 1950): 2–11.

5 Igarashi Takeshi, 'Peace-Making and Party Politics' *Journal of Japanese Studies* (1985): 341.

6 See Scalapino (1967): chs. 2 & 3; Paul Langer, *Communism in Japan* (1972) Stanford: chs. 2, 4, 5; J.A.A. Stockwin, 'The Communist Party of Japan' *Problems of Communism* (Jan./ Feb. 1967): 1–10; Swearingen and Langer (1952).

7 Swearingen and Langer (1952): 235; Langer (1972): 72; Lalima Varma, *The Making of Japan's China Policy* (1991) Delhi: 102.

8 Langer (1972): 50; Scalapino (1967): 88–90; P.A.N. Murthy, 'The Japanese Left and the Anti-Nuclear Movement' *International Studies* (Jan. 1964): 285.

9 Horie Muraichi, 'Chū-So yūkō dōmei to Nihon' *Zenei* (Apr. 1953): 43.

10 Ōmura Akira, 'So-Chū ryōkoku seifu no kyōdō sengen ni tsuite' *Zenei* (Dec. 1954): 47; *Tōkyō Shimbun* (13 Oct. 1954).

11 Stockwin (1968): 85; James Cary, *Japan Today* (1963) London: 48; Scalapino (1967): 96.

12 Nosaka Sanzō, 'Watashi no kaitō' *Chūō Kōron* (Nov. 1955): 125–6.

13 George Totten, *The Social Democratic Movement in Prewar Japan* (1968) New Haven.

14 Stockwin (1968): 37.

15 Iwamura Michio, 'Chū-So jōyaku to Nihon no tachiba' *Sekai Hyōron* (Apr. 1950) 5(4): 81.

16 See J.A.A. Stockwin, *The Japanese Socialist Party and Neutralism* (1968) Melbourne; Allan Cole, George Totten and Cecil Uyehara, *Socialist Parties in Postwar Japan* (1966) New Haven.

17 J.A.A. Stockwin, 'Positive Neutrality' *Asian Survey* (Nov. 1962): 38; Stockwin (1968): 71; Uezumi Minoru, 'Did [the] JSP's Policy Toward China Change?' *Japan Socialist Review* (1 Oct. 1962): 25–6; Cole, Totten & Uyehara (1966): 228.

18 Stockwin (1962): 38.

19 *Mainichi Shimbun* (13 Oct. 1954); Nomizo Masaru, 'Chū-So heiwa kōsei to Chōsen mondai no zento' *Jitsugyō no Sekai* (Dec. 1954): 22–3.

20 The Right-JSP sent Sone Eki, Kōno Mitsu, Sugiyama Motojirō, Matsumura Seiichi and Matsudaira Tadahisa: the Left-JSP was represented by Chairman Suzuki Mosaburō, Sata Tadataka, Sasaki Kōzō, Ashika Shikaichi and Nakada Yoshio. Cole, Totten and Uyehara (1966): 228 (n.32). See also: Yamaguchi Kikuichirō, et al., 'Chūkyō no jittai wa kō da' *Seikai Ōrai* (Dec. 1954): 129–30; 'Chūkyō Shisatsu Giindan no shūkaku' *Shūkan Asahi* (7 Nov. 1954): 13; Suzuki Mosaburō, 'Shin Chūgoku to Nihon Shakaitō' *Chūō Kōron* (Dec. 1954): 121.

21 Left-JSP, *Tōkatsudō* (10 Nov. 1954), cited in Cole, Totten & Uyehara (1966): 229. Similarly, the Right-JSP report suggested that Beijing 'might perhaps prove an important countervailing force in Asia against possible Soviet pretensions.' 'Chūgoku shisetsudan hōkokusho' *Jōhō Tsūshin* (1 Nov. 1954): 3–12, cited in Uezumi (1962): 25.

22 Stockwin (1968): 77; Morishima Morito, 'NisSo kōshō no genjō to tenbō' *Shakai Shugi* (Aug. 1955): 25.

23 Left-JSP, *Tōkatsudō* (30 Sept. 1955), cited in Ronald Dore, 'Left and Right in Japan' *International Affairs* (Jan. 1956): 22.

24 See: Cole, Totten and Uyehara (1966): 230; Morishima Morito, 'Chūka Jinmin Kyōwakoku to no kokkō juritsu ni tsuite' *Shakai Tsūshin* (1 July 1956), cited in Stockwin (1968): 84; Katsumata Seiichi, 'NitChū kokkō kaifuku no rosen' *Sekai* (Feb. 1957): 136–40; Donald Hellmann, *Japanese Foreign Policy and Domestic Politics* (1969) Berkeley: 114–9.

25 G. Totten and T. Kawakami, 'Gensuikyō and the Peace Movement in Japan' *Asian Survey* (May 1964): 839.
26 Murthy (1964): 283–4; J.Y.S. Cheng, 'Sino-Japanese Relations 1957–60' *Asian Affairs* (1977) 64(1): 72.
27 Murthy (1964): 284.
28 See: Seki Yoshihiko, 'Domestic Reorientation' *Journal of Social and Political Ideas in Japan* (Aug. 1964) 2(2): 51; Chae-Jin Lee, *Japan Faces China* (1976) Baltimore: 73, 77; *Nihon gaikōshi jiten* (1992): 767–8; P. Berton, P. Langer and R. Swearingen, *Japanese Training and Research in the Russian Field* (1956) Los Angeles: 193; *Shūkan Shinchō* (2 Oct. 1961); S.W. Simon, 'New Soviet Approaches to the Japanese Left' *Asian Survey* (June 1966): 324.
29 MC, Watanabe Roo, Yamaguchi Fusao, and William Sherman, 2 Mar. 1956, Box 8, 58-D-118 & 58-D-637, *Records of the Office of North East Asian Affairs: Japan, Subject Files, 1947–56, Confidential US State Dept. Special Files—Japan, 1947–56* (1990) Bethesda.
30 Scalapino (1967): 100.
31 'On the Historical Experience of the Dictatorship of the Proletariat' *Peoples Daily* (5 Apr. 1956) cited in Alfred Low, *The Sino-Soviet Dispute* (1976) Rutherford: 72.
32 Philip Mosely, 'The Moscow–Peking Axis in World Politics' in, Howard Boorman, et al., *Moscow–Peking Axis* (1957) NY: 222
33 Cole, Totten and Uyehara (1966): 225.
34 Stockwin (1968): 84.
35 The group's other 'founding fathers' were Nambara Shigeru, Ōuchi Hyōe, Nakajima Kenzō, Kaya Seiji, Hiratsuka Tsunejirō and Ichikawa Ennosuke. Kazami Akira, 'NitChū kokkō kaifuku no gendankai' *Sekai* (Feb. 1958): 123.
36 The committee's 21 members included vice-chairmen, Kodaira Tadashi, Yamahana Hideo, and Yoshida Hōsei, and Secretary-General Sasaki Ryōsaku. Cole, Totten and Uyehara (1966): 230–1.
37 Katsumata Seiichi, 'Chūgoku no hijū zōdai' in Ōkuma Nobuyuki et al., 'Sorezore no uketomekata,' *Chūō Kōron* (Mar. 1957, special Issue): 197.
38 On the latter point, there is some dispute as to exactly what Mao and Zhou said. See: *Asahi Evening News* (17 Apr.); *Japan Times* (23 Apr.); *Mainichi Daily News* (23 Apr.); *Yomiuri Shimbun* (22 Apr. 1957); Hatano Kenichi, 'Oku no te o dashita "NitChū fukashin jōyaku" Mō Takutō no Nihon seisaku ni noru!' *Nihon Shūhō* (15 May 1957): 52–3. See also: Shao Chuan Leng, *Japan and Communist China* (1958) Kyoto: 97–8; AmConGen Hong Kong to DOS, 693.94/5–2957, NA.
39 See, for example, the Zhou–Bulganin Joint Statement of 18 January 1957, the statement by Foreign Minister Shepilov on 12 February, and Khrushchev's 18 June interview with Hirooka Tomoo of *Asahi Shimbun*. Here the Soviet leader for the first time 'offered to urge the Chinese to revise [the Sino-Soviet] treaty [of alliance] in return for Japan's recognition [of the] PRC and North Korea and development of trade with them.' DOS, IR 8481, 6 June 1961, NA; Peter Jones and Sian Kevill, *China and the Soviet Union, 1949–84* (1985) Harlow: 8.
40 Naitō Tomochika, interview, 27 Nov. 1963, cited in Scalapino (1967): 106.
41 Sone Eki, 'Future Policy toward Communist China' *Japan Quarterly* (Oct./Dec. 1957): 432–35.
42 MC, Kawakami, Sone and Robertson, 2 Oct. 1957, 611.94/10–257, NA.
43 MC, Kawakami, Sone and Murphy, 3 Oct. 1957, 790.00/10–357, NA. When a promising young diplomat, Sone was a victim of the so-called 'Yoshida purge' at

MOFA following Hatoyama's purge by SCAP in 1946. Richard B. Finn, *Winners in Peace* (1992) Berkeley: 109.

44 DOS, IR 8481, 'Soviet Statements on Japan–USSR Relations' 6 June 1961, *OSS/ State Dept. Intelligence & Research Reports, Japan, Korea, South–East Asia & Far East* (1979) Washington.

45 Jones & Kevill (1985): 9–10.

46 Naoi Takeo, 'Sino-Japanese Deadlock' *New Leader* (29 Sept. 1958): 10.

47 'Shiga, Suzuki jomei mondai to Nikkyō rosen,' *Asahi Jānaru* (31 May 1964): 16.

48 Stockwin (1967): 5; Langer (1972): 51–2; Scalapino (1967): 101–2.

49 Hirotsu Kyōsuke, 'The Stategic Triangle: Japan' *Survey* (Jan. 1965): 128.

50 Scalapino (1967): 103.

51 See Chapter 4.

52 One newspaper commented that, 'Japan is not a small country that can be easily manipulated from abroad; it is a proud nation that does not scare easily.' Cited in Lawrence Olson, *Japan in Postwar Asia* (1970) London: 87.

53 Naoi (1958): 10. He also described Sino-Soviet military ties as 'strong'. *Asahi Shimbun* (16 Aug. 1958).

54 *Yomiuri Shimbun* (31 Aug. 1958).

55 'The Socialists and Communist China' *Japan Quarterly* (Oct./Dec. 1964): 412; Naoi (1958): 10; Horsey to Dulles, 15 Sept. 1958, 693.94/9–1558, NA; *Gekkan Shakaitō* (Oct. 1958): 19–20, cited in Cheng (1977): 78; *Asahi Shimbun* (12 Sept. 1958).

56 *People's Daily* (16 Sept. 1958) cited in AmConGen Hong Kong to Dulles, 693.94/9–1758, NA.

57 Patrick Malone, *Japan's Foreign Policy 1957 through 1967* (1969) Geneva: 34.

58 Kataoka Tetsuya, *The Price of a Constitution* (1991) Stanford: 193.

59 Lee (1976): 40.

60 Kataoka (1991): 193.

61 *Asahi Shimbun* (20 Nov. 1958); R.G. Boyd, 'China's Relations with Japan' *Australian Outlook* (Apr. 1960): 61–2; Kataoka (1991): 193; I. Morris, 'Japanese Foreign Policy and Neutralism' *International Affairs* (Jan. 1960): 7.

62 Fujiyama's 'positive wait and see' policy perhaps influenced the terminology. See Chapter 4.

63 Stockwin (1968): 89; Edward Seidensticker, 'Divisions in Japanese Socialism' *Soviet Survey* (Apr./June 1960): 64. In fact, there is some evidence to support such Socialist suspicions. According to anti-mainstreamer Kamiyama Shigeo's later testimony, a vigorous debate occurred at the JCP Central Committee's Fourth Plenum held in mid-January. The mainstream faction, which advocated that Japan should aim to achieve 'independence' first and 'neutrality' only later (supposedly the Chinese line), lost out to the group seeking 'independence' *through* neutrality (the Soviet position), although the former made its influence felt in the drafting and implementation process. Kamiyama Shigeo, 'An Open Letter to the JCP Leaders' 30 Aug. 1964, cited in Scalapino (1967): 108 (n.18).

64 Morris (1960): 16.

65 Stockwin (1962): 39.

66 Seidensticker (1960): 64.

67 Low (1976): 90–2.

68 Leonart to DOS, 19 May 1959, 693.94/5–1959, NA; Boyd (1960): 62–3.

69 The delegation included Katsumata Seiichi, Okada Sōji, Sone Eki, Nakazaki Toshi, Sata Tadataka and Tanaka Toshio.

70 *Asahi Shimbun* (28 Apr. 1959). See also, Stockwin (1968): 90–1.
71 MacArthur to Dulles, 14 Mar. 1959, 611.94/3–1459, NA.
72 Jain (1981 A): 227–9; Cheng (1977): 79.
73 Cole, Totten and Uyehara (1966): 235.
74 Kataoka (1991): 197–8.
75 For example, on 19 July, he declared that the Four-Power Collective Security Treaty could not be realised for the foreseeable future. MacArthur to DOS, 21 July 1959, 794.00/7–2159, NA.
76 Stockwin (1968): 91, 93.
77 Kamiyama in Scalapino (1967): 108 (n.18).
78 DOS, IR 8481, 'Soviet Statements Japan–USSR Relations' 6 June 1961, *OSS/ State Dept. Intelligence & Research Reports, Japan, Korea, South–East Asia & Far East* (1979) Washington.
79 Varma (1991): 102; Boyd (1960): 64; Rosemary Foot, 'New Light on the Sino-Soviet Alliance: Chinese and American Perspectives' *Journal of North–East Asian Studies* (fall 1991): 20; Jones and Kevill (1985): 15.
80 See, for example, 'Fu Shushō no Pekin hōmon' *Asahi Jānaru* (18 Oct. 1959): 29–31.
81 Text in *Contemporary Japan* (May 1960): 593–5.
82 'Smash the New Plot of War and Aggression of the US and Japanese Reactionaries' *People's Daily* (24 Jan. 1960), in *'Oppose the Revival of Japanese Militarism*' (1960) Beijing: 158.
83 On 7 February, the JCP Presidium declared it 'just' and completely consistent 'with the interests of the Japanese people.' *Akahata* (8 Feb. 1960).
84 *JT* (4 Mar. 1960).
85 Stockwin (1968): 104.
86 *JT* (4 Mar. 1960).
87 Stockwin (1968): 97.
88 Kurt Radtke, *China's Relations with Japan, 1945–83* (1990) Manchester: 133–4; DOS, IR 8481 (1961).
89 A 17-year-old rightist fanatic stabbed him to death. Cole, Totten and Uyehara (1966): 216.
90 *Gekkan Shakaitō* (Nov. 1960) cited in Uezumi (1962): 32.
91 Cole, Totten and Uyehara (1966): 216.
92 Taguchi Fukuji, 'Nihon Shakaitō ron' *Chūō Kōron* (Feb. 1961): 29–30.
93 *Shakai Shimpō* (18 Dec. 1960) cited in Stockwin (1968): 97.
94 Murthy (1964): 286.
95 Scalapino (1967): 118.
96 Totten and Kawakami (1964): 836.
97 Jones and Kevill (1985): 17–20.
98 Scalapino (1967): 106, 210.
99 Kasuga Shōjirō, interview, 26 Nov. 1963, cited in Scalapino (1967): 107.
100 Scalapino (1967): 106–7.
101 Low (1976): 110–5; Jones and Kevill (1985): 21–3.
102 P. Langer, 'Moscow, Peking, and Tokyo', *Unity and Contradiction,* K. London (ed.) (1962) NY: 229.
103 Scalapino (1967): 108–9.
104 Khrushchev told the delegates that if Japan's move towards neutrality were strengthened, the Soviet Union could resurrect the promise to Hatoyama concerning the Habomai and Shikotan Islands. E.E. Kutakov, *NisSo gaikō kankeishi* (1969) 3: 65.

105 Mao Zedong reassured the group that he still placed a higher value on the JSP (a 'direct ally') than on the LDP anti-mainstream ('indirect allies'), and hoped to see the cleavage within the latter continue to widen. He also agreed that there was no essential difference between Kishi and Ikeda. Lee (1976): 45; Radtke (1990): 135. On their return to Japan, members of the *Heiwa Dōshikai* mission argued that, 'Only American imperialism is the enemy of peace and national independence.' 'How to Break the Deadlock in Relations Between Japan and China' *Gekkan Shakaitō* (Feb. 1961): 84–90, cited in Uezumi (1962): 32. In response, Narita Tomomi, chief of the JSP Policy Planning Board and a close ally of Eda, agreed that 'American imperialism is undoubtedly an "enemy",' but he maintained that 'the immediate target is Japanese monopoly capitalism.' *Mainichi Shimbun* (8 Mar. 1961).

106 Uezumi (1962): 32; Radtke (1990): 155 (n.140).

107 *Japan Quarterly* (Oct./Dec. 1964): 413.

108 Stockwin, (1968): 105–7.

109 Ronald Dore, 'The JSP and "Structural Reform"' *Asian Survey* (Oct. 1961): 8. A delegation was sent to Moscow but its impact was minimal. Stockwin (1968): 97.

110 Sone Eki, 'Japan and the China Problem' *Japan Quarterly* (July/Sept. 1961): 279.

111 Wada Hiroo, 'Japan and the China Problem' *Japan Quarterly* (July/Sept. 1961): 277

112 Hakamada Satomi, *Akahata* (9 May 1961) cited in *Japan Socialist Review* (1 Oct. 1963): 32.

113 Iwama, who had attended the celebrations himself, also said that, 'efforts should be made to make the Eighth JCP Congress a success to meet the expectations of China.' 'Nikkyō, Chukyō rosen ni fumikiru' *Nihon Shūhō* (15 Aug. 1961): 59.

114 *Asahi Jānaru* (31 May 1964): 17.

115 In 1925, Kasuga studied for a year at Moscow's Eastern Workers' Communist University. G.M. Beckman and Genji Okubo, *The Japanese Communist Party, 1922–1945* (1969) Stanford: 368.

116 P. Langer, 'The JCP between Moscow and Peking', *Communist Strategies in Asia*, A. Doak Barnett (ed.) (1963) NY: 84–5.

117 Scalapino (1967): 111–2.

118 Others expelled included Central Committee members Yamada Rokuzaemon, Nishikawa Yoshihiko and Naitō Tomochika. Hirotsu (1965): 128; *Asahi Jānaru* (31 May 1964): 16.

119 Langer (1972): 52–3.

120 *Nihon Shūhō* (15 Aug. 1961): 59.

121 Scalapino (1967): 111.

122 *Tōkyō Shimbun* (2 Aug. 1961).

123 Uezumi (1962): 33.

124 Scalapino (1967): 119.

125 Murthy (1964): 287.

126 Stockwin (1968): 100.

127 Murthy (1964): 287

128 Kosaka Zentaro, 'Japan and Nuclear Weapons Tests' *Contemporary Japan* (Mar. 1962): 202–3.

129 J.S. Hoadley and Hasegawa Sukehiro, 'Sino-Japanese Relations, 1950–1970' *International Studies Quarterly* (June 1971): 139.

130 *Akahata* (1, 8 Sept. 1961) cited in Stockwin (1968): 100.

131 Totten and Kawakami: 837.

132 Eda Saburō, 'Kaku jikken akumade hantai' *Shakai Shimpō*, 24 Sept. 1961, cited in Stockwin (1968): 101.
133 Stockwin (1968): 101.
134 Jones and Kevill (1985): 24.
135 Langer (1963): 77, 87; Scalapino (1967): 136–7.
136 In September, Kasuga and Naitō formed a 'Preparatory Commission for a Socialist Reform Movement' and repeatedly lambasted the JCP leadership for becoming Beijing's stooge. Scalapino (1967): 138, 144.
137 *Akahata* (22 Nov. 1961) cited in Swearingen (1978): 108.
138 'For the Unity of the International Communist Movement and the Struggle Against Two Enemies' *Akahata* (29 Dec. 1961) cited in Swearingen (1978): 140–2.
139 Satō Noboru, 'Shakaishugi to chūritsu' *Shisō* (Oct. 1961): 34–43.
140 *Gekkan Shakaitō* (Dec. 1961): 4–28, cited in Stockwin (1968): 110.
141 The delegates' affiliations predetermined the outcome of the mission: members of left-wing factions comprised two-thirds of the delegates, with the *Heiwa Dōshikai* greatly over-represented. Stockwin (1968): 99.
142 Cole, Totten and Uyehara (1966): 235–6; Lee (1976): 64.
143 Full text in *Japan Socialist Review* (16 Jan. 1962): 1–7.
144 *JTW* (20 Jan. 1962).
145 Six months later, in a secret letter to Party Chairman Kawakami, Suzuki apologised for the Joint-Communiqué, and blamed members of the *Heiwa Dōshikai* for his reiteration of the Asanuma Statement. Kawakami decided that since the CEC had already given its approval, raking over the ashes would serve no purpose. After the House of Councillors' election, however, it was leaked (probably by the Eda faction), and Suzuki felt obliged to publicly retract his reaffirmation of the Asanuma Statement. Lee (1976): 65, 236; *Asahi Shimbun* (3, 4 Aug. 1962).
146 'New Phase of Neutrality Policy' *Japan Socialist Review* (10 Apr. 1962): 13.
147 Scalapino (1967): 147.
148 Langer (1963): 82.
149 Scalapino (1967): 144–6.
150 Scalapino (1967): 123.
151 A further 'donation' of 7.5 million yen for victims of Hiroshima and Nagasaki doubtless helped to reinforce China's position. Scalapino (1967): 124, 126.
152 Lee (1976): 65–6.
153 Murthy (1964): 288.
154 Scalapino (1967): 125.
155 Murthy (1964): 288–9.
156 Murthy (1964): 289; Totten and Kawakami (1964): 837.
157 Lee (1976): 66.
158 Eda Saburō, 'Japan–China Friendship and the Chinese Line' *Shakai Shimpō* (9 Sept. 1962) cited in ibid.
159 J.A.A. Stockwin, 'The JCP in the Sino-Soviet Dispute', *The Disintegrating Monolith*, J.D.B. Miller and T.H. Rigby (eds) (1965) Canberra: 145.

Notes for Chapter 7

1 Peter Jones and Sian Kevill, *China and the Soviet Union, 1949–84* (1985) Harlow, Essex: 26.

2 Robert Scalapino, *The Japanese Communist Movement, 1920–1966* (1967) Berkeley: 149.
3 Scalapino (1967): 150.
4 *Akahata* (25 Oct.; 7 Nov. 1962) cited in Scalapino (1967): 150, 152.
5 Paul Langer, 'The JCP Between Moscow and Peking', *Communist Strategies in Asia,* A. Doak Barnett (ed.) (1963) NY: 95 (n.17); Kurt Radtke, *China's Relations with Japan, 1945–83* (1990) Manchester: 144.
6 Scalapino (1967): 153.
7 Eda Saburō, 'Shakaishugi no atarashii bijyon' *Ekonomisuto* (9 Oct. 1962): 34.
8 Wada Hiroo, 'Chūritsu seisaku no zenshin no tame ni' *Chūō Kōron* (June 1962): 98–106.
9 *Japan Quarterly* (Oct./Dec. 1964): 413.
10 P.A.N. Murthy, 'Japan and the India–China Border Conflict' *International Studies* (July/Oct. 1963): 184.
11 Chae-Jin Lee, *Japan Faces China* (1976) Baltimore: 66.
12 Ibid.; Stockwin (1968): 115.
13 *Gekkan Shakaitō* (Mar. 1963): 133–4, cited in Lee (1976): 66; *JTW* (2 Feb. 1963); Hagihara Nobutoshi, 'Nihon Shakaitō e no gimon' *Chūō Kōron* (Mar. 1964): 73–4.
14 Ishibashi Masashi, 'On [the] Sino-Soviet Dispute' *Japan Socialist Review* (1 Feb. 1963): 32, 35.
15 'Focal Point of the Sino-Soviet Dispute' *Japan Socialist Review* (15 Feb. 1963): 1–9. The same issue carried 'Comments on the Sino-Soviet Dispute' by various union leaders, including Takaragi Fumihiko (chairman of *Zentei*, the All Japan Communication Workers Union) and Ōta Kaoru (chairman of *Sōhyō*). Both praised Khrushchev's 'courage' over Cuba. However, while Takaragi felt confident that the 'obvious conflict of opinion...between China and the Soviet Union...will naturally be solved', Ōta thought that the existence of 'a dispute between two clearly different policy lines' was 'extremely dubious'. He argued that China's hard line was merely an effort 'to divert attention from various domestic problems'. As regards the position of *Sōhyō*, Ōta was forthright: 'Sōhyō supports the "peaceful coexistence" line and in that sense stands as a rule on the same position with the Soviet Union (sic).' Ibid.: 10–12.
16 Sone Eki and Wada Hiroo, in Aichi Kiichi, et al., 'Watashi wa kō handan suru' *Chūō Kōron* (Mar. 1963): 156–9.
17 *Asahi Shimbun* (5 Mar. 1963).
18 *Asahi Shimbun* (24 July 1963).
19 *Japan Quarterly* (Oct./Dec. 1964): 410.
20 *Akahata* (24 Jan. 1963) cited in *JTW* (8 Feb. 1964).
21 *Akahata* (19 Feb. 1963) cited in *Japan Socialist Review* (1 Oct. 1963): 33.
22 'Chū-So tairitsu de yure ugoku Nikkyō' *Ekonomisuto* (20 Aug. 1963): 27.
23 Langer (1963): 89–90.
24 *Japan Quarterly* (Apr./June 1963): 147.
25 Scalapino (1967): 155.
26 Ibid.; Hirotsu (1965): 124.
27 *Ekonomisuto* (20 Aug. 1963): 27. According to a government source within the JCP, Miyamoto absented himself from the Central Committee's Sixth Plenum in June on grounds of ill health, but in fact he was afraid that by attending he would 'expose himself to the danger of being caught up in the Sino-Soviet conflict'. RAD, 'Data for Situation Appraisal No. 6' Enc. in AusEmbTok to DEA, 23 Sept. 1963, A1838, 3103/11/87 Pt.9, NAA.

28 Scalapino (1967): 157.
29 Jones and Kevill (1985): 31–45.
30 *Mainichi Shimbun* (10 Aug. 1963).
31 *JTW* (8 Feb. 1964).
32 *Akahata* (5 July 1963) cited in *Ekonomisuto* (20 Aug. 1963): 27.
33 *Akahata* (9, 10 July 1963) cited in *Journal of Social and Political Ideas in Japan* (Apr. 1965): 120.
34 *Akahata* (29 July; 4 Aug. 1963) cited in Scalapino (1967): 161.
35 *Akahata* (5 Aug. 1963) cited in *JTW* (17 Aug. 1963).
36 Stockwin (1965): 145.
37 Scalapino (1967): 159.
38 Totten and Kawakami (1964): 838; Murthy (1964): 293.
39 *Ekonomisuto* (20 Aug. 1963): 26.
40 Morton Halperin, *China and the Bomb* (1965) London: 57.
41 Murthy (1964): 293–4.
42 Scalapino (1967): 162–3.
43 Donald Zagoria, 'The State of the Parties: Asia' *Survey* (Jan. 1965): 96.
44 Kim Young Bae, *The JCP and the Soviet Union* (1974) Ph.D., University of Kansas: 163.
45 'Sino-Soviet Split and Present Condition of JCP' *Japan Socialist Review* (1 Oct. 1963): 34.
46 Scalapino (1967): 164.
47 Scalapino (1967): 162.
48 Murthy (1964): 294.
49 Hagihara (1964): 74.
50 Wada Hiroo, 'What Should Our Attitude be Toward the Moscow–Peking Conflict?' *Japan Socialist Review* (15 Aug. 1963): 15–29.
51 Wada denounced the JCP as the proverbial 'fox who borrowed authority from a tiger' for 'mechanically applying...an ideology based on the historical conditions of a foreign country [China] to a peace movement waged under the conditions in which Japan is actually placed.' Ibid.
52 Wada Hiroo, 'Chū-So ronsō to Shakaitō no tachiba' *Jiyū* (Oct. 1963): 2–9. Privately, however, Wada apparently described himself as a 'Tito-type Socialist'. Nutter (Tokyo) to SEA, 31 Dec. 1963, A1838, 3103/10/10/2, NAA.
53 Eda Saburō, 'Bei kyokutō seisaku no tenkan o' *Sekai* (Sept. 1963) 213: 83–4.
54 See Chapter 9.
55 *Japan Quarterly* (Oct./Dec. 1964): 410.
56 'Socialist Foreign Policy Vis-à-vis Sino-Soviet Dispute' *Japan Socialist Review* (15 Sept. 1963): 20–22.
57 *Japan Quarterly* (Oct./Dec. 1964): 410–1.
58 Narita also accused Moscow of 'stealing' the 'theory of peaceful revolution' from the JSP. '39th Central Committee of JSP' *Japan Socialist Review* (15 Oct. 1963): 34–6.
59 Hagihara (1964): 74.
60 Scalapino (1967): 165.
61 *Japan Socialist Review* (1 Oct. 1963): 35–6.
62 Rather more accurate was the analysis of Hirotsu Kyōsuke (*Kōan Chōsachō*). The following month he predicted that the rift would continue to grow and that 'If [the JCP] should prohibit free discussion concerning the Sino-Soviet dispute within the party...it

might lead the party to split'. Hirotsu Kyōsuke, 'Kokusai kyōsanshugi to Nihon Kyōsantō no tachiba' *Sekai to Nihon* (Nov. 1963): 23–4, 27.

63 Radtke (1990): 146.

64 Soeya Yoshihide, *Japan's Economic Diplomacy with China, 1945–1978* (1998) Oxford: 71.

65 Shiga claimed that, 'Although the test-ban treaty is far from ideal, it is of great benefit to the people of Japan and of all the world in that it will halt radioactive pollution of the atmosphere and curb further development of nuclear weapons.' *Asahi Jānaru* (31 May 1964): 12.

66 Hirotsu (1965): 123.

67 Scalapino (1967): 166–7.

68 Langer (1963): 88.

69 *Akahata* (10 Nov. 1963) cited in *JTW* (8 Feb. 1964). See also: Hirotsu (1965): 123–4; Scalapino (1967): 167–8.

70 L. Labedz & G. Urban (eds), *The Sino-Soviet Conflict* (1965) London: 65.

71 *JTW* (30 May 1964).

72 Hirotsu (1965): 129.

73 Peter Berton, 'The Soviet and Japanese Communist Parties' *Studies in Comparative Communism* (autumn 1982): 275.

74 Jones and Kevill (1985): 48–9.

75 Hakamada Satomi, 'Watakushi no sengoshi': 184–90, cited in Berton (1982): 276.

76 *Akahata* (10 Mar. 1964) cited in *JTW* (11 Apr. 1964). The author was reportedly Ueda Koichirō, elder brother of Fuwa Tetsuzō and a mainstream member of the Central Committee. *Asahi Jānaru* (31 May 1964): 15.

77 Scalapino (1967): 172–84.

78 Shimizu Shinzō, 'Gendaishi no naka no waga kakushin seiryoku' *Sekai* (Nov. 1963): 111–2.

79 Lee (1976): 47–8.

80 *Asahi Shimbun* (3 Mar. 1964).

81 Gerald Curtis, *The Japanese Way of Politics* (1988) NY: 142.

82 'Toward True Friendship between Japan and China' *Shakai Shimpō* (7 Mar. 1964) cited in *JTW* (14 Mar. 1964). An official CEC statement three days later reinforced the message.

83 *JTW* (28 Mar. 1964).

84 *JTW* (18 Apr. 1964).

85 *Japan Quarterly* (Oct./Dec. 1964): 413.

86 *JTW* (30 May 1964).

87 *Asahi Jānaru* (31 May 1964): 12–13.

88 Stockwin (1965): 138–9.

89 Hirotsu (1965): 129.

90 *JTW* (30 May 1964).

91 Hirotsu (1965): 125.

92 Zagoria (1965): 94.

93 Two later repented, but the rest were expelled in mid-November. Hirotsu (1965): 129.

94 Labedz & Urban (1965): 66; Scalapino (1967): 171.

95 Stockwin (1965): 146.

96 Mao labelled them 'nonsensical' and Zhou Enlai added that they were identical twins with the JCP's 'modern revisionists'. Lee (1976): 67.

97 See also Chapters 3 and 9.

98 Stockwin (1968): 124. Financial backers of the Sasaki faction like the Wasui Trading Company began to land lucrative contracts at the Canton trade fairs, whereas those supporting the Eda and Kawakami factions saw their business dry up. J.S. Hoadley and Hasegawa Sukehiro, 'Sino-Japanese Relations, 1950–1970' *International Studies Quarterly* (June 1971): 140.
99 Lalima Varma, *The Making of Japan's China Policy* (1991) Delhi: 95.
100 *JTW* (6 June 1964).
101 *JTW* (11 July 1964).
102 Zagoria (1965): 97.
103 Scalapino (1967): 232–3.
104 Hirotsu (1965): 126.
105 *JTW* (8 Aug. 1964); Zagoria (1965): 94.
106 *JTW* (8 Aug. 1964).
107 'The Puppet Theater in the Diamond Hotel' *Pravda* (1 Aug. 1964) cited in A. Kashin, 'The Defeat of the Pro-Soviet Faction of the JCP' *Bulletin of the Institute for the Study of the USSR* (Nov. 1964): 33.
108 Scalapino (1967): 235–6.
109 Scalapino (1967): 186–95; *JTW* (12 Sept. 1964).
110 See Chapter 9.
111 Jones and Kevill (1985): 91.
112 *JTW* (29 Sept. 1964).
113 *JTW* (10 Oct. 1964).
114 Stockwin (1968): 123; Lee (1976): 67.
115 *JTW* (24 Oct. 1964).
116 *JT* (22 Oct. 1964).
117 *JTW* (24 Oct. 1964).
118 Lee (1976): 67.
119 *JTW* (7 Nov. 1964).
120 Jones and Kevill (1985): 60.
121 *JTW* (24 Oct. 1964).
122 *Akahata* (17 Oct. 1964) cited in Hirotsu (1965): 130.
123 Jones and Kevill (1985): 60.
124 Hirotsu (1965): 126.
125 Scalapino (1967): 214–5, 224–5.
126 Berton (1982): 270.
127 *JTW* (17 Oct. 1964). In mid-July, the JCP joined with the JSP, *Sōhyō*, and 137 other organisations in planning joint action against escalating US involvement in the Vietnam War, and the Japanese government's support for it. This eventually developed into *Beheiren*, the very large and influential Japanese anti-Vietnam War movement. John Welfield, *Empire in Eclipse* (1988) London: 190.
128 *JTW* (12 Dec. 1964).
129 Hirotsu (1965): 130.
130 Stockwin (1968): 123–4.
131 Stockwin (1968): 115; Curtis (1988): 144–5.
132 Utsunomiya Tokuma, et al., 'Chūgoku no nashonaru intaresuto' *Gendai no Me* (Nov. 1964): 82, 85.
133 Fukui Haruhiro, *Party in Power* (1970) Berkeley: 236; Stockwin (1968): 116; Curtis (1988): 144–5.
134 Lee (1976): 68.

135 Varma (1991): 96.

136 Scalapino (1967): 262–5; J.A.A. Stockwin, 'JSP Under New Leadership' *Asian Survey* (Apr. 1966): 194–7. 'Hundreds of flowers of opinions are now blossoming within the [Japan Socialist] party, from a red one closest to the Chinese Communist line, through a pink one in favour of the Russian Communist line, to a yellow one supporting the line of the Socialist International.' Seki Yoshihiko, 'The Ideology of Socialist Groups and Parties in Japan since 1945' *St. Antony's Papers*, G.F. Hudson (ed.) (1967) 20, Oxford: 54.

137 Wada Takayoshi, *Asahi Jānaru* (18 Dec. 1966) cited in Stockwin (1968): 113.

138 Gilbert Rozman, *Japan's Response to the Gorbachev Era, 1985–1991* (1992) Princeton: 289.

139 William Griffith, *The Sino-Soviet Rift* (1964) London: 65.

140 *Asahi Shimbun* (22 Dec. 1965).

141 Hoadley and Hasegawa (1971): 137.

142 Fukui (1970): 235.

143 Scalapino (1967): 287.

144 During the 1960s, the JCP's share of the vote in Lower House elections steadily increased from 1.9% (1953) to 4.8% (1967). The party also claimed a huge increase in membership (from about 20,000 in 1955 to about 150,000). With a much looser party structure, the JSP was relatively stagnant by these measures of success: membership hovered around 50,000 for most of the decade and its share of the popular vote dropped from the high to the low twenties.

Notes for Chapter 8

1 'Chū-So dōmei wa Nihon ni dō hibiku' *Daiyamondo* (21 Feb. 1950): 12–13.

2 Iwamura Michio, 'Chū-So jōyaku to Nihon no tachiba' *Sekai Hyōron* (Apr. 1950): 78–83.

3 'Chū-So jōyaku to tai Nichi kōwa' *Sekai Jōsei Junpō* (Feb. 1950): 17–24; Hirano Yoshitarō, 'Chū-So yūkō dōmei jōyaku no Nihon ni oyobosu eikyō' *Joseisen* (Mar. 1950): 4–11; Kusano Fumio, 'Chū-So dōmei to Nihon e no eikyō' *Kumiai Undō* (Mar. 1950): 43–8; Takayama Gorō, 'Chū-So dōmei to Nihon no tachiba' *Jitsugyō no Nihon* (Feb. 1950): 58–9.

4 *Daiyamondo* (21 Feb. 1950): 12–13.

5 Kusano also claimed that 'Mao Zedong is not Stalin's running dog (sōku)'. Kusano (1950): 43–8.

6 Utsumi Teizō, 'Chū-So jōyaku no heiwateki kōka' *Daiyamondo* (21 Feb. 1950): 13–14.

7 *Asahi Shimbun* (16 Feb. 1950). See also: Hongō Gaichi, 'Soren to Chūkyō no kyokutō seisaku' *Chūō Kōron* (Mar. 1950): 81.

8 Takayama (1950): 58–9.

9 *Sekai Jōsei Junpō* (1950): 17–24,

10 Kusano (1950): 43–8.

11 *Sekai Jōsei Junpō* (1950): 17–24. See also 'Chū-So dōmei seiritsu to Nihon' *Tōyō Keizai Shimpō* (25 Feb. 1950): 3–4.

12 Similar answers were received regarding the Alliance's effect on maintaining peace in general. *Tōkyō Shimbun* (26 Feb. 1950).

13 For example, on 29 December 1950, United Press cited 'qualified sources in Tokyo' who believed that China's entry into the Korean War grew out of a political contest with Russia for control of the area north of the 38th parallel. *Evening Post*, 30 December 1950.

14 Bessho Jirō, 'Hokkaidō "kaihō henku"' *Kaizō* (10 Jan. 1952): 154–65.

15 'Which of the two camps will be split first?' 'The Communists will split first': 29.1%; 'Democrats will split first': 11.8%; 'Others': 16.9%; 'Don't Know': 26.2%; 'Don't Know, Red China': 15.5%. Sample: urban 1807; rural 1246. Reply: 87.2% (rural data weighted double in original survey). '*The World and Japan*' (15 August 1953), Enc. in Berger to DOS, 611.94/9–2253, NA.

16 *Yomiuri Shimbun* (5 Mar. 1953, evening).

17 Satō Shinichirō, 'Shiteyarareta no wa Soren ka Chūkyō ka' *Nihon Shūhō* (5 Dec. 1952): 7.

18 Sekai Mondai Kenkyūkai, 'Bei-So sekai seisaku no shindankai' *Chūō Kōron* (Apr. 1953): 65–74.

19 Tange Gorō, 'Chūkyō no kōgyō kensetsu no hōkō o saguru' *Ekonomisuto* (6 Mar. 1954): 24–7.

20 Hirasawa Kazushige, 'Chū-So wa dō deru: shinsekai senryaku e no tenkan' *Daiyamondo* (11 Oct. 1952): 48–50.

21 Ōhira Zengo, 'Katayotta Chūkyōkan o hai suru' *Jiyū no Hata no Moto ni* (Mar. 1953): 52.

22 Ishikawa Shigeru, 'Chū-So kankei o kettei suru yōin' *Soren Kenkyū* (Sept. 1953): 21.

23 Takeda Nanyō, 'Chūkyō–Soren ippentō no gendankai' *Soren Kenkyū* (Aug. 1953): 36–46.

24 Sano Hiroshi, 'Mosukō, Pekin, Tōkyō rosen' *Nihon oyobi Nihonjin* (Feb. 1954): 6–13; 'Soren heiwa kōsei no seikaku to mokuhyō' *Nihon oyobi Nihonjin* (Apr. 1954): 64–72.

25 Typically, one journal concluded, 'One cannot help but think that Sino-Soviet unity was strengthened internally and externally by the declaration'. 'Chū-So ryōkoku no tai Nichi yobikake' *Sekai to Warera* (Nov. 1954): 36–8.

26 Takahashi Masao, 'Chū-So seimei to daisan seiryoku no tachiba' *Shakaishugi* (Nov. 1954): 2–8.

27 Tachibana Yoshinori and Unno Minoru, 'Chū-So sengen no hamon to Yoshida toBei no shūkaku' *Jitsugyō no Nihon* (1954): 50–6.

28 Hirano Yoshitarō, 'Chū-So kyōdō sengen to Nihon' *Ajia Keizai Junpō* (Nov. 1954): 1–9; Maki Tadashi, 'Chū-So no tai Nichi sekkin no shini' *Jikei* (Dec. 1954): 82–5; *Mainichi Shimbun* (13 Oct. 1954).

29 According to a November 1954 poll, Communist China and the Soviet Union were 'liked' by 11.9% and 5.1% of respondents, respectively. They were 'disliked' by 21.3% and 37.3%. *Jiji nenkan* (1956): 320.

30 In June 1955, for example, a former vice-president of the *Tōa Kenkyūjo* (East Asia Research Institute) confidently predicted that 'the time will come when China parts ways with the CPSU.' Ōkura Kinmochi, 'NitChū-so no kankei o meguri' *Soren Kenkyū* (June 1955): 50. In contrast, a panel of well-known journalists concluded in August that 'while Communist China may have become a considerable "burden" [to the Soviets] economically and politically...they are sworn friends, and it is inconceivable that they will part company under present conditions.' Sakata Jirō, et al., 'Sobieto gaikō no teiryū' *Chūō Kōron* (Aug. 1955): 67.

31 Taiken, 'Chū-So kankei no kentō (2)' *Tairiku Mondai* (Aug. 1956): 29. See Appendix 4 for a list of *Taiken* members.

32 Doi Akio, 'Chūkyō shisatsu hōkoku' *Tairiku Mondai* (Nov. 1956): 9–12; 'Sashimukai Mō Takutō' *Bungei Shunjū* (Nov. 1956): 194.
33 Takenaka Shigehisa, 'Chūgokujin no tai So kanjō' *Soren Kenkyū* (Sept. 1956): 47.
34 Inoki Masamichi, et al., 'Chūgoku wa Soren to dō chigau ka' *Chūō Kōron* (Nov. 1956): 327.
35 Yamakawa Hitoshi, 'Shakaishugi e no michi wa hitotsu dewanai' *Chūō Kōron* (Dec. 1956): 153.
36 Maruyama Masao, *Thought and Behaviour in Modern Japanese Politics* (1963) London: 180–1, 212. Originally: '"Sutārin hihan" ni okeru seiji no ronri' *Sekai* (Nov. 1956), and postscript: *Gendai seiji no shisō to kōdō* (30 Mar. 1957): 366.
37 AmEmbTok to DOS, 19 Dec. 1956, 794.00/12–1956, NA.
38 Ōno Shinzō, 'Kuzureyuku Soren teikokushugi' *Nihon Shūhō* (15 Nov. 1956): 49.
39 Fujii Shōji, 'Dōyō suru Chūkyō to Ri Shōban no hokushin' *Nihon Shūhō* (5 Dec. 1956): 53, 57.
40 Doi Akio, 'NitChū-So no shōrai' *Nihon oyobi Nihonjin* (Jan. 1957): 9–11.
41 Taiken, 'Mō Takutō no mujunron wa Kyōsanken o yusubutte iru' *Tairiku Mondai* (Oct. 1957): 35–6.
42 Hatano Kenichi, 'NitChū-So bōeki kyōtei o nerau?' *Nihon Shūhō* (15 Feb. 1957): 16–17. See also: Iwamura Michio and Rōyama Masamichi.
43 Ōkuma Nobuyuki, et al., 'Sorezore no uketomekata' *Chūō Kōron* (Mar. 1957, special issue): 186, 192.
44 Komuro Makoto, 'Chūkyō-Soren kankei no jittai' *Soren Kenkyū* (Nov. 1957): 14, 19. For a list of *Soken* members see Appendix 3.
45 According to a November 1957 poll, Communist China and the Soviet Union were 'liked' by 2.0% and 1.3% of respondents, respectively. They were 'disliked' by 3.7% and 30.5%. *Jiji nenkan* (1959): 158.
46 Mushakoji Kinhide, 'The Changing Japanese Foreign Policy Attitudes in the 1960s' *Japan Institute of International Affairs Annual Review* (1970): 7.
47 See, for example, 'Namerareta Nihon' *Shūkan Tōkyō* (5 Apr. 1958): 3–11.
48 *Nihon Keizai Shimbun* (20 June 1958).
49 *Asahi Shimbun* (10, 20, 21 Aug. 1958).
50 Nanjō Tōru, 'Chū-So kankei no shindankai' *Soren Kenkyū* (Sept. 1958): 5.
51 Amō Eiji, 'Kyōsanken kenkyū' *Soren Mondai* (Dec. 1958): 16. Amō had been a vice-foreign minister during the war, with earlier diplomatic postings to the Soviet Union and China, and authored the infamous 'Amō plan' for China of April 1934. Classified as a Class 'A' war criminal, he was never tried, and later headed Japan's UN Association. See Appendix 5 for a list of founding Council of Sovietologists' members.
52 Ishikawa Tadao, 'Shakaishugiken ni okeru Chūgoku no yakuwari' *Chūō Kōron* (Nov. 1958): 89, 98.
53 'Shinshun ankēto' *Soren Kenkyū* (Jan. 1959): 44–54.
54 'Chūkyō tenbō' *Soren Kenkyū* (Apr. 1959): 49.
55 Inoki Masamichi, 'Chū-So no seiji kankei' *Soren Mondai* (Dec. 1959): 65–88. Participants in the seminar included Yamada Junji and Matsui Hidekazu (Eastern Europe Desk) and Nishizawa Kenichirō (acting head of the China Desk) from MOFA.
56 Doi Akira, 'Chūkyō yukidoke ni noreru ka' *Keizai Ōrai* (Nov. 1959): 125–9.
57 *Sankei Shimbun* (12 Sept. 1959) was unusual in emphasising that Moscow's appeal for a peaceful settlement of the Sino-Indian border dispute was an admonishment directed at Beijing, which showed that despite their close alliance the Communist powers were sometimes widely divided on important matters.

58 *Asahi Shimbun* (12, 13 Aug. 1959).
59 *Asahi Shimbun* (17 Oct. 1959).
60 'Fu shushō no Pekin hōmon' *Asahi Janaru* (18 Oct. 1959): 29–31.
61 Takaichi Keinosuke, 'Kakumei jūichi nenme no Chūgoku' *Sekai* (Dec. 1959): 95.
62 Hayashi Takuo, et al., 'Zuikō kisha no Ishibashi hō Chū hiwa' *Keizai Ōrai* (Nov. 1959): 135.
63 Hayashi (1959): 136.
64 Arai Takeo, 'Chūgoku ni dō tai subeki ka' *Nihon oyobi Nihonjin* (Dec. 1959): 15.
65 Suzukawa Isamu, et al., 'Heiwa kyōson e no taidō' *Gaikō Jihō* (Nov. 1959): 20–1.
66 Harako Rinjirō, 'Taigai seisaku o meguru Chū-So kankei' *Sekai Shūhō* (20 Oct. 1959): 32. See also Azuma Teruhiko, who related differing Sino-Soviet attitudes towards the status quo to their length of experience in building Socialism.
67 Marukawa Tatsuo, 'Kewashii NitChū dakai e no michi' *Soren Kenkyū* (June 1960): 54. Iwamura Michio clearly shared this view. Surveying the past decade of Sino-Soviet relations he anticipated no future problems. Iwamura Michio, '10 nenrai no Chū-So kankei' *Kokusai Seiji* (15 May 1960): 28–39.
68 'Chū-So no kuichigai' *Chūō Kōron* (Apr. 1960): 217–9. Similarly, for a staff writer with *Sekai Shūhō*, there was 'no basic clash of interests between them' even if there was 'a conflict of opinion...regarding the easing of world tension.' Inoue Shōzō, 'Chūkyō to yukidoke no bimyōna kankei' *Sekai Shūhō* (1 Jan. 1960): 47; 'Sekai o tsukiageru Chūkyō' *Sekai Shūhō* (28 June 1960): 44.
69 68 people replied of whom nearly half had also responded to the 1959 questionnaire. 'Shinshun ankēto' *Soren Kenkyū* (Jan. 1960): 42–55.
70 It was also felt that China eventually followed Soviet policy changes, although recently their positions seemed to have reversed. Taiken, 'Chū-So no tai Nichi seisaku' *Tairiku Mondai* (May 1960): 81. See also K. Alexandrov.
71 See, for example, S. Labin and C. Emmet, 'Is there a Sino-Soviet Split?' *Orbis* (spring 1960): 28–38.
72 Kiga Kenzō, 'Chū-So no tairitsu to Nihon' *Ronsō* (Feb. 1960): 61–7. See also Kubota Yasushi.
73 *Asahi Shimbun* (2, 3, 5 July 1960).
74 Hamano Masami and Shishikura Toshirō, 'Hyōmenka shita Chū-So ronsō' *Sekai Shūhō* (5 July 1960): 20–3.
75 Hamano Masami, 'Chū-So rikan no ugoki' *Tairiku Mondai* (Oct. 1960): 30–5.
76 *Soren Kenkyū* (July 1960): 41–2; (Aug. 1960): 4; (Sept. 1960): 5.
77 *Asahi Shimbun* (17 Aug. 1960). See Appendix 2 for a list of members.
78 See Chapters 3 and 5.
79 Maeshiba Kakuzō, 'Kaikyūteki shiten to jinruiteki shiten' *Ritsumeikan Hōgaku* (Sept. 1960): 214–38.
80 Eguchi Bokurō, 'Tairitsu suru Chū-So no riron to genjitsu' *Asahi Jānaru* (18 Sept. 1960): 14–19.
81 For a list of official participants see Appendix 6. While the only bureaucrat included on this list was Ōkita Saburō, then a junior member of the EPA, the observers included a large number of government personnel. Obata Misao, 'The Sino-Soviet Dispute' *Japan Quarterly* (Jan./Mar. 1961): 26.
82 H.F. Schurmann, 'The Third Sovietological Conference' *China Quarterly* (Oct./Dec. 1960): 102.
83 The other papers by Japanese were: Inoki Masamichi, 'Leninism and Mao Zedong Thought'; Miyashita Tadao, 'A Comparison of the Chinese and Soviet Economies';

Muramatsu Yūji, 'The Negotiation between Chinese Communism and Tradition During the Yennan Period'; Amō Eiji, 'Is International Communism Advancing in the Far East?'; Takahashi Masao, 'Communism in Japan'; Ueda Toshio, 'The "Two Chinas" and Japan'; Yamamoto Noboru, 'Japan's Communist bloc Trade' and Itagaki Yoichi, 'The Prospects for Nationalism, Democracy and Communism in South–East Asia'.

84 Onoe Masao, 'Factors Binding the USSR and Communist China', *Unity and Contradiction,* Kurt London (ed.) (1962) NY: 142–55; or in Japanese: 'Chū-So kankei no ketsugōteki yōso', *Soren to Chūkyō*, Ōa Kyōkai (ed.) (1962): 734–53.

85 Hirota Yōji, 'Chū-So kan no kiretsu ni tsuite' in Ōa Kyōkai (1962): 220–42, 167–9.

86 Kiga Kenzō, 'Chūkyō to Soren no aida no ketsugōteki yōso to taikōteki yōso' in Ōa Kyōkai (1962): 539–61.

87 Ishikawa Tadao, 'Chūkyō no tai Nichi seisaku' in Ōa Kyōkai (1962): 295–311.

88 Schurmann (1960): 113.

89 P. Langer, 'Moscow, Peking, and Tokyo' in London (1962): 223–30. Such views were not uncommon amongst US experts at this time. A. Doak Barnett even suggested that the Communist powers had 'closely coordinated the timing of their separate moves... toward...Japan'. A. Doak Barnett, *Communist China and Asia* (1960) NY: 371.

90 'Chū-So kankei no kokusai zemi' *Asahi Jānaru* (9 Oct. 1960): 105. See also, Schurmann (1960): 111; Obata (1961): 28.

91 Obata (1961): 29. See also, *Asahi Jānaru* (9 Oct. 1960): 104; Muramatsu Yūji, 'Chūkyō wa Yūgo no michi o ayumu ka' *Keizai Ōrai* (Nov. 1960): 65–71.

92 Taiken, 'Chū-So kankei no kentō' *Tairiku Mondai* (Nov. 1960): 16–34.

93 'Chū-So ronsō no honshitsu' *Sekai* (Nov. 1960): 207–12.

94 Zhou Jingwen, 'Chū-So tairitsu wa nai' *Sekai Shūhō* (1 Nov. 1960): 20.

95 Jin Xiongbo, 'Chū-So no antō wa tsuzuku' *Sekai Shūhō* (6 Dec. 1960): 56–7.

96 See Chapter 6.

97 Onoe Masao, 'Hachijūikkakoku kyōsantō sengen to Chū-So ronsō' *Kyōsanken Mondai* (formerly *Soren Mondai*) (Jan. 1961): 17–18.

98 'Chū-So no tairitsu wa kaishō shita ka' *Asahi Jānaru* (11 Dec. 1960): 77–9.

99 'Chū-So ronsō no tōtatsuten' *Ekonomisuto* (10 Jan. 1961): 6–16.

100 Kiuchi Nobutane, 'Gaikō no kokorogamae to kichō ni tsuite' *Keizai Rondan* (Feb. 1961): 10.

101 'Shinshun ankēto' *Soren Kenkyū* (Jan. 1961): 34–41.

102 Ōki Masato, 'Chū-So ronsō to Nihon teikokushugi' *Keizai Hyōron* (Jan. 1961): 50–61.

103 See Chapter 7.

104 Satō Noboru, 'Taisei no henkaku to heiwa kyōson' *Sekai* (Feb. 1961): 28–38.

105 Matsumoto Shigeharu, et al., 'Kawariyuku sekai to Nihon' *Jiyū* (Apr. 1961): 5–6.

106 Matsumoto Shigeharu, 'Gendai Nihon to kokusaiteki chii' *Chūō Kōron* (Oct. 1961): 35.

107 Doi Akio, 'Mondai no ōi Chū-So kankei' *Tairiku Mondai* (May 1961): 8.

108 'Chū-So kankei no genjō' *Soren Kenkyū* (Aug. 1961): 8.

109 Harako Rinjirō, 'Chū-So ronsō no shindankai' *Sekai Shūhō* (5 Dec. 1961): 30–5.

110 Harako Rinjirō, 'Chū-So kankei no jūrokunen' *Chūō Kōron* (Mar. 1962): 125, 132.

111 'Shinshun ankēto' *Soren Kenkyū* (Jan. 1962): 20–9. Unfortunately, the journal ceased publication in November 1962.

112 Watanabe Mikio, 'Fushigina sankaku kankei' *Keizai Ōrai* (Feb. 1962): 92–3.

113 *JT* (15 Feb. 1962).

114 *JT* (18 Feb. 1962).

115 *JTW* (17 Mar. 1962). The JCP had expelled another ten prominent intellectuals in early February. See Chapter 6.

116 William Ballis, 'A Decade of Soviet–Japanese Relations' *Studies on the Soviet Union* (1964): 152; 'Odoroki awateru Gaimushō' *Shin Shūkan* (17 May 1962): 26.

117 R.K. Jain, *The USSR and Japan* (1981[B]) New Delhi: 36.

118 See Chapter 5.

119 *Pravda* (27 Aug. 1963) cited in D. Petrov, 'Japan and the Mao Group's Foreign Policy' *International Affairs* (Moscow) (Dec. 1968): 32–3.

120 Asada Mistuteru, 'Chū-So ronsō to Nihon no sayoku' *Ronsō* (Apr. 1962): 84–91.

121 Kusano Fumio, 'Chū-So no ronsō to keizai kankei' *Ronsō* (Mar. 1962): 30–7.

122 Sekido Tatsuzō, 'Chū-So ronsō ni kanren shita Chū-So no tai Nichi dōkō to sono eikyō' *Tairiku Mondai* (Oct. 1962): 20–9.

123 Sakamoto Koretada, 'Chūgoku ni okeru kyōsanshugi to minzokushugi' *Chūō Kōron* (June 1962): 88–9.

124 Onoe even mentioned the possibility of a new Comintern being established to maintain unity. Onoe Masao, 'Chū-So riron tōsō no hitsuzensei to genkai' *Kokusai Seiji* (Apr. 1963): 68–70.

125 Iwamura Michio, 'Chū-So ronsō no ichikōsatsu' *Ajia Kenkyū* (July 1962): 1–20. In March, *Sekai* had reprinted an article on the dispute by these famous American Socialists. In it they declared: 'we have no doubt whatever that the Russians are right and the Chinese wrong.' And although they blamed the US for China's condition, the latter was nevertheless diagnosed as suffering from 'dogmatic leftism' and hence, 'the world should be grateful that China's foreign policy is subject to the moderating influence of the Soviet Union.' L. Huberman and P. Sweezy, 'The Sino-Soviet Dispute' *Monthly Review* (Dec. 1961): 337–46. Reprinted as 'Chū-So ronsō kakushin' *Sekai* (Mar. 1962): 64–71.

126 Harako Rinjirō, 'Chū-So maboroshi no wakai' *Jiyū* (July 1962): 58–65.

127 Robert Scalapino, 'The Left Wing in Japan' *Survey* (Aug. 1962): 110–11.

Notes for Chapter 9

1 'The Sino-Soviet Dispute and Japan' *Japan Quarterly* (Apr./June 1963): 144.

2 *Mainichi Shimbun* (4 Jan. 1963).

3 *Mainichi Shimbun* (21 Jan. 1963).

4 *Asahi Shimbun* (13 Jan. 1963).

5 *Sankei Shimbun* (9 Jan. 1963).

6 *Tōkyō Shimbun* (14 Jan. 1963).

7 *JTW* (5 Jan. 1963).

8 *JTW* (5, 19 Jan. 1963).

9 Seki Yoshihiko, 'Notes by the Editor' *Journal of Social and Political Ideas in Japan* (Apr. 1963): 78–9.

10 'Sensō to heiwa no mondai ni kan suru Chū-So no kenkai' *Gaimushō Chōsa Geppō* (Mar.1961): 26–53.

11 Kurihara Yukio, 'Chū-So ronsō no rekishiteki haikei' *Gendai no Me* (Mar. 1963): 34.

12 See, for example, Ikeyama Shigerō [Jūrō], 'Chū-So ronsō to taishū undō' *Gekkan Rōdō Mondai* (Apr. 1963): 116; Maeno Ryō and Tsuda Michio in Yamada Munemutsu, et al., 'Chū-So ronsō to kakushin jinei' *Gendai no Me* (Mar. 1963): 44.

13 Satō Noboru, 'Chū-So ronsō to kokusai kyōsanshugi undō' *Chūō Kōron* (Mar.1963): 102, Mori Kyōzō, 'Chū-So tairitsu kara nani o hikidasu ka' *Ronsō* (Mar. 1963): 7. See also, Nomura Kōichi, 'Tairitsuron ni tsuite futatsu, mitsu no gimon' *Asahi Janaru* (10 Mar. 1963): 10, Tsuda (1963): 45, Ishidō Kiyotomo, *Chū-So ronsōron* (20 July 1963): 208.

14 Terasawa Hajime, et al., 'Chū-So ronsō to Nihon no tachiba' *Fujin Kōron* (Mar. 1963): 98. Many other terms were used to a lesser degree, see the bibliography for examples.

15 Taiken, 'Chū-So tairitsu no kongen to sono yukue' *Tairiku Mondai* (Mar. 1963): 10. Outside contributors included Ōkawa Jirō (CRO), Hatano Kenichi, Yoshida Terao (Diet Library), Izaki Kiyota (*Kazankai*), and Doi Akira (*Shōwa Dōjinkai*). See also: Taniguchi Yasuji, 'Chū-So ronsō no shiten' *Gekkan Sōhyō* (Apr. 1963): 37; Yamazaki Isao, 'Chū-So ronsō o dō miru ka' *Ekonomisuto* (22 Jan. 1963): 41; Takasawa Torao, 'Chū-So ronsō to heiwa mondai' *Shakaishugi* (July 1963): 14.

16 Taniguchi (1963): 37.

17 See, for example, Taiken (Mar. 1963): 8–17; Saitō Takashi, '"Taikoku" no ronri to "jinmin" no ronri' *Chūō Kōron* (Feb. 1963): 55–6; Yamazaki Taketoshi, 'Chū-So tairitsu to Soren keizai no haikei' *Ronsō* (Mar. 1963): 16; Nakano Sumio, 'Chū-So ronsō ni kan suru ichikōsatsu' *Tairiku Mondai* (May 1963): 53; Nomura (1963): 10; Ikeyama (1963): 119–20; Aichi Kiichi, et al., 'Watashi wa kō handan suru' *Chūō Kōron* (Mar. 1963): 152–3; Ishikawa Tadao, 'Chū-So kankei no tenbō' *Kyōsanken Mondai* (May 1963): 33; Saitō Takashi, et al., 'Chū-So ronsō to gendai' *Sekai* (Mar. 1963): 36–68.

18 Taniguchi (1963): 37; Morinaga Kazuhiko, 'Shiro to kiiro no arasoi?' *Sekai Shūhō* (16 July 1963): 13.

19 Hirota Yōji, 'Mo Takutō ni kenri to tsugi ni kuru mono' *Ronsō* (May 1963): 7–10, 29.

20 See, Harako Rinjirō, 'Wakai no chō mienu Chū-So ronsō' *Sekai Shūhō* (12 Mar. 1963): 14; Yamazaki (Mar. 1963): 22; Ishikawa (1963): 29–38; Yamazaki Isao, 'Chū-So ronsō ni okeru jakkan no shudai' *Shisō* (Feb. 1963): 71; Harako Rinjirō, 'Bunretsu o fukameru sekai kyōsanshugi undō' *Ronsō* (Mar. 1963): 29–30. Interestingly, Harako considered the current rift only a partial vindication of the 'Titoisation' theories of the early 1950s, because Chinese nationalism was not content simply to break away from the Socialist bloc, it wanted to lead it.

21 See, for example, Shiina Rinzō in Aichi (1963): 155.

22 Hirota (May 1963): 22–3.

23 Mori (Mar. 1963): 14; Asahi Shimbun Chōsa Kenkyūshitsu, *Chū-So ronsō* (30 June 1963): 28.

24 See, Okuno Shintarō, in Aichi (1963): 152, Nishikawa Ichirō, 'Chū-So ronsō no kōsei' *Gekkan Shakaitō* (Mar. 1963): 91, Ishidō (1963): 14, Eguchi Bokurō, 'Chū-So ronsō to Nihonjin no tachiba' *Chūō Kōron* (July 1963): 48–57.

25 Satō (Mar.1963): 104, 110.

26 Kamei Katsuichirō, in Aichi (1963): 153.

27 See: Atsugi Morio, 'Chū-So ronsō no gendai to kaiko' *Rōdō Keizai Junpo* (11 Feb. 1963): 22; Fujita Shōzō and Takeuchi Yoshinori, both in Saitō, et al. (1963): 49, 64.

28 Ikeyama, in Yamada (1963): 55–6. For similar views see: Mitsuoka Gen, '"Chū-So ronsō" to Chūgoku zō' *Chūgoku Kenkyū Geppō* (May 1963): 1–22; Sakamoto Yoshikazu, 'Kakujidai no NitChū kankei' *Sekai* (June 1963): 21.

29 Taiken (Mar. 1963): 8–17.

30 '"Chū-So ronsō" Jimintō nimo tobihi' *Chūō Kōron* (Mar. 1963) 78. See Chapter 3.

31 Satō (Mar. 1963): 109; Fukuda, in Saitō, et al. (1963): 68.

32 Mitsuoka (1963): 1–22.
33 Shimizu Ikutarō, 'Chūgoku no kakubusō to Nihon' *Chūō Kōron* (Mar. 1963): 137.
34 Morinaga (1963): 12–13. See also Taiken (Mar. 1963): 17.
35 Ishidō (1963): 17, 20.
36 Ikeyama, in Yamada (1963): 49, 57. See also Nishikawa (1963): 91.
37 Ishidō (1963): 208.
38 Eguchi (July 1963): 48–50. See also Kurihara (1963): 43.
39 Saitō (Feb. 1963): 62–5; Saitō, et al. (1963): 63.
40 Asahi Shimbun Chōsa Kenkyūshitsu (June 1963): 29–30.
41 Fujita Shōzō in Saitō, et al. (1963): 49. See also Nomura (1963): 16.
42 Terasawa, et al. (1963): 105–6.
43 Taiken (Mar. 1963): 17.
44 Kawabata Osamu, 'Burujoa rondan ni okeru "Chū-So ronsō" to shūseishugisha no yakuwari' *Zenei* (May 1963): 22–9.
45 In June, the Prime Minister's Office asked nearly twice as many people a similar question—which bloc appeared militarily the stronger—and produced an almost identical result. Free world: 23%; Communist bloc: 13%; same: 26%; don't know: 38%. *Yoron chōsa nenkan* (1963): 69.
46 R.K. Jain, *China and Japan, 1949–80* (1981[A]) Oxford: 22.
47 P.A.N. Murthy, 'Japan's Changing Relations with People's China and the Soviet Union' *International Studies* (July 1965): 15.
48 *JTW* (31 Aug.; 14 Sept. 1963).
49 Jain (1981 A): 52, 69.
50 Robert Scalapino, *The Japanese Communist Movement, 1920–66* (1967) Berkeley: 163–4.
51 The Communist-controlled *Kyokutō* and *Nauka* bookshops in Kanda, Tokyo, also refused to stock Soviet publications. 'Sino-Soviet Split and Present Condition of JCP' *Japan Socialist Review* (1 Oct. 1963): 34
52 See Chapter 7.
53 See Chapter 3.
54 *JTW* (9 Nov. 1963).
55 *Nikkei Shimbun* (1 July 1963); *Asahi Shimbun* (22 June 1963); *Yomiuri Shimbun* (1 July 1963).
56 *JTW* (13 July 1963).
57 *Mainichi Shimbun* (7 Aug. 1963).
58 *Tōkyō Shimbun* (17 July 1963).
59 *Mainichi Shimbun* (15 July 1963). See also, *Sankei Shimbun* (23 July 1963).
60 *Asahi Shimbun* (6 Aug. 1963).
61 *Asahi Shimbun* (9 Sept. 1963).
62 *Mainichi Shimbun* (31 July 1963).
63 *Tōkyō Shimbun* (11 Sept. 1963).
64 *Sankei Shimbun* (23 July 1963).
65 *Sankei Shimbun* (30 Oct. 1963).
66 *JTW* (9 Nov. 1963).
67 See, for example, Somura Yasunobu, 'Chū-So tairitsu no kokusaiteki hamon' *Chūō Kōron* (Sept. 1963): 187.
68 Hayashi Kentarō, 'Chū-So ronsō no shinwa to genjitsu' *Jiyū* (Nov. 1963): 3.
69 He later became a member of the *Bōei Kenshūsho* (National Defence College) and an advisor to Prime Minister Satō Eisaku.

70 Wakaizumi Kei, *Amerika kara mita Soren to Chūkyō no shōrai oyobi Chū-So kankei* (8 Oct. 1963) LDP (internal party document.)
71 A possible exception was Saitō Takashi, who appeared to suggest that the rift basically came down to a disagreement over timing. 'Reisen no shindankai to nanboku mondai' *Sekai* (Jan. 1964): 130.
72 Taiken, 'Chū-So tairitsu no shōrai to sono eikyō' *Tairiku Mondai* (Sept. 1963): 21. See also: Nabeyama Sadachika, 'Chū-So ketsuretsu to Nihon no sayoku' *Keieisha* (Nov. 1963): 58; Mori Kyōzō, 'Bei-So sekkin to Chū-So no tairitsu' *Kokusai Mondai* (Sept. 1963): 18.
73 Iwamura Michio, '8 nenrai no Chū-So kankei' *Chūgoku Kenkyū Geppō* (Aug. 1963). See also: Eguchi Bokurō, 'Chū-So ronsō no rekishiteki igi to genzai no kokusai seiji ni okeru mondaiten' *Kokusai Mondai* (Sept. 1963): 5; Ichikawa Tajirō, 'Kokusai kyōsanshugi undō no nijū kōzō to Chū-So ronsō' *Kyōsanken Mondai* (Dec. 1963): 11.
74 '[Their] purpose is still to "bury" capitalism' he warned, the world was merely witnessing the 'agony of Communism's rebirth'. Kusano Fumio, 'Chū-So kankei no hitotsu no mikata' *Tairiku Mondai* (Nov. 1963): 23. See also Shigemori Tadashi, 'Chū-So kankei wa dō naru ka' *Tairiku Mondai* (Oct. 1963): 20.
75 Satō Noboru, 'Chū-So ronsō to Nihon no kakushin undō' *Chūō Kōron* (Sept. 1963): 194.
76 Interestingly, they blamed the rapid development of the ideological dispute into a national dispute on an 'almost complete lack of economic interdependence.' Satō Noboru and Sugita Masao, 'Chū-So ronsō to kokusai kyōsanshugi undō no shōrai' *Sekai* (Sept. 1963): 51–3, 56.
77 Satō (Sept. 1963): 194. Author and critic Yamakawa Kikue agreed that 'the demise of the Communist monolith...is a plus for the entire Socialist movement.' 'Kono me de mita Chū-So ronsō' *Bungei Shunju* (Sept. 1963): 87.
78 During 1973–7, Hayashi served as university president.
79 Hayashi (Nov. 1963): 9–11.
80 Shimizu Ikutarō, 'Atarashii rekishikan e no shuppatsu' *Chūō Kōron* (Dec. 1963): 36.
81 Inoki Masamichi, 'Kyōsanshugi to kokka no mondai' *Chūō Kōron* (Dec. 1963): 50.
82 Kusano (Nov. 1963): 22. See also, Taiken (Sept. 1963): 20–33, Eguchi (Sept. 1963): 4, Ichikawa (1963): 12.
83 *JTW* (10 Aug. 1963).
84 Mori (Sept. 1963): 12, 18–19.
85 Satō and Sugita (1963): 54.
86 Hayashi (Nov. 1963): 7.
87 Shigemori (1963): 23.
88 Mori Kyōzō, 'Nihon gaikō ni jishusei o motomu' *Jiyū* (Aug. 1963): 2–4. See also, Taiken (Sept. 1963): 31.
89 Wakaizumi (1963): 27, 32–3.
90 Satō (Sept. 1963): 201.
91 Mori (Aug. 1963): 2, 9. Nabeyama Sadachika noted how the actual Sino-Soviet rift differed from the Titoisation predicted by Yoshida and others back in 1950. Just when their argument had run out of steam 'China's intense struggle with the Soviet Union occurred.' Yet whereas 'Tito had an alternative and chose the US, Mao has no alternative', he would not come over to the West. Nabeyama (1963): 58. See also: Makiuchi Masao, 'Ajia ni okeru Chūkyō no seiryoku' *Kyōsanken Mondai* (Nov. 1963): 53; Kusano (Nov. 1963): 27.
92 *JTW* (10 Aug. 1963).

93 See, for example, Somura (1963): 190–2, Makiuchi (1963): 47–58, Mori (Sept. 1963): 18; Saitō (Jan. 1964): 131.
94 Somura (1963): 193.
95 Naikaku Chōsashitsu (1964): 52.
96 Shimizu Shinzō, 'Gendaishi no naka no waga kakushin seiryoku' *Sekai* (Nov. 1963): 112–3. See also: Satō (Sept. 1963): 194–201; Eguchi (Sept. 1963): 11,
97 Nabeyama (1963): 60.
98 Shimizu (Dec. 1963): 35.
99 Taiken (Sept. 1963): 32.
100 Taiken (Sept. 1963): 33.
101 Hayashi (Nov. 1963): 12.
102 Mishima Yukio, 'Tenka taihei no shisō' *Ronsō* (Sept. 1963): 40–2.
103 'The rift will become deeper' (48); 'the possibility of resolving the rift exists' (37); 'even a break in diplomatic relations is possible' or 'depending on circumstances a compromise is possible, but not for the foreseeable future' (12). Naikaku Chōsashitsu (1964): 51–2.
104 Makiuchi (1963): 51; Taiken (Sept. 1963): 27–8. See also: Kimura Hiroshi, 'Sakoku Sobieto no kaihō' *Chūō Kōron* (Dec. 1963): 92.
105 Shigemori (1963): 22.
106 Iwamura (Aug. 1963): 27; Shimizu (Nov. 1963): 111.
107 Wakaizumi (1963): 24.
108 Naikaku Chōsashitsu (1964): 50–1.
109 Satō and Sugita (1963): 52–3; Satō (Sept. 1963): 201.
110 Shimizu (Nov. 1963): 112.
111 Eguchi (Sept. 1963): 11.
112 *Tōyō Keizai Shimpō* (10 Aug. 1963).
113 Mori (Aug. 1963): 3, 6–7.
114 Hayashi Saburō, 'Jishu gaikō to bōei' *Keizai Ōrai* (Jan. 1964): 18–26.
115 Hayashi (1963): 5–9.
116 Taiken (Sept. 1963): 33.
117 *JTW* (29 Feb. 1964).
118 Jain (1981 A): 22.
119 30 million people ultimately signed the petition. Chae-Jin Lee, *Japan Faces China* (1976) Baltimore: 47–8.
120 Such undertakings became explicit in 1968. Kurt Radtke, *China's Relations with Japan, 1945–83* (1990) Manchester: 161; Nathaniel Thayer, 'Competition and Conformity', *Modern Japanese Organization and Decision-Making,* Ezra Vogel (ed.) (1979) Tokyo: 302.
121 *JTW* (23 May 1964); Murthy (1965): 15. See also, Chapter 5.
122 Sino-Soviet boundary negotiations had broken down two months earlier. Dennis Doolin, *Territorial Claims in the Sino-Soviet Conflict* (1965) Stanford: 42–4.
123 *JT* (2 Aug. 1964).
124 Doolin (1965): 47–57; William Griffith, *Sino-Soviet Relations, 1964–65* (1967) Cambridge, MA: 29–30
125 Doolin (1965): 68–72. He also suggested that the Habomais and Shikotan would be returned to Japan 'if the Americans will give back Okinawa'. Young C. Kim, *Japanese–Soviet Relations* (1974) Washington D.C.: 34. This did not please the Japanese government. *JTW* (26 Sept. 1964).
126 *Asahi Shimbun* (1 Apr. 1964).

127 *Sankei Shimbun* (2 Apr. 1964).

128 *Asahi Shimbun* (8 Apr. 1964).

129 Hirasawa Kazushige, 'Japan's Asian Policy' Lecture at the ANU, Canberra, 14 July 1964, A9564, 22/1, NAA. Later, however, Hirasawa claimed that he had just been trying to provoke Mikoyan to comment. Woodward to Horne, 20 July 1964, A1838, 3103/7/1/1, NAA.

130 *Yomiuri Shimbun* (13 July 1964).

131 See, for example, Kohtani Etsuo, 'Japan and the Sino-Soviet Conflict' *Bulletin of the Institute for the Study of the USSR* (Dec. 1964): 36 (The Japanese version was published in June 1964.)

132 Mutō Teiichi, 'Chūkyō ni tai suru warera no yūaikan' *Raito* (June 1964): 10.

133 Shimizu Ikutarō, 'Chū-So no hinkaku' *Chūō Kōron* (July 1964): 33, Taiken, 'Chū-So tairitsu no shindandan to sono eikyō' *Tairiku Mondai* (June 1964): 17, 24.

134 Doi Akio, 'Chū-So bunretsu to Nihon' *Tairiku Mondai* (Sept. 1964): 4.

135 Hayashi Kentarō, 'Sengoshi o dō miru Ka' *Chūō Kōron* (Sept. 1964): 82–4.

136 *Mainichi Shimbun* (25 Aug. 1964).

137 Asahi Shimbun Chōsa Kenkyūshitsu, *Chū-So taiketsu* (10 Aug. 1964): 35.

138 Tsuda Michio, '"Zenjinmin no kokka" ron hihan' *Yuibutsuron Kenkyū* (spring 1964): 5–18.

139 Nishi Yoshiyuki, 'Chū-So ronsō to Nihon no chishikijin' *Kikan Shakai Kagaku* (Sept. 1964): 256.

140 Shimizu (July 1964): 33.

141 Kohtani (1964): 37, Taiken (June 1964): 25. See also Mutō (1964): 11.

142 Taiken (June 1964): 25.

143 Doi (Sept. 1964): 7.

144 Kohtani (1964): 36–7. See also Nishi (1964): 252.

145 Mutō (1964): 10–13.

146 Kōsaka Masataka, 'Chūgoku mondai to wa nani ka' *Jiyū* (Apr. 1964): 39.

147 Tōyama Shigeki, 'The World and Japan' *Journal of Social and Political Ideas in Japan* (Apr. 1964): 111. Originally in Kinoshita Junji (ed.), *Chishikijin no shisō to kōdō* (1964).

148 Asahi Shimbun Chōsa Kenkyūshitsu (1964): 30–3.

149 Doi (Sept. 1964): 7.

150 Mutō (1964): 11–13.

151 Kōsaka (Apr. 1964): 45.

152 Kōsaka Masataka, 'Kaiyō kokka Nihon no kōsō' *Chūō Kōron* (Sept. 1964): 76–7.

153 Only eight months earlier, a group of Japanese Moscow correspondents had unanimously agreed that there was no likelihood of his stepping down. Tanihata Ryōzō, et al., 'Furushichofu no shidōryoku' *Chūō Kōron* (Feb. 1964): 258–75. On a possible reconciliation see *Asahi Shimbun* (16 Oct. 1964, evening); *JT* (25 Oct. 1964).

154 In December, one member of a *Taiken*-sponsored round-table discussion even suggested that Japan had provided the main channel linking the two! Takuya Kakuzō was referring to Shiga Yoshio's 'Nihon no koe' statement following his return from Moscow. Other participants pointed to domestic Soviet factors. Taiken, 'Chū-So kankei no kongo to sekai jōsei' *Tairiku Mondai* (Feb. 1965): 44. See Chapter 7.

155 Inoki Masamichi, 'Chū-So kankei no shindankai' *Kyōsanken Mondai* (Jan. 1965): 1–3.

156 Nakajima Mineo, 'Chū-So ronsō no shodanmen to gendai Marukusushugi' *Shisō* (Dec. 1964): 93; Sakamoto Koretada, 'Chū-So ronsō to kokkyō ryōdo mondai' *Kyōsanken Mondai* (Dec. 1964): 1–14; Ishidō Kiyotomo, 'Chū-So ronsō no tenbō' *Shisō no*

Kagaku (Nov. 1964): 76. Theories continued to proliferate in 1965: Shimizu Tōzō later blamed the 'root of the conflict' on 'Chinese chauvinism'. 'Sino-Soviet Polemics' *Review* (July 1965): 37. Onoe Masao pointed to Soviet efforts 'to preserve the Communist camp's unity' as a cause. 'Chū-So ronsō' *Rekishi Kyōiku* (Feb. 1966): 47. Uno Shigeaki claimed that 'US policy towards the Communist camp had an especially big influence'. 'Chū-So ronsō no dōkō' *Kokusai Mondai* (Jan. 1965): 22–9; a point hotly disputed by Doi Akio. Taiken (Feb. 1965): 44–53, 58.

157 'What do you think Sino-Soviet relations will be like in 1965?' 'Better' (17%), 'worse' (8%), 'no change' (24%), 'don't know' (51%). Sample: 2500, nationwide, Dec. 1964, *Jiji nenkan* (1966): 170.

158 'What do you think Sino-Soviet relations will be like in 1966?' 'Better' (3.6%), 'worse' (14.9%), 'no change' (27.7%), 'don't know' (53.8%). Sample: 2388, nationwide, Dec. 1965, *Yoron chōsa nenkan* (1965).

159 In May 1965, 811 Tokyo residents were asked 'how big an influence on the world did Khrushchev's retirement have?' 24% replied that it had a 'big influence' and another 35% 'some influence'. However, comparison with the figures for China's nuclear test—54% and 18% respectively—reveals that the latter was deemed to be of far greater significance. Also indicative was the response regarding the 'Vietnam problem': 62% and 17%. Tōkei Sūri Kenkyūjo, June 1965, *Yoron chōsa nenkan* (1965).

160 *Asahi Shimbun* (1 Nov. 1964).

161 'Increased danger' (29.4%), 'did not increase danger' (31.6%), 'don't know' (39.0%). *Shukan Jiji* (Nov. 1964).

162 'Japan–US Security Treaty should be strengthened' (22%), 'continue the Security Treaty as it is' (13%), 'conclude a Japan–US–USSR–PRC Non-aggression Pact' (12%), 'annul the Security Treaty and become an armed neutral' (10%), 'annul the Security Treaty and become a disarmed neutral' (8%), 'other' (1%), 'don't know' (34%). *Yoron chōsa nenkan* (1964).

163 *JT* (20 Dec. 1964).

164 Wakaizumi Kei, 'Chūgoku no kakubusō to Nihon no anzen hoshō' *Chūō Kōron* (Feb. 1966): 64.

165 Mushakōji Kinhide, 'Tachūshinshugi to Bei-Chū reisen no aida' *Asahi Jānaru* (18 Oct. 1964): 25. Also in, Utsunomiya Tokuma, et al., 'Chūgoku no nashonaru intaresuto' *Gendai no Me* (Nov. 1964): 87.

166 Kamiya Fuji, 'Nihon gaikō no "ririku" no tame ni' *Ushio* (Mar. 1965): 72.

167 Irie Michimasa, 'Chūkyō no kakuhoyū to Nihon no anzen hoshō' *Jiyū* (Dec. 1964): 83.

168 Kōsaka Masataka, 'Kokusai seiji no tagenka to Nihon' *Chūō Kōron* (Dec. 1964): 94–107.

169 Taiken (Feb. 1965): 44–61.

170 Utsunomiya, et al. (1964): 86.

171 'It has a rift (*tairitsu*) with the Soviet Union' (64.1%), 'It is not a free country (it is ruled by a Communist Party)' (68.1%), 'It does not have diplomatic relations with Japan' (54.1%), 'It is not a member of the UN' (54.1%), 'It has exploded nuclear weapons' (80%) 'It undergoes the Cultural Revolution' (69.4%). Asked to compare China and the Soviet Union, 16.2% liked China, 11.2% the Soviet Union, 2.3% liked both, 15.6% disliked both, and the rest could not say. However, this disguises an interesting generation gap: people over-40 liked China two-to-three times as much as the Soviet Union, people in their thirties only 2.3% more, and those in their twenties preferred the Soviet Union by 19.4% to 9.4%. Sample: 3000, nationwide, 24–5 June

1967, Kyōdō Tsūshinsha in 'Nihonjin no Chūgokukan' *Ajia Keizai Junpō* (Aug. 1967): 23–5.

172 Iida Momo, '"Chū-So ronsō" no shironteki bunkaronteki imi' *Shisō no Kagaku* (Nov. 1964): 86–99.

173 See, for example, Miyamoto Yoshio, *Chū-So ronsō no gairyaku to hihan* (1966); Kikuchi Masanori, et al., *Chū-So tairitsu* (1976); Kazawa Gō, *Chū-So tairitsu to sono haikei* (1978); Nakajima Mineo, *Chū-So tairitsu to gendai* (1978).

Bibliography

Official Publications

Chinese Government, *Oppose the Revival of Japanese Militarism* (1960) Foreign Languages Press, Beijing.

Japanese Government, Gaimushō, 'Sensō to heiwa no mondai ni kan suru Chū-So no kenkai' [Sino-Soviet Views Regarding the Issue of War and Peace] *Gaimushō Chōsa Geppō* (Mar. 1961) II(3): 26–53.

Japanese Government, Gaimushō, 'Statement Issued by the Foreign Office for the Purpose of Clarifying Japan's Position in the Korean Conflict' *Contemporary Japan* (July/Sept. 1950) 19(3): 463–69.

Japanese Government, Gaimushō, Ajia Kyoku, Chūgoku ka, *NitChū kankei kihon shiryōshū* [Basic Sources on Japan–China Relations] (1970) Kazankai.

Japanese Government, Gaimushō, Gaikō Shiryōkan, *Nihon gaikōshi jiten* [Dictionary of Japanese Diplomatic History] (1992) Yamakawa Shuppansha.

Japanese Government, Gaimushō, *Gaimushō Nenkan* [MOFA Yearbook] (Various years) Gaimushō.

Japanese Government, Gaimushō, Kokusai Shiryōbu, Shiryōka, 'Chū-So ronsō' [The Sino-Soviet Dispute] *Gaimushō Chōsa Geppō* (Aug./Sept. 1963) 4(8–9): 60–116.

Japanese Government, Gaimushō, Kokusai Shiryōbu, Shiryōka, 'Chū-So ronsō' [The Sino-Soviet Dispute] *Gaimushō Chōsa Geppō* (June 1964) 5(6): 69–111.

Japanese Government, Gaimushō, Kokusai Shiryōbu/Ōa Kyōkai, *Chū-So ronsō shuyō bunken shū* [Collected Documents on the Sino-Soviet Ideological Dispute, 1950–77] (1967–78: 4 volumes), Nikkan Rōdō Tsūshinsha/Hokutō Shuppan.

Japanese Government, Gaimushō, *Press Releases* (Annual, various years) Gaimushō.

Japanese Government, Gaimushō, *Waga gaikō no kinkyō/Gaikō seisho* [Diplomatic Bluebook] (1957–66: Annual) Gaimushō.

Japanese Government, Naikaku Chōsashitsu, '"Chū-So ronsō" no honshitsu' [The Essence of the 'Sino-Soviet Dispute'] *Chōsa Geppō* (Feb. 1961) 6(2): 1–10.

Japanese Government, Naikaku Chōsashitsu, 'Gendankai ni okeru So-Chū ronsō no shuyō ronten' [The Main Points at Issue in the Current Stage of the Sino-Soviet Dispute] *Chōsa Geppō* (Mar. 1963) 8(3): 50–65.

Japanese Government, Naikaku Chōsashitsu, 'NisSo [sic] ronsō ni tai suru kokunai no hannō' [Japanese Reactions to the Japan[sic]–Soviet Dispute] *Chōsa Geppō* (Aug. 1964) 9(8): 44–60.

Japanese Government, Naikaku Chōsashitsu, 'So-Chū kan no "ideorogii-ronsō" ni tsuite' [Concerning the 'Ideological Dispute' Between China and the Soviet Union] *Chōsa Geppō* (Oct. 1960) 5(10): 1–15.

Japanese Government, Naikaku Sōri-daijin Kanbō Kōhōshitsu, *Yoron chōsa nenkan* [Opinion Poll Yearbook] (Annual, various years) Ōkurashō Insatsuyoku.

U.S. Central Intelligence Agency, *C.I.A. Research Reports: China, 1946–76* (1982) UPA, Frederick, MD. (Microfilm).

U.S. Central Intelligence Agency, *C.I.A. Research Reports: Japan, Korea and the Security of Asia, 1946–76* (1983) UPA, Bethesda, MD. (Microfilm).

U.S. Government, *Declassified Documents Reference Series* (1975: Annual) Research Publications, Woodbridge, CT. (Microfiche).

U.S. Government, *John F. Kennedy National Security Files—Asia and the Pacific, 1961–63* (1993) UPA, Bethesda, MD. (Microfilm).

U.S. Government, *Lyndon B. Johnson, National Security Files—Asia and the Pacific, 1963–69* (1993) UPA, Bethesda, MD. (Microfilm).

U.S. Government, *Lyndon B. Johnson, National Security Files—USSR and Eastern Europe, 1961–63* (1993) UPA, Bethesda, MD. (Microfilm).

U.S. Government, *National Security Archive: The Cuban Missile Crisis, 1962* (1990) Chadwyck–Healey, Alexandria, VA.

U.S. House of Representatives, Committee on Foreign Affairs, Subcommittee on the Far East and the Pacific, *Report on the Sino-Soviet Conflict and its Implications* (14 May 1965) House Document 237, Washington D.C.

U.S. Office of Strategic Services/State Department, *OSS/State Dept. Intelligence and Research Reports, VIII—Japan, Korea, South–east Asia and the Far East Generally: 1950–61 Supplement* (1979) UPA, Washington, D.C. (Microfilm).

U.S. Office of Strategic Services/State Department, *OSS/State Dept. Intelligence and Research Reports, IX—China and India, 1950–61 Supplement* (1979) UPA, Washington, D.C. (Microfilm).

U.S. Office of Strategic Services/State Department, *OSS/State Dept. Intelligence and Research Reports, XI—Soviet Union, 1950–61 Supplement* (1979) UPA, Washington, D.C. (Microfilm).

U.S. State Department, *Confidential U.S. State Dept. Central Files—China, Internal and Foreign Affairs, 1950–59* (1985–87) UPA, Bethesda, MD. (Microfilm).

U.S. State Department, *Confidential U.S. State Dept. Central Files—Far East, Internal and Foreign Affairs, 1945–59* (1991) UPA, Bethesda, MD. (Microfilm).

U.S. State Department, *Confidential U.S. State Dept. Central Files—Japan, Internal Affairs, 1950–59* (1985) UPA, Bethesda, MD. (Microfilm).

U.S. State Department, *Confidential U.S. State Dept. Central Files—Soviet Union, Foreign Affairs, 1945–59* (1989) UPA, Bethesda, MD. (Microfilm).

U.S. State Department, *Confidential U.S. State Dept. Special Files—Japan, 1947–56* (1990) UPA, Bethesda, MD. (Microfilm).

U.S. State Department, *Confidential U.S. State Dept. Special Files—North–East Asia, 1943–56* (1990) UPA, Bethesda, MD. (Microfilm).

U.S. State Department, *Foreign Relations of the United States [FRUS]* (Annual, various volumes 1949–64) United States Government Publications Office, Washington, D.C.

U.S. State Department, *Records of the U.S. State Dept. related to U.S. Political Relations with Japan, 1950–59* (1987–9) Scholarly Resources, Wilmington, Del. (Microfilm).

U.S. State Department, *Records of the U.S. State Dept. related to Political Relations of Japan, 1955–59* (1989) Scholarly Resources, Wilmington, Del. (Microfilm).

U.S. State Department, *State Department Bulletin* (Various issues) Washington D.C.

Memoirs

Allison, John M. *Ambassador from the Prairie or Allison Wonderland* (1973) Houghton Miffin, Boston, MA.

Fujiyama Aiichirō, *Seiji waga michi* [My Political Path] (1976) Asahi Shimbunsha.

Furui Yoshimi, *NitChū jūhachi nen—isseijika no kiseki to tenbō* [Eighteen Years of Japan–China [Relations]: One Politician's Tracks and Prospects] (1978) Makino Shuppan.

Hatoyama Ichirō, *Hatoyama Ichirō kaikoroku* [Hatoyama Ichirō's Memoirs] (1957) Bungei Shunjū.

Ikeda Daisaku, *Chūgoku no ningen kakumei* [China's People's Revolution] (1974) Mainichi Shimbunsha.

Ikeda Masanosuke, *Nazo no kuni—Chūkyō tairiku no jittai* [Enigmatic Country: The True State of Continental China] (1969) Jiji Press.

Kennan, George F. *Memoirs, 1925–50* (1961) Atlantic, Little, Brown, Boston, MA.

Kennan, George F. *Memoirs, 1950–63* (1972) Little, Brown and Co., Boston, MA.

Khrushchev, N.S. *Khrushchev Remembers: The Glasnost Tapes* (1990) Little, Brown and Co., Boston, MA.

Nakasone Yasuhiro, *The Making of the New Japan* (1999) Curzon, Richmond, Surrey.

Ogawa Heishirō, *Chichi no Chūgoku to watashi no Chūgoku* [My Father's China and Mine] (Nov. 1990) Simul Press.

Okada Akira, *Mizutori gaikō hiwa—aru gaikōkan no shōgen* [The Secret History of Duck Diplomacy: A Diplomat's Testimony] (1983) Chūō Kōronsha.

Reischauer, Edwin O. *My Life between Japan and America* (1986) Charles Tuttle, Tokyo.

Tagawa Seiichi, *NitChū kōshō hiroku—Tagawa nikki—14 nen no shōgen* [A Secret Record of Japan–China Trade Negotiations: Tagawa's Diary—A 14–Year Testimony] (1973) Mainichi Shimbunsha, Toyko.

Utsunomiya Tokuma, *NitChū kankei no genjitsu* [The Reality of Japan–China Relations] (1963) Keisō Shobō.

Yoshida Shigeru, *Japan's Decisive Century, 1867–1967* (1967) Praeger, NY.

Yoshida Shigeru, *Kaisō jūnen* [Recollections of Ten Years] (1957–8) Shinchōsha.

Yoshida Shigeru, *The Yoshida Memoirs* (1962) Houghton Miffin, Boston, MA.

Monographs

ABC-Clio Information Services, *The Sino-Soviet Conflict: A Historical Bibliography* (1985) ABC-Clio, Santa Barbra, CA.

Ambroz, Oton, *The Realignment of World Power—the Russia–China Schism* (1972) Robert Speller, NY.

Andō Jinbē and Nishikawa Ichirō, *Furushichofu to Mō Takutō—Chū-So ronsō no mondaiten* [Khrushchev and Mao Zedong: Controversies in the Sino-Soviet Dispute] (30 June 1963) Gōdō Shuppansha.

Armour, Andrew J.L. (ed.) *Asia and Japan: The Search for Modernization and Identity* (1985) Athlone Press, London.

Asada Sadao, *International Studies in Japan: A Bibliographical Guide* (1986) Japan Institute of International Affairs, Tokyo.

Asahi Shimbun Chōsa Kenkyūshitsu, *Chū-So ronsō* [The Sino-Soviet Ideological Dispute] (30 June 1963) Asahi Shimbunsha.

Asahi Shimbun Chōsa Kenkyūshitsu, *Chū-So taiketsu* [The Sino-Soviet Confrontation] (10 Aug. 1964) Asahi Shimbunsha.

Asahi Shimbun, *Asahi nenkan* [Asahi Yearbook] (Annual) Asahi Shimbunsha.

Asahi Shimbun, *Gendai Nihon Asahi jinbutsu jiten* [Asahi's Who's Who of Modern Japan] (Dec. 1990) Asahi Shimbunsha.

Axelbank, Albert, *Black Star over Japan: Rising Forces of Militarism* (1972) Tuttle, Tokyo.

Baerwald, Hans H. *Party Politics in Japan* (1986) Allen and Unwin, Winchester, MA.

Ball, Desmond, Politics and Force Levels (1990) University of California, Berkeley, CA.

Barnds, William J. *The United States and Japan: Challenges and Opportunities* (1979) CFR/New York University Press, NY.

Barnett, A. Doak (ed.) *Communist Strategies in Asia: A Comparative Analysis of Governments and Parties* (1963) Praeger, NY.

Barnett, A. Doak, *China and the Major Powers in East Asia* (1977) The Brookings Institution, Washington D.C.

Barnett, A. Doak, *Communist China and Asia: A Challenge to American Policy* (1960) CFR/Vintage Books, NY.

Beckman, George M. and Okubo Genji, *The Japanese Communist Party 1922–1945* (1969) Stanford University Press, Stanford, CA.

Bedeski, Robert E. *The Fragile Entente: The 1978 Japan–China Peace Treaty in a Global Context* (1983) Westview Press, Boulder, CO.

Berton, P., P.F. Langer and G.F. Totten (eds), *The Russian Impact on Japan: Literature and Social Thought* (1981) University of Southern California Press, Los Angeles, CA.

Boorman, Howard L., Alexander Eckstein, Philip E. Mosely and Benjamin Schwartz, *Moscow-Peking Axis: Strengths and Strains* (1957) CFR/Harper, NY.

Borisov, O.B. and B.T. Koloskov, *Soviet–Chinese Relations 1945–70* (1975) Indiana University Press, Bloomington, IN.

Borton, Hugh, Jerome B. Cohen, William J. Jorden, Donald Keene, Paul F. Langer and C. Martin Wilbur, *Japan Between East and West* (1957) CFR/Harper, NY.

Brzezinski, Zbigniew, *The Fragile Blossom: Crisis and Change in Japan*, Harper and Row, NY (1972).

Buchan, Alastair, *The End of the Postwar Era: A New Balance of World Power* (1974) Weidenfeld and Nicolson, London.

Buck, James H. (ed.) *The Modern Japanese Military System* (1975) Sage Pubs, Beverly Hills, CA.

Buckley, Roger, *US–Japan Alliance Diplomacy, 1945–90* (1992) Cambridge University Press, Cambridge.

Bull, Hedley, *The Anarchical Society: A Study of Order in World Politics* (1977) Macmillan, London.

Burkman, Thomas (ed.) *The Occupation of Japan: The International Context* (1984) MacArthur Memorial Foundation, Norfolk, VA.

Cary, James, *Japan Today: Reluctant Ally* (1963) Pall Mall Press, London.

Chang, Gordon, H. *Friends and Enemies: the United States, China and the Soviet Union, 1948–72* (1990) Stanford University Press, Stanford, CA.

Chapin, William, *The Asian Balance of Power: An American View* (Apr. 1967) (Adelphi Paper 35) IISS, London.

Chapman, J.W.M., R. Drifte, and I.T.M. Gow, *Japan's Quest for Comprehensive National Security: Defence, Diplomacy, Dependence* (1983) Frances Pinter, London.

Chung, Chin O. *Pyongyang between Peking and Moscow: North Korea's Involvement in the Sino-Soviet Dispute, 1958–75* (1978) University of Alabama Press, AL.

Clough, R.N. *East Asia and US Security* (1975) Brookings Institution, Washington D.C.

Cohen, Warren I. (ed.) *Pacific Passage: The Study of American–East Asian Relations on the Eve of the Twenty–First Century* (1996) Columbia University Press, NY.

Cohen, Warren I. and Iriye Akira (eds), *The Great Powers in East Asia, 1953–60* (1990) Columbia University Press, NY.

Cole, Allan and Nakanishi Naomichi (eds), *Japanese Opinion Polls with Socio-Political Significance, 1947–1957* (1958) Tufts University, Medford, MA.

Cole, Allan B., George O. Totten and Cecil H. Uyehara, *Socialist Parties in Postwar Japan* (1966) Yale University Press, New Haven, CT.

Coox, A.D. and H. Conroy (eds), *China and Japan Search for Balance since World War One* (1978) ABC-Clio, Santa Barbara, CA.

Crankshaw, Edward, *The New Cold War: Moscow v. Pekin* (1963) Penguin Books, Middlesex.

Curtis, Gerald L. *The Japanese Way of Politics* (1988) Columbia University Press, NY.

Dittmer, Lowell, *Sino-Soviet Normalization and its International Implications, 1945–90* (1992) University of Washington Press, WA.

Doolin, Dennis J. *Territorial Claims in the Sino-Soviet Conflict: Documents and Analysis* (1965) Hoover Institution Press, Stanford, CA.

Dower, John C. *Empire and Aftermath: Yoshida Shigeru and the Japanese Experience, 1878–1954* (1979) Harvard University Press, Cambridge, MA.

Drifte, Reinhard, *Japanese Foreign Policy* (1989) Royal Institute of International Affairs, London.

Drifte, Reinhard, *Japan's Foreign Policy for the 21st Century: From Economic Superpower to What Power?* (1998) St. Antony's/Macmillan, Basingstoke.

Drifte, Reinhard, *The Security Factor in Japan's Foreign Policy, 1945–52* (1983) Saltire Press, Ripe, E. Sussex.

Duus, Peter (ed.) *The Cambridge History of Japan: Volume 6, The Twentieth Century* (1988) Cambridge University Press, Cambridge.

Edstrom, Bert, *Japan's Evolving Foreign Policy Doctrine: From Yoshida to Miyazawa* (1999) Macmillan, Basingstoke.

Ellingworth, Richard, *Japanese Economic Policies and Security* (Oct. 1972) (Adelphi Paper 90) IISS, London.

Ellison, Herbert J. (ed.) *Japan and the Pacific Quadrille: The Major Powers in East Asia* (1987) Westview Press, Boulder, CO.

Ellison, Herbert J. *The Sino-Soviet Conflict: A Global Perspective* (1982) University of Washington Press, WA.

Ellison, Herbert J. *The Soviet Union and North East Asia* (1989) University Press of America, Lanham, MD.

Emmerson, J.K. *Arms, Yen and Power: The Japanese Dilemma* (1971) Dunellen, NY.

Ferguson, Anthony, *Far Eastern Politics: China, Japan, Korea, 1950–75. An Index to International Political Science Abstracts Volumes 1–25* (1977) IPSA, Paris.

Finn, Richard B., *Winners in Peace: MacArthur, Yoshida and Postwar Japan* (1992) University of California Press, Berkeley, CA.

Floyd, David, *Mao Against Khrushchev* (1964) Praeger, NY.

Forsberg, Aaron, *America and the Japanese Miracle: The Cold War Context of Japan's Postwar Economic Revival, 1950–1960* (2000) University of North Carolina Press, Chapel Hill, NC.

Frankel, Joseph, *International Relations in a Changing World* (1979) (3rd ed.) OPUS, Oxford.

Frankel, Joseph, *The Making of Foreign Policy: An Analysis of Decision Making* (1962) Oxford University Press, Oxford.

Fukui Haruhiro, *Party in Power: The Japanese Liberal Democrats and Policy-making* (1970) University of California Press, Berkeley, CA.

Fukui Haruhiro, *US–Japan Consultations on Defense Cooperation* (Jan. 1983) UN Association of America, NY.

Furukawa Mantarō, *NitChū sengo kankeishi* [A History of Post-War Japan–China Relations] (1981) Hara Shobō.

Gaddis, John Lewis, *The Long Peace: Inquiries into the History of the Cold War* (1987) Oxford University Press, NY.

Gaddis, John Lewis, *We Now Know: Rethinking Cold War History* (1997) Clarendon Press, Oxford.

Gallicchio, Marc S. *The Cold War Begins in East Asia* (1988) Columbia University Press, NY.

Gartoff, Raymond L. (ed.) *Sino-Soviet Military Relations* (1966) Praeger, NY.

Giffard, Sydney, *Japan Among the Powers, 1890–1990* (1994) Yale University Press, New Haven, CT.

Gittings, John, *Survey of the Sino-Soviet Dispute, 1963–1967* (1968) Oxford University Press, Oxford.

Goncharov, Sergei N, John W. Lewis, and Xue Litai, *Uncertain Partners: Stalin, Mao, and the Korean War* (1993) Stanford University Press, Stanford, CA.

Goodby, James E., Vladimir I. Ivanov, Shimotamai Nobuo (eds), *"Northern Territories" and Beyond: Russian, Japanese and American Perspectives* (1995) Praeger, Westport, CT.

Gotoda Teruo, *The Local Politics of Kyoto* (1985) (Japan Research Monograph 7), Institute of East Asian Studies, University of California Press, Berkeley, CA.

Grant, Richard L. (ed.), *The Process of Japanese Foreign Policy: Focus on Asia* (1997) Royal Institute of International Affairs, London.

Greene, Fred, *Stresses in US–Japan Security Relations* (1975) Brookings Institute, Washington, D.C.

Griffith, William E. *Albania and the Sino-Soviet Rift* (1963) MIT Press, Cambridge, MA.

Griffith, William E. *Peking, Moscow and Beyond: The Sino-Soviet-American Triangle* (1973) (Washington Papers 6) Sage Publications, Beverly Hills, CA.

Griffith, William E. *Sino-Soviet Relations, 1964–65* (1967) MIT Press, Cambridge, MA.

Griffith, William E. *The Sino-Soviet Rift* (1964) Allen and Unwin, London.

Griffith, William E. *The World and the Great Power Triangles* (1975) MIT Press, Cambridge, MA.

Halperin, Morton H. *China and the Bomb* (1965) Praeger, NY.

Halperin, Morton H. *Sino-Soviet Relations and Arms Control* (1967) MIT Press, Cambridge, MA.

Halpern, A.M. (ed.), *Policies Toward China; Views from Six Continents* (1965) McGraw Hill, NY.

Hamaguchi-Klenner, Makiko, *China Images of Japanese Conservatives (LDP)* (1981) Mitteilungen de Institute fur Asien Kunde (123), Hamburg.

Hara Kimie, *Japanese–Soviet/Russian Relations since 1945* (1998) Nissan Institute/ Routledge, London.

Harding, Harry, *China and North–east Asia: The Political Dimension* (1989) University Press of America, Lanham, MD.

Hasegawa Tsuyoshi, Jonathan Haslam, and Andrew C. Kuchins, *Russia and Japan: An Unresolved Dilemma between Distant Neighbors* (1993) International and Area Studies, University of California, Berkeley, CA.

Hasegawa Tsuyoshi, *The Northern Territories Dispute and Russo-Japanese Relations* (1998) International and Areas Studies, University of California, Berkeley, CA.

Havens, Thomas R.H. *Fire Across the Sea: The Vietnam War and Japan, 1965–75* (1987) Princeton University Press, NJ.

Hellmann, D.C. *Japan and East Asia: The New International Order* (1972) Praeger, NY.

Hellmann, D.C. *Japanese Foreign Policy and Domestic Politics: The Peace Agreement with the Soviet Union* (1969) University of California Press, Berkeley, CA.

Hinton, H. C. *China's Turbulent Quest* (1972) Indiana University Press, Bloomington, IN.

Hinton, H.C. *The Bear at the Gate: Chinese Policy-making under Soviet Pressure* (1971) AEI-Hoover Policy Studies, Stanford, CA.

Hinton, H.C. *Three and a Half Powers: The New Balance in Asia* (1975) Indiana University Press, Bloomington, IN.

Hirano Yoshitarō, *Gendai Chūgoku to Chū-So kankei* [Contemporary China and Sino-Soviet Relations] (15 Jan. 1965) Keisō Shobō.

Hohenberg, John, *New Era in the Pacific: An Adventure in Public Diplomacy* (1972) Simon and Schuster, NY.

Holbraad, Carsten, *Superpowers and International Conflict* (1979) Macmillan, London.

Holsti, K.J. *International Politics: A Framework for Analysis* (1974) (2nd ed.) Prentice Hall, London.

Holsti, Ole P., P. Terrence Hopmann, and John D. Sullivan, *Unity and Disintegration in International Alliances: Comparative Studies* (1973) Wiley, NY.

Hosoya Chihiro (ed.), *Japan and Postwar Diplomacy in the Asia–Pacific Region* (1984) International University Japan, Niigata.

Howe, Christopher (ed.), *China and Japan: History, Trends and Prospects* (1996) Clarendon Press, Oxford.

Hsueh Chun-tu (ed.) *Dimensions in China's Foreign Relations* (1978) Praeger, NY.

Hudson, G.F., R. Lowenthal, and R. Mac Farquhar (eds), *The Sino-Soviet Dispute* (1961) China Quarterly, London.

Hunter, Janet E. *Concise Dictionary of Modern Japanese History* (1984) Kodansha, Tokyo.

Inoguchi Takashi and Daniel I. Okimoto (eds), *The Political Economy of Japan: Volume 2, The Changing International Context* (1988) Stanford University Press, Stanford, CA.

Inoguchi Takashi, *Japan's International Relations* (1991) Pinter, London.

Institute for the Study of Conflict, *Japan's Triangular Diplomacy* (1981) I.S.C, London.

Iriye Akira (ed.), *Mutual Images: Essays in American–Japanese Relations* (1972) Harvard University Press, Cambridge, MA.

Iriye Akira (ed.), *The Chinese and the Japanese* (1980) Princeton University Press, Princeton.

Iriye Akira and Warren I. Cohen (eds), *The United States and Japan in the Postwar World* (1989) University Press of Kentucky, Lexington, KT.

Iriye Akira, *Across the Pacific: An Inner History of American–East Asian Relations* (1967) Harcourt Brace and Wold, NY.

Ishidō Kiyotomo, *Chū-So ronsō ron—futatsu no shisō e no apurōchi* [A Theory of the Sino-Soviet Dispute: The Two Ideologies Approach] (20 July 1963) Aoki Shoten.

Ishii Akira, *Chū-So kankeishi no kenkyū, 1945–1950* [A History of Sino-Soviet Relations, 1945–50] (1990) Tokyo University Press.

Ishikawa Tadao, Nakajima Mineo and Ikei Masaru (eds) *Sengo shiryō: NitChū kankei* [Postwar Materials: Japan–China Relations] (1970) Nihon Hyōronsha.

Ishikawa Tadao, *Nihon no kokueki to Chūgoku no kokueki* [Japan's National Interest and China's National Interest] (1966) Ajia Chōsakai.

Ishikawa Tadao, *NitChū mondai shiken* [A Personal View of Japan–China Relations] (15 May 1973) Sakai Shoten.

Itoh Hiroshi (ed.), *Japan's Foreign Policy Making* (1982) State University of NY, Buffalo, NY.

Iwanaga Kazuki, *Images, Decisions and Consequences in Japan's Foreign Policy* (1993) Lund University Press, Lund, Sweden.

Jacobsen, C.G. *Sino-Soviet Relations since Mao: The Chairman's Legacy* (1981) Praeger, NY.

Jain, R.K. *China and Japan, 1949–80* (1981) (2nd ed.) Martin Robertson, Oxford.

Jain, R.K. *Japan's Postwar Peace Settlements* (1978) Radiant, New Delhi.

Jain, R.K. *The USSR and Japan, 1945–80* (1981) Radiant, New Delhi.

Jansen, Marius B. *Japan and China from War to Peace, 1892–1972* (1975) ABC-Clio Press, Santa Barbara, CA.

Jansen, Marius B. *Japan and Communist China in the Next Decade* (Dec. 1962) General Electric Co, Santa Barbara, CA.

Japan Center for International Exchange, *The Silent Power: Japan's Identity and World Role* (1976) Simul Press, Tokyo.

Jervis, Robert, *The Logic of Images in International Relations* (1970) Princeton University Press, Princeton, NJ.

Jiji Tsūshinsha, *Jiji nenkan* [Jiji Yearbook] (Annual, various years) Jiji Tsūshinsha.

Johnson, Chalmers, *MITI and the Japanese Miracle: The Growth of Industrial Policy, 1925–1975* (1982) Stanford University Press, Stanford, CA.

Jones, Peter, and Sian Kevill, *China and the Soviet Union, 1949–84* (1985) Longman, Harlow, Essex.

Jukes, Geoffrey, *The Soviet Union in Asia* (1973) Angus and Robertson, Sydney.

Kaplan, Morton A. and Mushakoji Kinhide, *Japan, America, and the Future World Order* (1976) University of Chicago/The Free Press, NY.

Kataoka Tetsuya (ed.), *Creating Single-Party Democracy: Japan's Postwar Political System* (1992) Hoover Institution Press, Stanford, CA.

Kataoka Tetsuya, *The Price of a Constitution: The Origins of Japan's Post-war Politics* (1991) Crane Russak, NY.

Katz, Joshua D. and Tilly C. Friedman-Lichtschein (eds), *Japan's New World Role* (1985) Westview Press, Boulder, CO.

Kawahara Hiroshi and Fujii Shōzō, *Nitchū kankeishi no kiso chishiki* [A Basic History of Japan–China Relations] (1974) Yūhikaku.

Kazawa Gō, *Chū-So tairitsu to sono haikei* [The Sino-Soviet Rift and its Background] (1978) Kyōikusha.

Kenkyūsha, *New Japanese–English Dictionary* (1974) Kenkyūsha, Tokyo.

Kennedy, Paul, *The Rise and Fall of the Great Powers* (1988) Fontana Press, London.

Kesavan, K.V. *Contemporary Japanese Politics and Foreign Policy* (1989) Radiant, New Delhi.

Kiire Ryō, *NisSo bōeki no rekishi* [A History of Japan–Soviet Trade] (10 Apr. 1983) Ningensha.

Kikuchi Masanori, Hakamada Shigeki, Shishido Yukata and Yabuki Susumu, *Chū-So tairitsu—sono kiban, rekishi, riron* [The Sino-Soviet Rift: Its Foundation, History and Theory] (30 Sept. 1976) Yūhikaku.

Kim, Ilpyong J. (ed.), *The Strategic Triangle: China, the United States and the Soviet Union* (1987) Paragon House, NY.

Kim, Young C. *Japanese–Soviet Relations: Interaction of Politics, Economics and National Security* (1974) (The Washington Papers II) Center for Strategic and International Studies, Georgetown University/Sage Publications, Washington D.C./Beverley Hills, CA.

Kodansha, *Japan: An Illustrated Encyclopedia* (1993) Kodansha, Tokyo.

Kosaka Masataka, *Options for Japan's Foreign Policy* (1973) (Adelphi Paper 97) IISS, London.

Koyama Uchihiro, *Sino-Soviet War* (1973) Tokyo Journal Centre, Tokyo.

Kurzman, Dan, *Kishi and Japan: The Search for the Sun* (1960) Ivan Obolensky, NY.

Kutakov, E.E. *NisSo gaikō kankeishi* [A History of Japan–Soviet Diplomacy] (1969) Tōkō Shoin [orig. (1962) Moscow].
Labedz, L. and G.R. Urban (eds), *The Sino-Soviet Conflict: 11 Radio Discussions* (1965) Bodley Head, London.
Lach, D.F. and E.S. Wehrle, *International Politics in East Asia since World War Two* (1975) Praeger, NY.
LaFeber, Walter, *The Clash: U.S.–Japanese Relations Throughout History* (1997) Norton, NY.
Langdon, Frank C. *Japan's Foreign Policy* (1973) University of British Columbia Press, Vancouver.
Langer, Paul F. *Communism in Japan: A Case of Political Naturalization* (1972) Hoover Institute Press, Stanford, CA.
Langer, Paul F. *Moscow, Peking and Japan—Views and Approaches* (12 Sept. 1960) Rand Corp. (P-2098), CA.
Lee, Chae-Jin, *China and Japan: New Economic Diplomacy* (1987) Hoover Institute, Stanford University Press, CA.
Lee, Chae-Jin, *Japan Faces China: Political and Economic Relations in the Post-war Era* (1976) Johns Hopkins University Press, Baltimore, MD.
Leng Shao Chuan, *Japan and Communist China* (1958) Doshisha University Press, Kyōto.
Lewis, John Wilson and Xue Litai, *China Builds the Bomb* (1988) Stanford University Press, Stanford, CA.
London, Kurt (ed.), *Unity and Contradiction: Major Aspects of Sino-Soviet Relations* (1962) Praeger, NY.
Low, Alfred D. *The Sino-Soviet Dispute: An Analysis of the Polemics* (1976) Fairleigh Dickinson University Press, Rutherford, MI.
Lowe, Peter, and Moeshart (eds) *Western Interactions with Japan: Expansion, the Armed Forces and Readjustment, 1859–1956* (1990) Japan Library, Folkstone, Kent.
Lu, David J. (ed.), *Perspectives on Japan's External Relations: Views from America* (1982) Bucknell University, Lewisburg, PA.
Macridis, Roy C. (ed.), *Foreign Policy in World Politics* (1976) (5th ed.) Prentice-Hall, Englewood Cliffs, NJ.
Maga, Timothy P. *Hands Across the Sea? U.S.–Japan Relations, 1961–1981* (1997) Ohio University Press, Athens, OH.
Maga, Timothy P. *John F. Kennedy and the New Pacific Community, 1961–63* (1990) Macmillan, London.
Malone, Patrick D. *Japan's Foreign Policy 1957 through 1967: Window to the West, Window to the East* (Apr. 1969) Graduate Institute of International Studies, Geneva.
Maruyama Masao, *Thought and Behaviour in Modern Japanese Politics* (1963) Oxford University Press, London.
Masuda Hiroshi and Hatano Sumio (eds), *Ajia no naka no Nihon to Chūgoku—yūkō to masatsu no gendaishi* [Japan and China in Asia: A Contemporary History of Friendship and Friction] (25 Oct. 1995) Yamakawa Shuppansha.
Masuda Hiroshi, *Anadorazu, kanshōsezu, hirefusazu—Ishibashi Tanzan no tai Chūgoku gaikōron* [Respected, Unhindered, Unbowed: Ishibashi Tanzan's Thoughts on China Policy] (1993) Sōshisha.
Masumi Junnosuke, *Contemporary Politics in Japan* (1995) Unviersity of California Press, Berkeley, CA.
Masumi Junnosuke, *Postwar Politics in Japan, 1945–1955* (1985) Unviersity of California, Berkeley, CA.

Mathieson, R.S. *Japan's Role in Soviet Economic Growth: Transfer of Technology since 1965* (1979) Praeger, NY.

Mayers, David Allan, *Cracking the Monolith: United States' Policy Against the Sino-Soviet Alliance* (1986) Louisiana State University Press, Baton Rouge, LA.

Mendel, Douglas H. *The Japanese People and Foreign Policy: A Study of Public Opinion in Post-Treaty Japan* (1961) University of California Press, Berkeley, CA.

Mendl, Wolf, *Issues in Japan's China Policy* (1978) R.I.I.A./Macmillan, London.

Miller, J.D.B. and T.H. Rigby, *The Disintegrating Monolith* (1965) ANU Press, Canberra.

Miyamoto Yoshio, *Chū-So ronsō no gairyaku to hihan* [An Outline and Critique of the Sino-Soviet Dispute] (15 Dec. 1966) Nikkan Rōdō Tsūshinsha.

Miyashita Tadao, *Development of the Trade Between Japan and Communist China* (1958) Japan Institute of Pacific Relations, Tokyo.

Morley, James W. *Forecast for Japan: Security in the 1970s* (1972) Princeton University Press, NJ.

Morley, James W. *Security Interdependence in the Asia Pacific Region* (1986) East Asia Institute, Columbia University/Lexington Books, Lexington, MA.

Morley, James W. *Soviet and Communist Chinese Policies toward Japan, 1950–57: A Comparison* (1958) Institute of Pacific Relations, NY.

Morris, Ivan, *Nationalism and the Right-wing in Japan: A Study of Postwar Trends* (1960) Oxford University Press, London.

Muraoka Kunio, *Japanese Security and the United States* (Feb. 1973) (Adelphi Paper 95) International Institute for Strategic Studies, London.

Nagai Yōnosuke and Iriye Akira (eds), *The Origins of the Cold War in Asia* (1977) University of Tokyo Press, Tokyo.

Nakajima Mineo, *Chū-So tairitsu to gendai* [The Sino-Soviet Rift and the Present Day] (10 Dec. 1978) Chūō Kōronsha.

Nakanishi Osamu, *Chūgoku to Soren—Chū-So Tairitsu to Shakai Shugi no Shōrai* [China and the Soviet Union: The Sino-Soviet Rift and the Future of Socialism] (20 Nov. 1979) Nihon Kōgyō Shimbunsha.

Nelsen, Harvey, W. *Power and Insecurity: Beijing, Moscow and Washington, 1949–1988* (1989) Lynne Rienner Pubs, Boulder, CO.

Nester, William R. *Japan and the Third World* (1991) Macmillan, Basingstoke, Hants.

Nester, William R. *Japan's Growing Power over East Asia and the World Economy* (1990) Macmillan, London.

Nester, William R. *The Foundations of Japanese Power* (1990) Macmillan, London.

Newby, Laura, *Sino-Japanese Relations* (1989) Royal Institute of International Affairs/ Routledge, London.

Newland, Kathleen (ed.), *The International Relations of Japan* (1990) Macmillan, Basingstoke, Hants.

Niizeki Kinya, *NisSo kōshō no butai ura—aru gaikōkan no kiroku* [Behind the Scenes at Japan–Soviet Negotiations: A Diplomat's Record] (20 Jan 1989) NHK Bukkusu.

Nimmo, William F. *Japan and Russia: A Reevaluation in the Post-Soviet Era* (1994) Greenwood Press, Westport, CT.

Nishihara Masashi, *The Japanese and Sukarno's Indonesia: Tokyo–Jakarta Relations, 1951–66* (1976) Hawaii University Press, Honolulu, HI.

Nixon, Richard, *Leaders* (1982) Warner Books, NY.

Nolte, Sharon H. *Liberalism in Modern Japan: Ishibashi Tanzan and his Teachers, 1905–60* (1987) University of California Press, Berkeley, CA.

Northedge, F.S. *The International Political System* (1976) Faber and Faber, London.

Ōa Kyōkai, *Soren to Chūkyō—Daisankai kyōsanken kenkyū kokusai kaigi hōkoku* [The Soviet Union and Communist China: Report of the Third International Conference on Communist bloc Research] (30 Nov. 1962) *Ōa Kyōkai*.

Ogata Sadako, *Normalization with China: A Comparative Study of U.S. and Japanese Processes* (1989) Institute of East Asian Studies, University of California, Berkeley, CA.

Okazaki Hisahiko, *A Japanese View of Détente* (1974) Lexington Books, Lexington, MA.

Olson, Lawrence, *Dimensions of Japan: A Collection of Reports Written for the American Universities Field Staff* (1963) American Universities Field Staff, NY.

Olson, Lawrence, *Japan in Postwar Asia* (1970) CFR/Pall Mall Press, London.

Osgood, Robert E. *Japan and the United States in Asia* (1968) (Studies in International Affairs 8), Washington Center of Foreign Policy Research, Johns Hopkins Press, Baltimore, MD.

Osgood, Robert E. *The Weary and the Wary: United States and Japanese Security Policies in Transition* (1972) (Studies in International Affairs 16) Johns Hopkins University Press, Baltimore, MD.

Ozaki, Robert S. and Arnold, Walter (eds), *Japan's Foreign Relations: A Global Search for Economic Security* (1985) Westview Press, Boulder, CO.

Packard, George R. *Protest in Tokyo: The Security Treaty Crisis of 1960* (1966) Princeton University Press, NJ.

Pempel, T.J. (ed.), *Policymaking in Contemporary Japan* (1978) Westview Press, Boulder, CL.

Pfaltzgraff, Robert L. and Jacquelyn K. Davis, *Japanese–American Relations in a Changing Security Environment* (1975) (Foreign Policy Papers 1(1)), Foreign Policy Research Institute/Sage Pubs, Beverly Hills, CA.

Radtke, Kurt Werner, *China's Relations with Japan, 1945–83: The Role of Liao Chengzhi* (1990) Manchester University Press, Manchester.

Rees, David, *Soviet Border Problems: China and Japan* (1982) Institute for the Study of Conflict (Study 139), London.

Reischauer, Edwin O. *Japan: The Story of a Nation* (1970) Knopf, NY.

Richardson, Bradley M. and Scott C. Flanagan, *Politics in Japan* (1984) Little, Brown and Co, Boston, MA.

Robertson, Myles L.C. *Soviet Policy Towards Japan: An Analysis of Trends in the 1970s and 1980s* (1988) Cambridge University Press, Cambridge.

Rose, Caroline, *Interpreting History in Sino-Japanese Relations: A Case Study in Political Decision-Making* (1998) Routlege, London.

Rosenau, James (ed.), *Domestic Sources of Foreign Policy* (1967) Free Press, NY.

Rothacher, Albrecht, *Economic Diplomacy between the European Community and Japan, 1959–1981* (1983) Gower, Aldershot, Hants.

Rōyama Michio, *The Asian Balance of Power: A Japanese View* (Nov. 1967) (Adelphi Paper 42) IISS, London.

Rozman, Gilbert, *Japan's Response to the Gorbachev Era, 1985–1991: A Rising Superpower Views a Declining One* (1992) Princeton University Press, NJ.

Saito Shiro, *Japan at the Summit: Japan's Role in the Western Alliance and Asian Pacific Cooperation* (1990) R.I.I.A./Routledge, London.

Sato Seizaburo, Koyama Kenichi and Kumon Shunpei, *Postwar Politician: The Life of Former Prime Minister Masayoshi Ohira* (1990) Kodansha, Tokyo.

Scalapino, R.A. *American–Japanese Relations in a Changing Era* (1972) (Washington Papers 2), Sage, Beverly Hills, CA.

Scalapino, R.A. (ed.), *The Foreign Policy of Modern Japan* (1977) University of California Press, Berkeley, CA.

Scalapino, R.A. and Junnosuke Masumi, *Parties and Politics in Contemporary Japan* (1962) University of California Press, Berkeley, CA.

Scalapino, R.A. *Asia and the Road Ahead: Issues for the Major Powers* (1975) University of California Press, Berkeley, CA.

Scalapino, R.A. et al., (eds), *Asia and the Major Powers: Domestic Politics and Foreign Policy* (1988) Institute of East Asian Studies, University of California, Berkeley, CA.

Scalapino, R.A. et al., *Asian Security Issues: Regional and Global* (1988) Institute of East Asian Studies, University of California, Berkeley, CA.

Scalapino, R.A. *Major Power Relations in North–East Asia* (1987) (Asian Agenda Reports 9) University Press of America, Lanham, MD.

Scalapino, R.A. *The Japanese Communist Movement, 1920–1966* (1967) University of California Press, Berkeley, CA.

Schaller, Michael, *Altered States: The United States and Japan Since the Occupation* (1997) Oxford University Press, NY.

Schaller, Michael, *The American Occupation of Japan: The Origins of the Cold War in Asia* (1985) Oxford University Press, Oxford.

Schonberger, Howard B. *Aftermath of War: Americans and the Remaking of Japan, 1945–52* (1989) Kent State University Press, Kent, OH.

Schram, Stuart, *Mao Tse-tung* (1966) Penguin, Harmondsworth, Middlesex.

Segal, Gerald (ed.), *The Soviet Union in East Asia: Predicaments of Power* (1983) Heinemann, London.

Segal, Gerald, *Normalizing Soviet–Japanese Relations* (1991) R.I.I.A, London.

Segal, Gerald, *The Great Power Triangle* (1982) Macmillan, London.

Shaw, K.E. *Japan's China Problem: Legal Analysis and Study of Policy (Marginal Position and Attitude during the Ikeda Period)* (1968) International Christian University, Tokyo.

Shigeta Hiroshi and Suezawa Shōji, *NisSo kihon bunsho shiryōshū* [A Collection of Basic Materials and Documents on Japan–Soviet [Relations]] (Nov. 1988) Sekai no Ugoki Sha.

Shimizu Hayao, *Nihonjin wa naze Soren ga kirai ka* [Why do Japanese Dislike the Soviet Union?] (10 Mar. 1979) Yamate Shobō.

Shiratori Rei, *Peace Research in Japan* (1970) The Japan Peace Research Group, Tokyo.

Sladkovsky, M.I. *China and Japan: Past and Present* (1975) Academic International Press, FL.

Smith, Anthony, *National Identity* (1991) Penguin, London.

Soeya Yoshihide, *Japan's Economic Diplomacy with China, 1945–1978* (1998) Clarendon Press, Oxford.

Stephan, John J. *The Kuril Islands* (1974) Clarendon Press, Oxford.

Stockwin, J.A.A, Alan Rix, Aurelia George, James Horne, Itō Daiichi and Martin Collick, *Dynamic and Immobilist Politics in Japan* (1988) St. Antony's/Macmillan, London.

Stockwin, J.A.A. *Divided Politics in a Growth Economy* (1982) (2nd ed.) Weidenfeld and Nicolson, London.

Stockwin, J.A.A. *The Japan Socialist Party and Neutralism: A Study of a Political Party and its Foreign Policy* (1968) Melbourne University Press, Melbourne.

Sudo Sueo, *The Fukuda Doctrine and Asean: New Dimensions in Japanese Foreign Policy* (1992) Institute of Southeast Asian Studies, Singapore.

Swearingen, Roger and Paul Langer, *Red Flag in Japan: International Communism in Action, 1919–1951* (1952) Harvard University Press, Cambridge, MA.

Swearingen, Roger, *The Soviet Union and Post-war Japan* (1978) Hoover Press, Stanford University, CA.

Tagawa Seiichi, *Matsumura Kenzō to Chūgoku* [Matsumura Kenzō and China] (1972) Yomiuri Shimbunsha.

Tanaka Akihiko, *Nitchū kankei 1945–1990* [Japan–China Relations, 1945–1990] (25 Apr. 1991) Tōkyō Daigaku Shuppankai.

Tanaka Shigeyuki, *Chū-So ronsō* [The Sino-Soviet Dispute] (20 Apr. 1967) Shakai Undō Kenkyūkai.

Thayer, Nathaniel B., *How the Conservatives Rule Japan* (1969) Princeton University Press, N.J.

The Japan Times, *What's What in Japan's Diet, Government, and Public Agencies* (1989) The Japan Times, Tokyo.

Thorp, Willard (ed.), *The United States and the Far East* (1962) (2nd ed.) American Assembly/ Prentice-Hall, Englewood Cliffs, NJ.

Totten, George, *The Social Democratic Movement in Prewar Japan* (1968) Yale University Press, New Haven, CT.

Tsurutani Taketsugu, *Political Change in Japan: Response to Postindustrial Challenge* (1977) David McKay, NY.

Varma, Lalima, *The Making of Japan's China Policy* (1991) Kalinga Pubs, Delhi.

Vimla, Savan, *The Sino-Soviet Schism: A Bibliography, 1956–64* (1971) Asia Publishing House, Bombay.

Vishwanathan, Savitri, *Normalization of Japan–Soviet Relations, 1945–70* (1973) Diplomatic Press, Tallahassee, FL.

Vogel, Ezra (ed.) *Modern Japanese Organization and Decision-Making* (1979) Tuttle, Tokyo..

Wakaizumi Kei, *Amerika kara mita Soren to Chūkyō no shōrai oyobi Chū-So kankei* (8 Oct. 1963) LDP (internal party document.)

Wakamiya Yoshibumi, *The Postwar Conservative View of Asia* (1998) LTCB International Library Foundation, Tokyo.

Walt, Stephen M., *The Origins of Alliances* (1987) Cornell University Press, Ithaca, NY.

Weinstein, M.E. *Japan's Postwar Defence Policy, 1947–68* (1971) Columbia University Press, NY.

Welfield, John, *An Empire in Eclipse: Japan in the Postwar American Alliance System* (1988) Athlone Press, London.

Welfield, John, *Japan and Nuclear China: Japanese Reactions to China's Nuclear Weapons* (1970) Australian National University Press, Canberra.

Westad, Odd Arne (ed.) *Brothers in Arms: The Rise and Fall of the Sino-Soviet Alliance, 1945–1963* (1998) Stanford University Press, Stanford, CA.

Whiting, Allen S., *Siberian Development and East Asia: Threat or Promise?* (1981) Stanford University Press, Stanford, CA.

Wight, Martin, *Power Politics* (1979) Leicester University Press, Leicester.

Wilson, Dick, *Asia Awakes: A Continent in Transition* (1972) Penguin, Middlesex.

Wilson, Dick, *The Sun at Noon: An Anatomy of Modern Japan* (1986) Hamish Hamilton, London.

Wolferen, Karel van, *The Enigma of Japanese Power: People and Politics in a Stateless Nation* (1989) Macmillan, London.

Yahuda, Michael, *China's Role in World Affairs* (1978) Croom Helm, London.

Yahuda, Michael, *The International Politics of the Asia–Pacific, 1945–1995* (1996) Routledge, London.

Yanaga Chitoshi, *Big Business in Japanese Politics* (1968) Yale University Press, New Haven, CT.

Yoshitsu, Michael M. *Japan and the San Francisco Peace Settlement* (1983) Columbia University Press, NY.

Young, Kenneth, T. *Negotiating with the Chinese Communists: The U.S. Experience, 1953–67* (1968) CFR/McGraw Hill, NY.

Zagoria, Donald S. (ed.), *Soviet Policy in East Asia* (1982) Yale University Press, New Haven, CT.

Zagoria, Donald S. *The Sino-Soviet Conflict 1956–61* (1962) Princeton University Press, NJ.

Zagoria, Donald S. *Vietnam Triangle: Moscow, Peking, Hanoi* (1967) Pegasus, NY.

Zhang, Shu Guang, *Economic Cold War: America's Embargo against China and the Sino-Soviet Alliance, 1949–1963* (2001) Woodrow Wilson Center Press/Stanford University Press, Washington, D.C./Stanford, CA.

Zhao, Quansheng, *Japanese Policymaking: The Politics Behind Politics: Informal Mechanisms and the Making of China Policy* (1993) Praeger, Westport, CT.

Doctoral theses

Bae, Kim Young, *The Japan Communist Party and the Soviet Union: Pattern of Coalition and Conflict, 1945–69* (1974) Ph.D. Thesis, Kansas University.

Itoh, Mayumi, *Japanese Perceptions of the Soviet Union: Japanese Foreign Policy Elites' Perceptions of the Soviet Union and Japanese Foreign Policy towards the Soviet Union* (1988) Ph.D. Thesis, City University, NY.

Maeno, J.R. *Postwar Japanese Policy toward Communist China, 1952–72: Japan's Changing International Relations and New Political Culture* (1973) Ph.D. Thesis, University of Washington, Seattle.

Odani Tsutomu, *Japan's Foreign Policy Making System: A Comparative Study of the Peace Agreement with the Soviet Union 1954–56 and the Rapprochement with the PRC, 1969–72* (1981) Ph.D. Thesis, University of Chicago.

Rhee, Sei Young, *The Impact of the Sino-Soviet Conflict on the Japan Communist Party, 1961–68* (1973) Ph.D. Thesis, University of Missouri.

Schulz, John J. *Japan and the Peace and Friendship Treaties with Moscow and Peking* (1980) D.Phil. Thesis, University of Oxford.

Soeya Yoshihide, *Japan's Postwar Economic Diplomacy with China: Three Decades of Non-governmental Experience* (1989) Ph.D. Thesis, University of Michigan.

Articles

Abe Keizō, Kunugi Teruo, Tamura Yūzō, Nishiyama Takichi, Watanabe Tsuneo, 'Nihon gaikō no jittai' [The Realities of Japanese Diplomacy] *Chūō Kōron* (Jan. 1964) 79(1): 112–25.

Aichi Kiichi, 'Japan's Legacy and Destiny of Change' *Foreign Affairs* (Oct. 1969) 48(1): 292–7.

Aichi Kiichi, Imanishi Kinji, Itō Sei, Iizuka Kōji, Okuno Shintarō, Kamei Katsuichirō, Kyūei Kan, Kuraishi Takeshirō, Shiina Rinzō, Suzuki Haruo, Sone Eki, Hirabayashi Taiko, Fujiyama Aiichirō, Wada Hiroo, 'Watashi wa kō handan suru—kakukai no ankēto—tokushū, shōten ni tatsu Chūgoku' [My Judgement is thus: A Special Questionnaire Focusing on China] *Chūō Kōron* (Mar. 1963) 78(3): 148–59.

Ajia Keizai Junpō, 'Nihonjin no Chūgokukan' [The Japanese View of China] *Ajia Keizai Junpō* (Aug. 1967) 693: 22–8.

Akashi Yasushi, 'Japan's Foreign Policy' *Yale Review* (Dec. 1957) 47(2): 198–218.

Akima Yoshio, Nakayama Masao, Nangō Saburō, Nishikawa Kumakichi, Matsumiya Yasuo, Yamamoto Naota, 'Chūkyō bōeki no zento wa akarui' [Bright Prospects for Communist China Trade] *Tōyō Keizai Shimpō* (1 Sept. 1956) 2743: 44–53.

Albright, David E. 'Sino-Soviet Conflict and the Balance of Power in Asia' *Pacific Community* (Jan. 1977) 8(2): 204–34.

Alexandrov, K. 'Japan and its Communist Neighbors' *Bulletin of the Institute for the Study of the USSR* (Apr. 1960) VII(4): 21–6.

Amō Eiji, 'Kokusai Kyōsanshugi wa ika ni shite kyokutō ni shinshutsu shita ka' [How has International Communism Advanced in the Far East?] *Soren to Chūkyō* (30 Nov. 1962) Ōa Kyōkai: 265–94.

Amō Eiji, 'Kyōsanken kenkyū' [Studies of the Communist bloc] *Soren Mondai* (Dec. 1958) 2(4): 1–17.

Ampiah, Kweku, 'Japan at the Bandung Conference: The Cat Goes to the Mice's Convention' *Japan Forum* (Apr. 1995) 7(1): 15–24.

Aono Hiroaki, 'Chū-So tairitsu to Nihon Marukusushugi' [The Sino-Soviet Rift and Japanese Marxism] *Kyōsanken Mondai* (Nov. 1964) 8(11): 1–18.

Aono Hiroaki, 'Marxism in Postwar Japan' *Review* (Tokyo) (June 1972) 33: 1–43.

Arai Takeo, 'Chūgoku ni dō tai subeki ka' [How Should We Cope with China?] *Nihon Oyobi Nihonjin* (Dec. 1959) 10(10): 10–18.

Arisawa Hiromi, Suzuki Kazuo and Takami Shigeyoshi, 'Kokomu no kabe o koete' [Surmounting the Obstacle of COCOM] *Sekai* (Dec. 1956) 132: 45–58.

Armstrong, J. David, 'The Soviet Union and the United States', *The Soviet Union in East Asia*, G. Segal (ed.) (1983): 31–49.

Arnold, W. 'Japan's Relations with China since 1978', *The International Relations of Japan*, Kathleen Newland (ed.) (1990): 121–46.

Aruga Tadashi, 'The Security Treaty Revision of 1960', *The United States and Japan in the Postwar World*, Iriye Akira and Warren Cohen (eds) (1989): 61–79.

Asada Mitsuteru, 'Chū-So ronsō to Nihon no sayoku' [The Sino-Soviet Dispute and the Japanese Left Wing] *Ronsō* (Apr. 1962) 4(4): 84–91.

Asahi Jānaru, 'Chūgoku no kakujikken setsu' [Rumours of a Chinese Nuclear Test] *Asahi Jānaru* (16 Sept. 1962) 4(37): 3.

Asahi Jānaru, 'Chūgoku no tai Nichi taido kawaru' [China's Changing Attitude towards Japan] *Asahi Jānaru* (11 Sept. 1960) 2(37): 76–8.

Asahi Jānaru, 'Chū-So kankei no kokusai zemi' [International Seminar on Sino-Soviet Relations] *Asahi Jānaru* (9 Oct. 1960) 2(41): 103–5.

Asahi Jānaru, 'Chū-So no tairitsu wa kaishō shita ka' [The Sino-Soviet Split is Settled]*Asahi Jānaru* (11 Dec. 1960) 2(50): 77–9.

Asahi Jānaru, 'Chū-So ronsō no ato' [Evidence of the Sino-Soviet Dispute] *Asahi Jānaru* (18 Sept. 1960) 2(38): 16–17.

Asahi Jānaru, 'Fu shushō Pekin hōmon' [Premier Khrushchev's Beijing Visit] *Asahi Jānaru* (18 Oct. 1959) 1(32): 29–31.

Asahi Jānaru, 'Kōno kōsō o nebumi suru' [The Kōno Plan Appraised] *Asahi Jānaru* (2 Sept. 1962) 4(35): 10–19.

Asahi Jānaru, 'NitChū kankei to Ikeda gaikō' [Japan–China Relations and Ikeda Diplomacy] *Asahi Jānaru* (15 Jan. 1961) 3(3): 8–13.

Asahi Jānaru, 'Shiga, Suzuki jomei mondai to Nikkyō rosen' [The Shiga and Suzuki Expulsion Problem and the JCP Line] *Asahi Jānaru* (31 May 1964) 6(22): 12–18.

Asanuma Inejirō, 'Shin Chūgokū mita mama kanjita mama' [The New China as I saw it] *Seikai Ōrai* (July 1957) 23(7): 86–91.

Asanuma Inejirō, 'Takaraka ni naru kokumin gaikō no shōri' [Shouting the Success of People's Diplomacy] *Nihon Shūhō* (15 May 1957) 406: 43–9.

Ashida Hitoshi, 'NisSo kōshō no zento' [The Future of Soviet–Japanese Negotiations] *Daiyamondo* (11 July 1955) 43(32): 12–16.

Atsugi Morio, 'Chū-So ronsō no genjō to kaiko' [The Sino-Soviet Dispute: Retrospective and Current State] *Rōdō Keizai Junpō* (11 Feb.–21 May 1963) 533, 534, 537, 538, 540, and 543: 22–6, 14–8, 22–6, 22–6, 18–22 and 8–12.

Azuma Teruhiko, 'Kuichigau Chū-So no taigai seisaku' [Foreign Policy Discord between the Soviet Union and China] *Soren Kenkyū* (Nov. 1959) 8(11): 18–21.

Baerwald, Hans H. 'The Diet and Foreign Policy', *The Foreign Policy of Modern Japan*, R.A. Scalapino (ed.) (1977): 37–54.

Ballis, William B. 'A Decade of Soviet–Japan Relations' *Studies on the Soviet Union* (1964) 3(3): 128–57.

Barnds, W.J. 'Japan and its Mainland Neighbours: An End to Equidistance?' *International Affairs* (1976) 52(1): 27–38.

Barnett, A. Doak, 'The United States and Communist China', *The United States and the Far East*, Willard Thorp (ed.) (1956): 98–157.

Barrass, Gordon and Richard Rochingham Gill, 'The Uncommitted Communist Parties', *The Sino-Soviet Conflict: 11 Radio Discussions*, Leopold Labedz and G.R. Urban (eds) (1965): 127–39.

Beer, Lawrence W. 'Some Dimensions of Japan's Present and Potential Relations with Communist China' *Asian Survey* (Mar. 1969) IX(3): 163–77.

Berton, Peter, 'The Soviet and Japanese Communist Parties: Policies, Tactics, Negotiating Behavior' *Studies in Comparative Communism* (autumn 1982) XV(3): 266–82.

Bessho Jirō, 'Hokkaidō "kaihō henku"' [Hokkaido's 'Liberated Zone'] *Kaizō* (10 Jan. 1952) 33(2): 154–65.

Blaker, Michael K. 'Probe, Push and Panic: The Japanese Tactical Style in International Negotiations', *The Foreign Policy of Modern Japan*, R.A. Scalapino (ed.) (1977): 55–101.

Borkenau, Franz, 'The Chances of a Mao–Stalin Rift: Will China's Communists take the Tito Road?' *Commentary* (Aug. 1952) 14(2): 117–23.

Borkenau, Franz, 'The Peking–Moscow Axis and the Western Alliance: How Really Hopeful for us are their Disagreements?' *Commentary* (Dec. 1954) 18(6): 513–21.

Borton, Hugh, 'The Relations of Japan to the Continent: China and South–east Asia' *Proceedings of the Academy of Political Science* (Jan. 1955) XXVI(2): 29–37.

Boyd, R.G. 'China's Relations with Japan' *Australian Outlook* (April 1960) 14: 50–68.

Brands, H.W. Jr, 'The United States and the Reemergence of Independent Japan' *Pacific Affairs* (fall 1986) 59(3): 387–401.

Brar, B.S. 'The Sino-Soviet Split and Retrospective Explanations: A Critique of Power-centric Analysis' *International Studies* (India) (Jan./Mar. 1966) 23(1): 1–20.

Brzezinski, Zbigniew, 'Threat and Opportunity in the Communist Schism' *Foreign Affairs* (Apr. 1963) 41(3): 513–25.

Buchan, Alastair, 'The End of Bipolarity in East Asia and the World System, Part I: The Superpowers and the Context' *Adelphi Paper* (Nov. 1972) 91: 21–30.

Bull, Hedley, 'The New Balance of Power in Asia and the Pacific' *Foreign Affairs* (July 1971) 49(4): 669–81.

Bungei Shunjū, 'NisSo gaikō hakusho' [A White Paper on Japan–Soviet Diplomacy] *Bungei Shunjū* (April 1955) 33(4): 68–85.

Burks, Ardath W. 'Japan's Relations with the Communist World' *Current History* (Apr. 1958) 24: 214–22.

Carlile, Lonny E. 'The Changing Political Economy of Japan's Economic Relations with Russia: The Rise and Fall of Seikei Fukabun' *Pacific Affairs* (fall 1994) 67(3): 411–32.

Chang Chun and Kawagoe Shigeru, 'Tōkyō kaidan' [A Tokyo Parley] *Kaizō* (Nov. 1952) 33(16): 54–62.

Cheng, Joseph Y.S. 'China's Japan Policy in the 1970s: The United Front and the "Four Modernizations"' *Asia Quarterly* (Jan./Mar. 1980) 27(1): 19–48.

Cheng, Joseph Y.S. 'Sino-Japanese Relations 1957–60' *Asian Affairs* (1977) 64(1): 70–84.

Chu Shao-hsien, 'The Chinese Communist United Front Operations in Japan and the Future of Peiping–Tokyo Relations' *Issues and Studies* (Taipei) (July 1972) VIII(10): 74–86.

Chu Shao-hsien, 'The Evolution of Japan's Peiping Policy' *Issues and Studies* (Taipei) (Dec. 1971) VIII(3): 16–29.

Chūō Kōron, '"Chū-So ronsō" Jimintō ni mo tobihi' [The 'Sino-Soviet Dispute' Spills Over into the LDP] *Chūō Kōron* (Mar. 1963) 78(3): 78.

Chūō Kōron, 'Chū-So no kuichigai—Amerika teikokushugi no hyōka' [Sino-Soviet Discord Over the Evaluation of US Imperialism] *Chūō Kōron* (Apr. 1960) 75(4): 217–9.

Clemens, W.C. 'The Nuclear Test Ban', *Sino-Soviet Relations and Arms Control*, M.H. Halperin (ed.) (1967): 145–67.

Cohen, Warren I. 'China in Japan–America Relations', *The United States and Japan in the Postwar World*, Iriye Akira and Warren Cohen (eds) (1989): 36–60.

Colbert, Evelyn, 'National Security Perspectives; Japan and Asia', *The Modern Japanese Military System*, James H. Buck (ed.) (1975): 199–215.

Commentator, 'The Normalization of Soviet–Japanese Relations' *International Affairs* (Moscow) (Nov. 1956) 1: 74–83.

Conolly, Violet, 'Sino-Soviet Conflict and the Far Eastern Region of the Soviet Union' *Journal of the Royal Central Asia Society* (June 1967) LIV: 146–50.

Conolly, Violet, 'Soviet–Japanese Economic Cooperation in Siberia' *Pacific Community* (Oct. 1970) 2: 55–65.

Coox, Alvin D. 'Japanese Attitudes toward the Soviet Union' *World Affairs Quarterly* (Jan. 1956) 26: 338–57.

Curtis, Gerald L. 'The Tyumen Oil Development Project and Japanese Foreign Policy Decision-making', *The Foreign Policy of Modern Japan*, R.A. Scalapino (ed.) (1977): 147–73.

Daiyamondo, 'Chū-So Dōmei wa Nihon ni dō hibiku' [How does the Sino-Soviet Alliance Affect Japan] *Daiyamondo* (21 Feb. 1950) 38(6): 12–13.

D'Cruz, V. 'Japanese Foreign Policy and the Cold War' *Australia Quarterly* (Sept. 1965) XXXVII(3): 35–48.

Demizu Koichi and Egashira Kazuma, 'Nishigawa gaikō no kūhaku nerau Soren to Chūgoku' [The Soviet Union and China Watch for a Vacuum in Western Foreign Policy] *Ekonomisuto* (30 Aug. 1960) 38(35): 32–7.

Dingman, Roger, 'The Anglo-American Origins of the Yoshida Letter, 1951–1952', *Perspectives on Japan's External Relations*, David J. Lu (ed.) (1982): 26–35.

Dingman, Roger, 'The Dagger and the Gift: The Impact of the Korean War on Japan' *Journal of American–East Asian Relations* (spring 1993) 2(1): 29–55.

Divine, Robert A. 'John Foster Dulles: What You See is What You Get' *Diplomatic History* (spring 1991) 15(2): 277–85.

Doi Akio, 'Chūkyō shisatsu hōkoku' [An Inspection Report on Communist China] *Tairiku Mondai* (Nov. 1956) 5(11): 2–31.

Doi Akio, 'Chū-So bunretsu to Nihon' [The Sino-Soviet Split and Japan] *Tairiku Mondai* (Sept. 1964) 13(9): 4–7.

Doi Akio, 'Chū-So hiyaku to Nihon' [Sino-Soviet Rapid Progress and Japan] *Tairiku Mondai* (Jan. 1959) 8(1): 4–7.

Doi Akio, 'Mondai no ōi Chū-So kankei' [Trouble-Ridden Sino-Soviet Relations] *Tairiku Mondai* (May 1961) 10(5): 4–9.

Doi Akio, 'NitChū-So no shōrai' [Japan, China, and the Soviet Union's Future] *Nihon oyobi Nihonjin* (Jan. 1957) 8(1): 6–13.

Doi Akio, 'Sashimukai Mō Takutō' [Face to Face with Mao Zedong] *Bungei Shunjū* (Nov. 1956) 34(11): 184–95.

Doi Akira, 'Chūkyō yukidoke ni noreru ka' [Can Communist China Agree to a Thaw?] *Keizai Ōrai* (Nov. 1959) 11(11): 122–9.

Doi Akira, 'Two Years Exchanges with China' *Japan Quarterly* (Oct./Dec. 1958) V (4): 435–51.

Dōkō, 'Chūkyō bōeki o meguru zaikai hiwa' [The Secret Story of Financial Circles' Trade with Communist China] *Dōkō* (June 1957) 4(6): 44–6.

Dore, Ronald P. 'Left and Right in Japan' *International Affairs* (Jan. 1956) 32(1): 11–26.

Dore, Ronald P. 'The JSP and "Structural Reform"' *Asian Survey* (Oct. 1961) 1(8): 3–15.

Dower, John W. 'Yoshida in the Scales of History' *Japan in War and Peace*, John W. Dower (1993): 208–41.

The Economist, 'All Orientals Together: Japan and China' *Economist* (London) (29 June 1963) 6253: 1351.

Eda Saburō, 'Bei kyokutō seisaku no tenkan o' [US Policy Towards the Far East] *Sekai* (Sept. 1963) 213: 83–4.

Eda Saburō, 'Shakaishugi no atarashii bijyon' [A New Vision of Socialism] *Ekonomisuto* (9 Oct. 1962) 40(41): 32–40.

Edstrom, Bert, 'The Internalisation of the Cold War in Japan' *Center for Pacific Asia Studies at Stockholm University Working Paper* (Sept. 1993) 33: 1–19.

Edstrom, Bert, 'Yoshida Shigeru and the Foundation of Japan's Postwar Foreign Policy' *Center for Pacific Asia Studies at Stockholm University Working Paper* (May 1992) 26: 1–25.

Eguchi Bokurō, 'Chū-So ronsō no rekishiteki igi to genzai no kokusai seiji ni okeru mondaiten' [The Sino-Soviet Dispute: Its Significance Historically and as an Issue in Current International Politics] *Kokusai Mondai* (Sept. 1963) 42: 4–11.

Eguchi Bokurō, 'Chū-So ronsō to Nihonjin no tachiba' [The Sino-Soviet Dispute and the Standpoint of the Japanese] *Chūō Kōron* (July 1963) 78(7): 48–57.

Eguchi Bokurō, 'Tairitsu suru Chū-So no riron to genjitsu' [Theory and Practice in the Rift between China and the Soviet Union] *Asahi Jānaru* (18 Sept. 1960) 2(38): 14–19.

Ekonomisuto, 'Chūkyō bōeki no genjō to kongo' [The Current State and Future of Trade with Communist China] *Ekonomisuto* (22 Nov. 1952) 30(35): 30–3.

Ekonomisuto, 'Chū-So ronsō no tōtatsuten' [The Sino-Soviet Dispute's Destination] *Ekonomisuto* (10 Jan. 1961) 39(2): 6–16.

Ekonomisuto, 'Chū-So sengen o dō uketoru ka' [How Should We Take the Sino-Soviet Joint Declaration] *Ekonomisuto* (23 Oct. 1954) 32(43): 24–6.

Ekonomisuto, 'Chū-So tairitsu de yure ugoku Nikkyō' [The JCP is Shaken by the Sino-Soviet Rift] *Ekonomisuto* (20 Aug. 1963) 41(33): 26–8.

Ekonomisuto, 'Kōsa suru futatsu no "tai Nichi rosen"' [Two Intersecting 'Policies Towards Japan'] *Ekonomisuto* (1 Jan. 1955) 33(1): 40–5.

Ekonomisuto, 'Meian kōsaku suru tai Kyōsanken bōeki' [A Mixture of the Bright and Dark in Trade with the Communist bloc] *Ekonomisuto* (8 Jan. 1955) 33(2): 20–9.

Ekonomisuto, 'NitChū bōeki kōshō to gyōkai no ugoki' [Sino-Japanese Trade Talks and the Moves of Japanese Industrial Circles] *Ekonomisuto* (23 April 1955) 33(17): 16–24.

Ekonomisuto, 'NitChū bōeki kyōtei no igi' [The Significance of the Japan–China Trade Agreement] *Ekonomisuto* (14 May 1955) 33(20): 20–3.

Ekonomisuto, 'NitChū bōeki saikai no gensō' [The Illusion of Japan–China Trade Resuming] *Ekonomisuto* (7 Feb. 1959) 37(6): 36–9.

Ekonomisuto, 'Shindankai ni haitta "Chū-So kokkō kaifuku"' ['Normalisation of Diplomatic Relations with China and the Soviet Union' Enters a New Stage] *Ekonomisuto* (6 Nov. 1954) 32(45): 16–17.

Ekonomisuto, 'Shinten suru tai NisSo kokkō kaifuku undō' [The Movement for Normalization of Diplomatic Relations with the Soviet Union Making Progress] *Ekonomisuto* (26 Feb. 1955) 33(9): 18–19.

Ekonomisuto, 'Takamaru NitChū bōeki sokushin undō—Kokkai no ugoki o saguru' [The Rise of the Japan–China Trade Promotion Movement: Probing Activity in the Diet] *Ekonomisuto* (13 June 1953) 31(24): 26–8.

Ekonomisuto, 'Tenkainan no NisSo bōeki shōdan' [Sluggish Japan–Soviet Trade] *Ekonomisuto* (4 June 1955) 33(23): 42–6.

Ekonomisuto, 'Zenmen chūzetsu shita NitChū bōeki' [The Total Suspension of Japan–China Trade] *Ekonomisuto* (24 May 1958) 36(21): 6–7.

Emmerson, John K. 'The Japanese Communist Party after Fifty Years' *Asian Survey* (July 1972) 12(7): 564–79.

Etō Shinkichi and Okabe Tatsumi, 'Chūka Jinmin Kyōwakoku tai Nichi hatsugen no naiyō bunseki' [Content Analysis of the People's Republic of China's Statements on Its Policy Towards Japan] *Chōsa Geppō* (Gaimushō) (Jan. 1965) 6(1): 1–7.

Etō Shinkichi, 'Evolving Sino-Japanese Relations', *Japan's New World Role*, Joshua Katz and Tilly Friedman-Lichtschein (eds) (1985): 49–65.

Etō Shinkichi, 'Post-war Japan–China Relations' *Survey* (autumn 1972) 18(4): 55–65.

Etō Shinkichi, 'Recent Developments in Sino-Japanese Relations' *Asian Survey* (July 1980) 20(7): 726–43.

Falkenheim, Peggy L. 'Eurocommunism in Asia: The Communist Party of Japan and the Soviet Union' *Pacific Affairs* (1979) 52(1): 64–77.

Falkenheim, Peggy L. 'Some Determining Factors in Soviet–Japanese Relations' *Pacific Affairs* (winter 1977–78) 50(3): 604–25.

Falkenheim, Peggy L. 'The Impact of the Peace and Friendship Treaty on Soviet–Japanese Relations' *Asian Survey* (Dec. 1979) XIX(12): 1202–23.

Fall, Bernard B. 'The "Third World"', *Sino-Soviet Rivalry: Implications for United States Policy*, Clement J. Zablocki (ed.) (1966): 181–93.

Foot, Rosemary, 'New Light on the Sino-Soviet Alliance: Chinese and American Perspectives' *Journal of North East Asian Studies* (fall 1991) X(3): 16–29.

Fujii Masuo, 'Chū-So ronsō no "hōhō" to "kanten"—Chūgokugawa kara mite' ['Method' and 'Point of View' in the Sino-Soviet Dispute: Seen from China's Side] *Shisō* (Feb. 1963) 464: 62–9.

Fujii Shōji, 'Dōyō suru Chūkyō to Ri Shōban no hokushin' [Agitating Communist China and Ree Sunman Northern Expedition] *Nihon Shūhō* (5 Dec. 1956) 389: 52–7.

Fujiyama Aiichirō, 'Jiyūshugi jinei no tachiba de ikkan shita gaikō rosen o iku' [The Free World's Stand: Towards a Coherent Diplomatic Strategy] *Daiyamondo* (22 Oct. 1957) 45(47): 30–2.

Fukuda Kanichi, 'Gendai Chūgoku to seiji ninshiki no mondai' [Contemporary China and the Political Recognition Problem] *Sekai* (Feb. 1967) 255: 25–52.

Fukuda Katsuichi, 'Chū-So ronsō o meguru Nihon Kyōsantō no ugoki' [Trends in the Japanese Communist Party Concerning the Sino-Soviet Dispute] *Kōan Jōhō* (Mar. 1964) 126: 1–8.

Fukui Haruhiro, 'Foreign Policy-making by Improvisation: The Japanese Experience' *International Journal* (autumn 1977) 32(4): 791–812.

Fukui Haruhiro, 'Policy-making in the Japanese Foreign Ministry', *The Foreign Policy of Modern Japan*, R.A. Scalapino (ed.) (1977): 3–35.

Fukui, Haruhiro, 'Tanaka goes to Peking: A Case Study in Foreign Policymaking', *Policy Making in Contemporary Japan*, T.J. Pempel (ed.) (1977): 60–102.

Funada Naka, 'Naze Chūkyō wa shin no kōryū o kobamu ka' [Why Does Communist China Reject True Exchange?] *Ronsō* (Oct. 1963) 5(10): 36–41.

Gaddis, John Lewis, 'Dividing Adversaries: The U.S. and International Communism 1945–58' *The Long Peace*, John Lewis Gaddis (1987): 147–194.

Gaddis, John Lewis, 'The Unexpected John Foster Dulles: Nuclear Weapons, Communism and the Russians', *John Foster Dulles and the Diplomacy of the Cold War*, R.H. Immerman (ed.) (1990): 47–77.

Galay, Nikolai, 'Monolithic Unity and the Cold War' *Bulletin of the Institute for the Study of the USSR* (May 1963) X(5): 3–18.

Gallicchio, Marc, 'The Kuriles Controversy: U.S. Diplomacy in the Soviet–Japan Border Dispute (1941–56' *Pacific Historical Review* (Feb. 1991) LX(1): 69–101.

Genda Minoru, 'Gai nomi ōkushite ri sukunashi—ryōkai shigatai Kenan Ronbun' [The Unconvincing Kennan Thesis does more Harm than Good] *Sekai Shūhō* (13 Oct. 1964) 45(41): 20–3.

Genda Minoru, 'Japan's National Defense' *Pacific Community* (Oct. 1970) 2(1): 30–48.

Genda Minoru, 'Kyokutō o odokasu Chūkyō no kakubusō' [Communist China's Nuclear Weapons Threaten the Far East] *Sekai Shūhō* (20 Aug. 1963) 44(34): 22–5.

Gittings John, 'Cooperation and Conflict in Sino-Soviet Relations' *International Affairs* (Jan. 1964) 40(1): 60–75.

Glaubitz, Joachim, 'Balancing Between Adversaries: Sino-Japanese Relations and Soviet Interference' *Pacific Community* (Oct. 1977) 9(1): 31–45.

Glaubitz, Joachim, 'Japan–Soviet Relations in the Contemporary World', *Europe and Japan: Changing Relationships since 1945*, Gordon Daniels and Reinhard Drifte (eds) (1986): 69–78.

Glaubitz, Joachim, 'Moscow–Peking–Tokyo: A Triangle of Great Power Relations' *Bulletin of the Institute for the Study of the USSR* (June 1971) XVIII(6): 20–33.

Graebner, Norman A. 'Eisenhower and Communism: The Public Record of the 1950s', *Reevaluating Eisenhower: American Foreign Policy in the 1950s*, Richard Melanson and David Mayers (eds) (1987): 67–87.

Griffith, William E. 'International Politics and the Sino-Soviet Dispute', *The Sino-Soviet Conflict: A Global Perspective*, H.J. Ellison (ed.) (1982): 131–46.

Guo Moruo, 'Nihon ni tai suru Chūgoku jinmin no taido' [The Attitude of Chinese towards Japan] *Chūō Kōron* (Dec. 1953) 68(14): 28–31.

Gushima Kanesaburō, 'Heiwa kyōson riron ni okeru Chū-So no tairitsu' [The Sino-Soviet Rift in the Theory of Peaceful Coexistence] *Hōsei Kenkyū* (10 Dec. 1963) 30(3): 1–15.

Hagihara Nobutoshi, 'Nihon Shakaitō e no gimon' [Some Doubts about the JSP] *Chūō Kōron* (Mar. 1964) 79(3): 61–76.

Hakamada Shigeki, 'Responding to Perestroika' *Japan Echo* (winter 1988) XV(4): 9–16.

Hall, Ivan P. 'Japanese Intellectuals' *Survey* (autumn 1972) 18(4): 74–94.

Halperin, Morton H. 'Sino-Soviet Nuclear Relations (1957–60', *Sino-Soviet Relations and Arms Control*, M.H. Halperin (ed.) (1967): 117–43.

Halpern, A.M. 'China and Japan since Normalisation', *Dimensions of China's Foreign Relations*, Hsueh Chun-tu (ed.) (1977): 104–25.

Halpern, A.M. 'China and Japan', *China in Crisis, Volume Two: China's Policies in Asia and America's Alternatives*, Tang Tsou (ed.) (1968): 441–63.

Hamano Masami and Shishikura Toshirō, 'Hyōmenka shita Chū-So ronsō—M–L shugi e no kaishaku futatsu ka' [The Sino-Soviet Dispute comes into the Open: Towards Two Interpretations of Marxism–Leninism?] *Sekai Shūhō* (5 July 1960) 41(27): 20–3.

Hamano Masami, 'Chūkyō no tai Nichi bishō gaikō' [Communist China's Smile Diplomacy Towards Japan] *Tairiku Mondai* (July 1964) 13(7): 59–64.

Hamano Masami, 'Chū-So rikan no ugoki' [Trends in Sino-Soviet Estrangement] *Tairiku Mondai* (Oct. 1960) 9(10): 30–5.

Hanai Hitoshi, 'Chū-So tairitsu (1958–1964 nen) sōgo sayō keiryō moderu ni yoru bunseki' [The Sino-Soviet Rift (1958–64): A Quantitative Interaction Model Analysis] *Kokusai Seiji* (1 Nov. 1970) 42: 37–55.

Harako Rinjirō, 'Bunretsu o fukameru sekai kyōsanshugi undō—nashonaru intaresuto no shikaku [The Split Deepens in the World Communist Movement: From the Viewpoint of National Interest] *Ronsō* (Mar. 1963) 5(3): 23–30.

Harako Rinjirō, 'Chū-So kankei no jūrokunen' [16 Years of Sino-Soviet Relations] *Chūō Kōron* (Mar. 1962) 77(3): 124–132.

Harako Rinjirō, 'Chū-So maboroshi no wakai' [The Illusory Sino-Soviet Reconciliation] *Jiyū* (July 1962) 4(7): 58–65.

Harako Rinjirō, 'Chū-So ronsō no shindankai' [The New Stage in the Sino-Soviet Dispute] *Sekai Shūhō* (5 Dec. 1961) 42(49): 30–5.

Harako Rinjirō, 'Japanese–Soviet Relations and Japan's Choice' *Pacific Community* (Oct. 1972) 4(1): 79–96.

Harako Rinjirō, 'Prospects for Relations with the USSR' *Survey* (autumn 1972) 18(4): 46–54.

Harako Rinjirō, 'Taigai seisaku o meguru Chū-So kankei' [Sino-Soviet Relations Concerning Foreign Policy] *Sekai Shūhō* (20 Oct. 1959) 40(42): 26–32.

Harako Rinjirō, 'Wakai no chō mienu Chū-So ronsō' [No Sign of Reconciliation in the Sino-Soviet Dispute] *Sekai Shūhō* (12 Mar. 1963) 44(11): 14–19.

Hasegawa Tsuyoshi, 'Japanese Perceptions of the Soviet Union 1960–85' *Acta Slavica Iaponica* (1987) V: 37–70.

Haslam, Jonathan, 'The Patterns of Soviet–Japanese Relations since World War II', *Russia and Japan: An Unresolved Dilemma between Distant Neighbours*, Hasegawa Tsuyoshi, Jonathan Haslam, and Andrew Kuchins (eds) (1993): 3–48.

Hatano Hirokazu, 'Sino-Japanese Relations Today' *Japan Quarterly* (July/Sept. 1968) XV(3): 309–15.

Hatano Kenichi, 'Chū-So kankei no rekishiteki tenbō' [A Historical Overview of Sino-Soviet Relations] *Soren Kenkyū* (Nov. 1952) 1(11): 8–17.

Hatano Kenichi, 'NitChū-So bōeki kyōtei o nerau?—Shū Onrai no ryokō kaban o saguru' [Aiming at a Japan–USSR–China Trade Agreement: Searching Zhou Enlai's Luggage] *Nihon Shūhō* (15 Feb. 1957) 397: 14–17.

Hatano Kenichi, 'Oku no te o dashita "NitChū Fukashin Jōyaku" Mō Takutō no Nihon seisaku ni noru!' [Mao Zedong Plays His Trump Card!—A 'Japan–China Non-Aggression Pact'] *Nihon Shūhō* (15 May 1957) 406: 50–3.

Hatoyama Ichirō, 'Nihon mezasu sekishoku kakumei' [Red Revolution Aimed at Japan] *Jimbutsu Ōrai* (July 1952) 1(7): 1–3.

Hatoyama Ichirō, 'Yoshida-kun no yarikata wa machigatte iru' [Yoshida's way of Doing Things is Mistaken] *Chūō Kōron* (Nov. 1954) 69(11): 172–5.

Hayashi Kentarō, 'Chū-So ronsō no shinwa to genjitsu' [Myth and Reality in the Sino-Soviet Dispute] *Jiyū* (Nov. 1963) 5(11): 2–23.

Hayashi Kentarō, 'Sengoshi o dō miru ka' [How to Approach Post-war History] *Chūō Kōron* (Sept. 1964) 79(9): 81–90.

Hayashi Saburō, 'Jishu gaikō to bōei' [Autonomous Diplomacy and Defence] *Keizai Ōrai* (Jan. 1964) 16(1): 18–26.

Hayashi Takuo, Shioguchi Kiichi, and Omura Tatsuzō, 'Zuikō kisha no Ishibashi hō Chū hiwa' [The Secret History of Ishibashi's China Trip According to the Accompanying Journalists] *Keizai Ōrai* (Nov. 1959) 11(11): 130–9.

Hellmann, Donald C. 'Basic Problems of Japan–South Korean Relations' *Asian Survey* (May 1962) II(3): 19–24.

Hellmann, Donald C. 'Japan's Relations with Communist China' *Asian Survey* (Oct. 1964) 4(10): 1085–92.

Hellmann, Donald C. 'Japan's Security and Postwar Japanese Foreign Policy', *The Foreign Policy of Modern Japan*, R.A. Scalapino (ed.) (1977): 321–40.

Hellmann, Donald C. 'The Confrontation with Realpolitik', *Forecast for Japan*, J.W. Morley (ed.) (1972): 135–68.

Hellmann, Donald C. 'The Impact of the Sino-Soviet Dispute in North East Asia', *Sino-Soviet Conflict: A Global Perpsective*, H.J. Ellison (ed.) (1982): 172–84.

Hewett, Ed A. and Levine, Herbert S. 'The Soviet Union's Economic Relations in Asia', *Soviet Policy in East Asia*, D.S. Zagoria (ed.) (1982): 210–8.

Hidaka Rokurō, 'Rekishi no kyōkun to risei no tachiba' [The Precepts of History and Dictates of Reason] *Tenbō* (Nov. 1964) 71: 12–33.

Hinton, Harold C. 'China's Attitude', *The Sino-Soviet Rift and Arms Control*, M.H. Halperin (ed.) (1967): 171–92.

Hirai Tomoyashi, 'Soren to "heiwa kyōson"—Chū-So ronsō e no hitotsu no apurōchi' [The Soviet Union and 'Peaceful Coexistence': One Approach to the Sino-Soviet Dispute] *Kokusai Seiji* (5 May 1966) 30: 72–91.

Hiramatsu Shigeo, 'Chū-So no "jinmin minshushugi" ron' [Chinese and Soviet Theories of 'People's Democracy'] *Hōgaku Kenkyū (Keiō Gijuku Daigaku)* (April, May and June 1964) 37(4, 5, 6): 75–89, 21–41 and 45–60.

Hiramatsu Shigeo, 'Chū-So tairitsu no haikei to genjitsu—Chū-So sensōron ni yosete' [Background and Realities of the Sino-Soviet Rift: On Sino-Soviet War Theories] *Ajia Kuōtarii* (July 1974) 6(3): 58–71.

Hirano Hiroshi, 'Saikin no NisSo kankei' [Recent Japanese–Soviet Relations] *Ajia Kuōtarii* (July 1972) 4(3): 39–53.

Hirano Yoshitarō, 'Chū-So Kyōdō Sengen to Nihon' [The Sino-Soviet Joint Declaration and Japan] *Ajia Keizai Junpō* (Nov. 1954) 232: 1–9.

Hirano Yoshitarō, 'Chū-So Yūkō Dōmei Jōyaku no Nihon ni oyobasu eikyō' [The Influence of the Sino-Soviet Treaty of Alliance and Friendship on Japan] *Jōseien* (Mar. 1950) 5(3): 4–11.

Hirano Yoshitarō, 'Nichi-Bei kankei no shōrai' [The Future of Japan–United States Relations] *Ekonomisuto* (19 Jan. 1957) 35(3): 26–30.

Hirasawa Kazushige, 'Chū-So wa dō deru—shinsekai senryaku e no tenkan' [Where are China and the Soviet Union Going: Conversion to a New World Strategy] *Daiyamondo* (11 Oct. 1952) 40(36): 48–50.

Hirasawa Kazushige, 'Japan's Emerging Foreign Policy' *Foreign Affairs* (Oct. 1975) 54(1): 155–72.

Hirosawa Kenichi, 'Chū-So ronsō to Nihon Shakaitō' [The Sino-Soviet Dispute and the JSP] *Ekonomisuto* (1 Mar. 1966) 44(8): 64–8.

Hirota Yōji, 'Chū-So kan no kiretsu ni tsuite' [Concerning Cracks Between China and the Soviet Union] *Soren to Chūkyō*, Ōa Kyōkai (30 Nov. 1962) 2: 220–42.

Hirota Yōji, 'Mō Takutō no kenri to tsugi ni kuru mono—Chū-So ronsō no honshitsu to Nihon no tachiba' [Mao Zedong's Rights, Claims, and Powers and What Comes Next—the Essence of the Sino-Soviet Dispute and Japan's Standpoint] *Ronsō* (May 1963) 5(5): 6–29.

Hirotsu Kyosuke, 'Kokusai Kyōsanshugi to Nihon Kyōsantō no tachiba' [International Communism and the Stand of the JCP] *Sekai to Nihon* (Nov. 1963) 3(11): 22–29, 39.

Hirotsu Kyosuke, 'The Strategic Triangle: Japan' *Survey* (Jan. 1965) 54: 123–30.

Hitchcock, D.I. 'Joint Development of Siberia: Decision Making in Japanese–Soviet Relations' *Asian Survey* (Mar. 1971) 11(3): 279–300.

Hoadley, J.S. and Hasegawa Sukehiro, 'Sino-Japanese Relations 1950–1970: An Appreciation of the Linkage Model of International Politics' *International Studies Quarterly* (June (1971) 15: 131–57.

Hōgen Shinsaku, 'Saikin no kokusai jōsei ni tsuite' [On the Recent International Situation] *Gaisei Kenkyū* (Jan./Feb. 1963) 2(1): 29–36.

Hōgen Shinsaku, 'Soren to kyōsanken no jittai wa kō da' [The Realities of the Soviet Union and Communist bloc] *Seikai Ōrai* (May 1961) 27(5): 40–54.

Hōgen Shinsaku, 'The Soviet Union's Global Policy and Japan–Soviet Relations', *Japan in the World*, Kajima Institute for International Peace (ed.) (1976): 51–67.

Holbraad, Carsten, 'The Triangular System' *Cooperation and Conflict* (1973) 8: 81–89.

Holland, William L. 'Japan and the New Balance of Power in the Far East' *International Affairs* (July 1952) 28: 292–7.

Hongō Gaichi, 'Soren to Chūkyō no kyokutō seisaku' [Soviet and Communist Chinese Far East Policy] *Chūō Kōron* (Mar. 1950) 65(3): 80–5.

Horie Masanori, 'NisSo bōeki o suishin suru mono habamu mono' [What Promotes and What Hampers Japan–Soviet Trade] *Chūō Kōron* (Dec. 1954) 69(12): 194–212.

Horie Muraichi, 'Chū-So Yūkō Dōmei to Nihon' [The Sino-Soviet [Treaty of] Friendship and Alliance and Japan] *Zenei* (Apr. 1953) 79: 41–6.

Hosoya Chihiro, 'Characteristics of the Foreign Policy Decision-making System in Japan' *World Politics* (Apr. 1974) XXVI(3): 353–69.

Hosoya Chihiro, 'From the Yoshida Letter to the Nixon Shock', *The United States and Japan in the Postwar World*, Iriye Akira and Warren Cohen (eds) (1989): 21–35.

Hsiao, Gene T. 'Some External Constraints in the Development of Sino-Japanese Relations', *Japan, America and the Future World Order*, M.A. Kaplan and Musakoji Kinhide (eds) (1976): 279–320.

Hsieh, Alice Langley, 'The Sino-Soviet Nuclear Dialogue 1963', *Sino-Soviet Military Relations*, R.L. Gartoff (ed.) (1966): 150–70.

Huberman, Leo and Paul M. Sweezy, 'The Sino-Soviet Dispute' *Monthly Review* (Dec. 1961) 13(8): 64–71. Translated as 'Chū-So ronsō kakushin' *Sekai* (Mar. 1962) 195: 337–46.

Hudson, G.F. 'Soviet Policy in Asia' *Soviet Survey* (June/July 1957) 16/17: 1–7.

Ichikawa Taijirō, 'Kokusai kyōsanshugi undō no nijū kōzō to Chū-So ronsō' [The Double Structure of the International Communist Movement and the Sino-Soviet Dispute] *Kyōsanken Mondai* (Dec. 1963) 7(12): 1–17.

Igarashi Takeshi, 'Peace-making and Party Politics: Formation of the Domestic Foreign Policy System in Postwar Japan' *Journal of Japanese Studies* (1985) 11(2): 323–56.

Iida Momo, '"Chū-So ronsō" no shironteki, bunkaronteki imi' [The Poetic and Cultural Meanings of the 'Sino-Soviet Dispute.'] *Shisō No Kagaku* (Nov. 1964) 32: 86–99.

Ikeda Masanosuke, 'Chūkyō no jittai o yoku mikiwamete' [Ascertaining the Actual Situation in Communist China] *Seikai Ōrai* (Nov. 1963) 29(11): 98–106.

Ikei Masaru, 'Sengo NitChū kankei no ichikōsatsu—Ishibashi, Kishi naikaku jidai o chūshin to shite' [A Study of Postwar Japan–China Relations: The Ishibashi–Kishi Cabinet Era] *Kokusai Gaikō Zasshi* (Nov. 1974) 73(3): 44–87.

Ikematsu Fumio, 'Japan–Soviet Relations' *Contemporary Japan* (Apr. 1957) 24(10–12): 558–69.

Ikeyama Shigerō [Jūrō] 'Chū-So ronsō to taishū undō' [The Sino-Soviet Dispute and Mass Movements] *Gekkan Rōdō Mondai* (Apr. 1963) 58: 116–21.

Inoki Masamichi, 'Chū-So kankei no shindankai' [The New Stage in Sino-Soviet Relations] *Kyōsanken Mondai* (Jan. 1965) 9(1): 1–3.

Inoki Masamichi, 'Chū-So no seiji kankei' [Sino-Soviet Political Relations] *Soren Mondai* (Dec. 1959) 3(4): 65–74.

Inoki Masamichi, 'Chū-So ronsō no shōten (1963–64' [Focal Points of the Sino-Soviet Dispute (1963–64] *Surabu Kenkyū* (1967) 11: 1–26.

Inoki Masamichi, 'Kyōsanshugi to kokka no mondai' [The Problem of Communism and the State] *Chūō Kōron* (Dec. 1963) 78(12): 50–8.

Inoki Masamichi, 'Leninism and Mao Tse-tung's Ideology', *Unity and Contradiction: Major Aspects of Sino-Soviet Relations*, Kurt London (ed.) (1962): 103–21.

Inoki Masamichi, 'Yōroppa kara mita Soren to Chūgoku' [The USSR and China Viewed from Europe] *Chūō Kōron* (Sept. 1957) 72(9): 140–7.

Inoki Masamichi, Nakanishi Tsutomu, Motohashi Atsushi, and Shishido Hiroshi, 'Chūgoku wa Soren to dō chigau ka' [How Does Communist China Differ from the Soviet Union?] *Chūō Kōron* (Nov. 1956) 71(12): 326–39.

Inoue Shōzō, 'Chūkyō to yukidoke no bimyōna kankei' [Delicate Relations between Communist China and the Soviet Union under a Thaw] *Sekai Shūhō* (1 Jan. 1960) 41(1): 41–7.

Inoue Shōzō, 'Sekai o tsukiageru Chūkyō—hanBei tōitsu sensen no kessei o yobikake' [Communist China Shakes the World: Advocates Formation of a Global Anti-American United Front] *Sekai Shūhō* (28 June 1960) 41(26): 44–7.

Inoue Toshikazu, 'Sengo Nihon no Ajia gaikō no keisei' [The Formation of Postwar Japanese Foreign Policy towards Asia] *Nihon Seiji Gakkai Nenpō: 1998* (27 Jan. 1999): 127–47.

Irie Keishirō, 'Tai Chū-So kokkō chōsei nani ga mondai ka' [What is the Problem Regarding the Sino-Soviet Diplomatic Readjustment?] *Sekai* (Nov. 1955) 119: 70–81.

Irie Michimasa, 'Chūkyō no kakuhoyū to Nihon no anzen hoshō' [Communist China's Nuclear Power and the Security of Japan] *Jiyū* (Dec. 1964) 6(12): 76–85. .

Iriye Akira, 'Chinese–Japanese Relations 1945–90' *China Quarterly* (Dec. 1990) 124: 624–38.

Ishibashi Masashi, 'On Sino-Soviet Dispute' *Japan Socialist Review* (1 Feb. 1963) 31: 32–7.

Ishibashi Tanzan, 'Fu Shushō tainingo no Soren ni nozomu' [Hopes for the USSR after Premier Khrushchev's Retirement] *Tōyō Keizai Shimpō* (24 Oct. 1964) 3195: 10–11.

Ishibashi Tanzan, 'Kyōsanshugi o sukutta heiwa kyōson' [Peaceful Coexistence Saved Communism] *Tōyō Keizai Shimpō* (31 Oct. 1964) 3196: 24–5.

Ishibashi Tanzan, 'NitChū fukkō to Chū-So ronsō ni tai suru watashi no mikata' [My Personal Views on the Restoration of Japan–China Relations and the Sino-Soviet Dispute] *Tōyō Keizai Shimpō* (16 Nov. 1963) 3141: 8–10.

Ishidō Kiyotomo, 'Chū-So ronsō no tenbō' [A View of the Sino-Soviet Dispute] *Shisō No Kagaku* (Nov. 1964) 32: 76–85.

Ishii Mitsujirō and Kiya Ikusaburō, 'Jimintō no funran o kiku' [Investigating Disorder in the LDP] *Seikai Ōrai* (Nov. 1956) 22(11): 38–45.

Ishikawa Shigeru, 'Chūgoku keizei no kaihatsu to shikō sakugo' [Trial and Error in China's Economic Development] *Sekai* (June 1963) 210: 28–37.

Ishikawa Shigeru, 'Chū-So kankei o kettei suru yōin' [Chief Determinants of Sino-Soviet Relations] *Soren Kenkyū* (Sept. 1953) 2(9): 21–6.

Ishikawa Shigeru, 'NitChū kokkō seijōka no keizaiteki igi' [The Economic Significance of the Normalization of Japan–Communist China Relations] *Ekonomisuto* (5 Jan. 1957) 35(1): 65–8.

Ishikawa Tadao, 'A Review of Japanese–Chinese Relations', *Japan in the World*, Kajima Institute of International Peace (ed.) (1976): 97–109.

Ishikawa Tadao, 'Chūkyō no tai Nichi seisaku' [Communist China's Japan Policy] *Soren to Chūkyō*, Ōa Kyōkai (30 Nov. 1962): 295–311.

Ishikawa Tadao, 'Chū-So kankei no tenbō' [Prospects for Sino-Soviet Relations] *Kyōsanken Mondai* (May 1963) 7(5): 29–38.

Ishikawa Tadao, 'Shakaishugiken ni okeru Chūgoku no yakuwari' [The Role of China in the Socialist Camp] *Chūō Kōron* (Nov. 1958) 73(11): 88–98.

Ishimoto Y. 'The Northern Territories and the Peace Treaty with the USSR' *Japan Institute of International Affairs Annual Review* (1965–68) 4: 37–49.

Ishiyama [Kenkichi] Chōsashitsu, 'Soren abura no shinshutsu de sekiyukai konran' [Oil Industry Confused by Advance of Soviet Oil] *Daiyamondo* (29 Jan. 1962) 50(5): 66–71.

Ishiyama Kenkichi, 'Kakutō no kōyaku o hyō suru' [Commenting on each Party's Election Pledges] *Daiyamondo* (11 Feb. 1955) 43(7): 12–16.

Ito Takashi, 'Shigemitsu Mamoru and the 1955 System', *Creating Single-Party Democracy*, Kataoka Tetsuya (ed.) (1992): 100–18.

Iwamura Haruhiko, 'Dokuritsu Nihon wa Soren to Chūkyō ni dō tachimukau ka' [How Should an Independent Japan Stand up to the Soviet Union and Communist China] *Keizai Shinshi* (July 1952) 7(7): 18–19.

Iwamura Michio, '"Chū-So ronsō" no ichikōsatsu' [A Study of the 'Sino-Soviet Dispute'] *Ajia Kenkyū* (July 1962) 9(2): 1–20.

Iwamura Michio, '10 nenrai no Chū-So kankei' [A Decade of Sino-Soviet Relations] *Kokusai Seiji* (15 May 1960) 12: 28–39.

Iwamura Michio, '8 nenrai no Chū-So kankei' [The Last 8 Years of Sino-Soviet Relations] *Chūgoku Kenkyū Geppō* (Aug. 1963) 186: 1–28.

Iwamura Michio, 'Chū-So jōyaku to Nihon no tachiba' [The Sino-Soviet Treaty and Japan's Standpoint] *Sekai Hyōron* (Apr. 1950) 5(4): 78–83.

Iwamura Michio, 'Chū-So kokkō seijōka no mondaiten' [Problems of Diplomatic Normalization with China and the Soviet Union] *Sekai to Nihon* (Mar. 1955) 15: 26–31.

Iwamura Michio, 'Chū-So to no kokkō kaifuku wa dekiru ka' [Can We Restore Relations with China and the Soviet Union?] *Ajia Keizai Junpō* (Jan. 1955) 238–9: 1–19.

Iwamura Michio, 'NisSo fukkōgo no NitChū kankei' [Japan–Communist China Relations after Normalization with the USSR] *Seikai Ōrai* (Jan. 1957) 23(1): 122–7.

Izumi Takayuki, 'Hiroshima Gensuikin taikai no kokusaiteki sokumen' [An International Perspective on the Hiroshima Anti-Bomb Conference] *Kokusai Mondai* (Sept. 1963) 42: 40–7.

Jacobsen, C.G. 'Strategic Considerations Affecting Soviet Policy toward China and Japan' *Orbis* (winter 1974) 17: 1189–1214.

Jan, George P. 'Japan's Trade with Communist China' *Asian Survey* (Dec. 1969) IX(12): 900–18.

Jan, George P. 'Party Politics and Japan's Policy towards Communist China' *Orbis* (winter 1971) 14: 973–91.

Jan, George P. 'Public Opinion's Growing Influence on Japan's China Policy' *Journalism Quarterly* (1971) 48: 111–9.

Jan, George P. 'The Japanese People and Japan's Policy toward Communist China' *Western Political Quarterly* (summer 1969) 22: 605–21.

Janaki, K. '"Hegemony Clause" or "Jishu Gaiko"?' *New Zealand International Review* (Mar./Apr. 1976) 1(2): 18–20.

Japan Quarterly, 'Assessing the Chinese Bomb' *Japan Quarterly* (Jan./Mar. 1965) XII (1): 12–16.

Japan Quarterly, 'Friendship with the Soviet Union' *Japan Quarterly* (Apr./July 1966) XIII(2): 143–6.

Japan Quarterly, 'Rapprochement with Peking?' *Japan Quarterly* (July/Sept. 1964) XI(3): 265–8.

Japan Quarterly, 'Soviet–Japanese Fishing Talks' *Japan Quarterly* (July/Sept. 1962) IX(3): 257–61.

Japan Quarterly, 'The Gromyko Visit' *Japan Quarterly* (Oct./Dec. 1966) XIII(4): 421–4.

Japan Quarterly, 'The Sino-Soviet Dispute and Japan' *Japan Quarterly* (Apr./June 1963) X(2): 144–8.

Japan Quarterly, 'The Socialists and Communist China' *Japan Quarterly* (Oct./Dec. 1964) X(4): 409–14.

Japan Socialist Party Press Bureau, 'Focal Point of the Sino-Soviet Dispute' *Japan Socialist Review* (15 Feb. 1963) 32: 1–9.

Japan Socialist Party, '[A] New Phase of Neutrality Policy' *Japan Socialist Review* (10 Apr. 1962) 11: 7–13.

Japan Socialist Party, '39th Central Committee of JSP—Arguments Focused on Peace Movement and Sino-Soviet Dispute' *Japan Socialist Review* (15 Oct. 1963) 48: 31–7.

Japan Socialist Party, 'Attitude of Business Toward Japan–China Trade' *Japan Socialist Review* (1 Dec. 1963) 51: 24–8.

Japan Socialist Party, 'France's Recognition of Peking and its Impact on Japan' *Japan Socialist Review* (1 Mar. 1964) 57: 18–22.

Japan Socialist Party, 'Japanese Trade Mission to Soviet Union and Development of Siberia' *Japan Socialist Review* (15 Aug. 1962) 20: 38–54.

Japan Socialist Party, 'Joint Statement JSP Delegation and Chinese People's Institute for Foreign Affairs' *Japan Socialist Review* (16 Jan. 1962) 6: 1–7.

Japan Socialist Party, 'Sino-Soviet Split and Present Condition of JCP—Complicated Attitude of JCP Leadership' *Japan Socialist Review* (1 Oct. 1963) 47: 30–9.

Japan Socialist Party, 'Socialist Foreign Policy vis-à-vis Sino-Soviet Dispute' *Japan Socialist Review* (15 Sept. 1963) 46: 20–2.

Japan Socialist Party, 'The Japanese Communist Party Firmly Entrenched in the Chinese Line' *Japan Socialist Review* (15 June 1964) 64: 46–52.

Jin Xiongbo, 'Chū-So no antō wa tsuzuku' [The Sino-Soviet Secret Feud Continues] *Sekai Shūhō* (6 Dec. 1960) 41(49): 56–7.

Johnson, Chalmers, '"Low Posture" Politics in Japan' *Asian Survey* (Jan. 1963) III(1): 17–30.

Johnson, Chalmers, 'How China and Japan See Each Other' [revised], *China and Japan: A Search for Balance Since World War One*, Alvin D. Coox and Hilary Conroy (eds) (1978): 5–16.

Johnson, Chalmers, 'How China and Japan See Each Other' *Foreign Affairs* (July 1972) 50(4): 711–21.

Johnson, Chalmers, 'MITI and Japan's International Economic Policy', *The Foreign Policy of Modern Japan*, R. Scalapino (ed.) (1977): 227–79.

Johnson, Chalmers, 'The Patterns of Japanese Relations with China 1952–82' *Pacific Affairs* (1986) 59: 402–28.

Johnston, Douglas M. 'Marginal Diplomacy in East Asia' *International Journal* (summer 1971) 26(3): 469–506.

Jorden, William J. 'Japan's Diplomacy between East and West' *Japan between East and West*, Hugh Borton, et al (1957): 240–97.

Kada Tetsuji, 'Oshaberi seiji to omoikosa gaikō no hiai' [The Misery of Gossip Politics and Thoughtless Diplomacy] *Nihon Shūhō* (5 May 1955) 325: 22–6.

Kajima Morinosuke, 'The Japan–US Treaty of Mutual Cooperation and Security: Its Relation to the Sino-Soviet Treaty of Friendship and Alliance', *Japan in Current World Affairs*, Kajima Institute of International Peace (ed.) (1971): 3–27.

Kameda Kōji, 'Gensuikyō taikai bunretsu no oshieru mono' [What we should Learn from the Split in the Anti-Nuclear Weapon Movement] *Tairiku Mondai* (Oct. 1963) 12(10): 24–7.

Kamiya Fuji, 'Nihon gaikō no "ririku" no tame ni' [For the 'Take-off' Stage in Japanese Diplomacy] *Ushio* (Mar. 1965) 57: 66–77.

Kamiyama Shigeo, '"Chū-So ronsō" to Nihon Kyōsantō' ['The Sino-Soviet Dispute' and the Japanese Communist Party] *Shisō No Kagaku* (Nov. 1964) 32: 100–10.

Kanazawa Masao, 'Japan and the Balance of Power in Asia' *Pacific Community* (Oct. 1972) 4(1): 71–8.

Kase Toshikazu, 'Japan's New Role in East Asia' *Foreign Affairs* (Oct. 1955) 34(1): 40–9.

Kashin, A. 'On the Fringe of the Bamboo Curtain, II' *Bulletin of the Institute for the Study of the USSR* (Dec. 1962) 9: 3–12.

Kashin, A. 'The Defeat of the Pro-Soviet Faction of the JCP' *Bulletin of the Institute for the Study of the USSR* (Nov. 1964) XI(11): 31–5.

Kasuga Shōjirō, 'Chō-So ronsō to Kyōsanshugi undō no kakushin' [The Sino-Soviet Dispute and Reform of the Communist Movement] *Kōzō Kaikaku* (Feb. 1963) 14: 2–14.

Kataoka Mitsugu, 'NisSo kokkō kaifuku seba—Soren no nerai wa doko ni aru' [The Soviets' Aim in Restoring Diplomatic Relations with Japan] *Keizei Ōrai* (Nov. 1956) 8(11): 6–10.

Katsumata Seiichi, 'NitChū kokkō kaifuku no rosen' [Strategies for Restoring Japan–China Diplomatic Relations] *Sekai* (Feb. 1957) 134: 136–40.

Kawabata Osamu, 'Burujoa rondan ni okeru "Chū-So ronsō" to shūseishugisha no yakuwari' ['The Sino-Soviet Dispute' and the Role of the Revisionist in the Bourgeois Press] *Zenei* (May 1963) 210: 22–9.

Kawakami Kenzō, 'Nichi-Bei-Ka Gyogyō Jōyaku to NisSo Gyogyō Jōyaku' [The Japan–US–Canada Fisheries Treaty and the Japan–Soviet Fisheries Treaty] *Kokusai Mondai* (May 1963) 38: 28–35.

Kazami Akira, 'NitChū kokkō kaifuku no gendankai' [The Present Stage of the Japan–China Normalisation Issue] *Sekai* (Feb. 1958) 146: 122–9.

Kazami Akira, 'Shin Chūgoku o sasaeru mono' [What Supports the New China] *Chūō Kōron* (Dec. 1953) 68(14): 38–41.

Kennan, George F. 'Japan's Security and American Policy' *Foreign Affairs* (Oct. 1964) 43(1): 14–28.

Kennan, George F. 'Polycentrism and Western Policy' *Foreign Affairs* (Jan. 1964) 42(4): 171–83.

Kesevan, K.V. 'Japan's Response to the Swing in US–Soviet Relations' *International Studies* (India) (Oct./Dec. 1974) 13(4): 677–93.

Kiga Kenzō, 'Chūkyō to Soren no aida no ketsugōteki yōso to taikōteki yōso' [Elements of Unity and Rivalry between Communist China and the Soviet Union] *Soren to Chūkyō*, Ōa Kyōkai (30 Nov. 1962) 1: 539–61.

Kiga Kenzō, 'Chū-So no tairitsu to Nihon' [The Sino-Soviet Rift and Japan] *Ronsō* (Feb. 1960) 2(4): 61–7.

Kiga Kenzō, 'Russo-Japanese Economic Cooperation and its International Environment' *Pacific Community* (Apr. 1973) 4(3): 452–70.

Kiga Kenzō, 'The Policy of Peaceful Coexistance and Soviet–Japanese Economic Relations' *Review* (Tokyo) (Mar. 1966) 8: 1–15.

Kim, Hong N. 'Deradicalization of the Japanese Communist Party under Kenji Miyamoto' *World Politics* (Jan. 1976) 28(2): 273–99.

Kim, Young C. 'Japanese Perceptions of Defense Issues: A Study of "Defense Influentials"', *Japanese and U.S. Policy in Asia*, Gaston Sigur and Y.C. Kim (eds) (1982): 15–44.

Kimbara Kazuyuki, 'The Development of Siberia and Japan' *Acta Slavica Iaponica* (1986) IV: 66–78.

Kimura Akio, 'Sino-Soviet Rapprochement. How Far Will it Go?' *Japan Quarterly* (July/Sept. 1983) XXX(3): 248–55.

Kimura Hiroshi, 'Basic Determinants of Soviet–Japanese Relations: Background, Framework, Perceptions and Issues' *Acta Slavica Iaponica* (1987) V: 71–92.

Kimura Hiroshi, 'Gorbachev and the Northern Territories' *Japan Echo* (winter 1988) XV(4): 11–23.

Kimura Hiroshi, 'Japan–Soviet Relations: Framework, Developments, Prospects' *Asian Survey* (July 1980) XX(7): 707–25.

Kimura Hiroshi, 'Sakoku Sobieto no kaihō' [The Opening Up of the Isolationist Soviet Union] *Chūō Kōron* (Dec. 1963) 78(12): 85–92.

Kimura Kihachirō, 'Daiyonji kyōtei kōshō no kihonten' [Focal Point of the Fourth [Japan–China Trade] Agreement Negotiations] *Ekonomisuto* (4 May 1957) 35(18): 20–3.

Kinbara Kazuyuki, 'The Economic Dimension of Soviet Policy', *The Soviet Union in East Asia*, G. Segal (ed.) (1983): 102–28.

Kinugasa Tetsuo, 'Heiwa kakumei to Chū-So ronsō' [Peaceful Revolution and the Sino-Soviet Dispute] *Shakaishugi* (Shakaishugi Kyōkai) (Oct. 1964) 156: 10–20.

Kirby, E. Stuart, 'The Stick and the Carrot' *Far Eastern Economic Review* (15 Oct. 1964) XLVI(3): 141–3.

Kishi Nobusuke, 'Japan in 1957' *Contemporary Japan* (Apr. 1957) XXIV(10–12): 553–7.

Kishi Nobusuke, 'Sōri kōho to iwarete' [As a Candidate for Prime Minister] *Bungei Shunjū* (Dec. 1956) 34(12): 74–83.

Kiuchi Nobutane, 'Gaikō no kokorogamae to kichō ni tsuite' [Concerning the Basis and Keynote of [Our] Diplomacy] *Keizai Rondan* (Feb. 1961) 7(2): 9–11.

Kiyomiya (sic), 'Chū-So ronsenba to kaesu—Mosukuwa no yūsu fōramu' [A Change of Scene in the Sino-Soviet Controversy: The Moscow Youth Forum] *Sekai Shūhō* (13 Oct. 1964) 45(41): 14–15.

Klein, Sidney, 'A Survey of Sino-Japanese Trade (1950–66' *The China Mainland Review* (Dec. 1966) II(3): 185–91.

Klinghoffer, Arthur Jay, 'Sino-Soviet Relations and the Politics of Oil' *Asian Survey* (June 1976) 16(6): 540–52.

Kohtani Etsuo, 'Japan and the Sino-Soviet Conflict' *Bulletin of the Institute for the Study of the USSR* (Dec. 1964) XI(12): 34–38.

Kohtani Etsuo, 'The Present Position of Moscow and Peking in the Communist bloc and in the Far East' *Bulletin of the Institute for the Study of the USSR* (Nov. 1969) 16: 11–18.

Kojima Shuichi, 'The Changing Japanese Perception of the Soviet Union as Seen in Postwar General-interest Magazines' *Kōnan Daigaku Sōgō Kenkyūjo* (1987–88) 16: 3–31.

Komuro Makoto, 'Chūkyō-Soren kankei no jittai' [The Substance of Sino-Soviet Relations] *Soren Kenkyū* (Nov. 1957) 6(11): 12–20.

Kondo (pseud?), 'NisSo Kyōkai' [The Japan–Soviet Society] *Zembō* (15 Sept. 1957) 59: 22–9.

Kōno Ichirō, 'Dorai ni mita Nihon no seiji—Ishibashi naikaku no mondai o warikitte kangaeru' [Japanese Politics Appear Dry: Clear Thinking on the Problem(s) of the Ishibashi Cabinet] *Bungei Shunjū* (Mar. 1957) 35(3): 126–35.

Kōno Ichirō, 'NisSo kōryū ni tsuite kokumin ni uttaeru' [My Appeal to the Nation Concerning Japan–Soviet Exchanges] *Chūō Kōron* (July 1962) 77(8): 190–7.

Kōno Ichirō, 'NisSo kōshō ni oite wareware no ito shita mono' [What We Sought in Japan–USSR Negotiations] *Chūō Kōron* (Dec. 1956) 71(13): 68–73.

Kōsaka Masataka, 'Chūgoku mondai to wa nani ka' [What is the China Problem?] *Jiyū* (Apr. 1964) 6(4): 30–45.

Kōsaka Masataka, 'Genjitsushugisha no heiwaron' [A Realist's Views on Peace] *Chūō Kōron* (Jan. 1963) 78(1): 38–49.

Kōsaka Masataka, 'Japan's Post-war Foreign Policy', *Papers on Modern Japan, 1968*, D.C.S. Sissons (ed.) (1968): 1–25.

Kōsaka Masataka, 'Kaiyō kokka Nihon no kōsō' [The Idea of Japan as a Maritime Nation] *Chūō Kōron* (Sept. 1964) 79(9): 48–80.

Kōsaka Masataka, 'Kokusai seiji no tagenka to Nihon' [Polycentrism in International Politics] *Chūō Kōron* (Dec. 1964) 79(12): 94–107.

Kosaka Zentaro, 'Japan and Nuclear Weapons Tests' *Contemporary Japan* (Mar. 1962) 27(2): 199–208.

Kosaka Zentarō, 'Nihon ni semaru chūritsuka seisaku' [Japan Pressured to Neutralize] *Seikei Shishin* (Aug. 1955) 2(8): 90–9.

Kosuge Shōzō, '"Chū-So ronsō" to Nihon no shūseishugi—Satō Noboru no ronbun ni tsuite' ['The Sino-Soviet Dispute' and Japanese Revisionism: Concerning the Satō Noboru Thesis] *Zenei* (Dec. 1963) 217: 93–103.

Kubota Yasushi, 'Chū-So fuwasetsu ni tsuite' [Concerning Sino-Soviet Discord] *Febian Kenkyū* (Mar. 1960) 11(3): 38–41.

Kubota Yasutarō, 'NitChū bōeki kōshō zasetsu no oshieru mono' [Lessons from the Collapse of the Japan–China Trade Talks] *Chūō Kōron* (Jan. 1958) 73(1): 124–35.

Kurai Ryōzō, 'Current Developments in Sino-Japanese Relations and Japanese Attitudes towards Communist China' *The Japan Annual of International Affairs* (1963–4) 3: 87–113.

Kurihara Yukio, 'Chū-So ronsō no rekishiteki haikei' [The Sino-Soviet Dispute's Historical Background] *Gendai no Me* (Mar. 1963) 4(3): 34–43.

Kusano Fumio, 'Chū-So dōmei to Nihon e no eikyō' [The Influence of the Sino-Soviet Alliance on Japan] *Kumiai Undō* (Mar. 1950) 5(3): 43–8.

Kusano Fumio, 'Chū-So kankei no hitotsu no mikata' [My Evaluation of Sino-Soviet Relations] *Tairiku Mondai* (Nov. 1963) 12(11): 22–7.

Kusano Fumio, 'Chū-So no ronsō to keizai kankei' [The Sino-Soviet Dispute and Economic Relations] *Ronsō* (Mar. 1962) 4(3): 30–7.

Labin, Suzanne and Christopher Emmet, 'Is there a Sino-Soviet Split?' *Orbis* (spring 1960) 4(1): 28–38.

Lafeber, Walter, 'Decline of Relations during the Vietnam War', *The United States and Japan in the Postwar World*, Iriye Akira and W.I. Cohen (eds) (1989): 96–113.

Langdon, Frank C. 'Japan's Liberal Democrats' Factional Discord on China Policy' *Pacific Affairs* (fall 1968) 41: 403–15.

Langer, Paul F. 'Japan and the Great Power Triangles', *The World and the Great Power Triangles*, W.E. Griffith (ed.) (1975): 271–320.

Langer, Paul F. 'Japan's Relations with China' *Current History* (Apr. 1964) 46(272): 192–8, 244.

Langer, Paul F. 'Moscow, Peking and Tokyo: Views and Approaches' *Unity and Contradiction: Major Aspects of Sino-Soviet Relations*, Kurt London (ed.) (1962): 207–32.

Langer, Paul F. 'The JCP Between Moscow and Peking', *Communist Strategies in Asia*, A. Doak Barnett (ed.) (1963): 63–100.

Lee, Chae-Jin, 'Factional Politics in the JSP: The Chinese Cultural Revolution Case' *Asian Survey* (Mar. 1970) X(3): 230–43.

Lee, Chae-Jin, 'The Making of the Sino-Japanese Peace and Friendship Treaty' *Pacific Affairs* (1979) 52(3): 420–45.

Lee, Chae-Jin, 'The Politics of Sino-Japanese Trade Relations 1963–68' *Pacific Affairs* (summer 1969) 42(2): 129–44.

Lowe, Peter, 'Challenge and Readjustment: Anglo-American Exchanges over East Asia 1949–53', *Conflict and Amity in East Asia*, T.G. Fraser and Peter Lowe (eds) (1992): 143–62.

Löwenthal, Richard, 'The Soviet Union, China and Japan' *Survey* (autumn 1972) 18(4): 30–7.

Maeda Hisao, 'The State of Japan–China Economic Relations and their Future', *Japan in the World*, Kajima Institute of International Peace (ed.) (1976): 111–27.

Maeda Yoshinori, 'Itashikayushi no NisSo fukkō—Okinawa henkan se so Beikoku saidai no kunō' [Delicate Japan–Soviet Normalization—Reversion of Okinawa is America's Biggest Headache] *Nihon Shūhō* (15 Nov. 1956) 387: 20–2.

Maeshiba Kakuzō, 'Kaikyūteki shiten to jinruiteki shiten—iwayuru "Chū-So ideorogii ronsō" ni tsuite' [The so-called 'Sino-Soviet Ideological Dispute' from the Viewpoints of Class and Humankind] *Ritsumeikan Hōgaku* (Sept. 1960) 34: 214–38.

Majima Kan, 'NisSo kokkō wa saikai sarete iku' [Soviet–Japanese Diplomatic Relations will be Reopened] *Chūō Kōron* (Mar. 1955) 70(3): 224–7.

Majima Kan, 'Shirōto gaikōron' [On Amateur Diplomacy] *Seikai Ōrai* (Oct. 1956) 22(10): 56–9.

Maki Tadashi, 'Chū-So no tai Nichi sekkin no shini' [The Real Motives Behind The Sino-Soviet Policy of Rapprochement with Japan] *Jikei* (Dec. 1954) 36(12): 82–5.

Makiuchi Masao, 'Ajia ni okeru Chūkyō no seiryoku—Chū-So ronsō to kanren shitemiru' [Chinese Communist Strength in Asia in the Context of the Sino-Soviet Ideological Dispute] *Kyōsanken Mondai* (Nov. 1963) 7(11): 47–58.

Mamoi Makoto, 'Basic Trends in Japanese Security Policies' *Foreign Policy of Modern Japan*, R.A. Scalapino (ed.) (1977): 341–64.

Marukawa Tatsuo, 'Kewashii NitChū dakai e no michi' [The Thorny Road to a Japan–China Rapprochement] *Soren Kenkyū* (June 1960) 9(6): 45–54, 78.

Matsueda Tsukasa and George E. Moore, 'Japan's Shifting Attitudes toward the Military: Mitsuya Kenkyū and the SDF' *Asian Survey* (Sept. 1967) VII(9): 614–25.

Matsumoto Shigeharu, 'Gendai Nihon no kokusaiteki chii' [Japan's Current International Position] *Chūō Kōron* (Oct. 1961) 76(10): 26–40.

Matsumoto Shigeharu, 'Japan and China: Domestic and Foreign Influences on Japan's Policy', *Policies Toward China: Views from Six Continents*, A.M. Halpern (ed.) (1965): 123–64.

Matsumoto Shigeharu, Paul Langer and Fukui Fumio, 'Kawariyuku sekai to Nihon' [The Changing World and Japan] *Jiyū* (April 1961) 3(4): 2–14.

Matsumura Kenzō, 'Bridging the Gap to China' *Japan Quarterly* (Jan./Mar. 1964) XI(1): 27–31.

Matsumura Kenzō, 'Chūkyō seikai no jinbutsu o kata[ru]' [Talks with Chinese Communist Political Leaders] *Seikai Ōrai* (Jan. 1963) 29(1): 74–82.

Matsumura Kenzō, 'Watashi no Ajia kan—NitChū kankei o chūshin ni' [My View of Asia: Concerning Japan–China Relations] *Shisō* (Jan. 1963) 463: 152–6.

Medvedev, Roy, 'The USSR and China: Confrontation or Detente?' *New Left Review* (Nov./Dec. 1983) 142: 5–29.

Mehnert, Klaus, 'Peking und Moskau' [Beijing and Moscow] *Osteuropa* (Nov./Dec. 1960) 10(11/12): 729–70.

Mendel, Douglas H. 'Japan Reviews Her American Alliance' *Public Opinion Quarterly* (spring 1966) 30(1): 1–18.

Mendel, Douglas H. 'Public Views of the Japanese Defense System', *The Modern Japanese Military System*, James H. Buck (ed.) (1975): 149–80.

Mendl, Wolf, 'Japan and China' *Survey* (autumn 1972) 18(4): 66–73.

Mendl, Wolf, 'Japan and its Giant Neighbours' *The World Today* (June 1983) 39(6): 206–15.

Mendl, Wolf, 'Keeping the Door Open: Some Considerations About Japanese Attitudes towards China in the Immediate Post War Era' *Proceedings of the British Association for Japanese Studies* (1976) 1(1): 151–68.

Miki Takeo and Kiya Ikusaburō, 'Jimintō shinkanjichō no kōsō o kiku' [The New LDP Secretary General Airs His Views] *Seikai Ōrai* (Mar. 1957) 23(3): 58–65.

Miki Takeo, Katsumata Seiichi, and Nosaka Sanzō, 'Atarashii tenkan ni dō taisho suru ka' [How to Deal With the New Turnabout] *Sekai* (May 1959) 149: 218–39.

Miki Takeo, Sata Tadataka, Kuroda Hisao, and Uramatsu Samitarō, 'NisSo kōshō daketsu to seikyoku no zento' [The Japan–Soviet Agreement and the Future Political Situation] *Sekai* (Dec. 1956) 132: 92–105.

Mishima Yukio, 'Tenka taihei no shisō' [An Ideology for a World at Peace] *Ronsō* (Sept. 1963) 5(9): 40–2.

Mitsuoka Gen, '"Chū-So ronsō" to Chūgoku zō' [The 'Sino-Soviet Dispute' and China's Image] *Chūgoku Kenkyū Geppō* (May 1963) 183: 1–22.

Miura Ryōichi, 'Chū-So kōsō to Nihon no sayoku seitō' [The Sino-Soviet Struggle and the Japanese Left Wing Political Parties] *Kikan Shakai Kagaku* (Aug. 1964) 4: 228–40.

Miyamoto Kenji, 'Chū-So dōmei to Nihon minzoku' [The Sino-Soviet Alliance and the Japanese People] *Atarashii Sekai* (Mar. 1950) 33: 2–11.

Momoi Makoto, 'Basic Trends in Japan's Security Policies', *The Foreign Policy of Modern Japan*, R. Scalapino (ed.) (1977): 341–64.

Mori Kazuko, 'Sino-Soviet Relations: from Confrontation to Cooperation' *Japan Review of International Affairs* (spring/summer 1988) 2(1): 42–66.

Mori Kyōzō, 'Bei-So sekkin to Chū-So no tairitsu' [The U.S.–Soviet Rapprochement and the Sino-Soviet Rift] *Kokusai Mondai* (Sept. 1963) 42: 12–19.

Mori Kyōzō, 'Chū-So tairitsu kara nani o hikidasu ka' [What can be Extracted from the Sino-Soviet Rift?] *Ronsō* (Mar. 1963) 5(3): 6–14.

Mori Kyōzō, 'Nihon gaikō ni jishusei o motomu—Chū-So ronsō to kakutei jōyaku ni yosete' [Demanding Independence in Japanese Foreign Policy: Under the Pretext of the Sino-Soviet Dispute and the Nuclear Test-Ban Treaty] *Jiyū* (Aug. 1963) 5(8): 2–9.

Mori Takanosuke, 'NisSo shinzen no itsuwareru seisō' [Japanese–Soviet Friendship's Deceptive Best Clothes] *Gendai no Me* (Aug. 1966) 7(8): 112–25.

Morinaga Kazuhiko, 'Shiro to kiiro no arasoi? Chū-So ronsō to Nihon no tachiba' [A Fight between Whites and Yellows? The Sino-Soviet Dispute and Japan's Standpoint] *Sekai Shūhō* (16 July 1963) 44(29): 12–13.

Morishima Morito, 'NisSo kōshō no genjō to tenbō' [The Present State of and Outlook for the Japan–Soviet Negotiations] *Shakaishugi* (Shakaishugi Kyōkai) (Aug. 1955) 49: 24–9.

Morley, James W. 'Japan's Image of the Soviet Union 1952–61' *Pacific Affairs* (spring 1962) 35(1): 51–8.

Morley, James W. 'Japan's Position in Asia' *Journal of International Affairs* (1963) 17(2): 142–54.

Morley, James W. 'The Soviet–Japanese Peace Declaration' *Political Science Quarterly* (Sept. 1957) 72: 370–9.

Morris, I.I. 'Foreign Policy Issues in Japan's 1958 Elections' *Pacific Affairs* (Sept. 1958) XXXI(3): 219–40.

Morris, I.I. 'Japanese Foreign Policy and Neutralism' *International Affairs* (Jan. 1960) 36(1): 7–20.

Mosely, Philip E. 'The Moscow–Peking Axis in World Politics' *Moscow–Peking Axis—Strengths and Strains*, Howard Boorman, et al. (1957): 198–227.

Mugino Ippei (pseud.), 'Gaimukanryō no seitai' [The Way of Life of Gaimushō Bureaucrats] *Jimbutsu Ōrai* (July 1955) 43: 26–31.

Mukohara Tatsuzō, 'Gaimushō: kō Bei ippentō—reizoku taisei no sentā o saguru' [MOFA: Taking the US Side—Investigating the Centre of the Dependency System] *Chūō Kōron* (Nov. 1954) 69(11): 92–100.

Muramatsu Yūji, 'Chūkyō wa Yūgo no michi o ayumu ka' [Will Communist China follow Yugoslavia?] *Keizai Ōrai* (Nov. 1960) 12(11): 65–71.

Murata Shōzō, 'Furui Chūgokukan e no keikoku' [A Warning to Our Old View of China] *Bungei Shunjū* (July 1955) 33(7): 56–63.

Murata Shōzō, 'NitChū kankei no genjō o ureu' [My Worries about the Current State of Japan–China Relations] *Sekai* (Nov. 1955) 119: 18–23.

Murata Shōzō, 'NitChū keizei kōryū no tenbō' [The Outlook for Japan–China Economic Exchange] *Sekai* (Feb. 1957) 134: 80–85.

Murthy, P.A. Narasimha, 'Gendai Shisō Kenkyūkai: The "Japanese New Left"', *International Studies* (India) (Oct. 1962) IV(2): 194–7.

Murthy, P.A. Narasimha, 'Japan and the India–China Border Conflict' *International Studies* (India) (July/Oct. 1963) V(1–2): 180–7.

Murthy, P.A. Narasimha, 'Japan's Changing Relations with People's China and the Soviet Union' *International Studies* (India) (July 1965) VII(1): 1–19.

Murthy, P.A. Narasimha, 'The Japanese Left and the Anti-Nuclear Movement' *International Studies* (India) (Jan. 1964) V(3): 281–95.

Mushakōji Kinhide, 'Nihon gaikōkan no shisō to kōdō' [The Thought and Behaviour of Japanese Diplomats] *Chūō Kōron* (Oct. 1961) 76(10): 332–40.

Mushakōji Kinhide, 'Tachūshinshugi to Bei-Chū reisen no aida—Kenan ronbun to Bandi enzetsu ni yosete' [Between Polycentrism and the US–China Cold War: On the Kennan Thesis and the Bundy Speech] *Asahi Jānaru* (18 Oct. 1964) 6(42): 20–5.

Mushakoji Kinhide, 'The Changing Japanese Foreign Policy Attitudes in the 1960s' *Japan Institute of International Affairs Annual Review* (1970) 5: 1–15.

Mutō Teiichi, 'Chūkyō ni tai suru warera no yūaikan' [Our Friendly Feelings Towards Communist China] *Raito (The Light)* (June 1964) 11(5): 8–14.

Nabeyama Sadachika, 'Chū-So ketsuretsu to Nihon no sayoku' [The Sino-Soviet Rupture and the Japanese Left Wing] *Keieisha* (Nov. 1963) 17(11): 58–61.

Nabeyama Sadachika, 'Chū-So tairitsu to Nikkyō no kiretsu' [The Sino-Soviet Rift and the Japanese Communist Fissure] *Kankō Rōdō* (15 Mar. 1963) 17(3): 11–13.

Nabeyama Sadachika, 'Chū-So tairitsu to Nikkyō' [The Sino-Soviet Rift and the JCP] *Kankō Rōdō* (15 July 1964) 18(7): 11–13.

Nakajima Mineo, 'China May Return to the Soviet bloc' *Japan Quarterly* (Apr./July 1983) XXX(2): 181–7.

Nakajima Mineo, 'Chū-So ronsō no shodanmen to gendai Marukusushugi [Various Perspectives on the Sino-Soviet Dispute and Contemporary Marxism] *Shisō* (Dec. 1964) 486: 88–97.

Nakajima Mineo, 'Chū-So ronsō shinkyokumen to Chūgoku' [The New Phase in the Sino-Soviet Dispute and China] *Ekonomisuto* (9 and 16 Apr. 1963) 41 (14, 15): 50–5, 44–52.

Nakajima Mineo, 'Japan's Policies toward the Soviet Union and China', *Japanese and U.S. Policy in Asia*, G.J. Sigur and Y.C. Kim (eds) (1982): 81–96.

Nakajima Mineo, 'The Sino-Soviet Confrontation in Historical Perspective', *The Origins of the Cold War in Asia*, Nagai Yonosuke and Iriye Akira (eds) (1977): 203–23.

Nakano Sumio, 'Chū-So ronsō ni kan suru ichikōsatsu' [A Study of the Sino-Soviet Dispute] *Tairiku Mondai* (May 1963) 12(5): 50–5.

Nakano Yoshio, 'NitChū kankei no akka to shimbun hōdō' [The Deterioration in Japan–China Relations and the Press] *Sekai* (July 1958) 151: 69–74.

Nakasone Yasuhiro, 'Fukami ni wa maru to yakedo' [Fall in the Deep End and Get Burnt] *Jitsugyō no Nihon* (1 Sept. 1954) 57(21): 47.

Nakasone Yasuhiro, 'Japan and the China Problem: A Liberal–Democratic View' *Japan Quarterly* (July/Sept. 1961) 8(3): 266–73.

Nakasone Yasuhiro, 'Nihon mo kazantai no ikkan' [Japan is also a Part of the Volcanic Zone] *Chūō Kōron* (spring 1957, special issue) 72(4): 198–9.

Nakasone Yasuhiro, 'Takai to jikai' [Disciplining Others and Oneself] *Chūō Kōron* (autumn 1956, special issue) 71(9): 164–5.

Nanjō Tōru, 'Chū-So kankei no shindankai' [A New Stage in Sino-Soviet Relations] *Soren Kenkyū* (Sept. 1958) 7(9): 4–7.

Naoi Takeo, 'Sino-Japanese Deadlock' *New Leader* (29 Sept. 1958) XLI(39): 9–10.

Nihon oyobi Nihonjin, 'NisSo kōshō to sayoku no senden katsudō' [Japan–Soviet Negotiations and Leftists' Propaganda Activities] *Nihon oyobi Nihonjin* (Aug. 1955) 6(8): 34–41.

Nihon Shūhō, 'Nikkyō, Chūkyō rosen ni fumikiru—Washinton no handan' [The JCP Plumps for Communist China's Strategy: Washington Concludes] *Nihon Shūhō* (15 Aug. 1961) 531: 59.

Niizeki Kinya, 'Soren sekai seisaku no gendankai' [The Present Stage of Soviet Global Policy] *Gaikō Jihō* (Nov. 1952) 111(1): 58–64.

Nishi Yoshiyuki, 'Chū-So ronsō to Nihon no chishikijin' [The Sino-Soviet Dispute and Japanese Intellectuals] *Kikan Shakai Kagaku* (Sept. 1964) 4: 241–54.

Nishihara Masashi, 'How much Longer the Fruits of the "Yoshida Doctrine"?', *Korea and Japan: A New Dialogue Across the Channel*, Hahn Bae-ho and Yamamoto Tadashi (eds) (1978): 150–67.

Nishikawa Ichirō, 'Chū-So ronsō no kōsei' [The Composition of the Sino-Soviet Dispute] *Gekkan Shakaitō* (Mar. 1963) 70: 86–95.

Nishimura Naomi, 'Watashi wa akaikoku Soren, Chūkyō o kō mita' [The Soviet Union and Communist China as I Saw Them] *Jitsugyō no Nihon* (1 Sept. 1954) 57(21): 44–5.

Nishizawa Tomio, 'Mosukuwa seimei no shūseishugiteki kaishaku—Satō Noboru shi no ronbun ni tsuite' [A Revisionist Explanation of the Moscow Declaration: Concerning the Satō Noboru Thesis] *Zenei* (Mar. 1961) 183: 44–55.

Nitze, Paul, 'Strategy in the Decade of the 1980s' *Foreign Affairs* (fall 1980) 59(1): 82–101.

Nobuhara Naotake and Akao Nobutoshi, 'The Politics of Siberian Development', *Japan's Economic Security*, Akao Nobutoshi (ed.) (1983): 197–215.

Noda Fukuo, 'The Left-wing Movement in Japan 1954–64' *Journal of Social and Political Ideas in Japan* (Apr. 1965) 3(1): 2–17.

Noguchi Yuichirō, 'Keizai nashonarizumu ron' [The Theory of Economic Nationalism] *Sekai* (Jan. 1965) 229: 53–62.

Nomizo Masaru, 'Chū-So heiwa kōsei to chōsen mondai no zento' [The Sino-Soviet Peace Offensive and Prospects for the Korean Problem] *Jitsugyō no Sekai* (Dec. 1954) 51(12): 22–3.

Nomizo Masaru, 'Hō So hō Chū no tabi' [Trips to the Soviet Union and China] *Sekai Shūhō* (21 Nov. 1955) 36(33): 68–9.

Nomura Kichisaburō and Kiya Ikusaburō, 'Ryōmen gaikō wa kanō ka' [Is a Two-Pronged Diplomacy Possible?] *Seikai Ōrai* (Oct. 1956) 22(10): 42–9.

Nomura Kōichi, 'Tairitsuron ni tsuite ni, mitsu no gimon' [Some Doubts Concerning Discussion of the Rift] *Asahi Janaru* (10 Mar. 1963) 5(10): 10–16.

Nonomura Kazuo, 'Japan–USSR Economic Relations', *Japan in the World*, Kajima Institute of International Peace (ed.) (1976): 69–96.

Nonomura Kunio, 'NisSo bōeki no shōrai to mondaiten' [Problems and the Future of Japanese–Soviet Trade] *Ekonomisuto* (25 June 1963) 41(25): 6–13.

Northedge, F.S. 'The Divided Mind of Japan' *Yearbook of World Affairs* (1957) 2: 156–83.

Nosaka Sanzō, 'Watashi no kaitō' [My Answer] *Chūō Kōron* (Nov. 1955) 70(11): 125–6.

Obata Misao, 'Sino-Soviet Dispute: Notes from Lake Kawaguchi' *Japan Quarterly* (Jan./Mar. 1961) 8(1): 25–32.

Ogata Sadako, 'Japanese Attitudes toward China' *Asian Survey* (Aug. 1965) 5(8): 389–98.

Ogata Sadako, 'The Business Community and Japanese Foreign Policy: Normalization of Relations with the PRC', *The Foreign Policy of Modern Japan*, R.A. Scalapino (ed.) (1977): 175–203.

Ōhara Sōichirō, 'Tai Chūgoku puranto yushutsu ni tsuite' [Concerning the Export of Plant to China] *Sekai* (Sept. 1963) 213: 103–08.

Ōhira Masayoshi, 'A New Foreign Policy for Japan' *Pacific Community* (Apr. 1972) 3(3): 405–18.

Ōhira Masayoshi, 'Diplomacy for Peace: The Aims of Japanese Foreign Policy' *International Affairs* (July 1964) 40(3): 391–6.

Ōhira Zengo, 'Katayotta Chūkyōkan o haisuru' [Communist China's One-Sided View Denounced] *Jiyū no Hata no Moto ni* (Mar. 1953) 1(3): 50–3.

Ohta Kaoru, 'Comments on [the] Sino-Soviet Dispute' *Japan Socialist Review* (15 Feb. 1963) 32: 10–11.

Okabe Tatsumi, 'Japan–China Relations', *Japan and Postwar Diplomacy in the Asia–Pacific Region*, Hosoya Chihiro (ed.) (1984): 297–315.

Okada Yuzurō, 'Japanese Intellectuals' *Journal of Social and Political Ideas in Japan* (Apr. 1964) 2(1): 2–7.

Okazaki Kaheita, Nishi Haruhiko, Matsumura Kenzō, Matsumoto Shigeru, and Uchida Kenzō, 'Nihon gaikō ni chūmon suru—NitChū kankei ni sokushite' [What is Desired of Japan's Diplomacy: Adapting Japan–China Relations] *Sekai* (June 1963) 210: 102–18.

Ōki Masato, 'Chū-So ronsō to Nihon teikokushugi' [The Sino-Soviet Dispute and Japanese Imperialism] *Keizai Hyōron* (Jan. 1961) 10(1): 50–61.

Ōkōchi Kazuo, 'Sōhyō ron ' [The General Council of Trade Unions of Japan] *Sekai* (Sept. 1955) 117: 63–73.

Ōkuma Nobuyuki, Kōno Ichirō, Fukumoto Kazuo, Koizumi Shinzō, Ōya Sōichi, Shimizu Ikutarō, Hirabayashi Taiko, Matsuoka Yōko, Katsumata Seiichi, and Nakasone Yasuhiro, 'Sorezore no uketomekata' [Several Reactions [to De-Stalinization]] *Chūō Kōron* (Mar. 1957, special issue) 72: 184–99.

Ōkura Kinmochi, 'NitChūSo no kankei o meguri' [Concerning Japan–China–Soviet Relations] *Soren Kenkyū* (June 1955) 4(6): 48–50.

Olson, Lawrence, 'In Ten Years, in Fifty Years: Comments on Chinese Trade, 30 October 1958' *Dimensions of Japan*, L. Olson (1963): 335–46.

Ōmori Minoru, 'Nihon gaikō no kihon gensoku o tou' [Questioning the Basic Principles of Japanese Diplomacy] *Chūō Kōron* (Jan. 1963) 78(1): 148–59.

Omura Akira, 'So-Chū ryōkoku seifu no kyōdō sengen ni tsuite' [Concerning the Sino-Soviet Joint Declaration] *Zenei*, 99(Dec. 1954): 46–50.

Ōno Shinzō, 'Kuzureyuku Soren teikokushugi' [Crumbling Soviet Imperialism] *Nihon Shūhō* (15 Nov. 1956) 387: 44–9.

Ōno Shinzō, Sono Akira, and Kim Ta-fu, 'Nihon o nerau heiwa kōsei' [Peace Offensive Aims at Japan] *Nihon Shūhō* (15 May 1953) 246: 30–9.

Onoe Masao, 'Chū-So riron tōsō no hitsuzensei to genkai' [Inevitability and Limits of the Sino-Soviet Theoretical Dispute] *Kokusai Seiji* (Apr. 1963) 21: 59–70.

Onoe Masao, 'Chū-So ronsō ni tai suru hitotsu no kaishaku' [One Interpretation of the Sino-Soviet Dispute] *Kokusai Seiji* (Oct. 1965) 29: 1–8.

Onoe Masao, 'Chū-So ronsō—sono rekishiteki igi to kokusai seiji ni okeru mondaiten' [The Sino-Soviet Dispute: Its Significance in History and International Politics] *Rekishi Kyōiku* (Feb. 1966) 14(2): 43–8.

Onoe Masao, 'Factors Binding the USSR and Communist China', *Unity and Contradiction,* Kurt London (ed.) (1962): 142–55.

Onoe Masao, 'Furushichofu no gaikō to Chū-So kōsō' [Khrushchev's Diplomacy and the Sino-Soviet Struggle] *Kyōsanken Mondai* (July 1965) 9(7): 21–39.

Onoe Masao, 'Hachijūikkakoku Kyōsantō sengen to Chū-So ronsō' [The Moscow Statement and the Sino-Soviet Dispute] *Kyōsanken Mondai* (Jan. 1961) 4(4): 10–18.

Ōnuma Kiichirō and Mishima Akira, 'Zōshin suru NitChū bōeki no jittai' [Increasing Japan–China Trade is a Reality] *Ekonomisuto* (27 Oct. 1956) 34(43): 22–30.

Oshima Yasumasa, 'Introduction' *Journal of Social and Political Ideas in Japan* (Aug. 1965) 3(2): 2–9.

Otake Heihachiro, 'NisSo kōshōgo no Kyōsanken bōeki' [Japan–Communist bloc Trade after the Negotiations with the USSR] *Jitsugyō no Nihon* (1 Sept. 1956) 59(21): 40–3.

Packard, George R. 'Living with the Real Japan' *Foreign Affairs* (Oct. 1967) 46(1): 193–204.

Park, Yung H. 'The Anti-Hegemony Controversy in Sino-Japanese Relations' *Pacific Affairs* (1976–7) 49: 476–90.

Park, Yung H. 'The Roots of Détente', *China and Japan*, A.D. Coox and H. Conroy (eds) (1978): 353–84.

Pempel, T.J. 'Japanese Foreign Economic Policy: The Domestic Bases for International Behaviour' *International Organization* (autumn 1977) 31(4): 723–74.

Petrov, D. 'Japan and the Mao Group's Foreign Policy' *International Affairs* (Moscow) (Dec. 1968) 12: 30–7.

Polaris, Jean, 'The Sino-Soviet Dispute: Its Economic Impact on China' *International Affairs* (Oct. 1964) 40: 647–58.

Pond, Elizabeth, 'Japan and Russia: The View from Tokyo' *Foreign Affairs* (Oct. 1973) 52(1): 141–52.

Prybyla, Jan S. 'Peking and Tokyo: Trade Without Recognition' *Twentieth Century* (autumn 1965) 19: 212–7.

Q. (pseud.), 'Tai So bōeki urabanashi' [The Inside Story on Trade with the Soviet Union] *Ekonomisuto* (18 Sept. 1954) 32(38): 20–1.

Qing Simei, 'The Eisenhower Administration and Changes in Western Embargo Policy Against China, 1954–58', *The Great Powers in East Asia, 1953–1960*, Warren Cohen and Iriye Akira (eds) (1990): 121–42.

Quigg, P.W. 'Japan in Neutral' *Foreign Affairs* (Jan. 1966) 44(2): 253–63.

Quigley, Harold S. 'Japan Between Two Worlds' *Far Eastern Survey* (Nov. 1956) 25(11): 168–74.

Rhee, T.C. 'Historical and Psychological Obstacles to Japan's Rapprochement with China' *Asia Quarterly* (Apr./June 1974) 19(2): 147–69.

Robinson, J.W. 'View from Peking: China's Policies towards the U.S., Soviet Union and Japan' *Pacific Affairs* (fall 1974) 45: 333–55.

Roucek, Joseph S, 'Changing Japanese Foreign Policy in Regard to the U.S. and Communist Countries' *Revue du Sud-est Asiatique* (1966) 2: 163–84.

Rōyama Masamichi, 'NitChū kokkō kaifuku mondai' [The Problem of Restoring Japan–China Relations] *Sekai* (Feb. 1957) 134: 73–79.

Rōyama Yoshirō, 'Sekaijō no hyōka o meguru Chū-So no ronsō' [The Sino-Soviet Dispute over their Judgements of the World Situation] *Shisō* (Dec. 1960) 438: 51–71.

Saeki Kiichi, 'Nihon no anzen hoshō o dō suru' [What to do about Japan's Security] *Ekonomisuto* (10 Oct. 1965, special issue) 43(43): 37–43.

Saeki Kiichi, 'Toward Japanese Cooperation in Siberian Development' *Problems of Communism* (May/June 1972) XXI(3): 1–11.

Saitō Motohide, 'Nichi-Bei Anpo Jōyaku kaitei to Soren no tai Nichi seisaku' [The Revision of the US–Japan Security Treaty and Soviet Policy toward Japan] *Hōgaku Kenkyū (Keiō Gijuku Daigaku)* (May 1980) 53(5): 65–86.

Saitō Motohide, 'The "Highly Crucial" Decision Making Model and the 1956 Soviet–Japanese Normalization of Relations' *Acta Slavica Iaponica* (1991) IX: 146–59.

Saitō Takashi, '"Taikoku" no ronri to "jinmin" no ronri' [The Logic of a 'Great Power' Versus the Logic of 'the People'] *Chūō Kōron*, 78(2), (Feb. 1963): 55–65.

Saitō Takashi, 'Reisen no shindankai to nanboku mondai' [The New Stage in the Cold War and the North–South Problem] *Sekai* (Jan. 1964) 217: 123–31.

Saitō Takashi, 'Risei no kenri o motomete' [Pursuing the Rights of Reason] *Gendai no Me* (Aug. 1964) 5(8): 66–73.

Saitō Takashi, Satō Noboru, Takeuchi Yoshimi, Fukuda Kanichi, and Fujita Shōzō, 'Chū-So ronsō to gendai—wareware wa dō uketomeru ka' [The Sino-Soviet Dispute and the Present Day: How Should We Deal With It?] *Sekai*, 207, (Mar. 1963): 36–68.

Sakai Haruyoshi, 'Kokusai kankyō to NitChū no zento' [The International Environment and the Future of Japan–China [Trade]]' *Ekonomisuto* (30 July 1955) 33(30): 24–30.

Sakamoto Koretada, 'Chūgoku ni okeru kyōsanshugi to minzokushugi' [Communism and Nationalism in China] *Chūō Kōron* (June 1962) 77(6): 82–9.

Sakamoto Koretada, 'Chū-So ronsō to kokkyō, ryōdo mondai' [The Territorial Issue in the Sino-Soviet Dispute] *Kyōsanken Mondai* (Dec. 1964) 8(12): 1–14.

Sakamoto Yoshikazu, 'A New Foreign Policy' *Japan Quarterly* (July/Sept. 1972) XIX(3): 270–80.

Sakamoto Yoshikazu, 'Kakujidai no NitChū kankei' [Japan–China Relations in the Nuclear Age] *Sekai* (June 1963) 210: 12–27.

Sakamoto Yoshikazu, 'Nihon gaikō no shisōteki tenkan—NikKan teikei ni okeru Bei-Chū taiketsu' [A Turnaround in Japanese Foreign Policy Thinking: Japan–South Korea Cooperation and the Sino-American Confrontation] *Sekai* (Jan. 1966) 242: 18–36.

Sakamoto Yoshikazu, 'Peaceful Coexistance in Asia: A Japanese View', *India, Japan, Australia: Partners in Asia?*, J.D.B. Miller (ed.) (1968): 111–27.

Sakata Jirō, Hayashi Saburō, Fujise Gorō, Maeda Yoshinori, and Matsumoto Shunichi, 'Sobieto gaikō no teiryū' [Undercurrents in Soviet Foreign Policy] *Chūō Kōron* (Aug. 1955) 70(8): 52–72.

Sano Hiroshi, 'Mosukō, Pekin, Tōkyō rosen' [Moscow, Beijing: the Tokyo Line] *Nihon Oyobi Nihonjin* (Feb. 1954) 5(2): 6–13.

Sano Hiroshi, 'Soren heiwa kōsei no seikaku to mokuhyō' [Characteristics and Aims of the Soviet Peace Offensive] *Nihon Oyobi Nihonjin* (Apr. 1954) 5(4): 64–72.

Satō Kikuo, 'Chūkyō kinyu kanwa no kōbōsen' [The Battle to Alleviate the China Embargo] *Sekai Shūhō* (5 Nov. 1957) 38(16): 16–22.

Satō Noboru and Sugita Masao, 'Chū-So ronsō to kokusai kyōsanshugi undō no shōrai' [The Sino-Soviet Dispute and the Future of the International Communist Movement] *Sekai* (Sept. 1963) 213: 50–9.

Satō Noboru, 'Chūkyō rosen ni miru sensō to heiwa' [The Communist Chinese Line on War and Peace] *Kokusai Mondai* (Sept. 1963) 42: 28–35.

Satō Noboru, 'Chū-So ronsō to kokusai Kyōsanshugi undō' [The Sino-Soviet Dispute and the International Communist Movement] *Chūō Kōron* (Mar. 1963) 78(3): 102–11.

Satō Noboru, 'Chū-So ronsō to Nihon no kakushin undō' [The Sino-Soviet Dispute and the Japanese Progressive Movement] *Chūō Kōron* (Sept. 1963) 78(9): 194–201.

Satō Noboru, 'Shakaishugi to chūritsu' [Socialism and Neutrality] *Shisō* (Oct. 1961) 448: 34–43.

Satō Noboru, 'Taisei no henkaku to heiwa kyōson—Mosukuwa seimei no rironteki shomondai to sono rekishiteki keifu' [Structural Reform and Peaceful Coexistence:

Theoretical Issues in the Moscow Statement and Its Historical Lineage] *Sekai* (Feb. 1961) 182: 28–38.

Satō Seizaburō, 'The Foundations of Modern Japanese Foreign Policy', *The Foreign Policy of Modern Japan*, R.A. Scalapino (ed.) (1977): 367–89.

Satō Shinichirō, 'Shiteyarareta no wa Soren ka Chūkyō ka' [Which is Outwitted, the Soviet Union or Communist China?] *Nihon Shūhō* (5 Dec. 1952) 230: 3–7.

Scalapino, Robert A. 'Japanese Socialism in Crisis' *Foreign Affairs* (Jan. 1960) 36(2): 318–28.

Scalapino, Robert A. 'Moscow, Peking, and the Communist Parties of Asia' *Foreign Affairs* (Jan. 1963) 41: 323–40.

Scalapino, Robert A. 'Perspectives on Modern Japanese Foreign Policy', *The Foreign Policy of Modern Japan*, R.A. Scalapino (ed.) (1977): 391–412.

Scalapino, Robert A. 'Relations between the Nations of the Pacific Quadrille', *Japan and the Pacific Quadrille*, H.J. Ellison (ed.) (1987): 5–27.

Scalapino, Robert A. 'The Left Wing in Japan' *Survey* (Aug. 1962) 43: 102–11.

Scalapino, Robert A. 'The Sino-Soviet Conflict in Perspective' *The Annals of the American Academy of Political and Social Science* (Jan. 1964) CCCLI: 1–14.

Scalapino, Robert A. 'The Sino-Soviet Relationship: Reflections upon its Past and Future' *Strategic Review* (fall 1977) 5: 45–63.

Scalapino, Robert A. 'The United States and Japan', *The United States and the Far East*, Willard L. Thorp (ed.) (1962) (2nd ed.): 11–73.

Schurmann, H.F. 'The Third Sovietological Conference' *China Quarterly* (Oct./Dec. 1960) 27(4): 102–13.

Seidensticker, Edward, 'Divisions in Japanese Socialism' *Soviet Survey* (Apr./June 1960) 32: 61–67.

Sekai Jōsei Geppō, 'Chū-So Jōyaku to tai Nichi kōwa' [The Sino-Soviet Treaty and Peace with Japan] *Sekai Jōsei Geppō* (Feb. 1950) 82: 17–24.

Sekai Jōsei Geppō, 'Chū-So kyōdō sengen to hōka daihyōdan no kaiken' [The Sino-Soviet Joint Declaration and an Interview with the Delegation Visiting China] *Sekai Jōsei Geppō* (Nov. 1954) 236: 1–11.

Sekai Mondai Kenkyūkai, 'Bei-So sekai seisaku no shindankai' [A New Stage in US–Soviet World Policy] *Chūō Kōron* (Apr. 1953) 68(4): 65–74.

Sekai Shūhō, 'Anpo chōin to NitChū-So' [Japan, China and the Soviet Union and the Signature of the Security Treaty] *Sekai Shūhō* (16 Feb. 1960) 41(7): 25–31.

Sekai Shūhō, 'Bishō gaikō no tenkai—Tai Nichi Sekkin de Chū-So Hariau' [The Development of Smile Diplomacy: China and the Soviet Union Vie for Better Relations with Japan] *Sekai Shūhō* (5 Nov. 1963) 44(45): 14–19.

Sekai to Warera, 'Chū-So ryōkoku no tai Nichi yobikake' [China and the Soviet Union Address Japan] *Sekai to Warera* (Nov. 1954) 33(11): 36–8.

Sekai, 'Chū-So no tai Nichi kankei seijōka no yobikake' [Appealing for the Normalisation of Soviet–Japanese and Sino-Japanese Relations] *Sekai* (Mar. 1955) 111: 2–7.

Sekai, 'Chū-So ronsō no honshitsu' [The True Nature of the Sino-Soviet Dispute] *Sekai* (Nov. 1960) 179: 207–12.

Sekai, 'Gensuikin taikai ni okeru "Chū-So Ronsō"' [The 'Sino-Soviet Dispute' at the Gensuikin Congress] *Sekai* (Oct. 1963) 214: 80–99.

Sekai, 'Shū Onrai kaikenki' [Interview with Zhou Enlai] *Sekai* (Dec. 1954) 108: 100–15.

Seki Yoshihiko, 'Domestic Reorientation' *Journal of Social and Political Ideas in Japan* (Aug. 1964) 2(2): 51–5.

Seki Yoshihiko, 'International Reorientation. (Notes by the editor)' *Journal of Social and Political Ideas in Japan* (Aug. 1964) 2(2): 79–82.

Seki Yoshihiko, 'Japan in Transition' *Journal of Social and Political Ideas in Japan* (Aug. 1964) 2(2): 2–10.

Seki Yoshihiko, 'Japanese Foreign Policy' *Journal of Social and Political Ideas in Japan* (Apr. 1966) 4(1): 2–10.

Seki Yoshihiko, 'Japanese Intellectuals: Their Role and Responsibility' *Journal of Social and Political Ideas in Japan* (Apr. 1964) 2(1): 79–86.

Seki Yoshihiko, 'Notes by the Editor' *Journal of Social and Political Ideas in Japan* (Apr. 1963) 1(1): 77–9.

Seki Yoshihiko, 'The Foreign Policy of Japan', *Foreign Policies in a World of Change*, Joseph E. Black and Kenneth W. Thompson (eds) (1963): 517–46.

Seki Yoshihiko, 'The Ideology of Socialist Groups and Parties in Japan since 1945' *St. Antony's Papers*, G.F. Hudson (ed.) (1967) 20, Oxford University Press, Oxford: 37–55.

Sekido Tatsuzō, 'Chū-So ronsō ni kanren shita Chū-So no tai Nichi dōkō to sono eikyō' [The Sino-Soviet Dispute and its Effect on Sino-Soviet Attitudes Toward Japan] *Tairiku Mondai* (Oct. 1962) 11(10): 20–9.

Sekido Tatsuzō, 'Furushichofu seisaku to Kōno Nōshō' [Khrushchev's Policy and Agriculture Minister Kōno] *Keizai Ōrai* (Aug. 1962) 14(8): 103–9.

Sekito Yoshimitsu, 'Gensuibaku kinshi undō to Chū-So ronsō' [The Japanese Anti-Nuclear Weapon Movement and the Sino-Soviet Dispute] *Shin Nihon Bungaku* (Aug. 1963) 18(8): 80–6.

Sen, Gupta B. 'Soviet Perception of Japan in the 1970s' *Pacific Community* (Jan. 1976) 7(2): 179–98.

Shigemori Tadashi, 'Chū-So kankei wa dō naru ka' [How Will Sino-Soviet Relations Develop?] *Tairiku Mondai* (Oct. 1963) 12(10): 18–23.

Shigemori Tadashi, 'Shiberia kaihatsu to NisSo bōeki' [The Development of Siberia and Japan–Soviet Trade] *Keizai Ōrai* (Feb. 1957) 9(2): 39–47.

Shima Shigenobu, 'Kaku Jikken Teishi Jōyaku chōin ni omou' [Thoughts on the Signature of the Nuclear Test-Ban Treaty] *Kokusai Mondai* (Sept. 1963) 42: 2–3.

Shimizu Ikutarō, 'Atarashii rekishikan e no shuppatsu' [A Start Towards a New View of History] *Chūō Kōron* (Dec. 1963) 78(12): 34–49.

Shimizu Ikutarō, 'Chūgoku no kakubusō to Nihon' [China's Nuclear Armament and Japan] *Chūō Kōron* (Mar. 1963) 78(3): 128–38.

Shimizu Ikutarō, 'Chū-So no hinkaku' [China and the Soviet Union's Guest of Honour] *Chūō Kōron* (July 1964) 79(7): 33.

Shimizu Izō, 'Kōka shita Chūkyō no tai Nichi gaikō' [Communist China's Japan Policy Hardens] *Seikai Ōrai* (Oct. 1957) 23(10): 20–5.

Shimizu Sayuri, 'Clarence Randall and the Control of Sino-Japanese Trade' *Journal of American and Canadian Studies* (Tokyo) (spring 1991) 7: 47–73.

Shimizu Sayuri, 'Perennial Anxiety: Japan–U.S. Controversy over Recognition of the PRC, 1952–1958' *Journal of American–East Asian Relations* (fall 1995) 4(3): 223–48.

Shimizu Shinzō, 'Gendaishi no naka no waga kakushin seiryoku' [Our Progressive Forces at the Present Stage of History] *Sekai* (Nov. 1963) 215: 111–22.

Shimizu Tōzō, 'Sino-Soviet Polemics—A Case of Quarrel à la Chinoise' *Review* (Tokyo) (July 1965) 5: 29–38.

Shin Shūkan, '"Akai sekiyu" sōdōki' [An Account of the Uproar over 'Red Oil'] *Shin Shūkan* (18 Jan. 1962) 2(2): 13.

Shin Shūkan, 'Kōno hō So no himitsu mokuteki' [The Secret Purpose of Kōno's Visit to the Soviet Union] *Shin Shūkan* (17 May 1962) 2(21): 25.

Shin Shūkan, 'Odoroki awateru Gaimushō—Gagārin rai Nichi yorokobu NisSo Kyōkai' [MOFA is Surprised, Japan–Soviet Association Happy at Gagarin's Visit to Japan] *Shin Shūkan* (17 May 1962) 2(21): 26.

Shinoda Yūjirō, 'Japan zwischen China und der Sovjetunion' *Europa Archiv* (1974) 29(9): 291–8.

Shinohara Hajime, 'The Leadership of the Conservative Party' *Journal of Social and Political Ideas in Japan* (Dec. 1964) 2(3): 40–5.

Shinsō, 'Gyakuten (shidashita) Nichi-Bei kōshō no uchimaku (chijimi sei zaikai)' [The Inside Story on the Turnabout in Japan–U.S. Negotiations] *Shinsō* (1 April 1955) 82: 15–23.

Shinsō, 'Nichi-Bei-So mitsudomoe no omowaku' [Japanese, American and Soviet Expectations] *Shinsō* (15 Mar. 1955) 81: 4–11.

Shūkan Asahi, 'Chūkyō Shisatsu Giindan no shūkaku' [The Rewards of the Diet Members' Communist China Inspection Group] *Shūkan Asahi* (7 Nov. 1954) 59(46): 13.

Shūkan Asahi, 'Ishibashi Tanzan—sono Hito to seisaku' [Ishibashi Tanzan: The Man and His Policies] *Shūkan Asahi* (30 Dec. 1956) 61(54): 4–9.

Shūkan Asahi, 'Yo nimo fushigina NisSo kōshō—Daresu adobarūn no imi suru mono' [Strange Japan–Soviet Negotiations: The Meaning of Dulles' Trial Balloon] *Shūkan Asahi* (9 Sept. 1956) 61(37): 12–14.

Shūkan Sankei, 'Chūkyō bōeki sokushin ni kitai—Yamamoto Kumaichi' [Expectations for Communist China Trade Promotion: Yamamoto Kumaichi] *Shūkan Sankei* (15 Mar. 1953) 56: 21.

Shūkan Shinchō, 'Fedorenko taishi no kyoshū' [The Fate of Soviet Ambassador Fedorenko] *Shūkan Shinchō* (4 Dec. 1961) 6(48): 24.

Shūkan Shinchō, 'Tanuki ana sōtokufu—Soren kōsei ni ugoku sekai chizu' [Badger's Den Government General: The Soviet Union Moves onto the Global Offensive] *Shūkan Shinchō* (5 Nov. 1956) 1(39): 52–5.

Shūkan Tōkyō, 'Namerareta Nihon—yukue fumei no hankachi gaikō' [A Fool is Made of Japan: Nothing More is Heard of Handkerchief Diplomacy] *Shūkan Tōkyō* (5 April 1958) 4(14): 3–11.

Shūkan Tōyō Keizai, 'Taiwan o meguru sei zaikai no omowaku' [The Political and Financial Worlds' Intentions Concerning Taiwan] *Shūkan Tōyō Keizai* (29 Feb. 1964) 3154: 38–43.

Sigur, Gaston J. 'Normalization and Pacific and Triangular Diplomacy', *The Chinese Connection and Normalization*, Chiu Hungdah and Karen Murphy (eds) (1980):

Simon, Sheldon W. 'Japan's Foreign Policy Adjustments to a Changing Environment' *Asian Survey* (July 1978) XVIII(7): 666–86.

Simon, Sheldon W. 'Maoism and Inter-party Relations: Peking's Alienation from the JCP' *China Quarterly* (July 1968) 35: 40–57.

Simon, Sheldon W. 'New Soviet Approaches to the Japanese Left' *Asian Survey* (June 1966) 6(6): 319–26.

Simon, Sheldon W. 'The Japan–China–USSR Triangle' *Pacific Affairs* (1974) 47(2): 125–38.

Sō Yōkichi, 'NitChū bōeki o ugokasu mono' [What Motivates Japan–China Trade] *Nihon oyobi Nihonjin* (Jan. 1957) 8(1): 62–8.

Somura Yasunobu, 'Chū-So tairitsu no kokusaiteki hamon' [The Sino-Soviet Rift's International Repercussions] *Chūō Kōron* (Sept. 1963) 78(9): 186–93.

Sone Eki, 'Future Policy toward Communist China' *Japan Quarterly* (Oct./Dec. 1957) 4(4): 430–9.

Sone Eki, 'Japan and the China Problem: A Democratic Socialist View' *Japan Quarterly* (July/Sept. 1961) 8(3): 279–87.

Sone Eki, Kitamura Tokutarō, Takahashi Masao, and Naoi Takeo, 'Soren to Amerika ni hasamarete' [Caught Between the U.S. and USSR] *Bungei Shunjū* (Dec. 1956) 34(12): 88–100.

Soren Kenkyū, 'Chūkyō tenbō' [Communist China View] *Soren Kenkyū*, 8(4), April 1959): 48–9.

Soren Kenkyū, 'Chū-So kankei no jittai o eguru' [Piercing the Reality of Sino-Soviet Relations] *Soren Kenkyū* (April 1952) 1(1): 39–44.

Soren Kenkyū, 'Chū-So no ichijiteki kyūsen' [A Temporary Sino-Soviet Truce] *Soren Kenkyū* (May 1962) 11(5): 16–17.

Soren Kenkyū, 'Chū-So no mujun kaishō fukanō—moto tasu tsūshinin ga ronhyō' [Sino-Soviet Contradictions Cannot be Resolved: A Former Tass Correspondent Comments] *Soren Kenkyū* (July 1962) 11(7): 51.

Soren Kenkyū, 'Kokusai jōsei ni tai suru Chū-So no kenkai' [Sino-Soviet Views on the International Situation] *Soren Kenkyū* (July 1960) 9(7): 41–4.

Soren Kenkyū, 'Mikoyan daiichi fukushushō to Nihon no jitsugyōkai daihyō to no kaidan' [First Deputy Prime Minister Mikoyan's Talks with Representatives of Japanese Business] *Soren Kenkyū* (Nov. 1960) 9(11): 46–58.

Soren Kenkyū, 'Shin daigishi no Soren kan—ankēto' [New Diet Members' Views of the Soviet Union: A Questionnaire] *Soren Kenkyū* (July 1958) 7(7): 13–17.

Soren Kenkyū, 'Shinshun ankēto' [New Year Questionnaire] *Soren Kenkyū* (Jan. 1961) 10(1): 34–41.

Soren Kenkyū, 'Shinshun ankēto' [New Year Questionnaire] *Soren Kenkyū* (Jan. 1955) 4(1): 36–49.

Soren Kenkyū, 'Shinshun ankēto' [New Year Questionnaire] *Soren Kenkyū* (Jan. 1960) 9(1): 42–55.

Soren Kenkyū, 'Shinshun ankēto' [New Year Questionnaire] *Soren Kenkyū* (Jan. 1959) 8(1): 44–54.

Soren Kenkyū, 'Shinshun ankēto' [New Year Questionnaire] *Soren Kenkyū* (Jan. 1962) 11(1): 20–9.

Soren Kenkyū, 'Soren tenbō—Chū-So kankei no genjō' [Soviet View: The Current State of Sino-Soviet Relations] *Soren Kenkyū* (Aug. 1961) 10(8): 4–8.

Soren Kenkyū, 'Soren tenbō—So-Chū kan no ronsō tsuzuku' [Soviet View: The Dispute Between the Soviet Union and China Continues] *Soren Kenkyū* (Aug. 1960) 9(8): 4–5.

Soren Kenkyū, 'Soren tenbō' [Soviet View] *Soren Kenkyū* (Sept. 1960) 9(9): 5–7.

Soren Kenkyū, 'Soren tenbō' [Soviet View] *Soren Kenkyū* (Sept. 1961) 10(9): 6–7.

Stephan, John J. 'Japan in the Soviet Mirror: The Search for Rapprochement' *Bulletin of Peace Proposals* (1982) 13(1): 61–6.

Stephan, John J. 'Japan–Soviet Relations: Patterns and Prospects', *Japan and the Pacific Quadrille*, H.J. Ellison (ed.) (1987): 135–59.

Stephan, John J. 'Soviet Policy in Asia (1945–51: An Overview', *Japan and Postwar Diplomacy in the Asia–Pacific Region*, Hosoya Chihiro (ed.) (1984): 59–99.

Stockwin, J.A.A. 'Japan and the Soviet Union', *Japan's Foreign Relations: A Global Search for Economic Security*, R.S. Ozaki and W. Arnold (eds) (1985): 67–84.

Stockwin, J.A.A. 'Japanese Attitudes to the Sino-Soviet Dispute' *International Journal* (1963) 18(4): 488–500.

Stockwin, J.A.A. 'JSP Under New Leadership' *Asian Survey* (Apr. 1966) VI(4): 187–200.

Stockwin, J.A.A. 'Positive Neutrality—The Foreign Policy of the JSP' *Asian Survey* (Nov. 1962) II(9): 33–41.

Stockwin, J.A.A. 'The Communist Party of Japan' *Problems of Communism* (Jan./Feb. 1967) XVI(1): 1–10.

Stockwin, J.A.A. 'The Japan Communist Party in the Sino-Soviet Dispute—From Neutrality to Alignment?', *The Disintegrating Monolith: Pluralist Trends in the Communist World*, J.D.B. Miller and T.H. Rigby (eds) (1965): 137–48.

Stockwin, J.A.A. 'Understanding Japanese Foreign Policy' *Review of International Studies* (1985) 2: 157–68.

Storry, Richard, 'Japan's Position as a World Power' *The World Today* (May 1965) 21(5): 217–22.

Storry, Richard, 'Options for Japan in the 1970s' *The World Today* (Aug. 1970) 26(8): 325–33.

Storry, Richard, 'The Best Course for Japan's Foreign Policy' *Pacific Community* (Jan. 1971) 2(2): 297–306.

Suganuma Fujio, 'Nihonjin no Chūgokukan' [The Japanese View of China] *Shisō* (Nov. 1961) 449: 115–21.

Suma Yakichirō, 'Chū-So o eguru' [Cutting to the Heart of China and the Soviet Union] *Soren Kenkyū* (July 1955) 4(7): 52–5.

Suma Yakichirō, 'Tai Chū-So kokkō wa kaifuku suru ka' [Will Diplomatic Relations with China and the Soviet Union be Restored?] *Tōyō Keizai Shimpō* (20 Dec. 1952, special issue) 12: 28–32.

Suma Yakichirō, Yamamoto Kumaichi, Zhu Chang, Kikikawa Tadao, Asakawa Kenji, Ishiyama Kenkichi, and Hoashi Kei, 'Mō Taku Tō jidai to Nihon no kiki' [The Age of Mao Zedong and Japan's Crisis] *Maru* (Oct. 1953) 6(10): 76–86.

Suzukawa Isamu, Komatsu Takeo, Watanabe Zenichirō, and Shimizu Toshio, 'Heiwa kyōson e no taidō' [Signs of Peaceful Coexistence] *Gaikō Jihō* (Nov. 1959) 968(16): 13–23.

Suzuki Kazuo, 'Shin dankai no NitChū bōeki' [Japan–China Trade at a New Stage] *Ekonomisuto* (17 Sept. 1963) 41(37): 42–5.

Suzuki Matsugorō, 'Kyōsanken bōeki ni odoru hitobito' [Supporters of Trade with the Communist bloc] *Jimbutsu Ōrai* (April 1955) 40: 53–56.

Suzuki Mosaburō and Utsunomiya Tokuma, 'Nihon no rieki to Chūgoku no rieki' [Japan's Interests and China's Interests] *Chūō Kōron* (1 Mar. 1962) 77(3): 134–43.

Suzuki Mosaburō, 'Shin Chūgoku to Nihon Shakaitō' [New China and the JSP] *Chūō Kōron* (Dec. 1954) 69(12): 117–21.

Swearingen, Rodger, 'Japanese Communism and the Moscow–Peking Axis' *The Annals of the American Academy of Political and Social Science* (Nov. 1956) 308: 63–75.

Tōyama Shigeki, 'The World and Japan' *Journal of Social and Political Ideas in Japan* (Apr. 1964) 2(1): 111–4.

Tachibana Jōhei, 'Fu Shushō no settoku wa seikō shita ka' [Has Secretary-General Khrushchev Proved Persuasive?] *Sekai Shūhō* (20 Oct. 1959) 40(42): 24–5.

Tachibana Yoshinori and Unno Minoru, 'Chū-So sengen no hamon to Yoshida toBei no shūkaku' [Ripples from the Sino-Soviet Declaration and the Fruit of Yoshida's US Visit] *Jitsugyō no Nihon* (1954) 57(26): 50–6.

Taguchi Fukuji, 'Nihon Shakaitō ron' [The Japan Socialist Party] *Chūō Kōron* (Feb. 1961) 76(2): 26–49.

Tairiku Mondai Kenkyūjo, 'Chū-So kankei no kentō (2)' [An Examination of Sino-Soviet Relations (Part 2)] *Tairiku Mondai* (Aug. 1956) 5(8): 6–31.

Tairiku Mondai Kenkyūjo, 'Chū-So kankei no kentō' [A Study of Sino-Soviet Relations] *Tairiku Mondai* (Nov. 1960) 9(11): 16–34.

Tairiku Mondai Kenkyūjo, 'Chū-So kankei no kongo to sekai jōsei' [Future Sino-Soviet Relations and the World Situation] *Tairiku Mondai* (Feb. 1965) 14(2): 44–61.

Tairiku Mondai Kenkyūjo, 'Chū-So no tai Nichi seisaku' [Sino-Soviet Policies Towards Japan] *Tairiku Mondai* (May 1960) 9(5): 72–82.

Tairiku Mondai Kenkyūjo, 'Chū-So tairitsu no kongen to sono yukue' [The Origin and Future Outlook of the Sino-Soviet Rift] *Tairiku Mondai* (Mar. 1963) 12(3): 8–17.

Tairiku Mondai Kenkyūjo, 'Chū-So tairitsu no shindandan to sono eikyō' [The Influence of New Steps in the Sino-Soviet Rift] *Tairiku Mondai* (June 1964) 13(6): 17–25.

Tairiku Mondai Kenkyūjo, 'Chū-So tairitsu no shōrai to sono eikyō' [Future Outlook and Influence of the Sino-Soviet Rift] *Tairiku Mondai* (Sept. 1963) 12(9): 20–33.

Tairiku Mondai Kenkyūjo, 'Kenan ronbun hihan' [A Critique of the Kennan Thesis] *Tairiku Mondai* (Dec. 1964) 13(12): 52–7.

Tairiku Mondai Kenkyūjo, 'Mō Takutō no mujunron wa Kyōsanken o yusubutte iru' [Mao Zedong's Theory of Contradictions Rocks the Communist Bloc] *Tairiku Mondai* (Oct. 1957): 35–6.

Takahashi Masao, 'Chū-So seimei to daisan seiryoku no tachiba' [The Sino-Soviet Declaration and the Stand of the Third Force] *Shakaishugi* (Shakaishugi Kyōkai) (Nov. 1954) 40: 2–8.

Takahashi Masao, 'Nihon ni okeru Komunizumu' [Communism in Japan], *Soren to Chūkyō*, Ōa Kyōkai (30 Nov. 1962): 340–64.

Takaichi Keinosuke, 'Chū-So tairitsu ni okeru Chūkyō no kihon rosen' [Communist China's Basic Line in the Sino-Soviet Rift] *Kokusai Seiji* (Oct. 1965) 29: 23–36.

Takaichi Keinosuke, 'Kakumei jūichi nenme no Chūgoku' [China 11 Years After the Revolution] *Sekai* (Dec. 1959) 168: 92–9.

Takane Masaaki, 'Economic Growth and the "End of Ideology" in Japan' *Asian Survey* (June 1965) V(6): 295–304.

Takaragi Fumihiko, 'Comments on [the] Sino-Soviet Dispute' *Japan Socialist Review* (15 Feb. 1963) 32: 11–12.

Takasaki Tatsunosuke, 'NitChū bōeki futatsu no rosen' [Two Lines on Japan–China Trade] *Seikai Ōrai* (Nov. 1963) 29(11): 88–97.

Takasaki Tatsunosuke, 'Shū On Rai to kaidan shite' [Meeting with Zhou Enlai] *Chūō Kōron* (Feb. 1961) 76(2): 246–52.

Takasaki Tatsunosuke, 'Watashi no mita Chūgoku' [China As I Saw It] *Asahi Jānaru* (15 Jan. 1961) 3(3): 14–21.

Takasawa Torao, 'Chū-So ronsō to heiwa mondai' [The Sino-Soviet Dispute and the Peace Problem] *Shakaishugi* (Shakaishugi Kyōkai) (July 1963) 141: 2–14.

Takaya Kakuzō, 'Chū-So dorojiai Hiroshima jitsuen o miru' [Sino-Soviet Mud-Slinging Demonstrated at Hiroshima] *Tairiku Mondai* (Oct. 1963) 12(10): 13–17.

Takaya Kakuzō, 'Chū-So kōsō to Nihon no sayoku jinei' [Sino-Soviet Hostilities and Japan's Leftist Camp] *Tairiku Mondai* (Aug. 1964) 13(8): 15–24.

Takayama Gorō, 'Chū-So Dōmei to Nihon no tachiba' [The Sino-Soviet Alliance and Japan's Standpoint] *Jitsugyō no Nihon* (Feb. 1950) 53(6): 58–9.

Takeda Nanyō, 'Chūkyō—Soren ippentō no gendankai' [The Current Stage of Communist China Taking the Soviet Union's Side] *Soren Kenkyū* (Aug. 1953) 2(8): 36–46.

Takenaka Shigehisa, 'Chūgokujin no tai So kanjō' [Chinese Peoples' Feelings towards the Soviet Union] *Soren Kenkyū* (Sept. 1956) 5(9): 44–7.

Takeuchi Yoshitomo, 'The Role of Marxism in Japan' *The Developing Economies*, V(4)(Dec. 1967): 727–47.

Takita Kazuo, 'Delighted Embarrassment' *Far Eastern Economic Review* (18 Aug. 1966) LIII(7): 309–12.

Tamura Kōsaku, 'Chūgoku no hikiageru o ketsui shita—Igirisu shōsha no kyōkun' [A Lesson from British Firms: They have Decided to Withdraw from China] *Tōyō Keizai Shimpō* (7 June 1952) 2527: 14.

Tamura Kōsaku, 'Kenan ronbun to NisSo Heiwa Jōyaku' [Kennan's Thesis and the Japan–Soviet Peace Treaty] *Tairiku Mondai* (Dec. 1964) 13(12): 46–51.

Tamura Kōsaku, 'Sino-Soviet Arsenal' *New Leader* (28 Nov. 1960) XLIII(46) section 2: 13–19.

Tanaka Takahiko, 'The Soviet–Japanese Normalisation and Foreign Policy Ideas of the Hatoyama Group', *Western Interactions with Japan: Expansion, the Armed Forces and Readjustment*, Peter Lowe and Herman Moeshart (eds) (1990): 105–14.

Tanaka Takahiko, 'The Soviet–Japanese Normalization in 1955–6 and US–Japanese Relations' *Hitotsubashi Journal of Law and Politics* (Feb. 1993) 21: 65–93.

Tange Gorō, 'Chūkyō no kōgyō kensetsu no hōkō o saguru' [Probing the Direction of Communist China's Industrial Construction] *Ekonomisuto* (6 Mar. 1954) 32(10): 24–7.

Tani Masayuki, 'Amerika no Chūkyō kan' [America's View of Communist China] *Tairiku Mondai* (Dec. 1957) 6(12): 37–43.

Taniguchi Yasuji, 'Chū-So ronsō' no shiten—Ronsō o dō uketomeru ka' ['The Sino-Soviet Dispute': How Should We Deal With It?] *Gekkan Sōhyō* (April 1963) 72: 35–9.

Tanihata Ryōzō, et al., 'Furushichofu no shidōryoku' *Chūō Kōron* (Feb. 1964) 79(2): 258–75.

Terasawa Hajime, Mori Kyōzō, Harako Rinjirō, and Kinoshita Junji, 'Chū-So ronsō to Nihon no tachiba' [The Sino-Soviet Dispute and Japan's Position] *Fujin Kōrōn* (Mar. 1963) 48(4): 98–106.

Thayer, Nathaniel, 'Competition and Conformity: An Inquiry into the Structure of Japanese Newspapers' *Modern Japanese Organization and Decision-Making*, Ezra Vogel (ed.) (1975): 284–303.

Togawa Isamu, 'Gaimudaijin wa 8 nin iru' [There are Eight Foreign Ministers] *Nihon* (June 1958) 1(6): 110–4.

Tokuda Noriyuki, 'China in World Politics' *Journal of Social and Political Ideas in Japan* (Dec. 1966) 4(3): 2–10.

Totten, George O. and Kawakami Tamio, 'Gensuikyo and the Peace Movement in Japan' *Asian Survey* (May 1964) IV(5): 833–41.

Toyama Shirō, 'NisSo, NitChū kokkō kaifuku no tadashii rikai no tame ni' [For a Correct Understanding of the Japan–Soviet and Japan–China Normalization Issue] *Zenei* (June 1955) 105: 36–43.

Tōyō Keizai Shimpō, 'Chū-So dōmei seiritsu to Nihon' [The Establishment of the Sino-Soviet Alliance and Japan] *Tōyō Keizai Shimpō* (25 Feb. 1950) 2411: 3–4.

Tōyō Keizai Shimpō, 'Kakutei Kyōtei chōin to Nihon no tachiba' [The Signing of the Nuclear Test Ban Treaty and Japan's Position] *Tōyō Keizai Shimpō* (10 Aug. 1963)3127: 4–5.

Tsou Tang, Najita Tetsuo, and Otake Hideo, 'Sino-Japanese Relations in the 1970s', *Japan, America and the Future World Order*, Morton Kaplan and Mushakoji Kinhide (eds) (1976): 49–87.

Tsuda Michio, '"Zenjinmin no kokka" ron hihan—Chū-So ronsō no isshudai ni yosete' [Criticism of the 'State of the Whole People' Theory: Commenting on an Issue in the Sino-Soviet Dispute] *Yuibutsuron Kenkyū* (spring 1964) 17: 5–18.

Tsukui Tatsuo, 'Anpo kaitei no ato ni kuru mono—Kyōsanken to no gaikō o dō suru ka' [Foreign Policy towards Communist bloc Countries after the Security Treaty Revision] *Seikai Ōrai* (Apr. 1960) 26(4): 56–61.

Tsurutani Taketsugu, 'Japan, China and East Asian Security' *Asia Quarterly* (July/Sept. 1973) 20(3): 221–42.

Tucker, Nancy Bernkopf, 'A House Divided: The United States, the Department of State, and China', *The Great Powers in East Asia, 1953–1960*, Warren I. Cohen and Iriye Akira (eds) (1990): 35–62.

Tucker, Nancy Bernkopf, 'American Policy toward Sino-Japanese Trade in the Postwar Years: Politics and Prosperity' *Diplomatic History* (summer 1984) 8(3): 183–208.

Uchiyama Kanzō, Kimura Kihachirō, Kuwabara Takeo, Takami Shigeyoshi, and Shiraishi Bon, 'NitChū fukkō wa dō susumetara yoi ka' [Sino-Japanese Normalisation: What is the Best Way to Proceed?] *Chisei* (Mar. 1957) 4(3): 31–9.

Uchiyama Masakuma, 'The Foreign Office of Japan Past and Present' *Keiō Journal of Politics* (1976) 2: 1–21.

Ueda Kōichirō, 'Sobieto gaikō no rironteki haikei' [The Rationale of Soviet Foreign Policy] *Chūō Kōron* (Jan. 1962) 77(1): 150–61.

Ueda Toshio, '"Futatsu no Chūgoku" to Nihon' ['The Two Chinas' and Japan] *Soren to Chūkyō*, Ōa Kyōkai (30 Nov. 1962): 365–77.

Ueda Toshio, 'The Outlook for Relations with Communist China' *Japan Quarterly* (July/Sept. 1966) XIII(3): 292–300.

Ueki Yasuhiro, 'Sengo NisSo kōshō to hiseishiki sesshokusha' [Post-war Japanese-Soviet Negotiations and Informal Contacts] *Kokusai Seiji* (Oct. 1983) 75: 81–97.

Uemura Shinichi, 'Taishōtekina futatsu no ronsaku—Bandi kōen to Kenan ronbun' [Two Diametrically Opposite Policy Prescriptions: The Bundy Speech and the Kennan Thesis] *Sekai Shūhō* (13 Oct. 1964) 45(41): 16–21.

Uezumi Minoru, 'Did [the] JSP's Policy Toward China Change?' *Japan Socialist Review* (1 Oct. 1962) 23: 24–37.

Uno Shigeaki and Yamagiwa Akira, 'Shiryō—Chū-So no ronsōten' [Sino-Soviet Points in Dispute (Materials)] *Chūō Kōron* (Sept. 1963) 78(9): 202–13.

Uno Shigeaki, 'Chū-So ronsō no dōkō' [Trends in the Sino-Soviet Dispute] *Kokusai Mondai* (Jan. 1965) 58: 22–29.

Urushiyama Shigeyoshi, 'Chū-So tairitsu to Nihon' [The Sino-Soviet Rift and Japan] *Kyōto Sangyō Daigaku Ronshū* (May 1976) 6(1): 40–56.

Ushiba Nobuhiko, 'Possibility of Expanding Trade with the Communist bloc' *Asian Affairs* (Ajia Kyōkai) (Mar. 1958) III(1): 71–9.

Utsumi Teizō, 'Chū-So Jōyaku no heiwateki kōka' [The Sino-Soviet Treaty's Peaceful Effect] *Daiyamondo* (21 Feb. 1950) 38(6): 13–14.

Utsunomiya Tokuma, 'Seifu no "seikan seisaku" ni hantai suru' [I Oppose the Government's 'Wait and See' Policy towards China] *Chūō Kōron* (Nov. 1959) 74(16): 44–51.

Utsunomiya Tokuma, 'Watashi no mita Chūgoku' [The China I Saw] *Ekonomisuto* (5 Feb. 1963) 41(5): 14–19.

Utsunomiya Tokuma, Katsumata Seiichi, Mushakōji Kinhide, and Takaichi Keinosuke, 'Chūgoku no nashonaru intaresuto' [China's National Interests] *Gendai no Me* (Nov. 1964) 5(11): 80–90.

Vinacke, Harold M. 'The Growth of an Independent Foreign Policy in Japan' *Pacific Affairs* (spring 1965) 38(1): 5–16.

Vishwanathan, Savitri, 'The Japan–China–USSR Triangle: A View from Tokyo' *India Quarterly* (April/June 1975) XXXI(2): 121–35.

Wada Haruki, 'Japanese–Soviet Relations and East Asian Security' *Japan Quarterly* (April/June 1983) XXX(2),: 188–92.

Wada Hiroo, 'Chūritsu seisaku no zenshin no tame ni' [For the Advance of a Neutralist Policy] *Chūō Kōron* (June 1962) 77(6): 98–106.

Wada Hiroo, 'Chū-So ronsō to Shakaitō no tachiba' [The Sino-Soviet Dispute and the Stand of the Socialist Party] *Jiyū* (Oct. 1963) 5(10): 2–9.

Wada Hiroo, 'Japan and the China Problem: A Socialist View' *Japan Quarterly* (July/Sept. 1961) 8(3): 273–9.

Wada Hiroo, 'What Should Our Attitude be Toward Moscow–Peking Conflict' *Japan Socialist Review* (15 Aug. 1963) 44: 15–29.

Wakaizumi Kei, 'Chūgoku no kakubusō to Nihon no anzen hoshō' [Chinese Nuclear Armament and the Security of Japan] *Chūō Kōron* (Feb. 1966) 81(2): 216–79.

Wakaizumi Kei, 'Japan's Dilemma: To Act or Not to Act' *Foreign Policy* (fall 1974) 16: 30–47.

Wakaizumi Kei, 'Japan's Role in a New World Order' *Foreign Affairs* (Jan. 1973) 51(2): 310–26.

Watanabe Akio, 'Japanese Public Opinion and Foreign Affairs: 1964–1973', *The Foreign Policy of Modern Japan*, R.A. Scalapino (ed.) (1977): 105–45.

Watanabe Mikio, 'Fushigina sankaku kankei—fukuzatsuna So-Chū-In no tairitsuten to mondaiten' [A Strange Triangular Relationship: Complicated Soviet-Sino-Indian Rifts and Problems] *Keizai Ōrai* (Feb. 1962) 14(2): 88–93.

Weinstein, Martin E. 'Is Japan Changing its Defense Policy?' *Pacific Community* (Jan. 1973) 4(2): 179–94.

Weinstein, Martin E. 'Japan and the Continental Giants' *Current History* (April 1971) 60(356): 193–9, 241–2.

Weinstein, Martin E. 'Strategic Thought and the US–Japan Alliance', *Forecast for Japan: Security in the 1970s*, J.W. Morley (ed.) (1972): 35–84.

Weinstein, Martin E. 'The Evolution of the Japanese Self-Defense Forces', *The Modern Japanese Military System*, James H. Buck (ed.) (1975): 41–63.

Welfield, John, 'A New Balance: Japan v. China?' *Pacific Community* (Oct. 1972) 4(1): 54–70.

Wilbur, C. Martin, 'Japan and the Rise of Communist China' *Japan between East and West*, Hugh Borton, et al. (1957): 199–239.

Wilbur, C. Martin, 'Some Findings of Japanese Opinion Polls' *Japan between East and West*, Hugh Borton, et al. (1957): 299–312.

Willis, David K. 'Japan in Asia: Rabbit, Porcupine or Tiger?' *Pacific Community* (July 1970) 1(4): 602–11.

Wright, Mary Clabaugh, 'Japan and China' *Monthly Review* (June 1955) 7(2): 67–74.

Yamada Hisanori, 'The Multipolarization of the Communist World and Japan', *Japan in Current World Affairs*, Kajima Institute of International Peace (ed.) (1971): 63–75.

Yamada Munemutsu, Tsuda Michio, Ikeyama Jūrō, and Maeno Ryō, 'Chū-So ronsō to kakushin jinei' [The Sino-Soviet Dispute and the Reformist Camp] *Gendai no Me* (Mar. 1963) 4(3): 44–57.

Yamaguchi Kikuichirō, Suma Yakichirō, Sasaki Kōzō, and Kōno Mitsu, 'Chūkyō no jittai wa kō da' [Communist China is Like This] *Seikai Ōrai* (Dec. 1954) 20(12): 126–43.

Yamakawa Hitoshi, 'Shakaishugi e no michi wa hitotsu dewanai—Furushichofu hōkoku to Ryū Shō Ki hōkoku o yonde' [There is not only One Way to Socialism: The Khrushchev–Liu Shaoqi Reports Examined] *Chūō Kōron* (Dec. 1956) 71(13): 151–63.

Yamakawa Kikue, 'Kono me de mita Chū-So ronsō—Chū-So no sokaku wa hajimatta koto dewanai' [My View of the Sino-Soviet Dispute: Sino-Soviet Alienation is Nothing New] *Bungei Shunjū* (Sept. 1963) 41(9): 84–7.

Yamamoto Kumaichi, 'Trade Problems with PRC' *Contemporary Japan* (Sept. 1958) XXV(3): 363–98.

Yamamoto Michio (pseud.), 'Chūgoku no yūjin ni tou' [Questioning China's Friends] *Tōa Jiron* (Jan. 1959) 1(1): 4–10.

Yamamoto Noboru, 'Nihon no Kyōsanken bōeki' [Japan's Communist bloc Trade] *Soren to Chūkyō, Ōa Kyōkai* (30 Nov. 1962): 378–96.

Yamamura Jirō, 'Nihon ni aru Chaina robii' [The China Lobby in Japan] *Jimbutsu Ōrai* (May 1954) 3(5): 84–9.

Yamauchi Takao, 'Chū-So ronsō to rondan no sekinin' [The Sino-Soviet Rift and the Responsibility of the Press] *Shin Nihon Bungaku* (Mar. 1963) 18(3): 107–9.

Yamazaki Isao, 'Chū-So ronsō ni okeru jakkan no shudai' [A Number of Themes in the Sino-Soviet Dispute] *Shisō* (Feb. 1963) 464: 71–83.

Yamazaki Isao, 'Chū-So ronsō o dō miru ka' [How Should We View the Sino-Soviet Dispute?] *Ekonomisuto* (22 Jan. 1963) 41(4): 38–46.

Yamazaki Masakazu, 'The Intellectual Community of the Shōwa Era' *Daedalus* (summer 1990) 119(3): 245–64.

Yamazaki Taketoshi, 'Chū-So tairitsu to Soren keizai no haikei' [The Sino-Soviet Rift and the Soviet Economic Background] *Ronsō* (Mar. 1963) 5(3): 15–22.

Yanagisawa Eijirō, 'Chū-So tairitsu ni okeru Soren no seisaku to tachiba' [The Sino-Soviet Rift and the Soviet Union's Policy and Standpoint] *Kokusai Seiji* (Oct. 1965) 29: 9–22.

Yasuhara Yoko, 'Japan, Communist China, and Export Controls in Asia, 1948–52', *Journal of Diplomatic History* (winter 1986) 10: 75–89.

Yasutomo, Dennis T. 'Satō's China Policy, 1964–66' *Asian Survey* (June 1977) XVII(6): 530–44.

Yobev, Stefan, 'Furushichofu to Mō Takutō no ideorogii no tairitsu' [Khrushchev and Mao Zedong's Ideological Rift] *Soren Kenkyū* (Sept. 1960) 9(9): 43–57.

Yokota Kisaburō, 'Chū-So to no kokkō chōsei—sono mondai to arikata' [Sino-Soviet Diplomatic Coordination: Problems and how it should be] *Sekai* (April 1955) 112: 55–63.

Yoshida Shigeru, 'Japan and the Crisis in Asia' *Foreign Affairs* (Jan. 1951) 29(2): 171–81.

Yoshimoto Takaaki, 'Mosha to kagami—aru Chū-So ronsō ron' [A Replica and a Mirror: A Theory of the Sino-Soviet Rift] *Shisō* (Oct. 1963) 472: 82–92.

Yoshimura Toshio, 'Smiling Revolutionaries' *Far Eastern Economic Review* (4 Sept. 1971) 73(36): 24–5.

Zagoria, Donald S. 'Sino-Soviet Conflict and the West' *Foreign Affairs* (Oct. 1962) 41: 171–90.

Zagoria, Donald S. 'The State of the Parties: Asia' *Survey* (Jan. 1965) 54: 89–104.

Zhou Jingwen, 'Chū-So tairitsu wa nai' [There is no Sino-Soviet Rift] *Sekai Shūhō* (1 Nov. 1960) 41(44): 20–7.

Index